The Salmon P. Chase Papers

Salmon P. Chase (1808–73)

Engraving by Max Rosenthal, Philadelphia, 1890.
Courtesy of the Chicago Historical Society.

The Salmon P. Chase Papers

VOLUME 5

Correspondence, 1865–1873

John Niven, Editor

Leigh Johnsen and James P. McClure,

Senior Associate Editors

Holly Byers Ochoa, Associate Editor

Kathleen Norman, Assistant Editor

The Kent State University Press

KENT, OHIO, AND LONDON, ENGLAND

Library of Congress Catalog Card Number 93-16217
ISBN 0-87338-618-3
Manufactured in the United States of America

07 06 05 04 03 02 01 00 99 98 5 4 3 2 1

Publication of this book has been supported in part by a grant from the National Historical Publications and Records Commission.

Library of Congress has cataloged volume 1 of this series as follows:

Library of Congress Cataloging-in-Publication Data
Chase, Salmon P. (Salmon Portland), 1808–1873.
The Salmon P. Chase Papers / John Niven, editor ; James P. McClure, senior associate editor ; Leigh Johnsen, associate editor ; William M. Ferraro, Steve Leikin, assistant editor[s].
p. cm.
Includes bibliographical references and index.
Contents: v. 1 Journals, 1829–1872
ISBN 0-87338-472-5 (cloth : alk. paper) ∞
1. Chase, Salmon P. (Salmon Portland), 1808–1873—Archives. 2. United States—Politics and government—1849–1877—Sources. 3. Legislators—United States—Archives. 4. Judges—United States—Archives. 5. United States. Congress. Senate—Archives. 6. Governors—Ohio—Archives. I. Niven, John. II. Title.
E415.6.C48 1993
977.1'03'092—dc20 93-16217

British Library Cataloging-in-Publication data are available.

JOHN NIVEN (1921–1997)

The publication of volume 5 of *The Salmon P. Chase Papers* concludes a distinguished and valuable scholarly enterprise. Sadly, John Niven, the series editor, died while the final volume was in press and even while he was researching a collective biography of Lincoln's cabinet. Professor Niven received his Ph.D. from Columbia University in 1954. As a student of Allan Nevins it is not surprising that his scholarly interest focused on the Civil War era and the writing of biography, most notably studies of Gideon Welles, Martin Van Buren, John C. Calhoun, and Salmon P. Chase. He also wrote *Connecticut for the Union* (1965) and *The Coming of the Civil War* (1989). Stepping outside the Civil War field, and perhaps reflecting his World War II service as a naval officer, he wrote *The American President Lines and Its Forebears, 1848–1984: From Paddle Wheelers to Container Ships* (1986). As a long-time professor of history at the Claremont Graduate School, he was a dedicated guide and mentor to a generation of students. He also enlisted the services of the editorial staff, who contributed so much to the success and value of the *Chase Papers* both in the microfilm and print editions. John Niven served the profession well in other areas, including a term as president of the Pacific Coast Branch of the American Historical Association. His wit and wisdom brightened many conferences and convention halls, and his passing is regretted by colleagues and friends.

John T. Hubbell
Director
The Kent State University Press

Contents

Acknowledgments

THE WORK NECESSARY to prepare this volume has of course involved more people than just the editors listed on the title page. In particular, an excellent group of students at Claremont Graduate University helped bring the volume to completion. Our thanks to John Walker, who verified texts of letters, researched annotation, and worked on various aspects of the volume; to Michael Vanderlan, Laura Pierce, and Dorran Boyle, who performed research and other tasks; and, for transcription or proofing of letters printed in this volume, to Scott Birrell, Maria Baglien, Peg Lamphier, Nora Farabaugh, Heather Wilson, Dorcas Hawker, Laura Morrow, and Krista Caufman.

Preparation of this volume was supported by: Claremont Graduate University; the National Endowment for the Humanities (NEH), an independent federal agency; and the National Historical Publications and Records Commission (NHPRC), a branch of the National Archives.

Michael Meier, research archivist of the NHPRC, assisted us with research questions and in obtaining illustrations for the volume. Edwin Hoyt graciously allowed us to reproduce pictures drawn by his grandmother, Janet Chase Hoyt. At Claremont Graduate University, Carol B. Gamble, Director of Budget and Business Affairs, has been of particular aid in the management of the project; and Jack Miles, former Director of the Humanities Center, went out of his way to locate funds for the support of graduate student assistants during the 1996–97 academic year. For their tenacity and patience, we are also grateful to the staff of the interlibrary loan office at Honnold Library of the Claremont Colleges and to the reference and government documents librarians of the colleges' libraries. Similar help came from staff at the genealogical research library of the Church of Jesus Christ of Latter-day Saints in Upland, California, and the Huntington Library in San Marino. Kenneth Wolf, professor of history at Pomona College, helped us make sense of a Latin phrase. Our appreciation also to Kimberlee Gillis-Bridges and the Writing Center of Claremont Graduate University for providing a key link in the transfer of computer files. Beverly Wilson Palmer at Pomona College has continued to be our valued colleague in historical editing. And as always we owe thanks to Linda Cuckovich, Joanna Hildebrand Craig, John Hubbell, Julia Morton, Will Underwood, and others at The Kent State University Press.

Chronology

1865 Lincoln's second inauguration (March)

Robert E. Lee and Joseph E. Johnston surrender last major Confederate armies; Lincoln assassinated; Andrew Johnson sworn into office (April)

Federal troops capture Jefferson Davis; Andrew Johnson issues proclamation of amnesty and authorizes Reconstruction in North Carolina (May)

Chase travels in former states of Confederacy (May–July)

Thirteenth Amendment becomes law, outlawing slavery throughout United States (December)

1866 Supreme Court strikes down "ironclad" oath in *Cummings v. Missouri* and *Ex parte Garland* (both in January) and *Garesche v. Missouri* (April)

Congress overrides Andrew Johnson's veto of the Civil Rights Act and recommends extension of national rights through passage of Fourteenth Amendment (April)

Andrew Johnson declares insurrection at end and restores civilian government throughout United States (August)

In re Turner, authored by Chase on circuit, invalidates Maryland legislation that permits system of indentured servitude in violation of Thirteenth Amendment and Civil Rights Act of 1866 (October)

In *Ex parte Milligan,* Supreme Court releases civilians imprisoned on suspicion of treason during Civil War, reaffirming force of habeas corpus (issued formally in December)

1867 Over Andrew Johnson's veto, Congress passes Tenure of Office Act, First Reconstruction Act, and Second Reconstruction Act (March)

Horace Greeley and others post $100,000 bond for Jefferson Davis (May)

Chase begins to hold circuit court in southern states (June)

Congress enacts Third Reconstruction Act over Andrew Johnson's veto (July)

Andrew Johnson defies Tenure of Office Act, dismissing Edwin M. Stanton as secretary of war (August)

1868 Congress passes Fourth Reconstruction Act (March)

Chase presides over impeachment trial of Andrew Johnson (March–May)

In Chicago, Republicans nominate Ulysses S. Grant and Schuyler Colfax as presidential and vice-presidential candidates (May)

Democratic national convention in New York denounces congressional reconstruction, considers Chase for presidential nomination, and selects Horatio Seymour and Frank P. Blair, Jr., as running mates; Fourteenth Amendment becomes law (July)

Democratic leaders contemplate Chase as replacement for Seymour (October)

Grant wins presidential election (November)

1869 Supreme Court dismisses charges of treason against Jefferson Davis (February)

William Sprague delivers controversial speeches on Senate floor, reveals strains in marriage with Kate Chase (March–April)

Supreme Court dismisses *Ex parte McCardle,* an appeal under habeas corpus, citing lack of jurisdiction; Chase declares Union "indestructible" in *Texas v. White* (April)

Chase purchases "Edgewood," estate on outskirts of Washington (September)

Ex parte Yerger, authored by Chase, extends Supreme Court's appellate jurisdiction (October)

1870 Chase writes majority opinion in *Hepburn v. Griswold,* denying Congress authority to require acceptance of greenbacks (February)

Fifteenth Amendment ratified, forbidding denial or abridgement of voting rights due to race (March)

Chase suffers stroke in New York (September)

1871 Chase's youngest daughter, Nettie, marries William Sprague Hoyt (March)

Knox v. Lee and *Parker v. Davis,* reverses *Hepburn v. Griswold,* declares Legal Tender Act of 1862 constitutional (May)

1872 In Cincinnati, delegates to Liberal Republican national convention reject Chase as presidential hopeful, nominate ticket comprised of Horace Greeley and Benjamin Gratz Brown (May)

Republican party names Ulysses S. Grant and Henry Wilson as running mates at national convention in Philadelphia (June)

Democratic national convention, meeting in Baltimore, accepts Liberal Republican nominees as presidential and vice-presidential candidates (July)

Grant wins reelection (November)

1873 In *Bradwell v. Illinois,* Chase dissents from Supreme Court decision that denies admission of female attorney to state bar (April)

Chase dies during visit to New York (May)

Introduction by John Niven

THIS VOLUME covers the period between Chase's nomination as chief justice of the U.S. Supreme Court on December 6, 1864, and his death in New York City on May 7, 1873. During these busy, tension-ridden years, Chase balanced his work on the Supreme Court with his never-ending quest for the presidency—a quest that would elude him. Thus, much of the correspondence involves politics and political issues.

For the Court and the nation, the transition from war to an uncertain peace posed a host of serious problems with few if any precedents that might serve as guides.

After Lee's surrender at Appomattox, and that of General Joseph E. Johnston's army at the Bennett House near Durham, North Carolina, most organized resistance came to an end. Chase had barely settled himself on the bench when John Wilkes Booth assassinated President Lincoln and Vice President Andrew Johnson became chief magistrate.

The hot war may have been at an end, but a cold war that had been smoldering between the executive branch and the Congress over the terms of peace began to flare up. A brief economic depression in 1866 sharpened the controversy as the Congress, driven by a radical faction of the dominant Republican party, challenged the new president on the burning issue of reconstructing the former Confederate states.

Mistakenly accounted an extreme radical in the popular mind, Chase sought to find a middle ground between presidential and congressional plans of Reconstruction. As head of the judicial branch in the nation's tripartite system of government, Chase was especially eager to brighten the public image of the court that the Dred Scott decision had tarnished; yet at the same time, he pursued career-long goals of equal rights for the more than three million African Americans, a vast majority of whom had been slaves.

During the war Chase's immediate objective had been the abolition of slavery everywhere in the nation. He applauded the Emancipation Proclamation but was troubled with the exemptions in that document. Lincoln had framed the proclamation as a war measure and had expressly stated where it would apply. The proclamation excluded those areas of the Confederacy that the Union army occupied, certain parishes of Louisiana, certain counties in Virginia, and the new state of West Virginia. The loyal slave states were exempted, though they were not specifically named. Soon after the proclamation took effect on January 1, 1863, Chase began urging the president to repeal the exemptions, but to no avail.[1] Despite Chase's continuing efforts in this regard, slavery would not be officially abolished throughout the nation until the ratification of the Thirteenth Amendment to the Constitution on December 18, 1865.

Before Lincoln's assassination, Chase was preparing himself for a fact-finding trip to the former rebellious slave states of the seaboard. Now, with President Johnson's approval, he visited coastal Virginia, North Carolina, the Sea Islands off the coasts of South Carolina and Georgia, Charleston, South Carolina, Florida, Cuba, and New Orleans. At various stopping places, he recorded his conversations with inhabitants and Union army commanders, and he made brief speeches to largely African-American audiences. In all, he sent seven lengthy letters to the president, which contained some of his observations on southern society, economy, and political views as well as his advice on Reconstruction. Because of space limitations the editors have selected only one of these letters to Johnson as an example.[2] The rest have been reprinted in Brooks D. Simpson et al., eds., *Advice After Appomattox: Letters to Andrew Johnson, 1865–1866: Special Volume No. I of the Papers of Andrew Johnson* (Knoxville, 1987).

Chase's views on Reconstruction had moved beyond the abolition of slavery to suffrage and other civil rights for the former bondsmen. But in the speeches he gave to his African-American audiences, he emphasized the practical aspects of emancipation. He advised his audiences and through them the entire adult African-American population to be industrious, to rely on education, whether formal or self-taught, and to be useful and productive members of their various communities. In short, if and when they were accorded a broad spectrum of civil rights, they could justify them and use them well.[3] Chase was criticized in the northern Democratic press for politicizing the Radical agenda on Reconstruction. His public speeches, however, were more paternalistic than partisan and were, if anything, quite traditional when measured against the social and economic standards of the day.

On his return to Washington, Chase revealed himself in his private correspondence to be closer to the congressional program of Reconstruction than his public utterances had indicated. In a letter to Senator Charles Sumner, he criticized Johnson's white-supremacist Reconstruction policy that relied primarily on loyalty to the Union. He thought it "a great mistake . . . a moral, political, & financial mistake." The people of the vanquished Confederacy, "were ready to accept, though of course reluctantly, universal suffrage."[4] As his correspondence with son-in-law William Sprague, Charles Sumner, John Sherman, and other political figures made plain, Chase considered that universal manhood suffrage was the key to Reconstruction policy. Recognizing, however, that such a goal had to be achieved through state action, he urged that the national government exert its power and influence to have the former Confederate states grant suffrage to all adult, male African Americans.[5]

Paradoxically, Chase adopted a more conservative stance in the advice he gave to the Joint Congressional Committee on Reconstruction, which was framing the Fourteenth Amendment. Chase's cautious position rested mainly on reducing the representation of those southern states that did not in their revised constitutions grant suffrage to their resident male African Americans. Later, when the committee and Congress adopted a much broader reduction of state power over civil rights and after their action had gained a favorable acceptance from the northern public, Chase supported the amendment. He hoped President Johnson would endorse it but was unable to persuade him to change his policy of opposition.[6]

When Chase tried unsuccessfully to mediate between a stubborn president and an increasingly radical Congress, he found himself and the Court faced with a series of politically charged cases involving the status of military rule in the South and its consequent impact on civil rights in northern states and on war powers in general. In many of the cases that came before the Court during this politically chaotic period, when peace terms in effect were being thrashed out for the defeated Confederacy, Chase was careful not to confront Congress with what he deemed to be questions of a political nature. Even in *Ex parte Milligan* (1868), where he concurred with the majority of the Court in nullifying a trial by military commission when the civil process was operative, he based his opinion on the congressional process, specifically the Habeas Corpus Act of 1863.[7] Yet in the *Test Oath Cases,* he dissented from the majority that struck down a Missouri law that made an "ironclad oath" a condition for resuming the practice of certain professions.[8] Privately, however, in a letter to the Radical senator from Missouri, Charles D. Drake, he regretted "that the Constitution of Missouri requires the oath it does, especially from persons not directly connected in functions with Government."[9] In swearing to such an oath, a person had to declare that he had no prior record of supporting or serving the Confederacy.

If Chase took a radical stand in joining Justice Samuel Miller's dissent on the *Test Oath Cases,* he must be adjudged more conservative in opposing the trial of Jefferson Davis for treason. The trial would have to take place in Virginia, where the alleged treason was committed, and was thus on Chase's judicial circuit. A civilian judge, Chase refused to hear any case while Virginia was under military control. He avoided adjudication and, in fact, determined that Davis would not be tried. When Congress circumscribed the Court's appellate jurisdiction, Chase convinced his colleagues in the *McCardle* case (1869) that it would not be appropriate at this time to challenge the legislation. But a year later in *Ex parte Yerger,* he persuaded the Court to defend its appellate jurisdiction.[10]

Chase's opinions on the circuit bench also underlined a drift toward a moderate stance on Reconstruction. Yet in a case that came before him on his circuit court duties, which included Maryland, Chase demonstrated that he would resist any incursion of state power that discriminated against former slaves in labor contracts. The case, *In re Turner* (1867), dealt with an apprenticeship contract binding an African-American, female minor that did not include certain benefits stipulated in apprenticeship for whites. To Chase that was a clear violation of the law. In a broad definition of civil rights, he stated that they were guaranteed by American citizenship and conferred by the Emancipation Proclamation, the Thirteenth Amendment, and the recently enacted Civil Rights Act on all former slaves irrespective of race or previous condition of servitude.[11]

The plaintiff did not appear, and in fact had relinquished his interest in the contract. Chase granted the petition for habeas corpus, thus releasing the apprentice from her obligation. Since there were no grounds for appeal to the Supreme Court, Chase failed to have his opinion debated at the highest judicial level and, as he had hoped, made the law of the land. A century later the Court in a civil rights case did just that in *Jones v. Alfred H. Mayer Co.* (1968), basing its conclusion on virtually all the points Chase had made.[12]

Chase's role as presiding officer in the impeachment trial of President Andrew Johnson was an important factor in Johnson's acquittal, but it cast Chase solidly and openly as a political moderate. During the impeachment trial he corresponded with such Democratic party leaders as Alexander Long, formerly a virulent antiwar congressman, and John D. Van Buren, a New York lawyer close to Democratic party leaders in the Empire State.[13] Despite his record as a Republican party stalwart, Chase was building support for the Democratic presidential nomination in 1868. His daughter, Kate Chase Sprague, acted as his campaign manager at the Democratic convention in New York City, but she and her coworkers were unable to prevail. New York governor Horatio Seymour was nominated for president and Frank Blair, at the time a bitter political enemy of Chase, for vice president. Chase lost much of his political credibility by his unsuccessful campaign. The harsh partisan attack on him, an attack that accused him of gross political apostacy, is seen in Theodore Tilton's scorching editorial entitled "A Folded Banner," in the April 16, 1868, issue of the popular religious paper the *Independent.*

To Chase, these attacks were unwarranted. Anyone who examined carefully his political past could see plainly that he had associated himself with the Democracy between 1849 and 1855 on almost all issues except slavery and its extension into the territories. What he had tried to do, he asserted, was to eliminate the slavery taint from the party of Jefferson and Jackson.[14] Chase's stand in 1868 would be in many respects the political core of the Liberal Republican movement of 1872; and, certainly, Chase's court decisions after the 1868 election reflect his states'-rights, hard-money, free-trade philosophy—all basic principles of the Democratic party since the Jackson administration.

Chase's opinion in the famous case of *Texas v. White* (1869) illustrated his political philosophy. There he sought an equilibrium between state and national power that equated civil rights for the blacks within the federal union.[15] In *Hepburn v. Griswold* (1870), he again adumbrated long-held monetary views that an exclusive specie basis for the national currency was essential, despite the circulation of over $400 million in greenback currency that he had supported as U.S. secretary of the Treasury during the war. And he managed to convince a majority of the Court to accept his hard-money views. The advent of two new justices to the Court with less restrictive monetary opinions formed a majority that overturned the *Hepburn* case, much to Chase's extreme disgust.[16]

Chase wrote no opinion in the *Slaughter House Cases* (1873), which moved the thrust of the Fourteenth Amendment toward states' policing powers. But in siding with the minority in that case, he supported an absolute, not relative, application of the amendment.[17]

By now Chase was a sick man. He suffered a crippling stroke in 1870. The burden of overwork and concern about the failing marriage of his daughter and her husband, William Sprague, had undermined his health. Sprague had become increasingly addicted to drink and indulged in affairs with other women. Nor had the high-spirited Kate spared her husband's feelings. Chase sought vainly to heal the breach, but well before he died Chase knew that the marriage from which he had expected so much could not be maintained.

Even his deeply felt concern for suffrage and other civil rights for African Americans seemed in jeopardy after the *Slaughter House Cases* shifted the emphasis of the Fourteenth Amendment to the states and away from the federal government.

This then, the last volume of Chase's papers, chronicles a tragic conclusion to a turbulent career, during which—for a quarter of a century—Salmon P. Chase was a towering figure on the American scene. A driven person, his basic principles were in the forefront of public morality, but sadly they never achieved permanence during his lifetime.

It was not so much his financial policies during the war (though they were crucial to ensure victory), nor his record as chief justice of the

United States that constituted his lasting contribution to the nation; rather, it was his stand against slavery and his insistence on equal rights before the law that became his most enduring monuments. *The North American Review,* in its April 1876 issue, almost three years after Chase's death, had it about right. "The impartial historian," said the *Review,* "will be compelled to award the largest measure of praise and glory to Mr. Chase, on the whole, as probably the wisest and most earnest of all of the workers against slavery in our country."[18] Although the documents represented in this volume deal primarily with politics and Reconstruction, the basic theme for the series, it seems to the editors, is best expressed in the preamble of the Constitution, the establishment of "a more perfect union." The framers were making a contemporary statement, but Chase and others of like mind accepted the phrase as a beginning in a timeless effort to improve the governance of the nation. Chase's career exemplifies his efforts to elevate and redefine the concept of freedom. He advanced the process toward a goal where all citizens irrespective of their racial or ethnic origin would enjoy freedom and protection under the law.

1. Roy P. Basler, ed., *The Collected Works of Abraham Lincoln,* 9 vols. (New Brunswick, N.J., 1953–55), 5:433–36; *Chase Papers,* 1:428–29, 4:110, 119, 147, 202, 225.

2. Chase to Johnson, May 17, 1865 (below).

3. Ibid.

4. Chase to Sumner, June 25, 1865 (below).

5. Chase to Sprague, Sept. 6, 1865; Chase to Sherman, Mar. 3, 1866 (both below); and Chase to Sumner, Oct. 20, 1865 (Chase Papers, Hist. Soc. of Pa.).

6. Chase to Stephen J. Field, Apr. 30, 1866; Chase to Jacob W. Schuckers, May 15, 1866 (both below).

7. 4 Wall. 132 (1866).

8. 4 Wall. 277 (1867).

9. Chase to Drake, Apr. 24, 1866 (below).

10. For *Ex parte McCardle* and *Ex parte Yerger,* see 6 Wall. 318 (1868) and 8 Wall. 85 (1869), respectively.

11. Harold M. Hyman, *The Reconstruction Justice of Salmon P. Chase:* In Re Turner *and* Texas v. White (Lawrence, Kansas, 1997); Bradley Tyler Johnson, ed., *Reports of Cases Decided by Chief Justice Chase in the Circuit Court of the United States Fourth Circuit . . . ,* intro. Ferne B. Hyman and Harold M. Hyman (New York, 1876; reprint, 1972), 157–61.

12. 392 U.S. 409 (1968).

13. Chase to Long, Apr. 8, 19, 1868; Chase to Van Buren, Mar. 25, Apr. 5, 1868 (all below).

14. Chase to William S. Rosecrans, Aug. 16, 1869 (below).

15. 7 Wall. 700 (1869).

16. For *Hepburn v. Griswold:* 8 Wall. 603 (1870). *Knox v. Lee* and *Parker v. Davis,* which reversed *Hepburn,* are published at 12 Wall. 457 (1871), and discussed in *Chase Papers,* 1:668–69.

17. Richard L. Aynes, "Constructing the Law of Freedom: Justice Miller, The Fourteenth Amendment, and the *Slaughter-House Cases,*" *Chicago Kent Law Review* 70 (1994): 627–88; 16 Wall. 273 (1870).

18. Isaac F. Redfield, "Chief Justice Chase," *North American Review* 251 (Apr. 1876): 339.

Editorial Procedures

THIS VOLUME brings to conclusion an edition that presents all of Salmon P. Chase's journals (in volume 1) and selected letters from his correspondence (volumes 2–5). Volume 5 covers a much broader chronological span than volumes 3 and 4, which printed selections of the very dense correspondence from Chase's service as secretary of the Treasury. The structure of the edition—with one book devoted to Chase's correspondence through 1857 (volume 2), most of the pages of two volumes documenting the period 1861–64 (volumes 3 and 4), and one volume covering the final eight and a quarter years of Chase's life (volume 5)—reflects the actual quantities of correspondence surviving from the major phases of his career. During his tenure as chief justice, Chase tended not to write many or long letters concerning cases before the Supreme Court, and his correspondence was considerably less dense than when he oversaw the Treasury during the Civil War. By far his most active period of correspondence represented in this book was the year 1868, when politics occupied much of his attention.

After the Civil War, Chase continued to use letterpress copies as a means of retaining files of the letters he wrote. In preparing this volume, the editors have at times had to rely on letterpress copies as the best or only representations of Chase's letters. During the postwar period Chase also used clerical assistance, most notably that provided by Eugene L. Didier in 1869–70, by David Demarest Lloyd in 1871–72, and, on a fill-in basis when Chase needed him and he was available, by Jacob Schuckers. These men, all of whom became published writers, acted as Chase's scribes and personal secretaries just as Schuckers and others—most notably Homer Plantz—had done as Treasury clerks during the war.

The stroke Chase suffered at the age of sixty-two afflicted his correspondence along with his flesh. For months after the paralytic attack in August 1870, he virtually ceased to write in his own hand. During his recuperation the infirm chief justice doggedly maintained his correspondence by dictation, applying a palsied signature to letters written out by a secretary.[1]

Gradually during 1871, Chase regained the strength and motor control needed to write his own letters. He recognized, however, that his writing betrayed the devastating effects of the stroke. "You see by my handwriting that I am not my old self," he confessed to John Work Garrett in March. "My weakness makes me write very slowly," he noted to Flamen Ball, his former law partner; yet "I flatter myself that my letters are more plainly written" as well as "fewer & shorter."[2] Even as his hand lost, with time, much of the shaking evident in the first letters he scrawled after the paralysis, his script retained a markedly tight quality. As Lloyd put it, after the stroke Chase's handwriting "was shorn of its curves." The resulting script was "plain and heavy, . . . very condensed and minute." It stood in contrast to an earlier handwriting that, while sometimes difficult to read, was in Lloyd's opinion "peculiarly elastic, delicate, and almost fanciful."[3]

After the stroke, fatigue—a new factor for Chase as a letter writer—influenced both the quality of his handwriting and his ability to compose long letters. "I think of much I should like to write," he confided to a friend late in 1872. "But it costs more labor than formerly & takes more time, and I have at present so little of the latter article."[4] Still, he was as dependent as ever on written correspondence to maintain relationships with friends, family, political allies, and professional colleagues. Working under the new conditions imposed by the stroke, he continued to write and receive letters on private and public affairs until his death in the spring of 1873.

TEXTUAL PROCEDURES

Our aim has been to reproduce the contents of each letter as its author intended it to be read by the recipient. For practical more than philosophical reasons, we do not indicate if words were interlineated or overwritten, nor reproduce text that was struck through or erased in the manuscript. In those unusual cases in which textual changes are of particular interest, we have reported the emendations in explanatory notes. Readers interested in the specific visual appearance of a letter or in the details of an author's emendations during composition, will want to consult the original manuscript or a facsimile on microfilm.

Uncertain readings, whether of portions of words or entire phrases, are shown in the same typeface as other text, but are enclosed in square brackets. The same style of bracket, if enclosing italic type, signals a message from the volume's editors, often relating to illegible text, such as [*illeg.*] or [*torn*]. Any square brackets found in the original documents are reproduced here as ⁅ ⁆ to distinguish them from the brackets introduced by the editors.

Spelling, capitalization, and punctuation are transcribed as they appear in the original documents. All abbreviations have been retained, and if any require explanation it is provided in explanatory notes. Superscript characters have been brought down to the line, with any mark that appears under them in the original shown here as a period. No punctuation has been supplied: if a mark of punctuation appears by itself in square brackets, it means the reading is uncertain, not that the editors have added the punctuation. In placing punctuation inside or outside of quotation marks we have tried to follow the manuscripts. If the original is ambiguous in such a case, we follow the rule for that mark of punctuation given in *The Chicago Manual of Style*. In Chase's day, clerks often placed opening quotation marks at the beginning of each line of a quoted passage. In such cases we show only the quotation marks at the beginning and end of the passage. Paragraphing has been retained as in the original manuscripts.

Words underlined in the manuscripts are printed in italic type. If underlined by more than one stroke, they appear here in small capitals. We follow the manuscripts in rendering signatures, including punctuation within them, but use small capital letters to set them off from the letters' texts. We have employed a virgule with space on either side, / , to indicate any spot where a sentence appears to end at the right edge of a manuscript page without punctuation or a paragraph break. Any ellipsis points in a transcription are part of the source text and have not been inserted by this volume's editors. Transcriptions from printed sources follow the originals except that signatures to letters from printed sources are rendered in the same standardized form used for manuscript originals. We do not attempt to reproduce all features of the typography or layout of printed documents or letterhead stationery.

A title heading at the top of each document indicates the letter's receiver (if Chase wrote it) or its author. Also at the head of each letter, a source note states the type of document, the collection and library in which the manuscript resides, and the reel and frame number where a facsimile may be found in the selective microfilm edition of Chase's papers (identified in source notes and other annotation as *micro*).[5] The word *autograph* in a source note means that the original letter is in its author's own handwriting.

ANNOTATION

Annotation to a document takes the form of numbered notes that follow the letter's text. The notes contain citations for sources of the information contained in them. We have reduced the bulk of these citations by using easily recognized abbreviations in citing manuscript repositories, including "Collec." for Collection, "Lib." for Library, "L.C." for Library of Congress, and "Hist. Soc. of Pa." for the Historical Society of Pennsylvania. Printed sources referred to more than once are cited in full at their first appearance and also in the bibliography. The latter contains, in addition, a list of certain frequently cited items, such as city directories and the *Dictionary of American Biography,* that are given in abbreviated form throughout the notes. Citations to printed reports of U.S. Supreme Court cases include volume number and abbreviated name of the court reporter, for instance, 8 Wall., the page on which the report begins, and the year of the decision (in parentheses). Biblical references in the notes are to the King James version. We have used G. Blakemore Evans et al., eds., *The Riverside Shakespeare* (Boston, 1974), for references to act, scene, and line numbers in the plays of William Shakespeare.

We have attempted to identify people who are mentioned in the letters but have not been identified in previous volumes. By design these identifications are succinct, intended not to provide a complete biography but to establish an individual's identity. In the index, boldface volume and page references point the reader to identifications that have appeared in earlier volumes.

For publication data about books and other printed sources, the editors have used, without citation in the notes, *The National Union Catalog: Pre-1956 Imprints,* 754 vols. (London, 1968–81); Winifred Gregory, ed., *American Newspapers, 1821–1936: A Union List of Files Available in the United States and Canada* (New York, 1936); Edna Brown Titus, ed., *Union List of Serials in Libraries of the United States and Canada,* 3d ed., 5 vols. (New York, 1965); *British Museum General Catalogue of Printed Books: Photolithographic Edition to 1955,* 263 vols. (London, 1965–66); and the databases of the Online Computer Library Center (OCLC) and the Research Libraries Information Network (RLIN). We have utilized the helpful compilation, *Historical Biographical Dictionaries Master Index . . . ,* 1st ed. (Detroit, 1980), edited by Barbara McNeil and Miranda C. Herbert, in locating biographical information, as well as a variety of concordances to assist in finding quotations and literary allusions.

1. A few letters were even signed with Chase's name "per Eugene L. Didier," as documented by letterbook copies of correspondence to Dr. John G. Perry on September 28 and in the first ten days of October 1870 (Chase Papers, L.C.).

2. Chase to Garrett, Mar. 8, 1871 (Garrett Papers, L.C.); Chase to Ball, Mar. 22, 1871 (Chase Papers, Cinc. Hist. Soc.). See also his April 20 letter to Gerrit Smith: "My handwriting, however, shews that I am not well physically" (Chase Papers, L.C.).

3. [David] Demarest Lloyd, "The Home-Life of Salmon Portland Chase," *The Atlantic Monthly* 22 (Nov. 1873): 528–29.

4. Chase to Whitelaw Reid, Dec. 26, 1872 (below).

5. John Niven, ed., James P. McClure, assoc. ed., and Patrick Delana, asst. ed., *The Salmon P. Chase Papers,* 43 reels with guide (Frederick, Md., 1987).

The Salmon P. Chase Papers

The Correspondence of Salmon P. Chase, 1865–1873

TO WILLIAM TECUMSEH SHERMAN

Autograph letter. William Tecumseh Sherman Papers, Library of Congress (*micro* 35:0512).

Washington Jany. 2, 1865.

Dear General[1]

In common with all loyal men I partake the gratitude and admiration inspired by the services of your army & yourself. My hopes of you at the beginning were great. They have been more than realized; and I trust that the country's debt to you is yet to be largely augmented.

But there is one feature of your military administration which gives pain to many, and, I think I perform the part of a true friend & infringe no rule of propriety in mentioning it to you.

I refer to the apparent harshness of your action towards the blacks. You are understood to be opposed to their employment as soldiers, and to regard them as a sort of pariahs, almost without rights. In your first report after opening communications with Gen Foster you spoke of the necessity of ridding your camp of the surplus negroes, mules &c.[2] I do not remember the exact words; but I do remember the regret I felt that an expression classing men with cattle found place in a paper, which cannot fail to be historical.

In my judgment negroes as men have the same natural rights as other men. The President has, by proclamation and as a military measure, enfranchised those who were held as slaves in the rebel states. The Attorney General, in a well considered opinion, has asserted the citizenship of those who are free.[3] And it seem to me not doubtful that, in the political reorganization of the states in insurrection, political, as well as natural, rights, must be conceded to a portion at least of the colored population. For myself, indeed, I freely say that I see no reason why all citizens may not vote subject only to such restrictions as are applicable to all irrespective of color. I feel sure that the justice and good sense of the People will at least demand the right of suffrage for all who are educated and all who have borne arms in the service of the Union.

Without this at least, I see no security against attempted reenslavement, against the most inhuman & cruel discriminations & treatment of the colored people as a class, or, indeed, against the ascendancy of the disloyal elements in the insurgent states, as soon as the military pressure shall be removed.

Doubtless you have thought much on these subjects. But may I not ask you to take them again into your consideration. May I not ask you especially to avoid any appearance of harshness or severity which does not represent or express your real sentiments & convictions. You have a great & most responsible position. Your example, for good or evil, will be followed by officers of lower character & less discretion. Your action will influence largely the destinies of multitudes. It is my anxious wish that it may command for you the lasting gratitude of all good men, and the approval of Him who is no "respecter of persons."[4]

With the sincerest respect & esteem,

Yours very truly
S P Chase

Maj. Gen. W. T. Sherman.

1. Maj. Gen. Sherman was assigned command over the military division of the Mississippi in March 1864. As supreme commander of Union forces in the West, he had recently finished his march through Georgia. In 1866, Sherman succeeded Ulysses S. Grant as lieutenant-general and from 1869 to 1883 served as commanding general of the U.S. Army. E. B. Long, *The Civil War Day by Day: An Almanac, 1861–1865* (Garden City, N.Y., 1971), 474; *DAB,* 17:95–97.

2. Brig. Gen. John Gray Foster commanded the Department of the South. Sherman first made personal contact with Foster on December 13, 1864, to discuss the impending attack on Savannah. "We have not lost a wagon on the trip," he wrote to Edwin M. Stanton the same day, "but have gathered a large supply of negroes, mules, horses, &c., and our teams are in far better condition than when we started. My first duty will be to clear the army of surplus negroes, mules, and horses." *DAB,* 6:550; Sherman to Stanton, Dec. 13, 1861, in *OR,* ser. 1, v. 44:701; Long, *Civil War Day by Day,* 609–10.

3. Chase refers to the Emancipation Proclamation, issued by Abraham Lincoln in its final form on January 1, 1863, and to an opinion from Attorney General Edward Bates written at Chase's request in November 1862. Chase to Bates, Sept. 24, 1862 (Attorney General's Papers, Gen. Recs., Dept. of Justice, Nat. Arch.); Bates to Chase, Nov. 29, 1862 (Letters Rec. from Exec. Officers, Gen. Recs. Treasury Dept., Nat. Arch.); Long, *Civil War Day by Day,* 306.

4. Acts 10:34.

TO SUSAN WALKER

Autograph letterbook copy. Chase Papers, Historical Society of Pennsylvania (*micro* 35:0508).

Washington Jany 2, 1865

My dr frd.[1]

Yr. very kind letter came a few days ago & gave me real pleasure. I thank you sincerely for yr. cordial words & I earnestly pray that I may be enabled to fulfil in some measure at least the hopes & expectations which so many seem to entertain.

I cant. agree with you on one point. You know what that is. My deliberate conviction is the other way. If I could think otherwise I shd.; but, however I may have wavered & sometimes acted my thoughts have always settled back into the firm assurance that there is but one right way & that there are no real exceptions.

Since I recd. your letter my dear Sister Helen has exchanged mortality for immortality. God was gracious in restoring to her so much of health & strength after that first terrible blow; but she never fully recovered.[2] The paralysis never wholly left the side which received the shock; though she cd. ride a little, walk a little, attend to some household duties, & enjoy the society of her family & friends. Had she been in ordinary health her constitution wd. probably have resisted the disease—inflammation of the lungs wh. at last proved fatal. She was attacked about a fortnight ago & died last Friday morning. I have recd. no letter since her death—only a brief telegram on that sad day—"Helen entered into rest this morning at half past one.

Her departure leaves me alone as that of your honored brother left you alone. There were eleven of us. One died in infancy—all the rest reached manhood & womanhood.[3] I alone remain waiting Gods time. May He enable me to wait with good hope.

You ask who wrote the lines I quoted in my last. You say they seem to haunt me. I thought you wd. recognize them as Tennyson's. They are from one of those beautiful little poems which make up In Memoriam.[4] I have read them a great deal & once committed several of them to memory. I suppose fr. yr. remark that I have quoted the verse in some former letter as well as in my last. It wd. not be strange. The sentiments it expresses have been much in my mind.

I feel pretty well & strong considering I am so close to my fifty eighth year. Eleven days more & I shall have completed fifty seven. But I live in more than the ordinary uncertainty of life. Several members of my family as you know have died very suddenly, & I cannot help feeling that I may be called in like manner. Ever since I was twenty years old I have thought something wrong about the region of the heart; &, although assured that there was no organic disease I have never been convinced that I was mistaken Latterly I think I perceive more certain indications. It may be there is no occasion for special uneasiness. It may be I shall reach the allotted term of three score & ten—now not remote, but it may be also that a year—a month—a week may bring the end of earth

It is natural that under these circumstances & left alone without brother or sister I shd. feel serious. But I do not wish to take any other views of my relations to time & eternity, to man & to God than I ought to take if I were sure to live a hundred years in uninterrupted health & vigor. In His sight "a *thousand* years are as one day;"[5] and I wd. fain be what He requires whether for one day or many years. I have always believed that the only way of life is through repentance and faith in Christ:

and while I mourn many deviations I cherish longings which encourage the hope that that I shall not finally lose it.

But I must not pursue these reflections. May God give you a happy new year & may all our new years be happy—& may the last—the unending year which we name Eternity, be the happiest of all

Sincerely your friend
S P Chase

1. Chase had known Walker since his settlement in Cincinnati and had practiced law with her brother, Timothy Walker, as a young man. The editors have inferred the letter's recipient based on similarities between its salutation and contents and those of a letter that Chase evidently wrote to Walker on March 17, 1865 (below), as well as its reference to events discussed in Chase to Walker, December 23, 1863, in *Chase Papers,* 4:224.

2. Chase's youngest sister, Helen Chase Walbridge, had suffered from paralysis since at least 1862. Henry Walbridge to Chase, June 5, 1862 (Chase Papers, L.C.).

3. One of Walker's brothers had evidently died in December 1863. Chase's siblings who survived childhood were, in order of birth: Hannah Ralston Whipple, Alexander Ralston, Abigail Corbet Colby, Dudley Heber, Janette Logan Skinner, Alice Jones Chase, Edward Ithamar, William Frederick, and Helen Chase Walbridge. Chase to Walker, Dec. 23, 1863, in *Chase Papers,* 4:224.

4. Alfred Tennyson, *In Memorium* (London, 1850).

5. 2 Pet. 3:8.

FROM WILLIAM TECUMSEH SHERMAN

Autograph letter on letterhead stationery. Chase Papers, Historical Society of Pennsylvania (*micro* 35:0534).

HEADQUARTERS, MILITARY DIVISION OF THE MISSISSIPPI,
In the Field, Savannah Jan 11 1865

Hon S. P. Chase.
Washington D.C.
My Dear Sir,

I feel very much flatterred by the notice you take of me, and none the less because you overhaul me on the negro question.[1] I meant no unkindness to the negro in the mere words of my hasty despatch announcing my arrival on the Coast. The only real failures in a military sense, I have sustained in my military administration have been the expeditions of Wm. Sooy Smith and Sturgis,[2] both resulting from their encumbering their columns with refugees. (negroes) If you can understand the nature of a military column in an enemys country, with its long train of wagons you will see at once that a crowd of negroes, men women and children, old & young, are a dangerous impediment.

On approaching Savannah I had at least 20000 negroes, clogging my roads, and eating up our substance.[3] Instead of finding abundance here I found nothing and had to depend on my wagons till I opened a way for vessels and even to this day my men have been on short rations and my horses are failing. The same number of white refugees would have been a military weakness. Now you know that military success is what the nation wants, and it is risked by the crowds of helpless negroes that flock after our armies. My negro constituents of Georgia would resent the idea of my being inimical to them, they regard me as a second Moses or Aaron.[4] I treat them as free, and have as much trouble to protect them against the avaricious recruiting agents of the New England States as against their former masters.[5] You can hardly realize this, but it is true. I have conducted to freedom & asylum hundreds of thousands and have aided them to obtain employment and homes. Every negro who is fit for a soldier and is willing I invariably allow to join a negro Regiment, but I do oppose and rightfully too, the *forcing* of negroes as soldiers. You cannot know the arts and devices to which base white men resort to secure negro soldiers, not to aid us to fight, but to get bounties for their own pockets, and to diminish their quotas at home. Mr Secretary Stanton is now here and will bear testimony to the truth of what I say.[6] Our Quarter master and Commissary can give employment to every negro (able bodied) whom we obtain, and he protests against my parting with them for other purposes, as it forces him to use my veteran white troops to unload vessels, and do work for which he prefers the negro.[7] If the President prefers to minister to the one idea of negro equality, rather than military success; which as a major [involves] the minor, he should remove me, for I am so constituted that I cannot honestly sacrifice the security and success of my army to any minor cause.

Of course I have nothing to do with the status of the negro after war. That is for the law making power, but if my opinion were consulted I would say that the negro should be a free man, but not put on an equality with the whites. My knowledge of them is practical, and the effect of equality is illustrated in the character of the mixed race in Mexico and South America. Indeed it appears to me that the right of suffrage in our Country should be rather abridged than enlarged.

But these are all matters subordinate to the issues of this war, which can alone be determined by war, and it depends on good armies, of the best possible material and best disciplined, and these points engross my entire thoughts.

With sincere respect & esteem
W. T. Sherman

Maj. Genl.

1. See Chase to Sherman, Jan. 2, 1865 (above).

2. On February 21, 1864, Confederate cavalry under Nathan Bedford Forrest defeated Union troops under Brig. Gen. William Sooy Smith (1830–1916) near Meridian, Mississippi. In the other battle, on June 10, 1864, Forrest routed Brig. Gen. Samuel Davis Sturgis at Brice's Crossroads, near Corinth, Mississippi. *DAB,* 17:367–68, 18:183; Long, *Civil War Day by Day,* 466–67, 519.

3. The siege of Savannah commenced on December 10, 1864. Long, *Civil War Day by Day,* 608, 613.

4. According to scripture, Moses and his older brother, Aaron (both 15th–13th century B.C.), led the Israelites out of Egypt in the Exodus. Geoffrey W. Bromiley, gen. ed.,

The International Standard Bible Encyclopedia, 4 vols. (Grand Rapids, Mich., 1982) 1:1–2; J. O. Thorne, ed., *Chambers's Biographical Dictionary,* rev. ed. (New York, 1969), 917.

5. Legislation of July 1864 permitted agents from the war-weary North to recruit soldiers in occupied regions of the South in order to fill state quotas. Sherman in particular detested the resulting system. Ira Berlin et al., eds., *Freedom: A Documentary History of Emancipation, 1861–1867,* ser. 2 (Cambridge, Eng., 1982), 76–78.

6. Edwin McMasters Stanton was secretary of war from 1862 to 1868. On December 20, 1869, the U.S. Senate confirmed Stanton's nomination as an associate justice of the Supreme Court, but he died shortly before taking his seat. *DAB,* 17:518–20.

7. Brevet Brig. Gen. Langdon Cheves Easton (1814–84) was Sherman's quartermaster from May 1864 to June 1865. *Appletons',* 2:292.

FROM GEORGE S. DENISON

Autograph letter on letterhead stationery. Chase Papers, Library of Congress (*micro* 35:0542).

Private

United States Custom House,
COLLECTOR'S OFFICE.
New Orleans, Jan. 13th 1865

My Dear Sir[1]

I have rec'd your letter of the 27th Dec. What you say of colored suffrage is doubtless correct, but it is difficult, if not impossible, to make these new Free State men who compose our Legislature, take the same view of it as you do. Of this matter I have fully spoken in previous letters.[2] Without being here you cannot easily understand how much these people have learned in regard to the colored man and his rights, and how much they have yet to learn.

When Gen. Banks[3] expressed himself to you as "decidedly in favor of the liberal extension of the right of suffrage to colored citizens"—he was doubtless sincere, but even he cannot soon remove the prejudices which the poor whites of the South have been acquiring during their whole lives. Only some strong political necessity will induce the Legislature to *extend* the right of suffrage, & if such extension was made a condition of the recognition of the State, it would probably be granted.

The inexpedient secession from the Free State movement, of Mr. Durant and his party, was very unfortunate.[4] I thought then & think now, that they should join with the others and control events as much as possible. But now instead of being able to do anything of consequence to the colored race, they have no voice.

I admire Mr. Durant and am sorry he is such a good hater. In speaking in a former letter, of Judge Whitaker as the only good man to be U.S. Judge, I did not think of Mr. Durant.[5] As you know them both however, it is not necessary for me to say more.

Gov. Hahn was elected last Monday, Senator for the term of six years from the 4th of next March,—as I said he would be.[6]

I learned from private sources—although it is not yet publicly known—that he has nominated for Chief Justice of the State, Judge Whitaker, & for Associate Justices; Heistand Ilsley & one other.[7] I know only Whitaker & Heistand—the others are from the country & have been confirmed by the Senate—but Whitaker & Heistand have not yet been confirmed. I think they will be however, although the Legislature pretend to have fears of their soundness on the Slavery question. The real reason of their hesitation is, that they wish to give these appointments into the hands of Gov. Wells when he comes into office,[8] for they perceive that there is a new power to disperse patronage, which they desire to propitiate.

Very Respectfully

Your Friend & Ob't Serv't
George S. Denison

Hon. S. P. Chase

1. Treasury special agent Denison, Chase's kinsman, held positions as a customs and internal revenue officer in New Orleans during the Civil War.

2. Chase's letter supported admission of senators and representatives from Louisiana to the U.S. Congress only after state legislators granted "the right of suffrage at least to colored soldiers & colored men who have sufficient intelligence to read." Chase continued: "Gen Banks has expressed himself to me as decidedly in favor of the liberal extension of the right of suffrage to colored citizens." Chase expressed similar sentiments in another letter to Denison on January 22. Chase to Denison, Dec. 27, 1864, Jan. 22, 1865 (Denison Papers, L.C.).

3. Nathaniel Prentice Banks, major general of volunteers, commanded U.S. troops in New Orleans, 1862–65, and represented Massachusetts in Congress, 1865–73. *DAB*, 1:578–80.

4. Thomas Jefferson Durant, a Louisiana attorney, and Benjamin F. Flanders led the radical faction of Louisiana's Free State party in opposition to moderates under Michael Hahn. The Radicals formally withdrew from the party's state nominating convention in New Orleans on February 1. Later in the year, Durant moved to Washington, D.C., where he pled regularly before the U.S. Supreme Court. Ibid., 5:543–44; *New York Times*, Feb. 2, 1864; Joel Gray Taylor, *Louisiana Reconstructed: 1863–1877* (Baton Rouge, 1974), 27–28.

5. John Smith Whitaker, formerly judge of New Orleans' Second District Court, was nominated chief justice of the state supreme court on January 10, but failed to win confirmation. *Biographical and Historical Memoirs of Louisiana . . .*, 2 vols. (Chicago, 1892), 2:451; *Journal of the Senate of the State of Louisiana* (New Orleans, 1864), 193, 194.

6. Owner of the New Orleans *Daily True Delta* and a former U.S. congressman, Georg Michael Decker Hahn had won election as governor of Louisiana in February 1864. Despite his recent victory, neither Hahn nor any other members of Louisiana's delegation took their seats in the Thirty-ninth Congress. *Bio. Dir. U.S. Cong.*, 180; *DAB*, 8:88.

7. The Louisiana senate had received nominations for Whitaker as well as New Orleans attorney Ezra Hiestand, John H. Ilsley of Ascension Parish, and Iberville Parish resident Zenon Labauve in executive session on January 10. The senate considered the nominations on January 12, but confirmed only Ilsley and Labauve. *Journal of the Senate*, 193, 194; Peyton McCrary, *Abraham Lincoln and Reconstruction: The Louisiana Experiment* (Princeton, 1978), 168.

8. Lieutenant Governor James Madison Wells became governor of Louisiana when Michael Hahn resigned in March 1865 and retained the post until June 1867. *DAB*, 19:642.

TO WENDELL PHILLIPS

Autograph letter. bMS Am 1953 (398), Houghton Library, Harvard University (*micro* 35:0587).

Private

Washington, Feby. 7, 1865.

My dear Sir,[1]

I have often regretted that talents so rare as yours were not devoted to more practical uses than that of the rostrum. I have wished for you at the bar, in legislative councils, in Administrations, & wherever else the hard work of reform was to be done; and have been, sometimes, not a little provoked by what seemed ungenerous & was unjust criticism upon those who were doing that work—most provoked, of course, when these criticisms were directed against me!

But a few days ago I read your speech in New York—your grand plea for universal suffrage and was forced to doubt whether, after all, you had not chosen your sphere of usefulness most wisely.[2] I felt, when reading your words as I did when I first read Milton's "Speech for the Liberty of Unlicenced Printing," which the "world will not willingly let die."[3] My heart said Amen to each glowing sentence, and bid me write you my earnest thanks for what you so nobly did.

I have had some trouble in bringing myself to do so; fearing misconception of my motives. But somehow I feel as if I must & so I write. Pray accept my thanks as those of one who feels most profoundly the absolute necessity of the action you recommend.

Since reconstruction was first thought of I have never doubted that a constitutional guaranty of universal suffrage or at least of suffrage for all loyal blacks who might be of sufficient education or had been in the national military service ought to be made an indispensable condition of the readmission of any rebel state to participation in the National Government. My own conviction is that universal is better & more practicable than any kind of limited suffrage, though I would not insist on the former, if it endangered the securing of the latter.

You will necessarily infer that the nominal state organizations of Louisiana & Arkansas, which exclude the mass of the loyal people from suffrage because of their complexions are exceedingly unsatisfactory to me. I have not ceased to remonstrate with our friends against their recognition as properly reconstituted states. To write or talk in this sense to somebody & to all I could, every day since this question became imminent, has seemed to me a duty.

It was with peculiar pleasure, therefore, that I read your brave defence of equal rights, guaranteed by equal laws, enacted under universal suffrage. It is most gratifying to observe the steady & rapid progress of opinion in the same direction. A few days ago I was in Baltimore, surrounded by some of the most able & influential young men in Maryland and was delighted by their general concurence in my views / There is a manifest change going on in Congress, greatly helped by the proposed Constitutional amendment.[4]

You may be of good courage therefore. Not many months will pass, I believe, before all yokes will be broken from all necks and universal suffrage will be recognized in the Constitution of every restored State as the only sure & perpetual safeguard against a new Slavery.

Yours very Truly
S P Chase

Wendell Phillips Esq

1. Phillips was a reformer and antislavery leader.

2. Speaking at the Cooper Institute on December 27, Phillips had criticized Louisiana's unwillingness to enfranchise former slaves before seeking readmission into the Union. "You cannot make the benevolence of the upper classes educate the lower," he asserted; "You can never educate four millions of blacks until you make the whites tremble at their power, by giving them the ballot." *New York Times,* Dec. 28, 1864.

3. John Milton, *Areopagitica; A Speech of Mr. John Milton for the Liberty of Unlicenc'd Printing, to the Parliament of England* (London, 1644). Chase's quotation paraphrases part of book one in Milton's *The Reason of Church-Government Urg'd against Prelaty . . .* (London, 1641). *Complete Prose Works of John Milton,* 8 vols. (New Haven, 1953), 1:810.

4. Chase evidently refers to a dinner party that he attended in Baltimore on the evening of January 31. Although passed by the U.S. Senate on April 8, the Thirteenth Amendment did not take effect until December 18, after ratification by the states. *Chase Papers,* 1:520; Long, *Civil War Day by Day,* 482, 696.

TO FRANCIS LIEBER

Letter in clerk's hand, signed by Chase. LI 1065, The Huntington Library (*micro* 35:0594).

Washington, Feb. 14th. 1865.

My dear Sir,[1]

I thank you for the copy you were kind enough to send me, of your letter to Senator Morgan. Allow me also, to thank you for your congratulations upon my appointment.[2] I think I may say without impropriety, that the cheers given by your *whole* household, for Rhode Island were worthily bestowed.

Upon matters which cannot possibly present a question for adjudication by the Courts, I feel as free to express my opinion as ever.

I have taken great interest in the extension of the right of suffrage to all Citizens, without distinction of color, in the States to be reorganized. I have no doubt that this great object can be attained through the loyal men of those States, if properly encouraged and supported by the National Government. It is within my knowledge that prominent citizens among them were very desirous, as a matter of self protection, to have the right of suffrage so extended; and I fear, that military interposition has done no good.

It is clear that, involved as the National Government is, in a civil war with the Rebel States, it can, and must, make peace upon some terms; & these terms must be agreed upon between the National Government and that body of citizens in each Rebel State, whom that Government is willing to recognize as competent to act for the State. One of these terms may be, and, in my judgment, should be, universal suffrage.

The Constitutional Amendment which you suggest, and which, I perceive, has already been introduced into Congress, would probably effect the same object.[3] One difficulty would be that of getting the necessary two-thirds in Congress; another, and even greater one, that of getting the necessary three-fourths of the States. Those who hold the right of suffrage already, will require a good-deal of education before they will freely share it with those, whom they regard as of an inferior class.

In the other way, as a condition of peace and as a measure of protection to all loyalists, white and black, in reconstituted states, it would be comparatively easy.

I have no time to write at length, or even with my own hand, and I fear, that, to one less clear-sighted than yourself, what I say would be uninteligible. You will, at once, apprehend my whole meaning, however imperfectly expressed.

With the greatest esteem & respect,

Yours very truly
S: P: CHASE

Dr. Francis Lieber
New York.

1. A noted legal scholar and doctor of philosophy, Lieber taught law at Columbia College in New York. *DAB,* 11:236–37.

2. Republican Edwin Denison Morgan represented New York in the U.S. Senate from 1863 to 1869. Lincoln nominated Chase as chief justice on December 6, and the U.S. Senate confirmed him later the same day. U.S. Senate, *Journal of the Executive Proceedings of the Senate of the United States* . . . (Washington, D.C., 1828–; reprint, New York, 1969), v. 14, pt. 1:1.

3. On February 6, Charles Sumner had proposed an amendment to the U.S. Constitution that, if ratified, would have based state representation in Congress on the number of males allowed to vote—rather than total population—and thus established an incentive for states to broaden the franchise. The Senate Judiciary Committee reported the proposal adversely on February 22. *Congressional Globe,* 38th Cong., 2d sess., 1864–65, 604, 980; *New York Times,* Feb. 10, 1865.

TO ABRAHAM LINCOLN

Autograph letter. Abraham Lincoln Papers, Library of Congress (*micro* 35:0632).

Washington, March 6, 1865.

My dear Sir,

I enclose the Circassian decision. An order or proclamation closing or restricting the ports will when military occupation is permanent, answer most of the purposes of blockade & be subject to no objection.

In the case of the Venice which I mentioned to you the Court held that the occupation of New Orleans must be considered as permanent from the 6th of May, on which day Gen. Butlers Proclamation was printed in the papers.[1]

As to Virginia I take the liberty of suggesting that it may be well that any Proclamation declaring the State no longer in insurrection should recite the fact of a continuous loyal State Government & confine the effect of the Proclamation to the counties acknowledging that Government & regularly represented in the Loyal Legislature, or hereafter acknowledging it & being so represented.[2]

Except one from West Virginia no cases have been heard on appeal from the Courts of either District of Virginia since the rebellion.[3]

Yours most truly
S P Chase

The President.

1. On January 30, Chase had delivered his first opinion as chief justice in *The Circassian,* a case that appealed the seizure on May 4, 1862, of a neutral vessel bound for Confederate New Orleans. The decision sustained the capture even though federal forces had taken the city on May 1. Maj. Gen. Benjamin Franklin Butler of Massachusetts, U.S. commander at New Orleans, placed the city under martial law with an order prepared on the same day but not published until May 6. *The Venice,* handed down on February 27, affirmed a decision by the U.S. District Court for the Southern District of Florida to restore a neutral vessel loaded with Confederate cotton. Chase and Lincoln had evidently discussed both cases earlier in the day. Howard K. Beale, ed., *The Diary of Gideon Welles,* 3 vols. (New York, [1960]), 2:253–54; Charles Fairman, *Reconstruction and Reunion, 1864–88, Part One,* vol. 6. of Paul A. Freund, gen. ed., *The Oliver Wendell Holmes Devise History of the Supreme Court of the United States* (New York, 1971), 37–38; Long, *Civil War Day by Day,* 206; *New York Times,* May 14, 1862; 2 Wall. 135, 258 (1865).

2. Andrew Johnson reestablished federal authority in Virginia through presidential proclamation on May 9, 1865, but did not make the distinctions that Chase suggested. *Statutes at Large,* 13:777–78.

3. On February 27, the Supreme Court had decided *Harvey v. Tyler,* a West Virginia case regarding a disputed land title. Fairman, *Reconstruction and Reunion,* 34; 2 Wall. 328 (1865).

TO SUSAN WALKER

Letterpress copy of autograph letter. Chase Papers, Historical Society of Pennsylvania (*micro* 35:0620).

Washington March 1865

My dear friend[1]

Daily, since the adjournment of the Court has it been in my thought to write you;[2] and daily have I allowed some other matter to be done first: until today I resolve to allow *nothing* to interfere with my purpose.

My first sensation after the adjournment & that terrible three months strain was taken off was a sort of stupid vacuity—a sort of sense of nothing to do—half agreeable, half irksome.— This lasted only a day or two & then I came back to the reality—that there was much to do; though with some power now to vary the doing & avoid the painful monotony of hearing, reading, thinking & writing on the same class of subjects & in the same way, all the time—morning, noon, evening & night.

I don't want you to understand that, on the whole, my present work is disagreeable to me. I have found all the Judges kind & their good will has, I think, constantly increased, as they have understood me better.[3] And the appreciation of the little I have really, with all my work, accomplished, by the bar & by the public has been all that I could wish. I did not expect so much; for I felt the difficulties of my [untried] position. Its very elevation would make failure the more conspicuous. I am glad & thankful that I cannot be said to have failed thus far.

Now comes another part of my work as yet untried—the Circuit. Doubtless you understand that every Judge of the Supreme Court has what are called circuit duties to perform / The whole country is divided into Districts—two for example in Ohio, the northern & the southern; one in Indiana; three in New York; one in Each of the New England states & so on. These districts are arranged in Circuits; and some one Judge of the Supreme Court is required to hold, with the District Judge a court at least once a year in each District of each Circuit. The Circuit to which I am assigned consists of Virginia, North Carolina, Maryland & Delaware—the same, which was assigned to the late Chief Justice.[4] The existing rebellion will relieve me from holding any courts in either District of Virginia or North Carolina for the present, leaving to me Maryland & Delaware. I go to Maryland next week and am trying to get ready for it: and this just now gives me work enough—[5]

Gov. Sprague & his sister left us this morning going to Rhode Island. Kate, Nettie & I compose the present family: quite the old triangle.[6]

I am sorry you could not come to the inauguration: though there was nothing but a crowd to see. Every body was grieved by the sad misconduct of Andy Johnson.[7] In my mind grief was the predominant sentiment; for I honor him greatly as one who risked every thing for his convictions. There are few who do. He I think has the martyr spirit [—]& wd. die for his. I hope he will fully retrieve himself.

Do you go East this Summer? & when? & which way? I hope the doctor is doing as well as he could wish & Mrs Doctor is well & happy.

Sincerely your friend
S P Chase

1. The editors have inferred the recipient and date of this letter from similarities between its salutation and those of Chase to Walker, January 2, 1865 (above), and Chase to Walker, December 23, 1863, in *Chase Papers,* 4:224, placement of the original in the letterpress volume, and a diary entry of March 17, 1865, in *Chase Papers,* 1:522, which mentions correspondence written to Walker on that date.

2. The Supreme Court had adjourned on March 10. Fairman, *Reconstruction and Reunion,* 85.

3. At this time, nine other judges besides Chase sat on the Court: John Catron, Nathan Clifford, David Davis, Stephen Johnson Field, Robert Cooper Grier, Samuel Freeman Miller, Samuel Nelson, Noah Hayes Swayne, and James Moore Wayne. Ibid., 2–4.

4. Former chief justice Roger Brooke Taney had died on October 12, 1864, after nearly three decades on the U.S. Supreme Court. *DAB,* 18:289, 292.

5. Chase arrived in Baltimore on Saturday, April 1, to preside over the Fourth Circuit Court and returned to Washington, D.C., on Thursday, April 13. Fairman, *Reconstruction and Reunion,* 2; *Chase Papers,* 1:522–28.

6. Catharine ("Kate") Jane and Janet ("Nettie") were Chase's two surviving daughters. Kate had married textile magnate William Sprague, U.S. senator from Rhode Island on November 12, 1863. Nettie wed William Sprague Hoyt on March 23, 1871. Sprague's sister was Almira Sprague, who later became the wife of Thomas Arthur Doyle. *Chase Papers,* 1:522; *New York Times,* Mar. 24, 1871; *DAB,* 17:473.

7. As chief justice, Chase administered the oath of office at Lincoln's second inauguration on March 4. Vice President Andrew Johnson, who held office as president from 1865 to 1869, delivered an incoherent speech at the ceremony that betrayed the effects of too much alcohol. *DAB,* 10:84, 88; *Daily National Intelligencer,* Mar. 6, 1865; Long, *Civil War Day by Day,* 647.

TO ABRAHAM LINCOLN

Autograph letter. Abraham Lincoln Papers, Library of Congress (*micro* 35:0697).

Baltimore, April 11, 1865.

My dear Sir,[1]

When all mankind are congratulating you, one voice, heard or not, is of little account; but I add mine.[2]

I am very anxious about the future: and most about the principles which are to govern reconstruction: for as these principles are sound or unsound so will be the work & its results.

You have no time to read a long letter; nor have I time to write one; so I will be brief.

And first as to Virginia.

By the action of every branch of the Government we are committed to the recognition & maintenance of the State organization of which Governor Pierpont is the head.[3] You know all the facts & recapitulation would be useless. There will be a pressure for the recognition of the rebel organization on condition of profession of loyalty. It will be far easier and wiser, in my judgment, to stand by the loyal organization already recognized.

And next as to the other rebel States:

The easiest & safest way seems to me to be the enrollment of the loyal citizens, without regard to complexion, and encouragment & support to them in the reorganization of State Governments under constitutions securing suffrage to all citizens of proper age & unconvicted of crime. This you know has long been my opinion. It is confirmed by observation more & more.

This way is recommended by its simplicity, facility &, above all, justice. It will be, hereafter, counted equally a crime & a folly if the colored loyalists of the rebel states shall be left to the control of restored rebels, not likely in that case to be either wise or just, until taught both wisdom and justice by new calamities.

The application of this principle to Louisiana is made somewhat difficult by the organization which has already taken place: but happily the Constitution enables the Legislature to extend the right of suffrage; and it is not to be doubted that, on a suggestion from the National Authorities that its extension to colored citizens on equal terms with white citizen is believed to be necessary to the future tranquillity of the country as well as just in itself, the Legislature will act promptly in the desired direction.[4]

What reaches me of the condition of things in Louisiana impresses me strongly with the belief that this extension will be of the greatest benefit to the whole population.

The same result can be secured in Arkansas by an amendment of the State Constitution; or what would be better, I think, by a new Convention the Members of which should be elected by the loyal citizens without distinction of color. To all the other states the general principle may be easily applied.[5]

I most respectfully but most earnestly commend these matters to your attention. God gives you a great place & a great opportunity. May He guide you in the use of them.

I noticed this morning your proclamation closing the ports & was glad to see it. I presume the law of forfeiture was well considered[6] & also the effect of discrimination against foreign vessels.

Most respectfully & truly Yours
S P Chase

The President

1. Chase had fifty copies of this letter, along with that of April 12 to Lincoln (below), printed for private distribution. Chase to John M. Schofield, May 7, 1865 (below); copy of printed letters, James Shepherd Pike Papers, Special Collections Department, Raymond H. Fogler Library, University of Maine, reproduced at *micro* 35:0699.

2. On April 9, the Confederate Army of Northern Virginia under Robert E. Lee surrendered to Ulysses S. Grant at Appomattox Court House, Virginia. Long, *Civil War Day by Day,* 670–71.

3. From 1861 to 1868, Francis Harrison Pierpont presided over the "restored" state of Virginia—that is, over territory of the state under federal control but outside the boundaries of West Virginia. *DAB,* 14:584–85.

4. Louisiana's new constitution, ratified on September 5, 1864, permitted enactment of liberal suffrage laws, but state legislators refused to extend the right to African Americans. African-American males were finally allowed to vote under the state's constitution of April 1868, ratified in accordance with the Reconstruction Act of 1867 as a prerequisite for the readmission into the Union. Ibid., 14:567; *Appletons' Annual Cyclopædia and Register of Important Events* . . . , 42 vols. (New York, 1862–1903), 4:479; Taylor, *Louisiana Reconstructed,* 47–48, 129, 152; Eric Foner, *Reconstruction: America's Unfinished Revolution, 1863–1877* (New York, 1988), 276–77.

5. As in Louisiana, African-American males in Arkansas received the franchise through the state constitution of April 1868, ratified to satisfy requirements for readmission imposed by Congress. Foner, *Reconstruction,* 276–77; Thomas S. Staples, *Reconstruction in Arkansas, 1862–1874* (New York, 1923; reprint, Gloucester, Mass., 1964), 241–42, 261.

6. By April 1865, federal military successes enabled the blockade to be lifted in selected southern ports. The proclamation restricted trade in other ports under authority

granted by legislation of July 13, 1861, which also prescribed conditions for forfeiture. *Statutes at Large,* 12:257, 13:753–54.

TO ABRAHAM LINCOLN

Autograph letter. Abraham Lincoln Papers, Library of Congress (*micro* 35:0701).

Baltimore, April 12, 1865.

My dear Sir,[1]

The American of this morning contains your speech of last evening. Seeing that you say something on the subject of my letter to you yesterday—reconstruction—, & refer, though without naming me, to the suggestions I made in relation to the Amnesty Proclamation, when you brought it before the Heads of Departments, I will ask your permission to add some observations to what I have already written.[2]

I recollect the suggestions you mention; my impression is that they were in writing. There was another which you do not mention and which, I think, was not in writing. It is distinct in my memory; though doubtless forgotten by you. It was an objection to the restriction of participation in reorganization to persons having the qualifications of voters under the laws of their several states just before rebellion.

Ever since questions of reconstruction have been talked about, it has been my opinion that the colored loyalists ought to be allowed to participate in it: and it was because of this opinion that I was anxious to have this question left open. I did not however say much about the restriction. I was the only one who expressed a wish for its omission; & I did not desire to seem pertinacious.

You will remember, doubtless, that the first order ever issued for enrollment with a view to reconstruction went to General Shepley & directed the enrollment of all loyal citizens; and I suppose that, since the opinion of Attorney General Bates, no one, connected with your administration, has questioned the citizenship of free colored men more than that of free white men.[3] The restriction in the amnesty proclamation operated as a revocation of the order to General Shepley:[4]—but, as I understood you not to be wedded to any particular plan of reconstruction, I hoped & believed that reflection & observation would probably satisfy you that the restriction should not be adhered to.

I fully sympathized with your desire for the restoration of the Union by the change of rebel slave States into Union free States; and was willing, if I could not get exactly the plan I thought best, to take the plan you thought best, & to trust the future for modifications. I welcomed, therefore, with joy the prospects of good results from the cooperation of General Banks with the Free State men of Louisiana. I think General Banks' error, & I have said so to him, was in not acting through instead of over the Free State Committee. This Committee had already shown itself disposed to a degree of liberality towards the colored people quite remarkable at that time. They had admitted delegates from the Creole colored population into their Free State Convention,[5] & had evinced a readiness to admit intelligent colored citizens of that class to the rights of suffrage. I have no doubt that great & satisfactory progress would have been made in the same direction had not the work been taken out of their hands. This created the impression that the advocates of general suffrage were to be treated with disfavor by the representatives of the Government. Discouragement & discontent were the natural consequences.

For one I was glad of all the good that was done; and, naturally, wanted more. So when I came to Washington last winter I saw Gen Banks; and, being now more deeply than ever persuaded of the necessity of universal suffrage, I begged him to write himself & to induce the Senators & Representatives elect from Louisiana to write to members of the Legislature and urge them to exercise their power under the constitution by passing an act extending suffrage to colored citizens.[6] I knew that many of our best men in and out of Congress had become thoroughly convinced of the impolicy and injustice of allowing representation in Congress to States which had been in rebellion and were not yet prepared to concede equal political rights to all loyal citizens. They felt that if such representation should be allowed & such states reinstated in all their former rights as loyal members of the Union, the colored population, would be practically abandoned to the disposition of the white population, with every probability against them; and this, they believed would be equally unjust & dangerous.

I shared these sentiments & was therefore extremely desirous that General Banks should take the action I urged upon him. I thought indeed that he concurred, mainly, in my views, & would to some extent at least act upon them. I must have been mistaken, for I never heard that he did anything in that direction.

I know you attach much importance to the admission of Louisiana; or rather to the recognition of her right to representation in Congress as a loyal state in the Union.[7] If I am not misinformed there is nothing in the way except the indisposition of her Legislature to give satisfactory proof of loyalty by a sufficient guaranty of safety & justice to colored citizens through the extension to loyal colored men of the right of suffrage. Why not then, as almost every loyal man concurs with you as to the desirableness of that recognition, take the shortest road to it by causing every proper representation to be made to the Louisiana Legislature of the importance of such extension.

I most earnestly wish you could have read the New Orleans papers for the last few months. Your duties have not allowed it. I have read them a great deal—quite enough to be satisfied that, if you had read what I have, your feelings of humanity & justice would not let you rest till *all* loyalists are made equal in the right of self protection by suffrage.

Once I should have been, if not satisfied, reasonably contented by suffrage for the more intelligent & for those who have been soldiers; now I am convinced that universal suffrage is demanded by sound policy and impartial justice alike.

I have written too much already & will not trouble you with my reasons for this conclusion. I shall return to Washington in a day or two & perhaps it will not be disagreeable to you to have the whole subject talked over

Truly & faithfully yours
S P CHASE

The President

1. Chase's rough draft of this letter is in his papers at the Library of Congress (*micro* 35:0704). Chase had fifty copies of the finished version and of his April 12 letter to Lincoln printed together for distribution to friends. See also note 1 for Chase to Lincoln, April 11 (above).

2. For the letter of the preceding day, see Chase to Lincoln, April 11, 1865 (above). Chase's earlier "suggestions" appeared in a letter written to Lincoln on November 25, 1863. Lincoln's speech, to a crowd that surrounded the White House in celebration of Lee's surrender, referred to responses by members of his cabinet to Lincoln's Proclamation of Amnesty and Reconstruction, issued on December 8, 1863. "One of them," said Lincoln, "suggested that I should then and in that connection apply the Emancipation Proclamation to the heretofore excepted parts of Virginia and Louisiana, that I should drop the suggestion about apprenticeship for freed people, and that I should omit the protest against my own power in regard to the admission of members of Congress." *Baltimore American,* Apr. 12, 1865; Basler, *Collected Works,* 7:53–56; *Chase Papers,* 4:202–3.

3. Stanton issued the orders to Brig. Gen. George Foster Shepley, military governor of Louisiana, 1862–64, on August 24, 1863. Attorney General Edward Bates's decision, written in November 1862, affirmed the citizenship of African Americans. Bates to Chase, Nov. 29, 1862 (Letters Rec. from Exec. Officers, Gen. Recs. Treasury Dept., Nat. Arch.); *DAB,* 17:79; *OR,* ser. 1, v. 26, pt. 1:694–95.

4. The proclamation recommended as "not improper" the maintainance of the same "general code of laws, as before the rebellion" in states seeking readmission. Basler, *Collected Works,* 7:56.

5. With reluctance, representatives admitted eighteen African-American delegates to its convention in Lyceum Hall on December 15, 1863. *Proceedings of the Convention of the Friends of Freedom, Held in Lyceum Hall, New Orleans, December 15th, 1863* (n.p., 1863), 5–6; *New York Times,* Dec. 27, 1863.

6. Male African-American Louisianans were finally allowed to vote under provisions of the state's constitution of April 1868. Taylor, *Louisiana Reconstructed,* 152, 158.

7. Legislation of June 25, 1868, readmitted Louisiana into the Union. *Statutes at Large,* 15:73–74.

TO CHARLES SUMNER

Autograph draft. Chase Papers, Historical Society of Pennsylvania (*micro* 35:0706).

Baltimore, Apl. 12, 1865.

My dear Sumner,[1]

Your letter is a real gratification. I rejoice in the Attorney General. He has been long on the right side; and cannot fail to be a great help to the cause.[2]

I *have* written to the President, & enclose you a copy of the letter, which I thought it best to retain.[3] Did I write too plainly? Please return the letter. I forbore writing till I *felt* I *must.*

His speech last night has just come under my eye.[4] His reference to *one* member of his cabinet, you will have readily divined was to me. He is correct, so far as my memory serves me, except in omitting to state, what he has doubtless forgotten, that I objected to the restriction of suffrage to persons qualified as voters by the laws in force before rebellion.

I rejoiced in the prospect afforded by Gen. Banks cooperation & aid, of an early organization of a Free State in Louisiana; but I did not dream that the practical work was to be taken out of the hands of the Free State Committee, but expected that the Committee would be mightily encouraged & the speedy accomplishment of its work promoted immensely by him. The *great* error was in setting it aside; and taking the back track on the question of suffrage. At least such was & is my judgment.

Most faithfully your friend
S P Chase

Hon. Charles Sumner.

How is Seward?[5]

1. Charles Sumner represented Massachusetts in the U.S. Senate, 1851–74.

2. Writing several days earlier, Sumner had reported on the president's visit to the occupied Confederate capital of Richmond on April 4 and 5, informing Chase that "on the main question" of black enfranchisement Lincoln was "reticent." "Why not write directly to the Presdt?" asked Sumner. "The Atty. Genl. is excellent," he asserted in reference to James Speed, a cabinet member from December 1864 to July 1866. "He & I agree entirely, & he is ready to do all that he can." Long, *Civil War Day by Day,* 666–67; Sumner to Chase, [Apr. 10, 1865], (The Huntington Library).

3. Chase to Lincoln, Apr. 12, 1865 (above).

4. That is, Lincoln's speech to celebrants shortly after Lee's surrender. *Baltimore American,* Apr. 12, 1865.

5. William Henry Seward, secretary of state, 1861–69, was recovering from a carriage accident that occurred on April 5. *Bio. Dir. U.S. Cong.,* 1792; Long, *Civil War Day by Day,* 667.

TO STANLEY MATTHEWS

Autograph letter. Chase Papers, State Historical Society of Wisconsin (*micro* 35:0718).

Washington, Apl. 14, 1865.

My dear Judge,[1]

The Commr. of Agr &c has sent me some seeds, & Sumner has put his name on some envelopes into which they are distributed & I send one to you more as a token of remembrance & a text for a short letter than for any good reason.[2]

Now there is the text; and the sermon shall forget it—no unusual occurrence.

We all feel very happy here in the prospect of the speedy return of peace. I hear of no rebel & no sympathizer with rebellion who does not consider the insurrection as effectually, though as yet only virtually quelled. Judge Campbell told the President at Richmond that he had expressed this opinion to Davis, Benjamin & Mallory just before they left Richmond, & they were silent.[3] It was the silence of despair.

Now comes the question of reconstruction. I was anxious that it should be provided for in advance eighteen months ago; and my plan was a very simple one. I proposed that the *loyal* citizens should be enrolled, either by voluntary action under a State Committee selected by an open public meeting, or by proper persons designated by the military authority; and that the citizens thus enrolled should elect delegates to a convention, which should conform the Constitution to the principles necessary to ensure future loyalty & peace & so prepare for a full restoration of all the privileges of a loyal state. Of course I contemplated no distinctions between colored & white loyalists. I was not able to get this plan adopted. And reconstruction has been made almost wholly a military job; with no good results so far. Louisiana is the only result as yet; and there the old secession element is rapidly gaining the ascendancy in consequence of the disfranchisement of the colored loyalists.

And now the President has given a sort of sanction, & a pretty strong one too, to the meeting of the rebel Legislature, with a view to its putting itself right by a simple declaration of submission & acquiescence in Emancipation.[4]

This greatly alarms those of us who want the hydra of rebellion killed not scotched; & there are signs of trouble. I hope they will all disappear; but I am uneasy.

I have been holding the Circuit Court in Baltimore.[5] There was little business & that little not important. A strong loyal sentiment prevails. With most of the loyal men it is very intense; and in a good many cases, naturally enough, vindictive. Many however have sons or brothers or other near relatives in the rebel armies, & are anxious for complete amnesty. Most of them would be glad to continue slavery.

But I must stop. Please let me hear from you.[6] What are your views of our future? What sentiments prevail in Ohio?

Yours faithfully
S P Chase

Hon Stanley Matthews

1. In April 1865, Matthews, an attorney and former Ohio state legislator, sat on the Superior Court of Cincinnati. In 1877, he won a seat in the U.S. Senate and, in 1881, was appointed an associate justice of the U.S. Supreme Court. *DAB,* 12:419; Charles Robson, ed., *The Biographical Encyclopædia of Ohio of the Nineteenth Century* (Cincinnati, 1876), 652.

2. Isaac Newton, the first U.S. commissioner of agriculture, had held his post since 1862. Chase also sent seeds to Mrs. Cary A. Trimble, the wife of a former Ohio congressman; Charlotte Ludlow Jones, a sister-in-law; Jane Auld, a niece; James T. Worthington,

an Ohio agriculturalist; Edward D. Mansfield, Ohio's commissioner of statistics; James Hall, a former judge and editor; Stephen S. L'Hommedieu, Cincinnati publisher and railroad magnate; Robert Hosea, Cincinnati merchant; and Thomas H. Yeatman, Cincinnati banker and industrialist and former U.S. Treasury employee. *Chase Papers,* 1:528; *DAB,* 13:472.

3. John Archibald Campbell of Georgia sat on the U.S. Supreme Court from 1853 to 1861. Since 1862, he had served as assistant secretary of war for the Confederacy. Campbell conferred with Lincoln on April 4 and 5, after President Jefferson Davis and the Confederate secretaries of state and navy, Judah Philip Benjamin and Stephen Russell Mallory, fled the city. *DAB,* 3:457–58; Long, *Civil War Day by Day,* 663–64, 666–67.

4. The precise nature of Lincoln's words to the Confederate legislature is uncertain. Writing on April 7, Campbell claimed that Lincoln had authorized the assembly to gather and to determine its willingness to administer U.S. laws. "I understand from President United States," wrote Campbell, "if the condition be fulfilled that no attempt will be made to establish or sustain any other authority." Lincoln, however, recalled matters differently. "I spoke of them not as a Legislature," wrote Lincoln to Godfrey Weitzel on April 12, "but as 'the gentlemen who have *acted* as the Legislature of Virginia in support of the rebellion. . . .' I dealt with them as men having power *de facto* to do a specific thing, to wit, 'to withdraw the Virginia troops, and other support from resistance to the General Government,' for which in the paper handed Judge Campbell I promised a specific equivalent, to wit, a remission to the people of the State, except in certain cases, the confiscation of their property." Basler, *Collected Works,* 8:406–7; John A. Campbell, *Reminiscences and Documents Relating to the Civil War during the Year 1865* (Baltimore, 1887), 41–44; Long, *Civil War Day by Day,* 667; *OR,* ser. 1, v. 46, pt. 3:656.

5. Chase returned to Washington, D.C., on April 13, having arrived in Baltimore on April 1 to preside over the Fourth Circuit Court. *Chase Papers,* 1:522–28; Fairman, *Reconstruction and Reunion,* 2.

6. See Matthews to Chase, April 19, 1865 (below).

TO WILLIAM SPRAGUE

Letterpress copy of autograph letter. Chase Papers, Historical Society of Pennsylvania (*micro* 35:0722).

Washington, April 14, 1865.

My dear Governor,

I came back last evening from Baltimore and found Katie pretty well—better than I feared, for she was not at all well when I went away.[1] She gratifies me this morning by reading a sentence from a letter of yours, in which you say that you are perfectly well & are pronounced handsome by all the ladies;—also that you have eschewed all liquor & cigars since returning home; except a glass at Anthony's,[2] which gave you a touch of dyspepsia, not felt till then. That was a friendly hint to you by your good genius. I don't mean whiskey, but nature. I strongly incline to think that exercise; open air, & regular & regularly good diet: will do more against dyspepsia than all the nostrums in the world.

I have been intending to write you ever since you went away; and can't give any good reason why I have not done so. I will do better hereafter if, this letter don't prove more than enough for you.

The President has been at Richmond![3] And every body has been on nettles to know what he was doing there. I fancy that he did very little except satisfy his own curiosity & gratify in some measure that of the public by sending telegrams to Stanton.[4] What little he did besides was, I fear, not well done.

Some days ago I learned from Sumner that the reports of encouragement given by Mr. Lincoln to Campbell & other rebels to [*illeg.*] the rebel legislature, & obtain a rescission of the Ordinance of secession, & to expect thereupon a recognition of the rebel state government as the legitimate state Government of Virginia were, in substance, warranted by the facts.[5] I still hoped that the case is not so bad: and the hope was strengthened by the news that on his return he sent for Pierpont, the Governor under the loyal organization. Today, however, appears, copied from the Richmond Whig, a call for a meeting of the General Assembly, elected under rebel auspices. This call is signed by some Senators, some Delegates, & some prominent citizens, & is sanctioned by the military Commander of Richmond acting, I have some reason to think, under the direct authority of the President.[6] If this be so Pierpont must have been sent for with a view to some arrangement to let in the rebel-loyal organization

All this seems to me management—& poor management. How much more simple & easy to say to the rebel Virginians: "Gentlemen, there is & has been all the while since you went into insurrection a loyal State Government of Virginia. To that Government you are bound to submit as much as to the Government of the United States. Gov. Pierpont will come to Richmond under the guaranty of the National Constitution. The Legislature will doubtless be elected in conformity with the constitution of the loyal State of Virginia; and the organization of the judiciary completed also in conformity with that constitution. If you desire to return to your allegiance & to secure full amnesty for rebellion, you will best show it by cordial acquiescence."

This would have settled every thing & on solid foundations. How strange that the President should hesitate about a course so direct & so plain: & prefer, or seem to prefer one so unfriendly to those who have abided in their loyalty & so dangerous.

But I am running on at too great length. Write me a good letter if you want more of this sort[7]

Faithfully & affectionately yours
S P Chase

Hon Wm Sprague

1. "Katie seems again to have a cough," Chase wrote to Sprague later in the month. "It makes me very uneasy about her." At this time, Chase's oldest daughter was pregnant with her first child, William Sprague, Jr., who was born in June. Chase to Kate Chase Sprague, June 24, 1865 (Chase Papers, L.C.); Chase to William Sprague, Apr. 30, 1865 (Chase Papers, Hist. Soc. of Pa.).

2. Sprague's colleague, Rhode Island journalist Henry Bowen Anthony, held a seat in the U.S. Senate from 1859 to 1884. *Bio. Dir. U.S. Cong.*, 542.

3. Lincoln visited the city on April 4 and 5. Long, *Civil War Day by Day*, 666–67.

4. On April 4, Lincoln telegraphed Stanton from City Point, Virginia, with news of military activity under Union generals Ulysses S. Grant, Godfrey Weitzel, and Philip Henry Sheridan. Basler, *Collected Works,* 8:385.

5. Sumner's letter recounted his own trip to Richmond, several days after Lincoln's. "Genl. Weitzel told us that the Presdt. had authorized him to convene the Va Legislature," wrote Sumner; "Stanton telegraphed to Genl. Weitzel that he must not hold any intercourse with Campbell. The Genl replied that he was instructed to do so by the Presdt." Sumner to Chase, Apr. 12, 1865 (Chase Papers, L.C.).

6. The address "To the People of Virginia" appeared in the *Richmond Whig* on April 12 under the authority of Maj. Gen. Godfrey Weitzel, whose troops had occupied Richmond on April 3. *DAB,* 19:616; *Daily National Intelligencer,* Apr. 14, 1865.

7. Sprague responded to Chase sometime before April 30. The letter, which the editors have not found, evidently contained an evaluation of William T. Sherman and warnings about possible dangers that Chase faced from conspirators in the Lincoln assassination. Chase to Sprague, Apr. 30, 1865 (Chase Papers, Hist. Soc. of Pa.).

TO JOHN DASH VAN BUREN

Letterpress copy of autograph letter. Chase Papers, Historical Society of Pennsylvania (*micro* 35:0734).

Washington, April 17, 1865.

My dear Sir,[1]

When you called at my house I was in Baltimore.[2] When I returned you had left Washington. I was sorry not to meet you, for I have never forgotten nor shall I ever forget your services or the spirit in which they were offered at the commencement of our great struggle.

I have you to thank for your financial article which you have been kind enough to send me.

That paper, to be a useful currency, must be made normally equivalent to coin by being made its actual representation I have never doubted. An emergency may justify, and, at the time when the legal tender act was passed did, in my judgment, actually justify the substitution of legal tender notes for coin.[3]

I never contemplated, however, any issue of such notes beyond the amounts which would be actually needed for the purposes of exchange, were the currency composed of coin & its equivalents. Nor has the amount of notes, which can be properly regarded as currency ever exceeded that limit. The largest amount ever issued was in round amounts four hundred & fifty millions: of which fifty millions were issued gradually in redemption of temporary deposits, and immediately put on course of reduction. Of the amount issued from ten to thirty millions—say an average of fifteen milions was constantly in the Treasury.

The extreme exigencies created by the vast expenditures of the war & the indisposition of Congress to impose the necessary taxes, excited a clamor for increased issues. This I resisted and made every effort in my power to raise the sums needed by loans. The embarrassments thrown in my way by unscrupulous opposition within & without the organization which supported the President hindered the success of these efforts and made them less fruitful than I hoped. I was compelled to use some expedients for payment of the Army & Navy, or see the defeat of all our efforts to save the integrity of the Republic. I adopted a middle course between the issue of more currency properly so called—that is notes not bearing interest, receivable for debts & made legal tender in payment—and the ordinary exchange of bonds for money by loans.

I issued notes bearing interest & made legal tender only for their face amount. I was aware, of course, that these notes would to some extent be used as currency—at first to a very great extent, but less and less as the interest should accumulate. The first issues [bore] an interest of five per cent & on a portion of them the interest was represented by coupons, payable every six months.[4] The coupon notes were issued in compliance with the wishes of the New York banks; a compliance which I had reason to regret. It was evident indeed that the periodical payments of interest would periodically make the notes simple legal tenders, & so increase from time to time the volume of currency & expose the Government & the business community to the evils of recurring inflation & contraction. To prevent this evil, which was magnified by interested parties but which was a real evil, I withdrew from the holders, by means of loans, a large amount, say sixty or seventy millions, before the maturity of the first coupons. The remedy was effectual: there was no expansion; but a contraction, at the time the expansion was expected.

At this time believing the rate of five per cent too low to secure the withdrawal of the notes from circulation as rapidly as was desirible & confirmed in my conviction of the impolicy of issuing legal tender notes with interest payable periodically, I determined on the issue of the Compound Interest Notes—that is notes made legal tender for their face, but bearing interest at 6% compounded semiannually for three years, & payable only at the expiration of that time.[5] These notes I intended to substitute for the five per cent legal tender notes, but I had no idea of increasing the volume already issued. On the contrary it was my purpose & expectation, if I could obtain the necessary legislation from Congress, to diminish it gradually until payments in specie could be safely resumed.[6] With a uniform national currency I believed, & yet believe, that resumption could be effected with less embarrassment than has heretofore attended such a condition in our own or any other country.

It was at this time that the differences between myself and our lamented President, over whose deplored death the whole nation is now weeping,[7] on the principles which should control appointments, led to my resignation.

After that the exigencies which had induced me to resort to interest bearing legal tenders induced my successor to issue the Compound notes & to increase the Certificates of Indebtedness far beyond my intention.[8] But there was still no increase of the Legal Tenders properly so called. The amount of these, in the Treasury & out of the Treasury in circulation, when I left the Dept., was about 430 mills: on the 31st of March 1865 it was $433,160,569. I had issued of Compound Interest notes about 15 millions & contemplated an additional issue in substitution for 5% notes withdrawn of about 40 millions. The amount issued on the 31st March was $[15]6.477.650. I do not remember the amount which I had issued of one & two years legal tender interest notes with & without coupons or the amount then actually withdrawn. The total amount issued, I think, was about 211.000.000 & the amount withdrawn, was about $80.000. No addition has, I believe been made to the issue & it appears to have stood on the 31st of March at 211,000,000,—with an amount withdrawn of 141.477.650; leaving outstanding $69,522,350. This whole amount is now due or nearly due & will be paid as presented or absorbed in the new loans.

This statement will show you the true condition of the currency, exclusive of that furnished by the State Banks & the National Banks. The rapid conversion of the former into the latter makes it certain that the currency of the country will soon be wholly national. I hope that the converted Banks will be required to substitute their National for their State currency, in which case no increase will arise from the issue of the former. It will be easy to prevent any increase at all by withdrawing, upon the issue of circulation to National Banks an amount of ordinary legal tenders equal to the excess of the National Bank notes issued over State Bank notes withdrawn &, if necessary, issuing in their stead compound notes which will gradually lose the character of currency & take that of debt.

So you see I think the currency now certain to improve, if the Treasy. Dept. is judiciously managed & not overwhelmed by excessive expenditure. I have great confidence in its present head; and I feel confident too that expenditures will be retrenched as fast as possible & soon brought within the resources supplied by revenue. Then borrowing will cease & reduction begin.

Your plan of substitution of gold accumulation for redemption will certainly improve the currency. The main objection to it is the danger of the custody of such accumulation. Who will keep it? Who will keep it safely? Who will keep the keepers. And does it not involve the annihilation of all Bank note currency, however safe, or [surely] convertible? And can such a revolution be achieved?[9]

I hardly know why I have written this long letter. I began intending only a few words. Topsy's explanation may answer "I spect it growed"![10]

Yours very truly
S P Chase

J. D. Van Buren Esq

1. Van Buren was a New York attorney and Democrat known to favor free trade and hard money. Early in the Civil War, he advised Chase on matters related to national revenue. *Nat. Cyc.*, 10:236.

2. Chase had returned to Washington, D.C., on April 13, after presiding over the Fourth Circuit Court in Baltimore. *Chase Papers*, 1:522–28; Fairman, *Reconstruction and Reunion*, 2.

3. Originally, legislation of February 25, 1862, authorized $150 million in legal-tender notes, also known as greenbacks, for use as legal tender except for duties and interest. *Statutes at Large*, 12:345–48.

4. Chase apparently refers to coupon bonds issued in accordance with the Ways and Means Act of March 3, 1863. Ibid., 12:709–10.

5. As with coupon bonds, Chase issued the compound-interest notes under authority of the Ways and Means Act of March 3, 1863. Ibid., 12:710.

6. Specie payments by many banks and the U.S. government ceased on December 30, 1861. Not until January 14, 1875, did Congress reauthorize the U.S. Treasury to pay government obligations in specie. Ibid., vol. 18, pt. 3:296; Long, *Civil War Day by Day*, 152.

7. Lincoln had died on April 15 of bullet wounds inflicted by actor John Wilkes Booth. *Chase Papers*, 1:528–31; Chase to Charlotte S. Eastman, Apr. 24, 1865 (below); Long, *Civil War Day by Day*, 677.

8. William Pitt Fessenden was Treasury secretary from June 1864 until March 1865. Hugh McCulloch presided in April 1865. Legislation of March 1, 1862, authorized the Treasury to issue certificates in return for deposits, payable one year later at the rate of 6 percent interest. *DAB*, 6:349; *Statutes at Large*, 12:352–53.

9. "Gold is less easily stolen than paper," wrote Van Buren in response to Chase's first concern; "It requires a horse and cart to carry away much gold: and hundreds of millions can as easily be guarded from loss as twenty millions. . . . I suggest for your consideration, that by withdrawing legal tenders & letting an issue of National Bank notes take their place, we are giving the people an inferior currency in exchange for a better one; likely to breed financial troubles." Van Buren to Chase, Apr. 21, 1865 (Chase Papers, Hist. Soc. of Pa.).

10. A paraphrase from chapter 20 of *Uncle Tom's Cabin:*

> "Have you ever heard anything about God, Topsy?"
> The child looked bewildered, but grinned as usual.
> "Do you know who made you?"
> "Nobody as I knows on," said the child, with a short laugh.
> The idea appeared to amuse her considerably; for her eyes twinkled, and she added,—
> "I spect I grow'd. Don't think nobody never made me."
>
> Harriet Beecher Stowe, *Uncle Tom's Cabin*, ed. Elizabeth Ammons (New York, 1994), 210.

FROM STANLEY MATTHEWS

Autograph letter. HM 20699, The Huntington Library (*micro* 35:0746).

Cincinnati Apl 19 1865

My dear friend:

I was very much gratified and flattered this morning by the receipt of your remembrance, implied in your note of the 14th and the accompanying package. Since it was written, what a shock the country has received![1] It is a great alleviation to my sense of the national calamity to observe, with what sublime faith in God and its own wisdom and destiny, the heart and mind of the people rebounds under stroke. It adds final proof to the many demonstrations of the past four years, that the people is the government. With them, I have great confidence that our future is safe: yet I am not also without great apprehensions and some forebodings.

You know I have not had unlimited confidence in Mr Johnson.[2] I hope that the circumstances which bring him into the Presidential responsibilities, will, if not reform his habits and change his character, at least hedge him with restraints, which will preserve his dignity and keep him from further outrages upon the public sense of propriety.[3] But aside from that, there are other causes of fear. Undoubtedly he hates the rebellion, and quite sufficiently, the rebel leaders, particularly the political plotters and agitators, who are chiefly guilty. But I fear he has no well considered, matured, statesman like constitutional views, of its relation to the State and Federal Governments. He talks a great deal about the ideas which lie at the basis of popular government, but does he really understand that there is no guarantee for personal civil liberty, but that of political liberty—universal suffrage; or if he does, has he the courage to stand by it. Perhaps to expect it from him is to judge him by too high a standard; and yet it seems to me, there is our principal means of safety. We can well afford to pardon every rebel, whether repentant or not, if we can effectually disarm and disable them, and nothing will do that, but to restore to the whole people the political power which they have usurped, monopolized and abused. I am for it without qualification and as the prime condition of the political reorganization of the rebel territory; but I am afraid even our communitities in the loyal states are not yet educated to this point of justice. But what I am most afraid of, as to Mr Johnson is that he lacks, not only in breadth of intellect, but in elevation of character—that he is not pure, lofty, disinterested. If this be so, we are certain to fall short of our proper gaol. But I hope for the best.

As to reconstruction, without adopting any particular theory or plan, I may say I certainly agree with your ideas in the main and as certainly dissent from the proceedings in Louisiana. My maxim would be to go slow—*festina lente.*[4] A masterly inactivity, is the medicine I should like to apply for the cure of Calhounism.[5] Let the national authority be exerted and administered over the conquered districts, by the military arm so far as necessary, by temporary civil organizations as far as practicable, until a spontaneous and natural growth of social order begets a local civil government able to fill the vacuum created by the rebellion, upon the true principles of American popular sovereignty. The new governments must grow and not be made: they must spring up from within, and not be forced from without; and to do this, will take time and the *vis medicatrix naturae.*[6]

The effect of the murder of the President, is in Ohio and will be universally, the utter extinction of every particle of sympathy with slavery and the rebellion. There have been manifestations of vindictiveness and revenge, which it will be the delight of demagogues to cherish and increase. But the sober thought of the wise people will be that slavery made the rebellion and murdered the President and starved our prisoners and has brutalized the community that has tolerated and sustained it, and it must be wiped away, every vestige of it and that without conditions and without delay. There will be no controversy further on the subject. The Democratic faction will not utter another, even feeble protest on the subject. On the whole, sad as I feel, I still feel able to thank God and to take courage.

Very sincerely

Your friend
STANLEY MATTHEWS

Hon. S. P. Chase
Washington City

1. See Chase to Matthews, April 14, 1865 (above), for the earlier note. Lincoln died of gunshot wounds on April 15. Chase to Charlotte S. Eastman, Apr. 24, 1865 (below); *Chase Papers,* 1:528–31; Long, *Civil War Day by Day,* 677.

2. Chase swore Andrew Johnson into office as Lincoln's successor on April 15. Chase to Charlotte S. Eastman, Apr. 24, 1865 (below); *Chase Papers,* 1:530.

3. Matthews apparently refers to Johnson's intoxication at Lincoln's second inauguration. Chase to Susan Walker, Mar. [17], 1865 (above).

4. "To hasten slowly," a motto attributed to the Roman emperor Augustus. Chase later used the phrase (in English) in a letter to Gerrit Smith, Feb. 13, 1873 (below). Anthony Cree, comp., *Cree's Dictionary of Latin Quotations* (Topsfield, Mass., 1978), 47; Hugh Percy Jones, ed., *Dictionary of Foreign Phrases and Classical Quotations,* new and rev. ed. (Edinburgh, [1963]), 44.

5. Prior to his death in 1850, John Caldwell Calhoun, venerated theorizer and spokesman of states' rights, had served as U.S. congressman and senator from South Carolina, vice president, and secretary of war. *DAB,* 3:411–19.

6. The "healing power of nature."

TO CHARLOTTE S. EASTMAN

Letterpress copy of autograph letter. Chase Papers, Historical Society of Pennsylvania (*micro* 35:0766).

Washington Apl. 24, 1865.

My dear friend,[1]

How I wish you were near me! Your *letters* are very pleasant and very kind, but I want *you.* If *your farm* were only in the vicinity of Washington instead of being on the seashore how nice it would be—for me.[2] Not so nice perhaps for you, & yet I do not see why you could not enjoy life just as well & be quite as useful here as in New England.

The shock of the Presidents assassination was fearful.[3] I had been exceedingly anxious about his course in respect to reconstruction and had written him two very earnest letters from Baltimore where I was holding the Circuit Court—one on Tuesday & the other on Wednesday.[4] Thursday afternoon I came over, with the intention of calling on him Friday.

Something induced me to defer the call till Saturday. That night of Friday, near midnight, a stranger[5] called at my door after I had retired & sat up [*two words illeg.*]. I told the servant to ascertain who he was & what he wanted; and was in a few minutes informed that the President had been shot. I could not believe it & directed the servant to ask the gentleman up to my bedroom. He came & told me the story very much as it afterwards appeared in the prints. I still thought it impossible to be wholly true; but all doubt was soon removed by three other gentlemen[6] who had fully informed themselves both as to the assassination of the President, but as to the attempted murder of Mr. Seward & his son.[7] My first impulse was to go to the scene; but it was so plain that I could be of no use, but would be rather in the way of those who might be, that I determined not to go. It was a night of horror.

No one could tell the extent of the conspiracy or the scope of it. As soon as possible guards were placed around the houses of all who were thought likely to be objects of assault, including my own.

The morning came with a heavy rain, as if the skies were weeping, and the Heavens had clothed themselves with mourning. I went up to Gov Sewards before breakfast, to learn what I could without disturbing any one. The President was already dead & the physicians at Mr. Seward thought it almost impossible that either he or his son could survive. There was a slight chance for Mr. S—none for Mr. F. S. The details of the attempted murder were horrible—six men[8] successively attacked—Mr. F. S—— felled by the assassin as he was forcing his way in to the Chamber—Mr. Seward assailed by the murderer, hindered by the resistance of one of the nurses—a soldier—who clung to his charge seriously & dangerously wounded—& just escaping immediately fatal blows in consequence of this hindrance—the strange escape of the assassin—how could such things be?

The Vice President had escaped as it would seem by the interposition of Providence. He was certainly included in the attempt; but the murderers failed to get at him as they designed. I called on him about nine. He was full of sorrow & anxiety. While I was with him the Secy of the Treasury & the Atto. General came in.[9] They said they were just about to go to my house to request my attendance in order to administer the oath to Mr. Johnston as President. How strange that seemed to me! I could not realize it. Just six weeks before—on a Saturday, wet, stormy & cold in the morning; but becoming bright & balmy & beautiful just as the President came on the platform, I administered to him the oath of office for the second term; & now I was to administer the same oath to his successor. The duty was performed with a heart as sad, as it had been joyous before. It all went with my lips as I said to Mr. Johns[on] "You are President; may God support, guide & bless you in your arduous duties." I left the room immediately afterwards & did not hear the remarks which the New President addressed to the gentlemen present.[10] You have, I, dare say [re]ad them. All he has since said is to the same purport.

All I have seen of him gives me the greatest hopes. His bearing is modest, firm & manly. His ideas agree very nearly with my own & of course I think them right. So in darkness there is light.

Before you receive this I shall probably be on my way southward.[11] It is my purpose to visit nearly all the towns on the Coast to New Orleans & then to come up the river. I shall probably be gone nearly or quite [a] month. Goodbye

Faithfully your friend
S P Chase

Mrs C. S. Eastman.

1. Chase and "Lottie" Eastman, the widow of a former Wisconsin congressman, had maintained a friendship for nearly a decade.

2. Eastman owned a small farm in the vicinity of Beverly, Massachusetts. *Chase Papers,* 1:483.

3. Lincoln had died early in the morning of April 15. In his diary, Chase also discussed events that surrounded Lincoln's assassination. Long, *Civil War Day by Day,* 677; *Chase Papers,* 1:528–31.

4. See Chase to Lincoln, April 11 and 12, 1865 (both above).

5. Elsewhere, Chase identified the "stranger" as "an employé in the Treasury Department." *Chase Papers,* 1:529.

6. All three men worked in the Treasury Department: William P. Mellen, a special agent; Homer Plantz, a clerk and one of Chase's secretaries during the Civil War; and Charles Manning Walker, the fifth auditor. Ibid.

7. On the night of April 14, Lincoln conspirator Lewis Thornton Powell Paine (or Payne) (c. 1845–65) broke into William H. Seward's quarters and attempted to assassinate him. Also wounded in the attack were Pvt. George Foster Robinson, a nurse, State Department messenger Emerick W. Hansell, and Seward's sons, Assistant Secretary of State Frederick William Seward and Maj. Augustus Henry Seward (1826–76), paymaster of the U.S. Army. *Appletons',* 5:473; *DAB,* 16:613; Francis Bernard Heitman, *Historical Register and Dictionary of the United States Army . . . ,* 2 vols. (Washington, D.C., 1903), 1:838; Long, *Civil War Day by Day,* 676; *New York Times,* Apr. 15, 20, 1865; *Wash. Dir. (1864),* 167; *Who Was Who in America, Historical Volume, 1607–1896 . . .* (Chicago, 1963), 400.

8. Seward and his son survived. Excluding Lincoln, the six victims were Seward, the four men attacked at his house, and Maj. Henry Reed Rathbone (1837–1911), who was a member of Lincoln's party wounded by Booth's dagger. *Appletons',* 5:185; *DAB,* 16:613, 620; *New York Times,* Aug. 16, 1911.

9. Hugh McCulloch had become secretary of the Treasury on March 9. He held the position until 1869, and from 1884 to 1885. McCulloch's companion was James Speed. *Bio. Dir. U.S. Cong.,* 18; *Chase Papers,* 1:530.

10. Johnson's brief speech included a request for assistance. "'Gentlemen, I shall lean upon you; I feel that I shall need your support,'" he reportedly said; "'I am deeply impressed with the solemnity of the occasion and the responsibility of the duties of the office I am assuming.'" *Washington Evening Star,* Apr. 15, 1865, 2d ed.

11. Chase had made plans to travel through states of the former Confederacy. Officially, he intended to investigate prospects for reopening federal courts and reviving trade. During the trip, which started on May 1 and ended nearly two months later, Chase took detailed notes for his diary and wrote frequently to Andrew Johnson, hoping to influence reconstruction policy. *Chase Papers,* 1:535–78; Simpson, *Advice After Appomattox,* 4–16.

TO KATE CHASE SPRAGUE

Autograph letter. Chase Papers, Historical Society of Pennsylvania (*micro* 35:818).

Beaufort N.C. May 5, 1865.

My dear Katie,

I finished my last letter as we were approaching Fortress Monroe.[1] It was about noon and a lovely day. The Perit, a large steamer from up the James had just arrived, and was discharging her passengers—some hundreds of rebel prisoners from Lees Army.[2] Some of our party talked with individuals among them. They [showed] the usual variety of tempers. Most of them, however, were thoroughly glad the war was over & that they were free from military duty. As usual they were ragged & dirty. A set of plantation negroes would not appear badly in comparison.

Among the gentlemen who came on board of our cutter was Major James the Quarter Master in charge of the Department, who was extremely civil.[3] On learning that we wished to visit the Freedmens Village at Hampton he sent for carriages—his own & another—and volunteered to accompany us. Nettie and I got into his double seated, one horse buggy, while the other gentlemen, Dr. Fuller, Mr. Reid, & the two Mr. Mellens followed in a two horse barouche.[4] The Major knew every thing & proved a very pleasant as well as very intelligent companion. He had married a Miss Janney of Columbus whom you may remember. She is a daughter of John Janney a good friend of mine & a most worthy gentleman.[5] The Major is himself a Pennsylvanian but his connexion with Ohio & my Ohio friends made him ready to serve me.

We went out over the old road, passing the houses of John Tyler,[6] Mallory and other residences of rebels now inhabited by better men or women. The Mission School, under the auspices of the American Missionary Society is, I believe, established in the Tyler House & Dr. McClellan, the able & efficient Surgeon in charge of all the hospitals in the vicinity, occupies the Mallory House.[7] A drive of about an hour brought us to the principal school. It was built, after a plan suggested by Gen. Butler in the form of a cross, each of the four arms being of equal length with a large space at their intersection, somewhat thus 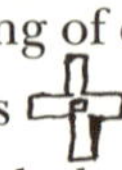. The square in the centre or intersection was occupied by a raised platform on which was the table of the Superintendent & chairs for visitors or others.[8] Standing on this platform we could keep a pretty good observation of the scholars dispersed in the four arms. Three of these were pretty fully occupied. One was not yet completed & the carpenters at work in it somewhat disturbed the school, or rather us the visitors. The seats, the desks, the slides for slates & the other conveniences for the scholars were if not so elegant quite as complete as in any school I ever visit. In each arm rows of seats extended back to the farthest side leaving on each side a space to move up & down; occupied also by a series of moveable arrangements which could be shut up as it were against the wall or expanded in a series of little recitation squares with a monitor for each mounted on his stool, and as conscious of his importance as a corporal. Every thing was done in military order. For example when we went in the children were engaged in some lesson under the charge of the monitors. Mr. Raymond for that was the name of the Superintendent took his place with us on the platform. "Attention Monitors"! Every little darkey was on his feet in an instant. "Take!"—all hands extended, "Stools!" All hands grasped stools "Place!" Stools elevated "Stools!" Stools all put one side in their places. Then came "Attention! School!" & all the children are on their feet: "March!" and they all, under the lead of their respective monitors, marched in perfect order to their rows of seats & stood expectant; the rank & file behind their several seats & the monitors at the end of each row. Then came the orders in obedience to which they were all seated & took their slates preparatory to writing. The drill had in it something ludicrous; but it was plain that it secured great promptitude, without confusion, & was calculated to make the children themselves orderly & methodical. We heard one class read and they read very well. Dr. Fuller made them a short address. Some specimens of hand writing were shown & they were very good. Mr. Day the principal of the Mission School & several ladies connected with it were present & manifested much interest

From this school we went to Hampton where Freedmens cottages have taken the place of the old aristocratic mansions—& in place of the old brick church where the first families worshipped of old there is a plain little chapel for Freedmens prayers & praise

Returning we took leave of the kind Major & went up to Norfolk. General Gordon met us at the wharf & took us to his house and to the old entrenched camp through which we passed as we went to Norfolk three years ago—right glad to find it abandoned & undefended.[9] I had a long talk with General Gordon about civil & military government & reorganization; taking good care to let him understand what part I thought the new made citizens must take in the latter.

It was dark when we returned from Norfolk & got on board the Wayanda, which was lying in the Roads to receive us.[10] Mr. Henriques, the commander & Mr Allen & Mr. OBrien the lieutenants had been very attentive & we were more than [have] sorry to exchange the Northerner for the Wayanda: which we found in by no means so perfect condition as Mr. Harrington thought it.[11] The after cabin however was very well arranged for myself & Nettie, and except the fear of seasickness we thought ourselves very well off.

Capt Merryman did not think it best to go out that night; but, at daylight Tuesday Morning, the 2d. we were under way.[12] The day was beautiful; but before breakfast time Nettie, (who by the way had lost her cloak & taken Ben Ludlow's military cape instead—we happened to meet him at Norfolk)[13] was too sick to eat. Mr. Reid was in the same condition & young Mr. Mellen also. The rest of us thus far remained very well. After breakfast however I felt some qualms which evidently had more connexion with the stomach than the conscience. But I did not get sick and could eat lunch & dinner with appetite which I felt it prudent to restrain. Poor Nettie however had a hard time. She got up very early & went on deck hoping to avoid the tiger: but she soon came down & took up her quarters on the floor & there remained all day, suffering greatly all the time & sometimes very much. At night she was better & came on deck for a while but when she came down would not take her berth. A nice mattress was arranged on the floor & she was made very comfortable & slept well. She was still sick in the morning & eat nothing till after we arrived here yesterday Morning. Then however she recovered at once. We had very pleasant weather around Cape Hatteras / The sky & air were all that could be desired: & but for the slight nausea I was as well as could be desired.

Early yesterday morning we arrived here. Poor Nettie could not be persuaded to get up until just before we came into the harbor: but we had hardly come to anchor before she was as bright as possible. Mr. Mellen & Dr. Fuller went over to Beaufort to take observations. They had not been gone long before Capt West of the Navy, Who is stationed here came along side in his cutter & coming on board asked us to visit his vessel the Orletta.[14] We complied nothing loth: and found her very nice though with rather contracted quarters. She is moored close along shore, so that a plank gangway reaches the beach. A few feet, two or three hundred perhaps from the water he has built a little frame of two rooms about ten by twelve each, in which he has established Mrs West, a handsome, sprightly, agreeable lady who received us with great kindness.[15] After a little talk with her we visited Fort Macon, one of our old fortifications seized by the order of the Gov. of N. Carolina before the state seceeded as the operation of inaugurating rebellion is facetiously called.[16] A young Massachusetts officer, Lt. Hinckley, was in command: and as attentive as possible. We saw where Burnsides' shells shattered the wall, & came so near exploding the magazine that the rebels thought it best to surrender.[17]

Returning to the boat we found our party who had been in Beaufort. They had seen some of the natives & had talked with them about the situation. One of them a Senator in the rebel Legislature, just returned, to his home which he left when our troops took possession, afterwards came to see me with the Clerk of the County Court[18] / They did not seem exactly to relish my suggestions about admitting the negroes to the ballot, & thought it wd. be better to let the Legislature (rebel [late] supposed Union now) assemble & call a Convention & bring the State back into the Union. They did not seem much surprised however when I told them that the Natl. Govt. could not consistently recognize any official body or individual who owed his position to rebel election or appt.; but must look directly to the people for reorganization. Our interview was pleasant. They [stayed] & lunched with us & then we started for Newberne. *Love to Wm.*

Your affectionate father
S P Chase

1. The letter, dated May 2, discussed the party's voyage from Washington, D.C., to a point two hours out of Fortress Monroe. Chase to Kate Sprague, May 2, 1865 (Chase Papers, Hist. Soc. of Pa.).

2. Possibly the *Thomas Perrit,* an infantry transport. *OR,* ser. 1, v. 43, pt. 2:628.

3. William Levis James of Pennsylvania, assistant quartermaster, presided over the Department of Virginia. Ibid., ser. 3, v. 5:346.

4. Richard Fuller, D.D., a native of Beaufort, pastored Baltimore's Seventh Baptist Church. Whitelaw Reid, a wartime reporter for the *Cincinnati Gazette* later gained notoriety as editor of the *New York Tribune* and author of *After the War: A Southern Tour. May 1, 1865, to May 1, 1866* (Cincinnati, 1866), an account based partly on observations made as a fellow traveler on Chase's southern trip. The other two passengers were William P. Mellen, and his son William S., who evidently clerked for his father.

5. Janney was an officer of the state bank of Ohio from 1851 to 1865.

6. Former U.S. president John Tyler, a secessionist, occupied the White House from 1841 to 1845. *Bio. Dir. U.S. Cong.,* 15.

7. Assistant Surgeon Ely McClellan (1834–93) received a brevet as major on May 9. Rossiter Johnson, ed., *The Twentieth Century Biographical Dictionary of Notable Americans . . . ,* 10 vols. (Boston, 1904; reprint, Detroit, 1968), vol. 7; *OR,* ser. 1, v. 46, pt. 1:1164.

8. Maj. Gen. Benjamin F. Butler commanded U.S. troops in and around Fortress Monroe from May to August 1861. U.S. Army chaplain Charles A. Raymond superintended public education in the District of East Virginia. A teacher named "Mr. Day" presided over the school. *Chase Papers,* 1:536; *DAB,* 3:358.

9. Maj. Gen. George Henry Gordon, commanded U.S. forces in Virginia's eastern district. For Chase's visit in May 1862, see *Chase Papers,* 1:336–44, 3:185–97.

10. The *Wayanda* was a steam-powered U.S. Revenue Service vessel. Ibid., 1:537.

11. Chase and his party had traveled on the *Northerner,* another Revenue Service steamer, since leaving Washington, D.C., on May 1. S. Allen O'Brien held a commission on board as second lieutenant. George Harrington had served as assistant secretary of the Treasury since 1861. Ibid., 1:535; U.S. Department of Transportation, *Record of Movements: Vessels of the United States Coast Guard, 1790–Dec. 31, 1933* (Washington, D.C., 1989), 478.

12. James H. Merryman, of the U.S. Revenue Service, commanded the *Wayanda.*

13. Benjamin Chambers Ludlow, Nettie's uncle, the brother of Chase's third wife, held the rank of brevet major general in the U.S. Army during the Civil War.

14. Lt. Comdr. William C. West captained the USS *Arletta,* a mortar schooner. *Chase Papers,* 1:538.

15. In his diary, Chase identified Mrs. West as the former "Miss Jamison of Maryland." Ibid.

16. John Willis Ellis (1820–61) governed North Carolina from 1858 to 1861. The state seceded on May 20, 1861. *DAB,* 6:106–8; Long, *Civil War Day by Day,* 76.

17. Fort Macon stood at the eastern tip of Borden's Banks, offshore Beaufort. Troops under Ambrose Everett Burnside, at that time brigadier general of volunteers, took the fort in April 1862 as part of his famous successful assault on the North Carolina coast. Ibid., 3:310; *OR Atlas,* plate 67, map 3.

18. The names of the senator and clerk were Michael F. Arendell, a physician, and James Rumley, respectively. *Chase Papers,* 1:538.

TO KATE CHASE SPRAGUE

Autograph letter. Chase Papers, Historical Society of Pennsylvania (*micro* 35:0822).

Beaufort Harbor N.C. May 5, 1865.

My dear Katie,

I closed my last letter with the close of my interview with the Beaufort gentlemen who called on me, just before we started for Newberne.[1] Capt West had been kind enough to arrange for our trip on the Railroad, & sent a tug to take us to Morehead City—a place so called in an anticipatory sort of way as the City exists as yet only on paper.[2] A few houses had been built there before the war & people resorted to it as a watering place in some numbers. It was also the terminus of the Railroad & the natural commercial point for the surrounding country, as there only was the water deep enough to allow vessels of considerable size to come up to the wharves.

But I dont mean to write Geography. We found a car awaiting us & soon were on our way. It was a very poor third class car, with only two or three whole panes of glass in its windows—but it was the best that could be furnished & we were content. The seats were bare boards no not exactly bare for they were covered with canvass so near in color & feel to boards that I actually did not know that the covering was there. "I thought her old gloves were on but twas her hands."[3] Just change this thus: "I thought I saw her hands but 'twas her gloves" & you get the idea. But if our car was poor the engine was good; our speed satisfactory; the road in fair condition; our company in good spirits; the air delightful; the day bright; and "all went merry as a marriage bell.[4] We reached Newberne about four in the afternoon, & found Gen Palmer at the Depot—with Col. Heaton & Commissioner French, & several other gentlemen waiting our arrival.[5] The General insisted on our accompanying him to his quarters on the banks of the Neuse—us now meaning my self & Nettie to whom add Dr. Fuller. Mr. Mellens, father & son, went with Mr. Heaton & Mr. Reid & Mr. Lowell to the Hotel.[6] After washing off the dust a little Nettie & I rode with the General to look at the Fortifications, and the Freedmens Village. The former are very interesting & I should think very strong. Most of the works are on the West bank of the Neuse; but there are some forts, one of which is called after me Fort Chase on the East bank.[7] The most striking feature in the defences is a rampart or earthen wall extending completely across the Peninsula formed by the Trent & the Neuse in the angle of which Newberne is situated—a very strong work making the town completely unassailable except by a very superior force. To these fortifications we have been twice or thrice indebted for the safety of Newberne against rebel attack. But the Freedmens Village is more remarkable than the Fortifications. It is a very large collection of small rude huts with little enclosures surrounding small patches of ground. These are arranged in perfect order, with wide streets running through them. You might fancy it a city in Africa: only there was nothing like a public building. In these houses are congregated the blacks who have fled from their old masters, to the number of several thousand. I did not learn the exact number. All the able bodied are just now in Government employment. They built their huts themselves & in all respects sustain themselves, with comparatively insignificant aid. Many of them, I was told, have accumulated small sums, & if land was for sale at cheap rates could buy & would be glad to buy small farms & go to work as farmers. These will probably get on pretty well; but there are many who only live from hand to mouth & these will be in great trouble when the government discharges them, as it soon must.

The poor white refugees seem in a condition even worse than that of the blacks.

So far last night—this morning, Saturday the 6th after an excursion first to the ancient town of Beaufort and then to the Revenue Cutter[8] ported here—I resume.

After our drive we returned to Gen. Palmers where we took tea. He lives in a house, which at the beginning of the war must have been the delightful residence of some well to do southerner. I heard the name but have forgotten it. Its front is on the Neuse, a broad beautiful stream, formerly dotted with the sails of a peaceful commerce, now thickly studded with vessels of war [&] their auxiliaries. On two sides there are fruit trees in full verdure & bearing & in the rear the servants quarters & kitchen. Every thing denoted substantial comfort, without luxury or great wealth. Col Heaton, do you remember as a Senator from Butler County during my first term as Governor[9] had invited me to his house after tea & therefore after tea we went—meaning this time Gen. Palmer, myself & Mr. Lowell who seemed to go along simply to see that no harm came to me for he left us at Mr. H's door. Here I met Mr. French—you remember his description of you and the convict to whom you carried a pardon[10]—and several other officers of the civil service. There were only two North Carolinians in the Room, one a rebel Colonel in rebel uniform on parol & the other an original Union man. The Colonel was now for Union on terms; & when asked what terms replied "Such terms as are satisfactory to my State." But he was by no means over confident. The "fight" is pretty thoroughly out of all the rebels, and the spirit can only be revived by gross injustice or very ungenerous treatment.

Nettie & I & Dr. Fuller slept at Gen. Palmers: and I slept well / The next Morning, yesterday May 5, was one of the most beautiful I ever saw. The air was balm; countless birds were singing; the skies were bright. Nothing could exceed the charm. Then came a delightful breakfast and at 8 we were off for Beaufort again, Gen P—— going down with us to see General Sherman just up from Savannah. He had sent me word that he wd. be glad to see me & as we found his steamer[11] lying at the Morehead City wharf we went directly on board. He was very hearty [in his] welcome & as frank & manly as possible / He feels very deeply wounded by the treatment he has received. He says he never received a word of advice or instruction from any body as to the course to be pursued & that the order to Grant of March 3d forbidding all negotiations about civil matters was never communicated to him.[12] All he knew was what Mr. Lincoln did at Richmond and that he said to himself when asked as to his wishes concerning Jeffn Davis that if he could get out of the county "*unbeknownst* to him" he would not be sorry.[13] Of course he thought he was pursuing the General line of policy approved by the President, & was governed in what he did by a simple wish to prevent the dispersion of Johnson's army into guerilla bands & to secure the earliest possible restoration of state organization & national authority. Our conversation was very interesting, though brief. He brought me and my party to the Wayanda in his tug and left us.

We hoped to get off immediately, but a strong gale from the south west had sprung up & the Captain[14] said it was simply useless to go out, for we should simply beat about without making any progress to the great discomfort of all on board. With this opinion it was idle to contend & we made up our minds to the situation hoping that the wind would go down before night. I spent the day writing the letter I have already sent to you & in other writing & in reading. In the afternoon upon Capt. West's invitation I went ashore & attempted a ride along the beach in his ambulance. It was a laughable apology for a ride. The wind was very high & the tide was nearly at full & coming in & the surf rolled in heavily, reducing the beach to the least possible strip, and often making it necessary to leave it & push through the sand. Most of our party left the wagon almost at starting & undertook to walk & pretty soon I did the same leaving only Nettie & Mrs West with Capt. W. who drove. Dr. Fuller & I walked some distance along the beach & then back. The surf was magnificent. I have never seen any thing like it, or rather any thing equal to it

As we returned we stopped at Mrs West's cottage where we met General Sherman again, just returned from a walk to Fort Macon.[15] There a little more chat & then back to the Wayanda & then after writing the first part of this letter to bed. Thus ended the 5th of May, our fifth day out. We are still weather bound.

This morning we expected surely to be on our way: but when I appeared on deck about light I was greeted with the same strong head wind—useless to go out. And so we are still here—it being now near ten at night. I have devoted the greater part of the day to a visit to the town of Beaufort & to talk with some of its leading citizens: and among them with the two who visited me yesterday. I found one gentleman, a Col Taylor, who readily assented to the proposition that the best security of the White Unionists would be found in the suffrages of colored unionists.[16] No other was so ready: but I am told that the little town is talking over the matter quite vigorously

This evening we had a visit from several gentlemen & ladies who brought us a basket of strawberries sent us by a Beaufort gentleman. But here I am;[17] good night

Most affy
S P CHASE.

1. In his diary, Chase identified the two "Beaufort gentlemen" as Michael F. Arendell, a physician, and James Rumley, clerk of the county court. *Chase Papers,* 1:538; see also, Chase to Kate Chase Sprague, May 5, 1865, note 18 (above).

2. William C. West had arranged for Chase and his youngest daughter to travel on the Atlantic and North Carolina Railroad. *OR Atlas,* plate 67, map 3.

3. Shakespeare, *As You Like It,* act 4, scene 3, lines 25–26.

4. George Gordon Byron, *Childe Harold's Pilgrimage: A Romaunt,* canto 3, stanza 21.

5. Maj. Gen. Innis Newton Palmer held a number of commands in North Carolina from 1862 to 1865. David Heaton, an Ohio politician and special agent of the U.S. Treasury Department, presided at New Bern. John R. French, a former Ohio state legislator, had recently received an appointment as a direct tax commissioner for North Carolina. *DAB,* 14:184; U.S. Senate, *Journal of the Executive Proceedings,* 13:488.

6. Russell R. Lowell, a former deputy U.S. marshall at Syracuse, New York, was special agent for the Treasury Department.

7. Others in the vicinity included Forts Amory, Anderson, Gaston, Rowan, Spinola, Stevenson, Totten, and Union. *OR Atlas,* plate 67, map 3.

8. The *Wayanda.*

9. Chase's first term as governor of Ohio lasted from 1856 to 1858. Elliott Howard Gilkey, *The Ohio Hundred Year Book: A Hand-Book of the Public Men and Public Institutions of Ohio* . . . (Columbus, 1901), 328.

10. As publisher of the *Painesville Telegraph,* John R. French had reported on a pardon that Kate delivered in March 1858 to "an old Polish exile" imprisoned for robbery. *Chase Papers,* 3:8–10; *Painesville Telegraph,* Mar. 11, 1858.

11. The *Russia,* a former blockade runner. *Chase Papers,* 1:538.

12. On April 18, Sherman and the Confederate general Joseph E. Johnston had signed a "Memorandum or basis of agreement" for the surrender of the Confederate Army of the Tennessee. President Johnson repudiated it, however, as an encroachment on issues related to Reconstruction policy. In accordance with Lincoln's order to Grant on March 3, Sherman and Johnston met again and, on April 26, agreed to a revised surrender identical to Lee's. Sherman was particularly upset at this time over Stanton's release of an account that described deliberations in which the cabinet had rejected the original agreement. Basler, *Collected Works,* 8:330–31; *DAB,* 10:146; Long, *Civil War Day by Day,* 678–79, 681–83; William T. Sherman, *Memoirs of General W. T. Sherman* (New York, 1990), 847–57.

13. The allusion to Richmond refers to Lincoln's meetings with John A. Campbell, discussed in correspondence to William Sprague on April 14 (above). As reported by Reid, who apparently witnessed the talk between Sherman and Chase, Lincoln prefaced his advice with a story about "an old temperance lecturer" willing to tolerate alcohol in his lemonade if added without his knowledge. "'Now General,' Mr. Lincoln concluded, 'I'm bound to oppose the escape of Jeff. Davis; but if you could manage to let him slip out unbeknownst-like, I guess it wouldn't hurt me much!'" Reid, *After the War,* 32–33.

14. That is, James H. Merryman.

15. Fort Macon stood at the eastern tip of Borden's Banks, offshore Beaufort. *OR Atlas,* plate 67, map 3.

16. Col. James H. Taylor was a local planter.
17. That is, at the foot of the page and out of room to write more.

TO EDWIN M. STANTON

Autograph letter. Edwin M. Stanton Papers, Library of Congress (*micro* 35:0826).

Beaufort N.C. May 5, 1865

My dear Sir,

How would it do to issue an order forbidding the calling of the freedmen, "contrabands", and the places where they are brought together in camps, "corrals." Words are things, & terms implying degradation help to degrade. Such an order, expressed as you know how, would correct a great evil & help those who need help.[1]

Here and at New Berne I have seen a number of the returned rebels—among them a Senator of the late rebel legislature & a Colonel in the rebel army paroled.[2] Evidently they would all like that restoration best which would give *them* most power & place; but they will, just as clearly, accommodate themselves to any mode of reorganization the National Government may think best—even including the restoration to the blacks of the right of suffrage which Slavery took from them about thirty years ago.

Sincerely yours
S P Chase

Hon E. M. Stanton.

It is clear to me that the National Government must *take* or *suggest* the initiatiative

1. The editors have not found evidence that Stanton issued the suggested order.
2. The former North Carolina state senator was Michael F. Arendell. Elsewhere, Chase identified the colonel as a "hotel keeper at Charlotte." *Chase Papers*, 1:538.

FROM WILLIAM TECUMSEH SHERMAN

Letterbook copy in clerk's hand. Generals' Papers and Books, Records of the Adjutant General's Office (Record Group 94), National Archives.

Head Qrs. Mil. Div. of the Miss—
Steamer Russia Beaufort Harbor.
May 6th. 1865 6 a.m.

Hon S. P. Chase—
Chief Justice U.S.—
Wayanda—
Dear Sir:—

On reaching this ship late last night I found your valued letter with the printed sheet which I have also read but not yet fully matured—[1] I am not yet prepared to receive the negro on terms of political equality, for the reasons that it will arouse passions and prejudices at the North, which superadded to the causes yet dormant at the South, might rekindle the War whose fires are now dying out, and by skilful management may be kept down. As you must observe I prefer to work with known facts, than to reason ahead to remote conclusions, that by slower and natural laws, may be reached without shock. By way of illustration; we are now weather bound. Is it not better to lay quiet at anchor till those white-cap breakers look less angry, and the South West wind shifts? I think all old sailors will answer, yes, whilst we impatient to reach our goal, are tempted to dash through at risk of life and property. I am willing to admit that the conclusions you reach by pure mental process may be all correct, but dont you think it better first to get the ship of State in some order, that it may be handled and guided? Now all at the South is *pure anarchy*. The Military power of the U.S. cannot reach the people who are spread over a vast surface of country. We can control the local State Capitals, and it may be slowly shape Political thoughts, but we cannot combat existing ideas with force. I say honestly that the assertion openly of your ideas as a fixed policy of our Government; to be backed by Physical power will produce new war, and one which from its desultory character will be more bloody and destructive than the last.

Our own armed soldiers have prejudices that right or wrong should be consulted, and I am rejoiced that you, upon whom devolves so much, are aiming to see facts and persons with your own eye. I believe you will do me the credit of believing that I am as honest, sincere, true & brave as the average of our kind, and I say that to give *all* loyal negroes the same political status as white "voters", will revive the war, and spread its field of operations. Why not therefore trust to the slower and not less sure means of Statesmanship? Why not imitate the example of England in allowing causes to work out their gradual solution, instead of imitating the French whose Political Revolutions have been bloody and have actually retarded the development of Political Freedom? I think the changes necessary in the Future can be made faster and more certain by means of our Constitution, than by any plan outside of it. If now we go outside of the Constitution for a means of change, we rather justify the rebels in their late attempt, whereas now as Genl. Schofield tells us the People of the South are ready & willing to make the necessary changes without shock or violence.[2] I who have felt the past War as bitterly & keenly as any man could, confess myself "afraid" of a new war: and a new war is bound to result from the action you suggest, of giving to the enfranchised negroes so large a share in the delicate task of "putting the Southern States in practical working relations with the General Government."[3]

With great respect—
(SIGNED.) W. T. SHERMAN—

Maj. Genl.

1. The editors have found two letters that Chase wrote to Sherman on May 5 (both William T. Sherman Papers, L.C.). One, to which Sherman refers in the document printed here, enclosed published copies of correspondence written to Lincoln on April 11 and 12 (both above) and offered Chase's perceptions of Andrew Johnson's attitude toward Reconstruction. "He would be gratified to have all loyal citizens participate in this work without reference to complexion," claimed Chase. The other letter, which enclosed an order of August 24, 1863, for George F. Shepley to "enroll all loyal citizens," advocated "boldness & decision guided by common sense & strict regard to rights" as "sure guides to safe results." *OR,* ser. 1, v. 26, pt. 1:694–95.

2. Since March, Maj. Gen. John McAllister Schofield had commanded the Department of North Carolina. In a communication from Raleigh on May 5, Schofield had encouraged "the government" to "make known its policy as to organization of State governments without delay. . . . The people are now in a mood to accept almost anything which promises a definite settlement," claimed Schofield. To him, the "all-important question" at the time was the fate of former slaves. *DAB,* 16:453; Schofield to Sherman, May 5, 1865, in *OR,* ser. 1, v. 49, pt. 3:405.

3. An apparent paraphrase from Lincoln's last public address, April 11, 1865: "We all agree that the seceded States, so called, are out of their proper practical relation with the Union. . . ." *Baltimore American,* Apr. 12, 1865.

FROM WILLIAM TECUMSEH SHERMAN

Autograph letter on letterhead stationery. Misc. War 1861–1865, Box 7, #599, New-York Historical Society (*micro* 35:0831).

Head-Quarters Military Division of the Mississippi,
On Board the Steamer Russia
Beaufort Har. N C. May 6 1865.

Hon S. P. Chase
On Board "Wayanda"
Dear Sir.

Your note with the letter of Instructions of the Secretary of War to Govr. Shepley of Louisiana is received and I thank you for the perusal.[1] I approve in my mind every word of those Instructions for it is a Well Established Principle & Practice that *During War* the Conqueror of a Country may use the local government & authorities already in existence, or create new ones subordinate to his Use. That is not the question now, for War has Ceased, and the question is to adapt legal Governments to Constitutional Communities which fully admit their Subordination to the National Authority. I have had abundant opportunities to know these Poeple both before the War, during its existence and since their public acknowledgment of submission. I have no fear of them armed or disarmed, and believe that by one single stroke of the pen nine tenths of them can be restored to full relations to our Government so as to pay taxes, live in Peace, and in War I would not hesitate to Mingle with them and lead them to battle against a National foe. But we must deal with them with frankness and candor, and not with doubt, hesitancy and prevarication. The nine tenths would from motives of self interest restrain the other Mischivous tenth, or compel them to migrate to Mexico, or some other country cursed with Anarchy & Civil War.

I return you the paper as you request and send you a copy of an order I make to my troops to counteract the effect of the insult so wantonly and unjustly, and so publicly inflicted on me by the Secretary of War. Of course this will soon lead to the closing my Military Career, and I assure you that I can have no aspirations to Civil favors, but will shun them with disgust. Indeed I have not yet thought whither I will cast my fortunes, but probably to some foreign land, if in my judgment events are drifting us further into another Civil or Anarchical War.[2]

That you may study the chances of changing the tone & character of a Poeple by Military occupation and Military Governors I invite your attention to the occupation of Spain by Napoleons best armies from about 1806 to the close of his career.[3]

With great respect

Your friend,
W. T. Sherman
Maj Gen'l

P.S. I feel additional confidence in the ability of the United States to rule the late Rebel States, by and through even their existing State Authorities by reason of the facts, that we now have possession of all forts, arms and Strategic Points— We have a vast politicial majority which Cannot be lost unless by seeming acts of oppression a reaction is created in their support.— Their resources are all gone, and their confidence in their leaders is turned to hate. With Moderation & Courage on our part Jeff Davis, Toombs, Cobb, Benjamin Slidell[4] and other Political leaders will receive less Mercy at the hands of their country men, than ours.— Where is the single act of severity ever shown to a Political Prisoner in our hands? To this hour the War Dept has sent me no orders to hunt for, arrest, or capture Jeff Davis, but on the Contrary as near as I know their wishes it is that he escape provided it be "unbeknown" to them.[5] But the Tribunal before which all conflicts must come at last, the Supreme Court, before whose decrees I and all Soldiers of my school bend with the veneration of Religion, is now surely safe to us on the "vexed questions" which led to our war and now threatens another. In it I hope is the "Anchor of Safety"—[6]

Again with respect & affection
W. T. Sherman

1. For Edwin M. Stanton's orders to George F. Shepley, issued on August 24, 1863, see Sherman to Chase, May 6, 1865, note 1 (above).

2. Sherman still smarted from Stanton's role in giving unfavorable publicity to Joseph E. Johnston's first surrender to Sherman. The editors have not found a copy of the proposed order, nor do they know whether Sherman actually issued it. Sherman remained in U.S. military service despite the threat and assumed general command of the U.S. Army on March 4, 1869. Chase's first letter to Kate Chase Sprague, May 5, 1865, note 12 (above); *Chase Papers,* 1:540; *DAB,* 17:97.

3. Napoleon dominated Spain from 1806 to 1813. His first abdication occurred in 1814. Thorne, *Chambers's Biographical Dictionary,* 931; C. W. Crawley, *War and Peace in an Age of Upheaval, 1793–1830,* vol. 9 of *The New Cambridge Modern History* (Cambridge, 1965), 267–335.

4. Robert A. Toombs, Confederate secretary of state; former U.S. Treasury secretary Howell Cobb, major general, C.S.A.; Judah P. Benjamin, attorney general for the Confederacy and, successively, secretary of war and state; and Confederate diplomat John Slidell. *DAB,* 2:182–83, 4:243, 17:210–11, 18:591.

5. Sherman alludes to a related story told by Abraham Lincoln, evidently discussed in Chase and Sherman's face-to-face talk, and recorded by Whitelaw Reid. See Chase's second letter to Kate Chase Sprague of May 5, 1865, note 13 (above). The editors have not found any evidence that Sherman received such orders prior to the capture of Davis on May 10. Long, *Civil War Day by Day,* 687.

6. Similar wording appears in Heb. 6:19.

TO WILLIAM TECUMSEH SHERMAN

Autograph letter. William Tecumseh Sherman Papers, Library of Congress (*micro* 35:0828).

U.S. Rev. Str. Wayanda, March[1] 6, 1865

Dear General,

I have always been thought a radical in principle & never have disclaimed the name; but I have tried to be conservative in working; & have generally got along without breaking things. This morning I met at Beaufort Col. Taylor, a gentleman of sixty, holder of a hundred & twenty five slaves before the war and a handsome estate in lands. He has come to the conclusion that it is best to restore the *old* Constitution of North Carolina under which *all freemen* voted,[2] & believes that that the Union & Union men will be *safest* with universal suffrage. I met others with different opinions, but none manifested any such feeling as would lead me to expect any renewal of troubles from the extension of the elective franchise to *all loyal citizens* & inviting all to participate in the work of reorganization.

The matter must be left to consideration & reflection. It is a clear duty to be frank & open; and this duty requires the National Government to say distinctly what, in its dictionary the words "loyal people" mean. The most obvious signification should, in my judgment be adopted. All loyal *men* must be taken as the synonymous expression. John Sherman has maintained this view, I am told, since the adjournment of Congress, in a speech in Ohio.[3]

But I will trouble you no further with these ideas. Time will try all opinions. Our ends are the same, permanent Union & permanent peace.

Let me, however, most respectfully but very earnestly advise against the publication of the General Order you have sent me. I cannot see that any good will come of it; but I fear some evil.[4]

My knowledge of the internal administration of the War Dept. for nearly a year past has been only that which all may gather from the journals; & of course I am not well enough informed to judge of the motives of recent action. I cannot believe however that it had its origin in any bad feeling towards you; so far as President Johnson or Secretary Stanton are concerned. Since my conversation with you I have seen more clearly the motives & views which governed you. I presume they do also; and will soon become more fully informed & more definitely impressed. I know what your feelings must be; but you are not required to do anything to ensure full justice to your acts & intentions both from the Government & the people.

I hope you will let time & reason do the work of your vindication & put the order, at least, in abeyance.

Pardon this expression of opinion on a matter of which you are so much the better judge. Your kindness in permitting me to see the order seems to warrant it.

You are a native of Ohio—a state which adopted me & has dealt most generously with me. Your honor & fame are therefore especially dear to me. Besides this your brother was my ablest & firmest supporter in my difficult financial administration; and my gratitude to him extends itself, in some sort, to you. So you must excuse my solicitude; not forgetting that it is that of one, a good deal older than you are, who has had a large experience, though less varied perhaps than your own.

Very truly your friend
S: P: CHASE

Maj. Gen. W. T. Sherman.

1. So in the original, although Chase wrote this letter in May, not March.

2. That is, in accordance with the state constitution of 1776, amended in 1835 to disenfranchise any "free negro, free mulatto, or free person of mixed blood, descended from negro ancestors to the fourth generation inclusive." *Revised Code of North Carolina, Enacted by the General Assembly at the Session of 1854 . . .* , (Boston, 1855), 13, 23.

3. John Sherman, William T. Sherman's younger brother, represented Ohio as a Republican in the U.S. Senate from 1861 to 1877. The younger Sherman sat on the Senate finance committee during the Civil War. Chase may refer to a speech delivered in Columbus on April 14, about five weeks after Congress adjourned, in celebration of Union victory. "As for the slaves," said Sherman, "or those who were formerly such, there is but one option.—They must be secured in their freedom in all time to come." *Bio. Dir. U.S. Cong.*, 175; *DAB*, 17:84–85; *Daily Ohio State Journal*, Apr. 15, 1865.

4. The editors have not found the order or any evidence that Sherman issued it. *Chase Papers*, 1:540.

TO JOHN M. SCHOFIELD

Autograph letter. John M. Schofield Papers, Library of Congress (*micro* 35:0840).

U.S. Steamer Wayanda, Beaufort Harbor
May 7, 1865.

Dear General,

Maj. Gen. Sherman has shewn me your telegram to him on the subject of the reorganization & government of North Carolina; & it has occurred to me that you might like to know the general views of those who think as I do.[1] I cannot perhaps put them before you with so little trouble or more distinctly than by sending you copies of two letters written by me to President Lincoln just before he was so foully murdered.[2] Some fifty copies were printed for the information of individuals—not for publication.

I have, since his accession, had several conversations with President Johnson & think myself authorized to say that he desires the earliest possible loyal reorganization of the late insurgent States.[3] He thinks that this reorganization should be the work of the people themselves, acting in their original sovereign capacity: and would be willing to aid their action in any proper way, as for example by the enrollment of all the loyal citizens preparatory to the election of delegates to a convention. In this enrollment he would prefer that the old constitutional rule in North Carolina, which recognized all freemen as voters, should be followed rather than the rule of the new Constitution, which excludes all freemen of color.[4] I think he is clear & settled in the opinion that no civil authority should be recognized which has its source in rebel election or appointment.

It may be that he has already issued an address or proclamation stating his views. He was considering the subject when I left Washington on the 1st inst. If no such document has appeared the information I now give may be useful to you.[5]

Permit me to suggest that you may find conference with General Cox on this class of subjects useful. I have known him well as a civilian, & have the highest opinion of his ability & judgment.[6]

Excuse me if you think any thing I have written intrusive or superfluous. I write only in the hope of being of some service to you & from interest in the important work of reorganization.

Yours very respectfully & truly
S P Chase

Maj. Gen. Schofield.

1. Chase apparently refers to Schofield's dispatch of May 5, discussed in Sherman's first letter to Chase of May 6 (above).

2. For the letters, see Chase to Lincoln, April 11 and 12 (both above). Lincoln had died on April 15. Long, *Civil War Day by Day,* 677.

3. The two men are known to have met at least five times since Johnson became president: on April 17, 18, 20, 26, and 29. "I have talked with him a good deal," Chase reported, "& believe that he does not materially differ from me unless as to the time of action." Chase to Theodore Tilton, May 1, 1865 (New-York Historical Society); *Chase Papers,* 1:531, 533–34.

4. As discussed in Chase's letter to William T. Sherman, [May] 6, 1865 (above), Johnson supposedly preferred North Carolina's constitution of 1776 to that of 1835.

5. Chase had pressed Johnson on the issue at their conference of April 29. The president finally revealed his views through two proclamations issued on May 29. The first, Johnson's famous Proclamation of Amnesty, offered pardons to all but fourteen categories of former Confederates, who could still apply for presidential pardons. The sec-

ond authorized Reconstruction to begin in North Carolina with a constitutional convention elected in accordance with antebellum regulations that excluded African Americans from voting. Chase to William Sprague, Apr. 30, 1865 (Chase Papers, Hist. Soc. of Pa.); Foner, *Reconstruction,* 183; *Statutes at Large,* 13:758–61.

6. At this time, Maj. Gen. Jacob Dolson Cox, a former antislavery legislator from Ohio, commanded a division of the Twenth-third Army Corps in support of Sherman. In 1866, Ohio voters elected Cox to a two-year term as governor. *DAB,* 4:476.

TO ANDREW JOHNSON

Autograph letter. Andrew Johnson Papers, Library of Congress (*micro* 35:0859).

Hilton Head, May 17, 1865.

My dear Sir,[1]

Since writing my last which I was obliged to bring here & which will go north with this on the Arago,[2] I have been at Charleston, on the Islands in this vicinity and in Savannah.

At Charleston, I saw a number of the most prominent citizens remaining in the town, among them the former Mayor Macbeth, Messrs Williams, a merchant & Phillips & Seymour, lawyers.[3] The same general fact is observable here as elsewhere—the utter absence of all *purpose* if not of all disposition to offer any further resistance to the Authority of the Union; and yet a strong desire to retain if possible the political ascendancy in their several states. A few and only a few comprehend & accept the new situation. They would like to reconstitute the state government to suit themselves; but will acquiesce in any plan you think best. Here as elsewhere I endeavored to impress on their minds the disposition of the Government to act with moderation & forbearance & through the people in the matter of reorganization, & I believe I have left, wherever, I have talked with the white citizens a better spirit than I found; though never holding back my own opinions as the necessity of universal suffrage for the best interests of all concerned. Of course, I have been careful to make them understand that the whole question of reorganization is in your hands, & that you will act according to your own best judgment, with a fixed determination to consult the best good of the whole country.

A number of colored people called on me after the white citizens had gone.[4] They were all anxious to know what their future was to be: and I endeavored to counsel them as well as I could. They attach very great importance to the right of voting—more perhaps than to any other except that of personal liberty. Gen. Saxton had arranged for a large meeting & requested me to attend it & I did so in company with General Gillmore. The number in attendance was very large & they were full of the most ardent loyalty. What I said to them may be pretty well gathered from the account in the Charleston Courier, which I enclose herewith. I had no opportunity to see the report until after I had reached Savannah, or I should have made it somewhat better.[5] The audience seemed quite as intelligent as a similar gathering in the north. The colored citizens of Charleston are more intelligent than elsewhere. Schools for free blacks have never been prohibited.

General Hatch, who commands the Department, may be fully relied on in any plan of reorganization, and will be able, I doubt not, to secure quiet acquiescence & ultimate cordial good will.[6]

On Saturday Morning I arrived here. General Gillmore arrived soon after & before noon General Saxton had reached Beaufort by a shorter route. There is a populous colored village on this Island, named Mitchell after General Mitchell.[7] The number of inhabitants is almost three thousand. They have a church, a minister, & schools. A few cultivate the soil in large & small parcels; most are in government employment; [but] all are doing well well—some very well.

On Sunday I went to Beaufort & thence across Ladies Island to St Helena's to the old Baptist Church to which the planter's families formerly resorted, with their black servants

A large School House has been built since the loyal occupation near the Church & between them under the interlacing branches of three or four enormous live Oaks, was a vast Congregation almost wholly of negroes. Dr. Fuller addressed them admirably. Quite a number of them had been his slaves, & the scene was a most interesting one.[8] I added a short exhortation to industry, temperance, truthfulness, & selfimprovement. I wish I had time to write or you to read a more particular description; but it is not possible.

In the afternoon I attended a similar meeting at Beaufort: but here the people were better dressed & a couple of thousand colored soldiers formed part of the audience. Dr. Fuller told them he differed from me as to the right of voting; as he would give it only to those who could read a chapter in the Bible; but said that it was certain they must have the right either with restriction or without it. Was not this something strange to be said in South Carolina, by an explanter to his ex slaves? Generals Gillmore & Saxton & a considerable number of other officers were present at both meetings.

The condition of the fields attracted much attention. Dr. Fuller said he had never seen such thorough cultivation or such promise of fine crops on St Helena. And the population seemed happy and thrifty.

On Monday I visited some of the schools: and was much gratified by the extreme anxiety which almost all manifested for education: all ages seem to feel it; the middle aged most.

Savannah—to which place I went night before last, spending yesterday there, was Charleston over again, except that there was no great meeting. A great desire was manifested to have one; but I would not consent; having determined to make no more addresses, fearing I might be taken for a politician or preacher rather than a Chief Justice. There were similar interviews with white & colored citizens; similar expressions of opinion from both classes; & similar schools.[9] I thought I observed, however, among some of the more active white citizens of the middle class, a greater apprehension of restored disloyalism & its ascendancy and a greater desire to be protected against it by the extension of suffrage to the colored citizens.

I find here this morning the New York Herald of the 13th. & Mr. Mellen has received the new trade regulations. The Herald refers to your address to Colored ministers but does not contain it.[10] I am very desirous to see it—I hope you gave some intimation of your purpose to extend the right of suffrage: or that if you did not you soon will. Every body will follow your lead; and I can only repeat my profound conviction that nothing will more exalt your character in the estimation of mankind.

Your order respecting further hospitality to insurgent vessels by foreign nations is to the point & most timely.[11]

Yesterday morning as we were going to Savannah, the steamer conveying Jefferson Davis & his companions came along side, & was made fast to our vessel.[12] Gen Gillmore asked me if I wished to see him; but I said, "No. I would not let any of our party see him. I would not make a show of a fallen enemy." I was dressing, & before I had finished the boats had parted company. As the telegraph operates from Macon to Washington you had doubtless received information of the Capture before we did. The arch leader of the rebellion is now in your hands. I congratulate you on the capture. It makes it impossible for insurrection to revive, & leaves to you only the task of restoring peace by reorganization.

I enclose a paper of practical suggestions, which seem to me worth considering so far as they have not already been considered. They can do no harm if they do no good—

Yours most truly
S P CHASE

The President

P.S. I enclose an order of General Gillmore, which, I think, will please you.[13]

Suggestions.

Trade.

The late regulations, in effect, restore the old condition as it existed before rebellion, except as to the export of Cotton & the collection of internal duties: but are unnecessarily complicated through a wish to avoid clashing with the act of Congress. Would it not be best to issue a short order, stating that within certain states—all the states east of the Mississippi—& that part of Arkansas & Texas occupied by National forces, the insurrection has so far ceased as to allow free internal trade & free export & import to & from other states.[14] This would greatly simplify the matter & be in substantial conformity with the legislation of Congress. Nothing in my judgment would contribute more to tranquillity & practical restoration.

Military Matters.

1. The objects of the war is twofold, (1) the suppression of armed insurrection; (2) the restoration of National relations through the reorganization of the state governments. The first is substantially accomplished: the second taxes nerve & brain.
2. As yet the rebels are disarmed only; not reconciled; hardly acquiescent: and there are no state governments to prevent outbreaks. Military supervision, for the present, therefore is indispensable.
3. Should not this military supervision be exercised in a mode as nearly analogous to that of State Government as possible: and to this end would it not be best to make each state a Department & each General commanding a Military Governor, in name as well as in fact; with a distinct declaration that the arrangement is temporary & only auxiliary to reorganization?
4. In the selection of Generals to command in the several States the greatest care should be used to find men suited to their work; thoroughly loyal to the Government and as ready to maintain the rights & promote the welfare of black as of white citizens. Success depends on this.
5. So far as I am able to learn Gen. Schofield in North Carolina may be well trusted with that State or Department. Should circumstances require his presence elsewhere Gen. Cox is admirably suited to the position. This Department is now under General Gillmore. I have met no officer who seems to me so well suited to his work: no one more able or more loyal in all respects or more thoroughly in sympathy with your own views. Should the Department be divided into State-Departments I should hope that he might be assigned to Georgia, where it seems to me he would be most useful. General Hatch or General Saxton would be excellent for Florida or South Carolina. General Saxton has had so much experience in the latter state that he would be most useful there.
6. Military Commanders being once established in each state reorganization would be easy. An order might at once be made for the enrollment of loyal white or black citizens & the mode of enrollment prescribed.[15]
7. Enrollment might be made either by Provost Marshalls, or what would seem to me a better mode by boards of loyal citizens in each county or other convenient place or precinct; who could administer the proper oath and make the necessary examination to be sure of loyalty & issue certificates of enrollment which should be evidence of right to vote.
8. The enrolled citizens should then be invited to vote for delegates to form a new constitution or amend the old: & the new amended con-

stitution should be submitted to them for ratification or rejection. The Convention of Delegates should also provide, in the event of ratification, for the election of Governor & other state officers & of Members of the Legislature & for the election or appointment of Judges & Justices of the Peace, & for the declaration of the results of these elections; & for the entrance upon their respective duties of the persons elected or appointed under the State Constitution.

9. The State Government being thus reconstituted all the political functions of the Military Commander would cease & his duties would be confined to the repression of disorder in aid of the state authorities; & the whole machinery of the National & State Governments would be once more fully restored & in practical operation.

10. This restoration of the late insurgent states to their national relations will be peace.

1. This letter and its enclosure were also published in Simpson, *Advice After Appomattox,* 26–31.

2. The *Arago* was an ocean steamer. Chase's party visited Charleston on May 11 and 12, and Savannah on May 16 and 17. In a letter written from occupied Charleston on May 12, Chase identified three categories of southern whites: "old conservatives" who favored slavery's restoration; "acquiescents," the "largest class," resigned to Reconstruction in any form; and "progressives" who advocated full civil rights for African Americans. In addition, he recounted details of a meeting on May 9 with a "colored deputation" in Wilmington, North Carolina. "They must work hard now;" Chase told his listeners, "get & save all they could, & await the future hopefully & patiently." Chase to Johnson, May 12, 1865 (Johnson Papers, L.C.); *Chase Papers,* 1:542–46, 548, 550–51.

3. Charles Macbeth, George Walton Williams, John Phillips, and Robert W. Seymour.

4. In his diary, Chase described members of the delegation as "all free & all able to read & write." *Chase Papers,* 1:547.

5. Brig. Gen. Rufus Saxton was military governor of the Department of the South, 1862–65. Maj. Gen. Quincy Adams Gillmore had commanded federal troops in the same department since 1864. As with other African Americans on this trip, Chase encouraged the congregation of Charleston's Zion Church to practice patience and diligence. "If you are patient and constantly show by your acts that you merit the right of suffrage, that you can safely be trusted with it, that in your hands it will be on the side of order and liberty and education, reasoning upon general principles," he told the audience, "I can safely say that you will get the elective franchise in a very short period." Chase and his companions visited Savannah on May 16 and 17. Ibid, 1:550–51; *Charleston Courier,* May 13, 1865; *DAB,* 7:295.

6. John Porter Hatch, a brigadier general of volunteers, actually presided over the district of Charleston. *DAB,* 8:393.

7. During the Civil War, Ormsby MacKnight Mitchel served in the federal army as a brigadier and major general of volunteers. In September 1862, he assumed command of the Department of South Carolina, where he died of yellow fever the following month. According to journalist Whitelaw Reid, "grateful negroes with a firm belief in [Mitchel's] friendship" named the settlement "Mitchelville" soon after the general's death. Reid, *After the War,* 89; Robson, *Biographical Encyclopædia,* 313–14.

8. Reid estimated that "between two and three hundred" of the former slaves had belonged to Fuller. "The grateful negroes had cherished the memory of Dr. Fuller, who had abandoned his lucrative legal practice to preach to them," wrote Reid. Reid, *After the War,* 102, 104.

9. According to Reid, Chase conferred with two delegations of African Americans in Savannah. The first was "headed by one or two preachers and a school-teacher." The second "consisted of blacks from the country, wearing coarse negro clothes instead of broadcloth, less graceful in their bearing, and less cultivated in their talk." Ibid., 143, 145.

10. The Treasury Department had issued new rules for domestic cotton trade on May 9. Three days later, Johnson delivered a speech to a group of visitors led by the Rev. E. Turner, D.D., president of the District of Columbia's National Theological Institute for Colored Ministers. According to the *New York Times,* the president reaffirmed his support for emancipation, but encouraged appreciation of unnamed "men in the South" who, despite being former slave holders, supposedly "felt a deep interest" in the welfare of African Americans. In addition, Johnson invited his listeners to find a new home better "adapted to their condition" if harmonious relations with whites in the U.S. proved impossible. To the *New York Herald,* the speech demonstrated Johnson's ability as "an experienced statesman." *New York Herald,* May 13, 1865; *New York Times,* May 12, 13, 1865.

11. On May 10, Johnson issued a proclamation that encouraged the "arrest" of all remaining Confederate raiders and threatened to close U.S. ports to ships of any nation that continued to extend "hospitality" to the "insurgent vessels." *Statutes at Large,* 13:757.

12. Troops from the Fourth Michigan Cavalry captured Davis and his entourage near Irwinville, Georgia, early in the morning of May 10. From there, the party headed toward Washington, D.C., under federal escort. Original members—aside from aides, guards, and servants—included Davis, his wife Varina Howell Davis (1826–1906), sister-in-law Margaret Graham Howell (b. 1842), personal secretary Burton Novell Harrison (1838–1904), Confederate postmaster general John Henninger Reagan (1818–1905), and Davis's four surviving children: Margaret Howell Davis (1855–1909), Jefferson Davis, Jr. (1857–78), William Howell Davis (1861–72), and Varina Anne Jefferson Davis (1864–98). When it reached Savannah, the party also included Confederate diplomat Clement Claiborne Clay (1816–82), Clay's wife Virginia Caroline Tunstall Clay (1825–1915), Vice President Alexander Hamilton Stephens (1812–83), and Lt. Gen. Joseph Wheeler (1836–1906) and his staff. The "steamer" to which Chase refers was the *Emilie* (or *Emelie*), a captured Confederate vessel of 458 tons. *Appletons',* 8:499–500; *DAB,* 4:170–71, 5:145–46, 15:432–34; 17:569–75; 20:50–52; Edward T. James, et al., eds., *Notable American Women, 1607–1950 . . .,* 3 vols. (Cambridge, Mass., 1971), 1:348–49; William Lytle, *Merchant Vessels of the United States, 1807–1868* (Mystic, Conn., 1952), 56; Monroe Haskell et al., eds., *The Papers of Jefferson Davis,* 9 vols. to date (Baton Rouge, 1971–), 2:248–49, 5:119; 6:110, 8:182; *OR,* ser. 1, v. 49:535–39.

13. Gillmore issued orders on May 14 that nullified actions by Confederate governors in Georgia, Florida, and South Carolina. In addition, he reaffirmed the free status of former slaves and urged "whites as well as blacks, to make such arrangements and agreements among themselves for compensated labor as shall be mutually advantageous to all parties." *OR,* ser. 1, v. 47, pt. 3:498–99.

14. Legislation of July 13, 1861, authorized the president to restrict commercial trade with areas declared in rebellion. Johnson had already issued an order on April 29 similar to that suggested by Chase. Omitted, however, was any reference to Arkansas and Texas. *Statutes at Large,* 12:257, 13:776–77.

15. Chase originally wrote *loyal citizens,* then added the words *white or black.*

TO EDWIN M. STANTON

Autograph letter. Edwin M. Stanton Papers, Library of Congress (*micro* 35:0875).

Fernandina, May 20, 1865.

My dear Sir,

If you have not seen my letters to the President I shall be very glad to have you take the trouble to read them.[1] They give the best views I have been able to form.

The general result is a thorough conviction that *universal suffrage* is essential to *thorough pacification,* and that the white population will acquiesce in this policy, without any serious opposition, if it is clearly announced, & firmly but kindly pursued.

I find every General I have met impressed by this conviction, except one.[2] Of course those who entertain it feel different degrees of certainty or expectation: but with almost all it is quite strong.

Among the generals I have met Gillmore is the ablest, most earnest, & most thoroughly in sympathy with the policy which you & I have always advocated. He seems to me the clearest headed administrative man I have met since I left Washington.

Nobody that I know of could so well fill his place here: but should the plan of making each state a Department, which seems to be on many accounts wisest, be adopted this Department must be subdivided. In that case Georgia will be the most important state.

I believe I mentioned in a short note written some days since my impression that Saxton will be the best Head of the Bureau of Freedmen.[3] He has succeeded well with the work you gave him to do & his experience acquired in it will be worth much.

My journey has taught me a great deal and I hope to learn much more, before it is ended. The deepest lesson yet is the immense capacity of the country, sure to be seen, under wise administration, in restoration and recuperation so speedy & so complete as to astonish the world.

Faithfully your friend
S P Chase

Hon E. M. Stanton.

1. Since leaving Washington, D.C., Chase is known to have written from Beaufort and Wilmington, North Carolina (May 4, 7, and 8), and Charleston and Hilton Head, South Carolina (May 12 and 17). On May 17, he also sent a letter of introduction in behalf of Richard Fuller. Additional correspondence, which the editors have not found, may have been sent on May 2 from Fortress Monroe, Virginia, according to *Chase Papers,* 1:537. Copies of all known letters are located in the Andrew Johnson Papers, Library of Congress, reproduced, except for Fuller's introduction, in Simpson, *Advice After Appomattox,* 17–31.

2. Evidently, William T. Sherman. See Sherman's letters to Chase of May 6, 1865 (above).

3. Legislation of March 3 had established the Freedmen's Bureau. On May 12, President Johnson appointed Brig. Gen. Oliver Otis Howard, U.S.A., who held the post from 1865 to 1872. John A. Carpenter, *Sword and Olive Branch: Oliver Otis Howard* (Pittsburgh, 1964), 224–25; *DAB,* 9:279–80; Long, *Civil War Day by Day,* 646; William S. McFeely, *Yankee Stepfather: General O. O. Howard and the Freedmen* (New Haven, 1968; reprint, New York, 1970), 25–26; *Statutes at Large,* 13:507–9.

TO CHARLES SUMNER

Autograph letter. Hampton L. Carson Collection, Rare Book Department, The Free Library of Philadelphia (*micro* 35:0880).

Jacksonville, Fla. May 20, 1865.

My dear Sumner

Yesterday I administered the oath of office to Mr. Adolph Mot, the first Mayor of the City of Fernandina, elected by black & white citizens.[1] Was not that an event?

Sometime ago the citizens had a meeting and the question whether the colored men should be allowed to vote was much discussed; finally the liberals carried it. The election for mayor was held soon after, and Mr. Mot was elected by a very handsome majority. He had not been sworn in when we stopped there yesterday, and I was asked to administer the oath; and was not at all loth to do so. Major General Gillmore; who is now visiting the Ports in Florida under his command, and whose guest I am on the Transport W. W. Coit—was present & several others officials & citizens. So Fernandina has a loyal mayor elected by a majority of *all* the loyal citizens. If all such elections result in the choice of such men the South will rapidly revive under universal suffrage. I do most earnestly hope that the President will see to it that it is not reorganized under hostile votes.

I was much gratified by what I saw at Fernandina. The place is small & much damaged by the waste of war, though exempt from conflagrations and bombardments. Cultivation is resumed to the full extent of the working force: and promises to be very productive. Mr. Mot is introducing the Vine—having already planted a respectable vineyard. He has made some olive oil superior in quality as he says to the best of France or Italy or Spain. He will do much for the Island [in this] way.[2]

The Schools seem to be doing very well. Gen. G—— & I visited two. They are composed of scholars of all ages & colors. Many of the colored soldiers attend and are striving very diligently for knowledge. The teachers are of that army of women—to whom this country owes more than it can ever pay & more than I fear it will ever be conscious of. The world has never seen such selfdenying and generous zeal for the education of a race as our American women have shewn.

Yulee called on me last night; having come in the day before.[3] He is very anxious about reconstruction: thinks that the whites, without any distinctions not made by the old state Constitution, should be entrusted with the work; admits that personal slaveholding is at an end, but wishes to substitute some form of compulsory labor; insists that the south will be Africanized & ruined if this is not done. General Gillmore showed him the order published this week which I daresay you will have seen before this letter reaches you.[4] It declares absolute freedom for all; hints at the possibility of suffrage for all; advises the ex-slavemasters to give fair wages & the negroes to work for fair wages; & expressly forbids all attempts at reorganization through the ex-rebel authorities whether executive or legislative. The perusal of it rather saddened Mr. Yulee: for he had been commissioned by the Governor of Florida,[5] with others, to proceed to Washn & confer with the President on reorganization

The boat which took Davis north[6] lay alongside of ours, made fast by lines, for some time a few mornings ago between Savannah & Fort

Pulaskie. But I did not see him. I did not wish to unless he asked it, & I presume he was not informed who were on our boat.

The officers who commanded under Sherman & are now occupying portions of Georgia & Florida are far from sound on the reorganization question. One at least had given aid to the capture of men as slaves[7] within the last few weeks, even to the extent of taking enlisted men from the ranks. I hope the President will lose no time in setting all this right. It is very important.

Gen Gillmore is the ablest, wisest, firmest and at the same time most conciliatory officer I have seen. He is thoroughly convinced of the safety & duty of giving to the loyal blacks the same rights of suffrage as is accorded to loyal whites & only waits full authority from Washington to put everything in the Dept. of the South on the best foundations.

Faithfully yours
S P CHASE

I hope to be in Washington again in about four weeks.[8]

1. Chase had known Adolphus Mot, a native of France, as a resident of Columbus, Ohio, during the 1850s.
2. Fernandina, Florida, sits on Amelia Island. *OR Atlas,* plate 145.
3. David Levy Yulee was a Southern businessman and former U.S. senator from Florida.
4. Chase refers to Gillmore's orders of May 14, mentioned in correspondence to Andrew Johnson on May 17, 1865 (above).
5. Confederate John Milton (1807–65) filled the post from 1861 until April 1, 1865, when he took his own life. *DAB,* 13:21.
6. The *Emilie* (or *Emelie*).
7. Chase originally wrote *recapture of slaves,* then altered the phrase to *capture of men as slaves.*
8. Chase returned to Washington, D.C., on August 17. Chase to Kate Chase Sprague, Aug. 17, 1865 (Chase Papers, Hist. Soc. of Pa.).

TO CHARLES SUMNER

Autograph letter. Chase Papers, Library of Congress (*micro* 35:0921).

Cincinnati, June 25, 1865.

My dear Sumner,

You wished me, if I remember rightly, to have the two letters I wrote to President Lincoln, published; and a few days ago I consented to allow one of the Editors of the Cincinnati Gazette to make use of them as you will see by the numbers of the paper sent with this note.[1]

I come home profoundly impressed with the conviction that President Johnson makes a great mistake in refusing to recognize the colored citizens as part of the people with which, in each state, he thinks himself not only authorized but bound to arrange the conditions of restoration.[2] It is a moral, political, & financial mistake. The vanquished rebels were ready to accept, though of course reluctantly, universal suffrage; a large portion of the loyal whites regarded it as essential to their own safety; the whole body of the colored citizens were anxious for it, & will never be satisfied or work contentedly without it. It is safe I think to estimate the commercial & financial value of the products of labor for five years with universal suffrage at not less than five hundred millions of dollars more than their probable amount without it. So does God tie together national duty & national prosperity.

I am grievously disappointed. But we must "bate no jot of heart or hope."[3] The People may set all right by refusing to states whose constitutions are made by a minority of the people & deny the right of so large a portion, & that the most loyal, of the same people, recognitions as restored members of the Union. If this hope also be disappointed we must work for the constitutional amendment & having obtained that renew our appeal to the People, which in the end will obey the instincts of humanity & the voice of justice.[4]

I expect to be at Narragansett Beach next week; where I should be so happy to meet you.[5] Narragansett Beach is the name of Governor Sprague's farm. The name of the Post Office is Wakefield. Let me find, at all events, a letter.

Yours faithfully
S P CHASE

Hon. Charles Sumner.

1. Copies of Chase's letters of April 11 and 12 (above) appeared in a column on June 24 signed by "Agate," Whitelaw Reid's pseudonym. *Cincinnati Daily Gazette*, June 24, 1865; *DAB*, 15:482.

2. The last segment of Chase's journey through the South ended on June 22 with his arrival in Cincinnati. President Johnson had issued proclamations on May 29 and June 13 that called for reconstruction of state governments in North Carolina and Mississippi based on antebellum constitutions that withheld the franchise from African Americans. Similar proclamations for Alabama, Georgia, and Texas followed on June 17 and 21. *Chase Papers*, 1:577–78; Foner, *Reconstruction*, 183; *Statutes at Large*, 13:760–62, 764–68.

3. John Milton, *Sonnett XXII*, lines 7–8. James Holly Hanford, *The Poems of John Milton*, 2d ed. (New York, [1953]), 187.

4. The Fifteenth Amendment, which went into effect on March 30, 1870, established equal voting rights throughout the nation. *Statutes at Large*, 16:1131–32.

5. The editors have not found any evidence that Sumner accepted Chase's offer, but the two men are known to have met in Boston on July 15. *Chase Papers*, 1:591.

TO JAMES SHEPHERD PIKE

Autograph letter. James Shepherd Pike Collection, Special Collections Department, Raymond H. Fogler Library, University of Maine (*micro* 35:0945).

Narragansett Beach July 8. 1865.

My dear Mr. Pike,[1]

On arriving here yesterday I found your letter of Apl. 19, which is not the less welcome because I find it was written under some misconception of what I wrote to Mrs P—— whose promise to you, by the way, of a letter to me was not kept as I wish it had been.[2]

I am afraid that I was not fortunate in the choice of expressions. If they conveyed, as it seems they did, any other sentiment than simple regret & pain that you had misunderstood my financial administration in some particulars & at a critical moment when I was almost overwhelmed by difficulties & anxieties of which you could know little or nothing, & had expressed yourself to the Secretary of State in terms of censure, which I thought, perhaps mistakenly, that he took a certain pleasure in immediately bringing to my special notice—certainly I remember no praise or cheer from any quarter that ever reached me through him—I say if they conveyed any other sentiment than this they conveyed more than I intended. Under ordinary circumstances what you said would have pained me less; but just then the persecutions of which I was made the object by those who claimed closest relations with the administration had reached their culmination, and my enemies, without cause, had succeeded in persuading Mr. Lincoln that certain appointments were essential to his reelection which I could not sanction without conscious disregard of public duty, & thus had brought about a state of feeling which made it impossible for me to remain in office & retain my self respect.[3] I cannot now recall what you said; but you will now easily comprehend how words which at another time would have moved me little, may well, at that time, have moved me much. You were one of my friends, most respected in his opinions & most trusted for sincerity; and I felt abandoned—and yet I *knew* in the depths of my understanding & conscience, that I was right in principle & in policy. Looking back now upon my whole financial administration I see no measure of importance which does not stand approved by my judgment, except my compliance with the wishes of the New York Banks in making the interest on a portion of the 5% legal tenders payable semiannually;[4] and I took good care to reduce the amount of this issue, by receipt & cancellation, so rapidly that little or no actual harm came of it.

Well, it is all over now. Accept my thanks for the kindness of your note. It is a comfort to me. It is also a comfort that my great aim to give the country a National currency—a permanent support to commerce & a steady stimulus & guaranty to labor—is being crowned with complete success. Had I remained at the Head of the Treasury, & been supported properly I should have resumed specie payments long since.[5] I wish Mr. McCulloch wd. now: This & its correlations are my only disagreements with him.

I have just returned from a long journey through the rebel states.[6] I visited Fortress Monroe, Beaufort, N.C., Newberne, Wilmington, Charleston, Hilton Head, Beaufort S.C. & the Sea Islands, Savannah,

Fernandina, Jacksonville, St Augustine Key West, Mobile, New Orleans, Vicksburgh, & so on up the Mississippi & the Ohio, by Cincinnati, Cleveland & New York, here. On the Mississippi I visited seven plantations; one that of a loyal planter & the other six in possession of the Government or its lessees / Among the six were those of Judge Rost, Gen. Dick Taylor, Jeff Davis, Joe Davis brother of Jeff & one of Gen Quitman.[7] I also visited Havana, Guines, & Matanzas in Cuba. Every where in the rebel states I gave special attention to the condition of the colored citizens and to the sentiments of the whites. Two things—or rather three things were conspicuous in the former class—eagerness for education, especially of the children; anxiety to own land; and desire for suffrage. I saw all sorts of emancipated people—the commonest field hands & the most intelligent mechanics & house servants. The Mechanics, & barbers compose their Aristocracy. From these come their preachers & their doctors. They have no use for lawyers. They have, however, not unfrequently, a sort of courts, but plaintiff & defendants manage their own causes.

Whereever our armies went, teachers followed. Some dedicated themselves & their property to the work;—some were sent by religious bodies;—some by Freedmen's Commissions under various names. Schools were opened almost as soon as the flag was displayed. It was a sort of educational army following the Military progress. And I suppose that nowhere in the world was there ever displayed such hunger for education as the colored people showed. Old & young flocked to the schools. The novelty of the thing of course had much to do with this: but though the novelty has worn off & the attendance, in places has a good deal diminished yet on the whole the interest has increased on more solid grounds & the aggregate attendance is greater than ever. Four years have made great changes in the educational condition of the blacks; but I expect wonders from the next four years. I wish I had time & space to go into details; but I have not. But I send you two pictures one representing a group of children liberated by the war, at school in New Orleans—the other a similar group at school in Natchez. I brought them home with me & meant to keep them; but they may do more good in your hands than in mine.

They are very anxious to be landholders. On the Sea Islands, under a plan of my own, the Government bought lands sold for taxes; divided them into small tracts, 10, 20 & so on up to 320 acres, & sells them to the colored people. Many of them have become owners in fee simple & are doing exceedingly well.[8] Others are laborers either for the Government or individuals. Some hold small offices, among them Robert Small who commands the steamer he brought out of Charleston now employed as a transport.[9] The whole of this population is about 15.000, of which about 3000 are in a town regularly organized with a very respectable municipal government. Gen. Saxton provided a Savings Bank for this population & the deposits exceed $150.000.00. On the Mississippi various systems have been tried. That which answers best is that of leaving plantations taken possession of by the government to the negroes in association. I visited Gen. Dick Taylor's plantation now cultivated in this way. It was never more productive of cotton & corn & never so productive of vegetables for ordinary domestic use. I do not know what policy will be adopted by the Govt. but I expected great things from the Freedmens Bureau under Gen. Howard.

I regret exceedingly that Prest. Johnson does not see his way clear to recognize the rights of the whole loyal people to vote in reorganization. He seems to me to make a mistake in disregarding the change wrought by the war in the citizenship, while he recognizes that change in the freedom, of the whole people. I enclose some letters which express my views & may interest you. I communicated them fully to Prest. J. before I went South.[10]

I have not been at Washington since my return. The mail this moment brings the news that the conspirators expiate their crime today on the scaffold. I sincerely hope we have now seen the last of Military Commissions. However warranted by laws of war or even indispensable, they should be resorted to as sparely as possible.[11]

Mr. Johnson has been really ill—but I hope is now out of danger if indeed he has been in danger. Mr. Stanton is much worse. Mr. Seward, escaped, almost by miracle, & his son, also, whom every body loves, are almost well again. We all mourn Mrs. Sewards loss: and sympathize with Mr. Seward in this sore bereavement.[12] Every body else seems well—but every body else hardly balance these.

I must not forget to tell you that I am a grandpa. Mrs Sprague has a fine son three weeks old & mother & child are in excellent health.[13] Nettie went with me on *"the round."*

Give my very best regards to Mrs P——. I wish she would write & that you would not let her writing make you omit it.

Sincerely & faithfully your friend,
S P CHASE

P.S. My address is *Washington City*[14]

1. So dated in the original, but actually written on July 7, 1865. Pike was an author, editor, and personal friend of Chase and, at this time, U.S. minister to The Hague. *Chase Papers,* 1:588.

2. Chase's longtime friend Elizabeth Ellicott had married Pike in 1855. In correspondence to her, written on March 17, Chase had described his distress over criticism of U.S. finances that appeared in a State Department dispatch authored by her husband. According to Chase, the report had lent support to adversaries intent on securing his resignation from Lincoln's cabinet—an event that transpired on June 30, 1864. Pike's response, written on April 19, acknowledged "profound concern" over "the progress of our

finances," but offered assurances of enduring friendship. Also included in the letter was a promise that "Lizzie" would write Chase "directly." Ibid., 1:236; Chase to Elizabeth E. Pike, Mar. 17, 1865 (James Shepherd Pike Coll., University of Maine); Long, *Civil War Day by Day,* 530; James Shepherd Pike to Chase, Apr. 19, 1865 (Chase Papers, Hist. Soc. of Pa.).

3. Chase and Lincoln disagreed in particular over the appointment of an assistant treasurer at New York and the collector of customs and general appraiser at the New York Custom House. Chase tendered his resignation on June 29, 1864. *Chase Papers,* 4:408–10.

4. The Ways and Means Act of March 1863 authorized 5 percent legal-tender notes with coupons, redeemable for interest every six months. *Report of the Secretary of the Treasury on the State of Finances, for the Year 1864,* 38th Cong., 2d sess., 1864, H. Ex. Doc. 3:18; *Statutes at Large,* 12:710.

5. "Nearly all of the State banks have voluntarily changed into national associations," reported the comptroller of the currency's annual report for 1865, "and it is a gratifying fact that this transformation has been accomplished without deranging the business of these institutions, or affecting essentially the volume of bank note circulation." Congress did not authorize the Treasury to resume specie payments until January 14, 1875. *Report of the Secretary of the Treasury on the State of Finances, for the Year 1865,* 39th Cong., 1st sess., 1865, H. Ex. Doc. 3:63; *Statutes at Large,* vol. 18, pt. 3:296.

6. Chase landed in Cincinnati on June 22. Between June 29, when he left that city, and July 4, he visited Columbus, Cleveland, and New York. He arrived at his older daughter's house in Rhode Island on July 6. *Chase Papers,* 1:577–78, 582–83, 586–87.

7. Pierre A. Rost and Richard Taylor, son of Zachary Taylor, hailed from St. Charles Parish, Louisiana. Mississippians Jefferson Davis, Joseph Emory Davis, an attorney, and John Anthony Quitman, a lawyer, soldier, and politician, owned plantations on the Mississippi River at Davis Bend. The "loyal planter" was evidently Thomas P. May, who lived near New Orleans. Ibid., 1:564, 570–71, 572.

8. Chase evidently refers to a recommendation that originated on June 7, 1862, with the direct-tax commissioners of South Carolina and that he officially endorsed on January 25, 1863. With Abraham Lincoln's sanction, Chase issued corresponding instructions to the tax commissioners on December 30, 1863. Ibid., 4:236–37; *Report of the Direct Tax Commissioners of South Carolina,* 37th Cong., 3d sess., 1862–63, S. Ex. Doc. 26.

9. In May 1862, Smalls (1839–1915), a former slave, had commandeered *The Planter,* a 300-ton Confederate steamer on which he served, and handed it over to the U.S. Navy. Soon after, Federal officials named him captain of the vessel. In 1875, Smalls entered the U.S. House as a congressman from South Carolina, where he stayed with one interruption until 1887. *DAB,* 17:224–25; *ORN,* ser. 2, v. 1:180.

10. As with other recent correspondents, Chase might have enclosed copies of letters written to Lincoln on April 11 and 12, 1865 (both above). Chase to John M. Schofield, May 7, 1865; Chase to Jacob W. Schuckers, July 7, 1865; and William T. Sherman to Chase, May 6, 1865 (all above).

11. Chase returned to Washington on August 17. According to the *Providence Daily Journal* of July 7, death warrants had been delivered on July 6 to George A. Atzerodt, David Edgar Herold, Lewis Thornton Powell, and Mary Eugenia Surratt, Lincoln assassination conspirators convicted by military commission. Despite widespread criticism, immortalized through Chase's concurring opinion in the case of *Ex parte Milligan* (1866), such trials continued through 1870. *Chase Papers,* 1:587–88; Chase to Kate Chase Sprague, Aug. 17, 1865 (Chase Papers, Hist. Soc. of Pa.); Fairman, *Reconstruction and Reunion,* 209–10; Mark E. Neely, Jr., *The Fate of Liberty: Abraham Lincoln and Civil Liberties* (New York, 1991), 176–77; *OR,* ser. 2, v. 8:696–700; 4 Wall. 132–42 (1866).

12. Edwin M. Stanton suffered from asthma throughout most of his life. William H. Seward and Frederick William Seward were recovering from wounds inflicted on the night of Lincoln's assassination. Frances Adeline Miller Seward (c. 1805–1866), the senior Seward's wife, had died on June 21 of "billious fever." According to the *Washington Evening Star* of that date, the disease was "doubtless" the result of "constant and untiring attendance upon her husband and son." Chase to Charlotte S. Eastman, Apr. 24, 1865 (above); Fletcher Pratt, *Stanton: Lincoln's Secretary of War* (New York, 1953), 12.

13. William Sprague, Jr., his father's namesake. *Chase Papers,* 1:579.

14. Pike had previously sent correspondence that never reached its destination. Chase might have included this postscript to help insure future deliveries. Pike to Chase, Apr. 19, 1865 (Chase Papers, Hist. Soc. of Pa.).

TO JACOB W. SCHUCKERS

Autograph letter. Chase Papers, Library of Congress (*micro* 35:0941).

Narragansett Beach
P.O. Wakefield, July 7, 1865.

My dear Mr. Shuckers,[1]

Both your notes have come & done me good. It is my greatest gratification—or among my greatest—that so many of the young men with whom I have been brought in contact manifest so much & so warm personal affection for me. Among these young men no one has a larger share of my own affection & respect than yourself.

Mrs Sprague & her boy are both doing very well—both indeed in excellent health.[2] If she knew of my writing she would send her best regards, for that *unjust judgment* has been reversed a good while. The boy is a "*brick*".

I wish I *could* give you some hints for a speech;[3] but I cant give any which will be of use. You will of course talk about the war; and its issues. A dumb man might be eloquent on such a theme. You will hardly forget the National Currency as one of those issues. I think it the greatest next to the Freedom of Labor: and it is an inexpressible satisfaction to me to know that my silent work is today a mainspring of prosperous commerce & a sure guaranty of just rewards to labor & so of active & fruitful industry. Isn't it good to think that every workman in the land is better off for my work.

A debatable issue yet but sure to come is Universal suffrage. If you speak of this insist that the American Idea is the *right* of every man, of full age & unconvicted of crime, to share in the government by the vote.

Mr. Johnson's mistake I think is in looking to the Constitutions of the States to ascertain the rights of citizens any more than the rights of Men. The *war* has made all men *free* & the *war* has made all men *citizens.* His duty is to look at *actual relations now*—not at legal relations five years ago. He has no right to say that the loyal blacks are not a part of the people. In saying that the loyal people constitute the state & must reorganize it & then saying that the loyal blacks shall have no part in the reorganization he seems to me to contradict himself.[4]

But my hope is that all will come right. Mr. Johnson will hardly interfere with Congress & Congress can pass a simple law of reorganization providing for the enrollment of all loyal citizens.[5] Even if this reorganization shall be confined to the whites & the states readmitted with Constitutions limiting suffrage to whites we must by no means despair. Truth will prevail at last. We shall probably have troubles which might be avoided by a wise policy, & we shall be delayed in recuperation & lose hundreds of millions which might be saved; but the just cause will triumph in the end.

Nothing can be gained by discontents & divisions. Let us all hold together & support the President just as far as we can. He will, in almost all things,—such at least is my confidence—coincide in judgment with the progressive men of the party. He will hold fast by the constitutional amendment; & this once adopted will be a fulcrum of immense value to movement & progress.[6]

At any rate patience, cheerfulness, hope—these will work the best results.

Thank you for that little article. I noticed it but did not know it was yours. It is a good thing to have friends correct errors & make good suggestions for the press.

I enclose a couple—or rather three letters which you may have seen. The second to Mr. Lincoln does not do justice to Gen Banks / I became satisfied of this at New Orleans. Had he not been superceded he would have done immense good. What about *our* book?[7]

Your friend Sincerely
S P Chase

1. Schuckers, an Ohio native and 1865 graduate of Albany Law School in New York, had worked as a clerk in the Treasury during the Civil War and served briefly as one of Chase's secretaries. Schuckers later became one of Chase's biographers.

2. Kate Sprague had given birth to Chase's first grandchild, William Sprague, Jr., on or around June 20. *Chase Papers,* 1:579.

3. A copy of this letter, in Schuckers's hand in the Chase Papers, Library of Congress, contains the following bracketed insertion at this point: "I had expected to make an address before my classmates of the Albany Law School."

4. Earlier in the summer, Johnson had taken measures to reconstruct former Confederate states relying on antebellum constitutions that disenfranchised former slaves. Recently, he had suggested that African-American votes could be manipulated and used against "the poor white man." "You and I know as to where the control of negro vote would fall," Johnson warned a South Carolina delegation on June 24; "When they come to talk about the elective franchise, I say let each State judge for itself." Chase to Charles Sumner, June 25, 1865 (above); *Statutes at Large,* 13:760–71; *Washington Evening Star,* June 26, 1865.

5. Equal voting rights on a national level were not fully established until ratification of the Fifteenth Amendment, which went into effect on March 30, 1870. *Statutes at Large,* 16:1131–32.

6. Chase anticipated ratification of the Thirteenth Amendment, which outlawed slavery, effective December 18, 1865. Long, *Civil War Day by Day,* 696.

7. Two of the letters to which Chase evidently refers were written to Lincoln on April 11 and 12, 1865 (both above). Earlier correspondence from Schuckers had discussed the possibility of a project to edit Chase's speeches, which evidently never materialized. Schuckers to Chase, Nov. 22, 1864 (Chase Papers, L.C.).

FROM QUINCY ADAMS GILLMORE

Autograph letter. Chase Papers, Historical Society of Pennsylvania (*micro* 36:0029).

Hilton Head S.C.
Aug. 22" 1865.

My dear Sir

I enclose a news-paper containing Gov: Perry's proclamation, & my Gen. Orders No 9 thereon.[1] You will see at a glance the gist of the matter. Gov: Perry had certain powers delegated to him viz: to take all necessary & proper steps for convening a convention to amend the old constitution of the State or present a new one.— He steps greatly beyond this, however, & proclaims the restoration to power of all the civil functionaries, upon their simply taking the amnesty oath.[2]— He does not require them to obtain pardon, even should they belong to the most obnoxious of the excepted classes.— I could not, from my interpretation of the terms of the Presidents proclamation appointing Gov: Perry,[3] allow the former civil officers to resume their functions, and therefore, in my order, restricted the powers of the "*Provisional Government,*" as the governor ambitiously styles himself, to those actually delegated to him. Martial law remains the only law throughout the state.—

If my course is right,—and I am very clear in my convictions that it is—, then Gen. Woods, if the newspaper reports are true, is all wrong in Alabama; for there, Gov: Parsons has assumed an attitude in every respect as unauthorized as Gov. Perry's,[4] & the military have been directed to support, & remain subordinate to, the newly restored civil funtionaries.—

I referred the matter to the War Dept, on the 1st. inst, and, in the mean time, every thing connected therewith remains in a state of quiet and very satisfactory abeyance.— I do not want instructions but prefer to let things remain as they are.— The colored people would be in a sad plight, if they were obliged to depend for justice upon the set of officials which Gov: Perry wishes to restore to power.—

Either Gen: Woods, or myself, is wrong.— We have had Gen. Carl Schurz here on an official visit. I enclose for your perusal a copy of a letter which I wrote him.[5]

I expect to be in Washington for one day sometime between the 5th. & 15th of next month, &, if you are there at that time, will call and see you. With respectful regards to your daughter I remain[6]

Very truly

Your obdt. Svt.
Q. A. Gillmore

Chief Justice S. P. Chase
Washington D.C.

1. South Carolina's Reconstruction had proceeded in accordance with a presidential proclamation issued on June 30. On July 20, Provisional Governor Benjamin F. Perry (1805–86) had issued orders to reorganize the state under terms that the *Charleston Courier* called "liberal and comprehensive." As explained below, Gillmore disagreed with selected portions, and in General Orders No. 9, issued on July 29, instructed troops under his command to facilitate only those parts "not inconsistent" with Perry's presidential commission. *Charleston Courier,* July 31, Aug. 5, 1865; *DAB,* 14:483–84; *Statutes at Large,* 13:769–71.

2. Andrew Johnson's Proclamation of Amnesty, issued on May 29, offered pardons to former Confederates who promised to "support, protect, and defend the Constitution of the United States, and the Union of the States thereunder," and "in like manner, abide by, and faithfully support all laws, and proclamations which have been made during the existing rebellion with reference to the emancipation of slaves." Among those excluded, however, were "all who are or shall have been pretended civil or diplomatic officers, or otherwise domestic or foreign agents, of the pretended confederate government." *Statutes at Large,* 13:758–59.

3. Perry's instructions, included within the presidential proclamation of June 30 to reorganize South Carolina, specifically referred to Johnson's Amnesty Proclamation of May 29. According to his commission, Perry was authorized to convene a state constitutional convention "composed of delegates to be chosen by that portion of the people of said state who are loyal to the United States, and no others." Ibid., 13:770.

4. Maj. Gen. Charles Robert Woods (1827–85) had commanded the Department of Alabama since June 27. Six days earlier, Andrew Johnson had appointed Lewis Eliphalet Parsons (1817–95) as provisional governor of the state. The instructions that Parsons issued on July 20 offered lenient terms similar to Perry's. *Appletons' Annual Cyclopædia,* 5:12–13; *DAB,* 14:268–69, 20:501–2.

5. Carl Schurz, previously a major general in the Union army, was traveling through states of the former Confederacy at the request of Andrew Johnson to report on conditions in the South. In September, Schurz commenced a career in journalism, and in 1868 won a seat to the U.S. Senate, where he represented Missouri until 1875. In his letter to Schurz, written on July 27, Gillmore assessed conditions in the South, which, in his opinion, required continued presence by U.S. troops to secure "the spirit of the Emancipation proclamation" and the organization of free labor. *DAB,* 16:468–69; Gillmore to Schurz, July 27, 1865 (Chase Papers, Hist. Soc. of Pa.), printed in *Documents Accompanying the Report of Major General Carl Schurz,* 39th Cong., 1st sess., 1865–66, S. Ex. Doc. 2, 47–49.

6. Gillmore was in Washington, D.C., on September 28, but did not meet with Chase. The greetings were intended for Chase's youngest daughter, Nettie, a teenager who still resided with her father. Gillmore to Chase, Sept. 28, 1865 (Chase Papers, Hist. Soc. of Pa.).

TO CHARLES SUMNER

Autograph letter. Chase Papers, Library of Congress (*micro* 36:0020).

Washington Aug 20, 1865.

My dear Sumner,[1]

I saw Harlan at church Sunday & a moment or two afterwards on the Street; but had no chance for talk. Stanton has called to see me—he alone of all the "Heads."[2]

I called on Mr. Johnson immediately on my return. It seemed to me that he was less cordial than before I went South. This perhaps was fancy. He wished to talk to me about the time, place & manner of the trial of Davis; but this did not seem to me a proper subject of conference between the President & Chief Justice & so I respectfully told him, and he readily as I thought assented.[3] So nothing passed except some general observations on his part about the necessity of doing something in the matter soon & on mine about the necessity of careful consideration of all steps to be taken by himself & the Cabinet & particularly the Attorney General.[4] He evidently did not wish to discuss other questions & indeed there was no time.

Mr. Stanton came to see me last Saturday night. He is unchanged, but does not feel inclined to urge the suffrage views on the President. He expressed some apprehension that the claims made by the Provisional Governors in several of the states that the military & especially the colored troops shall be withdrawn will be conceded. This seems to me hardly possible.

I have not seen a great many persons here. Among those I have seen there are very different opinions. Some insist that the President is trying an experiment only which is sure to fail & that he will either change the plan himself, or will agree cheerfully to have it changed by Congress; others think that he is convinced that the two races cannot exist together and is definitely opposed to allowing them suffrage where they are, and that he is preparing to make terms with those of the opposition who hold these opinions / There is a good deal which seems to confirm this latter supposition. And yet it is only this morning that Col Eaton[5] told me that he saw him yesterday and that he then confessed himself very decidedly as being himself in favor of universal suffrage. Perhaps the truth is that he is doubtful about the steps he is already taken & uncertain what course in the future will be safest & best.

Did you see Hitchcocks article in the Chronicle yesterday morning in defence of the action of the War Dept. in the matter of exchange of Prisoners. The defence seemed to me strong; but I was struck by the distinctness of the assertation that the cartel was based on the principle that there were two belligerents & by the language employed about "the two Powers."[6]

The account given by Prov. Govr.? Perry of his interviews with different members of the Administration, especially Mr. Johnson & Mr. Seward is not less singular. What do you think of it?[7]

I am glad that you are to preside at Worcester. You will *need* all your prudence, & *must not abate* anything of your courage & explicitness.[8]

Schenck at Chillicothe came out against negro suffrage! I was sorry to observe this. But Cox pitched his pipe to the Executive tune, & Schenck, I suppose, thought it safest to fall in. What lump and what leaven![9]

Sorry I am to say that I have not found the Bemis pamphlet. I wish I could.[10]

Write me fully.

Ever faithfully yours
S P Chase

Hon Charles Sumner

1. Chase clearly assigned a date of August 20 to this letter, but reference in its body to a newspaper article published two days later indicates that he actually wrote it on August 23.

2. On May 15, Andrew Johnson had appointed Iowa Republican James Harlan as secretary of the interior. Harlan resigned the post in 1866 and reentered the U.S. Senate, where he served 1855–64 and 1867–73. As explained below, Stanton met with Chase on August 19. *Bio. Dir. U.S. Cong.*, 1134.

3. Chase returned home from his southern trip on August 17, apparently in response to Johnson's request. Davis never did stand trial. Federal officials imprisoned him for two years at Fortress Monroe, Virginia, and released him on bail on May 13, 1867. Davis's case eventually reached the Supreme Court, but Chase and his brethren dismissed it on February 19, 1869, soon after Andrew Johnson took action that extended amnesty to the former Confederate president. Chase to Johnson, Aug. 12, 1865 (Johnson Papers, L.C.); Chase to Kate Chase Sprague, Aug. 17, 1865 (Chase Papers, Hist. Soc. of Pa.); *DAB,* 5:130; Fairman, *Reconstruction and Reunion,* 607–12; Johnson to Chase, Aug. 9, 1865 (Johnson Papers, L.C.).

4. James Speed.

5. Possibly John Eaton, assistant commissioner in the Washington area for the Freedman's Bureau, a colonel since 1863, and a recipient in March of a brevet as brigadier general. *DAB,* 5:609.

6. The article, written by Maj. Gen. Ethan Allen Hitchcock (1798–1870), commissionary general of prisoners of war, defended Edwin M. Stanton for arranging exchanges of captured black U.S. soldiers during the Civil War upon "principles applicable to the white troops." Ibid., 9:73–74; *Washington Daily Morning Chronicle,* Aug. 22, 1865.

7. On June 30, Andrew Johnson had appointed Benjamin Franklin Perry, a South Carolina Unionist, as provisional governor of his state. Soon after, Perry visited Washington, D.C., where he met with Postmaster General William Dennison, President Johnson, Treasury Secretary Hugh McCulloch, Secretary of State William H. Seward, Attorney General James Speed, and Secretary of War Edwin M. Stanton. According to Perry, Johnson expressed opposition to "any attempt on the part of Congress to control the elective franchise of a State." Perry's account of the other meeting depicted Seward as a sympathetic former fellow governor. *Statutes at Large,* 13:770; *Washington Daily Morning Chronicle,* Aug. 22, 1865.

8. Sumner presided over Massachusetts' state Republican convention in Worcester on September 14. *New York Times,* Sept. 15, 1865.

9. Robert Cumming Schenck, a former major general in the U.S. Army, was a Republican congressman from Ohio. On August 16, he addressed an assembly at Chilicothe, Ohio, en route to a military reunion at Scioto and Pike Counties. Schenck's speech expressed willingness to postpone debate over suffrage for African Americans. At present, he suggested, "there was no need for the Union party being disturbed by a discussion of the subject." Campaigning for the governorship of Ohio, Jacob Dolson Cox had recently expressed support for racially segregated political systems in Alabama, Florida, Georgia, and South Carolina. According to the New Testament, "a little leaven leaveneth the whole lump." 1 Cor. 5:6; Gal. 5:9; *New York Times,* Aug. 21, 1865; Eugene H. Roseboom, *The Civil War Era, 1850–1873,* vol. 4 of Carl Wittke, ed., *The History of the State of Ohio* (Columbus, 1944), 450.

10. Chase wanted to purchase a copy of George Bemis, *Hasty Recognition of Rebel Belligerency, and Our Right to Complain of It* (Boston, 1865). Sumner to Chase, Aug. 23, 1865 (Chase Papers, L.C.).

TO WILLIAM SPRAGUE

Autograph letter. Chase Papers, Library of Congress (*micro* 36:0076).

Washington, Sep. 6, 1865.[1]

My dear Governor,

I have written to Katie today & wrote her yesterday. So you see I keep up my part of the correspondence with the "Farm".[2]

But I must not on that account neglect to thank you for your last letter. It always does me good to get a letter from you.

I am afraid that whoever pays 20,000 for the Cove Farm will never see his money back again. It is hardly worth more than ten thousand. The other piece might I think be made to pay. What do you say to joining me in the purchase of one or the other. My means you know are not very abundant.[3]

Besides I have been lately making a little adventure. I have made it, as I always do, on faith. My old friend, Mr. Hanna, one of the most sagacious & careful men I know, told me some time ago of a gold operation of his from which he expected the very best results, & said that when it should be in a shape to *see through* he should offer an interest to me. He had before done a similar thing in respect to some railroad stock which turned out extremely well. So yesterday having got a letter from him offering me an interest of $3000, I took it and shall be disappointed if it does not turn out as the other did cent per cent during the year. I would offer the half of my little venture to you; but I should hate to be laughed at, if disappointed, and, besides, am already fancying your amusement at my small operation.[4]

I enclose a letter of Mr. Hannas in which he refers to another investment in the same sort of property. Perhaps you will not dislike to take an interest.[5]

There is nothing new here politically. I have seen the President, twice; Stanton, Dennison & Speed only have called on me.[6] In my last interview with the President he talked very freely about reorganization. I told him I supposed he had received my letters from the south[7] / He said he had & had preserved them all. He then went into an exposition of his views. The substance was this: the black of the south must either be absorbed into the general community as elements & integral portions precisely as the whites or they must be kept separate. If allowed to vote they will necessarily be so absorbed. Then the results must be looked at. They will naturally vote for men of their own color; and we shall have black members of the State Legislatures, & of Congress—maybe black Governors, & possibly—for it may even come to that a black President. Ought this to be thought of? Is it not a great deal better that the two races should be separated, & each control everything within their own limits? The blacks are entitled to their freedom; but have no claim to the right of suffrage. The arguments for it are popular but not sound. Suppose one should say Here are a great many young fellows of sixteen & eighteen who have fought bravely & done much service; ought they not to be allowed to vote sooner than rebels who have been amnestied & taken the oath? And so of the multitudes of noble women, who have risked so much & labored so devotedly. But nobody asks to have them vote. The races must separate. I offered myself to be their Moses, if no better one could be found.[8] No one is a sincerer friend & more willing to give them their rights than I. Here I could not help saying, "Really, Mr. President, you have thrown a new light on your offer to be the Moses of the Colored People. I supposed it was an offer to lead them out of their *condition* as Slaves, into a new condition of Freedom & Citizenship." I then went on to explain my views briefly: that the blacks were citizens of the United States & of the States in which they live; that under an appeal from the President to the People to reorganize, the blacks as part of the people had a right their fair share of influence & control in the work of reorganization; that the People meant *all* the People without respect to the color of the skin, &c. &c. He listened kindly. In the course of our talk he said After all we are not very far apart; we agree as to the continued existence of the States; the propriety of setting aside all authority derived from rebel appointment or election &, as to the natural rights of all men white or black." "Yes" I replied "there is a great of agreement; but there is also a difference & it occurs at a point from which I fear there will be a wide divergence. But we will talk further of this matter." Seward had just been announced & I left him. What do you think?

Are we all to go under or will Congress save the country?

Most affectionately yours,
S P Chase

Hon Wm Sprague.

1. Chase misdated this letter. In answer, Sprague acknowledged "your note dated the 6th, probably written the 4th." A date of September 5 is also possible, since Chase responded on that date to the letter from Joshua Hanna mentioned elsewhere in this letter. Hanna to Chase, Aug. 31, 1865; Sprague to Chase, Sept. 6, 1865 (both Chase Papers, L.C.).

2. The Spragues owned 350 acres in Narragansett, Rhode Island, that bordered the Atlantic Ocean. Chase is known to have corresponded with his oldest surviving daughter on September 4, 5, and 6. The letter of September 5 has not been found. That of September 4 expressed anxiety over the health of Kate and a servant, and it enclosed two pieces of correspondence: one from Maria Southgate Hawes, Kate's cousin, and another from Col. William Oliver Collins, of the U.S. volunteers, husband to a cousin of Chase's third wife, Sarah Bella, regarding the recent death of his son Lt. Caspar Wever Collins. "You need not give yourself the slightest uneasiness about it," Chase added in regard to Kate's anticipated arrival in Washington, D.C., "but rely on it that you will find everything when you return in tip top order." The letter of September 6 elaborated on household affairs and expressed disapproval of political setbacks "for the side of Freedom & Renovation" in Louisiana. Chase to Kate Chase Sprague, Sept. 4, 6, 1865 (Chase Papers, Hist. Soc. of Pa.); Chase to Charles Sumner, June 25, 1865 (above); *Chase Papers,* 1:244, 587; Agnes Wright Spring, *Caspar Collins: The Life and Exploits of an Indian Fighter of the Sixties* (New York, 1927; reprint, Lincoln, Nebr., 1969), 35–36, 53, 79–99.

3. "I fear this is too much," Sprague had written on August 28 regarding the price of the farm, which was located on a cove near his own property at Narragansett Beach. As alternatives, Sprague had suggested other farms for sale on the "hill" or close to nearby Narragansett Pier. Sprague to Chase, Aug. 28, 1865 (Chase Papers, L.C.).

4. Joshua Hanna, formerly of Pittsburgh, was a New York banker and businessman. His letter of August 31 offered Chase an interest in the Idaho Gold Quartz Company, whose returns later fell short of expectations. Earlier, Chase had invested in the Cleve-

land and Pittsburgh Railroad at Hanna's invitation. Chase to Jay Cooke, Sept. 14, 1866 (Cooke Papers, Hist. Soc. of Pa.); Chase to Hanna, Nov. 8, 1862 (Chase Papers, Hist. Soc. of Pa.); Hanna to Chase, Sept. 28, 1861, and Aug. 31, 1865 (both Chase Papers, L.C.).

5. "I have two or three Gold operations, . . ." responded Sprague; "All proving disastrous. So I am off from mines." Sprague to Chase, Sept. 6. 1865 (Chase Papers, L.C.).

6. Chase met with Johnson "immediately" after returning home from his southern trip on August 17, and with Stanton two days later. The editors have not discovered when the second meeting with Johnson occurred, nor when Postmaster General William Dennison and Attorney General James Speed called on Chase. Chase to Kate Chase Sprague, Aug. 17, 1865 (Chase Papers, Hist. Soc. of Pa.); Chase to Charles Sumner, Aug. [23], 1865 (above).

7. See Chase to Stanton, May 20, 1865 (above), for such correspondence prior to that date. Chase is known to have written two additional letters to the president—both from Florida—before returning home. The first, dated May 21, but most likely written on May 20, according to Chase's diary, summarized local politics in Fernandina. The other, dated May 23, offered impressions from Key West. Chase to Johnson, May 21, 23, 1865 (Johnson Papers, L.C.), reprinted in Simpson, *Advice After Appomattox,* 34–38; *Chase Papers,* 1:553.

8. Encouraged by former slaves, Johnson had assumed the title during a speech to "Colored Men" of Nashville on October 24, 1864. "If no other better shall be found," he reportedly said, "I will indeed be your Moses, and lead you through the Red Sea of war and bondage, to a fairer future of liberty and peace." Leroy P. Graf et al., eds., *The Papers of Andrew Johnson,* 13 vols. to date (Knoxville, 1967–), 7:251–53.

FROM JAMES A. GARFIELD

Autograph letter. Chase Papers, Library of Congress (*micro* 36:0130).

Hiram, O. Oct 4, 1865.

Hon S. P. Chase,
Dear Friend[1]

I was very sorry not to have seen you in Cleveland last week—but my ankle was so painful, after using at the Banquet in honor of the English Capitalist—that I got home as soon as I could[2] / I wanted to call, not only to pay my respects, but to learn from you what we have to hope from the policy now in favor at Washington. I am anxious to know whether the friends of Liberty and Union are to be greeted with Peace or War—when Congress assembles— The weak and timid course of our party in Ohio, has made me more reconciled to the accident which has kept me out of our Campaign—than I otherwise could have been— If we shall not be able to maintain the fight on the suffrage question alone—should we not make a preliminary resistance to immediate restoration and thereby gain time?

I hope you will have the time and inclination to write me your thoughts on this gravest of all questions.

With sincerest regards— I am

Very Truly Your Friend
J. A. Garfield

P.S. I have heard that Mr Hutchins is in Washington laboring to secure the removal of Mr Fassett, Col. of Int. Rev. for this Dist—and get some friend of his appointed in his place[3]— I can hardly think Mr McCullough would do it without my knowledge— Do you think there is any danger of such action? J.A.G.

1. In 1863, Ohio voters had elected Garfield to the U.S. Congress, where he served as a Republican until his inauguration to the presidency in 1881. *DAB,* 7:146–47.

2. Garfield had attended a dinner in honor of Sir Samuel Morton Peto, a British contractor and politician, on the evening of September 26. On the previous day Chase had arrived in Cleveland aboard the *Commodore Perry,* a new Revenue Service cutter, after a week of travel that included stops in New York and Buffalo. In Cleveland, he attended a "Christian Convention," called to establish a "National Society for Evangelization." Chase left the city around September 28, stopping "a few days" for "recreation among the islands of Lake Erie" before heading back to Washington on October 11. Chase to Edward L. Pierce, Oct. 14, 1865 (below); *Chase Papers,* 1:593–96; *Cleveland Plain Dealer,* Sept. 20, 25, 27, 28, 1865; *DNB,* 15:972–74.

3. John Hutchins, a Republican congressman from Ohio, 1859–63, practiced law in Warren. Henry Fassett collected revenue in Ashtabula, subordinate to Treasury secretary Hugh McCulloch. *Bio. Dir. U.S. Cong.,* 1239; *Register of Officers (1865),* 60.

TO ANDREW JOHNSON

Autograph letter. Andrew Johnson Papers, Library of Congress (*micro* 36:0132).

Washington, Thursday Evg, Oct 12, 1865.[1]

Dear Sir,

Your letter of the 2d., directed to Cleveland & forwarded to Sandusky, reached me there night before last.[2] I left for Washington yesterday morning and am just arrived.

To your enquiry whether a term of the Circuit Court of the United States for the District of Virginia will be held by myself or one of the Associate Justices of the Supreme Court during the autumn or early winter, I respectfully reply in the negative

Under ordinary circumstances the regular term, authorized by Congress would be held on the 4th Monday of November which, this year, will be the 27th. Only a week will intervene between that day and the commencement of the Annual term of the Supreme Court, when all the Judges are required to be in attendance at Washington. That time is too short for the transaction of any very important business.

Were this otherwise I so much doubt the propriety of holding Circuit Courts of the United States in States which have been declared by the Executive and Legislative Departments of the National Government to be in rebellion & therefore subjected to Martial law, before the complete restoration of their broken relations with the nation & the supercedure of the military by the civil administration, that I am unwilling to hold such courts in such states within my Circuit, which includes Virginia, until Congress shall have had an opportunity to consider and act on the whole subject.[3]

A civil Court in a district under Martial law can only act by the sanction and under the supervision of the Military power; and I cannot think that it becomes the Justices of the Supreme Court to exercise jurisdiction under such conditions

In this view it is proper to say that Mr. Justice Wayne, whose whole circuit is in the rebel states, concurs with me. I have had no opportunity of consulting the other Justices; but the Supreme Court has hitherto declined to consider cases, brought before it by appeal or writ of error, from Circuit or District Courts in the rebel portion of the country. No very reliable inference, it is true, can be drawn from this action, for circumstance have greatly changed since the Court adjourned; but so far as it goes it favors the conclusion of myself & Mr. Justice Wayne.

With great respect

Yours very truly
S P Chase

To
The President

1. This letter has also been published in Graf, *Papers of Andrew Johnson,* 9:231–32. A slightly different version appeared as well in the *New York Times,* Feb. 3, 1866.

2. Chase alludes to his recent trip to New York and Ohio, discussed in correspondence to James A. Garfield on October 4 (above). Two unsigned versions of the letter from Johnson are known to exist. One is a draft, written in the hand of Benjamin F. Butler, found among Butler's papers, (at the Library of Congress). The other, in an unknown hand, resides among Johnson's papers at the same repository, published also in Graf, *Papers of Andrew Johnson,* 9:161. Both versions suggested the possibility of prosecuting "high crimes and misdemeanors committed against the United States" within the District of Virginia and asked Chase whether he or any other Supreme Court justice intended to preside over the district court for that state in the autumn or early winter.

3. For additional details on Chase's reluctance, see his letters to Flamen Ball, May 12, 1866; George Washington Brooks, March 20, 1866; Horace Greeley, June 1, 1866; and Jacob W. Schuckers, May 15 and September 24, 1866 (all below). On March 2, 1867, Congress authorized the Supreme Court to assign circuits, and Chase assumed his duties in the South the following June. Chase to Janet Chase, June 7, 1867 (below); *Statutes at Large,* 14:433.

TO EDWARD L. PIERCE

Autograph letter. MS Am 1.65, Houghton Library, Harvard University (*micro* 36:0135).

Washington, Oct. 14, 1865.

My dear friend,[1]

I came home from Ohio Thursday Night & found your letter, and read the scrap enclosed.

That which relates Seward's conversation with Perry is characteristic.[2]

I agree with you in thinking that the Sumner-Fessenden feud should come to an end: but there is no cause for Sumner's wonder that mutual friends as Hooper & myself have not intervened.[3] I have done my best, in conversation, with both to bring about reconciliation, going certainly as far as I thought delicacy allowed in my suggestions. The difficulty is not so much in aversion to reconciliation as to making the first advance. Neither thinks *he* ought to. Each thinks the other wholly in the wrong. The fact doubtless, is that there is misconception on both sides—misconception too originating in feeling rather than reason & so, hard to be corrected. Either can well afford to make the first advance & to make it frankly & generously. If I were Sumner I think I should say to Fessenden, "You and I must have no quarrel. We represent the same general cause. You have your ideas & I mine. We will each respect the others & when we cannot agree differ with mutual confidence & respect. I honor your integrity & your abilities and will not allow any man to surpass you in cordial appreciation of your services." Fessenden would meet such an advance as that most frankly & cordially. If I were Fessenden I think I should say about the same things to Sumner; and I am sure Sumner would meet the advance with equal cordiality & frankness.

If the matter is not made up before the next Session I shall renew my efforts for reconciliation, & I know Mr. Hooper will do the same.

I have not yet seen a full report of the proceedings of your State Convention. I saw the conclusion of Sumner's speech in a column or two, excellent every way.[4] My daughters wrote me of your call at Narragansett & were sorry not to see more of you.

After the meeting of the Christian Convention at Cleveland, I gave a, few days to recreation among the islands of Lake Erie, eating grapes & catching black bass.

Best regards to Mrs P——[5]

Yours cordially
S P Chase

Edw L Pierce Esq

1. A Harvard graduate, associate of Charles Sumner, and former Treasury agent, Pierce had accepted an appointment as collector of internal revenue at Boston, a position he held from 1864 to 1866.

2. Benjamin F. Perry's controversial actions as provisional governor of South Carolina are discussed in Quincy Adams Gillmore's letter to Chase of August 22, 1865 (above).

3. Tensions had long existed between Charles Sumner, the idealistic chair of the Senate Foreign Relations Committee, and William Pitt Fessenden, Sumner's more practical colleague on the same committee. On April 27, 1864, Sumner and Fessenden exchanged personal recriminations on the Senate floor during an attempt by Sumner to amend a proposed banking act. Relations between the two senators were never again cordial in spite of efforts by friends like Samuel Hooper, Republican congressman from Massachusetts, 1861–75, to reconcile them. *Congressional Globe,* 38th Cong., 1st sess., 1863–64, pt. 2:1873, 1894–96; David Donald, *Charles Sumner and the Rights of Man* (New York, 1970), 143–45.

4. A detailed account of Massachusetts' state Republican convention, held in Worcester on September 14, appeared in the *New York Times* the following day. Also included in the piece was a transcription of the entire speech, which plead for national guarantees to secure equal rights for former slaves.

5. The convention, which commenced on September 27, had been called to organize a "National Society for Evangelization." Chase attended as part of a recent trip to

New York and Ohio. In April, Pierce had married Elizabeth H. Kingsbury (d. 1880) of Providence, Rhode Island. *Cleveland Plain Dealer,* Sept. 20, 1865; *DAB,* 14:576; James A. Garfield to Chase, Oct. 4, 1865 (above).

TO KATE CHASE SPRAGUE

Letterpress copy of autograph letter. Chase Papers, Historical Society of Pennsylvania (*micro* 35:0596).

Washington, [Oct]. 14, 1865.

My darling child

Your letter *did* come "just about in time" to give me "a welcome home". It came last night and I came the night before.

Do not trouble yourself at all about me. I am very well & doing very well. Mrs. Golden is a good enough cook; indeed, quite as good, I think, as Charlotte.[1] I am in no danger of starvation. Nor shall I want any silver from the Bank. I could get along *well enough* with the little I have: but what you have sent, will, when it comes be *very well.* Mrs Golden needs no money. I will supply whatever she wants. I shall have the muslin taken, perhaps, from one or two articles; but I prefer to have it remain on the rest. As to rooms, I propose putting most of the Library in the little room I slept in last winter; using the larger room as an office; and taking the room directly above that for a bedroom; or, if it will be more convenient to you I will go into the third story altogether, taking the three front rooms, putting the Library in the little room there, using the room above the present Library & office for office & the South East corner room for a bed room. The only inconvenience of this arrangement to me will be the necessity of seeing those who call on me down stairs in the sitting room or parlor.

Mrs Golden says she can make the red & green ingrain answer for a carpet for the servants sitting & dining room. She says she can make more out of it than the yellow carpet on the 2d. floor hall, which is too small.

It will be very difficult to get a second hand stove for the room such as you wish; but a good cooking stove can be had for $20, and a parlor cooking stove which would be better for a somewhat higher price say $30.

Mr. Walker has been here today with Mr. Woodward, about the back building, & while here measured the the fire places on the parlor floor.[2] I enclose his measurements which you will easily understand; but I will, to make sure, give you those of the Dining room fireplace. The height of that fire place from it's floor to the top of the arch is 2 feet 6½ inches & the width from wall to wall 2 feet 9 inches. The width of the hearth in front of the fireplace is 17 inches & its length four feet ten inches. Mr. Walker says that he has already sent you measurements for the carpets carefully noting the space to left out for the fireplaces.

Nothing has yet been done about the woodshed. Mr. Woodward has been very sick and narrowly escaped with life. He is not yet fully well. This accounts for some delay. Mr. Walker says the old woodshed in t[he cor]ner of the lot can be moved without any considerable expence; or he can build a new & better one either of one or two stories. He says he could build one of two stories, say 30 feet long by [18] wide, making a pair of stairs, leading to two plastered rooms in the 2d. story suitable for servants, with doors & windows for $[9]00. Such a building put up close to the house on the north side of your lot would shut of its 1st & 2d story windows looking into your yard. What shall be done?

Mrs Golden will have the Servants Hall put to rights by white washing, putting down the carpets &c &c & will have every thing arranged rightly, cleaning up the old laundry for Stewards room as you desire. I don't think she will need Cassie but will send for her if she does.[3]

Little Will is at home at his mothers, unwell. Frank is factotum now.[4] Mrs Golden will have a colored woman come to cook on Monday as she will have her hands full otherwise.

There I believe I have attended to all your charges. Write me what you wish done in the undecided matters or any thing else

Give abundant kisses to little Willie & love to the Governor & to the girls.

Your affectionate father
S P Chase

Mrs. K. C. Sprague

1. Mrs. Golden was evidently one of Chase's servants, comparable in culinary skills with Charlotte Ludlow Jones, his sister-in-law.

2. Possibly C. Woodward, a dealer in stoves and hardware, and one of several Walkers listed as carpenters in the city directory. *Wash. Dir. (1865)*, 353–54, 369.

3. A former slave, Catherine ("Cassie") Vaudry kept Chase's house in Washington, D.C.

4. Correspondence between Chase and his oldest daughter, possibly dating from the autumn of 1865, suggests that "Little Will"—not to be confused with the Spragues' infant son "little Willie" (mentioned elsewhere in the letter)—was a nickname for Chase's employee W. Albert Wells. Frank Bronaugh copied letters and maintained scrapbooks for Chase. Chase to Kate Chase Sprague, n.d. (Chase Papers, Hist. Soc. of Pa.).

TO LYMAN ABBOTT, JAMES M. MCKIM, AND GEORGE WHIPPLE

Letter in clerk's hand, signed by Chase, some alterations in Chase's hand. Rare and Manuscript Collections, Cornell University Library (*micro* 36:0168).

Washington D.C.
Nov 20th. 1865

Gentlemen,[1]

Nothing but imperative public duties would detain me from the meeting to be held to morrow evening under the auspices of the American Union Commission, the American Freedmen's Aid Commission, and the American Missionary Association. Its object, the relief of suffering at the South, without regard to color, must command the sympathy of all good and patriotic men.[2]

To suppress rebellion the American People put forth vast energies, counting neither treasure nor life dear in comparison with an undivided Country. And never, in the history of the world, was a civil war waged with so little rancor or vindictiveness on the part of the Nation against rebels. The people never forgot that success must be followed by the restoration, in due time and on just conditions, of the old relations between each state and the Union; and that, to the permanent and beneficial restoration of those relations, the reestablishment of fraternal sentiments between the citizens of all the States was indispensable. It is important now, that the people who have been in rebellion, should be thoroughly satisfied that the first wish of the loyal people, is the reestablishment of these sentiments.

The war has brought great changes. Among these the enfranchisement of four millions of Slaves is the greatest and most most momentous. The conversion of this vast population from bondmen into freemen and citizens imposes on the people of the States in which this wonderful revolution has taken place, on the people of the other States, and on the Government of the whole Country, new and peculiar duties. It is important that these new citizens should be assured that these duties will be neither evaded nor neglected.

How best to assure the white citizens of the States lately in rebellion, of the real good will of their fellow citizens of the loyal states, and of their readiness to afford active aid, where aid is wanted in relieving the necessities and repairing the injuries occasioned by the war; and how best to assure the colored citizens of those states of the country's great appreciation of their steady devotion to the National Authority, and of its purpose to promote, in every proper way their security and welfare, will doubtless engage the most earnest consideration of the meeting.

It is a welcome and significant sign of good, that the Associations which have devoted special efforts to different parts of the work of restoration and renovation, seem now likely to unite their means and activities in carrying forward the whole noble labor. The practical methods of usefulness,—whether in promoting true religion and sound education, or in relieving actual distress, or in encouraging industrial enterprise,—will be best considered, selected, and put in use, under such auspices. I cannot disguise my conviction that the surest and shortest road to permanent peace, settled order, sound credit, contented industry, and general prosperity in every state, is the frank recognition of the right of every citizen, white or colored, to protect his and his neighbor's freedom and promote his and his neighbor's welfare by his vote.

But I shall rejoice in seeing good done and in promoting the doing of it, in whatever measure or kind, and by whatever agency or authority.

We made war to save the Union. The Providence of God made our war for the Union, a war for Universal Freedom in America, and crowned it with success. Now comes the work of restoration and renovation. Let it be prosecuted with wise patriotism, sincere good will, and impartial justice, and who will dare doubt that God will crown this work also with success?

Yours very truly
S P Chase

Rev. Lyman Abbott
J. M. McKim, Esq
Rev. Geo. Whipple

1. In February, Abbott (1835–1922), noted later in life as a Congregational pastor and editor, had accepted a position as corresponding secretary of the American Union Commission, an organization formed in 1864 to assist southern Unionist refugees. Whipple (1805–76), another Congregational clergyman, and James M. McKim held similar posts in the American Missionary Association and the American Freedman's Union Commission, respectively. Augustus Field Beard, *A Crusade of Brotherhood: A History of the American Missionary Association* (Boston, 1909; reprint, New York, 1970), 316; *DAB,* 1:24–25; *New York Times,* Oct. 8, 1876; James M. McPherson, *The Struggle for Equality: Abolitionists and the Negro in the Civil War and Reconstruction* (Princeton, 1964), 5, 394, 398.

2. According to the *New York Times,* November 22, 1865, "perhaps five hundred persons" attended the gathering, which took place at the Brooklyn Academy of Music.

TO GEORGE BANCROFT

Autograph letter. Bancroft Collection, Massachusetts Historical Society (*micro* 36:0250).

Washington, Feb, 6 1866

My dear Mr. Bancroft,[1]

My delay would be inexcusable were it not for my incessant occupations & engagements. I write now after midnight.

The Proclamation of Apl. 15, 1861, was doubtless written by Mr. Lincoln himself. It bears on its face conclusive evidence of this in its style & diction.[2]

I hardly think that it was written before consultation with any member of his cabinet; though no such consultation probably changed it much in any respect.

He called the Heads of Departments together on Sunday the 14th April. I cannot now remember whether there was any prior meeting Saturday Evening; but my impression is that there was, & that the course to be pursued was then agreed on.[3]

At the meeting of Sunday the draft was submitted. There was some discussion as to the number of troops. My impression is that the number 75,000 was suggested by Mr. Seward. I remember that I suggested the 4th of July as the day for the meeting of Congress. There was some discussion also as to particular phrases & some other modifications of the original draft were made; but none of them were of material importance. The proclamation went to the country substantially in the same form in which it was drafted by the President with the hearty approval of of every member of his administration.

This Statement varies, you will see, somewhat from that attributed to me by Mr. Field; but there is no more difference than may be easily accounted for by the difficulty of remembering & repeating exactly what was said, in a conversation, no doubt casual & offhand.

Sincerely & faithfully

Your friend
S P CHASE

Hon Geo. Bancroft.

1. Bancroft was a diplomat, historian, and one of Andrew Johnson's confidants. *DAB,* 1:564–68.

2. Bancroft was evidently preparing a "Memorial Address on the Life and Character of Abraham Lincoln" for delivery before the House of Representatives on February 12. Lincoln's proclamation, issued one day after Fort Sumter's surrender, summoned 75,000 state militia troops for federal service and convened a special session of Congress, which opened on July 4. In a letter dated January 18, Bancroft had asked Chase about the accuracy of an assertion by New York politician David Dudley Field—supposedly originating with Chase—that Lincoln had issued the proclamation without consulting members of the cabinet. Ibid., 1:564–68; Bancroft to Chase, July 18, 1866 (Chase Papers, L.C.); Basler, *Collected Works,* 4:331–32.

3. As the Civil War started, Chase's associates in the Lincoln cabinet were Edward Bates (Justice), Simon Cameron (War), Montgomery Blair (Post Office), William H. Seward (State), Caleb B. Smith (Interior), and Gideon Welles (Navy). The Sunday meeting commenced at 10 A.M., after another session that lasted "the greater portion of the night previous." *Bio. Dir. U.S. Cong.,* 18; *New York Times,* Apr. 16, 1861.

TO JOHN C. HAMILTON

Letterpress copy of autograph letter. Chase Papers, Historical Society of Pennsylvania (*micro* 36:0266).

Washington Feb. 18, 1866.

My dear Sir,[1]

Accept my thanks for your very remarkable and very instructive paper. It contains some views which I felt it my duty to urge repeatedly upon the attention of our respected President very soon after his induction into office in April last;[2] and others either new to me or not heretofore sufficiently considered.

There are a very few expressions from which with my present lights I feel inclined to dissent. The most important of these perhaps is this, "defunct States," & this, "All the acts in the rebel states emanating & resulting from their acts (i.e. the acts of the "Provisional Governors") are merest nullities.

The official functionaries of the rebel states cannot, indeed, be recognized by the National Authorities. They vacated their offices by rebellion. But, I think, the States survive. They became *disorganized* by rebellion; not *defunct*. In consequence of rebellion, by Executive & Legislative acts, & by the recent Amendment of the National Constitution great numbers, in each of these states, have been raised from slaves to citizens.[3] These new citizens with the old now constitute the state. In the reorganization of the state & in the restoration of it to the Union all these citizens, not disqualified by persistent hostility to the National Government and its necessary policy of Enfranchisement, should be called to take part.

So far as actual reorganization has actually taken place in any rebel state, through the agency of Provisional Governors (for whose appointment I, like you, find no warrant) or otherwise, I am not disposed to regard it as null; though it may, I think, be set aside by Congress if judged best, and an enabling act, on right principles, substituted for Executive Proclamations and orders. At present, however, as it seems to me the Governors, Judges, & Legislatures deriving their authority from the recent elections must be regarded as exercising a valid authority, subject until complete peace & final restoration of Union relations to the control of National Military Authority & to the supervision of Congress.[4]

You see that I look on the *whole people* of each State as THE STATE; on each state which has been in rebellion as still imperfectly reorganized & as still subject to Military control, & national regulation in order to complete peace & complete reorganization; and on the Governments of these States, now existing, as capable of the valid exercise, in each branch Executive, Legislative & Judicial, of appropriate Governmental powers; so far as such exercise is not incompatible with the National policy still rightfully enforced by Military power.

But I must not prolong these observations, I do not know that I have expressed myself quite clearly; but I will ask you to receive with your usual kindness this brief note as an expression, however inadequate of the sincere respect & esteem with which I am always

Your friend
S P CHASE

Hon. John C. Hamilton

1. Hamilton was a New York attorney.

2. Chase evidently refers to a suggested address delivered to Johnson fourteen days after his swearing-in (April 15), which proposed that all southern loyalists be allowed to participate in Reconstruction regardless of "nativity or complexion." "An Address to the People of the United States," [Apr. 29, 1865] (Johnson Papers, L.C.); *Chase Papers*, 1:533–34; Long, *Civil War Day by Day*, 677.

3. Especially due to the Emancipation Proclamation, the First and Second Confiscation Acts—of August 6, 1861, and July 17, 1862—and the Thirteenth Amendment. *Statutes at Large*, 12:319, 589–92.

4. Balloting during the fall of 1865 had selected congressional, state, and local officers throughout the South. Foner, *Reconstruction*, 196–97.

TO JOHN SHERMAN

Autograph letter. John Sherman Papers, Library of Congress (*micro* 36:0278).

At Home[1] March 3, 1866.

My dear Mr. Sherman,

I find I cannot lay my hands on the Speech at the Cleveland Meeting as I thought I could.

The facts are briefly these: I had been invited to attend a Mass Meeting of citizens at Cleveland in reference to the imprisonment of some of the most respected citizens of Northern Ohio for alleged violation of the Fugitive Slave Act & had declined.[2]

On the morning of the day the meeting was to be held I was in the Governor's room at Columbus—I was then Governor of Ohio. A little after nine I received a telegram from Cleveland to the effect that trouble was feared & I must come. Hurrying to the depot I took the cars at once & reached Cleveland between two & three. The meeting was in progress & men's mind's were much excited. The tone of the speech which was being delivered was very strong.[3] My sympathies were warmly with the prisoners for I felt sure that they were unjustly imprisoned. But I thought it my duty to counsel moderation & forbearance & I did. I told the people that we must await judicial action & the ballot. I was more coldly received than I ever had been or have been since by a Western Reserve audience. But my counsels prevailed, & those who were then disposed to censure have since approved.

Of the resolutions of the meeting I know nothing.[4] I had nothing to do with them / I know, however, that I was never a nullifier nor a secessionist. I always claimed respect for the Judicial Tribunals of Ohio from the authorities of the National Government, & always insisted on respect for the Judicial Tribunals of the National Government by the authorities of the State.

A word further about my refusal to hold a Circuit Court in Virginia. I have never refused to hold a Circuit Court there. I have only said I was unwilling to do so until Congress could act on the subject of reorganization.[5] I need not have said this for after I received the Presidents letter there was time to hold a court there before the meeting of the Supreme Court in Washington. Mr. Justice Wayne & myself agreed that it would not become the Justices of the Supreme Court of the United States to hold courts in Districts in which martial law is maintained, & neither of us, therefore, held courts in the States lately in rebellion last summer & fall. I have always expected however that through the action of Congress & the Executive order & real peace would be so far reestablished during the present session that martial law might be either removed, or at least so modified that interference by the military authorities with the action of the Courts of Justice would no longer be deemed permissible.

Then courts may be held by the Justices of the Supreme Court without sacrifice of the consideration which seems to [be] due to them as the highest Judicial Officers of the Nation.[6]

Until then I shall be unwilling to hold such Courts; but shall obey whatever law Congress may enact on the subject.

Looking through Mr. Johnsons speech which you sent me I see he brings out somewhat into relief my dissent from the rest of the Judges on the subject of taking up the cases from the insurgent states.[7]

That dissent was not from calling the cases for argument. I was & am in favor of calling them[;] but not at this term. They had been passed four terms during the rebellion. I thought that before they should be taken up full notice should be given that parties might be prepared, and the court fully advised as to their present situation. I thought & still think that much injustice might be done by hasty action. I was opposed to taking up any cases at this term unless by consent or at least with full notice to party or counsel qualified under our rule or the rules of the inferior Court.

Certainly the question of hearing these causes has no connection with reorganization. The Circuits & Districts of the United States have not necessarily any dependence upon State lines or State organizations.

I have written in haste & I fear illegibly. You can use as many of the facts stated as you see fit, or pass Mr. Johnson's remarks without notice as you think best.

Of course you will make nothing like an apology for me. I take nothing back from my old condemnation of slavery & the fugitive slave law. I am for the Rights of Man, the Rights of the States, & the Supremacy of the Union.

Yours Faithfully
S P Chase

Hon John Sherman

1. Chase and the Spragues lived in the same house, at 6th and E Streets, until the fall of 1869. Chase to J. D. Hoover, Oct. 4, [1869]; Chase to Anna P. Hoover, Sept. 27 [1870] (both Chase Papers, L.C.); James M. Goode, *Capital Losses: A Cultural History of Washington's Destroyed Buildings* (Washington, 1979), 51–52.

2. The gathering, on May 24, 1859, protested the imprisonment of Simeon Bushnell, Charles Langston, and thirty-seven others for alleged complicity in the Oberlin-Wellington case, one of Ohio's most noted slave rescue incidents. According to one account, "the number of persons present upon the square to listen to the speakers was, at the lowest estimate, from ten thousand to twelve thousand." *Cleveland Plain Dealer,* May 25, 1859; Roseboom, *Civil War Era,* 346; Jacob R. Shipherd, comp., *History of the Oberlin-Wellington Rescue* (Boston, 1859; reprint, New York, 1972), 247–59.

3. The speaker immediately before Chase was Joseph M. Root, formerly a Free-Soil congressman from Ohio. "Stand steady," cautioned Root, "trust in God and keep your powder dry, and look for things that shall be." Ibid., 254.

4. Among the six resolutions adopted shortly before Root's speech were denunciations of the Dred Scott decision and the Fugitive Slave Law and an appeal for "an amendment of the federal judiciary system . . . so that the sovereignty of the States may be respected, and individuals guarded from oppression." Ibid., 253–54.

5. The sentence beginning *I have only said* is an interlineation. Chase wrote the next sentence, beginning *I need not,* at the bottom of the page and used an asterisk to indicate that it was to be a continuation of the interlineation. He also evidently meant to say that there was *no* time to hold a circuit court in Virginia before the commencement of the Supreme Court term. Regarding Chase's refusal, see his letters to Andrew Johnson, October 12, 1865 (above), George W. Brooks, March 20, 1866, Jacob W. Schuckers, May 15, 1866, and September 24, 1866 (all below).

6. Nine justices sat on the Supreme Court for half a decade after John Catron's death in May 1865. For an enumeration shortly before, see Chase to Susan Walker, March [17], 1865, note 3 (above). Fairman, *Reconstruction and Reunion,* 2–4.

7. Chase was the only member of the Supreme Court to dissent from a decision issued on February 21 to hear a series of cases from former Confederate states. To Reverdy Johnson of Maryland, speaking in the U.S. Senate on March 1, the majority opinion implicity acknowledged the restoration of those states to the Union. *Congressional Globe,* 39th Cong., 1st sess., 1865–66, 1111; *Daily National Intelligencer,* Feb. 22, 1866.

TO GEORGE WASHINGTON BROOKS

Letterpress copy of autograph letter. Chase Papers, Historical Society of Pennsylvania (*micro* 36:0303).

Washington, March 20, 1866.

My dear Judge,[1]

I fully agree with you as to the expediency and utility of restoring the Circuit as well as the District Courts of the United States, under the existing circumstances of the Country, wherever they formerly existed or may be authorized by Congress; in the States lately in rebellion.

My objections to the holding of Circuit Courts where the habeas corpus is still suspended & martial law is yet enforced do not apply with so much force to the District Judges as to the Chief Justice and Justices of the Supreme Court of the United States. I should waive them I think if I were a District Judge; but representing for the time as I do the Supreme Judicial Power of the Nation it has seemed to me best not to hold courts where my judicial action might come in conflict with the military power. As soon as the President who wields the Supreme Military power of the the Nation, shall think it wise & safe to revoke the suspension of the habeas corpus and with it martial law, as to all act of the Judicial Tribunals of the Nation my objection to the holding of courts by the Justices of the Supreme Court will be entirely removed, and I shall hold such courts in the Circuit assigned me, which as you know includes, at present Virginia & North Carolina.[2]

Meantime I advise you to hold the Circuit Court & make the necessary appointments to organize it, but make them [pro] tempore. If I were in your place I would do & if conflict with military power should occur, should submit for the occasion referring the matter to the President. Of course I should take care to avoid all [un]necessary conflicts.

Yours v[ery] truly
S P Chase

Hon G. W. Brooks
Dis. Judge &c &c

1. In January, the Senate had confirmed Brooks (1821–82), a North Carolina loyalist, as U.S. judge for the district that comprised his state. *DAB*, 3:77.

2. On April 2, Andrew Johnson issued a proclamation that declared the "insurrection" at an end and suggested in that statement the wisdom of restoring the writ. Chase remained dissatisfied, however, and pressed for an explicit statement to that effect. Not until June 1867 did he assume duties on circuit in the South. For more regarding restoration of the writ of habeas corpus, which Lincoln first suspended on April 27, 1861, see Chase's letter to Johnson, October 12, 1865 (above), and his letters to Flamen Ball, May 12, 1866; Horace Greeley, June 1, 1866; and Jacob W. Schuckers, May 15 and September 24, 1866 (all below). Chase to Janet Chase, June 7, 1867 (below); Long, *Civil War Day by Day*, 66; *Statutes at Large*, 14:812.

TO ELIZABETH ELLICOTT PIKE

Autograph letter. James Shepherd Pike Collection, Special Collections Department, Raymond H. Folger Library, University of Maine (*micro* 36:0305).

Washington, March 20, 1866

My dear Mrs Lizzie,

Show that to Mr. Pike and ask him if it is too familiar; and if he says "yes" tell him to prescribe the form of address. I was so used to calling you Miss Lizzie, that I cant realize that you can be anything more than Mrs Lizzie now.

Do you know that you never gave the name of your friend or her son, you most unmethodical of women. The President laughed a little at this, but took my memorandum for "Mrs Pike's friend's son": and I have had it in my mind to write to you for some time for a more *particular description*: and should have done so before many days had not your letter come & prompted an immediate reply.[1]

When I wrote you of the encouragement given by the President matters were in very different shape from the present. It is doubtful whether under existing conditions the encouragement given would have ripened into the fulfilment of your wishes.

It is very much to be regretted, I think, that Mr. Stevens & Mr. Sumner have excited the Presidents anger against the whole class of earnest men by remarks which he construed into personal assaults.[2] The necessary differences between him & Congress were sufficient to make it a duty to use all means of conciliation and cherish all sentiments of personal good will in order to avoid a breach, to which tendencies could not fail to develope themselves.

Mr. Johnson is not a New Englander nor a Pennsylvania & never was a Whig, but was a North Carolina man born, a Tennessee man by migration, a slaveholder & until he had to choose between union & Slavery, an upholder of Slavery. These things should have been more considered than they have been.

Not that this lack of consideration on one side excuses him on the other from the duty of fidelity to the great body of patriotic men by whom he was elected. He should adhere to the principles which he gave the country to understand that he held when he made his acceptance speech & when afterwards he addressed the Colored People at Nashville.[3] So far he has not done so, and I fear the probabilities of greater divergence are greater than those of reconciliation & future concord. I only do not despair. He has now before him the bill securing civil rights to negroes, I hope he will sign it— If he does, it may be an omen of good.[4]

I have been very hard at work this winter seeing fewer people than for many years during the same time. If I could make all my brother Judges think as I do on all important questions, I should like my present place very well. But that I can't expect, & I hate to see things go wrong, wrong, that is, according to my view. I try to console myself with the reflection that I may be wrong, that it may be all for the best &c but it don't amount to much.

Katie & Nettie are talking of going to Europe this summer. Gov Sprague can't go nor can I; and who will be found as a substitute I don't know. You speak of four months; and I infer that this is the term of your sojourn abroad: so you will be just about sailing when Katie arrives—if &c.[5] Of the four months one has nearly gone, and April, May & June remain. It will be a great pleasure to welcome you and dear Mr. Pike, back to your native land—how changed! and on the whole in spite of war & debt how much changed for the better! We need all our good men at home now more than abroad.

You will find me a good deal changed not I hope for the worse. I think more than ever on the things which never change except from glory to glory in infinite progress.

But I must close. I have snatched the moments for writing this from time which I had appropriated to preparation of an opinion. Goodbye & may Heaven abundantly bless you and your husband, whose friendship with yours is one of my most prized treasures.

Ever your friend
S P CHASE

Mrs Lizzie Pike.

1. Earlier, Pike had inquired about an appointment for the thirteen-year-old boy, who evidently sought admission to West Point. "The President did not exactly promise," replied Chase, "but he expressed himself in such a manner that I felt pretty sure that he intended to comply with my wishes in your behalf." Chase to Elizabeth Ellicott Pike, Dec. 23, 1865 (James S. Pike, Collec., Raymond H. Folger Lib. University of Maine); Elizabeth Ellicott Pike to Chase, Feb. 28, 1866 (Chase Papers, Hist. Soc. of Pa.).

2. On January 31, Pennsylvania Republican Thaddeus Stevens, a member of the Joint Congressional Committee on Reconstruction, had accused Johnson of "usurpation" for comments allegedly intended to discourage constitutional amendments that would have affected the basis of national representation. Charles Sumner had rekindled conservative enmity through "The Equal Rights of All"—oration, delivered in the Senate on February 4 and 5, which blasted an amendment supported by Johnson that would have disenfranchised African Americans. Intent on forming a moderate political coalition, Johnson

used the occasion to distance himself from the Radicals. Speaking on February 22, three days after he vetoed legislation to establish the Freedmen's Bureau, Johnson accused Stevens, Sumner, and Wendell Phillips of demonstrating hostility "to the fundamental principles of this Government" and of "laboring to destroy it." *Congressional Globe,* 39th Cong., 1st sess., 1865–66, 536, 649, 673–87; *DAB,* 17:624; Donald, *Charles Sumner,* 245–47, 254–57; *New York Times,* Feb. 23, 1866.

3. Johnson's acceptance speech for the Union party's vice-presidential nomination, delivered on June 9, 1864, expressed confidence in governance by citizens of "humble origins." "Traitors should take a back seat in the work of restoration," he added in regard to Reconstruction. Johnson expressed similar sentiments in his speech to "Colored Men" of Nashville, October 24, 1864, which also declared freedom for former slaves and announced his acceptance of a title as their "Moses." Chase to William Sprague, Sept. 6, 1865 (above); Graf, *Papers of Andrew Johnson,* 6:723–27, 7:251–53.

4. The Civil Rights Act of 1866 enumerated a list of rights held by all national citizens, defined as all persons born in the United States except Native Americans, and established legal mechanisms for enforcement. Johnson vetoed the measure on March 27, but Congress overrode him on April 9. *Congressional Globe,* 39th Cong., 1st sess., 1865–66, 1679; *Statutes at Large,* 14:27–29.

5. The Pikes returned to the United States on May 17 a total of five years' diplomatic service at The Hague. *DAB,* 14:596.

TO ROBERT G. CORWIN

Letterpress copy of autograph letter. Chase Papers, Historical Society of Pennsylvania (*micro* 36:0380).

Washington, Apl. 24, 1866.

My dear Corwin,[1]

At Washington I am almost if not quite as much in the fog as you are at Dayton.

Mr. Johnson's course just before the outbreak of the rebellion excited my gratitude & admiration; and, after Mr. Lincoln's administration was inaugurated, my duties, particularly in relation to Tennessee, brought me into somewhat special relations to him. I do not know that you are aware that in the earlier period of the rebellion I acted as a sort of assistant Secretary of War for Tennessee & Kentucky, & drew most of the orders under which Nelson, Rousseau & Johnson acted in organizing troops.[2]

All that I saw of Mr. Johnson then & until since his election confirmed my regard & respect for him. Sometimes I thought he was not quite prompt enough to recognize the part which Slavery had in the rebellion or our duties in respect to the Colored people. I was especially dissatisfied with his application to Lincoln to have Tennessee excepted from the Emancipation Proclamation & with his opposition to the employment of the Colored Soldiers.[3] But he became convinced that the exception was an error & that the Employment of the blacks in the army was a duty; & finally made his speech at Nashville, declaring the Colored People of Tennessee free & that loyal men white or black ought to Govern in the rebel states.[4] That was the most heroic utterance which had been made up to that time & it satisfied me completely.

So you may well suppose that when he became President my hopes were high & my confidence strong. What influences have prevailed with him since I do not know. I was disappointed when his proclamation for reorganization in North Carolina contradicted his Nashville Speech concerning black & white loyalists:[5] and every step he has taken since, in regard to that subject has increased the disappointment. Sometimes I think that if some of our friends have adopted a more conciliatory tone & had refrained from all harsh language he would not have gone exactly as he has; and yet when I think of the whole business, I don't feel at all sure of this

Whether there will be any turn I do not know. I cling to the hope that some ground may yet be found for common action: and am ready to do all I can, without advising the surrender of important principles, to promote it. But we cannot afford to surrender our ideas. We must have at least constitutional prohibition of payment of rebel debt or for emancipation of slaves & we must have, also, limitation of representatives by the number of those who are [not] disfranchised without charge of disloyalty or crime. My impression is that this is about all that can be had now: and this is a great deal. It does not secure universal suffrage at once; but it leaves the question open & under circumstances strongly favoring the most liberal action.

Your kind thoughts about me are natural, as we have long been friends.[6] I have not supposed that any [serious thought should be] entertained of my name in connexion with the next Presidency. Of course such a [position] offers vastly greater opportunities of usefulness than the one I now hold & nobody, [*illeg.*] unfit, would be likely [to refuse it]. But Providence [seems] to have led me to my present place [&] I am [*illeg.*]ly satisfied with [*nine? words illeg.*] of changing it [*eight? words illeg.*] [to see], something like the same call for my services in another, that led Mr. Lincoln to nominate me for this.

There—I think you now know my thoughts about as well as I know them myself. Write me when you can. Give my best regards to your wife[7] whose good will to good things I shall never forget & believe me

Sincerely & faithfully your friend
S P Chase

R. G. Corwin, Esq

1. Corwin, an attorney from Dayton, Ohio, had known Chase since at least the 1850s. *Chase Papers,* 1:304; *History of Warren County, Ohio* . . . (Chicago, 1882), 731–32.

2. William Nelson and Lovell H. Rousseau both attained the rank of brigadier general during the Civil War. Earlier, Chase had taken credit for securing Rousseau a colonel's commission in 1861 and for funding Nelson's efforts. *Chase Papers,* 3:80–88, 90–91, 4:345–46.

3. On December 4, 1862, Johnson and seven other Tennesseans had petitioned Lincoln for exemption from the preliminary Emancipation Proclamation of September 22.

Johnson's reluctance to recruit African-American soldiers dated from his appointment as military governor of Tennessee in April 1863. Berlin, *Freedom,* ser. 2, 123; Graf, *Papers of Andrew Johnson,* 6:85–86.

4. In the speech, delivered on October 24, 1864, Johnson had also assumed the title of "Moses" to former slaves. Graf, *Papers of Andrew Johnson,* 7:251–52.

5. Johnson's proclamation of May 29, 1865, authorized reorganization based on an antebellum constitution that disenfrancised African Americans. *Statutes at Large,* 13:760–61.

6. Writing on April 20, Corwin had expressed disappointment that Chase had not run for the presidency in 1864 and expressed hope that he would be a candidate in 1868. Corwin to Chase, Apr. 20, 1866 (Chase Papers, L.C.).

7. Eliza Bruen Corwin.

TO CHARLES D. DRAKE

Letterpress copy of autograph letter. Chase Papers, Historical Society of Pennsylvania (*micro* 36:0384).

Washington, Apl. 24, 1866.

My dear friend[1]

I should leave you to infer from my silence my reply to your note, in conformity with your intimation, if I did not feel, as the Friends say, impressed to write to you, as a friend from boyhood, a few words about the article you enclosed to me.[2]

From what source *any real information,* concerning the action of the Court, which is not announced from the bench, can be collected, I cannot imagine. If any Judge thinks himself at liberty to speak of what transpires in conference before such announcement, I do not know it. It is easy to suppose however, that conjecture may employ itself in assigning to this Judge, this opinion & to that Judge, that, and may proclaim its *guesses* as truths.

So far as I am concerned I am quite certain that no one knows my opinions in any case not yet decided and announced: and on the question which particularly interests the people of Missouri, I am free to say, I do not yet know it myself. It is too important a question to be disposed of under the pressure & in the hurry of the last days of a very laborious term; and I mean to devote to the careful consideration of the elaborate arguments and numerous authorities on both sides all the time I can command until my judgment is fully satisfied, & I mean that my conclusion shall be just what the Constitution & the great principles of public law require it to be & no other.

You see that the Republican had no ground for its *imputations*

Its *Statement* that I dissented from the majority in the Bank Tax Cases is correct. The dissent however was not mine more than that of Judge Wayne & Judge Swayne & was not from the *decision* but from an opinion on a point which though of great importance was not essential to the decision. In our dissent we followed as we thought the wisdom of Marshall[3] and the precedents, & are content to abide the judgment of the profession. I send you a copy. It may be thought of sufficient interest to the business community to be reprinted in one of your papers.

The Republican is quite right in saying that I am in favor of universal suffrage. I have said so a great many times during the last twenty years & expect to say so on all proper occasions. I believe, however, I have never manifested unseemly impatience & shown any want of respect for those who differ from me. I welcome all advances in the right direction; and if the direction is right am content to go with others, who propose to stop short of what I think the highest & best aims & results.

I thought it a very proper occasion to say something like this when at the late Centenary Meeting in New York I was invited look back & forward over the progress of a century past & to come. And I could hardly do less, it seemed to me, than to welcome the passage of the Civil Rights bill as an event and augury of that progress.[4]

I said nothing about its constitutionality or unconstitutionality. Some of its provisions I believe have never been assailed. When questions under it come before me, if they do come, I shall try to do my judicial duty. It is not at all impossible that under the peculiar circumstances which necessarily attend the close of a great civil war and a great social revolution, legislation, endeavoring to adjust new to old may overstep the boundaries of the Constitution. If I think so, it will be my clear duty, however I may approve the purposes & objects of legislation, to say so.

Before I close let me frankly express to you my regret that the Constitution of Missouri requires the oath it does, especially from persons not directly connected in functions with the Government.

I cannot think that any advantage, commensurate with [*illeg.*] attendant disadvantages, can be derived from the [req]uirement of such an oath, as a qualification for preaching, practicing law, or other like avocations. And I sincerely hope, if there be any practicable way in which this requirement can be either abrogated or reduced to such form that no reasonable exception can be taken to it by any loyal man, that the men who have made Missouri a free state will see that is adopted as the French say "avec le plus bref délai.[5]

Sincerely your friend
S P CHASE

Hon C. D. Drake

1. Chase had known Drake, a leading radical in Missouri's Unionist party, as a youth in Worthington, Ohio. From 1867 to 1870, Drake represented Missouri in the U.S. Senate. *Chase Papers,* 4:263; *DAB,* 5:425–26.

2. On April 19, the *Missouri Republican* ran an article that accused Chase of "carrying his radical and revolutionary politics to the bench of the Supreme Court, and allowing them to shape his opinions in every case that comes before that tribunal." For evidence, the newspaper cited his dissent in the *Bank Tax Case* (1865), which would have denied states the right to tax capital owned by national banks, and a speech delivered on April 9 to the Ladies Central Centenary Association of St. Paul's Methodist Church, New York, in

which he expressed support for the Civil Rights Act of 1866 and the enfranchisement of former slaves. According to the *Republican,* through "some artful management" Chase had also delayed formal announcement of the Court's decision against the Missouri test oath, a retrospective loyalty oath that covered actions of all public officers and certain private citizens, to limit voting and thus assist Radical candidates in state elections slated for November. Fairman, *Reconstruction and Reunion,* 46–48, 151–53; *New York Herald,* Apr. 10, 1866; 2 Wall. 200 (1865).

3. Chief Justice John Marshall presided over the U.S. Supreme Court from 1801 to 1835.

4. A congressional override of Andrew Johnson's veto enacted the legislation on April 9. *Statutes at Large,* 14:27–29.

5. "With the briefest delay."

TO STEPHEN J. FIELD

Letterpress of file copy in unknown hand. Chase Papers, Historical Society of Pennsylvania (*micro* 36:0392).

Washington. D.C.
April 30th 1866.

My dear Judge,[1]

It grieved me much to hear from your brother Mr Cyrus W. Field,[2] that you have been quite ill. I supposed that you were now in or very near California. You must take the best care of yourself not only for the sake of your family but of your country, which now needs true patriotism as well as legal learning upon the bench. I feel all the interest of warm personal friendship in your welfare. It is not in my nature to forget friends even when serious differences of judgment and political affinities come in to make separation; and no such differences come between us. Do you remember when just before the end of the term in the Spring of 1864 you met me on the Avenue and expressed your warm wish that I might fill the place I now occupy?[3] If you have forgotten it I have not nor shall I ever forget it. It took me by surprise; but was very grateful to my feelings.

What do you think of the plan of reconstruction or rather of completing reconstruction presented by the Committee of Fifteen?[4] To me it seems all very well provided it can be carried; but I am afraid that it is, as people say, rather too big a contract. So far as I have had opportunity of conversing with Senators and Representatives I have recommended to confine Constitutional Amendments to two points, (1) No payment of rebel debt and no payment for slaves, and (2) No representation beyond the constituent basis. And, as so many were trying their hands at form—I drew up these two amendments according to my ideas as follows: Article 14. Section 1. Representatives shall be apportioned among the several States, according to their respective numbers; but whenever in any State the elective franchise shall be denied to any of its inhabitants being male citizens of the United States and above the age of twenty-one years, for any cause[5] except insurrection or rebellion against the United States, the basis of representation in such State shall be reduced in the proportion which the number of male citizens so excluded shall bear to the whole number of male citizens over twenty-one years of age.

Section 2. No payment shall ever be made by the United States, for or on account of any debt contracted or incurred in aid of insurrection or rebellion against the United States; or for or on account of the emancipation of slaves

And I proposed further that the submission of this article to the States should be accompanied by a concurrent resolution to this effect "That, whenever any of the States, which were declared to be in insurrection and rebellion by the proclamation of the President of the U.S. dated July. 1. 1862,[6] shall have ratified the foregoing article, Senators and Representatives from such ratifying State or States ought to be admitted to seats in the Senate and House of Representatives respectively in the like manner as from States never declared to be in insurrection and rebellion; and that whenever the said article shall have been ratified by three fourths of the several States, Senators and Representatives ought in like manner be admitted from all the States."

It has really seemed to me that on this basis the completion of reorganization by the admission of Members in both houses of Congress would be safe; and I have greatly doubted the expediency of going beyond this. In two or three important respects the report of the Committee does go beyond this; (1) Prohibiting the States from interfering with the rights of citizens (2) Disfranchising all persons voluntarily engaged in rebellion till 1870 and (3) in granting express legislative power to Congress to enforce all the new constitutional provisions. Will not these propositions be received with some alarm by those who, though opponents of secession or nullification, yet regard the real rights of the States as essential to the[7] proper working of our complex system? I do not myself think that any of the proposed amendments will be likely to have injurious effects, unless it be the sweep of the disfranchisement: but I repeat that I fear the undertaking of too much; and I add that it seems to me that nothing is gained sufficiently important[8] and unattainable by legislation, to warrant our friends in overloading the ship with amendment freight.

But this letter is too long. Pardon and answer.[9] Have you read the opinion and the dissent in the Bank Tax Cases together? Yours cordially.

(SIGNED) S P CHASE.

Hon S. J Field
N.Y.

1. Supreme Court justice Field, a California immigrant, was on circuit in the West. *DAB*, 6:373–74; Field to Chase, June 30, 1866 (below).

2. Cyrus West Field, a New York merchant, had acquired fame for promoting the first Atlantic telegraph cable.

3. In 1864, the Supreme Court adjourned on April 18. *Daily National Intelligencer,* Apr. 20, 1864.

4. On April 30, a joint committee of Congress formally recommended passage of what became the Fourteenth Amendment. Its report also included recommendations to readmit states of the Confederacy after ratification, postpone payment of delinquent taxes, and bar specific categories of former Confederates from holding federal office. Serving for the U.S. Senate on the Joint Congressional Committee on Reconstruction were William P. Fessenden (Maine), James W. Grimes (Iowa), Ira Harris (New York), Jacob M. Howard (Michigan), Reverdy Johnson (Maryland), and George H. Williams (Oregon). The House members were John A. Bingham (Ohio); Henry T. Blow (Missouri); George S. Boutwell (Massachusetts); Roscoe Conkling (1829–88), Republican of New York; Henry Grider (1796–1866), Kentucky Democrat; Justin S. Morrill (Vermont); Democrat Andrew Jackson Rogers (1828–1900) of New Jersey; Thaddeus Stevens (Pennsylvania); and Elihu B. Washburne (Illinois). *Bio. Dir. U.S. Cong.,* 1094–95, 1735; *DAB,* 4:346–47; *House Journal,* 39th Cong. 1st sess., 1865–66, 636; *New York Times,* Apr. 30, 1866; *Report of the Joint Committee on Reconstruction . . . ,* 39th Cong., 1st sess., 1865–66, H. Rep. 30, iii.

5. Apparently Chase filled in portions of this faint word on the letterpress copy.

6. The proclamation also provided for penalties against owners of real estate in such states for delinquent taxes. *Statutes at Large,* 12:1266.

7. Word inserted, possibly by Chase.

8. Word inserted, possibly by Chase.

9. Field replied to Chase on June 30 (below).

TO WENDELL PHILLIPS

Autograph letter. bMS Am 1953 (398), Houghton Library, Harvard University (*micro* 36:0405).

PRIVATE

Washington, May 1, 1866.

My dear Sir,

Your note of the 23d. came duly & I send you some lines of good will accordingly[1]

I wish you could spend a day or two here before the meeting. Cannot you do so? It seems to me very important, that all true friends of impartial freedom, & impartial suffrage as its best security, should see eye to eye.

It has become clear that no measure securing immediate universal suffrage, whether in the form of constitutional amendment or act of Congress, can now be carried. For such an amendment the requisite three fourths of the States cannot be hoped for, even if the requisite two thirds could be obtained in Congress: and besides, its desirableness, unless sure of ratification, may be questioned, because of its implied negation of legislative power in Congress over the subject. The minds of men are not at all clear upon this question of the power of Congress; but the opinion that Congress may extend suffrage as a security of freedom evidently gains ground. It is hardly probable, however, that it has gained so much ground that an act providing for impartial suffrage could command a majority in each House; while it is certain that, if passed, it would be vetoed, & then could not command two thirds.

The opinion therefore is almost universal among our friends, & I agree with them, that the best that can now be done is to propose amendments of the Constitution which will smooth the path to future state legislation & contain no implied negation on the powers of Congress, and at the same time take away from the disloyalists of the south their best rallying cry and their best basis of organization against the liberals. The former of these objects is thought to be accomplished by the amendment which restricts representation in proportion to exclusion from suffrage and the latter by the prohibition of payment of rebel debt or compensation for slaves.[2]

You will note that the representation-amendt allows representation for citizens disfranchised for disloyalty and denies it for citizens disfranchised for color or race. In the former case it is allowed that the disfranchisement of rebels be not discouraged; in the latter denied that the enfranchisement of colored loyalists be encouraged.

My persuasion is very strong that the proposition to the states of these two amendments and their adoption will secure universal suffrage in the shortest time possible. I look for a great increase of opinion in favor of legislation by Congress on this subject, in all parts of the country & especially in the lately insurgent States. Every day more & more see that the safety of no really union man is safe except in the suffrage of all Union men.

I confess I do not feel so much interest in the Civil Rights amendment or in the Disfranchisement amendment.[3] The first seems to carry an admission that the Civil Rights *Act* lately passed by 2/3ds is unconstitutional & the second looks too much like a device for the security of mere party ascendancy. For my part I care a great deal more about Enfranchisement than Disfranchisement, and wish to see the Constitution free of every thing which can be safely left to legislation. And it seems to me clear that all the disfranchisement that is desirable can be accomplished by legislation.

I learn, however, that our friends in Congress are inclined to adopt the Report of the Committee very much as it was made. There is a good deal of diversity of opinion & agreement is hardly possible, unless some yield on points in respect to which they are not by any means satisfied.

One thing I insist on: that the Senate shall pass the bill giving Universal Suffrage in the District, which has already passed the House.[4] This will be an interpretation of the Amendments & make their practical results secure.

I don't know that I have made myself very clear. I wish you could come on.

Sincerely your friend
S P Chase

Wendell Phillips Esq

1. Phillips had invited Chase to the thirty-third annual meeting of the American Anti-Slavery Society, held in New York on May 8. Chase did not attend, but sent a letter that encouraged extension of the franchise to former slaves. *National Anti-Slavery Standard,* May 12, 1866; Phillips to Chase, Apr. 23, 1866 (Chase Papers, L.C.)

2. Chase refers to sections two and four of the amendment that the Joint Congressional Committee on Reconstruction formally proposed on April 30. *New York Times,* Apr. 30, 1866.

3. Section one of the joint committee's suggested amendment foreshadowed the famous "due process" clause of the Fourteenth Amendment. The third section barred "all persons who voluntarily adhered to the late insurrection" from voting for "Members of Congress, and for Electors for President and Vice-President of the United States" until July 4, 1870. *New York Times,* Apr. 30, 1866.

4. The Senate failed to pass the proposal during the first session of the Thirty-ninth Congress, but favorable action over presidential veto at the next session ensured enactment on January 8, 1867. *Statutes at Large,* 14:375–76.

TO FRANCIS B. CARPENTER

Autograph letter. Frank B. Carpenter Papers, Illinois State Historical Library (*micro* 36:0409).

Washington, May 2, 1866.

My dear Mr. Carpenter,[1]

Your letter of the 28th April came yesterday after I had acknowledged the receipt of your great Picture, and with your letter came one from Messrs Derby & Miller.[2]

My letter of acknowledgment is, I suppose all you or they want in the way of endorsement of what really needs no endorsement from any body; for it endorses itself. If you think best however you may insert in that letter these words, "The likenesses—I cannot judge that of myself—are excellent."

[But] I cannot say that I like the printed account of the painting which came with it. It says that it represents a Cabinet Meeting in July. Now so little important did any Cabinet Meeting in July relating to the proclamation seem to me, that not the slightest trace of such a meeting remains on my memory. Such a meeting must have been held, of course, for it seems that Mr. Lincoln spoke of it to you. And it is not surprising that I have forgotten it; for there was much talk which resulted in no action, &, of which, I took no account.[3]

I supposed it was your intention to represent the moment of decision—not of irresolution—not a scene of delay & postponement; but the scene when Mr Lincoln having convened the Heads of Departments said in substance, "I have considered every thing that has been said to me about the expediency of emancipation & have made up my mind to issue THIS PROCLAMATION: and I have invited you to come together not to discuss what is to be done; but to have you hear what I have written and to get your suggestions about form & style," adding, "I have thought it all over & have made a promise that this thing shall be done, to myself—& to God."[4]

The picture well represents that moment, which followed the reading of the Proclamation. It puts the two members who thoroughly endorsed & heartily welcomed the measure on the right of Mr. Lincoln; & the others, (who, though they now all acquiesced & Mr. Seward particularly made important suggestions, had hitherto doubted, or advised delay, or even opposed,) on the left.[5] It leaves every spectator's imagination free play. There is the great actor, Mr. Lincoln; and there is the great act, the Proclamation just read: and there are the Witnesses, the Heads of Departments. Mr. Seward may be considered as about to speak first, as was his right being Secretary of State & having precedence. The others are still thinking of what they have just heard, and the future it opens.

Such is my idea of the picture. It is a picture of "Lincoln reading the Emancipation Proclamation to the Heads of Departments." The printed account suggests the name "Mr Seward advising the postponement of the Emancipation Proclamation" and is hardly just to either Mr. Lincoln or Mr. Seward or yourself.

But all this is your concern not mine. I took my pen to acknowledge your letter & put in the sentence about the likenesses, & have been led into observation which I did not think of making when I began.

As always, your friend,
S: P: CHASE

F. B. Carpenter, Esq

1. Francis Bicknell Carpenter (1830–1900) was a portrait painter from New York. *DAB,* 3:510.

2. Carpenter had recently finished his famous painting of Lincoln reading the first draft of the Emancipation Proclamation to his cabinet. On April 28, the artist conveyed a proof taken from an engraving of the work, printed by New York publishing partners James Cephas Derby (b. 1818) and Norman C. Miller. *Appletons',* 2:146; Carpenter to Chase, Apr. 28, 1866 (Chase Papers, L.C.); *DAB,* 3:510; Derby, *Fifty Years Among Authors, Books and Publishers* (New York, 1884), 27, 489.

3. Carpenter had lived in the White House from February to July 1864 as he prepared for the painting. The essay was evidently his "Anecdotes and Reminiscences of President Lincoln," also printed as an appendix to Henry J. Raymond, *Life and Public Services of Abraham Lincoln . . .* (New York, 1865). Carpenter's discussion of the Emancipation Proclamation, based on Lincoln's recollections, appears on pages 759–66. The cabinet meeting, which is described in Chase's diary, occurred on July 22, 1862. Carpenter later

published another account of his visit, *Six Months at the White House: The Story of a Picture* (New York, 1866), which included Lincoln's impressions of the July meeting on pages 20–22. *Chase Papers,* 1:351–52.

4. Membership in Lincoln's cabinet had not changed since the Civil War started, with the exception of Edwin M. Stanton, who replaced Simon Cameron as secretary of war in January 1862. *Bio. Dir. U.S. Cong.,* 18.

5. In the picture, Chase and Edwin M. Stanton stand on Lincoln's right.

TO FLAMEN BALL

Autograph letter, corner with closing and signature has been removed. Chase Papers, Cincinnati Historical Society (*micro* 36:0444).

Washn. May 12, 1866

My dear Mr. Ball,[1]

Your note of the 9th came this morning. The letter with the notes & money came some time before.

I dont like to sell the 6th Street lot so low as $150 per foot; but I would take that price, cash, rather than remain in debt. I shall leave that matter entirely to your discretion; but would advise consultation with L'Hommedieu who knows the values in that vicinity. Whatever you do I shall be satisfied.

I do not know whether Davis will be tried or not. The Grand Jury at Norfolk found a bill this week & the next term of the Circuit Court will be held at Richmond in June.[2] I am not willing, as a member of the Supreme Court to hold Circuit Courts where martial law has not been abrogated or the habeas corpus restored. Some think that these things are accomplished by the proclamation of peace; but the fact that military commissions are still held & other like facts bring this conclusion into doubt. I have recommended to the President the issuing of a Proclamation distinctly & expressly declaring that the Habeas Corpus is restored & martial law abrogated in all cases within the jurisdiction of the Courts of the United States & as to all processes & proceedings of those courts: and he has this matter under consideration.[3] Should such a proclamation be issued there could be no question whatever as to any Executive influence operating upon the trial of any person charged with a crime against the United States. Nobody could allege such influence: and, in that case, I should feel at liberty to hold the Courts in Virginia & North Carolina, just as I have held them in Maryland;—for, in that case, there could be no imputation of Executive interference nor any possibility of unseemly conflict between judicial & military authority.

I do not wish to be understood as at all complaining of whatever course the President has taken or may take in the exercise of military authority / On the contrary I fully recognize his right to use that authority in the insurgent states according to his sound discretion; until peace shall be fully & completely restored by the restoration of that participation in national legislation which the rebel states refused when they rebelled, through the concurrent action of those states & of Congress. When Peace is so restored, Martial law will be abrogated & the Habeas Corpus restored without Executive Action. Until then the President may take, in reference to these subjects, such partial or general action as seems to him right.

I know nothing concerning the confirmation of the nomination of Stanbery. He is a great lawyer & would make a great judge. A bill has passed the House, however, limiting the number of Judges to nine & it is further proposed to limit the number to seven. Should the bill become a law there is no vacancy to fill & Should the proposed further measure become law no future vacancy can be filled till the number is reduced to seven.[4]

We have a letter from Katie this morning / She & Nettie are in London, & enjoying all they see. My own health is excellent. I shall hardly come west before fall.[5]

1. Ball, Chase's former law partner, held office as U.S. attorney for the southern district of Ohio during the Civil War and, starting in 1867, was a U.S. register for bankruptcy.

2. The indictment, which charged Jefferson Davis with treason, dated from May 8. Johnson, *Cases Decided by Chief Justice Chase,* 18–20.

3. Chase made the recommendation and presented a draft of the proposed proclamation in a meeting with the president earlier in the month or in April. Johnson never did take action in accordance with Chase's wishes, but satisfied the chief justice's concerns through another proclamation, issued on August 20, 1866, that declared the "insurrection" at an end and "civil authority" restored. Chase to Jacob W. Schuckers, Sept. 24, 1866 (below); *Statutes at Large,* 14:814–17.

4. On March 27, Johnson had nominated Cincinnati attorney Henry Stanbery to sit as an associate justice on the U.S. Supreme Court. Legislation approved on July 23 forbade any new appointments until total membership on the Court declined to six and, thus, doomed the appointment. On the same day, Stanbery became U.S. attorney general and remained at that post until March 1868, when he resigned to serve as chief counsel for the defense in Andrew Johnson's impeachment trial. *Statutes at Large,* 14:209; *DAB,* 17:498; U.S. Senate, *Journal of the Executive Proceedings,* v. 14, pt. 2:720.

5. Chase is not known to have traveled west until the fall of 1867. Chase to Richard C. Parsons, Sept. 28, 1867 (Chase Papers, Hist. Soc. of Pa.); Chase to William W. Warden, Oct. 8, 1867 (Andrew Johnson Papers, L.C.).

TO JACOB W. SCHUCKERS

Autograph letter. Chase Papers, Library of Congress (*micro* 36:0455).

Washington May 15, 1866.

My dear Schuckers,

I have tried this morning to rectify the "funny mistake" I made. Your name on the "bill" & probably Browns unusually *good* & *fine* hand misled me.[1]

It is a real satisfaction to know that you have no intention of leaving your profession, & that if the opportunity ever comes I may yet promote you "in the line."

What you say of Mr. Johnson is certainly very just. Those who oppose him are in part responsible for the present antagonism. But he could if he would put an end to it at once. The amendment to the Constitution proposed by the House is on the whole fair & just.[2] If there is something too much of it or some feature which he thinks objectionable I have no doubt Congress would readily yield to any suggested modification which would save the main points, no representation for non voters, & no payment of rebel debt or for slaves. I do not know why the President may not honorably & patriotically join in securing the adoption of these amendments. With his cooperation they can be adopted & the restoration of relations with the lately rebel states completed within three months.

I do not know yet that I shall hold any Court in Virginia or in North Carolina. It seemed to me, when I first read the Presidents Proclamation of Peace that it might be fairly construed as abrogating martial law & restoring the writ of Habeas Corpus; but subsequent orders from the War Department have put a different construction upon it, & I do not wish, as long as I with my brethren represent the Justice of the nation in its highest seat, to hold any Courts in the lately rebel states, until all possibility of claim that the judicial is subordinate to the Military power is removed by express declaration from the President.[3] My views are fully known to him, &, I hope, not unsatisfactory. They certainly are free from the slightest shade of intention to embarrass his action. I recognize absolutely & frankly all his rights & duties as the Executive Head of the Nation; and mean to perform mine as Head of the Judiciary with perfect fidelity to him & to the country.

Have you looked at the indictment against Davis? I see it is in print. If you have you have noticed that the offence is laid in 1854; and perhaps you may remember that Judge Field in the Chapman case in San Francisco decided that, under the act of July 17, 1862, participation in rebellion since the passage of that act is punishable by fine not exceeding $10.000 *or* imprisonment not exceeding 10 years, *or* both.[4] Judge Field is now in New York & perhaps you could get a copy of the opinion from him, if you feel any curiosity to examine it.

I was not aware of Col. Halpins preference till I received your letter.[5] I am much obliged to him for this mark of his good will. I do not doubt the right of the People to call any citizen to their service, either from the bench or the camp, or halls of legislation, or from from any other department of official duty or of private life. But I am not an aspirant for Presidential honors. The mention of my name, heretofore, in connexion with the nomination for the Presidency has always been productive of much more embarrassment than gratification to me, and in my present position I feel more than ever averse to any *such distinction.* Since I have been on the bench I have scrupulously avoided every thing like political action; unless it can be called political action to express my opinions on political questions, in conversation, with entire respect for those of others, & lend my advocacy to what seems to me right & just & beneficial without reference to party or partizan ends. I should do more of this sort of advocacy did I not see already how it is misconstrued.

I shall take great pleasure when I pass a Sunday in New York in going with you to your church.[6] Though, I dare say, the Herald and the World would see as a proof of my anxiety to conciliate Catholic votes. Some twenty six years ago when I was a member of the City Council of Cincinnati I divided my compensation between the Protestant & the Catholic Orphan Asylums;[7] and some of my friends seemed to think it a crime, which I had committed for the sake of popularity. But I believe they gave *that* up when they saw me for the sake of the principle of justice & freedom separate myself from a triumphant political party & go into the small & politically powerless organization which devoted itself to that principle. I live in the belief that other like imputations will perish. At any rate they will not deter me from doing what I believe right.

If I do not go to Europe in July, which is not impossible though improbable; and if I am not prevented by official duties I shall be much inclined [to] that trip up the lake.[8]

Your friend as always
S P Chase

J. W. Schuckers Esq

1. Schuckers and Thomas Brown, a special agent for the U.S. Treasury, were friends and possibly business associates. Schuckers to Chase, Nov. 13, 1866 (Chase Papers, L.C.).

2. On May 10, the House approved what became the Fourteenth Amendment in accordance with a recommendation that the Joint Congressional Committee on Reconstruction formally issued on April 30. Chase to Stephen J. Field, Apr. 30, 1866 (above); *New York Times,* Apr. 30, 1866; *Congressional Globe,* 39th Cong., 1st sess., 1865–66, 2545.

3. Chase refers to Johnson's proclamation of April 2. War Department orders issued soon after created the impression that martial law remained in effect. Chase discussed these and later developments regarding the writ of habeas corpus in correspondence to Horace Greeley, June 1, 1866; to Jacob W. Schuckers, September 24, 1866; and to Gerrit Smith, May 31, 1866 (all below). *New York Herald,* Apr. 12, 1866; *Statutes at Large,* 14:812.

4. A federal grand jury handed down the indictment in the U.S. Circuit Court for the District of Virginia in Norfolk, Virginia, on May 10. The document accused Davis of "traitorously" taking action in Richmond, Virginia, on June 15, 1864, "to subvert, and to stir, move and incite insurrection, rebellion and war against the said United States." In the case of *U.S. v. Greathouse et al.* (1863), the owners of the schooner *J. M. Chapman* were convicted of privateering. Section two of the Second Confiscation Act (of 1862) established the punishment for such behavior. For further discussion of the *Chapman* case, see Field to Chase, June 30, 1866 (below). Chase to Flamen Ball, May 12, 1866 (above); Fairman, *Reconstruction and Reunion,* 175–76; *New York Herald,,* May 12, 15, 1866; *Statutes at Large,* 12:590.

5. Charles Graham Halpine, an Irish-American journalist who served on the staff of Gen. David Hunter, had gained fame for reporting on Union army life as "Miles O'Reilly," a fictitious Irish soldier.

6. Schuckers was a recent convert to Roman Catholicism. Schuckers to Chase, Nov. 13, 1866 (Chase Papers, L.C.).

7. Chase had held a seat on the Cincinnati city council for one year beginning in April 1840. *Cincinnati Daily Gazette,* Apr. 8, 1840, Apr. 13, 1841.

8. The European trip never materialized, nor, to the editors' knowledge, did the excursion "up the lake."

TO GERRIT SMITH

Autograph letter. Chase Papers, Library of Congress (*micro* 36:0499).

Washington, May 31, 1866.

My dear friend,[1]

I am always glad to hear from you & am always certain of instruction from whatever you write, whether I find myself able to adopt your views or not.

It is yet uncertain when, if ever, I shall hold Courts in Virginia: but, if I ever do I shall try to know nothing in regard to any case that may be before me except the Constitution & the Law, & to put aside all consideration of persons, whether myself or others.

To me it has always seemed clear that the war was waged for the preservation & restoration of the Union. So long as separation was disputed there was something to preserve: so far as relations were interrupted & state governments disorganized there was much to restore. I have not been able to regard peace as fully reestablished until complete restoration, with substantial security in each state for the safety & security of all its inhabitants & especially of that portion whose freedom the Nation, during the war & as a war measure, pledged itself to maintain. To me, therefore, restoration of representation in Congress, & tranquillity & order based on full recognition of the freedom of that portion of the population, seem essential elements of a true peace.

Until such recognition the states to be restored must remain subject to such military control as is necessary to maintain freedom & order: and so long as that condition remains that military control must be supreme; and all courts must be either actual or quasi military Courts.

Now I have not been nor am yet willing to hold a quasi Military Court. When I hold a Court, the Military must be in proper relations to the judicial authority aids if needed to the execution of its process, but not however to direct the discharge of its functions.

I do not think complete restoration essential to the proper exercise of civil jurisdiction, in absolute freedom from possible military control. Such complete restoration will be accomplished only when the states are again represented in Congress & are in the actual performance of their duties as members of the Union. But the President may now, as it seems to me, with entire safety & propriety restore the habeas corpus & abrogate martial law, by express proclamation, in all cases where the National Courts have jurisdiction & as to all the proceedings & processes of those Courts.

When he thinks proper to do this I shall with divine permission, hold the Courts in the several districts of my Circuit within the rebellious states.

Several weeks ago I submitted to him the draft of a proclamation to this effect, but as yet he has not thought it proper to take any action.[2]

Congress is at work on reconstruction & will probably agree definitely early next week—perhaps even this week. So far as I can conjecture the result from indications, I do not expect the scheme which I would prefer: but I hope it will be one which will be adopted by the people, & will open the doors of Congress, to representat[ion] from the states which ratify, & will at least facilitate the result which I believe to be indispensable to safety & prosperity, equal justice secured by equal suffrage for all

Please make my best regards to Mrs Smith & to Col & Mrs Miller[3] & believe me

faithfully your friend
S P Chase

Hon Gerritt Smith

1. Smith was a former congressman from New York and, with Chase, a leader of long standing in the antislavery movement.

2. Johnson finally satisfied Chase's concerns with a proclamation issued on August 20, 1866, that declared civil government restored, but the chief justice did not begin to hold court on circuit in the South until June 1867. The meeting at which Johnson received the draft occurred in April or May 1866. Chase also discussed the need to restore the writ of habeas corpus in letters to George Washington Brooks, March 20, 1866; Andrew Johnson, October 12, 1865; Jacob W. Schuckers, May 15, 1866 (all above); and again to Schuckers, September 24, 1866 (below). Chase to Flamen Ball, May 12, 1866 (above); Chase to Janet Chase, June 7, 1867 (below); *Statutes at Large*, 14:814–17.

3. Smith's wife, Ann Carroll Fitzhugh Smith; his son-in-law, New York banker Charles Dudley Miller; and reformist daughter, Elizabeth Smith Miller.

FROM HORACE GREELEY

Autograph letter. Chase Papers, Library of Congress (micro 36:0502).

New York,
May 31, 1866.

My dear Sir:[1]

I presume you are aware that Messrs. O'Conor & Shea, counsel for Jefferson davis, will appear in Richmond on Monday next, at the opening of the U.S. Circuit Court there, expressly to move on the trial of their client, or at all events to procure an assignment of a time certain at which that trial shall take place.[2]

I write to beg you to be present on that occasion and to preside over the Court if possible; and, if any thing needs to be done to render it proper to do so, I am confident that an intimation from yourself to the Attorney General[3] will secure the requisite action.

You know, dear Sir, that our friend Judge Underwood will be out of his depth on such an occasion, and that it is indispensable that the bearing as well as the action of the Court shall be such as will command respect even where it fails to secure approval.[4]

I will say no more, but profoundly trust that the proceedings to be had on this occasion will be guided to a fit issue by yourself,

Yours,
HORACE GREELEY

Hon. S. P. Chase,
Washington, d.C

1. Greeley, editor of the *New York Tribune,* supported general amnesty for former Confederates and, in May 1867, signed Jefferson Davis's bail bond. In 1872, Greeley ran as the Liberal Republican party's unsuccessful presidential candidate. *DAB,* 7:532, 533.

2. New York attorneys Charles O'Conor (1804–84) and George Shea represented Davis. The court actually commenced on June 5. Ibid., 13:620–21; *Appletons',* 5:488; Johnson, *Cases Decided by Chief Justice Chase,* 20; W. Stewart Wallace, comp., *A Dictionary of North American Authors Deceased before 1950* (Toronto, 1951), 410.

3. James Speed.

4. A native of New York, John Curtiss Underwood (1809–73) had been judge of the U.S. district court for Virginia since January 1864. *DAB,* 19:113–14.

TO HORACE GREELEY

Autograph letter. Horace Greeley Papers, Library of Congress (*micro* 36:0505).

Washington June 1, 1866.

My dear Mr. Greeley,

I know nothing of what is proposed either by the Govt. or by the Counsel for Mr. Davis in respect to his trial.[1]

I have held courts regularly in the Districts, within my Circuit, in non-rebel states, so far as my business required my presence

In the Districts, in rebel states, I have not held courts, because in such states, as it seems to me, all courts must be either military or quasi-military until complete restoration under legislative action, or, at least, until restoration of the Writ of Habeas Corpus & abrogation of Martial law by Executive action.

The Duke of Wellington in Spain *required* the civil judges to hold courts subject to military supervision; and was doubtless right.[2] Our Government, during the rebellion, had no settled rule of action. Military provost courts were very generally resorted to; in some instances Provisional Courts were established like Judge Peabody's Court at New Orleans;[3] sometimes Military Commissions tried civil cases; & sometimes State & National Courts were put into partial action, but were regarded and are still practically subordinate to the Military power. Instances are not wanting where their acts have been nullified by military orders; and even in the late Charge to the Grand Jury, at Norfolk, Judge Underwood referred to the President & General Grant as, in some sort, authority for his action.[4]

Now I do not censure this. In flagrant war & until restoration of peace, in districts or states where military control is essential to the accomplishment of the objects of the War, the civil must needs be subordinate to the Military authority. And I have, in the interests of order & restoration, uniformly advised the District Judges to hold both the Circuit & District Courts of the United States &, in cases of conflict between civil & military jurisdiction, to yield or refer the matter to the President.

But the Chief Justice & Justices of the Supreme Court of the United States represent the HIGHEST JUDICIAL POWER of the Nation, which cannot, with propriety or decency, be subordinated to any military authority. In my judgment, therefore, so long as military authority is exercised at all in relation to process or proceedings of Courts of the United States, in the rebel states, neither I as Chief Justice nor any of the Associate Justices can properly hold courts there. Very recently military authority was so exercised in New Orleans over the proceedings of the Circuit Court of the United States held there by the District Judge. The action of General Canby in this business was, indeed, reversed; but the reversing order virtually asserted the Executive power to control the Court, by requiring that, in future cases, no military action should be taken, *except* under instructions from Washington.[5]

There will be no difficulty in the way of holding Courts where restoration is fully completed, under legislative action, by the acceptance, on the part of the insurgent states, of such terms as may be found needful to future security & harmony, & by renewed representation in Congress. For then Martial law must cease & the Habeas Corpus must be fully restored.

Nor, as I conceive, will there be any such difficulty whenever the President shall see fit to issue a Proclamation abrogating Martial law & restoring the Habeas Corpus in all cases of which the National Courts have jurisdiction.[6] The law clearly authorizes such a proclamation; and it would restore the proper relations between the National Courts & the Military authorities by requiring the latter to respect &, when required, aid in carrying into effect the decisions of the former, instead of controlling, revising or disregarding them.

It is said, I know, that the Peace Proclamation did, in fact, abrogate Martial law & restore Habeas Corpus; and that now, therefore, I or any of the Associate Justices of the Supreme Court, may properly hold courts as if no war had existed.[7]

I express no opinion concerning the effect of that proclamation. It is clear, however, that, if its effect is such as is asserted, all orders issued since in restraint of personal liberty or in the execution of martial law, except as to soldiers, sailors & other persons under military jurisdiction, are & must be held to be void. Repeated orders have been made since that Proclamation was issued, which are inconsistent with the suggested construction of it; & it is obvious what unpleasant consequences might follow if that construction should be established by adjudication.

I desire to avoid all causes of irritation or controversy. There is enough & too much division now.

Influenced by this feeling I submitted to the President some time ago a paper of which I enclose a copy proposing the abrogation of Martial law & the restoration of Habeas Corpus in all cases within the jurisdiction of the National Courts by express Proclamation.[8] He took the paper & seemed disposed to do whatever was needed to remove all obstacles to the full resumption of the exercise of National judicial authority in the insurrectionary region.

Since then he has had the matter, I suppose, under advisement. I hope the proclamation will be issued.

In that case I shall hold the Courts, with fixed determination, to see no persons in judgment, but only the Constitution, the law & the facts.

Sincerely your friend
S P Chase

Hon H. Greeley.

1. Chase was responding to Greeley's letter of May 31 (above).

2. Arthur Wellesley (1769–1852), First Duke of Wellington, commanded British and allied troops in Spain between 1809 and 1813 in opposition to forces under Napoleon I. *DNB,* 20:1081, 1088, 1098.

3. Charles Augustus Peabody, a former New York Supreme Court justice, sat on Louisiana's provisional court from the time of its formation on October 20, 1862. Later that year, he received an appointment as the state's chief justice.

4. Underwood had delivered instructions to the jury on May 8. *New York Herald,* May 10, 1866.

5. Maj. Gen. Edward Richard Sprigg Canby commanded federal forces in the vicinity of New Orleans. In April, troops under Canby had restrained a writ of sequestration secured by the Treasury Department to seize 500 bales of cotton. The judge in question was Edward Henry Durell, of Louisiana's eastern district. *DAB,* 3:469, 5:545; Heitman, *Historical Register,* 1:279; *New York Herald,* Apr. 30, 1866.

6. Andrew Johnson issued the proclamation that Chase sought on August 20, 1866. For other discussions of this issue, see Chase's letters to George W. Brooks, March 20, 1866; Andrew Johnson, October 12, 1865; Jacob W. Schuckers, May 15, 1866; Gerrit Smith, May 31, 1866 (all above); and again to Schuckers, September 24, 1866 (below). *Statutes at Large,* 14:814–17.

7. That is, the presidential proclamation of April 2, 1866. John Catron's death in May had left nine justices on the U.S. Supreme Court. For an enumeration of members, see Chase to Susan Walker, March [17], 1865, note 3 (above). Fairman, *Reconstruction and Reunion,* 2–4.

8. The meeting had occurred in April or May. Chase to Gerrit Smith, May 31, 1866 (above).

TO JANET CHASE

Autograph letter. Chase Papers, Library of Congress (*micro* 36:0514).

Washington, June 5, 1866.

My darling Nettie

I have not written journal wise the last week for one day seemed so like another that it seemed hardly worth while; but this morning I rose bright and early—more early than bright—at 5 A.M. & dressed myself as soon as possible in order to have time to write you a nice letter before breakfast, when I am to have the company of Mr. Fogg and Mr. Wood.[1]

The weather, all last week was delightful—rain enough to keep the streets in order and air & sun enough to make the temperature just about right. Now as I sit at my desk, in the Southwest corner of my library, just after six, the morning air comes in sweetly upon my forehead and the milk man is going by with his car, & our boy whistles on the pavement, and some birds join their notes from the trees, and a rooster puts in his crow, and the newsboy cries "Dai-l-y Chron-i-cle!, full account" of" something I don't understand what & "trial of Jeff Davis." The sun is under a cloud; but we can dispense with his smiles.

The Governor went away last Thursday night but I expect him this morning. Both the Senate & House adjourned from Thursday until Monday in respect to General Scott, whose funeral took place at West Point on Friday. Poor old man! All his renown has ended in the grave! No, not so; his services live, and his fame—the first worth much—the last now empty except as chronicle of the past.[2]

I have made it quite a rule for a week past to take a ride every evening, & generally after dinner. The horses need constant exercise to keep them in any thing like decent going order. My plan has been to take the Governor at the Capitol & any gentlemen he may invite, if before dinner; if after to pick up some friend in the neighborhood to go with us. Since he has been away I have filled his place with somebody else. Last Friday it was Mr. Sumner, & we went through Georgetown coming back across Rock Creek at Pierces mill & into the City on 14th Street. Saturday my companions were Judge Lawrence & Mr. Shellabarger & yesterday eveng it was General Hayes who accompanied me.[3]

Mr. Barréda called the other day, with Mr. Asta Buruagua & Mr. Molina—half South America in one coach.[4] Mr. [B]—— was pleased to hear of you having met Madame. He wants to sell his fine place at Newport Mrs B—— was offered, so Mr. Molina tells me, two hundred thousand dollars for it; but was afraid of Greenbacks.[5] Mr. B—— thinks she would have done well to take the money & put it in 5–20s and got the twelve thousand a year interest in gold—and I think so too: It makes me feel *slim* when I remember that all I have in the world would hardly do more than half pay for the Barréda House: and remember that so many have made immense fortunes in doing a little comparatively on commissions, of what I planned, put in action & supervised literally for nothing for my salary did not pay for my expences of living.[6] But this feeling is wrong. God gave me an opportunity to render service to my country, which perhaps no other man would have rendered, for hardly any body else had been trained to so much self reliance or to such readiness to do what seemed right & best simply because it was right & best. I am thankful for this opportunity; and it is a satisfaction to know that by some at least of my countrymen the service is appreciated.

Carpenters Picture—a large Engraving—of the Emancipation Proclamation has come & I have had it put in a handsome frame & hung in the hall surmounted by the portrait of Washington. Mrs Crawford has had all the pictures covered with—well I don't know the name of it—but it keeps the flies & other insects off.[7]

Grandma Smith is about as usual—pretty well, but rather feeble. I do not see that she changes at all.[8] Mrs Crawford is very attentive to her & we all try to promote her comfort.

After you left Brussells Mr. Sanford wrote telling how well you all looked, with compliments for each of you. It was a kind & thoughtful act & I felt much obliged by it.[9]

The principal topics of conversation are the Fenian Invasion of Canada; the Reconstruction; & the trial of Davis. A good many think that the Government makes rather a poor figure in its strictness with the Fenians & its zeal in the service of England, while the Canada Raids are so fresh in remembrance & the complete impunity given by the Canadians to the raiders, & the damages done by the Alabama & other British ships in the rebel service are not merely unpaid, but the mere consideration of our claims is contemptuously refused.[10] Perhaps our Government means to shame that of England by exact fulfilment of neutral obligations. I hope the British head will be sensible to these coals of fire.[11]

In a few days probably the Reconstruction programme of Congress will be completed & put before the Country. It is not likely to be very different from that now before the Senate: with which most of the Union men *are* well satisfied & nearly all profess to be. My opinion is that it covers too much ground, & proposes several propositions as amendments which are either already in the Constitution, or unnecessary to the main object, reorganization of the Union by the restoration on just terms of the States in rebellion. Still I see nothing which will do harm in the plan if adopted. I only fear that the number of propositions will afford points of attack, which need not have been exposed & may prevent the adoption or ratification of the amendment by the required number of States. We shall see. I hope the best.[12]

The trial of Davis will not be likely to take place before fall; but may take place sooner. I do not intend to hold Courts in rebel states until the question whether Martial Law is to be continued in practical force is settled by its absolute & complete abrogation at least so far as the National courts are concerned. I have thought that the President would probably issue a proclamation removing all doubts on this point. I expected it before now, but it has not appeared & I do not know whether it will. If none appears I shall delay holding courts until satisfied that a decision that Martial Law is at an end & the writ of Habeas Corpus in full efficiency will do no harm, by giving occasion to conflicts real or apparent between the judicial & the Military authorities[13]

There, that is about all I think of for this letter.

I am so thankful that God has so mercifully kept you all in health. Separated from you all by the breadths of the ocean I cannot help feeling a good deal of anxiety. It is a comfort to think that our father watches over us all. In a few days—before this letter reaches you—little Willie will have past his first birth day. Dear little boy! May God make him his child! In all your enjoyments, dear Nettie, do you remember Him who has been so precious to you & the precious Savior who died for you. Don't let the world take His place in your heart.

Kiss Willie for me & give my dearest love to Katie & kindest remembrances to Maggie[14] and to all friends, in which last category I include all who have shown kindness & courtesy to you.

Goodbye darling.

Your affectionate father
S P Chase

While we were at breakfast letters came from you at Brussels & from Katie at London, both very welcome, & both very good. You must illustrate more freely. Your pictures add life to your sketches.[15]

My objection to your dancing was to the waltz, which I presume is the almost universal dance in Europe. So I will withdraw it, & leave you to your own discretion. Exercise that however, & be careful to avoid persons and frivolities condemned by your own judgment & conscience. I want you to be an ornament of Society; but I want you be an ornament in the Christian sense.

Goodbye again. I shall enclose this letter to the Legation: and write also today to Katie care of Brown Shipley & co, & shall be glad to know which reaches you first.

1. Possibly E. B. Fogg and George Wood, Treasury Department employees. *Register of Officers (1865),* 18.

2. Winfield Scott, former general-in-chief of the U.S. Army, had died on May 29 at the U.S. Military Academy. *DAB,* 16:505; *New York Times,* May 30, 1866.

3. William Lawrence, previously a judge in Logan County, Ohio, and a Republican congressman, Samuel Shellebarger, and Rutherford Birchard Hayes—who had also served as a major general of volunteers and later became president—all of Ohio. *DAB,* 8:448–49.

4. Peruvian diplomat Federico L. Barreda, who in his career held posts in various European countries as well as the United States; Francisco Solano Astaburuaga Cienfuegos (1817–92), chargé d'affaires from Chile, 1861–67; and Luis Molina Bedoya (1820–73), Costa Rica's representative to the United States, 1855–66. Jordi Fuentes and Lía Cortés, *Diccionario Historico de Chile,* 2d ed. (Santiago, Chile, 1965), 46; Theodore S. Creedman, *Historical Dictionary of Costa Rica,* 2d ed., (Metuchen, N.J., 1991), 175; *Enciclopedia Universal Ilustrada Europeo-Americana,* 70 vols. (Barcelona, 1907–30), 7:910; *Wash. Dir. (1866),* 128.

5. Barreda's residence, called Beaulieu, overlooked the sea at Newport, Rhode Island. Antoinette F. Downing and Vincent J. Scully, Jr., *The Architectural Heritage of Newport, Rhode Island, 1640–1915*, 2d ed., rev. (New York, 1967), 138–39, plate 168; *Chase Papers*, 1:592–93.

6. Barreda advocated an investment in U.S. government bonds issued under the First Legal Tender Act of February 25, 1862, that matured in twenty years and were callable in five. The chief justice earned $6,500 annually. *Statutes at Large*, 10:655, 12:345–48.

7. The picture next to George Washington's portrait was Francis B. Carpenter's famous depiction of Lincoln's cabinet at the signing of the preliminary Emancipation Proclamation—a gift from the artist. Crawford evidently served on Chase's household staff. Chase to Carpenter, May 2, 1866 (above).

8. Mary Colton Smith was the mother of Chase's second wife, Eliza Ann, and the grandmother of his oldest surviving daughter, Kate.

9. Henry Shelton Sanford (1823–91) served as U.S. minister to Belgium, 1861–69. *DAB*, 16:348–49.

10. The Fenian Brotherhood, a militant Irish-American organization, supported Ireland's independence from Britain. In April, adherents staged an invasion of Canada at the island of Campobello, New Brunswick. U.S. troops played a prominent role stopping this and another more recent intrusion at Buffalo, New York, which ended on June 3. The *Alabama* was one of many British-built Confederate raiders that had preyed upon Union shipping during the Civil War. The United States and Britain did not settle claims over resulting damages until 1872. *Appletons' Annual Cyclopædia* 6:286–87; Adrian Cook, *The Alabama Claims: American Politics and Anglo-American Relations, 1865–1872* (Ithaca, 1975), 233–40; Brian Jenkins, *Fenians and Anglo-American Relations during Reconstruction* (Ithaca, 1969), 23–24, 134–46.

11. Rom. 12:20.

12. Chase had discussed the recommendations of the Joint Congressional Committee on Reconstruction in correspondence with Stephen J. Field on April 30 (above). The majority of the committee filed formal reports with the House and Senate on June 8. The minority issued reports in the lower and upper houses on June 19 and 22, respectively. *House Journal*, 39th Cong., 1st sess., 1865–66, 811, 866; *Senate Journal*, 39th Cong., 1st sess., 1865–66, 505, 563.

13. A presidential proclamation issued on August 20 declared the "insurrection" at an end and "civil authority" restored, and thus satisfied Chase's concerns. Chase, however, did not convene court in the South until June 1867. Chase to Janet Chase, June 7, 1867 (below); Chase to Jacob W. Schuckers, Sept. 24, 1866 (below); *Statutes at Large*, 14:814–17.

14. Maggie was William Sprague, Jr.'s nurse. Chase to Janet Chase, Mar. 27, 1867 (Chase Papers, L.C.).

15. Chase's youngest daughter had artistic talent and eventually became an illustrator of children's books. She and Kate had departed for Europe on April 4. *Chase Papers*, 1:608–9; *New York Times*, Nov. 20, 1925.

TO HORACE GREELEY

Autograph letter. Horace Greeley Papers, Manuscripts and Archives Division, The New York Public Library, Astor, Lenox and Tilden Foundations (*micro* 36:0512).

Washington, June 5, '66

My dear Sir,

The "Anxious" man can have a trial before Judge Underwood. That's one way: the Court will be a quasi-military court as I think under existing circumstances; but no question can be made of the regularity of the trial.[1]

Or, the President can say in one sentence Martial law is abrogated & the Habeas Corpus is restored in all cases within the jurisdiction of Courts of the United States & sign it Andrew Johnson.[2] That done Civil

Courts of the United States are no longer quasi military courts, but perfectly untrammelled Civil Courts. That done I should hold the Courts in Virginia & North Carolina, & try—whatever cases I should find on the docket. That's another way.

Or, States may accede to such terms of restoration as may be proposed by Congress, & then, *or otherwise,* order & peace may be so clearly reestablished as to justify the Courts in declaring the Habeas Corpus restored & the Martial Law abrogated, and all proceedings under Martial law affecting civilians unwarranted & null. In such circumstances also it would be my duty to hold the Courts & enforce the supremacy of civil over military authority, & I should do it.

The shortest, easiest &, in my poor judgment, the wisest way to the proper trial of important causes by the National Courts in the rebel states is that through a proper proclamation of the President & I yet hope that such a proclamation may be issued.

I am glad to read what you say about financial matters. The only way to resume is resumption. A fearless & sagacious Secretary would have resumed a year ago, & let contraction take care of itself. Contraction as a policy preliminary to resumption was a mistake. Of course the Fort Wayne Speech was a mistake. The Secretary meant right then; but the banks & circumstances were too many for him & he went on expanding in the worst way, not only by actual increase of circulation, but by allowing large deposits to accumulate in banks & loaned to the people. We have only seen, I fear, the beginning of the results.[3]

Faithfully yours
S P Chase

When do you finish your book & go a fishing?[4] I wish I could go too.

1. A recent presidential report described the nervous system of Jefferson Davis, a prisoner at Fortress Monroe, Virginia, as "deranged" and "excessively irritable." According to the report, "Want of sleep has been a great and almost the principal cause of his nervous excitability." Writing on May 31 (above), Greeley had urged Chase to attend the opening of the U.S. District Court for Virginia. *New York Tribune,* May 24, 1866.

2. Andrew Johnson finally issued a proclamation that met Chase's concerns on August 20. Chase to Jacob W. Schuckers, Sept. 24, 1866 (below); *Statutes at Large,* 14:814–17.

3. The *Tribune* had recently included articles that stressed the importance of resuming specie payments to drive paper currency out of circulation and thus diminish inflationary pressures. Treasury Secretary McCulloch's speech, delivered on October 11, 1865, acknowedged the importance of eventual specie resumption, but stressed the immediate need to contract the currency through congressional action to authorize purchase of legal tenders. Elsewhere, McCulloch also suggested divesting some notes of legal-tender quality. Modified forms of the proposals passed Congress and became law on April 12, 1866, despite criticism of their deflationary potential. Legislation of January 14, 1875, finally authorized the U.S. Treasury to resume specie payments, which did not fully occur until January 1879. Hugh McCulloch, *Men and Measures of Half a Century: Sketches and Comments* (New York, 1888), 201–4; *New York Times,* Oct. 15, 1865; *New York Tribune,* May 21, 24, 1866; Walter T. K. Nugent, *The Money Question during Reconstruction* (New York, 1967), 26–28; Robert P. Sharkey, *Money, Class, and Party: An Economic Study of Civil War and*

Reconstruction (Baltimore, 1959), 56–80; *Statutes at Large,* v. 18, pt. 3:296; Irwin Unger, *The Greenback Era: A Social and Political History of American Finance, 1865–1879* (Princeton, 1964), 401.

4. Greeley was evidently revising *The American Conflict* . . . , 2 vols. (Hartford, 1864–65).

FROM SAMUEL F. MILLER

Autograph letter. Chase Papers, Library of Congress (*micro* 36:0520).

Keokuk
June 5. 1866

Chief Justice Chase
My Dear Sir.

I call your attention to the statement of Mr. Johnson in the enclosed slip.[1] Whatever may be our guesses at the individual conclusions of the members of the court, it is certainly false that the court ever decided the case, or even took a vote upon it. Not only so but there are several members of the court, who have never as far as I know *expressed* any opinion on the subject.

A very animated political contest is now going on in the State of Missouri, between the radicals and their opponents; the latter including every returned rebel in the State.

This contest is looked upon by both parties as settling the future of that state for years to come, not only in its political relations, but as affecting the personal safety of the respective parties.[2]

In this contest the stringent character of the oath prescribed by the Missouri Constitution, which was before us in the case referred to by Mr. Johnson, is made a strong point in the attack upon the radicals; and the assertion; that the Sup. Court of the United States has decided it to be in Conflict with the Constitution of the United States is telling with fatal effect on the radicals.

Undoubtedly this was the purpose arrived at by the motion of Judge Field, that we should decide this case, and postpone the congressional oath case.[3] This move you will remember was defeated by my appeal to the court not to decide this case if they passed the other, which succeeded by the good feeling and sense of justice of our brother Grier.

Now shall this falsehood be permitted to work sucessfully its injurious effects or shall it be contradicted? The Honorable Mr. Hogan, is asserting the same thing every where in public speeches and so is Genl Blair.[4] It was certainly a violation of judicial propriety for any judge to state what Mr. Johnson says he knows, and I do not believe any Judge has said it, because it is false.

But it seems to me that while we may well feel restrained from stating what *did* take place; there is no wrong, but a manifest propriety in contradicting the assertion that the court has decided an important case, or an important principle where it has done no such thing.

I think if any of the radicals of reputable standing should ask me, I should feel bound to contradict the statement, but I beleive they are afraid to do so, lest the story of Johnson and Hogan might be confirmed.

I write this in private confidence, to learn your views of the matter, and also to suggest that such a confidential conversation between yourself and Senator Henderson, or Brown, or Genl Loan,[5] as would at least enable them to deny as boldly as Hogan and Johnson assert, might do a great deal of good without committing any impropriety; if you concur with me in the matter.

I have suffered this spring from fulness of blood in the head; but shall be through with my spring terms soon when I hope quiet will restore me.

With true regard I am

Your friend
SAM F. MILLER

P.S. I take it for granted that the word *minority* in the despatch is a misprint for majority.

Cant you say a word to some [senator or] mem. of the house for our judiciary bill?[6]

1. The "slip," a widely published letter of May 30 from Maryland senator Reverdy Johnson to Missouri congressman John Hogan, speculated on the two Missouri test oath cases pending before the Supreme Court: *Garesche v. Missouri* and *Cummings v. Missouri*. Attorney Alexander P. Garesche and John A. Cummings, a priest, were challenging provisions in the Missouri constitution of 1865—a document passed under Radical auspices—that required a retrospective oath of loyalty before either could practice his profession. In March, Johnson and David Dudley Field had argued before the Court that the law violated art. 1, sec. 10, of the U.S. Constitution as a bill of attainder in the nature of ex post facto legislation. "To this conclusion," claimed Johnson's letter, "a majority of the Court came, as was well known a few days before the close of the term. It was also known . . . ," he claimed, "that the failure to announce the decision was not because any one of the Judges constituting the majority then doubted upon the question, but I suppose that it was owing to the fact that the Judge selected to deliver the opinion had not time before the close of the term to prepare such a one as the importance and gravity of the question required. This will be done during the recess," Johnson asserted, "and that it will be delivered during the next term, I have no doubt." Formal disposition of the cases on January 14 (*Cummings*) and April 24 (*Garesche*), 1867, confirmed Johnson's predictions. *Appletons' Annual Cyclopædia*, 5:586–92; *DAB*, 9:120; Fairman, *Reconstruction and Reunion*, 144, 151–53, 240; *New York Times*, June 5, 1866; 4 Wall. 277 (1867).

2. In the election, which took place in November, 1866, Radicals triumphed over Conservatives by a margin of three to two. *Appletons' Annual Cyclopædia*, 6:526; *Daily National Intelligencer*, Nov. 16, 1866.

3. Congressional action of January 24, 1865, required all attorneys who practiced in federal courts to take the "ironclad" loyalty oath prescribed by legislation of July 2, 1862. A former Confederate official, Augustus Hill Garland, had petitioned for exemption

when applying for permission to practice before the U.S. Supreme Court. In *Ex parte Garland,* handed down the same day as *Cummings,* the Court found the legislation of 1865 unconstitutional. *DAB,* 7:150–51; Fairman, *Reconstruction and Reunion,* 134, 240; *Statutes at Large,* 13:424; 4 Wall. 333 (1867).

4. Democrats John Hogan (1805–92), who unsuccessfully sought reelection to Congress in 1866, and Francis Preston Blair, Jr., former Missouri congressman and brigadier general in the U.S. Army. Blair ran as the vice-presidential candidate for the Democratic party in 1868 and served as U.S. senator from Missouri, 1871–73. *Bio. Dir. U.S. Cong.,* 629, 1199; *DAB,* 2:333–34; 9:119–20.

5. U.S. senators John Brooks Henderson, who argued against Reverdy Johnson and David Dudley Field in the Missouri *Test Oath Cases,* and Benjamin Gratz Brown, both Unionists, and Republican congressman Benjamin Franklin Loan (1819–81), all of Missouri. *Bio. Dir. U.S. Cong.,* 1171, 1382; Fairman, *Reconstruction and Reunion,* 152.

6. The version of Johnson's letter in the June 1 edition of the *Daily National Intelligencer,* where it first appeared in print, does not include the word "minority." As explained in his response to Miller on June 9 (below), Chase discussed the pending legislation with William Lawrence, a member of the House Judiciary Committee.

TO SAMUEL F. MILLER

Letterpress copy of autograph letter. Chase Papers, Historical Society of Pennsylvania (*micro* 36:0538).

Washington, June 9, 1866.

My dear Judge

I have just received yours of the 5th, and thank you for it. [For] several days—indeed ever since I saw Johnson's letter to Hogan—[1] [I] have had it on my mind to write you on the subject.

The letter itself seemed to me a gross violation of all propriety, even if the facts were as stated by him. Where a court has agreed on its opinion—by a majority only especially—& for any cause thinks fit to postpone its announcement, I have always supposed it would be considered a breach of propriety for any Judge to state its substance, before delivered from the bench. I hardly know how to characterize the action of counsel who collects from conversation with Judges the supposed opinions of the several Members of the court, & then makes out by the comparison of numbers the judgment of the tribunal; and then invents an assignment to a particular Judge of the duty of writing the opinion

I have no memoranda of what took place: but my impression is that we took up & decided all the cases except the test-oath-for-lawyers case, under the act of Congress, & the two cases from Missouri,[2] one involving the Constitutionality of the test oath for lawyers & the other the Constitutionality of the test oath for Ministers required by the Constitution of Missouri. We had discussed the first case at great length; but had never taken up the two latter at all. Field, at last, moved to continue the first case till the next term & the motion prevailed by a majority of one: I then called the other cases, and expressed the opinion that as the first case had been continued these should be also. I forget whether any vote was taken on the question of present consideration. But you made a strong appeal against the taking of these up under the circumstances, and in the last hours of the term. Judge Grier on that appeal voted for postponement with Judges Swayne Davis, yourself & myself. Not only was there no decision; but so far as I recollection there was no consultation as to these cases.

I mean no consultation by the Court. If there was any by members of the Court, as a caucus or conference separate from the other Judges & with the intention of controlling the disposition of the causes I know nothing of it. I should be sorry to believe there was any such private arrangement or understanding for the decision of a case especially in the anticipation the regular conference & for the purpose of dictating its result.

You remember that I went to New York on the evening of the day we adjourned. Judge Clifford was on the cars & we had a good deal of talk. Among other things he told me that Judge Nelson told him either just before or immediately after we took our seats on the Bench the last day that Judge Grier had consented to withdraw his vote on postponement & the case could therefore be decided; to which he, Judge Clifford, replied that he should not have any thing to do with disturbing what was already settled. I could not help remembering the credit you had given Judge Grier for that vote & thought you ought to know the true state of facts.

Now I shall be very glad to have from you whose memory is so much more accurate than mine an exact account of what did actually transpire. It may be important that I be able to state the facts exactly hereafter.

As to Johnson's letter I see no reason why you should not state the fact that the case was never considered in consultation & never decided by the Court, in reply to an enquiry from any proper quarter. *I* have refrained from writing any such answer for publication though I have received several letters of enquiry; because it seems to have been assumed that I am in favor of sustaining the test oath requirements as entirely consistent with the National Constitution and such an answer would therefore be imputed to mere partizanship. My conscience would acquit me, for nothing is the object of more earnest desire with me than to know the sense of the Constitution just as it was known by those who made & adopted it, & to declare this sense—just this & this only—in every case that comes before us. I have only said in conversation that the record shows that the two Missouri causes are continued *under advisement* & that I know nothing that contradicted that statement. In only one letter to a friend in St Louis have I said that no such decision was made by the Court; whatever may have been concluded out of the Court by Judges among themselves: and this was in private to avoid the imputation I have mentioned. Your position would relieve you from such an imputation; or if not absolutely so, such an imputation would have far less weight & credit in your case than in mine.[3] I shall speak to Henderson whom I have already referred to the record on the subject. He was counsel on one side & Johnson on the other, & has a right to know that Johnson has had no information which was denied to him.

I am very sorry to read of your indisposition. You must not run any risks of hard work. What do you say to going up to Lake Superior in July—say from 1st to 19th or later say from 20 July to 16 August. I am thinking seriously of it & we could meet at Detroit or (better) Cleveland.[4]

The Judiciary Committee of the House have the Court bill under consideration. It has been in the hands of my friend Judge Lawrence of Ohio as a sub committee who has conferred freely with me, and it is now in a very satisfactory shape. If the Committee agree to the amendment & the House sanction the bill I think the whole country will be benefitted.[5]

Please give my best regards to Mrs Miller & your daughter.[6] My children are in England now.

With sincerest esteem

Your friend
S P CHASE

Hon. Sam. F. Miller

1. Reverdy Johnson to John Hogan, May 30, 1866, discussed in Miller to Chase, June 5, 1866 (above).

2. In his letter to Chase, June 5, 1866 (above), Miller had discussed *Ex parte Garland,* which challenged congressional legislation of January 24, 1865, as well as *Garesche v. Missouri* and *Cummings v. Missouri,* which questioned the constitutionality of the Missouri test oath.

3. In his letter to Charles D. Drake, April 24, 1866 (above), Chase had addressed allegations of using his judicial position to promote partisan politics. Chase no doubt felt that Miller would be perceived as an impartial source. Fairman, *Reconstruction and Reunion.* 155–56.

4. The visit to Lake Superior never materialized. On July 14, Chase left for a vacation in New England and returned to Washington on September 6. *Chase Papers,* 1:612–33.

5. The House Judiciary Committee had nine members: Massachusetts congressman George S. Boutwell, who retained his seat until 1869 and then served as Treasury secretary, 1869–73; Burton Chauncey Cook (1819–94) of Illinois; Chase's friend, William Lawrence; Daniel Morris (1812–89) of New York; Andrew Jackson Rogers; Maryland congressman Francis Thomas (1799–1876); Pennsylvania congressman Thomas Williams; James Falconer Wilson (1828–95) of Iowa, chair of the committee; and Frederick Enoch Woodbridge (1818–88) of Vermont. Chase was concerned about two proposed pieces of legislation. As introduced by Ira Harris, S. 103 would have created an intermediate court of appeals for each circuit; but the bill died in the House Judiciary Committee after passage in the Senate. H.R. 334, which became law on July 23, 1866, limited the size of the Supreme Court to seven justices. *Bio. Dir. U.S. Cong.,* 821, 1535, 2083; Chase to Miller, June 15, 1866 (below); *DAB,* 18:429–30, 20:331–32; Fairman, *Reconstruction and Reunion,* 160–61; *Statutes at Large,* 14:209.

6. Justice Miller and Elizabeth Winter Reeves Miller, his wife of nine years, had two daughters: Lida M., and another who eventually wed Irvine Miller of Springfield, Ohio.

Two other surviving daughters from an earlier marriage—whose names are unknown—became the wives of George B. Corkhill of Mt. Pleasant, Iowa, and W. F. Stocking of New York. Charles Noble Gregory, *Samuel Freeman Miller* (Iowa City, 1907), 62–63.

TO SAMUEL F. MILLER

Letterpress copy of autograph letter. Chase Papers, Historical Society of Pennsylvania (*micro* 36:0554).

Washington, June 15, 1866.

My dear Judge,

It is very important,—if it is important that adequate salaries should be paid to the Judges of the Supreme Court that the number of Judges should be reduced prospectively as vacancies may occur, to seven. I think that the salaries of the highest Judicial Officers of the nation ought not to be less than that of the highest Military officers: and, at least, an approximation might be made if the number were not so large, and especially if by the reduction of the number the means of increase would be ultimately supplied.[1]

If you concur in this view please write to Wilson and press it on him, without naming me in this connexion however.[2]

There is one connexion, though, in which it may be well to name me. The House Judiciary Committee has before it the Judiciary bill from the Senate and in respect to this I should like to have Wilson confer with me freely. So far it has been in the charge of Judge Lawrence, who has now been called home by the illness of his father.[3] Your relations as friend and con[stitu]ent to Wilson will warrant you in asking him to confer with me and your knowledge of me will warrant you in assuring him that I shall be most happy to give any assistance in making the bill what it ought to be.

Your friend cordially
S P Chase

If you think it wise pray write to Swayne & Davis to write to any members they are on such terms with, as to make it proper.[4]

1. Chase's annual salary was $6,500, and that of his brethren was $6,000. On May 4, the House had passed legislation to create the rank of general of the U.S. Army, with yearly remuneration of $17,640. The Senate approved the bill on July 17, and it became law eight days later. *Congressional Globe,* 39th Cong., 1st sess., 1865–66, 2393, 3858; Fairman, *Reconstruction and Reunion,* 166; *Statutes at Large,* 10:655, 14:223.

2. In a letter to Chase, June 27, 1866 (below), Miller reported on resulting correspondence with James Falconer Wilson, chair of the House Judiciary Committee and Miller's congressional representative.

3. Chase had discussed S. 103, the ill-fated proposal to create intermediate appellate courts, in his letter to Miller, June 9, 1866 (above). The father of William Lawrence, a former Ohio jurist, was Joseph Lawrence. *DAB,* 11:52.

4. In a letter to fellow justice David Davis, written on June 28, Miller expressed disapproval of Chase's involvement in the pending legislation—a sentiment that Miller echoed in correspondence written directly to Chase on June 27 (below). Fairman, *Reconstruction and Reunion,* 165.

FROM SAMUEL F. MILLER

Autograph letter. Chase Papers, Library of Congress (*micro* 36:0602).

Keokuck
June 27. 1866

My Dear Chief Justice.

On my return from St Paul last night I found yours of the 13th instant concerning the library additions, and also that concerning the legislation of Congress affecting the court and the Judges.[1]

In regard to the additions to the library, I have no suggestions to make except it be to remind you that a list was made out winter before last by Judge Swayne and Clifford which I think you have and which met the general approval of the court. So far as my personal wishes are concerned I think the reports of decisions on the circuit, would be more useful to me in my room, than any other class of works.

I have written by the same mail that carries this to Wilson on the matters that you suggest.

I fear our Judiciary bill will fail. The session draws near its close. The bill had full consideration in the Senate. Judge Harris submitted it repeatedly to the Judges, and it was approved by all except Clifford[2]

If it is attempted to remodel it now, at the close of the session, with no opportunity to consult either the Judges of the Supreme or District courts, it may be doubted if it will succeed or if it will be generally satisfactory.

The bill as it passed, the Senate had the approval of all the district judges, of all the Judges of the Sup Court but one—Clifford. Can it be hoped that serious changes can now be introduced in the house, without dissatisfaction and danger of defeat. Besides the Senate as a body, is much more inclined to respect the views of the members of our court than the House, and it was there you could have exerted yourself to perfect the bill, with more success. If this fails I shall trouble myself no more with efforts to procure legislation. I have suggested to Mr Wilson, that he should call on you on the subject, and have also made mention of the matter of salaries in connection with a reduction of the number of the Judges. I have done this with some reluctance, as I have a great indisposition to seem to ask for legislation for mere personal advantages to myself—

But in reference to the Judiciary bill I have been painfully conscious of the delay of Justice in the Sup. Court. I commenced agitating the subject before you came on the bench, in a long communication to the

Chairmen of the Judiciary Com. of both houses.[3] I thought when I left Washington there was strong prospect of fair fruit for these exertions, in the passage of the Senate bill. I am of course aware that no bill can embody all that every person may desire. But as none of the court expressed dissatisfaction with that bill, except Clifford, as it passed the Senate with nearly unanimity I had some ground to hope it would be accepted by the house, and pass. I know not what modifications you wish to urge. From your sound sense I infer they must be wise ones. If they result in defeating the bill, either by delay or by the contests they provoke I shall doubt if they are worth that sacrifice.

You will excuse this frankness as that quality is one of the great pleasures of our intercourse. I am so deeply interested in the passage of the bill I could not say less

Your friend
SAML F. MILLER

1. See Chase to Miller, June 15 (above), in regard to pending legislation to create an intermediate court of appeals. The editors have not located the letter concerning "library additions."

2. Ira Harris of New York, who chaired the Senate Judiciary Committee, had authored the appellate court legislation. *Congressional Globe*, 39th Cong., 1st sess., 1865–66, 11; Fairman, *Reconstruction and Reunion*, 160.

3. Congressman James Falconer Wilson and Senator Ira Harris.

FROM STEPHEN J. FIELD

Autograph letter. Chase Papers, Library of Congress (*micro* 36:0617).

San Francisco
June. 30: 1866.

Hon. Salmon P. Chase
Chief Justice of U.S. Supreme Court.
My dear Sir,

I received a day or two since the correspondance between Mr. Hogan of the House of Representatives, and Reverdy Johnson in relation to the supposed action of the Supreme Court in the Missouri Test oath cases.[1] I read the letter of Mr. Johnson with amazement, both at the strange character of his statements, and the singular indelicacy of giving them publicity,—even if they were in fact true. As we are aware no decision was reached in the cases—the only vote taken being on the question of the postponement of their consideration until the next term. As announced by you on the last day of the session they were held over under advisement. Mr. Johnson has evidently confounded the action of the court in the military commission cases with the supposed views of some of the judges in the Missouri cases.[2] The conduct of Johnson is indefensible—more—it merits severe rebuke. How foolish he would appear if the decision of the Court should be different from what he supposes it will be, or if a reargument should be ordered. I suppose he got what he knows on the subject from Judge Nelson with whom he was very intimate—mingled up however with other matters. I do not regret that I was never intimate with him.[3]

The proposed amendments to the Constitution, prepared by the Committee on reconstruction, and passed by Congress appear to me to be just what we need.[4] I think all members of the Union party can unite cordially in their support. If the President withhold his approval he will sever all connection with the Union party. Two things are certain—the American people do not intend to give up all that they have gained by the war—and they do intend that loyal men shall govern the country.[5]

I see that Davis has been indicted for treason alleged to have been committed in 1864; and I take the liberty of enclosing to you a charge of mine in a case of treason tried in this city in 1863. I would call your attention to some observations upon the act of July 17. 1862 which you will find on pages four and five.[6]

I owe you many thanks for your letter of April 30th. received in New York a few days before I left for California, and for the very kind and friendly expressions it contains.[7] I remember well the conversation I had with you in 1864 on the subject of your appointment to the place you now occupy. But I have never told you of my interview on that subject with President Lincoln—nor of the telegrams and letters sent to Washington from California urging your appointment immediately after the death of Chief Justice Taney.[8] I will some day speak to you of them. I did indeed feel very solicitous for your appointment, and I always rejoiced, and do now rejoice that you were appointed. I know of few persons who could have filled the position so well—of none who could have filled it better.

I have been holding Court, for the last three weeks, and shall probably be occupied either here or in Oregon or Nevada until October. I commenced my term here with ninety six cases on the calendar, some of which are of great importance & difficulty

I see your friend Gen. McDowel every few days, and he always has a kind word for the Chief Justice.[9]

I am very truly your friend & obedient St
STEPHEN J. FIELD

Hon. S. P. Chase
Chief Justice of
U.S. Sup. Court

1. Field referred to Reverdy Johnson's published letter of May 30 to John Hogan. Samuel F. Miller to Chase, June 5, 1866 (above).

2. In March, the Supreme Court had heard arguments in the case of *Ex parte Milligan*. The petitioner, Lambdin P. Milligan, challenged the legal jurisdiction of military commissions that had convicted him and two other civilian Peace Democrats in Indiana for dis-

loyalty during the Civil War. The Court's ruling, announced on April 3, agreed with the petitioners and ordered their release. A formal decision was not rendered until December 14. Fairman, *Reconstruction and Reunion,* 143–44, 192–96, 207–11; 4 Wall. 132–42 (1866).

3. Field had special reasons for concern about confidentiality since his brother, David Dudley Field, had joined Reverdy Johnson in court to argue against the test oaths. Carl Brent Swisher, *Stephen J. Field: Craftsman of the Law* (Washington, 1930), 142.

4. On June 16, a joint resolution of Congress proposed passage of revisions that, together, comprised the Fourteenth Amendment. Chase discussed work of the committee that made the recommendation in letters to Stephen J. Field, Apr. 30, 1866; Jacob W. Schuckers, May 15, 1866; and Janet Chase, June 5, 1866 (all above). *Statutes at Large,* 14:358–59.

5. President Johnson had already signaled disapproval in a message to Congress on June 22 and soon after repudiated the amendment entirely. The political results matched Field's expectations and similar concerns that Chase expressed to William G. Brownlow on July 2 (below). Foner, *Reconstruction,* 260–61; *Message from the President of the United States . . . ,* 39th Cong., 1st sess., 1866, S. Ex. Doc. 57.

6. A federal grand jury had indicted Jefferson Davis on May 8. Chase was already familiar with *U.S. v. Greathouse et al.* and its relationship to the Second Confiscation Act. Chase to Flamen Ball, May 12, 1866; Chase to Jacob W. Schuckers, May 15, 1866 (both above); Johnson, *Cases Decided by Chief Justice Chase,* 18–20.

7. Chase to Field, Apr. 30, 1866 (above).

8. Roger Brooke Taney had died on October 12, 1864. *DAB,* 18:289.

9. In 1864, the War Department assigned Ohio native Irvin McDowell, a major general of volunteers during the Civil War, to duty in San Francisco. Ibid., 12:29.

TO WILLIAM G. BROWNLOW

Letterpress copy of autograph letter. Chase Papers, Historical Society of Pennsylvania (*micro* 36:0626).

Private

Washington, July 2, 1866.

Dear Governor,

Your two letters—the last with a copy of your proclamation convening the Legislature—were duly received and gave me much satisfaction.[1]

It amazes me that the President takes ground against the amendment. He does not, so far as I understand, except to any one of the propositions it embodies: indeed, at different times & in different manners, he has expressed substantial approval of every one of them. Nor can any body doubt that the ratification of this amendment will lead to the immediate adoption of his [*illeg.*] [policy.] The admission of loyal members—Senators & Representatives—from the lately rebel States [will hasten] the day of complete restoration and with it the return of tranquillity [& prosperity] to the whole country.

It does seem to me that every patriot should at once get to work to secure the earliest possible adoption of the amendment after which there will be room enough for the reorganization of parties upon the new issues which the times present.

It seems to me that the President is taking a course such as his *enemies* would wish him to take. He cannot be strong against the body of the men who elected him, rallying almost unanimously for the amendment. He cannot be strong when [putting] himself *against* the earliest practicable restoration of all practical relations between the lately insurgent states & the States which have maintained allegiance to the Union. Nothing is more certain to my mind than that he will be abandoned before twelve months go round by those who now hang upon his skirts & stimulate him to quarrel with his best friends.

I may be mistaken. It is not possible for me to give so much thought to political subjects as I formerly did. This note is written in great haste for I need all my time for other work. It seems to me however that from my position outside of the whirl I can judge as truly of the course and results of events as if I were actually in it. Most gladly would I have seen the President make himself so dear to all the faithful men who sustained Mr. Lincoln during the War, (and wanted, I know, to sustain Andrew Johnson,) that no one could have turned them from his reelection. Most sorrowfully do I witness his alienation from them & theirs from him. And I think I see the future in his failure and in the triumph of the cause, still so dear to the hearts of the people of Union & Freedom. I would rather see his success, if it could be harmonized with the success of that cause. I have been & am his friend; for I cannot forget the last five years—but my country is, as she has ever been, dearer to me than any friend personal or political.

Most heartily do I wish you success in your present endeavor to obtain a fair expression of the loyal legislature of Tennessee upon the amendment / Most anxiously do I hope, apart from all political considerations whatever, that the amendment may be ratified. If I know my own heart I desire the peace & prosperity of the Southern States as much as I do that of the Northern or Western. I proved this when immediately after Johnstons surrender I advised the removal of all restrictions upon trade; & the cessation of all attempts to collect cotton & other property for the Government, as abandoned or captured, leaving it to those who held it, subject to such individual claims, if any, as might be recognized & enforced by the courts; and the use of all possible means to aid the whole people in reestablishing prosperity on solid foundations.[2] I entertain the same sentiments now. And it is precisely because I do entertain these sentiments that I desire that the same Gracious Providence which has thus far guarded & guided us may bless your efforts to bring about complete peace & truest fraternal relations between Tennessee and the States from which she has been for a time divided in sentiment & action.

Sincerely yours
S P Chase

His Excellency
Wm G. Brownlow
Governor of Tennessee

1. The editors have located only one of the two letters that Brownlow, governor of Tennessee since 1865, had recently authored. Written on June 20, it informed Chase of a recent proclamation that convened a special session of the Tennessee legislature on July 4 to consider ratification of the Fourteenth Amendment. "I think we can pass the Amendments," he predicted, in spite of opposition inspired by Andrew Johnson. "His treachery is ruining us in the South," claimed Brownlow of the president. Tennessee's senate and house ratified the amendment on July 11 and 17. *Appletons' Annual Cyclopædia,* 6:728–29; Brownlow to Chase, June 20, 1866 (Chase Papers, L.C.).

2. Chase had apparently offered the advice to President Johnson in meetings sometime between the surrender of Joseph E. Johnston, on April 26, 1865, and issuance of an executive order three days later that removed selected trade restrictions. *Chase Papers,* 1:533; Graf, *Papers of Andrew Johnson,* 7:669.

TO SAMUEL F. MILLER

Letterpress copy of autograph letter. Chase Papers, Historical Society of Pennsylvania (*micro* 36:0638).

Washington, July 3, 1866.

My dear Judge,

Yours of the 27th came yesterday.[1] I will observe your wishes in directions to the Librarian about books. The list prepared by Judges Swayne & Clifford (or Field) would cost about six hundred dollars, and as only about $200 can be hoped for I wanted each one's advice. I have had replies only from yourself and Davis, and he leaves everything open. So unless I get more explicit directions from our other brothers I will leave all purchases to be made after we meet again: only keeping back as much of the appropriation as I can, for application to books for rooms. For myself I mean to get the Reports on the Circuit & in Districts if the money will go so far.

You are quite right about the Court Bill.[2] No amendments should be suffered to interfere with its passage and this is what I say to our friends on the Committee.

The three amendments which I feel most concerned in are (1) the Appointment of a Marshal for the Court by the Chief Justice with the sanction & approval of the Court (2) the reduction of the number of Judges to 7 by direction that no new appointments of Associates be made till the number reduced to that figure (3) application of money saved by reduction to increase of salaries. I am quite willing to give them all up rather than lose the bill.

The greatest danger, however, is not from amendments but from delay. The Judiciary Committee has not been called since the bill was referred to it, & the opposition of some of the Eastern Members makes it impossible for the Committee to get consent to report it out of order. Lately there has been even a majority against it in Committee: but that majority has been overcome so far that it will be reported. What Wilson[3] sa[id] to me yesterday led me to hope that it would be rep[ort]ed today: and it may be—or may have been for it is now about 4 P.M. If actively pressed it need not fail but my fears are greater than my hopes. If once through the House it will be safe.

This morning I had a letter from Wallace[4] in which he spoke of Griers paralytic affection as quite serious, though it did not at all affect his mind, nor indeed any part of his body save his lower limbs. He says that brother G—— bears the calamity bravely. He has gone to the sea-shore & I shall try to visit him.

What did you do about Johnsons letter? I heard there was a paragraph in one of the Missouri papers stating that there was no decision & no consultation on the authority of a Western Judge. Was it on yours?

A day or two ago I received the following telegram from Judge Field "Have read with amazement Reverdy Johnsons letter to Hogan on Missouri case. Does it require any notice from Judge. Please answer"[5] / I suppose "Judge" means "Judges." I have not replied, hardly knowing what to say. Johnson's statement may well *amaze* any body, unless there was, what I will not believe, a secret arrangement among five of the Judges that the Congress-Attorney-oath case[6] should be postponed, and that the Missouri oath cases should be decided against the oath without any opportunity for fair consultation among the Judges, and one or more of the parties understanding was sanguine enough to take the success of the scheme for certain & spoke of what was agreed to be done as a fact accomplished. If you can imagine any other explanation of Johnsons confident assertion that the conclusion of the majority was well known. If it be true as he says that a judge was selected to prepare the opinion this also must have been agreed on in the caucus! Is this possible? Can it be possible? On the other hand how could Johnson have manufactured the story from whole cloth?

Your sincere friend
S P Chase

Mr. Justice Miller

1. Miller to Chase, June 27, 1866 (above).

2. That is, S. 103, the proposed appellate court legislation that died in the House Judiciary Committee. Fairman, *Reconstruction and Reunion*, 161.

3. James Falconer Wilson, chair of the committee.

4. John William Wallace was reporter of the U.S. Supreme Court from 1863 to 1875. Limited by paralysis, Associate Justice Robert C. Grier resigned from the Supreme Court on February 1, 1870. *DAB*, 7:613.

5. Field's telegram to Chase, dated June 30, expressed alarm over Reverdy Johnson's letter of May 30 to John Hogan, discussed in Samuel F. Miller to Chase, June 5, 1866 (above).

6. *Ex parte Garland*.

TO WILLIAM SPRAGUE

Autograph letter. Chase Papers, Historical Society of Pennsylvania (*micro* 36:0656).

Cornish N.H. July 25, 1866

My dear Governor,

Your two letters reached me here in my native town & gave me a great deal of pleasure.[1] Nothing is so cordial to me as the assurance of reciprocal love and mutual trust between you and Katie. It is one of my greatest delights to think her worthy of you, and to know that your affection for her is such that she cannot do too much to prove her worthiness.

I think very well of your idea of studying law. It is an excellent disciplinary study; but it will impose a very considerable tax on your time & patience. As you will not intend to practice, however, the tax will be tolerable. The outlines of doctrine, which comprehend all the details—these being innumerable as the waves of the ocean & the swells & falls of the land—are broad & general like the boundaries of continents empires & states. The most general book I know of is Walker's Elements of American Law.[2] You will find the last edition I presume—and last editions are generally best—in the Congressional Library. After Walker naturally comes Kent; and, if you desire to look farther into the sources of jurisprudence, I would then recommend Blackstone.[3] These books would demand a year's diligent reading, giving about six weeks to each & reading some history, English & American, in connexion. At the end of the year and indeed at the end of every month of the year you would find your labor richly repaid. It will give me very great pleasure to read over these books at the same time and talk of their contents with you & aid you as far as I can.

You ask what I wish in connexion with the household; and I don't know how to answer. You seem to think that I am too reticent in the expression of my wishes, & would be better pleased if it were otherwise. The truth is that I have so few positive wishes or preferences that it is difficult for me me to express any. I want you to do just as you think best and it will be the easiest thing in the world to suit me for I shall be suited with whatever you do. If you think best to transfer the household to the Farm,[4] and incline yourself to go to the Plains with Sherman, who tells me, he expects you,[5] I will go there occasionally in August and see that all goes right. If on the other hand you think it best for it to remain at Washington, I will go there for a week or two in September. My courts will keep me pretty busy probably in October & November. My present notion is to pass the month of August in New England, just when I find it most agreeable: to go to Ohio; to pass the first two weeks of September there; and then to go hard at work on my cases: and I can accomplish most by taking rooms on Capital Hill & studying in our Conference Rooms.[6] It will, therefore, be equally convenient for me whether the transfer to the Farm takes place or not. I think, as the question of economy need not be considered being equally balanced, I should let Mrs Smith[7] & Mrs Crawford decide transfer or no transfer, simply because I should be too indifferent to decide it myself.

I see that the Bill reducing prospectively the number of the Judges is in the hands of the President. It is hardly possible that he can veto such a bill as that. Years ago in 1855 I advocated this reduction in the Senate

& my proposition had votes from all sections of the country & from the best men. It cannot therefore be considered as prompted by a wish to reduce executive patronage; on which need alone might the President be inclined to use the veto as repelling an attack on his rights. If it should be vetoed I hope it will be passed notwithstanding.[8]

The salaries are left untouched.[9] I must regret this. No Judge can now live & pay his travelling expenses on his salary. Its amount practically is not as large as it was at the organization of the Government. That of the Chief Justice should be at least 12000 & that of each Associate 10.000. They would then be no more, relatively, than they were when fixed by Congress at their present amount. Can't this increase yet be provided for on the general appropriation bill or some other. Consult Johnson, Hindricks & Trumbull & see What can be done.[10]

I had a very pleasant visit at Dartmouth, and day before yesterday after passing three days nearly with my friends in Royalton came down to Windsor; dined with Mr. Evarts & passed the night under his hospitable roof, &, after driving with him over his farm, came here, where I am the guest of Mr. Pike, a well-to-do farmer, assessor for this Congl. District, and his handsome & accomplished wife.[11] Last night all Cornish, with large delegations from the neighboring towns came to pay me their respects. You know I am a native of this town, & this was their welcome. Two bands of Music, one of Cornish & the other from Hartland—across the river in Vermont—volunteered their cooperation, and we had a pleasant time. They tried to get a Speech out of me, but I was resolutely dumb, except for ordinary conversation. I am credibly informed that if Cornish could decide I would be President!!

A letter reaches me here from my friend Yeatman of Cincinnati, who says he has sent me two cases of Sunshine in place of the two that were Spoiled. I enclose the Express receipts. Please send one case to your mother[12] with my best regards & six bottles from the other to Mr. Evarts; by Express prepaying the Express Charges. His Address is Hon William M Evarts Windsor, Vt. I forget his middle name. Harrison Morgan can give it or it can be easily learned from the State Dept.[13] Let the other six bottles be put where they will keep well for Katie.

Most affectionately
S P Chase

1. Chase had arrived in New England on July 14 and remained there on vacation until early September. *Chase Papers,* 1:612–30.

2. Chase apparently meant an *Introduction to American Law, Designed as a First Book for Students* (Philadelphia, 1837), a popular volume authored by his former law partner, Timothy Walker. *DAB,* 19:363.

3. James Kent, *Commentaries on American Law* (1826–30), and William Blackstone, *Commentaries on the Laws of England* (1765–69).

4. Chase refers to the 350-acre estate the Spragues owned at Narragansett, Rhode Island.

5. Perhaps William T. Sherman, who had attended commencement at Dartmouth College with Chase. *Chase Papers,* 1:612, 613, 614, 615.

6. In the basement of the Capitol, beneath the robing room. Fairman, *Reconstruction and Reunion,* 65.

7. Mary Colton Smith.

8. President Johnson had actually signed the legislation two days earlier. *Statutes at Large,* 14:209.

9. Chase had also discussed the need for a salary raise in correspondence to Samuel F. Miller, June 15, 1866 (above).

10. Senators Reverdy Johnson, Thomas Andrews Hendricks of Indiana, and Lyman Trumbull of Illinois.

11. Chase visited Hanover, New Hampshire, July 17–19, and attended commencement at his alma mater. His entourage evidently included niece Eliza Chase Whipple and Israel Otis Dewey, a former merchant and postmaster at Hanover. In Royalton, Chase apparently stayed with one of several families descended from his aunt and uncle, Rachel Chase Denison and Dr. Joseph A. Denison, Sr. Windsor was the hometown of Helen Minerva Wardner Evarts, the wife of William Maxwell Evarts, U.S. attorney general from July 1868 to March 1869. *Chase Papers,* 1:613–17; *DAB,* 6:216.

12. Fanny Morgan Sprague.

13. A political associate of Secretary of State William H. Seward, Evarts had represented the United States on diplomatic missions to England in 1863 and 1864. *DAB,* 6:216.

TO BENSON J. LOSSING

Autograph letter. Anson Conger Goodyear Collection, Manuscripts and Archives, Yale University Library (*micro* 36:0684).

Providence, R.I. Aug. 24, 66

My dear Sir,

Your letter addressed to me at Washington has followed me to New England.[1]

The question addressed by Mr. Lincoln to the members of the Cabinet was substantially this Ought Fort Sumter to be provisioned? To this question Mr. Blair & myself replied in the affirmative, & I as well as Mr. Blair was frequently called to consultation as to the mode of accomplishing that purpose. My impression at the time was that the Fort might be provisioned, especially if the despatch of provisions should be accompanied by by a clear & distinct declaration of the purposes of the Government without occasioning open hostilities.[2] I do not think that Mr. Lincoln anticipated open War as the result. I certainly did not. That was the madness of the rebels through which God appointed the destruction of their scheme.

I have read much of the first volume of your History & with great pleasure. It seems proper however to say that it strikes me as an important omission that so little is said on the financial measures by which means were provided for the war & safeguards established against convulsion & distress on the return of Peace. As Secretary of the Treasury, I aimed at three leading objects 1. To provide means for daily disbursements by securing prompt exchanges of the credit of the Nation for the Material of War and Means of Administration 2. To provide a uniform national currency which would prevent commercial & financial disturbances at the close of the War, & 3 To establish a funding system by which the whole debt might be early consolidated into two great loans the 10–40s[3] & the 5–20s and ultimately into one at the lowest rate of interest & consequently with the least possible pressure on the resources of the nation and individual citizen. I accomplished all these objects; or at least so far as I did not accomplish them myself I made practicable & easy their accomplishment by others.

It is not of much importance to me personally whether these things find a place in contemporary history or not. Posterity will judge them rightly. Still it is not a matter of indifference with me, nor as I think is it a matter of little moment without reference to which competent judgments may be formed concerning our great struggle. I write in haste but am,

Yours very truly
S P Chase

Benson J. Lossing Esq.

P.S. When you visit Washington I shall be happy to see you & give you any information I can.

1. An engraver, editor, and author from New York, Benson John Lossing (1813–91) was revising the first volume of his *Pictorial History of the Civil War in the United States of America,* 3 vols. (Philadelphia, 1866–68), for publication as a new edition. Written on August 8, while Chase vacationed in New England, Lossing's letter inquired about the accuracy of an assertion by Francis Lieber that Postmaster General Montgomery Blair was the only member of Lincoln's cabinet who favored "making an attempt to strengthen Fort Sumter garrison at all hazards" early in 1861. *DAB,* 11:421–22; Lossing to Chase, Aug. 8, 1866 (Chase Papers, L.C.).

2. For Chase's formal response to Lincoln, see Chase to Lincoln, March 16, 1861, in *Chase Papers,* 3:53–54. Lincoln's offer to South Carolina governor Francis Wilkinson Pickens, sent through State Department clerk Robert S. Chew, echoed Chase's recommendation. "I am directed by the President of the United States to notify you that an attempt will be made to supply Fort-Sumpter with provisions only;" read the message of April 6, 1861, "and that, if such an attempt be not resisted, no effort to throw in men, arms, or amunition, will be made, without further notice, or in case of an attack upon the Fort." Basler, *Collected Works,* 4:323–24.

3. U.S. government bonds authorized by the Ways and Means Act of March 3, 1863, payable in ten to forty years from date of sale. *Statutes at Large,* 12:709–10.

TO JACOB W. SCHUCKERS

Autograph letter. Chase Papers, Library of Congress (*micro* 36:0748).

Washn. Sep. 24, 66

My dear Mr. Schuckers,

Many thanks for your kind & most welcome letter.

I rejoice that the Mower is like to prove so great a success, and sincerely hope that your springing hopes will not be cut down like the grass. By the way where's that interest I was to have? I should not have the least objection to have my salary doubled; &, just now see no great likelihood that Congress will double any except their own![1]

My recollection about the potatoes is nil: nor do I remember about saying by way of comparison with Mrs Macaulay[2] that you ought to see Mrs Eastman. But I remember Mrs M—— and how elegant she was, and I hope she is so still. Mrs Eastman was & is a very dear friend—not of the style of Mrs M—— so that I should care to challenge a comparison between them—but a sweet & lovely woman, unaffected & unpretending, good looking enough, though no longer Young, to be pleasant to the eyes, and intelligent enough though not learned, to be an agreeable talker, The papers show their *usual* impudence in connecting my name with hers: (I have seen no such reference:) but as it *is* usual & has been displayed several times before in ascribing to me matrimonial intents on the most trivial occasions & sometimes no occasion at all, I do not mind this instance. You may, however, contradict, verbally, every report you see or hear of this sort concerning me (if you think it worth while) until you hear from me that I have actually determined again to enter or have already entered the bonds of matrimony. I don't absolutely renounce the idea, and I know no one better calculated to make the happiness of a home than the dear friend I have mentioned, with whom and in whose neighborhood I have passed some delightful days this last summer. She makes her home with another dear friend of Mine Mrs Rantoul whose guest I was for several days, and I saw much of her also while a guest at several other of those charming residences along the shore;[3] but I am still and still likely to remain a widower. Why should I think of anything else, being a grand father. Ought there not to be a law against grandfathers being married to any but grandmothers?! Can you send me the paper you refer to?

By the way when you come to Washington let it be after the 10th or let me know before hand that you are coming earlier. Otherwise I may be absent. You must stay with me & shall have some of those beautiful toasted potatoes when you come & may eat them with your fingers if you like.

The papers are talking again, I see about the trial of Davis. Perhaps you would like to know a few facts and you may let Mr. [Young] know them too, if you please.[4] If you were here I would explain every thing fully & let you take it down in short hand,—but I have not time now & I hate to write anything. No wonder you think, my hand is so bad.

Well the few facts.

1. The Chief Justice has no more to do with the trial of Jeff. Davis than any other Justice except that it happens that he was allotted or assigned to the Circuit in which Virginia is to accommodate Judge Swayne who desired to be assigned to the Circuit in which Ohio is.

2. The Chief Justice when he holds a Court tries what cases he happens to find on the docket, if they are for trial. It makes no difference to him who the parties are; his duty is to administer the law.
3. The Chief Justice has never enquired & never will enquire what cases are to come before him except in the regular course & way. He neither seeks nor shuns the responsibility of trying Jeff. Davis or any other man.
4 The Chief Justice has held three terms of the Circuit Court for the District of Maryland since his appointment nearly two years ago. There were indictments for treason pending at the first term and except in certain cases, where the accused individuals have been pardoned, they are pending yet.[5] But the Government has not thought proper to proceed to trial in any of these cases. If the Govt. had desired a judicial exposition of the law of treason, it might have been had from the Chief Justice at either of these three terms; in April or November 1865 or in Apl. 66.
5. Early last Spring Bradley Johnson a double traitor, if treason consists in levying war against his state as well as the U. States was arrested in Maryland for treason & was held to bail by the District Judge. Gen. Grant requested to have him discharged without bail, on the ground that he was not liable to arrest or trial, because he had been paroled at the time of the surrender of Lee or Johnston; and the President, thereupon, ordered the discharge through the Attorney General &, On motion of the District Attorney under direction of the Attorney General the District Judge directed the discharge.[6] I will not express any opinion on the propriety of this interference with the course of judicial proceeding. It prevented the expression of a judicial opinion upon the effect of military paroles upon liabilities to punishment for treason or other crimes.
6. The Chief Justice held no court in Virginia in 1865 because the writ of habeas corpus was suspended & martial law enforced within its limits;[7] and in his judgment, all courts in a region under martial law must be quasi military Courts, and it was neither right nor proper that the Chief Justice or any Justice of the Supreme Court of the United States—the highest tribunal of the Nation & the head of one of the coordinate Departments of the Government should hold a court, subject to the Control or Supervision of the Executive Department, exercising military power / In this opinion, I believe, all lawyers of reputation, of whatever political opinions, concur.
7. Soon after the Adjournment of the Supreme Court in April last the President issued a proclamation the effect of which seemed to the Chief Justice to be the abrogation of Martial law & military government & the restoration of the writ of habeas corpus in all the states except Texas, & he determined, therefore, to hold the Circuit Court

at the ensuing May term in Virginia;—but various Executive orders inconsistent with the conclusion that Military government had ceased, soon followed the proclamation & led to an apprehension that the construction put upon it was not intended by the President.[8] The Chief Justice, therefore, reconsidered his purpose to hold the Circuit Court.

8. Desirous, however, to omit no duty, the Chief Justice called on the President in April or May and requested him to issue a proclamation of which a draft was submitted declaring, in unequivocal terms, that martial law was abrogated & the writ of habeas corpus restored in all cases of which the Courts of the United States had jurisdiction & in respect to all processes issuing from such courts. This was not done.
9. Subsequently however another proclamation was issued affirming the restoration of peace throughout the whole country,[9] which has, as yet, been followed by no orders asserting the continuance of Military government. Under this proclamation therefore it seems fair to conclude that martial law & Military government are permanently abrogated & the writ of habeas corpus fully restored. and this conclusion warrants the holding of Courts by the Chief Justice & associate Justices as the law may direct.
10. There is no act of Congress however which authorizes the holding of any Circuit Court in Virginia until the November Term,—the 4th Monday in November,—unless the Chief Justice shall order a Special term, as he is authorized to do by an act of the last Session.[10] The Chief Justice will no doubt, order a Special term if the District Attorney & the Attorney General represent to him that it is needed for the due administration of public justice.[11]
11. An act of the last Session of Congress changes all the Circuits, (except the first & second which include the Districts in New England & New York,)[12] & reduces the number from ten to nine: but it neither makes nor authorizes any allotment of the Chief Justice or Justices to these new circuits: and it is very doubtful whether the old allotment gives any jurisdiction to hold courts in the Districts which happen to remain in the same Circuit numerically as at the time of that allotment; while it is quite Certain that neither the Chief Justice nor any Justice can exercise jurisdiction in any Circuit except by allotment or assignment under an act of Congress.

    It is, therefore; very doubtful whether the Chief Justice can hold any Court in Virginia until after some further legislation by Congress making or authorizing allotments to the New Circuits.[13]
12. The absence of the Chief Justice or a Justice of the Supreme Court from any Circuit does not, however, prevent the holding of Circuit Courts; for the law provides expressly that in the absence of a Justice

> of the Supreme Court the Circuit Court may be held by the District Judge. Circuit Courts have, accordingly, been held in all the Circuits within the rebel states by the District Judges, ever since the reestablishment of the authority of the United States and the appointment of District Judges. These Courts, during Military government, were held, of course, subject to military control & supervision, to which, under the circumstances District Judges might more properly submit than the Justices of the Supreme Court. Of course any trial which might have taken place, the Chief Justice or an Associate Justice being present, might have taken place, with equal jurisdiction & equal effect, the Chief Justice or an Associate Justice being absent.

I had no idea this statement would be so long. And yet many details are omitted. But I believe it is clear & will enable you to understand the whole case & make others understand it.

I deeply—deeply regret the Presidents course. I verily believe that had he taken the course I ventured to recommend to him on those several occasions the great shame & disaster of a brush between him & Congress might have been averted. Had he done what I first recommended when the whole field was clear, & recognized *all* loyal men as citizens & entitled to part in the work of reorganization, *nothing* could have prevented his reelection.[14] I am sure he had not a sincerer or more disinterested friend than I was. Even now I cherish no unkind sentiment. My worst wish is that he may see the truth & obey it.

I notice all you say about the possibility that in the selection of the next candidate the public attention may turn to me. I will not affect indifference to such a possibility / I think I understand the wants of the country in its various relations of duty & interests pretty well & should like to try my hand in raising her name & fame & prosperity. But I know how uncertain such things are, & I do not set my heart upon it. Let what come may I mean to be quiet and content, doing my duty as it lies before me as well as I can, & leaving wholly to others the question whether I shall be called to the discharge of any other.

When you have that $10.000 a year, if I have as much I will resign & we will go to Europe together!

Meantime the pay of the Crier is only $4 or $5 per day;[15] but it is a good place for any young gentleman who wants to spend a winter in Washington. He must be a gentleman.

Faithfully your friend
S P Chase

1. Schuckers had an interest in the Hoit Mowing and Reaping Machine Company of New York. In October, Chase purchased four hundred shares, from which Schuckers expected a return of 5 percent. Chase's yearly salary as chief justice was $6,500. Schuckers to Chase, Oct. 20, 30, 1866 (Chase Papers, L.C.); *Statutes at Large,* 10:655.

2. Mary E. Macaulay ran the school in New York attended by Chase's youngest daughter, Janet.

3. Charlotte S. Eastman lived with Jane Elizabeth Woodbury Rantoul of Beverly, Massachusetts. Chase had visited the area from July 28 to August 15. *Chase Papers,* 1:620–25.

4. Evidently, John Russell Young (1840–99), the noted journalist who became managing editor of the *New York Tribune* in 1866. *DAB,* 20:630–31.

5. In 1865 alone, twenty-five indictments had been handed down in Maryland for treason or conspiracy. James G. Randall, *Constitutional Problems under Lincoln* (Urbana, 1951; reprint, 1964), 97.

6. Maryland native Bradley Tyler Johnson (1829–1903), who was arrested on March 26, 1866, had attained the rank of brigadier general in the Confederate army prior to the surrenders of Robert E. Lee and Joseph E. Johnston on April 9 and 26, 1865, respectively. Johnson won his freedom on April 5, 1866, as a result of Ulysses S. Grant's request, dated March 30, 1866. Respectively, the district judge of the court in Baltimore, attorney general, and district attorney were William F. Giles, James Speed, and William J. Jones. *DAB,* 10:90–91; *Daily National Intelligencer,* Mar. 28, Apr. 6, 1866; Graf, *Papers of Andrew Johnson,* 10:335–36; Long, *Civil War Day by Day,* 670–71, 682–83.

7. On his own, President Lincoln suspended the writ of habeas corpus on April 27, 1861, and at various other times during the Civil War. Congressional authority for suspension did not come until March 3, 1863. Long, *Civil War Day by Day,* 66, 79, 90, 270–71, 325, 409.

8. President Johnson's proclamation, issued on April 2, actually preceded the adjournment, which occurred on April 3, 1866. Chase had previously discussed his uneasiness in letters to Johnson, October 12, 1865; Flamen Ball, May 12, 1866; George Washington Brooks, March 20, 1866; Horace Greeley, June 1, 1866; and Jacob W. Schuckers, May 15, 1866 (all above). "Minutes Supreme Court U.S. Jan. 8, 1866 to Feb. 28, 1867" (National Archives).

9. Johnson issued the proclamation on August 20, 1866. *Statutes at Large,* 14:814–17.

10. In accordance with provisions of H.R. 334, which became law on July 23, 1866. Ibid., 14:209.

11. The district attorney for Virginia was Lucius H. Chandler, an unsuccessful claimant to a seat in the Thirty-eighth Congress. Henry Stanbery had held the post of attorney general since July. *Bio. Dir. U.S. Cong.,* 177; *DAB,* 17:498; Graf, *Papers of Andrew Johnson,* 8:387.

12. That is, H.R. 334.

13. Legislation of March 2, 1867, granted the authorization. *Statutes at Large,* 14:433.

14. Chase evidently refers to his meeting with Johnson on April 29, 1865, in which he urged the president to issue such a statment. Recently, Johnson and Congress had come to blows over two major initiatives designed to protect the civil rights of former slaves: a bill to extend the life of the Freedmen's Bureau (vetoed on February 19) and the Civil Rights Act (passed over Johnson's veto on April 19). In June, Johnson had also aligned himself with those who opposed passage of the Fourteenth Amendment. *Chase Papers,* 1:533; Chase to William Sprague, Apr. 30, 1865 (Chase Papers, Hist. Soc. of Pa.); *DAB,* 10:86; Foner, *Reconstruction,* 260–61.

15. Legislation of February 26, 1853, established the court crier's pay at two dollars per day. *Statutes at Large,* 10:165.

TO NOAH H. SWAYNE

Letterpress copy of autograph letter. Chase Papers, Historical Society of Pennsylvania (*micro* 36:0771).

Washington, Sep. 29, 1866

My dear Judge,

I have been hoping to see you in Washington, but I now despair of it until the term shall bring you.

Enclosed with this you will find a brief, but tolerably full statement of the law concerning the organization of Circuits & Allotments together with some of the allotments actually made.[1]

I have looked through the whole of the Statutes and examined all the allotments, & am now pretty well acquainted with the Organization of our Court & of the Circuits, considered historically & in the light of legislation.

So far as I can see the legislation having reference to allotment by the President or requests from the Chief or an Associate Justice to any one of the Justices to hold Courts in a Circuit other than that to which allotted has no application to the present difficulty.

My best judgment on the law & facts embraced in the Statement may be summed up in the following propositions

1. The Justices of the Supreme Court have no Circuit Court jurisdiction except when assigned or allotted to particular Circuits in pursuance of [law].

2. Congress, exercising its general legislative power may [create] & alter Circuits & make [such] assignment or allotment of the Chief & Associate Justices [to such] Circuits as may seem to it expedient.

3. Unless Congress sees fit to interpose, it is the duty of the Supreme Court under the act of 1802, or, in the specified cases, of the President, to make such assignment or allotment upon the appointment of a new Chief or an additional Associate Justice.[2]

4. Upon an addition to the number or an alteration in the Constitution of Circuits the Court has no power of allotment under the act of 1802 or other than such as may be conferred by the act making such addition or alteration.

5. Every allotment made by the Court must have have relation to the Circuits as they exist at the time. No such allotment warrants the exercise of Circuit Court jurisdiction by the Chief or any Associate Justice in any other than that allotted to him (except in certain cases on request, not requiring consideration here) and therefore not in any Circuit created or altered after such allotment.

6. Under the allotment made in 1864 the Chief & Associate Justices have not jurisdiction to hold Circuit Courts in the Circuits constituted anew by the act of July 23, 1866.[3]

Please give me the benefit of your best judgment on these propositions. I have not confidence enough in my own to feel perfectly sure; and want to be either confirmed or set right by yours.

So far as my preferences are concerned, I should *like* to hold the Courts in the 4th Circuit, and should do so had not the alteration been made which quite destroys its identity with that to which I was allotted.

Yours most sincerely
S P Chase

Hon Noah H Swayne

1. Passage of H.R. 334 reconfigured U.S. circuit courts but did not include provisions for another allotment of Supreme Court justices—a feature covered in S. 103, the failed Senate proposal. In this letter, Chase responded to another from Swayne that questioned the authority of the justices to preside in circuit due to what Chase's note called the resulting "difficulty." Legislation of March 2, 1867, resolved the issue by providing the Court with limited authority to make allotments. A facsimile of a letterpress copy of Chase's statement, most of which is illegible, can be found at *micro* 36:0773. Chase repeated the substance of his position in letters to David Davis, October 4, 1866 (below), and in a statement to other members of the Court dated October 5, 1866 (Chase Papers, Hist. Soc. of Pa.). Fairman, *Reconstruction and Reunion,* 172–75; *Statutes at Large,* 14:433; Swayne to Chase, Aug. 14, 1866 (Chase Papers, Hist. Soc. of Pa.).

2. The legislation became law on April 29, 1802. *Statutes at Large,* 2:156–67.

3. That is, H.R. 334. The allotment had been made in December 1864. Chase to David Davis, Oct. 4, 1866 (below).

TO DAVID DAVIS

Letter in clerk's hand. Davis Papers, Illinois State Historical Library (*micro* 36:0788).

Washington D.C. October 4th. 1866.

My dear Sir,

Doubts expressed by several of our brethren in respect to the jurisdiction of the Chief Justice and Associate Justices in the Circuits established by the Act of July 23d 1866,[1] have induced me to give a pretty careful consideration to the subject the results of which I desire to submit to your judgment.

The question may be stated thus:

What is the effect of the Act of Congress approved July 23d. 1866, "to fix the number of Judges of the Supreme Court of the United States, and to change certain judicial circuits," upon the circuit jurisdiction of the Chief Justice and Associate Justices of the Supreme Court?

A short review of the legislation relating to the organization of Circuits and the Courts to be held in them seems necessary to a satisfactory answer to this question.

It is to be borne in mind that the Chief Justice and Associate Justices are commissioned only as Judges of the Supreme Court. Whatever jurisdiction they may possess as Judges of the Circuit Courts is superadded by Congress to their proper powers and must be limited to the times, places and conditions prescribed by law.

The first Circuits, three in number, were created by the Act "to establish Courts of the United States," in 1789.[2] This Act required that the Circuit Courts should be held by two Justices of the Supreme Court and the District Judge of the proper District. Under it no allotment was necessary or was made. Whatever Justices attended the Circuit Court had jurisdiction.

The Act of Feb 13. 1801, wrought a revolution in the original Circuit Court system and relieved the Justices of the Supreme Court from all Circuit Jurisdiction.

This was changed was changed by the Act of 1802, which reimposed upon the Justices Circuit Court duties, and a special assignment of the Chief Justice and Associate Justices to the six several Circuits which it created. Under this Act no Justice had Circuit Jurisdiction in any other Circuit than that to which he was specially assigned or allotted.[3]

To preserve this policy of special assignment or allotment, it was made the duty of the Court, upon every subsequent appointment of a Chief Justice or Associate Justice, to make a new allotment and enter it on record; in default of which, and, also, for the time between an appointment and allotment, the President was authorized to allot. Every allotment lawfully made by the Court or the President, was made *binding* until another allotment.

No allotment was made under this Act until 1812.

During the ten years which intervened no alterations were made in the six Circuits created by the Act of 1802: but in 1807, by Act Feb 24 a new Circuit, the 7th., was organized; and authority was given for the appointment of an additional Justice, who was assigned by the Act, until otherwise allotted, to the new Circuit.[4]

Some changes were also made by Congress in the assignment of Justices; the Court taking no action in these assignments, whether made for convenience, or on occasion of new appointments,—of which there were two, one in 1804 and one in 1806.[5]

In November 1811, however, two additional appointments were made,[6] and no assignment of the Justices was made by Congress. The Court therefore, at its next term in February 1812, proceeded to make the allotment required by law.

Since 1812 the *Court* has often exercised this power upon the *appointment* of an *additional Chief Justice or Justice,* to which occasions it seems limited by the Act of 1802.[7]

Since 1812, also, very material *alterations* have been made by *Congress in the Circuits,* either by addition of new or change of old; in 1820, 1837, 1842, 1862 and 1863;[8] but no allotment appears to have been made by the *Court* after such *alterations,* unless in virtue of some clause in the law, directing "allotments" to be made "by the Court as heretofore;" or as in the Act of August 16th. 1842, specially requiring a new allotment.

The first allotment, in 1812, was as follows:

1st. Circuit: The Districts of New Hampshire, Massachusetts, Rhode Island: Mr Justice Story.

2d. Circuit: The Districts of Connecticut, New York, Vermont: Mr Justice Livingston.

3d Circuit: The Districts of New Jersey, Pennsylvania: Mr Justice Washington.

4th Circuit: The Districts of Maryland, Delaware: Mr Justice Duvall.

5th Circuit: The Districts of Virginia and North Carolina Mr Chief Justice Marshall.

6th Circuit: The Districts of South Carolina and Georgia. Mr Justice Johnson.
7th Circuit: The Districts of Ohio, Kentucky and Tennessee. Mr Justice Todd.

The last allotment was made at December Term 1864.

By the Acts of July 15th 1862 and March 3d 1863, most of the old Circuits were materially altered and new Circuits were created and power was given, by the usual special provision, in like cases, to the Supreme Court to make allotments. An unimportant modification was made also by the Act of January 28th 1863.

Under former Acts and these Acts, and the allotment of December Term 1864, the Circuits were constituted as follows:
1st. Circuit The Districts of Maine New Hampshire, Massachusetts Rhode Island: Mr Justice Clifford.
2d. Circuit: The Districts of New York, Vermont, Connecticut: Mr Justice Nelson.
3d. Circuit: The Districts of Pennsylvania and New Jersey: Mr Justice Grier.
4th Circuit: The Districts of Delaware, Maryland, West Virginia, North Carolina: Mr Chief Justice Chase.
5th Circuit: The Districts of South Carolina, Georgia, Alabama, Mississippi, Florida: Mr Justice Wayne.
6th Circuit: The Districts of Louisiana, Arkansas, Kentucky, Tennessee, Texas: Mr Justice Catron.
7th. Circuit: The Districts of Ohio and Michigan: Mr Justice Swayne.
8th Circuit: The Districts of Illinois and Indiana: Mr Justice Davis.
9th Circuit: The Districts of Missouri, Iowa, Kansas, Minnesota, Wisconsin: Mr Justice Miller.
10th Circuit: The Districts of California and Oregon. Mr Justice Field.

This statement shows how steadily the policy of legislation, begun in 1802 to make Circuit Court jurisdiction depend on allotment or assignment to a particular Circuit has been persisted in.

The only apparent exceptions are where a Justice allotted to one Circuit may exercise jurisdiction in another, upon request by the Justice allotted to such other Circuit, or under certain circumstances by the Chief Justice. These apparent exceptions, however, are only apparent for the request, under the law, operates as a temporary allotment.

The cases in which new allotments by the Court or assignments by the President are required, are of two classes:

(1) When new appointments are made. The Act of 1802 provided for this class of cases.

(2) When the Circuits are changed by addition or alteration. This class of cases has been uniformly, with perhaps one exception, provided for in the law making the changes.

The intent of Congress and the constancy with which it has been adhered to, is illustrated by the Act of August 16th 1842, which made important changes in the organization of four Circuits without any change in number, and expressly provided that it should not take effect until after a new allotment made by the Court. This provision seems to imply the want of jurisdiction under a former allotment, after a change in the constitution of the Circuit to which that allotment was made.

The Act of July 23d 1866, may be best examined with this course of legislation in view.

It reduces the number of Circuits from ten to nine; and, leaving the first and second unchanged, constitutes the remainder as follows.

3d Circuit: Of the Districts of Pennsylvania, New Jersey, and Delaware.

4th Circuit: Of the Districts Maryland, West Virginia, Virginia, North Carolina, South Carolina.

5th Circuit: Of the Districts of Georgia, Florida, Alabama, Mississippi, Louisiana, Texas.

6th Circuit: Of the Districts of Ohio, Michigan, Kentucky, Tennessee.

7th Circuit: Of the Districts of Indiana, Illinois, Wisconsin.

8th Circuit: Of the Districts of Minnesota, Iowa, Missouri, Kansas, Arkansas.

9th Circuit: Of the Districts of California, Oregon, and Nevada,

This Act may have been framed in view of the probable passage of another Act, which had passed the Senate and was then pending in the House of Representatives, and established intermediate Courts of Appeal in the several Circuits, and provided for the assignment of the Chief Justice and Associate Justices to them[9]

However this may be, the Act must be construed without reference to any such supposition.

It makes no assignment or allotment of the Chief Justice and Justices, nor does it authorize any: and it necessarily repeals all inconsistent legislation.

It is not inconsistent with the legislation which established the First and Second Circuits, nor with the allotments to them of the Justices who preside in their Circuit Courts.

But it seems to be inconsistent with the Acts by which all the other Circuits were organized.

Under the former Acts there was a tenth Circuit composed of the California, Oregon and Nevada Districts. These Districts now compose the Ninth Circuit. Is not, then so much of former Acts as established the Tenth Circuit therefore repealed? And is not the allotment of Mr Justice Field to that Circuit annulled? Can that be upheld as an allotment to the Ninth Circuit though composed of the same Districts?

So the Eighth, to which Mr Justice Davis was allotted, was composed of the Indiana, Illinois and Wisconsin Districts; while the Eighth Circuit constituted by the Act is composed of Minnesota, Iowa, Missouri, Kansas and Arkansas. It is the Seventh Circuit under the Act that is composed of the Districts which formed the Eighth under former laws: can the former allotment to the Eighth give present jurisdiction to the Seventh?

So Mr Justice Miller was allotted to the Ninth, all the Districts of which are now made part of and, with the addition of the Arkansas District, constitute the Eighth.

All the other Circuits, also, are materially changed in their constitution: the Third by addition of the Delaware District: the Fourth by *detaching* the Delaware and adding the South Carolina Districts: the Fifth by detaching the South Carolina and adding the Texas Districts: and the Sixth by detaching the Texas and Arkansas, and adding the Ohio and Michigan Districts.

All the Circuits under the Act, except the First and Second, are other and different Circuits than those to which the Chief Justice and Justices of the Supreme Court were allotted.

Must not the Act which established them be regarded as inconsistent with the Acts by which those other and different Circuits were constituted? It seems so to me; and if so, those Acts are repealed, and the allotments to those Circuits give no jurisdiction in the Circuits as they now exist.

If these views are unsound, I am desirous to have corrected. Will you them a thorough examination and let me have the benefit of your judgment? I have submitted the substance to our Brother Swayne, and shall immediately send a duplicate of this letter to each of the other Justices.[10]

Yours very truly[11]

1. Chase refers to H.R. 334.
2. *Statutes at Large,* 1:73–94.
3. Among other provisions, the act of February 13, 1801, required the Supreme Court to meet in Washington, D.C. The act of April 29, 1802, repealed legislation of the previous year. Ibid., 2:89, 156–67.
4. Legislation of February 24, 1807, created a place on the Supreme Court for a sixth associate justice, which Thomas Todd (1765–1826) occupied after confirmation on March 2, 1807. *DAB,* 18:574–75; U.S. Senate, *Journal of the Executive Proceedings,* 2:54.
5. William Johnson (1771–1834) and Henry Brockholst Livingston (1757–1823) confirmed on March 2, 1804 and December 17, 1806, respectively. *DAB,* 10:128–29, 11:312–13; U.S. Senate, *Journal of the Executive Proceedings,* 1:466, 2:45.
6. Gabriel Duval (1752–1844) and Joseph Story both won confirmation on November 18, 1811. *Appletons',* 2:277; U.S. Senate, *Journal of the Executive Proceedings,* 2:190.
7. *Statutes at Large,* 2:158.
8. In accordance with legislation of March 30, 1820; March 3, 1837; August 16, 1842; July 15, 1862; and January 28, 1863. Ibid., 3:554–55; 5:176–78, 507; 12:576, 637, 794–95.
9. S. 103 had died in the House Judiciary Committee.
10. Chase had written to Swayne on September 29 (above). "My judgment is entirely clear," replied Swayne on October 2, "that the Judges, whose circuits have been changed in their numbers, can not respectively hold Courts in them—in the existing state of the

law—and also that I can not hold the Court in the 6th Circuit by vertue of a request from you." Responding on October 22, Davis concluded that he could not legally hold court in his own circuit, the seventh. "But where the number of the circuit was unchanged, and the only change was in taking off one district, and adding on another," he continued, "I thought that there was no difficulty." Chase's letters to Clifford, Field, Grier, Nelson, and Miller, all of which were dated October 6, enclosed statements written on October 5 that repeated the substance of his correspondence to Davis and Swayne. Of those who responded, Grier, Miller, and Nelson either concurred with Chase or for other reasons doubted the legality of holding district courts. Only Clifford disagreed. Chase to Clifford, Oct. 6; Chase to Field, Oct. 6 ; Chase to Grier, Oct. 6; Chase to Nelson, Oct. 6 ; Clifford to Chase, Oct. 13; Davis to Chase, Oct. 22; Grier to Chase, Oct. 9; Miller to Chase, Oct. 11; Nelson to Chase, Oct. 18; Swayne to Chase, Oct. 2 (all Chase Papers, Hist. Soc. of Pa.).

11. Although the letter was not signed, a recipient's endorsement indicates that it was "Recd & ansd."

TO BENJAMIN RUSH COWEN

Autograph letter. Benjamin Rush Cowen Papers (VFM 1448), Ohio Historical Society (*micro* 36:0938).

Washington, Nov. 8, 1866.

My dear General,[1]

I was very much gratified a short time since by receiving a letter from you expressing continued friendship and giving your views of the recent elections.[2]

Since that letter was written the elections of Tuesday have crowned the great work which had been then so auspiciously begun.[3] Except in Maryland the People have every where vindicated Congress, and have made every scheme of usurpation impossible. It is a most wonderful result, when the conditions are considered, especially in New York. Every where the loyal party had to contend with the Administration which itself had placed in power; but in New York it had to contend also with the defection & active opposition of its own most trusted Chief & Champion, and all the weight of his personal influence & political connexions. That Governor Fenton has been reelected notwithstanding all this proves more signally perhaps than any other event of the whole canvass, how fixed & ineradicable is the determination of the country not to restore to the late rebel states their political power in the Government without complete guaranties against renewed abuses.[4] I hope, also, it indicates a determination equally fixed that the newly made citizens shall have a voice in the governments under which they are to live.

I am much disappointed in Maryland. There is every reason to believe that the loose registration under the auspices of Gov. Swann, and the looser morality taught by Reverdy Johnson that the oath of loyalty prescribed by the Constitution is unconstitutional and, therefore, may be taken falsely with a good conscience, contributed largely to the result[5]—indeed secured it at this time—but, after all, the fear among the ignorant and debased of negro elevation & suffrage, & the hatred among the Aristocracy, so called, of those who "freed the nigger" and assailed their ascendancy are strong, very strong elements in all the exslave states. It will require the influence of a national administration thoroughly committed and sincerely attached to the new ideas to counterbalance & overcome permanently these influences. What I regret most just now is the loss of Cresswell from the Senate. He has proved himself so true & able that a very deep interest has been concentrated upon him.[6]

I agree with you entirely in your view of the canvass in Ohio. I am sure that our success depends on bold yet temperate adherence to radical views. My own experience, during successive canvasses of the state, in 1855, 1856, & 1857 as well as in 1860 convinced me that very earnest advocacy of fundamental principles, when seen to be sincere & logical, never hurt our cause in any county, as much as it helped it. Truth is very strong when presented without passion.

It is perfectly clear to my mind as it is to yours that we *ought* to have declared for impartial suffrage a year ago: and that *now* we are shut up to the issue of the Constitutional amendment,[7] leaving suffrage for after consideration & advocacy. At present the shortest road to impartial suffrage seems to lie through the amendment. Still this winter may disclose other paths; and the shortest to that result, which will not also lead to defeat in 1868, is doubtless the best. I may add that even defeat in 1868 would be better than such a compromise either in respect to principles or men as would make apparent victory real disaster.

I thank you heartily for your expressions of confidence in me & of wishes that the choice of our friends for a standard bearer in the next canvass may fall on me. I will not deny that I should be greatly gratified by such a proof of public esteem; and especially by the support of Ohio, once already given me by the voice of her Convention, but neutralized & made impotent by what I must always regard as ungenerous and unloyal action in some of the districts. I shall be content, however, if any competent man is selected in whose hands the great interest of freedom & our organization will be perfectly safe.

Do not be silent hereafter, if for no better reason than the fear of "boreing" me. It gives me very great pleasure to hear from you, and need not fear writing too often.

Your friend most cordially
S P Chase

Gen. B. R. Cowen

1. Cowen (1831–1908), a former clerk in the Ohio House, served as a brigadier general of volunteers during the Civil War and adjutant general of the state from 1864 to 1868. In November 1866, he also chaired the executive committee of Ohio's Union party. Cowen to Chase, Oct. 12, 1866 (Chase Papers, L.C.); *Who Was Who,* 1:266–67.

2. Cowen's letter of October 12 analyzed Benjamin F. Butler as a potential presidential candidate and offered impressions of the state's "most closely contested campaign" in October, a victory for the Republican party. "My own opinion is that we made a mistake in

not declaring for impartial suffrage a year ago," he asserted. Cowen expressed confidence in Chase: "I still look to you as 'our Moses . . . ,'" wrote Cowen, "and trust the people may yet call you to guide them out of the terrible wilderness into which their own folly has led them." In closing, Cowen attributed an interruption in correspondence to his unwillingness to "bore any one in any way." *Appletons' Annual Cyclopædia,* 6:604; Cowen to Chase, Oct. 12, 1866 (Chase Papers, Hist. Soc. of Pa.); *New York Times,* Oct. 11, 1866.

3. On November 6, elections had been held in twelve states: Delaware, Illinois, Kansas, Maryland, Massachusetts, Michigan, Minnesota, Missouri, Nevada, New Jersey, New York, and Wisconsin. As explained in the text of this letter, Republicans triumphed in all except Maryland. *New York Times,* Nov. 4, 1866.

4. Secretary of State William H. Seward maintained close ties with President Johnson and had attempted, with others, to form a new party of conservatives and moderates. Reuben Eaton Fenton had won his first election as governor of New York in 1864. *DAB,* 6:326, 16:620; Foner, *Reconstruction,* 264.

5. Chase had known Thomas Swann, governor of Maryland since January, as a law student in Washington, D.C., during the 1820s. Swann had removed Republican police commissioners and replaced them with conservatives soon after taking office. Maryland's "ironclad" oath, authorized by a new state constitution, dated from January 1865. As counsel, Johnson had opposed Maryland's test oath in *Thomas Anderson v. the Board of Registration of the Fourth District of Montgomery County* and stated his position on the constitutionality of state oaths in general in *Cummings v. Missouri* and *Garesche v. Missouri. Appletons' Annual Cyclopædia,* 5:526, 527; 6:471, 472; *Chase Papers,* 1:8; *DAB,* 18:238; Samuel F. Miller to Chase, June 5, 1866 (above).

6. John Angel James Creswell, a staunch supporter of emancipation, male suffrage, and the Civil Rights Act of 1866, had represented Maryland in the U.S. Senate since March 1865. *DAB,* 4:541.

7. The Fourteenth Amendment.

TO HORACE GREELEY

Autograph letter. Horace Greeley Papers, Library of Congress (*micro* 36:0969).

Washington, Nov. 21, 66

My dear Mr. Greeley,

It is good news that I hear that our friends in New York mean to send you to the Senate: and that we are not likely to be disappointed this time. So mote it be.[1]

I have thought you wd. like to know from me direct, the facts of my interviews with the President.

He has indicated, on several occasions, within this month & the last days of October that he would like free comparison of views with me, and I have seen him several times. At the first interview he urged his own policy, of restoration, without condition except ratification of the Freedom-Amendment already agreed to,[2] & with representation subject to no restriction except loyalty [*torn*] Senators & Representatives elected to be judged of by [*torn*] House separately. I told him that my convictions were that the true Course for him & the Country was that he should recommend the ratification of the Congress-Amendment. If, as every body expected, the November Elections should go in favor of it, he might yield his views to the popular decision, without discredit, & not only without discredit but with honor.[3]

Circumstances prevented any other interview till last week: when we had two more. Meantime it had become evident that a portion at least of those who opposed us at the polls had become satisfied that some concession must be made to the popular demands, &, unwilling to take the Con[stl.] Amendt. just as it had been proposed, were inclined to ask for the substitute of Universal or Manhood Suffrage & Universal Amnesty for the second & third clauses of the amendt. and, so modified urge its ratification.[4]

Accordingly at these two interviews I strenuously advised that, if he could not recommend the ratification of the amendment as it stands, he should recommend its ratification with a clause ensuring Universal Suffrage with Universal Amnesty.

I saw no reason to think that any impression was made on his mind. He fell back on the position of immediate restoration of political participation in the Government to the ex rebel States & avowed opposition to any more amendment while representation was denied to [twelve] states.

So I came away with little or no hope except in the Providence of God & in the Constancy of ou[r] people & their representatives.

Sincerely your friend
S P Chase

Hon Horace Greeley.

1. Greeley ran for the Republican nomination, but lost to Roscoe Conkling. Glyndon G. Van Deusen, *Horace Greeley: Nineteenth-Century Crusader* (Philadelphia, 1953), 348–49.

2. That is, the Thirteenth Amendment, in effect since December 18, 1865. *Statutes at Large,* 13:774–75.

3. Congressional elections for the Fortieth Congress, which Republicans won overwhelmingly, were considered a referendum on the proposed Fourteenth Amendment. Foner, *Reconstruction,* 267.

4. The second clause of the Fourteenth Amendment provided for congressional apportionment and reduced the national representation of any state that denied the franchise to qualified males. The third clause barred from public office those who had previously sworn allegiance to the United States and participated in rebellion.

TO WAGER SWAYNE

Letterpress copy of autograph letter. Chase Papers, Historical Society of Pennsylvania (*micro* 36:0999).

Washington, Dec. 4, 1866

My dear General,[1]

It always gives me pleasure to see you, talk to you, and hear from you. Your last letter from Montgomery gave me special gratification as it indicates that the Legislature of Alabama is still disposed to act with deliberation.[2]

My conversations with the President to which you refer were not at all satisfactory.[3] He was kind enough to invite the interview or rather interviews & we talked very freely. He was courteous & kind & seemed to entertain a real personal goodwill & respect for me, which I sought to deserve by reciprocal personal respect & good will, and by entire frankness.

He expressed the most positive convictions that his policy of immediate recognition of the restored condition of the lately rebel states by the admission of their loyal Senators & Representatives to seats to the Senate & House was soundest & ought to be adopted while I urged upon him the fact that the opposite policy of Congress had received the endorsement of the people & that it was for him the part of patriotism & wisdom to recommend to those states the ratification of the Constitutional Amendment. I made no impression upon him in this direction and then I suggested what several leading gentlemen had suggested to me the possibility of a modification of the amendment by substituting for the second section—the apportionment clause—a section declaring all men of sound mind & unconvicted of crime & over twenty one years of age electors, & for the third, or disfranchisement section or more properly speaking qualified amnesty section, one providing for general amnesty. But neither did this suggestion meet with favor / He summed up all by saying that he could not favor any amendment proposed by a Congress in which only a part of the States were represented.

This position, of course excludes all agreement between the President & Congress as to amendments: for Congress claims to represent & does in fact represent the whole country & proposes terms of restoration of political power to a part which has been in rebellion & in contumacious abdication of its share of that power.

I am sure that the wisest course for Alabama to pursue is to ratify the amendment. The refusal to ratify which has thus far been the course of the ex rebel states has produced a very bitter state of feeling in the states which have ratified or will ratify. What Congress may do under the influence of their indignant constituencies is hard to predict. Certainly no terms of restoration more favorable than the amendment. Let the amendment be ratified & let Universal Suffrage be conceded, & I think the generosity of the Country may be safely trusted for the removal of the disabilities imposed by the 3rd Section if not from all, at least from almost all on whom it is imposed. And who would not prefer removal of a disability to a pardon.

I do not think that in the present temper of the people universal suffrage & universal amnesty can be looked for as a substitute for the amendment. Certainly Congress will propose nothing of the sort, if present indications may be relied on. Nothing short of a proposition to amendment the amendment by substituting these measures for those of the 2d & 3d Sections, coming from the ex rebel states would secure consideration for such a proposition. I repeat ratification is the best solution / Let those who will be temporarily affected by it show their gratification by advocating the measure & all will be well

Of course you may show this if you think good can be done but it must not be printed.

Yours most truly
S P Chase

1. The son of Chase's colleague, Noah H. Swayne, Wager Swayne held a rank as major general of volunteers in the U.S. Army. In December 1866, he was also an assistant commissioner in Alabama for the Freedmen's Bureau. *DAB,* 18:240–41.

2. Swayne's letter of November 27 reported that Alabama's legislature had postponed action on the Fourteenth Amendment until January 15, 1867, when "it will probably be ratified." "There is a quite general and somewhat outspoken preference for immediate suffrage," he continued, "with a more general amnesty." Swayne also hinted that Chase should suggest such a course to President Johnson. Swayne to Chase, Nov. 27, 1866 (Chase Papers, L.C.).

3. In regard to the interviews, see Chase to Horace Greeley, November 21, 1866 (above).

TO ROBERT C. KIRK

Letterpress copy of autograph letter. Chase Papers, Historical Society of Pennsylvania (*micro* 36:1003).

Washington December 5, 66

My dear Kirk,[1]

Your letters are always welcome but just now I have little time for reply for our court has opened & I am much pressed.[2]

At one of my three interviews with the President within the last few weeks I happened to meet Seward.[3] I had been talking to the President of your services & the propriety of devoting a sentence in the Message to the good will & justice of the Argentine Govt. in the settlement of the claim you arranged—& when Seward came mentioned it to him. I found him dead set against it, & had to give up the case. It is too bad[4]

I do not know that the greatest favor my friends could do me would not be to leave me where I am, without any effort to place me elsewhere. It is impossible however not to feel grateful for the good will & confidence they manifest. In that gratitude you must take a good share. I do not see that any thing can now be done beyond the frank expression of preferences, and taking care[,] that Ohio is not divided again so as to lose her legitimate influence.[5] I shall be glad to hear from you what you learn of the indications of public sentiment. I don't want my name used at all unless Ohio is decidedly for me; for I am entirely content where I am & should be if I had no public position at all.

Sincerely your friend
S P Chase

Hon. R. C. Kirk

1. Kirk (b. 1821) had served as lieutenant governor of Ohio from 1859 to 1861. As U.S. minister to Argentina, 1862–66, he negotiated a settlement of claims by U.S. citizens against Argentinians. *Nat. Cyc.*, 12:440.

2. Kirk had written from Mt. Vernon, Ohio, on November 30, shortly after returning from Argentina. "If I can do any thing at any time to promote your interest let me know," he offered. Kirk went on to express reluctance to resume his diplomatic post. "I have been very badly treated," he complained without explanation. Kirk to Chase, Nov. 30, 1866 (Chase Papers, L.C.).

3. Chase discussed the interviews in a letter to Horace Greeley, November 21, 1866 (above).

4. The final version of President Johnson's annual message to Congress, delivered on December 3, failed to mention either Argentina or Kirk's services. *Congressional Globe,* 39th Cong., 2d sess., 1866–67, appendix, 1–5.

5. Radicals and conservatives in Ohio's Union party were divided over suffrage for African Americans. Roseboom, *Civil War Era,* 449–57.

FROM WAGER SWAYNE

Autograph letter on letterhead stationery. Chase Papers, Library of Congress (*micro* 36:1008).

Headquarters, District of Alabama,
Montgomery, Ala., Dec. 10. 1866.

Hon. Cheif Justice Chase
Washington, D.C.
My dear Sir

I have a great deal to thank you for in the very kind tenor of of your favor of 4th. inst., and its interesting and valuable statements.[1]

Before it reached me, my own mind had settled on the same conclusion you express. The rapid growth of purpose to enforce at all hazards the Congressional plan of restoration, its power, and the measures proposed to that end, made an impression here, which made it seem to many of us wise to attempt immediate ratification.

Accordingly, on Thursday Morning was sent in the Message of which I sent you a copy. It produced a marked sensation, but no sensible recoil. That night we thought we should succeed, we seemed to be in full possession of the senate. The strain however was severe, such as only could be due to the threatening programme of a Territorial government with indefinite results.[2] For it was undeniable that the people, ignorant, proud, and without mail facilities were not yet up to the necessity, and would be severe upon whoever should act favorably without consulting them. And yet so vivid was the memory of '60–'61, that this dread would have been overcome.[3]

Unfortunately, a dispatch had gone to Governor Parsons, asking counsel.[4] It came, emphatic that the Amendment be at once rejected, and that the Legislature meet again in January. I dont believe this had the inspiration of the President, yet it was openly asserted that it had. The cry was raised "we cant desert *our* President," and quite soon it was plain that a vote was unavoidable, and that the measure would be lost. Then all those who were willing to hazard their positions on the consequences of success fell into line and we were left with scarce a force to muster. But they went home with sad hearts.

When they come back, they'll be prepared for either course. Meanwhile the Governor, I think, will follow up the new direction. He goes to night to Florence, where he lives, and probably will speak this week at Huntsville and Tuscumbia. Then he expects to go to Washington, and others with him, to confer, and see the ground, and to fend off a possible disruption. I still hope we may ratify when he comes back.

A week ago, a bill was introduced resembling Stewart's proposition.[5] That is the programme seems to have been to amend the constitution of this State according to impartial Suffrage, and then ask representation leaving the amnesty question in the hand of Congress. This I am told is popular, and the Member is sustained by his constituents.

My friends who go to Washington desire your acquaintance. I bid them go, because I like to swell the number of your friends.

Present me very kindly to the ladies, when you write. I am, gratefully and respectfully,

Yours
WAGER SWAYNE

1. See Chase to Swayne, Dec. 4, 1866 (above).

2. On December 6, Alabama governor Robert Miller Patton (1809–85) had reversed a position he had taken previously and issued a statement urging the state legislature to ratify the Fourteenth Amendment. On December 5, Congress had approved a resolution to study the "expediency" of reorganizing states of the former Confederacy as federal territories. "There is an unmistakable purpose on the part of those who control the National Legislature to enforce at all hazards their own terms of restoration," complained Patton. *Appletons' Annual Cyclopædia,* 6:11, 12; *Congressional Globe,* 39th Cong., 2d sess., 1866–67, pt. 1:11; *Nat. Cyc.,* 10:434.

3. Alabama's secession convention, which was chosen in December 1860 and convened in January 1861, encountered intense criticism for not submitting its ordinance of secession to the electorate for ratification. *Appletons' Annual Cyclopædia,* 1:10.

4. Lewis Eliphalet Parsons, provisional governor of the state from June to December 1865, helped organize opposition in Alabama to ratification of the Fourteenth Amendment. *DAB,* 14:268–69.

5. William Morris Stewart (1827–1909), U.S. Senator from Nevada, 1864–75, introduced the joint resolution on March 16, 1866, but the Senate postponed action on April 4. Ibid., 18:13–14; *Congressional Globe,* 39th Cong., 1st sess., 1865–66, 1437, 1755.

TO JOSEPH MEDILL

Letterpress copy of autograph letter. Chase Papers, Historical Society of Pennsylvania (*micro* 37:0008).

Private

Washington, Jany 2, 1867.

Dear Mr. Medill,[1]

Many happy New Years to you & yours! By this time you have read the two opinions in the Milligan Case; and will have been able to form a clear opinion on what was said & done.[2]

One word about the Mott case cited in the able article you sent me. That was a case arising under Military Law enacted by Congress, under the Constitutional grant of power to make rules & regulations for the *Government* of the National forces: and the correctness of the decision has never been disputed.[3] A proceeding under an act of Congress, clearly constitutional, is a very different thing from a proceeding under Executive Order asserted to be of paramount authority to an act of Congress. It will be an evil day for this Country when the wisdom of the framers of the Constitution is disregarded & the Executive recognized as Superior to the Legislative authority.

Your friend
S P CHASE

J. Medill Esq

1. Medill, a Republican journalist formerly of Ohio, edited and published the *Chicago Tribune.*

2. The Supreme Court's decision in *Ex parte Milligan,* decided formally in December 1866, included two opinions: one that David Davis wrote for the majority and another that Chase authored, which agreed with Davis's conclusion but used different reasoning about suspension of habeas corpus. Fairman, *Reconstruction and Reunion,* 207–11.

3. On December 29, the *Chicago Tribune* had published an editorial that discussed the case of Jacob E. Mott, a New York resident fined after the War of 1812 for having "failed, neglected and refused to rendezvous and enter the service of the United States," in violation of orders issued by the governor of his state. The resulting case, *Martin v. Mott,* eventually reached the U.S. Supreme Court, and Joseph Story authored its decision in January 1827. Story's opinion affirmed the legitimacy of congressional action, which dated from February 28, 1795, to call forth the militia in cases of national invasion in accordance with art. 1, sec. 8 of the U.S. Constitution. *Statutes at Large,* 1:424–25; 12 Wheat. 19 (1827).

TO JOHN W. THOMPSON

Letterpress copy of autograph letter. Chase Papers, Historical Society of Pennsylvania (*micro* 37:0063).

N.W. Corner 6th & E. Streets, Jany 30, 1867

Sir,[1]

I left the Capitol this afternoon with Professor Henry of the Smithsonian Institution in the car which started at 3 or just after.[2] Neither of us happening to have tickets or small change, I asked the conductor for a package of tickets & offered a five dollar bill, the smallest I had, in payment. He replied "I can't touch that. I then told him I would pay for both tomorrow. He refused, but a gentleman in the car was kind enough to pay for me & Professer H—— [&] myself fortunately had pennies enough to pay for him. The conductor seemed to me rude & unnecessarily strict; but supposing a good deal of strictness required by the rules of the Road, I said nothing & thought little of the matter.

I was obliged to leave at 12th Street &, just before coming to it, went to the rear platform & told the conductor I wanted to get out at the next Street. He paid no attention & I was obliged to ring the bell to stop. Probably the signal was wrong for the car kept on. Under the impression it would stop, however, I jumped down, as passengers frequently do, but the street being covered with ice I was obliged to run or rather allow myself to be dragged several paces before the car was stopped by the conductor. I just escaped a bad fall.

A man on the platform with the conductor seemed to enjoy the thing very much.

Knowing how important proper conductors are to the comfort of passengers & to the success of your road, in which though not interested I have taken a lively interest, I have thought it best to report this matter to you.

Very respectfully yours
S: P: CHASE

President Thompson
Metropolitan R.R. Co.

1. As indicated later in this letter, Thompson was president of the Metropolitan Rail Road Company, a Washington streetcar company incorporated in 1864. DeB. Randolph Keim, *Keim's Illustrated Handbook: Washington and Its Environs* . . . 4th ed. (Washington, D.C., 1874), x; *Wash. Dir. (1867)*, 87, 547.

2. Physicist Joseph Henry was first secretary and director of the Smithsonian Institution.

TO ROBERT A. HILL

Letterpress copy of autograph letter. Chase Papers, Library of Congress (*micro* 37:0117).

Washington, March [1],[1] 1867

My dear Judge[2]

I thank you for your letters. They are very interesting to me and though I am necessarily a not very good correspondent I hope you will continue to write often.[3]

It seems to me that you have pursued a very wise course. Your charge to the Grand Jury was exactly what it should have been. The Civil Rights Bill is as important to the prosperity of the Whites as it is to the security of the blacks. It is greatly to be desired that the course of the High Court of Errors will verify your anticipations.

It is deeply to be lamented that the Legislatures of the Several Southern States did not ratify the Constitutional amendment. Prompt ratification would have ensured complete restoration in my judgment. The refusal to ratify has resulted, as I expected, in a more stringent measure. I am glad to see that Gov. Brown of Georgia re[co]mmends to the people the acceptance of the new bill [& org]anization under it by universal suffrage.[4] If I were [a] Southern man I should follow this lead. Universal Suffrage is sure to come & the sooner it is conceded the sooner will all political questions be settled. Then no objection can exist to the ratification of the amendment—as required by the new bill—and prompt organization & ratification will certainly lead to the early modification if not complete removal of the disabling clause of the amendment.[5] If I had been in rebellion I would rather owe my restoration to political privileges to the removal of a disability by the people through Congress than to a pardon by the President. And if those who were leaders would now lead in restoration, preferring the welfare of the people & the states to their own aspirations or sensibilities for the present, I am very sure they would do the best possible thing for their states & for themselves.

For one I am exceedingly anxious for the complete recovery of the Southern States from the evils of the war. They are a most important part of the Country. Their prosperity is the prosperity of the whole. I know that the path of restoration is a hard one: but with wise men difficulty & even harshness is better than permanent or long continued distraction.

The decision of the majority of the Court is law until reversed and you do right in conforming your action to it.[6] I do not regard it as denying the right of Congress to require the oath as a prerequisite to entering on the duties of an office where the appointment has been made since the act: but only as denying the right to impose the oath as a condition of continuing to exercise an office or profession. I may be mistaken in this but such is my understanding.

Hoping that you will find your new residence at Oxford agreeable and thanking you warmly for all your expressions of kindness which I cordially reciprocate I remain

Very truly & respectfully

Your friend
S P Chase

Hon Robert A. Hill
District Judge U. States
Jacinto,
Mississippi

1. In the original, Chase evidently wrote over the 2 with a *1*.

2. Andrew Johnson had made Jacinto, Mississippi, resident Robert Andrews Hill (1811–1900) a U.S. district judge in 1866. *DAB*, 9:44–45.

3. Hill corresponded regularly with Chase on legal affairs in Mississippi. His most recent letter, written on February 20, told of his impending move to Oxford, Mississippi, and discussed a recent charge to a grand jury in Jackson in which he "commented in very strong terms on all the State laws in any way restricting the civil rights of the colored population, holding the civil rights law, constitutional, and directing prosecutions against those who have violated it. . . . The Circuit Judges so far as I have heard sustain the act of Congress," wrote Hill in regard to the Civil Rights Act of 1866; "I am inclined to the opinion that a majority of the Supreme Court, or High Court of Errors and Appeals as it is termed, will do the same thing[.]" The letter also asked whether the Supreme Court's decisions in *Cummings v. Missouri* and *Ex parte Garland* nullified the "ironclad" oath required by legislation of July 2, 1862. Hill to Chase, Feb. 20, 1867 (Chase Papers, L.C.).

4. Joseph Emerson Brown (1821–94) governed Georgia from 1858 to 1865. Overriding President Johnson's veto, Congress had passed the first of four Reconstruction acts on March 2. The law divided all former Confederate states except Tennessee into five military districts under commanders empowered to use the U.S. Army to protect life and property. Also outlined were the requirements needed for congressional recognition of new state governments, including ratification of the Fourteenth Amendment and creation of new state constitutions that authorized suffrage for African Americans. A second, supplementary bill, which Chase authored and Congress passed over President Johnson's veto on March 23, provided processes to achieve the goals of its predecessor. *DAB,* 3:141–43; Fairman, *Reconstruction and Reunion,* 318, 324–26; *Statutes at Large,* 14:428–29, 15:2–4.

5. As ratified, sec. 3 of the Fourteenth Amendment disqualified certain former Confederate officers from holding federal or state office unless permitted by act of Congress.

6. Chase refers to *Cummings v. Missouri* and *Ex parte Garland.*

TO ISAAC N. ARNOLD

Letterpress copy of autograph letter. Chase Papers, Library of Congress (*micro* 37:0114).

Washington, March 2, 1867

My dear Sir,[1]

I have nothing of Mr. Lincoln's which seems proper for publication at this time; unless it be what he said to the Cabinet at the final reading of the proclamation of Emancipation. I hardly know whether this should be published; but if on reflection I think it may be, it was promised to Mr. Owen for his book before I knew of your intended publication.[2]

The draft of a proclamation to which you refer as submitted to the President by me was very brief and not at all "a grand paper."[3] It is remarkable for nothing except for the concluding paragraph, which, with some modification, Mr. Lincoln adopted as his concluding paragraph.

The paragraph as I wrote it was as follows: And upon this act sincerely believed to be an act of justice warranted by the Constitution [& an act of duty demanded by the circumstances of the country,] I invoke the considerate judgment of mankind & the gracious favor of Almighty God."

Mr. Lincoln struck out the words in brackets & inserted instead "upon military necessity".

Hoping to see you before long I remain

Very sincerely your friend
S P Chase

Hon. I. N. Arnold.

1. Arnold, a former Illinois congressman and Treasury auditor, had authored *A History of Abraham Lincoln and the Overthrow of Slavery* (Chicago, 1866). Earlier, Chase had corresponded with Arnold about possible errors and omissions in the volume, which emerged later as *Sketch of the Life of Abraham Lincoln* (New York, 1869). *DAB,* 1:369; Chase to Arnold, Feb. 9, 1867 (Chase Papers, Hist. Soc. of Pa.); Chase to Arnold, Feb. 18, 1867 (Chase Papers, L.C.)

2. In his diary, Chase had recorded impressions at the final reading of the Emancipation Proclamation, which had occurred in cabinet on September 22, 1862. Robert Dale

Owen, antislavery leader and freedmen's advocate, was working on a biography of Lincoln that he never completed. *Chase Papers,* 1:393–95; Richard William Leopold, *Robert Dale Owen, A Biography,* (Cambridge, Mass., 1940), 396–97.

3. For the complete text of Chase's draft, see Chase to Lincoln, Dec. 31, 1862, in *Chase Papers,* 3:350–51.

TO ROBERT M. PATTON

Letterpress copy of letter, portion in Chase's hand and portion recopied in clerk's hand. Chase Papers, Library of Congress (*micro* 37:0135).

Washington, D.C. March 11th 1867.

Dear Governor,

I received sometime since your telegram in respect to the probable action of Congress in relieving you, being Governor, from disability in case of the ratification by the Alabama Legislature of the Constitutional Amendment.[1] I did not reply because I had no information which would warrant the expression of an opinion; and because at the time I received your telegram Congress was about acting on the Military Bill so called, which has since become a law notwithstanding the objections of the President.[2]

This law has in some respects changed the aspect of affairs. Had the Constitutional Amendment been adopted as you recommended, there is little room for doubt that the ratifying States would have been promptly allowed representation in Congress and the disabling clause would have been so modified as to relieve very many,—all, indeed, who should manifest a sincere and hearty good will to the Union and the National Government. The rejection of the amendment made the recent law inevitable; as all foresaw who understood the condition of things.[3]

And now it seems to me that the advice given by Ex Gov. Brown of Georgia is the best for all the unrepresented States. The sooner they avail themselves of the mode of obtaining representation given in the Act the better it will be for all concerned. To be sure the terms of restoration are somewhat more stringent than the mere adoption of the [amendment]; [but except] that full representation with full suffrage is substit[uted] instead of partial representation with partial suffrage all the terms not included in the amendment cease to be operative after restoration & restoration is [*illeg.*] on compliance with the act. So then, really, the only difference of a permanent nature between the ratification of the amendment as prescribed by the act and ratification without reference to it is in the settlement of the question of suffrage. And is it not best that this question be settled? Will it not interfere with the prosperity & progress of the states so long as it remains unsettled. When settled & with representation restored won't a great revival of material prosperity take place. Capital will flow in to stimulate labor; and all parts of the country will take hold once more in active efforts for the good of all.

Nor have I the least doubt that the kind feeling which now finds expression in the appropriation of a million of dollars (I wish the sum were five Millions & believe it would be the best possible investment for the sum) for the relief of destitution in the unrepresented States would find further expression in the relief of many & perhaps nearly or quite all from the disability imposed by the amendment.[4]

Let there be trust, confidence & loyalty & all will be well.

Very truly Yours
S P Chase

Gov. Patton of Alabama

1. Alabama did not ratify the Fourteenth Amendment until July 13, 1868. *Appletons' Annual Cyclopædia,* 8:17–18.

2. That is, the First Reconstruction Act of March 2, 1867.

3. On February 18, the Alabama legislature formally refused to ratify the Fourteenth Amendment or to enlarge the franchise through an amendment to the state constitution. In accordance with terms of the First Reconstruction Act, military supervision commenced on April 1 under John Pope of the Third Military District and Wager Swayne, Pope's subordinate in charge of Alabama. *Appletons' Annual Cyclopædia,* 7:16–17.

4. On March 9, the Senate had passed S.R. 16, a resolution that appropriated $1 million for implementation of the First Reconstruction Act. Subsequent congressional action reduced this amount to $500,000. *Congressional Globe,* 40th Cong., 1st sess., 1867, 39–48, 274, 281–82; *Statutes at Large,* 15:29.

TO HORACE GREELEY

Autograph letter. MA 6041 (3), The Pierpont Morgan Library, New York (*micro* 37:0001).

My dear Mr. Greeley,[1]

Reid showed me a letter from you the other day, and I presume has seen you ere this and assured you of my wish to do all I can to benefit a paper which has rendered such invaluable service to the cause of Freedom & Right.

I was glad to see your articles on resumption.[2] If I had time I would look up the facts of the last six years & lay them in order before you. I was often accused of expansion but I never went beyond the original limit of 450 millions, nor beyond 400 mill except in an emergency.[3] The expansion by *adding* the National Currency to the Greenback currency instead of substituting the former for the latter took place after I left the Dept

Would you like to see the list of persons recommended for Register in New York. The number is large & increasing. I wish you wd. advise Congress to repeal the clause putting the nomination on me.[4]

Your friend sincerely
S P Chase

Hon H Greeley

1. A letterpress copy of this document is in Chase's papers at the Library of Congress (*micro* 37:0139). The date assigned to that copy (in a different hand) and the document's location in the letterpress volume indicate that Chase wrote the letter on March 14, 1867.

2. On March 7 and 8, the *New York Tribune* had published editorials critical of assertions that the United States lacked sufficient reserves of domestic gold to resume specie payments. "We believe the Government might safely resume to-morrow," countered the editorial of March 8, "that the reserve of specie is sufficient—that even if it should prove otherwise and the Treasury be forced to suspend again—there would be no panic, and that the premium on Gold would henceforth be nominal only."

3. The Ways and Means Act of March 3, 1863, set the limit of $450 million for Treasury notes. *Report of the Secretary of the Treasury on the State of the Finances for the Year 1866*, 39th Cong., 2d sess., 1866–67, H. Ex. Doc. 4, 41; *Statutes at Large*, 12:710–11.

4. Legislation of March 2 turned U.S. district courts into courts of bankruptcy and authorized the chief justice to nominate at least one register in bankruptcy for each congressional district. Chase objected to the additional duties, however. With his sanction, the Senate debated a bill introduced on March 21 to repeal this provision and referred it to the Senate Judiciary Committee, where it died. *Statutes at Large*, 14:517–18; *Congressional Globe*, 40th Cong., 1st sess., 1867, 241, 277–281; *New York Times*, Apr. 9, 1867; *New York Tribune*, Mar. 27, 1867.

FROM JOHN D. VAN BUREN

Autograph letter. Chase Papers, Historical Society of Pennsylvania (*micro* 37:0322).

New York City
63. West 9th. St.
June 1 1867

Dear Sir

I am greatly obliged by your attention in sending me for persusal your letter of August '64 to Mr. Fessenden, which, in compliance with your request, I herewith return. I have read it with great interest.[1] It proves that the great details of the then difficult financial situation were well and clearly written down *in your head*. Without going into details of your plan of operations, upon some of which I might possibly not agree with you, one sentence proves that you knew in what direction & by what means to find relief, to wit: "the sale of 7.30s [and the 10/40s] should be *pushed* in every possible way. I have already suggested a General Agent and with or without such an Agent, the most *liberal* and active advertising and the most *liberal* encouragement to purchasers for resale and to the National Banks acting as Agents." The great point was to keep the government coffers well filled always with ready money; AT ANY NECESSARY COST to this end; it was of secondary importance what *rate of interest* you paid or *what compensation* was paid to necessary agencies. If this principle had been well fostered in your mind at the beginning you would have carried us through the war *paying specie all the time*. I do not mean to flatter you; I have too much respect for your intellect for that. In my judgment, you made some serious mistakes—I say it with entire respect. But you were suddenly rushed into the greatest financial task by far that has ever fallen upon a statesman. It was natural you should look for advice from what are called "practical financiers"—bank-presidents and bankers. You had not passed thirteen years in immediate business contact with them as I had and learned their hollowness of head and heart as a class. With some honorable exceptions (very rare) they know no more of finance than the horse in a cider-mill does of the principles of cider-making; and their habits of daily minute money shaving makes it impossible for them to give a public man advice in money matters, except with reference always to their own prospects of making money out of his transactions. I am satisfied that if *you* had been continued in the Treasury till now, that the government would now be paying specie,[2] its credit twenty per cent better in Europe and at home than it is now, the business of the country in a much better condition and consequently the revenues more flourishing and the future certain and solid. I seriously fear now a disgraceful and disastrous future; the present Secretary cannot even learn, as all wise men do, from his own proved blunders.[3] As a distinguished economist of this country (perhaps the most celebrated by the voluminous quantity of his writings)[4] said in a private letter I saw a few months ago, "the Secretary is costing the country more than the war". I never agreed with this economist (who is a great protectionist) before; but in this sentiment I concur emphatically.

With great respect

Your friend & Obedient Servant
JNO D VAN BUREN

Hon. S. P. Chase

1. See Chase to William Pitt Fessenden, August 27, 1864, in *Chase Papers,* 4:424–28.
2. Specie payments did not fully resume until January 1879. Unger, *Greenback Era,* 401.
3. Hugh McCulloch replaced Fessenden as Treasury secretary in March 1865. Chase had previously criticized McCulloch in correspondence to Horace Greeley, June 5, 1866 (above).
4. Possibly Henry Charles Carey, a prominent Philadelphia economist, founder of the American School of political economy and advocate of protectionist, soft-money policies. *DAB,* 3:487–89; Unger, *Greenback Era,* 50–58.

FROM WAGER SWAYNE

Autograph letter on letterhead stationery. Chase Papers, Library of Congress (*micro* 37:0335).

Head-Quarters District of Alabama,
Montgomery, Ala., June 3d. 1867.

Hon. Chief Justice Chase
Washington D.C.
My dear Sir

Many thanks for your kind and valued letters. That of May 20th. I deferred answering until I could make definite reply to the suggestions it contained. I had previously about made up my mind that the conduct of Judge Busteed in the discharge of his duties made it impossible for me to do otherwise than avoid him.[1] Upon receipt of your letter I considered the matter carefully, and felt a little among members of the bar, as a result of which I concluded that you might be right in ascribing his faults merely to strong impulses and that if he would turn over a new leaf the past might be ignored.

So I told him quite frankly, that in view of your letter, our relations should hereafter be determined by himself. That if he would henceforth pursue a course which all men should approve I would stand by him and support him warmly. This met with an emphatic and cordial response. He promised to clear out one or two of the rascals who yet hang about his court, and to do something which I asked him to befriend the Union Men of Mobile, to lend them his court room to meet in. He also intimated that he would not insist upon his preference for a man of bad character for Register of this District. Thereupon, to make up his quarrel with the colored people and to give him countenance, I took him with me to a colored barbecue and appeared with him in public. That afternoon I was obliged to go to Atlanta. When I returned I found that he had broken out again, and had been acting like a madman. The members of the bar, most of them being compromised by the rebellion, had been employing reporters of known loyalty to take down his proceedings, a bar meeting had been held, and a formidable project of impeachment was already underway. I think that they are right, and I can of course have no more to do with him. I have not told him so in express terms, but I mean to if it is necessary. Somebody ought to tell him to resign.

Meanwhile I do not see that you need do anything more than not to write to him, (though I am quite willing he should know the entire contents of this letter,) until you have information from more than one source. I would have written you before but it was noon of Saturday when I came back to my office from Atlanta, and this is Monday Morning.

Tomorrow we shall organize the Republican State Convention of Alabama, and the town is full of delegates, so I am full of interruptions.[2] I shall be glad to send you any further information you desire. I have written in some haste.

Very respectfully and truly yours
WAGER SWAYNE

1. Richard Busteed had held the post of U.S. district judge in Alabama since the fall of 1865. Since then, he had quarreled with U.S. military officers about the suspension of habeas corpus and established a record of erroneous judicial decisions. On May 14, Busteed incurred the distrust of African Americans for allegedly exercising inadequate vigilance at a meeting over which he presided that degenerated into a race riot. *Appletons'*, 1:476; *Appletons' Annual Cyclopædia*, 7:22–26; Fairman, *Reconstruction and Reunion*, 828–32; Thomas McAdory Owen, *History of Alabama and Dictionary of Alabama Biography*, 4 vols. (Chicago, 1921), 3:272.

2. Alabama's biracial Union Republican convention assembled in Montgomery on June 4. *Appletons' Annual Cyclopædia,* 7:25.

TO JANET CHASE

Autograph letter, unsigned. Chase Papers, Library of Congress (*micro* 37:0338).

Raleigh, N.C. June 7, 1867

My darling Nettie,

Here in Raleigh, a pretty, & very old town, named in honor of Sir Walter, I am holding with the District Judge a Circuit Court of the United States.[1] I came day before yesterday from Richmond, where I had spent the afternoon of the preceding day, having left Washington in the Morning. I had a very pleasant journey here. The sail down the Potomac to Aquia Creek was delightful. The air was cool & bracing and all the prospects charming. At Aquia the contrast with what it was during the war was striking. Then there was a city of frame offices for Commissioners & Quarter Masters, frame buildings, for stores; officers quarters & barracks; a city of war. Now only a small building in which the Cars from Fredericksburg arrive & depart. Then great wharves stretched out into the water and along the shore. Now the small landing receives the boat from Washington.

We found the cars very nice & comfortable. The General Agent, Mr. Walker, had come down with to ensure a pleasant trip for me & took charge of me on the boat & to Richmond Petersburgh, Weldon & Warrenton, only forty miles or thereabouts from Raleigh, where his duties obliged him to leave me. I had Frank with me also and, of course, did not lack attention.[2]

Our rid to Richmond took me for the first fifteen miles—from Aquia to Fredericksburgh—over pretty well known ground. I had traversed it when McDowell was encamped there & afterwards when Hooker was in command.[3] Traces of the Military occupation were visible in many places. We made no stop at Fredericksburgh, but passed quickly through the lines of rifle pits which made Lees defences at the time of the unfortunate battle directed by Burnside; lost, I fear, through the ill will or indifference of his subordinates.[4] Then we traversed the route of Grants March; and across the Chickahominy & its swamps into Richmond.[5] There old memories mingled with more recent impressions; I rode out & visited Gamble Hill, the old residence of the Cabells & thought of pleasant days in Richmond long, long ago, & the beautiful women & worthy & able men I met there.[6] Belle Isle was in full view, where our brave soldiers suffered so horribly. And I went to Libby Prison & all through it & remembered our brave officers who were confined there and among them your Uncle Israel, whom I hope you have met with Lud Jones or will meet in Europe.[7] And I was shown where our brave, patriotic, & ingenious fellows worked out a long underground passage & effected,—some of them, not all, alas!—their escape. And I went to the Davis House—the Presidents House of the Confederacy, which Mr Davis left one Sunday and Mr. Lincoln entered the next Tuesday.[8] And many other places & buildings I saw, of more or less interest, too tedious to mention.

We left Richmond before day light and were in historic Petersburgh at breakfast before five. Then we passed again through Lees lines of defence & then through Grants lines of attack. There they stretch away right & left for miles & miles, line after line. They look still formidable.

Southward still to Weldon & now on Shermans lines of march. But we soon left them on our way to Raleigh. At Warrenton Mr. Walker left me, going back to Weldon.

When we reached Raleigh I was surprised to see a great crowd gathered at the depot. I soon found it was a great gathering of the Freedmen to welcome me! How strange the Revolution which made this possible in Raleigh! The Union League & some other associations were out with music & banners. Some white gentlemen were there with two or three carriages in one of which I was taken to the Hotel preceded by the League & the band & followed & surrounded by the dark visaged mass.

The rest of my experience in Raleigh thus far you must learn from the slips which I enclose. They will be interesting to my children at least. They are from the Raleigh Standard.[9]

Almost all the leading men of the state are here—many of them leaders too in the rebellion. They have all called on me & treat me with great respect & consideration; and I talk to them about their errors & the rebellion just as I talk in Washington.

Goodbye for the present my darling.

1. Raleigh, or Ralegh (c. 1552–1618), English explorer, naval commander, and writer, claimed the entire Atlantic coast of North America for the British crown in 1584. Chase and George Washington Brooks, U.S. district judge for North Carolina, opened the session in the senate chamber of the state capitol on June 6. Chase's opening comments described this circuit court as the first of any to meet "within the insurgent states" after Andrew Johnson ended military rule in the South and Congress authorized reallocation of circuits among the Supreme Court justices. *DNB*, 16:629, 632–33; *Raleigh Tri-Weekly Standard,* June 8, 1867.

2. Probably Frank Bronaugh, a young man who performed secretarial duties for Chase.

3. Chase met Irvin McDowell at Fredericksburg on May 24–25, 1862. The visit with Joseph Hooker occurred at the general's camp near Falmouth, Virginia, on May 21–22, 1863. *Chase Papers,* 3:205, 4:37.

4. Union troops under Ambrose Burnside sustained heavy losses at the battle of Fredericksburg on December 13, 1862, and were forced to retreat before Robert E. Lee. Long, *Civil War Day by Day,* 295–96.

5. Ulysses S. Grant's famous march on Richmond began at the Rapidan River on May 3, 1864, and traveled south and east to culminate in the Battle of Cold Harbor, June 1–3, 1864. Ibid., 491–515.

6. Chase probably visited Gamble's Hill in Richmond sometime between 1827 and 1829, when he studied law under William Wirt. Wirt's wife, Elizabeth, was the daughter of

Robert Gamble, for whom the hill was named. Elizabeth's sister, Agnes, was married to former Virginia governor William H. Cabell. *Chase Papers,* 1:4–7; Alexander Brown, *The Cabells and Their Kin,* (Cambridge, Mass., 1895), 255–56.

7. Belle Isle Prison, the largest Confederate prison in Richmond, held noncommissioned officers and privates. Richmond's Libby Prison, which accomodated commissioned officers, was the site of "the largest and most sensational escape of the war," which occurred on February 9, 1864, when 109 men tunneled out, only 59 of whom reached Union lines. Nettie had evidently traveled to Europe sometime during the winter, and Kate had followed in April. Chase hoped that his daughters would meet Israel Ludlow—the brother of Chase's third wife, Sarah Bella, and a captain in the Fifth Regular U.S. Artillery—and Ludlow Ap-Jones, the son of Sarah Bella's sister, Charlotte Chambers Ludlow Jones. Chase to Janet Chase, July 11, 1867 (below), and Mar. 27, 1867 (Chase Papers, L.C.); Chase to William H. Seward, Apr. 20, 1867 (Misc. Letters of the Dept. of State, Record Group 59, Nat. Arch.); Long, *Civil War Day by Day,* 462; *OR,* ser. 2, v. 6:474–76, 544–46, 1087–89, 8:80–81.

8. Jefferson Davis evacuated the White House of the Confederacy on Clay Street on April 2, 1865. Lincoln toured defeated Richmond, including the Davis house, on April 4. William C. Davis, *Jefferson Davis: The Man and His Hour,* (New York, 1991), 605; Long, *Civil War Day by Day,* 663–66.

9. Chase stayed at the Yarborough House. The *Raleigh Tri-Weekly Standard* of June 8, apparently the source of Chase's "slips," described the reception which took place on June 5, and printed his brief speech. "Let freedom come with peace," Chase challenged listeners, "and with freedom let there come the assurance that the rights of all are the best, and, indeed, the only guaranty of the welfare of all."

FROM JOHN GLANCY JONES

Autograph letter. Chase Papers, Library of Congress (*micro* 37:0341).

Private

Reading
7 June 1867

My dear Sir[1]

Your Speech, & the events, which transpire at Raleigh with the Tribune, N.Y.s, comments, will strike the South, most favorably, especially, preceded as they are by the attacks of the NY Herald— The NY. Times & Weed's Evening Journal,[2]

These three Papers, are governed solely by Greeleys, "coup-de-etat" in capturing the conservative element—& inviting its co-operation with the friends of universal suffrage, & no slavery.— They are so hostile to Greeley, that antagonism to him is the ruling motive—right or wrong— Grant is, brought out by them, but to follow such a lead is not a lingering death but instantaneous suffocation—[3]

Seward, must adhere to the *President*—& Weed, can neither, lead, for the old Abolition element—the democracy or the radical Republican element— [4] The fact is he is without a party— I have a recent letter from Stephens of Georgia, who asks me to explain, these phenomena. Genl. Longstreets last letter is significant[5] / The South of his class, cannot follow any lead that refuses, to recognize impartial suffrage & this is the element of Southern Power as a unit, which will control the National democratic convention in making its nomination— In Penn we have the word white in our Constitution,[6] we are a States Rights, party,

& claim that suffrage is a state question; we will probably nominate Judge Sharswood for our candidate for the Supreme Court vice Chf. Woodward; our Platform will be *hostile to negro suffrage* & rallying to our state constitution—but, with a predetermination to, *submit* to universal suffrage, when it is forced upon us by *constitutional Authority;*[7] the South will be a unit on the question that suffrage shall be universal or that they must be relieved, & the rest will be taken care of by the logic of events; The most Powerful of all Agents: when, based upon sound, principles—

The public mind is bewildered North & South— The National Conventions are a year off[8]—Congress will not meet until Dec.—& nothing can lead public sentiment out of chaos—but the *Press:* Many of the leading Journals have private ends in view—personal ambition & private grievances; will designedly mislead the public mind & this brings me again to the important point; the *Press*—your friends must move; *Col Thomas, talks well, means well but he is too slow* to comprehend & act;[9] A Press, to *talk ideas, with proper foresight* & commitment to the logic of events, "nolens volens" should be established instantly in places where ideas, will be looked for— The Penna Dem Convention, will meet next Tuesday: a State Ticket & Platform will be in the field, Then the Press must move; on this point let us have *decision at once*— I write to A H Stephens to day to answer his letter; In July I meet Letcher, Lee & Hampton, (Wade) at White Sulphur Va—[10] so also Ex Prest Pierce at Newport, & Judge Parker, Schell & Hoffman at West Point— all looks well[11]

Truly yours
J. GLANCY JONES

Hon S P. Chase
chf Jus S.C.U.S.

1. Jones (1811–77), a Democrat, had served as deputy attorney general for Pennsylvania and U.S. minister to Austria under President James Buchanan. *Appletons',* 3:467.

2. The *New York Tribune* of June 6 and 7 covered Chase's arrival in Raleigh, North Carolina, which coincided with a goodwill visit from Andrew Johnson, and carried texts of speeches delivered on June 5 and 6. Chase discussed the first in correspondence of June 7 to his daughter Nettie (above). The other, which Chase delivered before the U.S. circuit court for North Carolina, explained the opening of that court on June 6 as the first in the South since the end of martial law. On both occasions, Chase spoke in conciliatory terms about "the restoration of every State to equal rights and benefits in the Union" and "restoring our whole country." "We wish no more howling or gnashing of teeth," wrote the *Tribune* in endorsement; "It will only bring discomfort, unrest, endless toil, and trouble. We want hearty peace, confidence, nationality." The "attacks" to which Jones alludes evidently refer to critical comments that greeted the release of Jefferson Davis from imprisonment at Fortress Monroe as a result of $100,000 that Horace Greeley and others posted as bail on May 13. *Albany Evening Journal,* May 30, 1867; *DAB,* 10:86; *New York Herald,* May 14, June 5, 1867; *New York Times,* May 16, 1867; Van Deusen, *Horace Greeley,* 352–54.

3. The *Albany Evening Journal* of May 30 praised "the wise moderation of General Grant," who had recently expressed willingness to accept the Republican nomination for president in 1868.

4. The influence of Weed, one of Seward's closest allies and editor of the *Albany Evening Journal* from 1830 to 1863, had diminished in Republican circles since Lincoln's

death. Weed moved to New York City in 1863, and in 1867 assumed editorship of the *Commercial Advertiser. DAB,* 19:598–99.

5. Former Confederate vice president Alexander H. Stephens had been paroled in October 1865. In January 1866, Georgia elected him to the U.S. Senate, but Congress refused to seat representatives from states not formally readmitted into the Union. Stephens spent the next two years writing *A Constitutional View of the Late War Between the States*..., 2 vols. (Philadelphia, 1868, 1870). James Longstreet, previously a general in the Confederate army, had written twice to the editor of the *New Orleans Times,* most recently on April 6, urging Southerners to accept their defeat and to work with the Republican party to put whites rather than blacks in positions of leadership. *DAB,* 17:574; Jeffry D. Wert, *General James Longstreet* (New York, 1993), 410–12.

6. Pennsylvania's constitution of 1790, art. 3, sec. 1, extended voting rights only to "every white freeman of the age of twenty-one years." *The Constitution of Pennsylvania*... (Philadelphia, 1874), 5.

7. George Sharswood (1810–83), a Philadelphia district court judge, became the Democratic nominee for the Pennsylvania Supreme Court and won election in October. George Washington Woodward was chief justice of the state supreme court, 1863–67, and a Democratic congressman from 1867 to 1871. Pennsylvania's Democratic convention, which met in Harrisburg on June 11, acted in accordance with Jones's expectations. "We proclaim as usurpation and outrage the establishment of negro suffrage in any of the States by the coercive exercise of Federal power," read the resulting platform, "and we shall resist to the last resort the threatened measures of the leaders of the Republican party to interfere by acts of Congress with the regulation of the elective franchise of the State of Pennsylvania." *Appletons' Annual Cyclopædia,* 7:619–20; *Bio. Dir. U.S. Cong.,* 2086; *DAB,* 17:28–29.

8. The Republican national convention convened in Chicago on May 20, 1868. The Democrats assembled in New York on July 4. *Appletons' Annual Cyclopædia,* 8:744, 747.

9. William B. Thomas had served as an officer in Pennsylvania's 192d Volunteer Infantry Regiment and as U.S. collector of customs at Philadelphia.

10. Democrat John Letcher (1813–84) served as U.S. congressman from Virginia, 1851–59, and governor of the state, 1859–64. Wade Hampton, previously a South Carolina state senator, ended the Civil War as a lieutenant general in the Confederate army. Robert E. Lee and his family had gone to the White Sulphur springs in Greenbrier County, West Virginia, for health reasons. *DAB,* 8:214–15, 11:192; Douglas Southall Freeman, *R. E. Lee, A Biography,* 4 vols. (New York, 1934–35), 4:323–24.

11. Former Democratic president Franklin Pierce had retired to New Hampshire after leaving office. In 1867, Amasa Junius Parker (1807–90), a candidate for governor of New York on several occasions, lectured at Albany Law School. Augustus Schell (1812–84), an attorney and businessman, had held the post of U.S. collector of customs at the port of New York during the presidency of James Buchanan. John Thompson Hoffman (1828–88), a leading Tammany Hall politician, won election to the mayoralty of New York in 1865 and 1867 and, in 1868, was chosen governor of the state. *Appletons',* 5:417; *DAB,* 14:214–15, 579, 9:113–14.

TO DAVID DAVIS

Letterpress copy of autograph letter. Chase Papers, Library of Congress (*micro* 37:0352).

Washington June 24, 1867

My dear Judge,

I have thought you might like to hear from me, and to know what my impressions are of North Carolina. And I have an inclination to write you, because—well, because I like you; and my esteem for you & confidence in you have been growing all the time we have been together—barring that time when you seemed to suspect me of some unfairness; which my conscience told me I was not & would not on any account be guilty of—in that matter of notice to lawyers in the Southern Cases.[1]

Well—let all this pass—I think we understand each other now and it shant be my fault, if we ever fall out again even for an hour

But now as to North Carolina. I believe I met as many of the leading men of all ways of thinking as any body ever met before in the same time; and I must say that I found them on the whole very well disposed. Not that I think they like the situation *per se;* or that they would allow suffrage to the negroes if they did not feel they must; or even that Slavery would not be reestablished, if the whites could have the question put to them & decided by them on a free canvass with no restraint on passions & prejudices. But they have made up their minds that Slavery cant be reestablished, and a majority of the good & thinking men—and there are about as many such in North Carolina as anywhere—are glad of it; and they have made up their minds that the negro must vote, and a larger majority are satisfied that this is right & on the whole for the best interests of all; and they have made up their minds finally that the present situation is the best attainable until they come back into full communion through the door Congress has left open.

Almost all were glad that we decided the Mississippi and Georgia cases, & decided them as we did.[2] I did not hear of one single man who found fault. All men's thoughts were on being once more represented in Congress by Senators and Representatives and partaking in the Government of the Country & in the benefits of Government. They don't like Military Government, especially when it takes a legislative turn: but very many, & I think most, would dislike to have military power wholly withdrawn. My hope & expectation is that they will hold a Convention; frame a Constitution to which no reasonable exception can be taken; have it approved by Congress & ratified by the People; and elect under it Governor, & Legislature, & Representatives to Congress, & that the Legislature will elect Senators and that the good old North State will be back in her place by Spring. I long to see her back and all the states back, and real harmony founded on real justice & general good will once more.

I send you a copy of an opinion which I delivered to a bar all ex-rebels save one.[3] I hope you will like it. Perhaps you have seen it already. Did you see the brief Address to the bar? Please write me & tell me all about yourself[4]

Cordially yours
S P Chase

1. In February 1866, Chase and Davis had disagreed over the fate of four cases: *Andrews v. Hensler, De Sobry v. Nicholson, Newell v. Norton and Ship,* and *Simpson v. Dall*—all appealed from southern courts but held in abeyance during the Civil War. In Chase's view, the inability of previous attorneys of record to take the loyalty oath prevented them from pleading before the Supreme Court and thus required new notices sent to "qualified" counselors "under the existing rules" before proceedings commenced. Davis and the majority disagreed, however, and permitted the cases to be heard "on proof of notice

by either party to the other or to the counsel of such other party appearing of record in this Court or to the attorney of record in the Court which the case is brought." Fairman, *Reconstruction and Reunion,* 135–37; 3 Wall. 257, 420, 460 (1866); 6 Wall. 254 (1867).

2. In April, Mississippi and Georgia had filed motions in the Supreme Court to prevent implementation of the First and Second Reconstruction Acts through two cases that were nearly identical: *Mississippi v. Johnson* and *Georgia v. Stanton.* The Court dismissed Mississippi's motion on April 15 and Georgia's on May 13, and issued formal explanations for both on February 10, 1868, that cited its inability to prevent the chief executive from enforcing congressional action suspected of being unconstitutional. Fairman, *Reconstruction and Reunion,* 378–94; 4 Wall. 475 (1867); 6 Wall. 50 (1867).

3. That is, all except one of the attorneys were former Confederates. The "opinion" to which Chase refers was *Shortridge et al. v. Macon,* issued on circuit in North Carolina earlier in the month. In it, Chase affirmed the continuity of federal sovereignty over the Confederacy during the Civil War and maintained the right of Northern creditors afterward to collect debts in the South incurred before secession. The decision includes an allusion to recent pardons offered through "legislative or executive authority" to all former Confederates, except some "of the greatest offenders." Fairman, *Reconstruction and Reunion,* 861–63; *New York Times,* June 22, 1867.

4. Davis responded on August 12. "The little matter of notice to attorneys, on which we differed, and which for the moment may have affected our feelings toward each other, has been long forgotten," he wrote. Chase had delivered his speech before the U.S. district court in Raleigh, North Carolina, on June 6. John Glancy Jones to Chase, June 7 (above); Davis to Chase, Aug. 12, 1867 (Chase Papers, L.C.).

TO HORACE GREELEY

Letterpress copy of autograph letter, portion recopied in clerk's hand. Chase Papers, Library of Congress (*micro* 37:0366).

Washington D.C. June 25 1867.

Dear Mr Greeley,

How could you!

Don't the Constitution say, what shall constitute "treason." Isn't it "Levying war"? Didn't the rebels "levy war"? Didn't they, then, "commit treason"?[1]

Read that part of Websters Speech in reply to Hayne in which he describes the consequences of nullification.[2] You will find no hint that nullifiers, pursuing their nullification to civil war, ceased to be traitors on becoming engaged in such a war.

But no matter what he said. There is the Constitution and it is so plain that it cant be made plainer.

Now what is the business of a Court? To fritter away plain words by arbitrary interpretation? or, to declare their obvious meaning, and leave to the political departments of the government the duty of applying the proper mitigations?[3]

I saw no ground on which the rebel acts of sequestration could be set aside,[4] if the *de facto* character of the rebel government were admitted; for it is the universal rule that the acts of a defacto government, done during its existence as such, are valid. And there is no middle ground between a defacto government, and a treasonable combination of rebels in arms, every exercise of whose pretended authority against the government is treason.

It was necessary therefore to meet & dispose of the question of treason; for treason or no treason [was the very] [*illeg.*] of the matter.

What the political powers should do is plain enough. And Congress has been liberal, & the President has been more than liberal. Congress will, I think, be more liberal still when the rebel states come back [to] their duties with constitutions guarantying all rights, & with [*illeg.*] that will guaranty [*illeg.*]. I should not be at all surprised if when the states have thus returned to their duties, Congress should adopt your doctrine of universal amnesty.[5]

Meantime dont let us by construction cut out the law: but take it as it is, & conform it at last to the highest of all laws "whose voice is the harmony of the world."[6]

Yours cordially
S P Chase

Hon H. Greeley

Since writing this letter I have seen a headnote in the Commercial in which some part of my opinion is referred to as "an [adroit] thrust at Greeley."[7] *You* know better. You know—at least I hope you know—how earnest & sincere is my attachment to you. In political matters I generally accept your views: but in questions of law I am and must be a mere judge; or be dishonest.

1. Greeley had faulted the reasoning behind Chase's decision in *Shortridge* in a *New York Tribune* editorial printed on June 24. According to Greeley, the opinion inappropriately denounced all armed opposition to the federal government and failed to recognize the legitimacy of widespread unrest provoked by genuine grievances—evident, for example, in events that led up to the American Revolution. The U.S. Constitution defines treason in art. 3, sec. 3.

2. In their famous debates of 1830, U.S. senators Daniel Webster and Robert Young Hayne discussed the results of unilateral attempts by states to nullify national laws. "To resist by force the execution of a law, generally, is treason," asserted Webster on January 27. Charles M. Wiltse, et al., eds., *The Papers of Daniel Webster,* 14 vols. (Hanover, N.H., 1974–86), 1:344.

3. In the original, the first page of the letter ends with the words *political departments* in this sentence. The letterpress copy failed to produce a legible image of Chase's manuscript, and a clerk recopied the page's text.

4. In *Shortridge,* the defendant claimed that sequestration of his note, authorized by action of the Confederate congress on August 30, 1861, and February 15, 1862, absolved him of any legal obligation to pay his debt. *The Statutes at Large of the Provisional Government of the Confederate States of America . . .* (Richmond, 1864), 201–7, 260–66; *New York Times,* June 22, 1867.

5. Greeley had advocated universal suffrage for the South since November 1866. According to him, Congress would repeal the third, disabling section of the Fourteenth Amendment if states of the former Confederacy granted broad sufferage on their own. *New York Tribune,* Nov. 10, 1866.

6. A paraphrase from Richard Hooker, *Of the Lawes of Ecclesiasticall Politie* (London, 1593), book 1, chap. 16, sec. 8.

7. Chase's alleged "thrust" at Greeley was a passage from *Shortridge:* "Nor can we agree with some persons distinguished by ability and virtues, who insist that when rebellion

attains the proportions and assumes the character of civil war, it is purged of its treasonable character, and can only be punished by the defeat of its armies and disappointment of its hopes, and the calamities incident to unsuccessful war." Elsewhere, Chase claimed that the passage referred to Gerrit Smith, but suggested as well that "perhaps it had a little reference" to Greeley. *Cincinnati Commercial,* June 22, 1867; Chase to Smith, June 25, 1867 (below).

TO GERRIT SMITH

Autograph letter. Chase Papers, Library of Congress (*micro* 37:0371).

Washington, June 25, 1867.

My dear friend,

I wish I were with you & dear Mrs Smith on the beautiful banks of Lake Geneva; instead of under these sweltering heats of Washington.[1]

Many thanks for your commendation of my opinion, at least of its style & general correctness. Laudari a laudato in old Latin;[2] but the gratification of it is ever fresh.

You are entirely right in supposing my reference to men "distinguished by abilities & virtues" meant you. Perhaps it had a little reference also to our friend, whom you so justly style in your late paper, the great American Editor, though I am not sure that he ever put forth the doctrine as expressly as you have.[3]

Nor indeed have I understood you as maintaining that those who engaged in rebellion did not commit treason as defined by the Constitution; but rather that there is some general principle of universal law, which overrides the language of the Constitution in the case of a great civil war.[4]

I do not think that there is such a principle and I do recognize my obligation as a Judge to declare the law as I find it written in the Constitution. "Courts" as I remarked "have no policy,"[5] & I might have added "Courts have no pardoning power & no right to exercise political discretion." As Governor of Ohio, I pardoned many a man whom had I been judge I should have felt bound to sentence to the Penitentiary. And the President & Congress in the exercise of political power and discretion can whenever they think fit proclaim universal amnesty. And I agree with Macaulay in thinking the grandest trait in the character of William was that which made him so earnest in his endeavors to procure parliamentary amnesty for the Jacobites after the Revolution of 1688, & finally led him, when the time came, to prepare & carry the Act of Grace[6]

Besides you think the conclusion correct: and as a matter of law I do not [be how] it can be sustained except upon the premises. There is no middle ground between Treason & *de facto* Government: and *de facto* Government involves the validity of its acts during its existence. If the rebels levying war against the Government were not traitors, secession was a valid act; and our war was one of conquest.

I had no time to elaborate these points in an opinion in an opinion; nor have I now: but I am sure of them.[7]

Nor can any harm come of my doctrine. It leaves the power & duty of amnesty in full vigor.

I see in the Tribune of yesterday a criticism, friendly enough, upon my position. It is well written too but it won't stand the test of sound principles of interpretation.[8]

I must tell you that I received your letter on bailing Jefferson Davis at Raleigh either just before or just after I pronounced the opinion. I read it with great pleasure: and my heart went along with you through the whole of it. I don't know that I agreed with you in every proposition but there were few in which I did not.

I gave one of the two copies to an ex-confederate officer to read; who after reading it wanted it that he might lend it to others.[9] The other I gave to my associate Judge Brooks; a true hearted & earnest man; who before I left him had given it quite a circulation. I doubt if any two copies you printed will have had more readers before worn out.

The colored people are doing well at Raleigh. One in particular James H Harris, educated at Oberlin & since quite a traveller having been to Liberia & Sierra Leone, is doing a great deal. He is a remarkable orator & a man of sense.[10] By the way you could not put $50 or $100 to a better use than sending it to him to aid in paying his expences. I have sent him $50 since I came back.[11]

The schools are prosperous & the churches full. Just thinking of the Chief Justice at an African Church in Raleigh seated between a Union officer & an ex member of Stonewall Jacksons staff![12]

Best regards to Mrs Smith & your son[13] & believe me

Most sincerely yours
S P Chase

Hon Gerrit Smith

1. Smith and his wife, Ann Carroll Fitzhugh Smith, lived in Peterboro, New York, not far from Geneva, on Seneca Lake. *DAB,* 17:270.

2. *Laudari a viro laudato:* "to be praised by a man who is himself praised." Jones, *Dictionary of Foreign Phrases,* 64.

3. Chase's opinion in *Shortridge et al. v. Macon* mentions such "distinguished" people. Chase denied that the phrase referred to Greeley in a letter written to him on the same day (above). However, Smith's "paper," *On the Bailing of Jefferson Davis* (Peterboro, N.Y., 1867), an explanation for signing the former Confederate president's bail bond, identified Greeley as "the Great American Editor." Johnson, *Cases Decided by Chief Justice Chase,* 51.

4. "The law of war knows no treason," asserted Smith's essay; "I add that treason ceases just when and where the acknowledgment of belligerent rights begins. Reason teaches this. Humanity teaches this. The political liberalists of Europe beseech us to believe this." Smith, *Bailing of Jefferson Davis.*

5. A quotation from *Shortridge et al. v. Macon. New York Times,* June 22, 1867.

6. William III (1650–1702) ruled England from 1689 to 1702. The Act of Grace, issued in May 1690, pardoned all but "a few great criminals" among the Jacobites, partisans of

James II and the Stuarts, who lost power during the Glorious Revolution of 1688. To British historian Baron Thomas Babington Macaulay (1800–1859), who praised the king for "immutable resolution that the glory of the great deliverance which he had wrought should not be sullied by cruelty," the act was one of William's "noblest and purest titles to renown." *DNB,* 12:410, 21:306, 312, 321; Macaulay, *The History of England from the Accession of James II,* 6 vols., ed. Charles Harding Firth (London, 1914), 4:1828–30.

7. In *Ex parte Milligan,* Chase issued a minority opinion on the scope of war powers within the Court's overall decision for the plaintiff.

8. Chase discussed the criticism, which appeared in the newspaper's edition of June 24, in his letter to Greeley of June 25 (above).

9. Chase refers to David Miller Carter (1830–79), a former colonel on the staff of Confederate general Thomas Jonathan (Stonewall) Jackson and an attorney who was admitted to practice in the court that Chase and George W. Brooks reopened on June 6. *OR,* ser. 4, v. 2:248; *Raleigh Tri-Weekly Standard,* June 8, 1867; *Dictionary of North Carolina Biography,* 5 vols. to date (Chapel Hill, 1979–), 1:333.

10. Formerly a teacher with the Freedmen's Aid Society, Harris (1832–91) was one of North Carolina's most prominent African-American politicians. Harris helped form North Carolina's Republican party, later served as a state legislator for several terms, and for years held posts as an alderman and tax collector for Raleigh. *Dictionary of North Carolina Biography,* 3:53.

11. Sometime before August, Smith sent Harris—through Chase—a check of unknown amount. Chase to Harris, Aug. 2, 1867 (Chase Papers, L.C.).

12. On June 9, Chase attended services at the African Methodist Church, and on June 16 at the Second Baptist Church, another African-American church. With him on June 9 were former Confederate officer David M. Carter; Massachusetts native Nelson Appleton Miles (1839–1925), a colonel in the regular U.S. Army and veteran of service with the Army of the Potomac; and two officers from Miles's Fortieth Infantry Regiment: Maj. Dewey and Lt. Granger. *Raleigh Tri-Weekly Standard,* June 11, 18, 1867; *DAB,* 12:614–15; Thomas H. S. Hamersly, *Complete Regular Army Register of the United States, 1779–1879* (Washington, D.C., 1881), 206, 404, 471.

13. Gerrit and Ann Smith's son was Green Smith (1842–86). *Guide to the Microfilm Edition of the Peter Smith Papers, 1763–1850, and Gerrit Smith Papers, 1775–1924* (Glen Rock, N.J., 1974), 86.

TO JOHN RUSSELL YOUNG

Letterpress copy of autograph letter. Chase Papers, Library of Congress (*micro* 37:0376).

Washington, June 26, 1867.

My dear Mr. Young,

Your kind note is just received.

Your reference to the absence of Mr. Greeley leads me to suppose that you are probably the author of the article criticizing my recent opinion in Georgia.[1] It was too kind in its tone to make me feel very bad: but I am so sure that its logic is wrong & that the conclusion of the opinion in which the Tribune concurs, cannot be defended except upon the premises which it does not admit, that I could not help writing a few lines to Mr. Greeley, which please take as addressed to yourself.[2] Of course I want nothing of this by talk in the paper.

I seldom read the Herald. I should if I were in a position which required me to acquaint myself with all that could be said against as well as for my public action. But I am in no such position and its causeless

& persistent personal hostility is better unread than read. I know that it can do me no real harm.

One of its chief correspondents, when I was Secretary, menaced me with its displeasure if I did not give him some special advantages in respect to departmental intelligence. My only reply was, "The Herald did not make me & I do not believe that it can unmake me".

As to the National Banks, I do not regard these as *perfect institutions,* nor their managers as anything extraordinary in the way of Saintship. But I believe them well adapted to the commercial wants of the country,—much better than so many local banks,—and that they are managed with as much honesty & intelligence as any equal number of other corporations whether manufactury or commercial. What I expected of them, they do & do it satisfactorily. They furnish a national currency; which could not have been secured in any way, so certainly or so permanently or with so little disturbance of existing interests, as by their establishment and the conversion of the local banks into national. I dare say the system can be improved; but it is not every tinker who can improve it

I notice what you say about Mr. Johnson. On this subject I should like to compare views with you in a friendly talk.

I must say frankly that I see no ground for thinking that the President has not intended to carry out the Reconstruction acts in good faith: or that the Attorney General has not honestly sought to ascertain & state their true meaning.[3] I do not concur in the Attorney General's opinions on some of their most important particulars; because I start with the premises that Congress has full power to govern the rebel States until they accept terms of restoration which will ensure future loyalty, the fulfilment of national obligations; the repudiation of all rebellion & the obligations of rebellion; & the security of all rights for all men; and that the acts of Congress [of Congress] must be construed, with reference to these ends, liberally: whereas the Atto General starts with the premises that the acts are punitive & must be construed strictly. But I have known him long; am sure of his great legal abilities; & equally sure that he is an upright & loyal man.

I don't want to see Congress *set aside* the provisional State Governments.[4] It would be a very mischievous measure, in its effects on private rights; and lead to much litigation, & very seriously retard, I fear, the restoration of order & prosperity to the South.

Congress may very well provide that the Military commanders may remove state officials, who put themselves in the way of reconstruction & that their successors be elected by *universal suffrage;* but I would not have military commanders authorized to appoint these successors, unless temporarily, nor would I have them diverted from their proper work under the acts to the work of legislation on matters of property & business.

My observation in North Carolina fully satisfied me that Congress acted wisely in recognizing the existing governments as provisional governments & that all will go well if it adheres to the general policy of the acts.

I have written too much,—for I have been obliged to write hastily. My old motto was "Freedom & union, without compromise". It is so still

By the way I must mentioned that one of the best republicans I met in N.C.—an active & influential member of the State Committee—was a member of Stonewall Jackson's staff & is disfranchised.[5]

Very cordially your friend
S P CHASE

John R. Young, Esq.

1. Chase evidently meant to write *Shortridge,* rather than *Georgia.* The *Tribune* supported the Court's decision to dismiss *Georgia v. Stanton,* but found fault with Chase's opinion in *Shortridge et al. v. Macon. New York Tribune,* May 17, June 24, 1867.

2. See Chase to Greeley, June 25, 1867 (above).

3. Congress passed the First and Second Reconstruction Acts over President Johnson's veto. Attorney General Henry Stanbery published his opinion on May 24. *New York Times,* May 27, 1867; *Statutes at Large,* 14:429, 15:4.

4. The First Reconstruction Act declared civil governments in the ten unrepresented southern states provisional only and gave Congress authority to "at any time abolish, modify, control, or supersede" them. Ibid., 14:429.

5. David M. Carter helped organize the state's Republican party. *Dictionary of North Carolina Biography,* 1:333.

FROM WAGER SWAYNE

Autograph letter on letterhead stationery. Chase Papers, Historical Society of Pennsylvania (*micro* 37:0383).

Head-Quarters District of Alabama,
Montgomery, Ala., June 28. 1867.

My dear Sir

I wrote you in some haste just at the close of our Convention, meaning to write you about matters of more general interest so soon as the multitude of strangers had left town, but was deterred by your absence at Raleigh.[1]

We are now engaged in registering the voters of this State, but as yet we have not sufficient data for general conclusions of much value. It is however apparent that the colored vote if undivided will control this State in the election of all Legislative bodies, such as the convention, owing to its concentration in the more populous counties. The white minority in these, which will be actually unrepresented, is yet sufficient to take from the aggregate white vote its natural preponderance in the State.[2]

Again there seems to be a growing feeling against a convention. This has its rise in part from the hope of a reaction North in favor of the

Democratic party, the success of which is watched with the same interest as the success of the rebel arms while hostilities prevailed.[3] The greater part of this people however would ignore this alternative and seek the shortest practicable settlement; but for a growing sense of the necessity for military supervision. Instances of violence to individuals, the results of which have shown how easily a collision of the races could be precipitated here, and how serviceable in such cases is the proximity of troops, have made an impression which is continually appealed to. A few there are who feel that these conditions, with the added presence of an element of ruffianism which would still delight in persecuting loyal men, and take the risk of punishment by civil law; that these together demonstrate the unfitness of this people to be left to themselves on any terms at present. To what extent these influences will prevail we cannot yet anticipate with certainty but I have still a hopeful expectation that the State will vote for reconstruction. Not that the difficulty last mentioned has not great weight with me, but I think that committed as this country is to that plan of self government of which it is the illustrious exponent, it is worth considerable risk to bring our entire territory again under its homogeneous operations.

The prospective meeting of Congress has of course peculiar interest to us.[4] The contest as to who may vote and who may not does not seem to me fraught with important results. But there is one aspect which is extensively discussed and has had serious consideration. Before the war, up to its very opening, a man must generally have been a Union Man, in Alabama, to be elected to office. During the war, men of that feeling sought small offices also to keep out of the Army, often to make use of their position to help and protect Union men. These men are generally disfranchised and there is a feeling that a rule might be adopted which without releiving any considerable number of the opponents of reconstruction would convert very many of our friends from passive well-wishers into serviceable candidates and efficient helpers. The precise terms of such a rule are undetermined, but the better opinion is that persons who can take an oath 1. to having voted against secession, 2, to having two years before the close of the war desired the supremacy of the United States, as in the North Carolina bill,[5] 3, to being in favor of reconstruction now, might well be releived from all except the operation of the test oath. With this it is thought to be unwise to interfere at present. For my own part I should be very glad if some such rule might be adopted at the July session, and I am quite sure that any effort made in that direction would secure grateful appreciation here and the approbation of good men every where. We could make excellent use of it to counteract the injury which threats of confiscation do us in exciting enmity and recklessness.

I would not intrude on you so long a letter except after consultation and from a strong sense of the weight of your opinion.

Our convention was an eminent success, and so far there is no appearance of opposing organization. What we have most to fear is "No Convention".[6]

Very respectfully and truly yours
WAGER SWAYNE

Hon. Cheif Justice Chase
Washington D.C.

1. Alabama's state Republican convention, which met on June 4 and 5 while Chase presided over the U.S. circuit court in North Carolina, endorsed congressional action on Reconstruction. *Appletons' Annual Cyclopædia,* 7:25–26.

2. The Second Reconstruction Act provided federal officials like Swayne with the authority and mechanisms to register voters and organize state constitutional conventions in states of the former Confederacy. *Statutes at Large,* 15:2–4.

3. As expected, Democrats made significant gains throughout the North in elections held during the fall of 1867. In the South, massive registration of new African-American voters bolstered the fortunes of the Republican party. Foner, *Reconstruction,* 314–15.

4. Swayne anticipated the first session of the Fortieth Congress, which convened on July 3. *Bio. Dir. U.S. Cong.,* 183.

5. Legislation that Congressman Thaddeus Stevens introduced on December 13, 1866, to reorganize North Carolina (H.R. 882) included such a provision, but Congress never voted on the bill. *House Journal,* 39th Cong., 2d sess., 68.

6. Alabamans who opposed congressional Reconstruction convened a "state conservative convention" in Montgomery on September 4. On October 1–3, voters throughout the state elected delegates for a constitutional convention, which gathered in Montgomery on November 5. Voters ratified the resulting document, which modified Alabama's existing constitution to conform with the First Reconstruction Act, on February 4, 1868. *Appletons' Annual Cyclopædia,* 7:28–35, 8:16.

TO THEODORE TILTON

Letterpress copy of autograph letter. Chase Papers, Library of Congress (*micro* 37:0408).

Washington, July 9, 1867

Dear Mr. Tilton,

I see no objection to your using the letters which Mr. Bailey put into your hands, as you say, "in part & discreetly."[1]

If any names are used, they should, of course, not appear in print.

I hope you will say nothing, in connexion with them, unkind of President Johnson. The letters were written with anxious desires that he might take a line of action, which would make him the great leader of Freedom & Progress. I greatly regret that he did not take it for his own sake & the country's: but he did not. His error was its own punishment. I make no reproaches, & wish none made in connexion with any correspondence of mine with him, at a time when I thought we were nearly agreed

He assures me now that he is in favor of universal suffrage; and, *I think,* regrets the past. He has so far as I can see executed in good faith the reconstruction acts ever since the veto. He certainly was not to blame for calling for the opinion of the Atto General on points as to which the Generals were in doubt & asked for instructions: nor can he be blamed for agreeing with the attorney general on points of construction.[2] I am glad that Congress has come together & will make plain what was, in the judgment of able & good men obscure: and I shall be sorry if they attempt supersede the President in the Command of the Army, or to make the District Generals superior to all civil authority as well as all military. For I do not think this necessary to the great end for which the country longs restoration on the basis of justice & equal rights, firmly secured by Constitution & laws. So far Congress has acted with great [wisdom]. If it acts with less wisdom, or, what I think, [no] wisdom now, I shall console myself by the reflections that its [ends] are just & noble & that in a few months, with wisdom & prudence & firmness in action, we shall have doubled the cape & entered the *Pacific* Sea.

I enclose you as "germane to the matter"[3] a couple of letters which I addressed to Mr. Lincoln the last week of his life. The second one was read probably on the morning of the day of assassination / He read it to Mr. Speed that morning.[4]

Sincerely your friend
S: P: CHASE

Theodore Tilton Esq

I go to Albany tomorrow, but cannot stop in New York. I may, as I return; in which case I hope to see you

1. Tilton, editor of the *Independent,* had requested permission to publish quotations from letters written to President Johnson during Chase's trip to the South in the spring of 1865. "This plan is so exactly like the one finally adopted by Congress that I would like to make the fact apparent to the public," wrote Tilton of suggestions in regard to Reconstruction. Tilton had obtained the documents from John F. Bailey, a Treasury clerk and agent during the Civil War. *Chase Papers,* 1:535–78; Chase to Andrew Johnson, May 17, 1865 (above); Simpson, *Advice After Appomattox,* 4–38; Tilton to Chase, July 2, 1867 (Chase Papers, Hist. Soc. of Pa.).

2. President Johnson vetoed the First and Second Reconstruction Acts on March 2 and 23, 1867, respectively. Henry Stanbery's highly critical opinion of both bills, which Chase discussed on June 26 in correspondence with John Russell Young (above), dated from May 24. On June 12, Stanbery published another opinion on the same legislation that analyzed the powers and duties of military commanders. According to Stanbery, the Second Reconstruction Act should be construed strictly. "It is a grant of power to military authority, over civil rights and citizens, in time of peace," he wrote; "It is a new jurisdiction, never granted before, by which in certain particulars and for certain purposes, the established principle, that the military shall be subordinate to the civil authority, is reversed." *Appletons' Annual Cyclopædia,* 7:659–65; *New York Times,* Mar. 4, 24, May 27, 1867; *Statutes at Large,* 14:428–30, 15:2–5.

3. Shakespeare, *As You Like It,* act 5, scene 2, lines 158–59.

4. See Chase to Lincoln, April 11, 12, 1865 (above).

TO JANET CHASE

Autograph letter. Chase Papers, Library of Congress (*micro* 37:0417).

Albany, July 11, 1867

My dear, darling Nettie,

I have just attended the wedding of Miss Clara Harris with Col. Rathbone at her fathers in this city.[1] A few days ago I received a very kind

In this detail from a photograph of Abraham Lincoln's second inaugural on the steps of the Capitol in March 1865, Chase is the second figure seated to the right of the president, who stands at the small podium delivering his speech. Chase administered the oath of office to Lincoln that day, as he did to Andrew Johnson the next month, after Lincoln's assassination, and to Ulysses S. Grant in 1869 and 1873. *Courtesy of the National Archives.*

FRANK LESLIE'S ILLUSTRATED NEWSPAPER

Entered according to the Act of Congress in the year 1867, by FRANK LESLIE, in the Clerk's Office of the District Court for the Southern District of New York.

No. 652—VOL. XXVI.] NEW YORK, MARCH 28, 1868. [PRICE 10 CENTS. $4 00 YEARLY. 13 WEEKS $1 00.

JUDGE NELSON ADMINISTERING THE OATH TO CHIEF JUSTICE CHASE, AS PRESIDING OFFICER OF THE COURT OF IMPEACHMENT, IN THE SENATE CHAMBER, WASHINGTON, D. C., ON THE 5TH MARCH. FROM A SKETCH BY JAS E. TAYLOR.—SEE PAGE 19.

In March 1868, at the start of the Senate's impeachment trial of Andrew Johnson, Associate Justice Samuel Nelson gave Chase (on the right, with a short-lived ruff of chin whiskers) the oath as presiding officer. *Courtesy of the Library of Congress.*

This Thomas Nast cartoon, "A Wild-Goose Chase," which appeared in *Harper's Weekly* on July 4, 1868, depicts Chase using support for universal suffrage as an attempt to win the Democratic presidential nomination. *Courtesy of the Library of Congress.*

Chase's daughter Janet ("Nettie," born 1847) as she appeared at age sixteen. In 1871 she married William Sprague Hoyt, cousin of her half-sister Kate's husband, William Sprague. *Courtesy of Edwin C. Hoyt.*

Nettie's artistic depiction of Edgewood, the house purchased by Chase in 1869. He did not move there until 1871, after the property was extensively renovated. Located in the District of Columbia but outside the Washington city limits of the time, it was two and a quarter miles north of the Capitol. *Courtesy of Edwin C. Hoyt.*

Another drawing by Nettie shows Chase's study and law books at Edgewood. *Courtesy of Edwin C. Hoyt.*

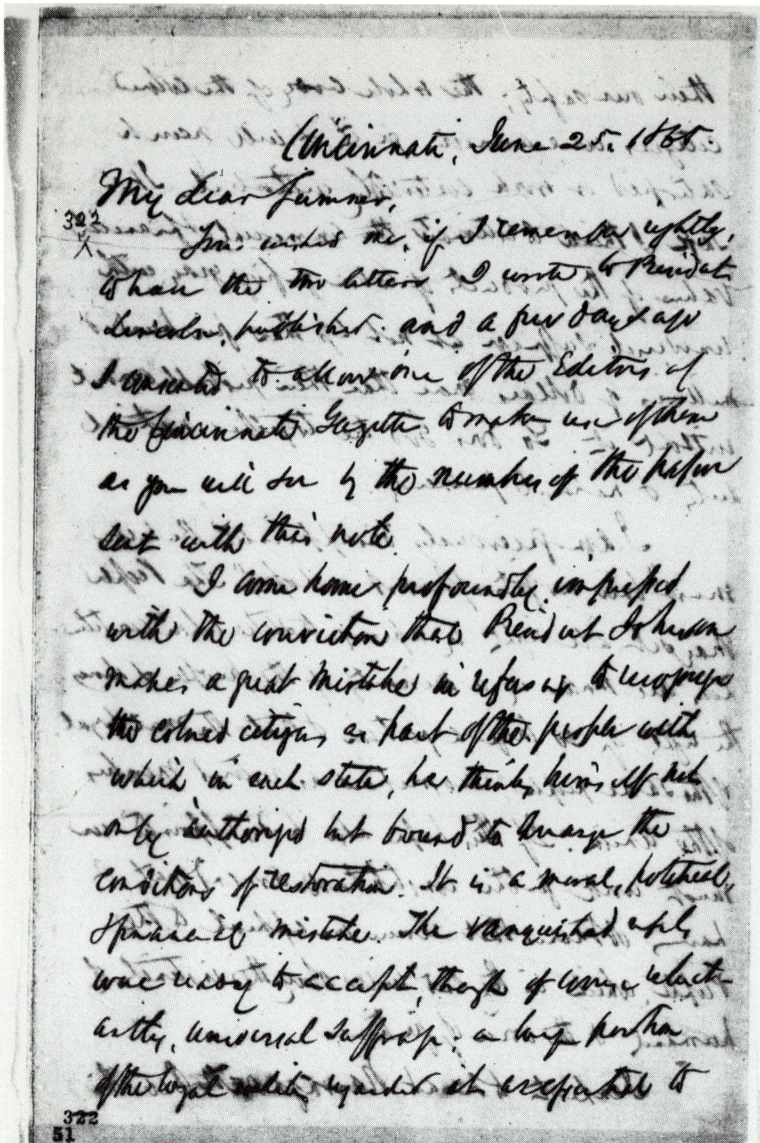

Cincinnati, June 25. 1865.

My dear Sumner,

You wished me, if I remember rightly, to have the two letters I wrote to President Lincoln published; and a few days ago I consented to allow one of the Editors of the Cincinnati Gazette to make use of them as you will see by the number of the paper sent with this note.

I came home profoundly impressed with the conviction that President Johnson makes a great mistake in refusing to recognize the colored citizens as part of the people with which in each State, he thinks himself not only authorized but bound to arrange the conditions of restoration. It is a moral, political & financial mistake. The vanquished whites were ready to accept, though of course reluctantly, universal suffrage: a large portion of the loyal whites regarded it as expedient to

322

51

Chase's handwriting, while difficult to read, showed strength in this June 25, 1865, letter to Charles Sumner. *Courtesy of the Library of Congress.*

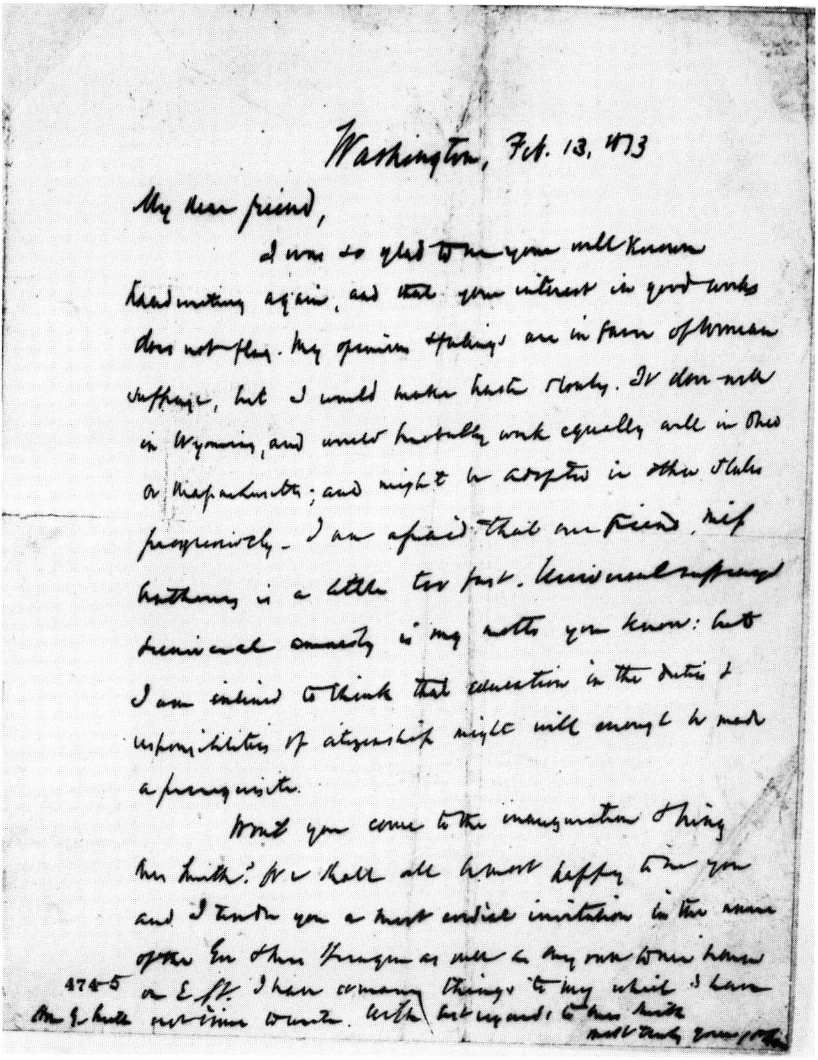
Washington, Feb. 13, 1873

My dear friend,

I was so glad to see your well known handwriting again, and that your interest in good works does not flag. My opinions & feelings are in favor of woman suffrage, but I would make haste slowly. It does well in Wyoming, and would probably work equally well in Ohio or Massachusetts; and might be adopted in other States progressively. I am afraid that our friend, Miss Anthony is a little too fast. Universal suffrage & universal amnesty is my motto you know: but I am inclined to think that education in the duties & responsibilities of citizenship might well enough be made a prerequisite.

Won't you come to the inauguration & bring Mrs Smith? We shall all be most happy to see you and I tender you a most cordial invitation in the name of the [illegible] as well as my own to our house

4745 on E St. I have so many things to say which I have [illegible] not time to write. With best regards to Mrs Smith

most truly yours [illegible]

By 1873, as evidenced in this letter to Gerrit Smith, Chase had recovered the ability to write that he had all but lost after a stroke in 1870, but the strength was no longer there. He died less than three months after this February letter was written. *Courtesy of the Library of Congress.*

Late in his life, Chase's face showed the effects of age and ill health. *Courtesy of the National Archives.*

note from her inviting me to be present on the occasion, & the friendship the Judge has constantly shown for me induced me to come. The day has been lovely. The air fresh & almost cool; the breezes gentle but full of life; the sky just clouded enough to break by shadows the continuity of sunshine. And the company was very agreeable. I met several whom I had before met at Washington and a good many whom I had never seen. I made myself as agreeable as I know how, and every body made himself or herself agreeable to me. So the hour went by pleasantly enough. There were a good many enquiries about my daughters, & when I expected them &c. &c. Col. Rathbone & his bride will sail on Saturday in the Ville de Paris and I hope you will meet them and be very kind & cordial to them.[2]

I left Washington Tuesday Evening, & had my usual experience on a Sleeping car. From ten to half past four I slept about two thirds of the time in variable quantities. My compagnon de voyage was a young Mr. Cummins, of Oregon, to whom I had an opportunity of showing a kindness some half dozen years ago, and who is now bent on securing for me the support of all the Pacific States in the next Presidential nomination.[3] And it does look now that, if there were no military names before the public, the choice of the people might fall upon me. But very many seem to think that the nomination of a military candidate is a predestinated event, which must take place anyhow, and against which it is useless to make opposition. There are it is true many who think otherwise and who are zealous for me. But there are other non-military men who have also zealous friends; and I can easily see that I am not much more likely to be preferred than I was in 1860 or 1864. So I make myself contented,—or try to. It is true that it does seem to me that that I could accomplish, if I had the power, much that would be beneficial to the country and I am not insensible to the distinctions of the Chief Magistricy. But if the people dont want my services, I have no right to complain & if the distinctions are not to be mine, I shall, by no means repine. No man has any *claim* to such distinctions in a country like ours.

Congress is engaged in amending the reconstruction laws. It is to be hoped, and I think the hope will be realized, that the amendments will be so framed as to ensure the earliest possible reorganization, under Constitutions securing to all equal rights & equal security for rights. It is not likely that the session will continue beyond next week.[4] Gov. Sprague left Washn the night before I did. He was called home to a meeting of the Trustees of Brown University who have much trouble in finding a Prest to succeed Dr. Sears.[5] He will return I suppose this week. I think of going to Saratoga tomorrow. I was never there; and being so near propose to take the opportunity of nearness, if I can find one or two of like inclinations. Next week I expect to be in Washington again to finish some work which still requires attention. No letter from any of you last week or, so far, this. May our Heavenly Father watch over you all; so prays your loving father on Earth.

S. P. C.

1. Clara Harris (d. 1883) was the daughter of New York senator Ira Harris, a former member of the state supreme court. On the night of Lincoln's assassination, Clara sat in the presidential box at Ford's Theatre with Henry R. Rathbone, who was wounded in the attack. In 1883, after years of depression, he killed his wife and attempted suicide. *New York Times,* Dec. 28, 1883.

2. Chase's daughters were in Europe. The destination of the mail steamer, *Ville de Paris,* was Havre, France. Ibid., July 13, 1867; Chase to Janet Chase, June 7, 1867 (above).

3. Indiana native John Cummins (1838–1916) had served in the legislatures of Oregon and Idaho. From 1865 to 1866, he was U.S. collector of internal revenue in Idaho, and in 1866 received an appointment to the territory's supreme court, where he remained until 1868. *Register of Officers (1865),* 61; *Who Was Who,* 1:284.

4. Congress had several proposals on its agenda to amend the first two Reconstruction Acts. The most notable, which became law on July 19 over presidential veto, rejected the narrow interpretation expressed in Henry Stanbery's opinion of June 12, affirming instead broad discretionary powers for district military commanders and extending to voter registration boards authority to decide who could vote. The first session of the Fortieth Congress recessed on July 20, then resumed on November 21 and continued to December 1. *Bio. Dir. U.S. Cong.,* 183; *Congressional Globe,* 40th Cong., 1st sess., 1867, 466, 480; *Statutes at Large,* 15:14–16.

5. Barnas Sears, D.D., LL.D., had resigned in April after twelve years at the post. In September, the trustees appointed George Ide Chace (1808–85), Ph.D., LL.D., as interim president. The permanent successor of Sears, Alexis Caswell, D.D., LL.D., served from February 1868 until 1872. *Appletons',* 1:562, 5:447; *DAB,* 3:570–71; Walter C. Bronson, *The History of Brown University, 1764–1914* (Providence, 1914), 366–67.

TO HORACE GREELEY

Letterpress copy of autograph letter. Chase Papers, Library of Congress (*micro* 37:0443).

Washn. Aug. 5, 1867

My dear Mr. Greeley,

I do not know that you are not much better informed as to public matters here than I am: but it is well enough that, in your position, you should know what I am about to tell you.

The President sent for me last Friday morning and I went to the White House between nine & ten. He received me kindly as he always does & soon went, as his way is, directly to the matters upon his mind.

He declared most expressly that he had executed & meant to carry out the reconstruction acts in perfect good faith; but was much dissatisfied with Gen. Sheridans action. He censured especially the letter of General S—— to General Grant, in which he spoke of the President as hostile to the legislation of Congress, & of the Attorney Generals construction of it as forming a highway for [perjury]. He thought it insubordinate & [*illeg.*]able that such a letter should be sent to the Commanding General, & published at New Orleans & New York almost before mailed, & [never] communicated to him officially even to this day.[1] He censured Sheridan, also, for his course in other respects—in removal of [*four words? illeg.*] & appointing Levee Commissioners—[*six words? illeg.*] [and he] intimated very plainly his intention to remove him & put Hancock in his place.[2]

After hearing, what he had to say I asked him if he wanted my views, [&] he said that was what he wanted [*illeg.*] for. And then I told him what I thought very plainly, very much as follows: The People had set their hearts on the restoration of the rebel states with full guaranties for future peace, order, & security, especially by universal suffrage: his Vetoes had created a general impression north & south that he was hostile to this purpose;[3] this impression had been partially removed by his action in carrying the laws into execution; but the reference of the applications of the District Generals for [instru]ctions to the Attorney General, and his opinions,[4] had revived & intensified this impression, encouraging the enemies of reconstruction, discouraging its friends in the unrestored states, & inflaming the people in the other states. This had made the meeting of Congress a necessity, & the new law & the new veto had caused him to be looked on more & more as opposed not to the [policies] only, but to the objects which the people favored. Under these circumstances it was, I thought, exceedingly undesirable to make a new issue by displacing General Sheridan. I did not argue with him the fitness of General Sheridans acts, farther than to express my decided opinion that [Monroe], [*two words? illeg.*] ought to have been put on trial for their part in the Massacre—but I urged that any interference with Gen. S—— could & would work only evil.[5]

Of course I give only a faint sketch of what was said on both sides, merely summing up the substance instead of trying to repeat words or preserving any thing of the conversational character [of] the discussion.

He had expressed no decided determination when I left him but as three days have now elapsed and nothing has been done I hope the idea has been abandoned. Every member of his Cabinet, I am informed, (not by him however,) is against interference. And I earnestly hope that there will be none.[6] The country wants all its energies now for the [*illeg.*] work of restoration, without the distraction of a another[7] hot conflict with the President.

In the course of our talk the President intimated that he thought of putting Gen Grant temporarily at the head of the War Dept, to which of course nobody would object, except that it would imply the displacement or resignation of Mr Stanton. I took the liberty of expressing a quite decided opinion that no change would benefit the country or ought to be made.[8]

Of course I do not wish anything of what I have written should be made public: but, while [you will not refer] to anything said in this letter, it may [be you will] write [somewhat] differently with this knowledge than you would without it.[9]

Sincerely yours
S P Chase

1. Maj. Gen. Philip Henry Sheridan governed the fifth military district, comprised of Louisiana and Texas, from New Orleans. Copies of correspondence that he wrote to Commanding Gen. Ulysses S. Grant on June 22 appeared the following day in the *New Orleans Daily Picayune* and *New York Times*. The letter complained about orders from President Johnson to extend the deadline for voter registration in the fifth district to August 1. Sheridan also criticized Attorney General Henry Stanbery's legal opinion of June 12 on the First and Second Reconstruction Acts as "opening a broad macadamized road for perjury and fraud" and characterized President Johnson's attitude toward them as "bitter antagonism."

2. Democrat John T. Monroe, the unrepentant Confederate mayor of New Orleans, had won reelection with presidential sanction in March 1866. Monroe's alleged complicity in the riot of July 1866, discussed elsewhere in this letter, and his hostility toward Union officers encouraged Sheridan to dismiss him one year later. In June 1867, Sheridan had removed Louisiana's governor, James M. Wells, and the city's levee commissioners for supposedly misusing public money for partisan ends. President Johnson restored the commissioners, however, and on August 19 reassigned Sheridan to command the Department of the Missouri. Johnson then appointed Maj. Gen. George Henry Thomas in Sheridan's place, but Thomas declined due to poor health. One week later, the president assigned Maj. Gen. Winfield Scott Hancock instead. *DAB*, 17:81; Holli, *Biographical Dictionary of American Mayors*, 258; *New York Times*, June 9, Aug. 5, 21, 31, 1867.

3. By 1867, Johnson had established a record of opposition to congressional reconstruction. Congress had overridden his most recent veto—of the Third Reconstruction Act—on July 19. *DAB*, 10:86; *Statutes at Large*, 15:14–16.

4. In correspondence to Theodore Tilton on July 9 (above), Chase had explained that district generals had wanted clarifications, which resulted in Henry Stanbery's opinion of June 12.

5. Heightened political tensions between Conservatives and Radicals in New Orleans had erupted on July 30, 1866, into a riot that involved former soldiers and killed thirty-seven people, most of whom were African Americans who had assembled for a convention of Radicals. Evidence of police complicity with the attackers fueled discussion about the administrative practices of Louisiana governor James M. Wells, President Johnson, and Sheridan, who was visiting Texas when the riot occurred. *Appletons' Annual Cyclopædia*, 7:454–59; Foner, *Reconstruction*, 262–63; *New Orleans Riots*, 39th Cong., 2d sess., 1866–67, H. Rept. 16.

6. Johnson's cabinet officers at this time were Orville Hickman Browning (Interior), Hugh McCulloch (Treasury), Alexander Williams Randall (Post Office), William H. Seward (State), Henry Stanbery (Justice), Edwin M. Stanton (War), and Gideon Welles (Navy). *Bio. Dir. U.S. Cong.*, 18.

7. Chase originally wrote *a hot*, then inserted *another* without cancelling *a*.

8. By displacing Stanton, Johnson would have challenged the Tenure of Office Act, which Congress passed over his veto on March 2, 1867. The bill required Senate concurrence for the removal of any cabinet member during the term of the president who appointed him. On August 12, Johnson suspended Secretary of War Stanton and offered the job to Grant instead, taking advantage of a provision in the law that permitted the president to act unilaterally when the Senate was not in session and to seek approval when Congress reconvened. Johnson's refusal to accept Senate rejection of the ouster after it gathered again in November helped set the stage for impeachment proceedings against him the following year. *Bio. Dir. U.S. Cong.*, 183; *DAB*, 7:498, 17:520; Foner, *Reconstruction*, 333–34; Graf, *Papers of Andrew Johnson*, 12:476–77; *Statutes at Large*, 14:430–32.

9. On August 7, the *New York Tribune* included an editorial that accused President Johnson of wanting to remove Sheridan because of his success at organizing a state government in Louisiana dominated by Radicals.

TO BENJAMIN F. FLANDERS

Autograph letter. Special Collections, Dartmouth College Library (*micro* 37:0486).

near Boston, Sep. 3, 1867

My dear Governor,[1]

It is said that you intend to resign in case of Hancock's assuming command in the Louisiana District. I hope this is not so. The President has acted with strange disregard of public opinion in his interference with General Sheridan, whose best act, in my judgment, was the appointment of yourself[2] / But I do not think your sense of duty will allow you to resign. Honest men & capable at the same time, are not so numerous that the country can afford to spare you & your first duty is to the country. You must not resign.

Sincerely your friend
S P CHASE

His Excellency
B. F. Flanders

1. Philip H. Sheridan had appointed former Treasury agent and Unionist congressman Benjamin Franklin Flanders as military governor of Louisiana in June 1867. Six months later Flanders resigned. *Appletons',* 2:478.

2. Johnson had replaced Sheridan with Winfield S. Hancock as commander of the Fifth Military District late in August. Chase to Horace Greeley, Aug. 5 (above); *DAB,* 17:81; *New York Times,* Aug. 21, 30, 1867.

TO DANIEL SICKLES

Letterpress copy of autograph letter. Chase Papers, Library of Congress (*micro* 37:0493).

Washington. Sep. 19, 1867.

Dear General,[1]

Coming home I found some of your orders which had been forwarded to me, I suppose, by your direction.[2]

Thanking you for the courtesy, I seize the occasion to say that my esteem & admiration for you, excited by your patriotic services during the war, is undiminished, and your services since in a civi-military capacity command my gratitude as they do that of our countrymen in general. While I say this from the heart, I must say just as much from the heart that I think it was a mistake that you did not at once, upon information of what had occurred at Wilmington direct your subordinates to refrain from all interference with the process of the Courts of the United States. The reconstruction acts, in my judgment, contemplated no such interference, and I never doubted, until I saw your order to the contrary, that on this point your judgment agreed with mine.[3]

You need no assurance, I hope, that had my advice been taken & followed you would have been continued at your post & sustained, except on the single point, I have indicated, in an admn. which seemed to me just, able, & sure to conduct to early restoration on the plan prescribed by Congress.[4]

Sincerely yours
S P CHASE

Maj. Gen. D. E. Sickles

P.S. This note is, of course, not for publication; but I desire that your friends & mine may, so far as may be convenient, understand my real views & sentiments.

1. In 1865, President Johnson had appointed Sickles, a former New York congressman and major general in the Union army, military governor of the Carolinas. In March 1867, Sickles became commander of the Second Military District, which comprised North and South Carolina, under terms of the Second Reconstruction Act. *Appletons' Annual Cyclopædia,* 7:690; *DAB,* 17:150–51.

2. The nature of Chase's complaint in the text of this letter suggests that one of the documents received was General Orders No. 10, issued by Sickles on April 11, 1867. Section two of the order suspended collection processes for debts incurred between December 1860 and May 15, 1865. *Appletons' Annual Cyclopædia,* 7:547–48; *General Orders—Reconstruction,* 40th Cong., 2d sess., 1867–68, H. Ex. Doc. 342, 39.

3. In June, while on circuit in Raleigh, North Carolina, Chase had awarded judgments in civil debt cases against defendants from Wilmington, but the town's military commandant prevented the deputy marshal from serving writs of execution. Sickles balked at reversing himself and was removed on August 13. Maj. Gen. Edward R. S. Canby replaced him on August 26. *Appletons' Annual Cyclopædia,* 7:547–48; *General Orders—Reconstruction,* 40th Cong., 2d sess., 1867–68, H. Ex. Doc. 342, 60; Joseph G. de Roulhac Hamilton, *Reconstruction in North Carolina* (Gloucester, Mass., 1964), 231–32.

4. That is, in accordance with the Reconstruction Acts.

FROM R. STOCKETT MATHEWS

Autograph letter. Chase Papers, Library of Congress (*micro* 37:0544).

Private.

Baltimore Nov. 7. 1867

My Dear Governor,[1]

Now that the elections are over, and the worst disasters have proven not more serious than expected—only defeats of mismanaged parties, and not the extinction of recuperative principles—I can sit down, and fulfill a wish, which frequent absences and the work of the campaign, have delayed already too long[2]— You have heard—or perhaps may have seen that the *American* has placed at its head, the name of General Grant, as the preference of the Republicans of Maryland, as their candidate for the Presidency. Mr Fulton, the Editor of that paper—without Consultation with the leading members of an organization, and without their knowledge, offered in the last State Convention a resolution commending Genl Grant, as the most fitting candidate, and that resolution was Carried, almost *sub silentio* against seventeen dissenting votes.[3] Since then, no remonstrances on my part have availed to modify the determination of Genl Grant's friends to mislead our people, through the *American,* and to impose upon them a concession to the necessity of such a nomination. Not only do I not concur with them in their views and oppose and regret their premature and unwise importunity, in that direction—but I am quite sure, independent of my personal regard for you—that our party could com-[4] no worse blunder than to accept at the hands of timeservers, and trimmers the nomination of a man who, however meritorious as a soldier, and reliable as a patriot, in other respects, is not distinguished for the possession of those great attributes of strong conviction, and earnest advocacy of progressive principles, which ought to be recognized in the foremost man of our party. You know how real is my faith in you, and how earnestly I hope to see you at the head of the Nation—not for your own sake alone—but that the deepest needs of our civilization may be met as far as one able man can help their fulfillment, and I write to you now, to ask you if there is any way in which I can cooperate with your friends in arresting the panic-stricken clamors of timid and selfish men in their outcry in favour of a military Candidate— You can command my services in any way—I do not often volunteer to show my regard for public men—and this letter is an exception to my whole political life—but I am profoundly anxious to see one man during my time, in charge of our perplexing affairs—with brain enough, and heart enough for his epoch. Please let me hear from you—[5]

Your's very truly
R. STOCKETT MATHEWS.

1. Mathews (1827–90), an attorney from Baltimore, had served as a Maryland legislator and federal elector. In 1867, he became register in bankruptcy for the state's third congressional district. Mathews represented his city at the Republican state convention on October 10. *Baltimore: Its History and Its People,* 3 vols. (New York and Chicago, 1912), 2:325–28; *Baltimore American,* Oct. 11, 1867.

2. In balloting on November 5—the first election under Maryland's new constitution—Democratic candidates won all seats in both branches of the state legislature as well as the governorship. *Appletons' Annual Cyclopædia,* 7:479–80.

3. Charles C. Fulton, editor of the *Baltimore American,* made the suggestion at the Republican state convention on October 10. According to the proposal, which actually passed by a margin of 64–18, "The Republicans of Maryland, in convention assembled, recommend to the Republican party of the Union Gen. Ulysses S. Grant as their candidate for President of the United States." The newspaper suggested Grant for president "subject to the decision of the Republican National Convention." In Latin, "subsilentes" indicates silence—literally "under silence." *Baltimore American,* Oct. 11, 1867.

4. Mathews evidently intended to write *commit,* but neglected to complete the word after hyphenating at the turn of a page.

5. "I frankly confess myself much disappointed by the action of the Maryland Unionists," replied Chase on November 12; "If I have ever omitted one opportunity to serve & aid them when I had power, or, in or out of power, failed in earnest sympathy with their noble & generous aims, I do not remember the occasion: and, now I shall not complain that they seem inclined to seek new friendships, if the new prove better & surer for the great cause of equal rights & exact justice for all men, than the old." Chase to Mathews, Nov. 12, 1867 (Chase Papers, L.C.).

TO GILBERT PILLSBURY

Letterpress copy of autograph letter. Chase Papers, Library of Congress (*micro* 37:0550).

Washington, Nov. 12, 1867

My dear Sir,

Your letter of the 24th would have been answered much earlier had I not been so much pressed by engagements & hindered by absence from Washn.[1]

It is, of course, out of my power to frame a Constitution for you, & happily it is not necessary. The old Constitution will no doubt be the groundwork of the new. The wisest men I see, whose friendship for the newly enfranchised citizens may be depended on seem agreed in the opinion that the fewer the alterations beyond those absolutely necessary to adapt the new Constitution to the new conditions, the better it will be for all concerned. This opinion may be summed up, well enough perhaps, in this way.

The new Constitution should contained

1st An express prohibition of slavery

2nd A distinct recognition of the necessity of universal education, and an emphatic injunction to the Legislature to provide the necessary means

3rd A clear declaration that all adult male citizens, unconvicted of crime, may vote & be elected to any office, with such exceptions only of persons engaged in the late rebellion as are necessary to secure the beneficial practical working of the government under the new Constitution and suitable provisions for the removal of disabilities in proper cases.

4th Such modifications of the judicial system as are required to ensure impartial justice to all men without respect to color or condition.

These are all the changes I think of or have heard mentioned as desirable: and these to be sure are great changes. The Convention will need great wisdom, [*illeg.*]tion & firmness. I hope, earnestly, for its complete success.[2] The enemies of renovation as essential to restoration are hoping for its failure / Many anxious eyes & thoughts will wait upon it, in this & other lands, God grant that the result may be a new proof that the best of all governments is self government.

Very truly your friend
S P Chase

Gilbert Pillsbury Esq

1. Pillsbury, formerly of Massachusetts, had written from Charleston, South Carolina, on behalf of the Union League and Union Republican party. "We desire draft of a Constitution," he wrote in anticipation of elections on November 19 and 20 for delegates to a state constitutional convention, "as complete in all its parts as may be, and as well suited to our wants as the most thorough legal judgement can devise." Pillsbury's letter also included an expression of confidence that Republicans would select Chase as their

presidential nominee in 1868. *Appletons' Annual Cyclopædia,* 7:700; Pillsbury to Chase, Sept. 24, 1867 (Chase Papers, L.C.).

2. South Carolina's constitutional convention gathered in Charleston on January 14, 1868. The resulting document, which voters ratified on April 14–16, 1868, incorporated the points that Chase suggested. *Appletons' Annual Cyclopædia,* 7:700, 8:695, 697; *Revised Statutes of the State of South Carolina* . . . (Columbia, S.C., 1873), 19, 37, 39–40, 43, 44.

TO HORACE GREELEY

Letterpress copy of autograph letter. Chase Papers, Library of Congress (*micro* 37:0567). Fragment of autograph letter. Personal Misc.—Salmon P. Chase, Manuscripts and Archives Division, The New York Public Library, Astor, Lenox, and Tilden Foundations (*micro* 30:0733).

Washn. Nov. [19],[1] 1867

My dear Mr. Greeley,

I feel as the Quakers say impressed to write you about the Finances.[2]

There are few who understand what my work was. It may be set under three heads.

1. To establish satisfactory relations between the public credit and the productive industry, of the country—in other words to obtain supplies

The suspension of the banks put an end to the first & most obvious resort, loans of gold, & made new methods indispensable.

Then I resorted to Legal Tender Notes, made them a currency, & borrowed them as cash[3]

The patriotism of the people came in aid of the plans of the Treasury & the Legislation of Congress, and the first great object was made secure

2. To provide against disastrous [*illeg.*][4] [on the return] of peace.

This could only be done by providing a National Currency.

There were about 1500 state Banks in existence who wanted to make their own paper the currency of the country

This I resisted & confined my loans to greenbacks but I could not drive out their currency, nor indeed did I think it exactly honest to deprive them of it without giving an equivalent

To neutralize their opposition to a national currency and make them allies as far as possible instead of enemies in my endeavor to secure one I proposed the National Banking System:[5] and before I left the Department its success was assured.

The National Banks were certain to be useful in many ways but my main object was the establishment of a National Currency.

This saved us from panic & revulsion at the close of the war, and is of inestimable value to the men of labor & the men of business indeed to every class.

3. The third division of my work was the provision of a funding system.

It was unavoidable that every resource of credit should be used. I borrowed money every way I could at reasonable rates. The form which suited one lender did not suit another, and the Army & Navy wanted every dollar that could be raised in every form.

Hence many temporary loans—Certificates of deposit / Certificates of Indebtedness, 7.30 notes,[6] compound interest notes, Treasury notes payable after 1 & 2 years &c &c

But it was necessary to have funding loans into which all these temporary loans might be ultimately merged. To this end I established the 5–20 loan & the 10–40 loan.[7] My belief was that after the [51]4.000000 of the 5–20 loan had been taken,[8] that the additional amounts needed could be obtained by the 10–40 loan & the temporary loans; but was ready to resort to the 5–20s in case of emergency. I did get 73. millions on the 10–40 loan, & my successors got about 120 millions more at par, & I have never[9] been able to see any good reason for making the 7.30 currency notes subsequently issued convertible, at the holders option, into 5–20s instead of 10–40s. Lenders of course preferred the former, bearing 6% in gold to the latter bearing only 5%; and lenders were rather more favored[10] after I left the Department than before. And so indeed were brokers; for Jay Cooke got nearly or quite twice as large commissions under Fessenden & McCulloch as I allowed him.

You can see how this funding system of mine has worked if you take up the last Statement of the Public Debt—[11]

I haven't it at hand but the condition is something like this 1200.000.000 5–20s; 200.000000 10/40. 200.000.000[12] 81s payable now after 14 years which *can then*[13] easily be put into 10–40s; other loans (all temporary) say 500.000.000[14] of which 3/4ths consists of 7.30s all convertible & certain to be converted into 5–20s & the other 1/4 may be easily converted into 10–40s, & say 400.000.000[15] Greenbacks including fractional currency—making the aggregate debt of 2500.00000.[16]

So you see the whole debt except the 81s is already funded or sure to be [very soon] in 5–20, 6%s or 10–40 5%s.

Can there be a better funding system? I don't believe it.

Yet there is talk of a new funding loan!

The object is to catch gudgeons by *apparently* yielding to the popular clamor for taxation on bonds.

The way is to offer a new 6% loan, with reservation of right to tax not exceeding 6%[17]—in other words a non-taxable 5% loan: and it is proposed to make this a long loan say 30 years. It will be magnificent for brokers, bankers, & lenders, but death on the people. Of course such a loan can be negotiated; for a 5%, 30 year loan untaxable is worth more in the market than any loan now outstanding; and nothing is more certain in the future than Government will be paying within five years 5 10 & even 15% for the privilege of paying its debt before maturity.

I want specially to call your attention to this. It may be well enough to make the loan, in the form proposed, if the clamor for taxation will be satisfied by it; but why make it for *20* or *30* years, instead of adhering to the 10–40 plan, by which the debt is[18] redeemable at any time after 10 years & thus kept under the control of the [*illeg.*].[19] I have no doubt that, if our finances are properly managed, we can borrow within 10 years at 4%, or 5 with right to tax 1/5, as easily as we can now borrow at 5 or 6 with right to tax 1/6. Why bind ourselves to pay interest for 30 years, when it is not only unnecessary, but certain to entail a heavy additional expence, in the form of premiums for redemption.

But enough though I could add much more.

Yours cordially
S P Chase

P.S.[20]

Perhaps you have not had your attention particularly directed to the fact that when I negotiated at par the 73 millions of 10–40, five per cents the currency was much less inflated than it has been ever since & is now. The issues of the greenbacks and the indisposition of Congress to tax the State Bank Currency out of circulation caused almost all the inflation that took place under my administration. The late inflation does not seem to me excused by public exigencies. The greenbacks should have been retired nearly or quite *pari passu* with the issuing of National Bank Notes & the equilibrium preserved.

The comparative inflation will appear from a Statement of the Circulation on the 30 June 1864, when I left the Department & on the 30 June 1866.[21]

June 30, 1864

U.S. Notes, (greenbacks) 431.178.670.81
Fractional[22] & Postage Currency 22.894.877.25
National Bank Notes (say) 30.000.000
Total National Currency 484.073.548.06
Add 1 year Treasury Notes 44.520.00
" Compound Int. Notes 15.000.00
Total issues used more or less as currency 59.520.000
State Bank Circulations (say) 100.000.000
Total 643.593.548.06

June 30, 1866

U.S. Notes, (greenbacks) 400.619.206
[*illeg.*] Postage Currency 27.070.876.96
National Bank notes (say) 292.671.753
Total National Currency 720.361.835.96
Add Compound int notes more or less used as curry. 15.901.214

State Bank Circulation 46.533.060
Total 792.796.209.96
Increase in 1866 149.202.661.10

1. In the original, the date appears to be *20* altered to *19,* or vice versa. As bound in the letterpress volume, the letter falls between others of the twelfth and the twentieth. On Nov. 26, 1867, Greeley's *Tribune* printed this letter in the guise of a communication of Nov. 19 from "Our Special Correspondent," reporting information gained in conversation with Chase. In the *Tribune* the letter has new text at its beginning and end, the first-person voice of the manuscript has been converted to third person, and there are other changes of wording. Variations between the manuscript and the version in the *Tribune* will not be noted here unless they pertain to substantive material that is difficult to read in the original.

2. By tradition, the Friends' doctrine of the Inner Light stressed the immanence of God's Spirit and its capacity to prompt action among humans. Elbert Russell, *The History of Quakerism* (New York, 1942), 48–53.

3. Major American banks and the U.S. government suspended payment of specie on December 30, 1861. Congressional action of February 25, 1862, authorized $150 million in such notes (greenbacks) to be used as legal tender except in payment of duties and interest. Long, *Civil War Day by Day,* 152; *Statutes at Large,* 12:345–48.

4. The version printed in the *Tribune,* which in some places alters the wording of the manuscript, has *results* here. The word on the letterpress copy could be *inflation.*

5. The national banking system emerged from the National Currency Act of February 25, 1863, developed further through the National Currency Act of June 3, 1864. *Statutes at Large,* 12:665–82, 13:99–118.

6. According to legislation of July 17, 1861, the notes bore yearly interest of 7 3/10 percent, payable semiannually. Ibid., 12:259.

7. The first Legal Tender Act of February 25, 1862, authorized 5–20 bonds. The U.S. government started to issue 10–40 bonds in accordance with the Ways and Means Act of March 3, 1863. Ibid., 12:345–48, 709–10.

8. Congress authorized a total of $511,000,000 in 5–20 bonds. *Appletons' Annual Cyclopædia,* 4:373.

9. The text of the letter to this point is available only in the form of the letterpress copy. The fragment at the New York Public Library begins with the next word and continues through the signature.

10. In the fragment, but not on the letterpress copy, the text from *into 5–20s* through *more favored* is set off by two *x*s in the margin.

11. The Treasury secretary's most recent report, issued on December 3, 1866, included a statement of the public debt as of June 30. *Report of the Secretary of the Treasury . . . 1866,* 38–43.

12. In the fragment but not on the letterpress copy, a *5* appears above the 2 of this figure. The *Tribune* gives the number as $200,000,000.

13. These words are not underlined in the letterpress copy. The expression "81s" referred to twenty-year bonds sold under legislation of July 17, 1861. *Statutes at Large,* 12: 259–61.

14. In the fragment but not on the letterpress copy, there are two *x*s in the margin alongside the two lines in the manuscript beginning *81s payable* and ending with this figure.

15. Chase evidently wrote *375* for the first three digits, then formed *400* over them; in the fragment he also wrote *400* again above the line. The text in the *Tribune* gives the figure as 400,000,000.

16. That is, 2,500,000,000. In June 1862, Congress had authorized use of postage stamps and fractional paper currency for payments of less than one dollar. *Statutes at Large,* 12:592.

17. So in the original; *one percent* in the *Tribune.*

18. In the fragment, an *x* appears in the margin next to the line beginning with this word.

19. The version in the *Tribune* has *people* here. Chase appears to have written one word over another—*nation* and *public* are possibilities, but not *people.*

20. The fragment lacks the page with the postscript, which is given here from the letterpress copy.

21. The editors have not located either statement. According to later estimates, the total value of currency in circulation among the loyal states as of June 1864 and June 1866 was $1,073,600 and $1,834,500, respectively. Wesley Clair Mitchell, *A History of the Greenbacks with Special Reference to the Economic Consequences of their Issue: 1862–65* ([Chicago], 1903), 179.

22. The *Tribune* here has *Fractional and.*

TO GEORGE WASHINGTON BROOKS

Letterpress copy of autograph letter. Chase Papers, Library of Congress (*micro* 37:0553).

Washington, Nov. 20, 1867

My dear Judge,

I had the pleasure today of receiving yours of the 16th, and regret as much as you do that I cannot be with you at Raleigh during the approaching term; but I must give the next week to other duties. I half promised Judge Underwood that I would go to Richmond to charge the Grand Jury on the 25th, but I do not now see that it will be possible.[1]

No suggestions of importance occur to me as to the Charge proper to be made at Raleigh. It may be well to remind the people that there is such a crime as treason & to give the Grand Jury the law on the subject as modified by the act of 1862. I incline to the opinion expressed by Mr. Justice Field in the Chapman case that under that act the offence of leving war against the Government may be committed under three heads 1. Under the old [law] levying war whether by domestic force or giving aid & comfort to enemies punishable with death 2. Under the act of 1862 by giving aid & comfort to enemies punishable with death or fine & imprisonment at the discretion of the [Court] 3. Under the same act exciting or engaging in rebellion punishable by fine not over 10.000 or imprisonment not over 10 years or both.[2] I am afraid that the settled principles of construction will oblige the Courts to construe the word enemies as embracing foreign enemies only; though I much doubt if that was the actual meaning of of Congress. Of course you will charge pretty strong against Counterfeiting, revenue frauds & the like, by no means forgetting offences against the reconstruction laws,[3] which I agree with you in regarding as constitutional in their general object & leading provi[sions] if not altogether so.

I am very sorry to read your account of Carter. He ought to have held out.[4]

As to the Habeas Corpus writs applied for I am clear that you did right in allowing them. I presume proper returns will be made: That should be insisted on. If the return shows a detention warranted by the reconstruction acts the parties should be remanded—otherwise they should be discharged.[5]

As you failed to give me the satisfaction of seeing you in Washington during the summer, through illness which I much regret, I shall hope for it now that you are happily well again during the winter.

With great esteem & respect
Your sincere friend
S P Chase

Hon. G. W. Brooks

Best regards to all Raleigh friends

1. Chase did not attend the opening of the court, but sent Underwood a draft of the charge. Chase to Underwood, Nov. 23 and 24, 1867 (Underwood Papers, L.C.); *New York Times,* Nov. 27, 1867.

2. Art. 3, sec. 3, of the U.S. Constitution defines treason and leaves punishment to the discretion of Congress. Chase had discussed the Second Confiscation Act, which became law on July 17, 1862, and Stephen J. Field's opinion in *U.S. v. Greathouse et al.,* also known as the "Chapman case," in correspondence of May 15, 1866, to Jacob W. Schuckers (above).

3. To date, the first three Reconstruction Acts.

4. On November 4, David M. Carter, Republican organizer and former Confederate officer, had delivered a speech against congressional reconstruction. *Raleigh Tri-Weekly Standard,* Nov. 12, 1867.

5. Legislation of February 5, 1867, which amended the Judiciary Act of 1789, expanded the authority of federal courts to issue writs of habeas corpus on appeal to the U.S. Supreme Court. Fairman, *Reconstruction and Reunion,* 448; *Statutes at Large,* 1:73–93, 14:385.

TO THOMAS W. CONWAY

Printed copy. *New York Tribune,* September 19, 1870.

My Dear Sir:[1] I have received your kind letters, and am much obliged for the information they convey. I am particularly touched by the proofs they afford of the attachment and confidence of the colored people. I have always said that to possess the affection and true respect of the poor and the oppressed is a worthier object of ambition than any official position, even the highest. In that ambition I am glad to know I am not likely to be disappointed. I may be mistaken, but I really believe that I have been credited with more ambition for place than I feel. Not that I possess any uncommon indifference to the gratification derived from distinction, but, to me, great place has always been chiefly valuable as great opportunity for useful service.

No one can foresee the future. Congress has adjourned, and the members have gone home to confer with their constituents.[2] When they return, I presume they will take hold of their work vigorously. Opinions differ as to what is best to be done. On one point there is little real division. All seem agreed that the Reconstruction policy of Congress must be ardently pursued, and that the earliest possible restoration of the Southern States to their old relations, upon the basis of Universal Suffrage and Equal Rights, is most desirable. I feel more anxiety on this point than any other, because, this point once secured, all others may be reckoned as secured. The rights of labor, and the interest of labor, are at the basis of all sound policy, and nothing is so important to theirs as the right to vote for the laborer.

Sincerely yours,
S. P. CHASE.

P.S.—I have never advocated Universal Suffrage and Immediate Amnesty to All. I have said that Universal Suffrage would reconcile comprehensive lenity with tranquillity and prosperity. I would have no more disfranchisement after the complete establishment of Universal Suffrage than is absolutely necessary to secure the new order of things, and the new State Constitutions against overthrow. Those lately in rebellion have no more right to destroy the country by ballots than by bullets.

As to the trial of Jefferson Davis, the amount and kind of misrepresentation is astonishing. The facts are simple. I neither seek nor shun the responsibility of trying anybody. (My purpose is to do my duty as a Judge, honestly and faithfully, turning neither to the right nor the left.) While military authority was supreme in the South, as an incident of the war, and anybody could be tried by military commission, no Justice of the Supreme Court could properly hold a Court there. This state of things lasted from the surrender of Lee, in April, 1865, till the final suppression of the Rebellion was proclaimed, in 1866.[3] Meantime, in July, 1866, an act of Congress, by changing the Circuits, had deprived the Justices of the Supreme Court of jurisdiction in the Southern States, and jurisdiction was not restored until March, 1867, when Congress passed the necessary act.[4] Of course, from July, 1866, to March, 1867, neither the Chief-Justice, nor any other Justice, could try anybody in Virginia. Any editor of any newspaper would have as much right. At the time the act of March, 1867, was passed, the Supreme Court was sitting in Washington, and the Chief-Justice was bound to be there, but he wrote to the District Judge at Richmond, Va., that he would come down and join him in holding the Court, as soon as the Supreme Court adjourned in May.[5] Jefferson Davis, however, was brought before the District Judge and bailed in May, before the Supreme Court adjourned. This seems to have been done by a sort of consent, and it was done without any conference with the Chief-Justice, and was a matter of which he had no control. The counsel of both sides were informed by the District Judge that the Chief-Justice would come in a few days and if a trial had been desired on either side, it could have been then had in that very month of May.[6] In October, 1867, an adjourned term having been appointed to be held at Richmond on the 13th of November, the Chief-Justice caused the parties to be notified that he would attend at that time, in order that the trial might take place, if parties were willing. He did accordingly attend, but the parties were not ready. This was in November, 1867. Since then the Chief Justice has been obliged to attend the Supreme Court at Washington. One thing is certain, there has been no term at Richmond since the capitulation of Lee, which the Chief Justice could have attended, at which he has not attended; and another thing is clear, that the trial of Jefferson Davis might at any time have taken place, that is, since his capture in May, 1865, either by military commmission, when military commissions were being held for the trial of offenders under the authority of the President, or by a court held by the District Judge. The Chief Justice, therefore, is in no sense or in the least degree responsible for the delay which has taken place. Until last May he could not try him, and since then he has always been ready.

S. P. CHASE.

Washington, Jan. 1, 1868.

1. Conway, a Baptist minister, former army chaplain, and assistant commissioner for freedmen, eventually became superintendent of schools for Louisiana. Johnson, *Twentieth Century Biographical Dictionary,* vol. 2.

2. The second session of the Fortieth Congress was in recess from December 21 to January 6. *Congressional Globe,* 40th Cong., 2d sess., 1867–68, 317.

3. Lee surrendered on April 9, 1865. President Johnson finally issued a proclamation that satisfied Chase on this point on August 20, 1866. Chase to Jacob W. Schuckers, Sept. 24, 1866 (above); Long, *Civil War Day by Day,* 670–71; *Statutes at Large,* 14:814–17.

4. The bill that deprived Chase and his brethren of jurisdiction was H.R. 334, which became law on July 23, 1866. Congress supplied the remedy through legislation of March 2, 1867. *Statutes at Large,* 14:433.

5. Chase had written to Underwood on May 13, in response to a letter of May 10 regarding accomodations in Richmond. Chase to Underwood, May 13, 1867; Underwood to Chase, May 10, 1867 (Chase Papers, L.C.).

6. Horace Greeley, Gerrit Smith, and eleven others posted bail of $100,000 for Davis on May 13, 1867. At that time, Lucius H. Chandler, U.S. district attorney for Virginia, and New York attorney William M. Evarts represented the government. Davis's attorneys were George Shea and Charles O'Conor. According to a record of proceedings, Chase had written to Underwood "intimating his intention to come to this city if any important cases are likely to be tried." Johnson, *Cases Decided by Chief Justice Chase,* 43–52.

TO HENRY B. WALBRIDGE

Autograph letter. Chase Papers, Historical Society of Pennsylvania (*micro* 37:0597).

Washington, Jany 2, 1868.

My dear brother,[1]

I have been waiting for a proper mood in which to write you; and the New Year has come & finds me as much pressed & bothered as the old did. I pray however for a quiet & loving heart & try to keep down the troublesome emotions & all wrong feelings.

At any rate I wont longer delay writing to you. I thank you heartily for sending me the photographs of dear Helens monument & of your church. The monument is very appropriate indeed: but I thank God that it can cover nothing but what is mortal. In fact what is best in a monument is what is most spiritual. The memories it evokes, the feelings it stirs, the aspirations that it excites makes the stone live. And the dear one that is gone before lives the best life of all. May it be our blessed priviledge to attain that life.

We are getting old. You are so many years my junior that I dare say you do not feel it as I do. But my sixtieth year is nearly completed: and *I* enter upon the last of the seven decades allotted to man. I do not expect to complete it. Whether I do or not I want to leave absolutely and with entire satisfaction in the hands of God. I desire to have no will of my own in respect to it.

I am glad to hear that your children give you so much comfort. Assure them all of my affectionate remembrance. You are right in supposing that it was not because of any lack of affection or desire that I did not visit Toledo when I was last in Ohio. My visit had two objective points voting at Cincinnati & spending a day or two with Jane Auld & her children at Conneaut. I went no where out of the lines to & from these points and had not time to go any where & still get back to Baltimore to hear a cause there set for a particular day.[2]

My duties as Judge are rather irksome. If I had been appointed younger, & before becoming so deeply concerned in political matters & so largely identified with political measures, I should have liked the position better than any other. I am not dissatisfied with it now; but should the people see fit to call me to administrative duties, which I do not really expect, I should be better suited. If not I shall try to be contented, &, whether I remain where I am or find myself induced to resign & take other more active employment, shall endeavor to do my whole duty.

It gave me real pleasure to receive your kind letter & I do wish you would write me oftener & tell me about your family, your church, & yourself.

Katie & her boy & Nettie with myself make up our present household. Governor Sprague is in Rhode Island looking after his business, which is immense. Nettie is an earnest member of the Church: by communion: Katie & her boy by baptism; Katie by sincere belief, but not by Communion yet. I sometimes wish she & her husband, who is all kindness to her, were poorer & less immersed in this world.

But goodbye: and believe me
Always & most affectionately

Your brother
S P Chase

Rev. H. B. Walbridge

1. Walbridge was rector of Trinity Protestant Episcopal Church in Toledo, Ohio, and the widower of Chase's sister Helen Maria, who had died in December 1864. Walbridge had included photographs of his church and of Helen's monument in a letter written to Chase on December 4, 1867. Harvey Scribner, ed., *Memoirs of Lucas County and the City of Toledo . . .* (Madison, Wisc., 1910), 303; Walbridge to Chase, Dec. 4, 1867 (Chase Papers, L.C.).

2. The December letter from Walbridge mentioned five children: Alice, Dudley, Hunt, Lillie, and Willie. Chase's trip to Ohio lasted from late September to early October and included a visit with Jane, his niece, and her two surviving daughters, Alice and Amy. The case that Chase heard in Baltimore was *In re Turner,* decided in favor of Elizabeth Turner, an African American, on October 16, 1866. The decision struck down an apprenticeship system permitted by Maryland's constitution of 1864 as a violation of the Thirteenth Amendment and the Civil Rights Act of April 9, 1866. Chase to Richard C. Parsons, Sept. 28, 1867 (Chase Papers, Hist. Soc. of Pa.); Fairman, *Reconstruction and Reunion,* 1309; Hyman, *Reconstruction Justice,* 123–39; Johnson, *Cases Decided by Chief Justice Chase,* 157–61; *New York Times,* Oct. 17, 1867; Walbridge to Chase, Dec. 4, 1867 (Chase Papers, L.C.).

TO HORACE GREELEY

Autograph letter. Horace Greeley Papers, Manuscripts and Archives Division, The New York Public Library, Astor, Lenox and Tilden Foundations (*micro* 37:0608).

Private

Washington, Jany 17, 1868.

My dear Sir,

Among my best treasures I prize your esteem and among my best sources of gratification I place your confidence: and I thank you most gratefully for the expressions of both in last weeks Independent. Shall I confess of the weakness of a wish to see it in the Tribune?[1]

I agree with you most fully that no man has any claims upon the Presidency or any other office. When a man has done all he can for his country, if he need not confess himself "an unprofitable servant," he must admit that he has only "done that which it was his duty to do."[2] And I can say honestly that I would rather be thought worthy of high position & not have it, than to have it & not be thought worthy. And my fears that I should not prove equal to the great trust are such that I shall find no great difficulty in accepting a popular decision adverse to the wishes you so kindly express.

As an argument your article seems to me the best presentation of "the case" it is capable of; except perhaps that the provision of the means for paying the army & navy might be put more as a ground of acceptability to the soldiers and sailors, and in this way the argument of availability might be met. My own conviction is that a party which has ideas & principles which make it really strong is always strongest when it trusts them fully & that he is most available as its candidate who most fully represents them. But I know that this is not equally the view of politicians—I mean the professional sort—and I see that the present set of the current runs as they would have it. I have some faith, however, yet in arguments addressed to sober sense and earnest faith. But such arguments to avail much must be strongly put like yours, & be given line upon line & precept upon precept.[3]

Apart from all questions of men, however, & above them all stands the great question whether the states shall be reorganized upon the Congressional plan with universal suffrage. This, at present, seems to me the one thing needful. I am afraid that the additional bill giving the new powers to General Grant will delay rather than advance reconstruction.[4] It will certainly tell powerfully against the Republicans in the approaching elections. It is certain to me that the people dont like military domination. True a majority of our friends like it, because they like whatever seems most hard on the rebels. But a large minority dislike it, & they drop out of the ranks one by one & two by two, until the majority of the people is on the other side. It would have been a vast improvement in reconstruction policy if the Military District Commanders had substituted by appointment or election (all voting) loyal state officers for disloyal in the provisional governments & then sustained the civil authorities without organizing a single military commission. Then no bills for injunction would have been brought by Georgia or Mississippi,[5] & no case of habeas corpus would have come from Mississippi. As things now are I believe that if Congress would just pass a bill embodying these ideas—(1) Power to the State reconstruction Conventions to admit to suffrage in the question of adopting the state Constitution & all future elections such as they see fit; (2) Payment of the expenses of Convention including a moderate per diem for members for not more than twenty days, with a resolution that the work of constitution making be finished within that time & (3) power to the Conventions to fix a short day for taking the vote on ratification, & the same or another short day for the election of State Officers & Legislatures, so as to secure the earliest possible representation of the states in the Senate & House—that nothing more would be needed. Despatch is the one thing needful just now. Constitutions which simply add to the old provisions universal suffrage; such a moderate disfranchisement of rebels as will secure for universal suffrage a fair trial; & an injunction on the legislature to provide universal education; & moreover wipe out such clauses as in any way countenance the old system of slavery, these would do the work. All else may be safely left to legislatures & future conventions. Much delay may lose all.

Are you quite sure that it is best to give such praise to the practical enforcement of the tenure of office bill & to Gen. Grant for his course.[6] There is no doubt that many of our best men question the constitutionality of that act. It is said that Senator Wade is of their number.[7] And is it wise to multiply questions of constitutional law for the Courts. Have we not enough to do in carrying out the reconstruction acts, & in meeting the demands of the Country for some acceptable financial measures. Is it not wisest to reach our ends now with as little rough friction as possible?

But I dare say I have written more than you will read. If you get as far as this paragraph read enough more to be assured that I shall not be at all mortified if you dont answer any of my questions. But I do commend all of them to your patient thought.

Most sincerely yours
S P CHASE

Hon H. Greeley

1. On January 16, Greeley had published an article in the *Independent* that compared Chase and Ulysses S. Grant as presidential candidates. "No man's services in putting down the Rebellion were more essential, more important, than those of the man who devised and gave effect to the measures whereby our Federal Treasury was kept in working order," wrote Greeley of Chase. "Gov. Chase has for twenty years stood up for Equal Rights, irrespective of color," continued Greeley in endorsement; Grant, however, "has kept quiet, while such conspicuous Grant oracles as *The Times* and *The Commercial Advertiser* have persistently assailed Impartial Suffrage." The *New York Tribune* reprinted Greeley's article on January 18.

2. "We are unprofitable servants: we have done that which was our duty to do." Luke 17:10.

3. "But the word of the Lord was unto them precept, precept upon precept; line upon line, line upon line; here a little, *and* there a little; that they might go, and fall backward, and be broken, and snared, and taken." Isa. 28:13.

4. On January 20, the House passed H.R. 439, a supplementary Reconstruction act, which would have given the general of the army authority to remove and appoint civil officers in provisional state governments and to carry out "any and all acts" formerly prerogatives of district military commanders. The proposal eventually died in the Senate. *Congressional Globe,* 40th Cong., 2d sess., 1867–68, 476, 1431.

5. The "bills for injunction" were *Mississippi v. Johnson* and *Georgia v. Stanton,* which Chase discussed in correspondence to David Davis on June 24, 1867 (above). The "case of habeas corpus" refers to *Ex parte McCardle,* a suit that reached the Supreme Court in December 1867. One month earlier, U.S. military officials had arrested William H. McCardle, editor of the *Vicksburg Times,* for publishing articles that, among other alleged faults, disturbed the peace. McCardle had requested a writ of habeas corpus under legislation of February 5, 1867, that allowed such appeals directly to federal courts. The Supreme Court heard the case between March 2 and 9, 1869, and unanimously dismissed it on April 12, 1869, for want of jurisdiction after Congress revoked permission to appeal. Fairman, *Reconstruction and Reunion,* 415, 437–38, 448–451, 492; 6 Wall. 318 (1868); 7 Wall. 506 (1869).

6. Chase had expressed concern about President Johnson's challenge to the Tenure of Office Act in a letter to Greeley dated August 5, 1867 (above). In accordance with the act, the Senate had refused to accept the ouster of Secretary of War Edwin M. Stanton, which the *Tribune* noted with approval on January 14. To the paper, Ulysses S. Grant's subsequent surrender as interim secretary of war was "one of the most admirable examples of the subordination of the military to the civil power which the history of America or of the world affords." *New York Tribune,* Jan. 14, 16, 1868.

7. Benjamin F. Wade of Ohio was a Radical Republican and, at this time, president *pro tempore* of the Senate. *DAB,* 29:305.

TO THE UNITED STATES SENATE

Letter in clerk's hand, signed by Chase. Records of Impeachment Proceedings against Andrew Johnson, Records of the Fortieth Congress, Records of the U.S. Senate (RG 46), National Archives.

To the Senate of the United States:

Inasmuch as the sole power to try impeachments is vested by the Constitution in the Senate, and it is made the duty of the Chief Justice to preside when the President is on trial, I take the liberty of submitting, very respectfully, some observations in respect to the proper mode of proceeding upon the impeachment which has been preferred by the House of Representatives against the President, now in office.[1]

That when the Senate sits for the trial of an impeachment it sits as a Court, seems unquestionable.

That, for the trial of an impeachment of the President, this Court must be constituted of the members of the Senate, with the Chief Justice presiding, seems equally unquestionable.

The Federalist is regarded as the highest cotemporary authority on the construction of the Constitution; and in the sixty-fourth number the functions of the Senate "sitting in their judicial capacity as a court for the trial of impeachments" are examined.

In a paragraph explaining the reasons for not uniting "the Supreme Court with the Senate in the formation of the Court of Impeachments" it is observed that "to a certain extent the benefits of that union will be obtained from making the Chief Justice of the Supreme Court the President of the Court of Impeachments, as is proposed in the plan of the Convention, while the inconveniences of an entire incorporation of the former into the latter will be substantially avoided. This was, perhaps, the prudent mean."[2]

This authority seems to leave no doubt upon either of the propositions just stated.

And the statement of them will serve to introduce the question upon which I think it my duty to state the result of my reflections to the Senate, namely, At what period, in the case of an impeachment of the President, should the Court of Impeachment be organized under oath as directed in the Constitution?

It will readily suggest itself to anyone who reflects upon the abilities and the learning in the law which distinguish so many Senators, that besides the reason assigned in the Federalist, there must have been still another for the provision requiring the Chief Justice to preside in the Court of Impeachment. Under the Constitution, in case of a vacancy in the office of President, the Vice President succeeds; and it was doubtless thought prudent and befitting that the next in succession should not preside in a proceeding through which a vacancy might be created.

It is not doubted that the Senate, while sitting in its ordinary capacity, must necessarily receive from the House of Representatives, some notice of its intention to impeach the President at its bar; but it does not seem to me an unwarranted opinion, in view of this constitutional provision, that the organization of the Senate as a Court of Impeachment under the Constitution, should precede the actual announcement of the impeachment on the part of the House.

And it may perhaps be thought a still less unwarranted opinion that articles of impeachment should only be presented to a Court of Impeachment; that no summons or other process should issue except from the organized Court, and that rules for the government of the proceedings of such a Court should be framed only by the Court itself.

I have found myself unable to come to any other conclusions than these. I can assign no reason for requiring the Senate to organize as a Court under any other than its ordinary presiding officer, for the later proceedings upon an impeachment of the President, which does not seem to me to apply equally to the earlier.

I am informed that the Senate has proceeded upon other views; and it is not my purpose to contest what its superior wisdom may have directed.[3]

All good citizens will fervently pray that no occasion may ever arise when the grave proceedings now in progress will be cited as a precedent; but it is not impossible that such an occasion may come.

Inasmuch, therefore, as the Constitution has charged the Chief Justice with an important function in the trial of an impeachment of the President, it has seemed to me fitting and obligatory, where he is unable to concur in the views of the Senate, concerning matters essential to the trial, that his respectful dissent should appear.

S: P: Chase
Chief Justice of the United States

Washington,
March 4th, 1868.

1. Art. 2, sec. 3, of the U.S. Constitution outlines the duties of the chief justice in cases of presidential impeachment. On February 24, the House had voted to impeach Andrew Johnson for "high crimes and misdemeanors," and had drawn up eleven articles of impeachment for presentation to the Senate on March 3. Central to the charges was an alleged violation of the Tenure of Office Act for removing Edwin M. Stanton as secretary of war and replacing him with Maj. Gen. Lorenzo Thomas on February 21 without the Senate's advice and consent. *Congressional Globe,* 40th Cong., 2d sess., 1867–68, supp., 3–5.

2. Alexander Hamilton first published the piece on March 7, 1788. *The Federalist,* ed. Jacob E. Cooke (Middletown, Conn., 1961), 439–45.

3. The Senate did not organize as a court of impeachment until March 5, having received articles of impeachment adopted in the House on March 2 and 3. Meanwhile, a select committee of seven—appointed by president *pro tempore* Benjamin F. Wade, a longtime antagonist of Chase and next in presidential succession—handled related Senate

business. As a legislative body, the upper chamber passed rules for the proceedings on March 2, then adopted them in its judiciary capacity on March 6. *Chase Papers,* 3:246–49, 312–14; *Trial of Andrew Johnson, President of the United States . . .*, 3 vols. (Washington, D.C., 1868), 1:3–15.

TO SAMUEL C. POMEROY

Copy of letter in hand of Jacob Schuckers. Chase Papers, Historical Society of Pennsylvania (*micro* 37:0625).

Private.

Thursday morning, Mar. 5.

Dear Sir,[1]

I respectfully suggest the adoption of the resolution enclosed today. Nothing more seems to me necessary till after the organization of the Court.

The Mem. are for the consideration of yourself and the Court.

Yours Sincerely
S. P. Chase.

Hon. S. C. Pomeroy.

Resolved, That a Committee of two be appointed by the Chair who shall, on behalf of the Senate, request the attendance of the Chief Justice of the United States in the Senate Chamber at one o'clock tomorrow, in order to the organization of a High Court of Impeachment for the trial of the President.[2]

Mem:

After the Court shall have been organized all irregularities may be cured perhaps by an order of the Senate, directing the Secretary to communicate to the Court such papers as have been brought to the Senate by the Ho. of Rep., including the original message of impeachment and the articles.

What right or duty has the Chief Justice connected with the trial of a *Vice President* upon whom the powers and duties of the office of President shall have devolved. *His authority* to preside is *expressly limited* to the case where the "*President* of the United States is tried."[3] If Mr. Johnson is not, in fact, President, how can the Chief Justice preside?

1. On March 4, president *pro tempore* Benjamin F. Wade had appointed Samuel Clarke Pomeroy of Kansas to a three-member committee charged with responsiblity for conducting Chase to the Senate chambers to begin the impeachment proceedings. *Trial of Andrew Johnson,* 1:10.

2. The committee actually included three members: Pomeroy, Republican Henry Wilson of Massachusetts, and Charles Rollin Buckalew (1821–99), Democratic senator from Pennsylvania, 1863–69. Ibid.; *DAB,* 3:225–26.

3. In accordance with art. 1, sec. 3, of the U.S. Constitution.

TO JOSEPH E. SNODGRASS

Letterpress copy of autograph letter. Chase Papers, Library of Congress (*micro* 37:0634).

Washington, Mar. 16, 1868

My dear Doctor,[1]

I thank you for the new proof of your old friendship which your letter affords. Those who opposed slavery & the domination of the slave power when it cost something to do so, can afford the censures of new zeal which risks nothing & may gain much.

The writer of the Antislavery Standard is unknown to me.[2] What motives prompted his misrepresentations is equally unknown, nor do I think worth while to enquire after the person or his motives. If he errs honestly he will probably see his error some time or other & be sorry for it; if dishonestly nothing can be gained by enquiry. Corrected in one he would invent another calumny.

As to the Chief Justice being the ally of Mr. Johnson it is a [flat] absurdity. Since his proclamation of a provisional government for North Carolina, in order to reconstruct on the white basis, I have been a steady opponent of his plans.[3] And I have been just as steady a friend to the Congressional policy of reconstruction so far as it contemplated equal rights for all secured by equal constitutions & laws. But I do not believe in military domination any more than I do slaveholding oligarchy: nor do I believe that any thing has been accomplished by military supremacy in the rebel states that could not have been as well if not better accomplished by civil supremacy authorized & regulated by Congress with military subordination / But I prefer even military domination for a time itself controlled & directed by Congress[,] with an honest [reference] to restoration of the states to full participation in the Government with suffrage secured to all who will not seek to withhold it from others, to any such plan as that proposed by the President.

While I have condemned the Presidents attempts to impose on the colored population of the South, the rule of the ex rebel white population, and his hostility to the Congressional reconstruction I have not thought it necessary to revile him. I do not quarrel with people about matters on which I differ from them. I like manly & frank dealing even between vehement political opponents. I have, therefore, called on the President when official propriety has required[—]three or four of these occasions have been at his request; others have been on public occasions. Once & once only have I called to know if I could friends who had done faithful service in the war. On several occasions when I have met the President public matters have been themes of conversation; & I believe I never failed in what I thought my duty on such occasions. I urged him by every argument that I could think of to abandon his opposition to Congressional reconstruction & to universal suffrage. At the last of these interviews, now, months ago, he complained of Seward & Stanton and intimated his purpose to remove them. I told him plainly what I thought of it and what the people would think of it and warned him of the danger of the avalanche.[4]

I do not deny that sympathy with him had something to do with my actions. I remembered his loyalty at the outset of the war & his patriotism all through the war and I longed to have him retrace his steps. But I could do nothing / I believe however that he sees that my purpose was an honest purpose & not stimulated by personal hostility, & therefore felt a certain degree of respect & perhaps regard for me. It was not enough to induce him to spare my friends from removal, but it led him, doubtless, to pay me the compliment of attending that reception of mine to which the correspondent referred.[5]

Now that is all of my intercourse with the President. I tell you for your own satisfaction and information. Let it go no farther. I will not defend myself against calumny except by my acts.

And in the present heated temper of the public mind I cannot hope to escape a great deal of honest censure. My duties are judicial. What I honestly believe the Constitution & laws to sanction or condemn that I must fearless sanction or condemn. I am of no party on the bench. If I believe an act or part of an act of a Republican Congress to be unconstitutional I must say so. If a man whom Republicans would gladly see condemned has rights and I must judge the rights shall be [respected]. And so of the Democrats. I expect to please neither at all times. But God helping me I will do my duty, sorry only that limited powers do not allow me to do it better.

Good bye.

Sincerely your friend
S P Chase

[Dr.] J. E. Snodgrass.

1. Chase had known Joseph Evans Snodgrass, M.D., since 1848, when he edited an antislavery newspaper in Baltimore. Snodgrass to Chase, Dec. 12, 1864 (Chase Papers, L.C.).

2. "Brandon," an author in the *National Antislavery Standard,* published his piece on March 14. "Salmon P. Chase, mad with the Presidential fever and desperate in the consciousness of baffled plans, meanly jealous of Wade, and, perhaps, cherishing the forlorn hope of a Democratic nomination, joins forces with the enemy, and stands as the Presidential ally," claimed the author; "His carping letter to the Senate, his refusal, at first, to obey the mandate to appear as its presiding officer, and his decisions of the following day, are but the first unfolding of a plot to obstruct and defeat, as far as possible, the conviction of the President."

3. Presidential reconstruction started on May 29, 1865, with proclamations that declared general amnesty and authorized North Carolina's Reconstruction. Foner, *Reconstruction,* 183.

4. Since Lincoln's death, Chase is known to have met with Andrew Johnson several times in April and once in August 1865, late in April or early May 1866, and early in August 1867. Chase to Flamen Ball, May 12, 1866; Chase to Horace Greeley, Aug. 5, 1867;

Chase to Jacob W. Schuckers, Sept. 24, 1866; Chase to Charles Sumner, Aug. [23], 1865 (all above); Chase to Kate Chase Sprague, Aug. 17, 1865 (Chase Papers, Hist. Soc. of Pa.); *Chase Papers,* 1:531, 533–34.

5. According to "Brandon," President Johnson and his daughter had attended a party that Chase held on the evening of March 4, the day before impeachment proceedings started. "Few who were present with me will soon forget the significant looks which passed from face to face through those brilliant and crowded rooms," wrote the author, "as the unusual event of the President of the United States attending an evening reception of the Chief-Justice was fully realized." *National Anti-Slavery Standard,* Mar. 14, 1868.

TO JOHN D. VAN BUREN

Copy in clerk's hand with corrections by Chase. Chase Papers, Historical Society of Pennsylvania (*micro* 37:0646).

Private.

Washington, March 25, 1868.

My dear Sir,

I return the letter which you were kind enough to send me.[1]

The disposition to which it refers will doubtless prove ephemeral, and is not, I fancy, very general.

I am neither candidate nor aspirant for any political place or distinction. I am anxious only so to discharge the duties which my office of Chief Justice imposes upon me as to secure the approval of my own conscience, and, if it may be so, that of impartial and just men.

In the excited times through which we are now, unhappily, passing, it is not to be expected that the faithful performance of these duties will meet the wishes of any party. And he who strives most earnestly so to perform them may easily make mistakes which will, by partizans, be called by a harder name.

I am prepared for all this, but one circumstance does give me some concern.

The extent of the power of the Chief Justice is vastly misconceived. In the Supreme Court he is but one of eight Judges, each of whom has the same powers as himself. His judgment has no more weight, and his vote no more importance, than those of any other of his brethren. He presides, and a good deal of extra labor is thrown upon him. Thats all.

In the Senate when the President is tried, even upon the theory of those who claim that it is his duty to vote upon all questions, he would be only one of the fifty odd Judges. Upon the theory that he simply takes the place which the Vice President fills when other civil officers are tried and has no more authority as Judge than the Vice President would have as Judge; he can only vote in the case of a tie. His duty is limited except in that case to the decision of questions of order and perhaps of incidental questions as to evidence; an important duty to be sure, but not a source of power—since every decision is subject to be overruled by the Senate.

In fact it is only as a Circuit Judge that the Chief Justice, or any other Justice of the Supreme Court has, individually, any considerable power; and even then it is not active power, but only authority to declare what the law is by which the active power of others should be regulated.

I hope that so far as it may be in your power you will set this matter right. You may do much good, and render an acceptable service to many in this way.[2]

Thanking you, as I have had many occasions before to do, for your constant kindness and personal friendship, believe me with full reciprocation of it all,

Yours very truly,
S. P. CHASE.

Col. Jno. D. Van Buren.

1. The letter, which has not been found, included a discussion of emergent support for Chase as a presidential candidate. Chase to Van Buren, June 25, 1868 (below).

2. Van Buren might have played a role preparing an article that appeared in the *New York World* on April 1 in defense of Chase's conduct. Chase to Van Buren, Apr. 5, 1868 (below).

TO MURAT HALSTEAD

Autograph letter. Misc. Mss., Chase, Salmon P., New-York Historical Society (*micro* 37:0652).

PRIVATE

Washington, March 26, 1868.

My dear Mr. Halstead,[1]

Yesterday a friend sent me a number of the Gazette in which I found greatly to my surprise a sort of ex cathedra article on my views & position. I learn from Reid today that he wrote a private letter to Smith the other day giving him briefly what he supposed to me my general notions as he gathered them from my talk; and that Smith expanded what he wrote into the Gazette Article.[2]

I have no great objection to it except that it attributes to me some assumption that I have never felt or expressed and that it undertakes to express my views when I have given no warrant to any one to speak for me; and certainly do not desire to be brought in that way before the public. I don't converse for the press.

How idle to say that "We are able to state" that democrats have talked about the nomination of the Chief Justice "without consulting his views." As if I had any business with what democrats please to talk about; or as if it were of consequence to them whether they consulted my views or not.

And then "one thing is certain & for this we have the highest authority that if the Democrats run Mr. Chase they must come to him &

stand upon his platform. He will not go to them." I certainly never gave any authority for saying this; nor ever said any thing of the sort. It is not my way of talking about men or parties.

Again;—"It may further be stated that Mr. Chase has given no encouragement whatever to the leaders who have been using his name in this connection." The form of expression carries the totally incorrect idea that it is made upon my authority & even at my instance. The fact is that no democratic leader has even thought it worth his while to speak to me on the subject; and I have had no occasion either to encourage or discourage the use of my name.

Your good opinion & constant friendship has great value for me, & I thought therefore that I would let you know exactly how this thing came about, and how unwarranted the Ex cathedra tone of the Article is. I should have had no objection to it, but for this tone. If it had purported to be a mere speculation based on a general knowledge of character it would have been very well: for in most respects it is about right.

But does Mr. Smith reflect what an immense wall he puts between my views and those which now prevail in the Republican Party when he says that I have not changed my mind as to those *military features* of the reconstruction laws? Mine for the Minimum of military government—theirs for the Maximum;—mine against the laws of war & military commissions in peace,—theirs for both: mine for restoration with universal suffrage & universal amnesty, theirs only for universal suffrage & large disenfranchisement.

The truth is that I had, as you said, ceased to think of the Presidency & was perfectly content to have my name taken out of the list of supposed candidates, & now it gives me no pleasure to see my name brought forward again.[3] I am no candidate or aspirant for any political position or distinction. I simply want to do my duty faithfully & impartially. I do not hope to please any party. I dont expect always to please myself. Still I am obliged to act, in a [new] & difficult place, and without experience. All I can say is that I will not to please any body do anything which I do not at the time of doing it believe to be fit & right to be done.

One thing I don't like. Many seem to think that the Chief Justice sitting upon the Trial of the President has some great power. The truth is he has very little. He has only that which the Vice President would have, if the Chief Justice were impeached & tried. What the extent of that power is is somewhat debated. The Constitution seems to limit it to the ordinary duties of a presiding officer extended perhaps to the decision of questions of evidence. And this limitation has the sanction of the practice in every case hitherto tried. Thus limited he can only vote when there is a tie & not at all on the final question: and every decision he makes on order or evidence is subject to be overruled by the Court.

And I am inclined to the opinion that this is the correct view. So I may see much that I disapprove without any power to correct it

I leave much unsaid; but must take room to congratulate you on the suppression of Myers.[4]

Cordially your friend
S P Chase

1. Halstead, a Republican, owned and edited the *Cincinnati Commercial*. *DAB*, 8:163.
2. Whitelaw Reid was apparently in Washington to report on impeachment proceedings for the *Cincinnati Gazette*, in which Richard Smith owned an interest. The article discussed "talk" among "leading" Democrats about Chase as the presidential nominee of their party. "To use Mr. Chase as the candidate of that party would require a radical change in his principles or in the principles of the men who now represent the Democratic part of this country.," claimed the piece. Ibid., 15:483; *Appletons'*, 5:584; *Cincinnati Daily Gazette*, Mar. 23, 1868.
3. The *Cincinnati Commercial* supported Chase as the Democratic presidential nominee, leaving "The question to be decided whether the Democracy have the sagacity to accept the situation and the leader, adapt themselves to the times, and recognize in Chase the coming man." *Cincinnati Commercial*, Mar. 23, 1868.
4. On January 22, Halstead's paper had accused Cincinnati attorney M. W. Myers of bribing the city council to secure Covington, Kentucky, a contract for municipal water. Soon after publication, Myers filed a libel suit, which had recently resulted in a hung jury. *Cincinnati Commercial*, Mar. 21, 22, 1868.

FROM CHARLES G. HALPINE

Autograph letter on letterhead stationery. Charles Graham Halpine Collection (#7719), Clifton Waller Barrett Library, Special Collections Department, University of Virginia Library (*micro* 37:0660).

REGISTER'S OFFICE,
HALL OF RECORDS.
City and County of New York.
April 1st. 1868.

My dear Chief Justice:[1] I have the honor to acknowledge the receipt of your letter dated the 26th. instant, which has just come to hand; and thank you very respectfully for the same. The points given in it shall be used to such advantage as I can put them, in your interest; but their source shall be kept as private as you wish—indeed, as they would have been without your warning of "strictly private" at the top. Let me say that, in conversation with Mayor Hoffman half an hour ago, he expressed his conviction that the Demc. & conservative party would have "to unite on Chase as their only hope of success"—and this from Hoffman is important; as he is only a tube through which more important organ-players whistle popular music.[2] Certainly the *Herald* has not been unfriendly to you of late—I mean within the past fortnight; as I have written nearly all the articles in which your name occurred: and I further know Mr. Bennett wishes you to be pressed for the Presidency: but he is so fitfull and uncertain that I could not find myself for his continuing steadfast to this or any other programme.[3] Greeley, I know, for he told me so at dinner yesterday week, is deeply chagrined at the apparent necessity ("a necessity of bad faith & cowardice", was my rejoinder,) which makes Grant the Radical nominee; for I tell you frankly, and indeed have so said in my paper, that as between Chase for the Radicals and Pendleton for the Democrats,—there are 25,000 Democrats in this City alone who would vote for Chase,—myself included.[4] That Pendleton himself will be nominated, I do not think; but the contest will lie in our Convention between some equivalent for Pendleton—some man of his or similar antecedents & present platform—and the more loyal and moderate Conservatives who will (I hope,) press your name, or some name of your equivalent. To win, we must get back the old free-soil vote, represented by the *Evening Post,* (Wm. Cullen Bryant & Parke Godwin,)[5] in this City; and to win back that free-soil Democratic element, your name is certainly the most available we have offered. With kindest & most respectful remembrances to Mrs. Sprague & the Governor,

Believe me always to remain,

Your Obliged friend & Servant
CHAS. G. HALPINE

Hon Salmon P. Chase
Chief Justice United States.

1. Halpine, a famous Civil War journalist, had gained prominence as a Democratic political reformer and editor of the reform journal *Citizen* after retiring from the army in 1864. In 1866, he successfully ran against Tammany Hall, gaining election as register of the County and City of New York. *DAB,* 8:161.

2. John T. Hoffman was the Democratic governor of New York.

3. Recent articles in the *New York Herald,* the paper of James Gordon Bennet, Sr., tended to support Chase's role in the impeachment proceedings, but disparaged as "silly talk" suggestions that Chase run as the Democratic presidential nominee. "Mr. Chase would do as the candidate of an intermediate party," claimed the *Herald* on March 29, "but a jump at once from the radical to the democratic camp is out of the question." *New York Herald,* Mar. 22, 23, 28, 29, 1868.

4. George Hunt Pendleton, a former Cincinnati congressman, was a Peace Democrat during the Civil War and George McClellan's vice-presidential running mate in the election of 1864. Pendleton had recently fallen out of favor with eastern Democrats for advocating redemption of 5–20 bonds in greenbacks rather than coin. *DAB,* 14:420.

5. William Cullen Bryant, a former Free Soil Democrat, edited the *New York Evening Post* with his son-in-law, Parke Godwin. Ibid., 3:203.

TO GERRIT SMITH

Autograph letter. Chase Papers, Library of Congress (*micro* 37:0663).

Washington, Apl. 2, 1868

My dear friend,

Thanks for your generous words addressed to Mr. Tilton. They do me good. May God help me to justify your confidence[1]

The subject of the Presidency has become distasteful to me. Some will say, "Sour grapes:" and there may be some ground for the application of the proverb.[2] But I really think that I am not half so ambitious of place as I am represented to be. Certainly I never used any of the ordinary means to get place. I worked for ideas & principles & measures embodying them, & with all citizens of like faith & aims; and was always quite willing to take place or be left out of place as the cause, in the judgment of its friends required. And I am certainly entirely content now to be left out of consideration in connexion with the Presidency

My desire at present is perform the duties of President of the Senate sitting as a Court of Impeachment faithfully & impartially. My constant prayer is for guidance & strength, for wisdom & courage; and I trust I shall be kept from making any serious mistakes.

My position is peculiarly difficult. As the Chief Justice my whole duties, except in the single case of impeachment, connect me with another body. Coming into the Senate to preside I feel and am felt as a sort of foreign element. The Senate like all other bodies has a good deal of Esprit de Corps. I as Chief Justice look for my powers & duties in the Constitution and very naturally find myself disagreeing as to their nature & extent from many senators. So far these differences have been attended by no disagreeable results. The majority has substantially sustained my views & I have tried to avoid every claim which could be, as I thought [fairly] called in question.

Mr. Sumner's motion yesterday alarmed me.[3] The question at once forced itself upon me "What will be my duty in case the Senate by denying to me the casting vote which belongs to the President of the Senate sitting as a Court of Impeachment refuses in effect to recognize my right to preside. Happily I was not compelled to decide this question.

I hope that your health is good, & that you are enjoying your delightful home. How I should like to drop in upon you.

I suppose Col. & Mrs Miller are abroad. Your son, I presume, is with you.[4] I shall like to have you write me more about yourself & your family goings on.[5]

1. The March 19 edition of Theodore Tilton's *Independent* had included an allusion to "great temptations" that might deter Chase from impartial justice in the impeachment proceedings. "As well may it be feared that Heaven will be transmuted into Hell as that Chase will lose his integrity," responded Smith the following week. *Independent,* March 19, 26, 1868.

2. In Aesop's fable, "The Fox and the Grapes," the fox pretends not to want grapes beyond his reach, claiming that they are "sour." *Aesop's Fables* (New York, 1941), 51.

3. Charles Sumner had introduced measures on March 31 and April 1 that would have disqualified the chief justice from voting on any question in the trial or to break a tie. The Senate defeated both proposals. *Trial of Andrew Johnson,* 1:185–88.

4. Elizabeth Smith Miller and Charles Dudley Miller were Smith's daughter and son-in-law. Gerrit Smith's son was Green Smith.

5. A letterpress copy in the Chase Papers at the Library of Congress shows the signature and receiver's name.

TO JOHN D. VAN BUREN

Copy in clerk's hand with interlineation by Chase. Chase Papers, Historical Society of Pennsylvania (*micro* 37:0669).

Washington, April 5, 1868.

My dear Sir,

I see nothing in the article you sent me to object to; but am much obliged both to Mr. Marble and yourself for it. It will do much to disabuse the public.[1] Here my position is well understood; and no one, on either side, except perhaps a few over zealous partizans, desires or expects anything of me except the honest and impartial discharge of my duties as presiding officer. In this expectation, I trust no one will be disappointed.

In the McCardle case I agreed with all the Judges except two (Grier and Field), who have made public their dissent, that it would not become the Supreme Court to *hasten* their decision of an appeal for the purpose of getting ahead of the legislation of Congress.[2] The Constitution gives the Supreme Court jurisdiction on appeals only "with such exceptions and under such regulations as the Congress shall make."[3] Congress, therefore, had the undoubted right to except such cases as that of McCardle from its appellate jurisdiction; and it would have been, as we thought, an indecency to run a race in the exercise of *that* jurisdiction with the Legislature.

Whether Congress can *oust* an appeal already taken and perfected is another question. There are cases which support this view; but I should have been glad to have had the question argued. I was not present when it was decided to postpone the argument of it to the next term, having been necessarily absent in the Court of Impeachment all the week. I had previously proposed an adjournment to June, but met no support.

It was especially desirable to me to have the case decided; for it is highly probable that I shall meet the question on the Circuit; and I should feel better if I had a decision to guide and support me.

As to the North Carolina case no one, I think, will now doubt, that had I been in the District when the process of the Court was interfered with by the military, the judicial authority would have been maintained.[4] I hardly think that Gen. Sickles would have arrested me for directing the commencement of the usual criminal proceedings against the officer who resisted the process. Certainly no fear of the consequences would have deterred me from the performance of my duty.

Most earnestly do I long for the complete restoration of peace and union. I see no practical choice except between restoration on the basis of universal suffrage and universal amnesty, and restoration on the basis of universal suffrage for the blacks[5] and partial suffrage and partial disfranchisement of the whites. My own judgment is that all ought to be allowed to vote, and that everybody ought to be willing to allow the right to everybody else. If Mr. Johnson had insisted on this, we should have escaped all our present trouble. If this disposition could now be wrought into the Southern mind, peace and prosperity would speedily return, and intellect and character would again be welcomed to the lead. Is this too much to hope for?

Sincerely and Cordially yours,
S. P. Chase.

Col. John D. Van Buren.

1. Manton Malone Marble (1835–1917) was owner and editor of the *New York World.* On April 1, the newspaper carried an editorial that defended Chase's impartiality as presiding officer in the impeachment proceedings and as a Supreme Court justice, especially in the case of *Ex parte Garland,* which Benjamin F. Butler, a Republican congressman since 1867, had assailed during the impeachment trial on March 31. *DAB,* 12:267.

2. The Supreme Court had taken *Ex parte McCardle* under advisement on March 9, pending a proposal in Congress to revoke the habeas corpus legislation of February 5, 1867, that had enabled McCardle to make his appeal. The Court dismissed the case on April 12, 1869, after passage of the measure. A report in the *Daily National Intelligencer,* March 30, 1868, identified Stephen J. Field and Robert C. Grier as the only adversaries to the postponement. Fairman, *Reconstruction and Reunion,* 467–81, 492.

3. Art. 3, sec. 2.

4. Chase discussed the case in correspondence to Daniel Sickles on September 19, 1867 (above).

5. The phrase *for the blacks* was inserted as an interlineation.

TO ALEXANDER LONG

Autograph letter. Alexander Long Papers, Cincinnati Historical Society (*micro* 37:0677).

Private & confidential

Washington, Apl 8. 1868.

My dear Sir,[1]

Your letter marked "strictly confidential" has been received. You hardly need any assurance that the injunction will be scrupulously observed.[2]

It would please me to know the author of the article you enclosed: and it does please me to be assured that you have no regrets for the part you took in my election to the Senate in 1849. If you will turn to the Congl. Globe Debates in the Senate of Apl. 9, 1853 you will find the view I took of that election and its results; which will, I think, interest you now.[3] It may interest you, also, to read again, if you have ever read it at all, my letter to Mr. Breslin on the subject of Union between the Old Line & the Independent democracy written during the summer after that election. You will find it in the Congressional Globe 1849–50 Part 1, p. 135. You will see, if you read Mr. Butler's Speech, especially its second paragraph, & what immediately follows the letter, that he feared that Union.[4] It is in my belief today that if that Union had taken place all our calamities would have been avoided; or if, that be too strong, that civil war & national debts would at least have been escaped; and yet that universal freedom would have been assured, if not as soon, yet without very great delay & with the concurrence of the States most interested.

Nothing would now gratify me more than to see the Democracy turn away from past issues, & take for its mottoes, Suffrage for all; amnesty for all; good money for all; & security for all citizens, at home against military despotism and abroad against governmental invasion.

But I am neither aspirant nor candidate myself. I want no more political distinction or position. All I desire is courage & wisdom to do my immediate duty, now & in the future.

Very truly yours
S P Chase

Hon. Alexander Long.

1. A former Ohio legislator, Long represented his state in Congress from 1863 to 1865. In 1868, he served as a delegate to the Democratic National Convention. *Bio. Dir. U.S. Cong.*, 1386.

2. Long had written on April 6, enclosing a letter to the editor of *West and South,* a Democratic newspaper from Cincinnati, that endorsed Chase as the party's presidential candidate. "I believe that the nomination of Mr. Chase as the sole candidate in opposition to Gen. Grant, besides affording a fair assurance of a constitutional President, will also afford a fair assurance of a constitutional House of Representatives," wrote "R."; "I believe that it is the only way in which such an assurance can be realized." Long's own letter offered additional encouragement: "I have never found it necessary, publicly or otherwise, to ask God to forgive me for my votes in the Ohio Legislature in the winter of 1848–9," he wrote in regard to Chase's first senatorial election, "and I shall not be in the least disappointed now to See the whole party unfurl the banner under which a few of us then marched, wheel into line and become enthusiastic in being lead to victory by a general they have so long and so often denounced as well as the few men who assisted in giving him his first position." Stephen Gutgesell, ed., *Guide to Ohio Newspapers, 1793–1973: Union Bibliography of Ohio Newspapers Available in Ohio Libraries* (Columbus, 1974), 87; Long to Chase, Apr. 6, 1868 (Long Papers, Cinc. Hist. Soc.); *West and South,* Apr. 4, 1868.

3. Long later informed Chase that the author was Cincinnati journalist Henry Reed. Chase's victory in 1849 had resulted from a controversial arrangement between a handful of antislavery Free-Soil Ohio legislators, who held a balance of power, and their more numerous Democratic counterparts. On April 9, 1853, California senator John B. Weller had attacked the arrangment as "a dishonorable bargain." "I have ever preferred—and all the acts of my life will prove it," countered Chase, "action with a minority in defense of principles, to action with a majority, and to any position which a majority can confer, in disregard of principles." *Congressional Globe,* 32d Cong., 3d. sess., 1852–53, appendix, 328, 329; Long to Chase, Apr. 11, 1868 (Long Papers, Cinc. Hist. Soc.). For more on the election, see *Chase Papers,* 2:213–19, 222.

4. John G. Breslin was speaker of the Ohio House on July 30, 1849, the date of Chase's letter. "I am a democrat, unreservedly," wrote Chase, "and I feel earnestly solicitous for the success of the democratic organization and the triumph of its principles." Chase read the letter from the Senate floor on January 10, 1850. Senator Andrew Pickens Butler of South Carolina responded that Chase and other antislavery Independent Democrats intended to "proscribe the South, or to presume on desertion and treason." *Chase Papers,* 2:249–52; *Congressional Globe,* 31st Cong., 1st sess., 1850, 135–36.

TO THEODORE TILTON

Autograph draft. Chase Papers, Historical Society of Pennsylvania (*micro* 37:0679).

Washington, Apl. 9, 1868.

My dear Mr. Tilton,

You asked last evening for the points on which I have found myself in disagreement with a number of Senators since the House determined on the impeachment of the President: and perhaps I cannot use an hour better than in giving you a brief account of this disagreement, not for the press, but for your own information if not satisfaction.[1]

On the Friday 21st of Feby. Mr. Stanton communicated to the House of Representatives the letter of the President removing him from the office of Secy of War and notifying him of the appt. of Gen Thomas ad interim. C. Globe 1867–8 p 1326[2]

On the same day a resolution for impeachment was introduced by Covode & referred to the Reconstruction Committee

Ib. 1329-30[3]

On Saturday the 22d. the Reconstruction Committee made their report. It embodied the President's letter, of removal (Feb. 21 '68) to Stanton and his letter of appointment of the same date to Thomas & concluded with a resolution of impeachment.[4]

There was debate until late Saturday night or sometime Sunday C.G. 1360 m.c. Morng when the House took a *recess* till Monday at 10: and adjourned the Saturdays Session at one minute before 12 on Monday the 24th & at [once] resumed its Session & [contd.] the debates[5]
At 5 P.M. under the p. q. the resolution was adopted; C.G. 1400 m.c. & immediately thereafter, under that p. q. & a resolution suspending the rules & interdicting [dilatory] motions, two other resolutions one for the appt. of a Com of two to impeach the Prest. at the bar of the Senate & the other for a Committee of Seven to prepare & report articles of impeachment were forced through.[6]

On the next day Tuesday the 25th the Committee of two Stevens & Bingham appeared in the Senate, & formally impeached the President of high crimes & misdemeanors in Office & notified the Senate that the H.R would exhibit articles & demanded that the Senate take order for the appearance of the President to answer

No notice of this appearance had been given to the Senate; it was not organized for the trial of an impeachment; the Prest. pro tempore[7] was in the chair; & he, who could not under the Constitution preside in the trial, answered for the Senate, "the Senate will take order in the premises."

Thereupon Mr. Howard moved the reference of the Message of the House to a Select Committee of Seven to consider & report thereon.[8]

Mr. Bayard at once called the attention of the Senate to the fact that the Senate had no authority to act as a legislative body in relation to a question of impeachment; that the first step on receiving notice of [an] intended impeachment, in which light he considered the communication from the House, was to to resolve the Senate into a Court, with, in this case, the Chief Justice presiding[9]

1. The House passed resolutions of impeachment on February 24. *Trial of Andrew Johnson,* 1:2–3.

2. The letter that appointed Lorenzo Thomas as secretary of war *ad interim* actually appeared on pages 1326–27.

3. Congressman John Covode represented Pennsylvania. Members of the House Committee on Reconstruction included Fernando Cortez Beaman (1814–82) of Michigan, James Burnie Beck (1822–90) of Kentucky, Ohio congressman John A. Bingham, Massachusetts congressman George S. Boutwell, James Brooks of New York, Illinois congressman John Franklin Farnsworth (1820–97), New York congressman Calvin Tilden Hulburd (1809–97), and Halbert Eleazer Paine (1826–1905) of Wisconsin. *Bio. Dir. U.S. Cong.,* 594–95, 596, 1229; *DAB,* 3:77–78, 14:148–49, 16:284–85.

4. *Congressional Globe,* 40th Cong., 2d sess., 1867–68, 105.

5. Ibid., 1360, 1369, 1382.

6. "P.q." is an abbreviation for "privileged question." Thaddeus Stevens and John A. Bingham constituted the committee of two. The other congressional committee was composed of John A. Bingham, George S. Boutwell, George W. Julian of Indiana, John Alexander Logan (1826–86) of Illinois, Thaddeus Stevens, New York congressman Hamilton Ward (1829–98), and James F. Wilson. Ibid., 1400–1402; *Bio. Dir. U.S. Cong.,* 2006; *DAB,* 11:363–64.

7. Benjamin F. Wade.

8. Members of the committee formed at the request of Michigan senator Jacob M. Howard were Roscoe Conkling, George Franklin Edmunds of Vermont, Howard himself, Reverdy Johnson, Oliver Hazard Perry Throck Morton of Indiana, Samuel C. Pomeroy, and Lyman Trumbull. *Congressional Globe,* 40th Cong., 2d sess., 1867–68, 1406.

9. Senator James Asheton Bayard represented Delaware. The Senate adopted rules for the court of impeachment on March 2 and started proceedings on March 5, with Chase presiding. Ibid., 1568–1603; *Trial of Andrew Johnson,* 1:6, 12–15.

FROM TIMOTHY O. HOWE

Autograph letter. Chase Papers, Library of Congress (*micro* 37:0592).

Monday P.M.[1]

Sir[2]

For the first time since this trial Commenced, so far as I remember, I addressed to You as the Presiding Officer, a few moments since a question[3]

I put the question in entire good faith

I wished to be made certain as to whether the record showed that a Certain fact had been put in evidence by one Side or the other—I thought the question material to a correct decision of the pending question—

Certainly if the *Managers* had proved that the Office of Secy ad interim had been tendered by the President to Genl Sherman *I* should hold it Competent for respondent to prove what was said at the time[4]

But if that fact was put in evidence by the respondent I thought they could not prove accompanying declarations—

Manifestly then it was important to my vote that I should know how the record stood—

You broadly insinuated to the Court & the Auditors that my question as to the State of the record was an Argument upon the record—[5] In that, You did me injustice which I must believe was not intended & which I hope you will correct—

I am

Very Respy

Yours

T. O. Howe

Hon S. P. Chase

1. According to the impeachment record, the incident described below occurred on April 13, 1868. *Trial of Andrew Johnson,* 1:520.

2. Howe was a senator from Wisconsin.

3. Proceedings started formally on March 5, but opening arguments were not delivered until March 30. *Trial of Andrew Johnson,* 1:11, 87.

4. The issue at hand was the admissibility of a question posed to William T. Sherman, a witness supposedly offered the post of secretary of war. Howe had asked "whether the fact that this office was tendered to the witness on the stand was a fact put in by the defence or by the prosecution. My own recollection," he explained, " is not very distinct about it, and I am not sure that I am right." Ibid., 1:520.

5. "The Chief Justice must remind the senator that no debate is in order unless there be a motion to retire for conference," warned Chase. Ibid., 1:520.

TO ALEXANDER LONG

Autograph letter. Alexander Long Papers, Cincinnati Historical Society (*micro* 37:0685).

Washington, Apl. 19, 1868

My dear Sir,

My reply to your last note has been somewhat delayed. My time as you may readily imagine is much occupied.[1]

It appears to me quite unlikely that such a union, as is essential to success, can be brought about among those who agree in opposition to military commissions and military ascendancy in the government.

The Democratic Party, no doubt, could ensure such a union by proclaiming anew its old creed of Equal & Exact Justice for all men and declaring itself for the full restoration of the States, now unrepresented, on the basis of universal suffrage & universal amnesty, but against military government & military commissions, & the whole train of related doctrines such as State suicide, State subjugation, confiscation and the like. Of such a union, so brought about I should certainly desire the success. I should wish as earnestly now as I did in 1849 for the success of the Democracy united on such a basis. I could not wish otherwise & be faithful to my antecedents.

With these sentiments I should not be at liberty to refuse the use of my name on the contingency you refer to. I see, however, very slight indications that such a contingency will occur; and I have, certainly, no desire for a nomination. I greatly prefer to remain disconnected from all political responsibilities save that of casting my vote.

I have no doubt however that such a union as you desire would be attended with complete success. Nor is there any reason stronger than prejudice why it should not take place. The restoration of the Southern States on the basis of universal suffrage is now certain. Every one of them will have adopted constitutions, recognizing the right of every citizen, not disfranchised, to vote before the present Congress ends;[2]—most of them certainly & all of them probably before the Presidential election. The United Democracy, frankly conceding the permanence of these Constitutions & the rights of suffrage secured by them, and appealing to the sentiments of justice and generosity & enlightened interest for universal amnesty & the removal of all political disfranchisements, would carry two thirds if not more of these States: whereas, without the union suggested & upon the antiquated issues the Democratic Party can hardly hope to carry one of them, and its success seems impossible.

But enough of this. The impeachment draws to an end. The arguments will probably be concluded this week. Whether the Senate will proceed at once to vote or take time for conference & deliberation no one can say. The course thus far pursued would indicate an immediate vote. I hazard no conjucture as to the result but I think it safe to say that if the vote were deferred for six weeks, until after the Chicago nomination, conviction would be impossible.[3]

The Senate in my opinion, made its gravest & most injurious mistake yesterday, when it refused to receive the testimony of the Heads of the Departments.[4]

Under his oath to *preserve, protect* & *defend* the Constitution,[5] the President is bound to disregard an act of Congress which, in his honest judgment, attacks and impairs the Executive power confided to him by the Constitution, at least so far as may be necessary in order to obtain a judicial determination of the question of its constitutionality. If he is right in his judgment it is Congress that violates the Constitution in passing the act;—not the President who disregards it for such a purpose. Otherwise we have a despotism under the worst possible form—that of the hydra.

The President then if he honestly believed the tenure of office act unconstitutional committed no misdemeanor but performed a duty, in in disregarding it in order to obtain a judicial decision; and it was his clear right to put in evidence of the sincerity of his belief & of the purpose of his action; and certainly no evidence on these points could be so valuable as that of the Heads of the Departments, with whom he advised on the whole subject, if not on the particular act charged.

Necessarily therefore I held the evidence admissible & was surprised by its exclusion. It is difficult to see how Senators who voted for its admission can reconcile themselves to vote for conviction. But many things do take place of which one may say the same thing.

I am glad to know who wrote the article you enclosed to me / I greatly honor Mr. Reeds abilities & his independence of thought, & wish I could give him some better evidence of it than words.[6]

But I must close this already too long letter—remaining,

Very truly yours,
S: P: CHASE

Hon. Alexander Long.

1. On April 11, Long had responded to Chase's letter of April 8 (above). "Thousands of anxious hearts are instinctively turning to you," he asserted in regard to the Democratic presidential nomination; "Would it not be a duty you owe to your country, to the cause of freedom, free government and civil liberty, to accept?" Long's letter proposed a united Democratic movement behind Chase, "with the constitution for a platform and amnesty for all, good money for all, Security for all citizens at home against military despotism and abroad against governmental invasion." Long to Chase, Apr. 11, 1868 (Long Papers, Cinc. Hist. Soc.).

2. The second session of the Fortieth Congress ended on November 10. By then, Congress had voted to restore seven southern states to the Union: Tennessee (July 24, 1866); Arkansas (June 22, 1868); and Alabama, Florida, Louisiana, North Carolina, and South Carolina (all June 25, 1868). In 1870, Congress voted to readmit Virginia (January 26), Mississippi (February 23), Texas (March 30), and Georgia (July 15). Each state was required to ratify the Fourteenth Amendment prior to readmission, in accordance with the First Reconstruction Act. *Bio. Dir. U.S. Cong.*, 183; *Statutes at Large,* 14:364, 428–29; 15:72–74; 16:62–63, 67–68, 80–81, 363–64.

3. The final vote—in favor of aquittal—occurred on May 16. The Republican party held its national convention in Chicago, May 20–21. Chase to Clark Williams, May 16, 1868 (below); *Chicago Tribune,* May 21, 22, 1868; *Trial of Andrew Johnson,* 2:486–87.

4. The Senate rejected the admissibility of the testimony as evidence by a vote of 20–29. *Trial of Andrew Johnson,* 1:693.

5. Art. 2, sec. 1.

6. In his letter of April 11, Long had identified jounalist Henry Reed as the writer of the article from the April 4 edition of *West and South,* sent to Chase on April 6. Chase to Long, Apr. 8 (above), Long to Chase, Apr. 11 (Long Papers, Cinc. Hist. Soc.).

TO GERRIT SMITH

Autograph letter. Chase Papers, Library of Congress (*micro* 37:0688).

Washington, April 19, 1868

My dear friend,

Many thanks for your two kind notes & for the article on the casting vote in which you so admirably stated the true doctrine.[1] Nettie also desires to thank you in her own behalf for your remembrance of her & I enclose her note.

The trial of the President draws towards its end. The evidence will doubtless be closed tomorrow & it is not improbable that the first speech on the part of the Managers will be made. If the Senate adheres to its resolution to allow only two arguments on each side I do not see how the discussion can be protracted beyond the week, unless the Senate retire for consultation among themselves

To me the whole business seems wrong: and if I had any option under the Constitution I would not take part in it. But the President is on trial & the Constitution is express that "when the President is tried the Chief Justice shall preside."[2]

Nothing is clearer to my mind than that acts of Congress not warranted by the Constitution are not laws. In case a law, believed by the President to be unconstitutional, is passed, notwithstanding his veto, by the requisite two thirds majority, it seems to me that it is duty to execute it precisely as if he held it to be constitutional, except in the case where it directly attacks & impairs the Executive power confided to him by the Constitution. In that case it seems to me to be the clear duty of the President to disregard the law, so far at least as may be necessary in order to bring the question of its constitutionality before the Judicial Tribunals.

Until the late rebellion a broad distinction was always made between the oath of office required of the President & the oath required of other officers. That of the President is prescribed by the Constitution itself: "I do solemnly swear that I will faithfully execute the office of President of the United States & will to the best of my ability *preserve, protect* and *defend* the Constitution of the United States. That of other officers was prescribed by law—the first ever enacted under the Constitution—& follows almost literally its direction "I do solemnly swear that that I will *support* the Constitution of the United States.[3]

The Test oath Act of 1862 introduced for the first time into the oath to be administered to other officers than the President the word "defend" in addition to the word "support".[4]

How can the President fulfil his oath to preserve, protect & defend the Constitution, if he has no *right* to *defend* it against an act of Congress sincerely believed by him to have been passed in violation of it?

To me therefore it seems perfectly clear that the President had a perfect right & indeed was under the highest obligation to remove Mr. Stanton, if he made the removal, not in wanton disregard of of a Constitutional law, but with a sincere belief that the Tenure of Office Act was unconstitutional & for the purpose of bringing the question of its Constitutionality before the Supreme Court. Plainly it was a proper & peaceful, if not the only proper & peaceful mode of protecting & defending the the Constitution.

I was greatly disappointed & grieved, therefore, when the Senate, yesterday, excluded the evidence of the Members of the Cabinet as to their consultations & decisions, (in some of which Mr. Stanton took a concurring part,) and the advice given by them to the President in pursuance thereof.[5] I could not conceive of evidence more proper to be received or more appropriate to enlighten a Court as to the intent with which the act was done: and accordingly ruled that it was admissible.

The vote, I fear, indicated a purpose which, if carried into effect, will not satisfy the American People, unless they are prepared to admit that Congress is above the Constitution

Have you looked at the questions, whether in the event of conviction the President pro tempore of the Senate is an "officer" who under the Constitution can "*act* as President"? & whether if such an "officer" he must *remain* such while acting as President? My own mind answers the last question in the affirmative & inclines to a negative answer to the first—

It seems to me that you ought to give the public the American view of these questions, if you can find time to consider them.

Faithfully & affectionately your friend
S P Chase

P.S. I suppose you have seen Mr. Tilton's "folded banner.[6] He came to Washington some ten days or two weeks ago & sought a conversation with me and I talked freely with him. I dare say he thought that what I said warranted the opinions he expressed. I do not: but if it did it was certainly an abuse of hospitality to build & publish such conclusions on the basis of a private conversation.[7]

1. Smith's recent publication, *Has the Chief Justice a Casting Vote?* (Peterboro, N.Y., 1868), cited evidence from the Constitution to answer its leading question in the affirmative.

2. Art. 1, sec. 3.

3. The president's oath is included in art. 2, sec. 1, of the U.S. Constitution. Congress mandated the oath for other officers in legislation of June 1, 1789. *Statutes at Large,* 1:23.

4. The bill became law on July 2, 1862. Ibid., 12:502.

5. Chase elaborated on this point in correspondence of the same date to Alexander Long (above).

6. In "A Folded Banner," an editorial that appeared in the *Independent* of April 16, Theodore Tilton renounced his support for Chase as a presidential candidate. "We now have reason to believe that Mr. Chase would not accept the Republication nomination, even if it were tendered," wrote Tilton; "We have equal reason to believe, also, that he would accept the Democratic nomination, if it could be tendered on a platform not inconsistent with his well-known views of Negro suffrage." In Tilton's view, the *Independent* had "no right any longer to solicit the Republican party to unfurl at their head the banner of his name."

7. Chase explained himself at greater length in a letter to Tilton written on the same date (below).

TO THEODORE TILTON

Copy by Jacob W. Schuckers. Chase Papers, Historical Society of Pennsylvania (*micro* 37:0691).

Strictly private.

Washington, Ap'l 19, 1868.

Dear Sir,

Your article, under the caption "A Folded Banner," was very different from anything which your conversation with me foreshadowed.

You visited me at my house and invited a conversation. I was glad to see you as I have always been; and my esteem for you and trust in you were such that I talked with you very freely. I little thought that I was on trial before an Editor, and that he was about to pronounce a sentence upon me, *ex cathedra,* according to the supposed result of his investigations. Had I been aware of that I should, probably, have followed a great military example and observed a prudent silence.[1]

I had seen, with perfect content, so far as I was concerned, the Republican preference concentrating upon General Grant. I had observed also new shibboleths of republican faith invited and demanded, in the hot contentions of the time, which I could not frame my lips to pronounce. I felt, therefore, that whatever might be my obligation to support Republican candidates because of my agreement with the majority of the party on the great point of equal rights protected by equal suffrage, I could not myself properly represent it as its candidate. And so I said to you that I could not take the Republican nomination if I could have it. I knew I could not have it, even were General Grant out of the way, if I proclaimed my opinions on impeachment, military commissions, military government, and the like; and I wanted no nomination with concealed or unavowed opinions, and, indeed, wanted no nomination at all. For this reason, I said I would not take the Republican nomination if I could have it. I had said it to nobody else. I said it to you because I felt like saying it, and thought you knew me well enough to believe me.— I certainly never dreamed of a proclamation by you in The Independent based upon it. I knew very well that everybody who should think I had made such a declaration to you, and did not know me intimately, would characterize it, coming as it must have come, from one who had not and knew he had not the least chance of receiving the nomination, in very uncomplimentary terms.

I was still more surprised by your confident expression of opinion that I would accept the Democratic nomination. I refused to say to you that I would not accept it. But I did not say that I would, nor did I say anything to that effect. I have never sought or expected it. I have never thought it in the least degree likely that it would be offered to me. It would have been ridiculous in me to say that I would not accept what had not been offered, and was not likely to be. It would have savoured strongly of a vanity and presumption justly offensive, and from which, at least, I hope I am free.

What you said led me to suppose that you agreed with me in opinion that the Chief Justice presiding in the Senate has the same right as the Vice President when presiding in that body, and I expressed a wish that you would express that opinion in The Independent. You said you would and your article does contain a sentence to that effect.

For this and for your declaration that I am not likely to abandon any of the ideas and principles on which I suppose your former preference for me was based, I beg you to accept my thanks. I regret that you saw fit to withdraw that preference with such a flourish of trumpets. You might have said with truth that I was neither candidate nor aspirant for any nomination; and that the Independent did not think it useful to urge any further consideration of my name. I do not think you had any right to make any other inference from my conversation with you; and if the conversation did warrant any other inference by you I do not think you had a right to use a private conversation for that purpose.

I write frankly just as I spoke frankly. I do not believe that you will hereafter reflect with complacency upon your article. But I do not desire to have another written based on this note, *which is exclusively for your personal information, and not for that of the readers of the Independent.* I am content to be read out of the Republican party. I can afford to be, so long as I retain my old principles and my old fidelity to the cause of the oppressed and the needy. I regret only that Theodore Tilton took upon himself the office of reader, and that he read the sentence in a way which, taken in connexion with the *leaded* and leading article of some weeks ago and his remarks to me concerning it, strikes me as peculiarly ungracious and unwarranted.

And so I remain, regretfully yours,
S. P. Chase.

Theodore Tilton Esqr.

1. Tilton's editorial appeared in the April 16 *Independent.* Chase's correspondence to Tilton of April 9 (above) suggests that the visit occurred on the evening of April 8. Chase also expressed outrage over the editorial in his letter of April 19 to Gerrit Smith (above).

TO HENRY W. HILLIARD

Autograph letter. Chase Papers, Library of Congress (*micro* 37:0696).

Washington, Apl. 27, 1868

Dear Sir,[1]

Some days since I received, from an unknown hand a paper containing a letter of yours which I read with great interest

My acquaintance with you when we were both in Congress, you in the House and I in the Senate was very slight; but slight as it was I take occasion from it to write you a few lines suggested by your letter.

Ever since the war closed I have been very anxious for the earliest practicable "restoration of the states of the South to their proper relations to the other states of the Union." I adopt your own statement of the problem to be worked out; because I agree with you in the opinion that "these states have never been other than states within the Union since they became parties to the federal government"; & that "the several ordinances of secession were only so many declarations of independence"; and that the failure "to maintain their assertion of independence, in the conflict of arms that followed left those states still within the Union."

The point on which I probably differ from you is this: the people for whom & through whom these states were to be reorganized at the close of the war was not the same people as that which existed in them when the war began.

In my judgment the refusal of the proprietary class, if it may be so called, to recognize this *fact* with its legitimate and, indeed, logical consequences, and the convictions of large majorities in the states which adhered to the National Government in respect to it, has caused most of the trouble of the last three years.

I have not time to go at large into this subject; but I may say briefly that emancipation came to be regarded by these majorities as a military necessity; that the faith of the nation was pledged by the proclamation of Emancipation to maintain the emancipated in people in the possession & enjoyment of the freedom it conferred; that to this end the amendment of the Constitution prohibiting slavery throughout the United States was proposed & ratified; that, becoming freemen, the emancipated people became necessarily citizens; and that as citizens they were entitled to be consulted in respect to reorganization & to the means of self protection by suffrage.

This is a very brief but I think a perfectly correct statement of what may be called, for the sake of brevity, the northern view of this matter. It would perhaps be more correct to call it the loyal view north & south, using the word loyal as distinguishing the masses who supported the national government from the masses who opposed it during the war.

Now the particular matter to which I wish to draw your attention is whether policy & duty do not require the class which I have called proprietary, meaning thereby the educated & cultivated, men of the south whether property holders or not, to accept this view fully & act upon it.

Is it possible to doubt that, had this view been accepted and acted upon three years ago after the surrender of Lee & Johnson,[2] the southern states would have been richer by hundreds of millions, & that long ago universal amnesty & the removal of all disabilities would have prepared the hearts of men on both sides for a real union? Can it be matter of question that the colored voters, finding in the better classes true friendship, evinced by full recognition of the rights and practical acts of good will, would have gladly given to these classes substantially their old lead in affairs, directed now however to Union & not to disunion; to the benefit of all & not exclusively to the benefit of a class?

I observe that you say that "the attempt to carry on the government with the privilege of universal suffrage incorporated as one of its elements is full of danger". Danger is the condition of all governments; because no form of government ensures wise & beneficial administration. But I beg you to consider, Is there not a greater danger without than with universal suffrage. You cannot make suffrage less than universal for the whites, & will not the attempt to discriminate excite such jealousies & ill feelings as will postpone to a distant future what seems so essential, namely restoration of general good will of & the bringing into lead, the educated men & men of property, & so securing the best & most beneficial administration of affairs for all classes. Take universal suffrage & universal amnesty & all will go well. Can you, my dear Sir, devote your fine powers to a better work than complete restoration on this basis?

Very truly yours
S: P: CHASE

1. Henry Washington Hilliard (1808–92) represented Alabama in Congress from 1845 to 1851. During the Civil War, he served in the Confederate army and attained the rank of colonel. Other, slightly different versions of this letter appeared with Chase's permission in the *New York Times* and *New York Tribune* on November 19 and 21, 1868, respectively. *DAB*, 9:54–55; Hilliard to Chase, Nov. 27, 1868 (Hilliard Papers, Special Coll., LSU Libraries, La. State Univ. and Agricultural and Mechanical Coll.).

2. Confederates troops under Robert E. Lee and Joseph E. Johnston surrendered on April 9 and 26, 1865, respectively. Long, *Civil War Day by Day*, 670–71, 682–83.

TO KATE CHASE SPRAGUE

Autograph letter. Chase Papers, Library of Congress (*micro* 37:0718).

Washington, May 10, 1868.

My dear dear Katie,

I am ashamed that your affectionate letter has remained so long unanswered; but you know how prone I am to procrastination, and what excuses—(not sufficient however I admit)—I have lately had for it.

But my duties connected with the Impeachment are nearly over, and I *will* write you a few words today:

The Governor tells me that you will probably leave Narragansett very soon. He is anxious about you, and talks of going south with you as soon as the trial is ended. If he does go I will and go at once; so if you incline that way and wish Nettie to go with you please write her immediately and come home.

I was dreadfully frightened about your cold, and very uneasy about your going north when you did. The Governor says you have found the Narragansett air too bracing and his uneasiness increases mine. You *must* take care of yourself.

How I wish you would take a different view of your social duties, & cease exposing yourself, by attending those wretched night parties. You could do so, I think, & lose nothing in any respect.

Most of all I long to see you an earnest christian woman—not only religious but happy in religion. I realize painfully how far short I come of my own ideal; but I am not on that account the less desirous that you should excel where I fail. One thing I am sure of that true faith in Christ is the only thing on earth really worth having; and the only thing that we can carry from earth.

How I do love you my darling! My whole heart seems to go towards you while I write and tears come into my eyes. How wrong it is for those who love not to express their love. I remember how often you have felt hurt by my apparent indifference to what interested you: and I feel sorry that I ever occasioned any such feelings to you. I see now in your husband something of that which I blame on myself. But I know how strong my love really was, and I know how strong his is. And I am very glad that, while you have sometimes forgotten that the happiness of a wife is most certainly secured by loving submission & loving tact, you, generally, conquer by sweetness. I never saw him so much affected as by the difference that occurred between you just before you went away. He was almost unmanned—moved to tears. I have not thought it best to refer to it; but try to make my society pleasant for him & hope I succeed. You must *love away all his reserve*—and help yourself to do so by reflecting how generous, self sacrificing & indulgent a husband he has been to you. How few husbands would consent to such absences, & be at once so liberal & thoughtful. If he were only a true Christian he would be nearly perfect.

The final question on the impeachment is ordered for Tuesday—day after tomorrow, and it is probable that it will then be taken.[1] My own judgment & feeling favors acquittal; but I have no vote & do not know how the Senators will vote. It seems to be that there is very little balance of probability either way. It is not impossible that something may occur to postpone the question a day or two. It will require parts of two days probably to complete the vote when begun. The question is to be taken on each article and it may be that some articles will be divided. The form of the question to be put by me on each article to each Senator is "Mr Senator ——— How say you? Is Andrew Johnson President of the United States guilty or not guilty of a high misdemeanor as charged in this article?": and each Senator must rise in his place & answer "guilty" or "not guilty." It will take about half a minute for each Senator & there are fifty four Senators—say 25 minutes to each article & there are 11 articles, making with the time required for reading about 6 hours. Shan't I be tired?

Goodbye my darling—kisses & dear love for Willie—don't let him forget grandpa.

Your affectionate father
S P Chase

1. The Senate postponed voting on the articles of impeachment until May 16, and agreed to cast ballots first on article 11, which charged Johnson with violating the Tenure of Office Act and for "devising and contriving . . . to prevent the execution" of the Reconstruction and Army Appropriations Acts of March 2, 1867. Passage required a two-thirds majority, but the article failed by a margin of 35–19. *Trial of Andrew Johnson,* 2:486–87.

TO CLARK WILLIAMS

Letterpress copy of autograph letter. Chase Papers, Library of Congress (*micro* 37:0736).

Washington May 16, 1868.

My dear Sir,[1]

I was glad to see your handwriting once more. I do *not* quite agree with you. To me the most important thing seems to me—not that Mr Johnson should be acquitted, or convicted,—but—that his Judges, the Senators of the United States, should render an honest & impartial judgment according to constitution & the laws upon the facts proved before them. In what I have done as presiding officer I have endeavored to be & I believe I have been perfectly unbiased.

I had written thus far when the time came for me to go to the Capitol, whence I have just returned. You have already learned the result of the vote on the [11]th article on which the Senate required the question to be put first; thirty five declaring the President guilty & nineteen declaring him not guilty; so that there not being two thirds voting guilty he was declared acquitted.[2] I was under the impression, that the result would be the other way until the vote had been taken: with one exception, I had never heard any Senator, who had not pronounced his opinion in [committee], ever intimate what his vote would be on this article; and yet if you were to believe what is published in the papers you would imagine that I had contrived the whole thing.[3]

The truth is that conviction, which should be a judicial, has assumed very much the character of a party question; and here in my judgment is the chief danger to our country.

What possible harm can result to the country from the continuance of Andrew Johnson [nine] months longer in the Presidential chair, compared with that which must arise if impeachment becomes a mere mode of getting rid of an obnoxious President. What would be thought of a jury or a court which would convict or sentence a man to the penitentiary, because of "general cussedness" to use the current phrase without sufficient proof of specific charges of offenses or crimes. Suppose the proof insufficient of crimes definitely charged could the jury convict? Suppose the proof sufficient but the facts alleged not to constitute the crimes charged, what court would sentence. If any body brought a suit against you would you be satisfied with the Court or the jury which would find & adjudge against you without good warrant in law & in fact?

But I have written more than I intended. All I meant to say when I began was that I fear you do not allow sufficiently for honest differences of judgment, and that your old friend is still just what you always took him to be and that nobody shall fail of having a fair and impartial trial in any tribunal when he presides, if your friend has the power of securing it to him.

Faithfully yours
S P Chase

Clark Williams Esq

1. Chase had known Williams, evidently a Cincinnati attorney, since the 1840s.
2. The Senate had voted earlier in the day. *Trial of Andrew Johnson,* 2:486–87.
3. Rumors circulating in the press placed Chase and the Democrats at the center of a plot to destroy Republican unity and acquit Johnson. *New York Times,* May 14, 1868; *New York Tribune,* May 14, 1868; *Wilkes' Spirit of the Times,* May 16, 1868.

TO HORACE GREELEY

Letterpress copy of file copy in clerk's hand. Chase Papers, Library of Congress (*micro* 37:0740).

Private.

Washington, May 19th 1868.

My dear Sir— I am very sorry to see in The Tribune of yesterday a statement that "He"—the Chief Justice—"decided the vote of Mr. Van Winkle. He did his utmost—happily in vain—to carry off Messrs. Anthony and Sprague. We doubt that Mr. Henderson would have voted as he did but for the Chief Justice's exertions."[1]

I appeal from Horace Greeley thus informed to Horace Greeley better informed.— More lies seem to be afloat about me than I thought invention capable of. I have not interchanged a word with Mr. Van Winkle on the subject of impeachment that I remember, and my acquaintance with him is very slight. I have not exerted myself to influence anybody one way or the other. Until yesterday, when I happened to fall in with him on the street, all my conversation with Anthony would not occupy ten minutes. Sprague was not influenced by me, nor did I seek to influence him. Henderson took his dinner—he is a near neighbor[2]—twice with Sprague and myself during the trial, but I am sure that I gave him no advice nor sought in any way to control him, *and could not if I had.* The stories about dinner are mere bosh, and so are the stories about rides, except that there is a grain of fact sunk in gallons of falsehood.[3] On particular points in occasional talks with Senators I have expressed my opinion just as I should in talk with you, but I certainly have not sought to make converts to my views, and just as certainly I had no idea when I put the question on the XIth Article what the result would be. I thought it doubtful and very doubtful with the probability in favour of conviction. I had no information whatever how any Senator would vote; I mean of those who had not read opinions or declared them in the Senate, except of course that I did not doubt how Sumner, Drake, and those of that sort would vote.[4]

I care very little for clamour. But I have felt greatly enriched by your friendship and good opinion, and know I have done nothing which should entail the loss of either. I have kept my oath on the trial, and have done nothing from partiality or hostility.

Your article of May 9, "Counsel in Extremity," was just and kind, only overrating me.[5] I have not made a step from my platform and your platform of universal suffrage and universal amnesty. I am looking for nothing in the political way. I believe myself to be, as you say, "a thorough democrat, according to the true definition of that much abused term," and nothing would more rejoice my heart than to see the democratic party conforming its policy to democratic ideas and principles. I do not expect it to do so this year; but it may, for this is a day of revolution. Whether it does so or not, I ask nothing from it or any other party.

Perhaps there is little use in writing this note. In the tempest there is little chance of hearing. And when this note reaches you the shouts from Chicago will be filling your ears.[6]

So let me end by assuring you that I am in no whit changed in my devotion to the ideas and principles which you have approved, and that I can never change in my gratitude for your friendship—not *past,* I hope—and for the support with which you have aided me in my endeavors to serve the country.

Most truly yours,
S. P. CHASE.

Hon H Greeley

1. Peter Godwin Van Winkle (1808–72), the last unknown vote in alphabetical order, was a Republican senator from West Virginia, 1863–69. Van Winkle's "not guilty" vote—a last-minute decision—secured Johnson's acquittal on article 11 of impeachment. "The man who has done more than all others . . . to secure this result, is Chief Justice Chase," claimed the *Tribune* on May 18. According to the paper, Chase had attempted to recruit Rhode Island senators Henry Bowen Anthony and William Sprague, Sr., as well. Senator John B. Henderson represented Missouri. R. W. Bayless, "Peter J. Van Winkle and Waitman T. Willey in the Impeachment Trial of Andrew Johnson," *West Virginia History* 13 (Jan. 1952): 85; *DAB,* 19:219–20.

2. Henderson's address was 448 E Street. Chase and the Spragues lived at 6th and E until the fall of 1869. Chase to Janet Chase, June 5, 1866 (above); *Daily National Intelligencer,* May 16, 1868.

3. According to the May 16 edition of *Wilkes' Spirit of the Times,* Chase had lobbied the two West Virginia senators, Peter Van Winkle and Waitman Willey, at a personal dinner. The paper also reported another, similar dinner and a three-hour conversation with Anthony, and afternoon rides with Henderson and Indiana senator Thomas A. Hendricks.

4. Senators Charles Sumner and Charles Daniel Drake were outspoken proponents of Johnson's impeachment. *DAB,* 5:425, 18:212.

5. According to the article, Chase was "one of the ablest—perhaps the very ablest—of our country's statesmen." "Were Mr. Chase nominated and cordially supported by the Democrats," wrote Greeley, "we believe he would come nearer to beating Gen. Grant than any other living man possibly could."

6. The Republican national convention met in Chicago on May 20 and 21, unanimously choosing Ulysses S. Grant as its presidential standard-bearer on the first ballot. Delegates selected Speaker of the House Schuyler Colfax of Indiana as his vice-presidential running mate on the sixth ballot. *Chicago Tribune,* May 21, 22, 1868.

TO JAMES GORDON BENNETT

Draft in Chase's hand. Chase Papers, Library of Congress (*micro* 37:0759).

Private

Washington, May 22, 1868.

My dear Sir,[1]

I cannot any longer forbear saying to you how much I feel myself indebted for the kind things which the Herald has lately said of me[2]

It is a particular gratification since they give me an opportunity of saying to you directly how much I valued your son's patriotic services & the generous tender of his yacht to the Treasury Department at the beginning of the war. I wanted to do this when he retired from the service, but about that time, something, I don't know what, drew upon me the wrath of the Herald, & I did not wish to do or say any thing which might be construed into an effort to stay or mitigate its censures.[3] My Scotch blood rebels against asking or seeming to ask quarter.

Before that time the Herald had given me important support in my efforts to get money for the war, and I had more than once sought an opportunity of expressing my appreciation of it, but never found you in your rooms when I called for that purpose.

Let this suffice for the past. I only want it understood. And now after thanks for present kind words let me say that a remark in your columns a few days ago to the effect that I have undertaken to engineer the movement for my nomination to the Presidency does me injustice, I have done no such thing, & shall do no such thing.[4]

What was said in the Herald some short time before that I had ceased to think of being a candidate was the exact truth.[5] There was a time when I thought that I might be nominated, and I dont deny that a nomination would have gratified me; but I assure you that I never desired it so much as to make me at all discontented when the probability of it disappeared.

Since then new measures & new questions are agitated; new complications have arisen, & new duties have devolved upon me. In the discharge of these duties I have not looked nor can I look either to the right hand or to the left. I have not hoped nor do I hope to satisfy partizan politicians; I expect to satisfy the demands of my own judgment & conscience & am not without a pretty confident belief that what I have done & may do will meet the approval of enlightened & important men in the long run. With these views I cannot be an aspirant for political office—not even for the highest. The responsibilities & dangers of the Presidency repel more than its distinctions or even its opportunities for usefulness attract me. So I have preferred to be entirely quiescent in respect to the recent discussions in which my name has been brought forward. If they result in any thing more than mere discussion it will be beyond any expectation & without any procurement of mine. But I am none the less grateful for every generous word you have uttered & trust you will never have occasion to regret it.

And now will you not allow me to say a few words on a subject which seems to me infinitely more important to the country than the question who shall be president?

In the Spring of 1865, early in May, the Herald, with great sagacity, declared itself in favor of equal suffrage as the best basis for restoration of the southern states. I urged the same view upon President Johnson, & on all southern gentlemen I met in my journey through those states at that time.[6] I took the simple ground that the people of each state was entitled to be consulted in the work of reorganization, & that the people in May 1865 was not the same people as in December 1860 having been then constituted of white freemen only & now being constituted of white & colored citizens together; & that it was vain to expect the most productive labor from disfranchised & therefore discontented laborers. I estimated the annual production of labor of disfranchised at fully a hundred millions less than the production of the same labor, fully enfranchised. The estimate, it is now evident, was too low. Intelligent southern business men have declared to me their opinion that if the reconstruction question had been settled at once on the basis of equal suffrage that the south would now be more than three hundred millions richer than she is. Quiet & order would have been fully restored; capital would have flowed in; all branches of enterprize & industry would have been invigorated, the beneficent influence would have been every where felt, and the country would have been spared the whole contest between the [President and Congress and all its evil] consequences.[7]

Now eight of the eleven ex rebel states have adopted constitutions guarantying universal suffrage.[8] Some of these constitutions, for example those of North Carolina & Georgia contain no disfranchising provision; and all of them, I believe, provide practicable methods for relieving disabilities. The other three states will doubtless soon be restored under similar provisions.

Now might not the grand idea in the spring of 1865 be very well resumed in the Herald?[9] The time seems very favorable & the good that may be accomplished is immense. If the democratic party were wise it would go beyond instead of falling behind the Chicago declarations on the subject of suffrage.[10] Very many of the ablest colored men in the south are sensible of the dangers of having all the colored voters on one side politically and wish for some action of the democratic party which will allow them to act with it. What they want especially is to secure the new Constitutions from attempts to set aside by amendment or otherwise the suffrage provisions. These being safe from assault by either party it is reasonably certain that colored voters [*illeg.*] would act with the democrats to secure democratic majorities in most if not all those states.

It is my firm belief that simple assurance to all parties, north & south & white & colored that the new regulation of suffrage will not be disturbed except so far as may be needful to give full effect to universal amnesty & removal of disabilities on account of insurrection will do more to restore prosperity to the South & ensure prosperity to the whole country than any other one measure that can be named.

I should be delighted to see the Herald advocating this wise & noble policy

With sentiments of much respect & much obligated, believe, my dear Sir,

Yours very truly
S P Chase

James Gordon Bennett Esq

1. In 1867, Bennett had turned over control of the *New York Herald* to his son, James Gordon Bennett, Jr. *DAB,* 2:199.

2. An editorial published in the *New York Herald* on May 18 promoted Chase as the Democratic presidential candidate because of his candidacy's potential to unite conservative Republicans and "sensible" Democrats and to defeat Grant. Chase, claimed the article, "is now on the conservative side of the great issue of the day—the conflict between the power of the national legislature and the constitutional prerogatives of the Executive and Judiciary."

3. Third Lt. James G. Bennett, Jr., served in the U.S. Revenue Service from May 14, 1861, to May 11, 1862, onboard the *Henrietta,* a donated yacht named after his mother. On May 18, 1862—one week after Bennet resigned—the *New York Herald* criticized Chase for his efforts in the Port Royal Experiment. "His schemes for making educated saints of the contrabands at Hilton Head have resulted in nothing but expense, failure and the personal chastisement of Chase's man Friday, the Reverend Pierce," claimed the paper regarding Chase's assistant, Edward L. Pierce. *ORN,* ser. 1, v. 12:576; Don C. Seitz, *The James Gordon Bennetts, Father and Son: Proprietors of the* New York Herald (Indianapolis, 1928), 182; U.S. Department of Transportation, *Record of Movements,* 32, 470.

4. "There is a break in the republican party," reported the *New York Herald* on May 16; "It is given out that the Chief Justice himself is the chief engineer in this enterprise."

5. An article of May 7 had called Chase "the people's candidate for the Presidency," "the man who now stands above party." "Having apparently dismissed the Presidency from his thoughts," claimed the paper, "he is immeasurably nearer to that high office now than he ever was during the years he sought it."

6. "The concession of negro suffrage in the reconstruction of the insurgent States will effectually spike the last gun of the Northern abolitionists," the *New York Herald* had argued on May 3, 1865, "and will expel or neutralize the fire-eating political elements of the South for all time to come." Chase had taken a similar position in his letter of May 17, 1865, to Andrew Johnson (above).

7. Words are missing in the original draft manuscript due to a tear between the words "between the" and "consequences." The final letterpress copy in another's hand (also in the Chase Papers, L.C.) was used to obtain the missing words and to confirm other readings in this transcription.

8. The eight southern states with universal male suffrage were Alabama, Arkansas, Georgia, Florida, Louisiana, North Carolina, South Carolina, and Tennessee. Texas, Mississippi, and Virginia had not yet revised their constitutions. *Appleton's Annual Cyclopædia,* 8:35–36, 269–70.

9. Chase's suggestion apparently went unheeded. On June 5, the *New York Herald* referred to African Americans as "an ignorant and excitable race." "We firmly believe that both the former slaveholders of the South and their emancipated slaves would gradually have adapted themselves to their new relation to each other . . . if fanatical intermeddlers had not wickedly sown the seeds of a dreadful conflict of races," asserted the paper.

10. According to the second resolution of the Republican platform, accepted in Chicago on May 21, "the question of suffrage in all the loyal States properly belongs to the people of those States." *Chicago Tribune,* May 22, 1868.

TO AUGUST BELMONT

Letterpress copy of file copy in clerk's hand. Chase Papers, Library of Congress (*micro* 37:0807).

Private and confidential

Washington, May 30, 1868.

My dear Sir,[1]

It would show a want both of sensibility and sense if I did not reply to your frank and generous letter of yesterday at once and without reserve.

For more than a quarter of a century I have been in my political views and sentiments, a Democrat; and I still think that, upon questions of finance, commerce, and administration generally, the old democratic principles afford the best guidance.

What separated me, in former times, from both parties was the depth and positiveness of my convictions on the slavery question. On that question I thought the Democratic party failed to make a just application of democratic principles, and regarded myself as more democratic than the democrats. My old friend General Cass would sometimes say to me, when we served together in the Senate,[2] "Why, Chase, you are as good a democrat as any of us;" and I would answer, "I am sorry, General, that I cannot return the compliment by saying that you are as good a democrat as I am."

In 1849 I was elected to the Senate by the united votes of the old line democrats and the independent democrats, and subsequently made earnest efforts to bring about a union of all democrats on the ground of the limitation of slavery to the States in which it then existed and non-intervention in those States by Congress. Had that union been effected it is my firm belief that the country would have escaped the late civil war and all its evils. I [wish] you could find time to read a letter of mine to the democratic Speaker of our Ohio House of Representatives written at that time. It is printed in the Congl. Globe of 1849–50, part 1, page 135, in connection with a speech of Mr. Butler of So: Carolina, and it will give a clearer idea of what I then thought and still think than I can convey in a letter.[3]

The slavery question, as you say, is now settled. It has received a terrible solution; but it has a successor in the question of reconstruction, and this question partakes largely the nature of that.

I never favoured interference by Congress with Slavery in the States; but as a war measure Mr. Lincoln's proclamation of emancipation had my hearty assent; and I united, as a member of his administration, in the pledge it made to maintain the freedom of the enfranchised people.

This pledge has been partly redeemed by the constitutional amendment prohibiting Slavery throughout the United States; but its perfect fulfilment requires, in my judgment, the assurance of the right of suffrage to those whom the Constitution has made freemen and citizens.

Hence I have been and am in favour of so much of the reconstruction policy of Congress as bases the reorganization of the State Governments in the South upon universal suffrage.

I do not doubt the authority of the National Government under that clause of the Constitution which requires the United States to guaranty to each State in the Union a Republican form of Government, to provide for the reëstablishment of such governments by the people of the several States whose governments were disorganized by rebellion.[4] I think that President Johnson was right in regarding the Southern States, except Virginia and Tennessee, as being, at the close of the war, without governments which the United States Government could properly recognize[5]— without governors, judges, legislators, or other State functionaries; but wrong in limiting, by his reconstruction proclamations, the right of suffrage to whites and only such whites as had the qualifications he required.[6]

On the other hand, as it seems to me, Congress was right in not limiting, by its reconstruction acts, the right of suffrage to whites; but wrong in the exclusion from suffrage of certain classes of citizens and all unable to take its prescribed retrospective oath, and wrong also in the establishment of arbitrary[7] military governments for the States and in authorizing military commissions for the trial of civilians in time of peace. There should have been as little military government as possible; no military commissions; no classes excluded from suffrage; and no oath except one of faithful obedience and support to the Constitution and laws and of sincere attachment to the Constitutional government of the United States.

But it has been and is impossible to get these reconstruction acts amend[ed;] nor is it desirable, in my opinion, to delay the restoration of these States to their proper places in the Union under the Constitutions recently adopted in some of them and likely soon to be adopted in the others. The coloured people of [the] South are unanimous in their desire for such restoration, because these constitutions secure to them the right of suffrage and thereby the means of [self-]protection against injustice. And there seems no reason to apprehend that any class of white citizens will be prejudiced by such restoration.

I have considerable information concerning the feelings of Southern coloured voters; and, if the white citizens hitherto prominent in affairs will simply recognize their right of suffrage and assure them against future attempts to take it from them, I am sure that those citizens will be welcomed back to their old lead with joy and acclamation. Nor do I doubt that if the democratic party will give such assurance in any way that they can understand and rely on, a majority if not all the Southern States may be carried for the democratic candidates at the next election.

I am glad to know that many of the more intelligent Southern democrats agree with me in these views and are willing to accept universal suffrage and universal amnesty as the basis of reconstruction and restoration. They see that the shortest way to revived prosperity, possible only with contented industry, is universal suffrage now and universal amnesty with removal of all disabilities as speedily as possible through the action of the State and National Governments.

I have long been a believer in the wisdom and justice of securing the right of suffrage to all citizens by state constitutions & legislation.[8] It is the best guaranty of the stability of institutions and of the prosperity of communities. My views on this subject were well known when the Democrats elected me to the Senate in 1849. It was also known, I suppose, that I had no desire to force them into premature and useless discussion, but was quite content with holding them and declaring them on proper occasions as my personal opinions without making them or having opposite opinions made a political test.

I have said too much, perhaps, on this subject; but I could not honourably answer such a letter as yours, and leave any room for misapprehension.

I sympathize fully with the apprehension, now so widely prevailing, of danger to our institutions from the aggressions of Congress upon the Executive and Judicial Departments of the Government,—not likely in my judgment to end, if successful, without subversion of the Senate by the House. I am no believer in military government for any of the States; nor in military commissions for the trial of civilians in time of peace; nor in arbitrary government of any kind. I long most earnestly for the removal by genuine acts of kindness and sincere goodwill of all traces of the unkindness and the illwill which have sprung from the rebellion and hinder real union and true prosperity. I would eradicate, if possible every root of bitterness. I want to see the Union and the Constitution reëstablished in the affections of all the people. And I think that the initiative should be taken by the successful side in the late struggle. Let magnanimity attend success and benefits console defeat. Towards these ends I am willing to do all I can in office and out of office, with a party or without a party.

I have now answered your letter as I think I ought to answer it. I beg you to believe me—for I say it in all sincerity—that I do not desire the office of President nor a nomination for it. Nor do I know that, with my views and convictions, I am a suitable candidate for any party. Of that my coun[trymen] must judge. If they think fit to require such services as I can render, [they] are, without doubt, entitled to them. If they have no requisition to make upon me I shall be entirely content.

Excuse this long letter, which I have not had time to make shorter, and believe me with the sincerest respect and esteem,

Yours very truly,
S. P. Chase

A. B.

1. Belmont was a prominent New York City banker, diplomat, and Democratic party activist, who opposed George Pendleton as the current front-runner for the Democratic presidential nomination. Foner, *Reconstruction*, 339.

2. Democratic Lewis Cass twice represented Michigan in the U.S. Senate, 1845–48 and 1849–57.

3. Chase had discussed both his letter of July 30, 1849, to John G. Breslin and Andrew Pickens Butler's related speech in correspondence to Alexander Long, April 8, 1868 (above).

4. Art. 4, sec. 4.

5. The phrase beginning with "which" was added as an interlineation to the text.

6. Proclamations that President Johnson issued in May and June 1865 offered pardons to certain categories of former Confederates and authorized Reconstruction to begin in Alabama, Georgia, Mississippi, North Carolina, and Texas on the basis of suffrage for white males only. *Statutes at Large*, 13:760–62, 764–68.

7. In the text, *despotic* is ruled through and *arbitrary* written above it.

8. The phrases *the right of* and *by state constitutions & legislation* were inserted as interlineations to the text.

TO JACOB W. SCHUCKERS

Autograph letter. Chase Papers, Library of Congress (*micro* 37:0831).

Richmond, June 3, 1868.

My dear Schuckers,

I forgot, in my letter of yesterday, to say that I left behind, by accident some papers enclosed in an envelope & relating to some matters in North Carolina, sent from the Attorney General's Office. Please have this envelope redirected to me here & forwarded at once.[1]

The trial of the Davis case was continued till next term; but the entry of the order of continuance was deferred until a new bond for appearance could be made. An agreement between Mr. Evarts & Mr. O'Conor that the case should not now be called for trial was read in which a wish was expressed that some day should be fixed. On this paper a motion for continuance was made. I enquired if the counsul present were ready for trial independently of that paper. In answer it was stated for the Government that Mr. Chandler the District Attorney could not be present & proceed, now, in consequence of the very imminent danger of his wife; (who was supposed to be dying yesterday) that his associate counsel could not [proceed] in his absence & besides the accused Mr Davis was not in Court. The consel for Mr Davis stated that the absence of Mr Davis was occasioned by his understanding founded upon the agreements between the counsel in New York that the case would not be tried this month; and that they preferred a continuance to the next regular term rather than an adjournment till October. I said that it would suit me better to attend some time during October if not obliged at that time to be in some other District; but I thought that under the circumstances the counsel for the accused had a right to have the case continued if they insisted on the motion; and that I would attend on the [fourth] Monday of November, and remain until obliged to attend the Supreme Court at Washington. So *the* trial did not come off. It was simply impossible to bring it on.[2]

You may make a statement to this effect if you think it worth while for the Intr.[3] There is a much improved state of feeling here among gentlemen; but the old bitterness is still vehement among the ladies. I saw today Gov. [Letcher] in the Court Room & Gen. Lee and quite a number of the notabilities of the Rebellion in the Marshalls office as I came out of the Court, & Gen. Wise, Gen. Bradley Johnson & a good many more came to see me in the Judges room.[4] A few have also called at the house. They all greet me kindly; but there is a sad state of things growing out of their past hostility to suffrage & the consequent alienation of the colored people; & the white disfranchisement policy of Congress,[5] the natural fruit of black disfranchisement by the whites

Cordially yours
S P Chase

J. W. Schuckers Esq

1. Schuckers evidently served as Chase's private secretary. Chase's letter of June 2 asked Schuckers to order a check of $100 for Jane Auld, his niece, and told of encountering two former Confederate officers in Richmond "all willing to take universal suffrage & universal amnesty." On June 6, Shuckers sent the papers originally from the office of Orville H. Browning, who served as U.S. attorney general from March 13 to July 20, 1868. *Bio. Dir. U.S. Cong.*, 18; Chase to Schuckers, June 2, 1868, and Schuckers to Chase, June 6, 1868 (both Chase Papers, L.C.).

2. William Evarts, lead prosecutor, and Charles O'Conor, defense counsel, agreed on May 28 to postpone the trial of Jefferson Davis until the fall term. On June 3, Chase granted the continuance and renewed Davis's bail bond. On the same day, Henry Horatio Wells (1823–1900), the newly appointed military governor of Virginia, represented the prosecution, since Evarts had already left Richmond, while Fulton Anderson (1820–74), a

Mississippi attorney and former state legislator, counseled Jefferson Davis. The U.S. attorney general for Virginia was Lucius H. Chandler. Chase elaborated on the background of the Davis case in another letter of the same day to Milton Sutliff (below). Graf, *Papers of Andrew Johnson,* 8:387; Haskell, *Papers of Jefferson Davis,* 4:136; Johnson, *Cases Decided by Chief Justice Chase,* 79–80; *New York Times,* June 4, 1868; Robert Sobel and John Raimo, eds., *Biographical Directory of the Governors of the United States, 1789–1978,* 4 vols. (Westport, Conn., 1978), 4:1647.

3. The editors have not found any evidence that Schuckers prepared such a statement for the *Daily National Intelligencer.*

4. John Letcher, Henry Alexander Wise (a former general in the Confederate Army) and Bradley T. Johnson had returned to private legal practice after the war. Since September 1865, Robert E. Lee had served as president of Washington College. The U.S. marshall in Richmond at this time was Charles Van Winkel. *DAB,* 11:127–28, 192; Sobel and Raimo, *Biographical Directory,* 4:1644; U.S. Senate, *Journal of the Executive Proceedings,* 16:185, 198.

5. The Fourteenth Amendment and the First Reconstruction Act included provisions that disqualified certain former Confederates from political participation. *Statutes at Large,* 14:429.

TO MILTON SUTLIFF

Autograph letter. Norton Family Autograph Collection, MS 4025, Western Reserve Historical Society (*micro* 37:833).

Richmond, June 3, 1868.

My dear Judge,[1]

Your extremely kind & very welcome letters have been both received—the last, here, to day.[2]

I have noticed the movement for bringing out my name by the democrats: and many gentlemen, some of them of great note & influence have spoken to me on the subject: but it has never appeared to me as a thing likely to be really done. To say nothing of the natural and general wish of the democratic party to be represented, in the coming national canvas, by one much more identified with them in party connexion than I have been, it has seemed to me well nigh impossible to get over the difficulty created by the almost universal commitment of the party to hostility to the colored people. My whole life has been devoted to what I believed to be genuine democratic ideas; and to their practical application, so far as practicable under the constitution, by the securing to every man all his natural rights, & to all men equality of political rights without regard to race or color. I have lost none of my faith in these ideas, nor any of my sinse of obligation to give them practical effect. How can the democrats nominate me & at the same time maintain their exception, as I think it, to the practical application of democratic ideas. I have as yet seen no way to overcome this difficulty

On the question of currency there would perhaps be as little difficulty in reconciling my ideas with those of the party, as there will be in reconciling those of different Sections of the party with each other. The country shrinks from repudiation; a large body of the people are obviously discontented with the idea of two currencies one for the bondholder & the other for the workingman, and this discontent will not be removed by payment of the principal of the 5–20s in greenbacks while interest on the national debt continues to be paid in coin & other obligations are paid in paper; the remedy seems to be in having good money for all: and I believe resumption not only practicable, but certain to prove highly beneficial. It has been too long delayed by unreasonable fears of consequences.

It is not difficult for me to estimate calmly the obstacles to the bringing forward of my name by the democrats; for I really do not desire any nomination. Not that I apprehend defeat in case of nomination. On the contrary I am sure that the accession of strength which would be ensured in that event would make success certain. But the office does not seem to be desirable. The annoyances and perplexities and difficulties which attend it at all times would, in the present situation of the parties & the country be multiplied many fold for me. I should strive to do my duty both towards those who elected me & to the country, & it seems a task too great for me. So I have deliberately made up my mind that the nomination is, for me, an undesirable thing. This makes me very willing to think it an unlikely if not impossible thing.

I came here to try Mr. Davis. A year ago I was ready to come, on the adjournment of the Supreme Court certain to take place within four or five days. Then the action of counsel in having him brought into Court, & getting the case continued while I was obliged to be in Washington prevented the trial. Last fall determined to give an opportunity for trial I had the counsel notified that I would attend here in November. I attended accordingly & neither side was ready. Now I am here again; and again there is an arrangement by counsel which postpones the case.[3] If I were President I would proclaim a general amnesty to every body of all political offences committed during the late rebellion. Such an amnesty would not interfere with the punishment of ordinary crimes against person or property committed during rebellion; nor with any exlusion from suffrage or office under acts of States or of Congress. I can see no good to come, at this late day, from trials for treason. I would rather engage in trials of mutual good will and good help.

There seems to be a great improvment here, in the temper of the men who took part in the rebellion. That of the ladies, I fear, is as implacable as ever. There is great embarrassment in business and impoverishment. If they would only consent to complete justice to the colored man, I fully believe that a large part of their trouble would be relieved. My faith in universal suffrage & universal amnesty, always strong, is strengthened by all I see & hear.

Faithfully your friend
S: P: CHASE

P.S. I have said nothing about the impeachment. I was satisfied with the result: but I was terribly lied about. I dont remember one truth except that I thought impeachment unwise & conviction on the articles & proof, unwarranted.[4]

1. A former Free-Soil state representative, Sutliff was chief justice of the Ohio Supreme Court from 1858 to 1863. In 1868, he practiced law in Warren, Ohio. Robson, *Biographical Encyclopædia,* 129; Sutliff to Chase, May 28, 1868 (Chase Papers, L.C.).

2. Sutliff had written on May 28, encouraging Chase to run as a Democratic candidate for the presidency and to support a platform that included "*general amnesty & universal suffrage,* and, to go to the *letter of the law,* in redeeming the bonds as redeemable, paying the bond holders in the same legal currency paid to the soldiers for their $13. per month." "If your nomination *could* be *once made,* on *such* a *platform as suggested,*" wrote Sutliff, "this senate I believe would be *as safe* for *you,* as it was in 64. for Lincoln." Sutliff to Chase, May 28, 1868 (Chase Papers, L.C.).

3. Posting of a $100,000 bail bond released Jefferson Davis on May 13, 1867, three days before the Supreme Court adjourned. On November 26, attorneys on both sides agreed that the trial would begin on March 26, 1868. The most recent delay led to a new date scheduled for November 23, 1868. Chase also discussed the Davis case in correspondence of the same date to Jacob W. Schuckers (above). Johnson, *Cases Decided by Chief Justice Chase,* 42–80; "Minutes Supreme Court U.S. Y April 1, 1867 to Mar. 24, 1868" (National Archives).

4. Chase expressed similar sentiments in a letter to Horace Greeley on May 19 (above).

FROM WILLIAM CULLEN BRYANT

Autograph letter. Chase Papers, Historical Society of Pennsylvania (*micro* 37:0867).

Roslyn, Long Island June 13, 1868.

My dear Sir,

It has been suggested to me by persons well-affected towards you, that I should write to you on the subject of your becoming a candidate for the Presidency. I hesitated at first, but have at length concluded to write, for the reason that what I have to say can at least do no mischief. I wish it to be understood that what I write has no reference to the part which the Evening Post may take in the approaching election, but is simply a personal and confidential communication from friend to friend. Whomever that journal may support for the Presidency it cannot fail to pursue a course towards you dictated by a high respect both for your character and your talents.

You are about to become if you please the candidate of the democratic party for the office of President of the United States. The older leaders of that party who have their prejudices against negro suffrage to over come, will be drawn into this measure by the younger men who are inclined to more generous views, and by such of the older leaders as care nothing for principles but every thing for party supremacy. It is in your power, relying upon the support of these two classes to dictate the platform of principles on which you are to be nominated. The tide is rushing so swiftly and strongly in that direction, that those who would, cannot resist it, and would submit silently to any declaration of principles necessary to be put forth in order to secure your assent to what the party so much desire. So eager, so resolved, in fact has the party become, to make you their candidate, that they would be willing, I do not doubt, to regard the question of equal and impartial suffrage without distinction of color, as already decided by the voice of the nation, to accept it as a condition from which there is no escape, and viewing it thus, inscribe the doctrine upon the party banner. By requiring them to do that you would settle a question which it is disgraceful to the democratic party to keep alive, and by no means honorable to the country,—a question in regard to which the course taken by the recognized leaders of that party had been simply an assertation of the principles upon which aristocratic rule depends in every country cursed with an aristocracy.

As the democratic party now stands, with the strenuous opposition of its public men to negro suffrage, in any shape, the success of that party in the elections, whether federal or local, is in fact a denial of negro suffrage in the states where those elections are held, and is every where so understood. If the platform on which you are nominated should be silent on that question it will be inferred that your success is the success of a party pledged to refuse to the colored race the right to vote. This inference cannot be avoided, save by an explicit pledge to allow the right. So earnestly are the people in favor of permitting the race lately emancipated to take part in making and administering the laws under which they are to live, that I firmly believe it impossible for any party which does not declare itself in favor of that policy to elect its candidate to the Presidency, or for any man to be its candidate who has been known as a friend of negro suffrage without largely losing their esteem.

I was impressed by the manly tone of your letter lately published in the newspapers.[1] If you can induce the democratic party to adopt a declaration of principles in conformity with that letter you will have performed a service for which the country and the friends of humanity and liberty will be grateful, and whether you be successful or not in the competition for the Presidency, your name will be held in honor. What I desire—and what I am sure many others desire is, that such a platform of principles should be adopted by those who support you, that no man, who has the welfare of his race at heart, whether in this country or elsewhere, will regard with sorrow the return of that party to power.

Accept and excuse, I pray you, what I have written as the words of one who writes with a sincere respect for you personally, and with an ancient wish for the welfare of our common country.

I am, dear sir.

very truly yours.
W. C. BRYANT.

Hon. Salmon P. Chase.—

1. Bryant evidently refers to a letter that Chase wrote to Thomas W. Conway on May 25, 1868, in defense of himself as presiding officer during Andrew Johnson's impeachment trial. "They may denounce and abuse me and read me out of the party, if they choose," wrote Chase. "I will follow my old lights, not the new. . . . It would . . . gratify me exceedingly," he added, "if the Democratic Party would take ground which would assure the party against all attempts to subvert the principle of universal suffrage established in eight, and to be established in all of the Southern constitutions." Copies of the correspondence appeared without the recipient's name in the *New York Times* and *New York Tribune* on June 10. Chase to Conway, May 25, 1868 (Chase Papers, L.C.).

FROM JOSIAH PRENTICE TUCKER

Autograph letter. Chase Papers, Library of Congress (*micro* 37:0888).

27 State St Boston June 15th 1868

My dr Sir[1]

Having occasion to go to New York last week, I complied with a circular invitation of Mr John Welsh and others of Phila and attended a meeting at the Continental Hotel on the 10th inst, called as the circular indicated "for the purpose of taking into consideration the propriety of presenting your name as a candidate for President of the United States." You have undoubtedly already been advised of its action, attendance &c.[2] Good harmony prevailed at the meeting, and especially upon one point viz. that you was the man best qualified in every particular for the position: the resolutions unanimously approved show this. If I can be allowed to criticise the meeting and its effect, I should say that its strength would have been much increased by a different class of originators; simply for the reason that from observation, I conclude that they were not of the first and substantial men of the Country, but rather Politicians of medium grade, and office seekers. To have met my desires and hopes, they should have been men who have been unknown in political circles as aspirants for office, men who represent the great commercial and financial interests of the Country, and whose manifest interest and action would have indicated prominently to the masses that they were satisfied that the time had come when the whole future prosperity of the Country demanded that we should have a statesman at the head, rather than a General whose sole prominence and ability thus far shown is of a military character; such a meeting in my humble judgment would have resulted in much good, I am not prepared to say that the one held will be of no benifit, but I am fearful, As you I presume know, it was resolved to select a committee of one hundred men from the different States to press your name upon the attention of the Convention to be held in New York on the 4th prox. If care and judgment is used in selecting this committee it can do much good. It was left to me to name those for New Hamp and this state / I shall endeavor to have good men, and have the advice of shrewd men in their selection.

Mr Haven is quite disgusted that his name should have been used (without his consent), as Vice Prest at a ratification meeting the other evening,[3] There is a strong open feeling among a handsome majority of the people in favor of your being the next President of the United States, The only question is? how to secure unanimity of action among such, I have faith that it will be done. If nominated on such a Platform as I feel confident you would have, the question of election seems to me beyond a doubt, The Delegation from N.H. are not against you, and several are openly in favor of your nomination; the same feeling exists among the Delegates from this State, I have good reliable information that those from Connecticut and New Jersey are stronger still in favor. There are many Republicans who would go in heartily, but who now stand back on account of lack of confidence that the Convention of the 4th will ever be induced to nominate you, when this is once done, they will show themselves at the ballot box, Mr. Tappan has said that if you were nominated he should not do any thing against you and that you are the *best* man for Prest. Unless I am much mistaken, Mr Fogg would be glad to join such a movement, "he is anxious"[4] / I could name many others of less prominence in N,H. I hope this will reach you at Washington, and that you are in good health. We are all well at home. Please give much love to Mrs Sprague and Miss Nettie and Willie. Hoping that the Democratic Convention at N. York will see the benifit of doing a good deed after many bad ones during the last ten years.

I am Yours Very Truly & Respectfully
J. P. Tucker

To
Hon S. P. Chase C.J.
Washington D.C.

1. Tucker, the husband of Chase's niece, Hannah Ralston Whipple, had worked as a customs surveyor in Boston and New Orleans.

2. The Continental Hotel was located at the corner of Chestnut and South 9th Street in Philadelphia. Chase learned about the gathering in a letter of June 10 from George F. Gordon, an appointed secretary. The major resolution of the meeting expressed support for Chase's presidential candidacy and resolved "that a committee of one hundred be appointed to promote his nomination by the Democratic convention at New York on the 4th of July next." The circular's signers were Welsh (1805–86), a Philadelphia entrepreneur and philanthropist; William Freame Johnston (1808–72), former Whig governor of Pennsylvania; and John W. Frazier (b. ca. 1837), who had worked as an internal revenue assessor in Philadelphia. *Appletons'*, 3:460; Graf, *Papers of Andrew Johnson,* 10:652; *DAB,* 19:647; *Phila. Dir. (1868–69),* 394; Gordon to Chase, June 10, 1868 (Chase Papers, L.C.); *Philadelphia Inquirer,* June 11, 1868.

3. Massachusetts Republicans had tapped Boston banker Franklin Haven, Sr., as vice president of a meeting on June 10 in support of Ulysses S. Grant and Schuyler Colfax. Haven to Chase, June 12, 1868 (Chase Papers, L.C.).

4. Mason Weare Tappan, at this time a Republican, represented New Hampshire in Congress, 1855–61. George Gilman Fogg, another Republican, served as U.S. senator from the same state, 1866–67. *Bio. Dir. U.S. Cong.,* 1010, 1910–11.

TO GERRIT SMITH

Autograph letter. Chase Papers, Library of Congress (*micro* 37:0903).

Washington, June 17, 1868.

My dear friend,

I have read your circular with great pleasure not merely because of the unshaken confidence it shows you still repose in me, but for its noble protest against the spirit of inconsiderate reviling now so general.[1]

The New York nomination gives me no uneasiness / It is said that the Convention will be willing to declare universal suffrage a principle of the democratic faith to be applied in the states by the states respectively under the constitution of the United States. If the nomination is offered me on that or an equivalent basis will it not be my duty to accept it? If not offered I, certainly, shall be entirely content. That it will be seems, to me, unlikely

It was wonderful to me lately in Richmond to observe the fast progress made in the south towards a recognition of the fact that universal suffrage is their surest guaranty of prosperity.[2] I am more than ever satisfied that the most generous course towards our fellow citizens lately in arms against is the wisest. This helps them mightily to see the wisdom of justice to the black citizens. The law of love prevails with them more than the edicts of force.

I wish I could tell you all I heard & saw in Richmond. But I have not time now; and I fear I shall not be able to make you a visit in Peterboro this summer; though I will certainly, if I go over the Central Railroad this summer diverge far enough to see you at your home.[3]

Those good and true men who now manifest so much distrust of me and seem so harsh in their judgments will perhaps see more clearly in time and reverse their judgments. If not I must console myself with the assurance of my own conscience, that I have, in nothing censured by them departed from my clear convictions of duty; & with the assurance also which comes from you and many more likeminded in respect to faith in Human Rights that they see nothing in what I have done or declared inconsistent with that faith.

With best regards to Mrs Smith and the other members of your family, I am more & more

Affectionatley your friend
S P Chase

Hon Gerrit Smith

I enclose a photograph which I beg you to ask Mrs Miller to accept[4]

1. On June 12, Smith had published a paper entitled *Destroy Not Man's Faith in Man! Accept the Right Man, Whichever Party Nominates Him!* (Peterboro, N.Y., 1868). The essay dis-

missed as "calumnious and contemptuous" attacks against Chase as presiding officer at Andrew Johnson's impeachment trial and expressed preference for Ulysses S. Grant and Schuyler Colfax, the presumed Republican presidential and vice-presidential candidates. "Neverthless if contrary to my expectations, the Democrats shall have the wisdom to nominate the Chief Justice," wrote Smith, "and along with him a gentleman of similar views and spirit—a gentleman honest both toward the Nation's creditors and toward the negro—I shall prefer to vote for the Democratic Candidates."

2. Recently, Chase had returned from a two-week visit to Richmond, Virginia, on circuit court business. Chase to Jacob W. Schuckers, June 3, 1868 (above), and June 2, 9, 1868 (Chase Papers, L.C.); Ira Harris to Chase, June 13, 1868 (Chase Papers, Hist. Soc. of Pa.).

3. The New York Central Railroad ran between Albany, New York, and Buffalo, stopping at Syracuse, near Smith's home in Peterboro. Henry V. Poor, *History of the Railroads and Canals of the United States of America . . .* (New York, 1860), 272.

4. Chase had enclosed a photograph of himself for Smith's daughter, Elizabeth Smith Miller. Smith to Chase, June 20, 1868 (Chase Papers, Hist. Soc. of Pa.).

TO JOHN D. VAN BUREN

Letterpress copy of autograph letter. Chase Papers, Library of Congress (*micro* 37:0925).

Private & confidential

Washington June 17, 1868.

My dear Sir,

Your letter with the note enclosed in the same envelope reached me at Richmond when I was much occupied by an important criminal trial, at the close of which I returned to Washington[1]

The letter to which the note refers was written hurriedly and was given to the press without any authority and in gross breach of propriety. I do not however regret the fact of its publication for so far as it goes it expressed my sentiments correctly. I do follow my old lights not the new: and my old lights were the maxims of Jefferson on the subject personal rights, administrative economy & general policy.[2]

I am surprised that your friend should have any doubts as to my zeal for the interests of the white laboring masses. No platform can be constructed by men of common sense in the recognition & support of the rights of labor which will not be cordially [accepted] by me. One great Motive with me in originating a national currency was that the working man might no longer be defrauded of [his savings] through being obliged to receive for them the paper of irresponsible banks which might perish in his hands. And it is not the least among the arguments for the speediest possible return to specie payments[3] that the Wages of labor will then be paid in gold or its equivalent. While I insist on the honest fulfilment of all national obligations I want but one currency for the working man and the bondholder. I am glad to know that a vast number of working men are directly & indirectly holders of bonds also, and I wish that [every] one of them was.

I give prominence to the question of restoration of the states lately at war with the Government on the basis of universal suffrage and general amnesty solely because that question now most profoundly engages public attention, and, unless the democratic Convention takes ground on it satisfactory to the great numbers of republicans who are disinclined to follow the new lights and are really democratic in general sympathy, will constitute the main issue of the impending Canvass. I have no doubt either that a wise solution of this question will more largely contribute to the increase of national, state & individual welfare & prosperity than any other one thing that can be done.

It has been stated to me that a considerable [*illeg.*] of Democrats will be satisfied with the disposition of the question in the platform by a resolution recognizing universal suffrage as a democratic principle the application of which in the states is to be left to the states themselves under the Constitution of the United States. I have been told that such a resolution would be acceptable & would be accepted. If so the Suffrage question may be easily disposed in a manner which would give offence to none. Such a resolution followed by one in favor of universal Amnesty & the removal of all disabilities on account of participation in the rebellion would make a platform upon the reconstruction question of immense strength. It should of course be accompanied by a resolution against Military government for any states of the Union and against the trial of citizens by Military Commission

I hear indirectly from New York that Mr. Belmont is dissatisfied with a letter which I wrote to him in answer to one from him and that he has used my letter to him in such a way as to create some dissatisfaction.[4] I wish you would read this letter. It was written frankly in response to a very kind letter from him;[5] and I hoped that it would give satisfaction. You will find that it contained nothing which I have not said to you.

You will remember the opinion which I expressed to you of the movement in favor of my nomination when it first began to develope itself: that it was limited to a few persons & would prove ephemeral.[6] It has turned out otherwise: but I have never been insensible to the great difficulty of accomodating the democratic platform to the new conditions of states & individuals & in such a manner as to recall to the party, with immense additional numbers, those who have been more or less separated from it in action by the questions growing out of slavery.

I desire far more to see a united Democracy, united upon the impartial application of democratic principles to all questions & measures,—than to have any nomination[7] from it. Indeed as I have often said I do not wish for any position for myself. I long to see our country restored, misrule arrested, & prosperity revived in all parts of our land. The Democratic Party has now a great opportunity.

Faithfully your friend
S P CHASE

Col. John D. Van Buren

You enquired in your letter how Mr. Pendleton & his friends are affected towards me. I cannot say as to Mr. P——. Our personal relations have always been friendly. He is a thorough gentleman as well as an able statesman, though as I think cheap interest is better than cheap money we don't quite agree financially. *His* friends in Ohio, are, I believe to a very considerable extent my friends also, with however a preference for him. What does the World mean?

1. Chase had left Richmond, Virginia, in the middle of June. Van Buren's recent letter, dated June 9, returned a note originating with Chase that discussed popular support in Ohio for his presidential candidacy and that reported similar sentiments in New York and Michigan. In addition, Van Buren told of promoting Chase with the acting editor of the *New York World* and of encouraging cooperation with Democratic leaders. "Of course it will not do to put your name in the Convention to be fought over as competing with Pendleton or any other regular Democrat," warned Van Buren; "It must be done by a degree of general assent, ripened over between this & 1st of July by the present popular warmth for you." Ira Harris to Chase, June 13, 1868; Van Buren to Chase, June 9, 1868 (Chase Papers, Hist. Soc. of Pa.).

2. The letter, which Chase wrote to Thomas W. Conway on May 25 (Chase Papers, L.C.), had appeared in the *New York Times* and *New York Tribune* on June 10 without the name of the recipient. William Cullen Bryant had also discussed the letter in correspondence to Chase on June 13, 1868 (above).

3. Congress reauthorized specie payments on January 14, 1875. *Statutes at Large*, v. 18, pt. 3:296.

4. See Chase to August Belmont, May 30, 1868 (above). The editors have not located the letter that Belmont wrote.

5. The words *from him* are an interlineation by Chase on the face of the press copy.

6. The opinion was expressed in a letter that Chase wrote to Van Buren on March 25, 1868 (above).

7. Chase wrote *whatever* as an interlineation on the face of the press copy, then struck through it.

TO JAMES LYONS

Letterpress copy of file copy in clerk's hand. Chase Papers, Library of Congress (*micro* 37:0913).

Washington, June 18th, 1868.

My dear Sir,[1]

I reply with as little delay as possible to your kind note of the 16th.[2]

What I said at your table was without affectation. I do not desire a nomination for the Presidency. I have therefore written no letters for publication, for such letters would be regarded as evidence of such a desire.

In conversation, however, and in some private letters, my views have been freely stated; and I have no objection to say to you what I think on the topics mentioned in your letter; and you are quite at liberty to quote what I say to such gentlemen as you see fit, but I do not want to go into print at this time.

And first of universal suffrage. I am, as you supposed, in favour of it as the best security of popular institutions and the surest guaranty of general prosperity. It seems to me especially desirable in the Southern States to ensure a contented and industrious labouring population, and to remove all distrust felt by the coloured citizens of their former masters and of the educated classes to which they generally belong, and in this way bring the ability and character of the South once more into the lead. But while this is my personal judgment, I welcome gladly every advance towards the general object by free concessions of impartial, if not universal suffrage.

Of the reference of the suffrage question to the States, there can be no doubt in general of the wisdom and expediency. I am not prepared, however, to say that Congress under the 13th and 14th amendments, should the latter be ratified as now seems certain,[3] will not have *any power* in relation to suffrage in the States, nor can I say that in those States whose governments became involved in the war, the question of restoration, at its close, could not be properly referred to the whole body of citizens without distinction of colour. Whether Virginia was one of the States without a government, when the war ended, which the National Government was bound to recognize as a valid and subsisting government, may well be questioned.

Of the wisdom and indeed of the necessity of a general amnesty and of the removal of all disabilities imposed on the people of the Southern States I have no doubt whatever. Complete reconciliation between those who adhered to the National Government and those who sought to establish an independent confederate government, is indispensable to national tranquillity and prosperity, and the policy of amnesty and removal of disabilities will contribute largely to their reconciliation. It will, moreover, bring into useful public service a vast amount of intellect, character, and patriotism now excluded from it.

The restoration of all the States to the Union with the abolition of all military government and control should take place as speedily as possible. It never seemed to me necessary in order to the reorganization of the State governments to put any of the Southern States under military government, and such government is certainly unwarranted by the genius of American institutions. And much more even are military commissions to try civilians in time of peace to be condemned.

I am exceedingly anxious for the restoration of prosperity, and its increase beyond all former example in the Southern States. It is my firm belief that a frank and full recognition by the educated classes of the coloured citizens' right to vote will prove the very best means of bringing about this result. This recognition will ensure a speedy general amnesty and the removal of all disabilities. Suffrage will give assurance of safety and protection to labour; amnesty will provide men fit for public trust. Can there be anything better? Will not patriots bury the past, recognize the present, and provide for the future?

I shall be glad to hear from you: and with the assurance of warm appreciation of your personal kindness, and that my best efforts, in whatever position, will be contributed to the work of restoration and peace, I remain,

Very truly yours,
S. P. CHASE.

Hon. James Lyons.

June 18. P.M. Wrote note explaining non-authorization of statement of "replies to distinguished democrats" printed in papers ("Constl. Union") and explain[ing] that I merely stated what I had heard mentioned by democrats & proper elements of a platform likely to unite the greatest number.[4]

1. Lyons (1801–82), a Richmond lawyer and former Confederate congressman, was one of Jefferson Davis's attorneys. Jon L. Wakelyn, *Biographical Dictionary of the Confederacy* (Westport, Conn., 1977), 293.

2. Chase and Lyons had apparently met earlier in June when Chase held circuit court in Richmond. In his letter, Lyons requested an elaboration of four major elements in Chase's "platform," as outlined later in this letter: universal suffrage, state control of voter qualifications, amnesty, and abolition of military rule in the South. "Although not an advocate of universal suffrage for either whites or blacks," wrote Lyons, "I could not withhold my support from a statesman of great ability and experience who does advocate it, but concedes to the States the right to decide whether it shall prevail within their limits or not." Lyons to Chase, June 16, 1868 (Chase Papers, L.C.).

3. The Fourteenth Amendment took effect on July 28, 1868. *Statutes at Large,* 15:708–11.

4. The paragraph beginning *June 18* was added in Chase's hand in the letterbook, presumably referring to a postscript he appended to the Lyons letter, but not copied verbatim by his secretary. Chase's message evidently yielded a notice dated June 18, that appeared in various papers around June 20—including the *Washington Constitutional Union*—and supposedly reflected "elements" discussed "in convention with prominent Democrats" on June 17. Added to the points discussed in the Lyons letter was a suggestion that "taxes should be reduced as far as practicable; collected impartially and with strict economy, and so apportioned to bear upon wealth rather than upon labor." Slightly different versions of the list appear in *Mr. Chase's Views,* a circular apparently printed in July 1868 (Oran Follett Papers, Cin. Hist. Soc.); *New York Times,* June 20, 1868; Jacob W. Schuckers, *The Life and Public Services of Salmon Portland Chase* (New York, 1874), 567. Charles H. Coleman, *The Election of 1868: The Democratic Effort to Regain Control* (New York, 1933; reprint, 1971), 136–37.

TO WILLIAM CULLEN BRYANT

Letterpress copy of autograph letter. Chase Papers, Library of Congress (*micro* 37:0922).

Washington June 19, 1868

My dear Sir,

It was at Richmond where I was holding the Circuit Court that your kind letter of the 13th reached me.[1] It gave me great satisfaction in one respect; for it proved that recent events have not impaired the esteem with which you have long honored me; and which I have ever felt to be a true & great honor. To have lost that would indeed have been a great calamity.

The movement for my nomination has taken me entirely by surprise: and I cannot even now persuade myself of the reality of it; or rather I cannot imagine that it will develope into such strength as will produce any important result on the action of the Convention of the 4th.[2] It is pretty obvious that a large number of the northern democrats are wearied of the formulas under which, for the last ten years, they have been led to defeat; and that very many of the southern men long for peace & restoration on almost any terms which will ensure to them amnesty & complete removal of disabilities, and which are not in themselves dishonorable. All these would gladly accept me as a candidate believing that through the election of a citizen holding my ideas of restoration on the basis of universal suffrage & universal amnesty peace & prosperity would be most certainly restored to the country and the party so established upon true democratic principles as to afford a just hope of a continued ascendancy, unless forfeited by corruption & maladministration hereafter.

But to these progressives in the Democratic Party a large body of the democrats are very hostile [*illeg.*]; and those anti progressives will most probably control the Convention; and another period of four years [*illeg.*] will probably be necessary to bring the progressives into the ascendancy.

So you perceive that it is not likely to be at all in my power to exercise any material influence upon the platform to be adopted next month. Nobody, now, I am glad to find expects me to desert the logical application of democratic ideas which I have ever labored to make real in the government. This application might be sufficiently assured by the incorporation into the platform of one of two forms of expression—either restoration on the basis of universal suffrage and universal amnesty, without any declaration one way or the other about suffrage in the states, or recognition of the fact that universal suffrage is a democratic principle the application of which is to left in the states under the constitution, to the states themselves without saying any thing more about restoration except to declare in favor of general amnesty & the removal of all disabilities on account of [insurrection]. Upon a platform in either of these forms of expression I might, I suppose, honorably accept a nomination, and I have no doubt that this practical settlement of the question would be hailed with great satisfaction as the harbinger of restored Union & peace & prosperity. It is hardly extravagant to say that such action as this would be speedily followed by a large advance in the value of property throughout the south. On all other questions there is no substantial difference between me and other democrats who do not propose repudiation.

I do not expect any result personal to myself from the action of the 4th of July convention. If any comes it will surprise me not less than the movement which has already taken place. The movement itself, however, will not be without result. It has shown a liberality & progressiveness of sentiment among democrats which cannot fail to have an auspicious influence upon the future: and it has given to the country a better knowledge than it has hitherto had of my true character & sentiments, and will [enable] hereafter to speak to the southern educated classes on the great questions which [expecially] concern those states with freedom & with the certainty of a respectful & very often kindly hearing. It may enable in this way to do as much real good as I could do in a higher position. With this I ought to be & shall be content.

It would be interesting to you I think if I could relate to you the conversations I had in Richmond. They indicated a great advance in the right direction, and gave me great hopes of the future.

Very faithfully your friend
S P Chase

Wm. Cullen Bryant, Esq

1. See Bryant to Chase, June 13, 1868 (above).
2. That is, the Democratic national convention, which convened in New York on July 4. *New York Herald,* July 5, 1868.

FROM WILLIAM CULLEN BRYANT

Autograph letter. Chase Papers, Library of Congress (*micro* 37:0968).

Roslyn, Long Island
June 23d 1868.

My dear Sir.

I thank you for your letter of the 19th, which is admirable in every respect. When I wrote to you the tide was running so strongly in your favor here—that is to say in New York—that it seemed to me impossible for the Convention of the 4th of July to avoid nominating you for the Presidency.[1] You have surveyed the ground from a higher point of view and with a more comprehensive vision.

Parties will probably require another term of four years to adjust themselves to the new state of things consequent upon the civil war, and the reduction of the rebellion. In some way or other the policy of equal suffrage—that is to say, suffrage without distinction of color, must be accepted sooner or later by both parties as the permanent policy of the country—as not only just but necessary to its domestic peace.

There is much in what you say of the power of influencing public opinion at the South which your present relation to political parties will give you, I have no doubt that the power will be exercised in such a manner as to add to the obligation which your country already owes you.

I am, dear sir,

very truly yours.
W. C. BRYANT.

Hon S. P. Chase.

1. Chase's letter of June 19 replied to Bryant's of June 13, 1868 (both above), written in anticipation of the Democratic national convention. *Appleton's Annual Cyclopædia,* 8:747.

TO JOHN J. CISCO

Letterpress copy of autograph letter. Chase Papers, Library of Congress (*micro* 37:0977).

Confidential

Washington June 25, 1868.

My dear Mr. Cisco,[1]

A thousand thanks for your kind letters. With this you will receive a more formal note which you can show if you think it advisable.[2] But *don't let it get into print.* It is impossible to guard against misconstruction.

I expect to send a letter to Col. Van Buren this evening.[3] Please show him my note to you & read mine to him. I have entire confidence in him & in you; but doubt exceedingly the utility *of any publication* at this time.

You both know my views perfectly and can explain them to others better than I can write them.

Ever your friend,
S P CHASE

John J. Cisco Esq

1. Cisco, a Democrat, had resigned his post as assistant U.S. Treasury secretary at New York in 1864. Since then, he had owned and operated a bank on Wall Street. *New York Times,* Mar. 24, 1884.

2. Cisco had written from New York on June 1 to report a groundswell in favor of Chase as the Democratic presidential candidate. "I have been watching and aiding it now for three weeks or more," wrote Cisco, "and am satisfied it has gained strength very rapidly and is now gaining every day." Cisco followed with another letter on June 23 that Chase addressed directly in his "more formal note" of June 25 (below). Cisco to Chase, June 1, 1868 (Chase Papers, L.C.); Cisco to Chase, June 23, 1868 (Chase Papers, Hist. Soc. of Pa.).

3. Chase's letter of June 25 to John D. Van Buren, who served during the Civil War as paymaster-general of New York, is printed below. *Nat. Cyc.,* 10:236.

TO JOHN J. CISCO

Letterpress copy of autograph letter. Chase Papers, Library of Congress (*micro* 37:0975).

Washington, June 25, 1868.

My dear Sir,

The declaration to which you refer was not published with my sanction as an expression of my views.[1] The propositions contained in it had been stated to me by democrats, as suitable to be embodied, with other declarations, in a platform on which all opponents of centralized Government at Washington & of military domination in the states might very well stand; & I repeated them as such in conversation with some other democrats. In this way they got into print; and I am quite willing to abide by them for I see nothing to object to in either of the propositions.

But I have no idea of putting them forth as a platform. The construction of a platform is for other hands than mine.

I saw the so called declaration in the journals; but kept no paper containing it. A friend, however, has made a copy of it for me today which I enclose.

Yours very faithfully
S P Chase

John J. Cisco, Esq

1. Writing on June 23, Cisco had asked Chase to verify certain "declarations" printed in "one or two" unnamed newspapers purported to mirror Chase's own views upon "public questions now prominent." "The masses of the Democratic party seem to find these quite in accord with their own," added Cisco; "so much so that your name is, wherever I go, spoken of by Democrats with the warmest approval for the Presidential nomination." Chase's response in this letter refers to the unauthorized statements to which he alluded in correspondence to James Lyons on June 18. Early in July, the proposed platform expanded to encompass a total of fifteen points. Chase to John D. Van Buren, July 3, 1868 (below); Cisco to Chase, June 23, 1868 (Chase Papers, Hist. Soc. of Pa.); *Mr. Chase's Views; New York Times,* June 20, 1868; Schuckers, *Life and Public Services,* 567–70.

TO JOHN D. VAN BUREN

Autograph draft. Chase Papers, Historical Society of Pennsylvania (*micro* 37:0978).

Washington, June 25, 1868.

My dear Sir,

It is my habit to be quite unreserved in the expression of my opinions in private conversation, and it is, perhaps, an unavoidable consequence that I am often much misrepresented. Sometimes too letters written off hand, in reply to particular statements or enquiries, are allowed to go the press, in violation of the implied pledge not to make public, any thing said or written in private, always held inviolable among honorable men; and misapprehensions of such letters whether printed entire or in part must frequently occur.

I must leave such misrepresentations & misapprehensions to be corrected by the tenor of my life. My acts are the best interpreters of my words.

You and I have not always thought alike. Both of us however supported Mr. Van Buren as democrats in 1848;[1] and it is my belief now that if the doctrines which we then maintained had been accepted by the whole democratic party and by the country the slavery question would have found a pacific Solution & there would have been no civil war. Since then we have differed in political action. Your views of duty have connected you with the democratic party; mine have identified me in general political action with the union or republican party though by no means approving of some things done particularly in respect to arbitrary arrests & forcible interference with the press. Notwithstanding our differences, however, you came, as a volunteer, to my aid, when at the onset of the war I found myself in charge of the Treasury Department, with immense responsibilities & small resources.[2] I have ever been grateful for the timely support you then most disinterestedly & patriotically gave me.

Now the War has passed away and the work of restoration & renovation is upon us. The north has suffered little; but the south has suffered immensely. The first desire of my heart is the restoration of true peace & abundant prosperity to the south; and cordial reconciliation to each other of all who in the late civil war have taken adverse sides. Nor do I think that reconciliation, cordial & complete, between brave & honorable & patriotic men need be difficult. My best efforts will certainly be dedicated to that object.

Nor do I think that you and I are likely hereafter to differ much upon public questions. Events, beyond our control, are taking out of the national politics those topics of discussion on which we have most widely differed.

I am as firm as ever in my belief that suffrage in the southern states ought to be extended to the colored citizens as well as to the white. The reason is plain. These citizens in those states constitute almost exclusively the great class of agricultural laborers. Like other laboring men they can have but a very precarious security against oppressive legislation, or even against the violence of the ill disposed unless they have some voice in public affairs. Nor have I any doubt that this security to them will be a vast advantage to the whole communities of which they form a part. Will not the whole south & the whole country feel the advantage of more contented, better applied, & more productive labor? Will not property throughout the south become at once & progressively more valuable? And can any one doubt that interest & old attachments will give the support of these voters to those who by experience, intelligence & character are best qualified to lead in the conduct of affairs.

To enable them to do so and as a measure dictated equally by policy & justice all disfranchisement & all disabilities on account of participation in rebellion should cease at once. A general amnesty for all political offences should be granted by the National & the state governments.

Whether I am right or wrong in my views as to suffrage events as I have just said seem to be taking questions of this class out of national politics. However men may differ as to the means by which restoration is accomplished the fact seems certain that all or nearly all the southern states will soon be restored to their full relations with the General Government under constitutions which recognize general suffrage & in several of the states, I am glad to see, contain no disfranchising clauses.

(Can congress interfere to reverse this? Certainly not, without violation of the principle in my judgment both sound & wise which leaves suffrage to regulation by the states.) Can the Supreme Court set aside these Constitutions? Not without disregard the doctrine asserted at the last term that political questions are to be determined by the political authorities.

I agree with you that the tendency to centralization of power at Washington & especially in the House of Representatives is a very serious evil perhaps the great evil & danger of our time. It is indispensably necessary, in my judgment, to the preservation of our institutions and indeed ultimately of our Union, that the several coordinate departments of the Government, the Executive the Judiciary & the Legislative be maintained in their full constitutional authority without encroachment by either upon the other. I agree also with you in the opinion that there is now pressing need of an administration of public affairs which will restore the Jeffersonian doctrines & practice. With these restored, corruption [must be] be arrested; public expenditures diminished; taxes reduced & more fairly adjusted; the rights of labor and laboring men fully maintained; [cheap interest, our present] greatest financial [want secured], & [christian] faith reconciled with equality of [*illeg.*].

To these ends it will be necessary that all military domination over the civil authorities and all trials of citizens by military commissions shall every where cease, & entire control of government, both in organization & administration remitted to the people. If there is any excuse for the assumption of unconstitutional authority in time of war there is no excuse for such assumption in time of peace. We cannot live outside of the Constitution: we must live within it & under it. There only is Freedom safe.

Nor while security & prosperity at home is thus provided for, may our rights or our duties in respect to other nations be forgotten. No nation can command respect among nations which, while observing scrupulously the rights of others, does not resolutely maintain its own. Every American citizen, native or nationalized, in every part of the world, must feel himself protected from all aggression by that citizenship as by an impenetrable shield.

I have thus traced for you rapidly with a [*illeg.*] general views. I make no secret of them. At the same time I do not wish now to get into print. The recent use of my name has taken me entirely by surprise. But I cannot ignore it: and am not willing even even to seem to seek a nomination for the office with which it is connected. I am entirely content where I am & with the opportunities of usefulness which my present position affords. But it will augur a glorious future for our country if the democratic party, obeying its own great law of progress & forgetting the things which are behind shall press forward to the things which are before in earnest efforts to reestablish government on the solid basis of equal rights, exact justice & constitutional liberty.

Yours most truly,

To/ Col. John D. Van Buren
(But not sent).[3]

1. Former president Martin Van Buren ran for the presidency in 1848 on the antislavery Free-Soil ticket. *DAB,* 19:156.

2. John D. Van Buren gave Chase financial advice throughout the Civil War beginning in the summer of 1861. Van Buren to Chase, Apr. 21, 1865 (Chase Papers, Hist. Soc. of Pa.).

3. Van Buren's name and the notation below it are in Jacob Schuckers's handwriting.

FROM JOHN D. VAN BUREN

Autograph letter. Chase Papers, Historical Society of Pennsylvania (*micro* 37:0987).

private

N York
June 25 /68

Dear Sir

I sent the draft of letter as a bare suggestion for *your* judgment on all points. I do not think any letter necessary or useful now. So far as I can judge, the phrase about suffrage which begins the so called platform lately published in the papers at Washington & here is satisfactory to our people—the same phrase as was in your last letter to me.[1]

But, as I said to you in the beginning of this movement in one of my letters, the consent of Pendleton is essential before the Convention meets.[2] With that consent now, your nomination would be certain. Without it, I almost give it up. Your name cannot come in as a *competing Democratic candidate.* Have you no friend who can go to Pendleton and secure his consent at once? *He* cannot be nominated. New York will protest. Believe me the popular desire for you does not abate—but a move among the leaders is necessary. Pendleton is the one now essential.

In talking with Tilden, bear in mind that though not opposed absolutely to you, he has never yielded to the impulse in your favor and he will do nothing except from cold calculation.[3]

Yours truly
JNO D VAN BUREN

please say if you received yesterday a letter from me *in pencil*—only the fact of its receipt.

Don't answer my letters unless when necessary / Save your time

1. Chase authorized Van Buren to prepare a platform for his candidacy, evidently sometime late in June or early July. "Universal suffrage is a recognized Democratic principle, the application of which is to be left under the Constitution of the United States to the States themselves," read the first element of the platform published on June 20. Similar wording appears in Chase's letter of June 17 to Van Buren (above). Chase to John J. Cisco, June 25, 1868 (two letters, above); Chase to Van Buren, July 2, 1868, and Van Buren to Chase, July 2, 1868 (both Chase Papers, Hist. Soc. of Pa.); Coleman, *Election of 1868,* 136–37; *New York Times,* June 20, 1868.

2. Van Buren to Chase, June 9, 1868 (Chase Papers, Hist. Soc. of Pa.).

3. Samuel Jones Tilden chaired New York's state Democratic committee, 1866–74. *DAB,* 18:539.

FROM SAMUEL WARD

Autograph letter on letterhead stationery. Chase Papers, Library of Congress (*micro* 37:0997).

Office of Webster & Craig
No. 29 Nassau Street,
New York 26th. June 1868

My dear Sir/[1]

I reached Mr. Tilden's house at 8 this am & had an hour's talk with him in wh I learned that thus far such of the Ohio men as have appeared here evince individual bull-headedness & a want of Cohesion & concert of action. They are inaccessible to approaches & no one man nor any group of men seems empowered to act for the Whole.

Mr. Tilden will start with Mr. Van Buren for Barnums at 8 am tomorrow—will see you at about 4 PM and return by the 9 PM train.[2]

Mr. Seymours, masterly speech skilfully eludes any reference to Candidates— [3] Van Buren is his most trusted friend—

Yours faithfuly
S. W

His Honor
Ch. Justice Chase

1. Ward (1814–84), a New York financier and author, was a lobbyist in Washington during the presidency of Andrew Johnson. *DAB,* 19:439.

2. Chase had traveled to Baltimore for unknown reasons. Samuel Jones Tilden and John D. Van Buren planned to meet him there at Barnum's City Hotel. Chase to Hiram Barney, June 26, 1868 (Chase Papers, Hist. Soc. of Pa.); Writers' Program, Maryland, *Maryland: A Guide to the Old Line State* (New York, 1940), 226.

3. Horatio Seymour twice served as governor of New York, 1852–54 and 1862–64, and ran unsuccessfully for president on the Democratic ticket in 1868. Seymour's speech, delivered at New York City's Cooper Institute on June 25, covered a range of anticipated issues in the next presidential election, but ignored the position of any specific Democratic candidate. *DAB,* 17:7–8; *New York Times,* June 26, 1868.

TO THOMAS EWING, JR.

Printed copy. *New York Herald,* July 6, 1868.

JULY 1, 1868.

Please say to your friend that he is entirely right as to my views of suffrage and States rights.[1] What I desire for the Southern States is peace and prosperity, with all disfranchisements and disabilities removed and all rights restored to all citizens. But the practical disposition of the question of suffrage, as well as all other domestic questions, is for the people of the States themselves, not for outsiders. On this question I adhere to my old States rights doctrines. In the event of nomination and success I trust I should so act that neither the great party which makes the nomination, nor the great body of patriotic citizens whose coöperation would insure success, would have any cause to regret their action. It is an intense desire with me to see the democratic party meeting the questions of the day in the spirit of the day, and assuring to itself a long duration of ascendancy. It can do so if it will.

Yours truly,
S. P. CHASE.

1. Chase wrote this letter in response to published correspondence from former U.S. senator Thomas Ewing, Sr., of Ohio, to his son, Thomas Ewing, Jr. (1829–96), a Washington attorney and an attendee at a Soldiers' and Sailors' Convention in New York that ran concurrently with the Democratic national convention. The letter from Ewing, Sr., dated June 22, discussed Chase's position on suffrage and state jurisdiction. "Chase is in favor of two things—the constitution of the United States and the rights of the States under it and suffrage without distinction of race," wrote the elder Ewing; "and I think he has never said he would violate the first in order to secure the last, and it is not an inconsistency or a departure from principle to refuse the attainment of an end, however desirable, by an assumption of ungranted powers." The *New York Herald* of July 6 identified the sender and recipient of the June 22 document only as "a distinguished statesman of Ohio" and "a gentleman in this city." *Mr. Chase's Views,* 4, includes partial copies of both letters. Chase to John D. Van Buren, July 8, 1868 (Chase Papers, Hist. Soc. of Pa.); *DAB,* 6:238–39; Thomas Ewing, Sr., to Thomas Ewing, Jr., June 22, 1868, and Chase to Thomas Ewing, Jr., July 1, 1868 (both Ewing Papers, L.C.); Fairman, *Reconstruction and Reunion,* 539–40.

FROM KATE CHASE SPRAGUE

Autograph letter. Chase Papers, Historical Society of Pennsylvania (*micro* 38:0019).

94. Fifth Avenue
New York. 2 July /68

Dearest Father,

Your dear loving letter came this morning— Don't pray worry yourself about me— I feel perfectly well, & don't cough at all[1]— The perfect quiet & rest, I find here, is perfectly delightful to me. Mr. Hoyt's family are all at Astoria but one or the other of its members come in to see me every day— Amasa is here & working with all his might.[2] The young men are the life of this movement— Things look a good deal clearer, & A. insists that *he* "will know to-night which way the cat will jump"— The point now is to select *the* man to be spokesman in the convention— Governor Seymour, Mr. Van Buren, insists,—Gov S—— is the guest of Mr. Van B— is perfectly sincere in his intention under no circumstances to be a Candidate— He would like to be permanent President of the Convention, but thinks it would be discourteous to the Inst, & Gov. Bigler, or Mr. Richardson of Ill—— are talked of, nothing is settled, however, as to that.[3] Mr. Belmont has bought out a German, & goes into the Convention as a Delegate.[4]

Mr. Hunter, Col Cabell, Bradley Johnson, & Gilmer, have been sent for to-day— It is thought they would be useful[5]— *Edgerton* of Ills. is as bitter as gall, & swears he would not vote for you under any circumstances—this from Mr. H—— Smith—but such men are very rare.[6] The popular voice here is all one way, most singularly enthusiastic. I have been afraid they would get up a popular demonstration prematurely, & give undue offense to the Western delegates. The Pendleton men are very fractious. I enclose a P—— Green-back[7]— I think of spending Sunday at Narragansett, with dear little Willie. I shall be obliged to go back to Washington & shall return with the Governor, when he comes from R.I—

I am glad to hear of Nettie & her safe arrival in Cinti. I wrote her there.

I am glad you are not going to be greatly disappointed if the nomination is not for you— I should like to see this bright jewell added to your crown of earthly distinction, & *I believe it will* be. But we can love & be very happy & just as proud of you with-out it. Will the *Country* do as well

Devotedly your daughter
KATIE

1. Chase had demonstrated special concern in the past over his daughter's coughing, remembering no doubt that Kate's mother and stepmother, Eliza and Belle, had both suffered from tuberculosis. *Chase Papers,* 2:271–275, 279; Chase to William Sprague, Apr. 30, 1865 (Chase Papers, Hist. Soc. of Pa.); Noah Worcester to Chase, Sept. 5, 1842 (Chase Papers, L.C.).

2. New York businessman William Sprague Hoyt, a second cousin of William Sprague, married Chase's youngest daughter, Janet (Nettie), in March 1871. Astoria, which later became part of Queens, borders the East River. Amasa Sprague, the business partner and brother of Chase's son-in-law, lived in Cranston, Rhode Island.

3. On opening day, July 4, 1868, delegates chose Horatio Seymour of New York to be the president of the Democratic national convention. William Bigler (1814–80) and William Alexander Richardson were former U.S. senators from Pennsylvania and Illinois, respectively. *DAB,* 2:264; *New York Herald,* July 6, 1868.

4. August Belmont, a delegate-at-large, chaired the national executive committee of the Democratic party and delivered the welcoming address on July 4. *New York Herald,* July 5, 1868; Stewart Mitchell, *Horatio Seymour of New York* (Cambridge, Mass., 1938), 417.

5. Henry Coalter Cabell (1820–89) of Virginia, a former colonel in the Confederate army, was the son of William H. Cabell, brother-in-law of Chase's legal mentor,

William Wirt. John H. Gilmer (b. 1812) practiced law in Richmond, Virginia, and had served as a state senator. Brown, *Cabells and Their Kin,* 252, 258, 586–87; Graf, *Papers of Andrew Johnson,* 9:250; Henry C. Cabell to Chase, Feb. 4, 1871, and Chase to Gilmer, July 14, 1868 (both Chase Papers, L.C.).

6. Newspaper reports of the convention make no mention of any Illinois delegate named Edgerton. Hamilton Smith, a coal and cotton entrepreneur from Indiana and one of Chase's Dartmouth College classmates, might have meant Joseph Ketchum Edgerton (1818–93), Democratic congressman from Indiana, 1863–65. *Bio. Dir. U.S. Cong.,* 950; *New York Herald,* July 6, 1868.

7. George H. Pendleton, the major western contender for the Democratic presidential nomination, had fallen out of favor among hard-money eastern Democrats for supporting redemption of 5–20 bonds in greenbacks. *DAB,* 14:420.

TO JOHN D. VAN BUREN

Autograph letter. Chase Papers, Cincinnati Historical Society (*micro* 38:0028).

Washington, July 3, 1868

My dear Colonel,

A friend (40 5th Av.) writes me asking if I would not be satisfied with the substitution of the words "That a broad basis of suffrage is a democratic principle," for the first clause of the suffrage resolution in your platform.[1] I will answer to you and telegraph him to see you: and I shall be greatly obliged if you & Mr. Craig will join as my interpreters.[2] Understanding each other you may reach by similar impressions quite different men & classes.

To me personally the change requested would be indifferent; but it would probably cost tens of thousands of votes by the openings it would give to attack. My name can only be of service to the country in the present crisis by forming a link of connexion between the body of the Democratic Party as now constituted, & a multitude of Republicans ready to accept democratic ideas on all other questions, and asking only that their principles on the question of suffrage be respected and yet not asking that they be carried into effect by the national government.

My friend also says "I think you consider the reconstruction acts of Congress as unconstitutional, as the Supreme Court would probably decide." I certainly should not oppose what the Supreme Court might decide: but no such decision has yet been made. Military commissions in states where the Courts are open have been held to be unconstitutional:[3] and it may perhaps be not unreasonably be inferred that military government in states, permanently established by acts of Congress would also be held to be unconstitutional / But whether such governments, temporarily provided, for the purpose of securing to the whole people of a state as early an opportunity as possible of reorganizing their state governments disorganized by rebellion is quite a different question / My own opinion is that "the establishment & continuance of such governments," even for that purpose, is "unwise, unnecessary,

& inconsistent with the true principles of civil liberty."[4] I do not go any farther than that. A general declaration in the platform that the reconstruction acts are unconstitutional would doubtless suit a great many; but it would be taken as a declaration of a determination to set aside by force the constitutions under which Senators & Representatives from three of the southern states have already been admitted to seats in Congress, & will certainly be shortly admitted from six more; &, probably, before the election from all.[5] Success with such a declaration is simply out of the question. It would band the whole republican party in adhesion to the Chicago ticket; and drive to their standards a large number of citizens north & south, who would prefer Gen. Grants platform "Let us have peace" to the platform which such a declaration would make "Let us have war." It is easy to gain any thing that is desirable without attempting to set aside these constitutions. Justice & good will will give to the educated classes of the south the lead of the colored masses; & with that secured all beneficial amendments will be practicable.

You can show this to Mr. Craig; but use it only so far as others are concerned, for your own information in the interpretation of my views

Faithfully your friend
S P Chase

P.S. I send you a few letters wh. may interest you—they are specimens only— Dr Dupérier was a great planter & is now a member of the La Legislature.[6] His letter is valuable as showing what class of men wd. be alienated by an attempt to overthrow the new state constitutions

1. Van Buren was preparing a platform for Chase's candidacy. On June 25, Van Buren had signaled acceptance of the suffrage resolution in the statement printed in the *New York Times* on June 20. The opening of the resolution read: "Universal suffrage is a democratic principle. . . ." The fourth item of the fifteen-point platform that eventually emerged asserted that "all public and private interests repose most securely on the broadest basis of suffrage." *New York Times,* June 20, 1868; Chase to Van Buren, July 2, 1868 (Chase Papers, Hist. Soc. of Pa.); *Mr. Chase's Views,* 2; Schuckers, *Life and Public Services,* 568; Van Buren to Chase, June 25, 1868 (above).

2. In the convention, James B. Craig represented New York's second district. *New York Herald,* July 6, 1868.

3. According to the Supreme Court's decision in *Ex parte Milligan,* formally decided on December 17, 1866. 4 Wall. 132–42 (1866).

4. Identical wording appears in the seventh item of Chase's final fifteen-point platform. *Mr. Chase's Views,* 2–3; Schuckers, *Life and Public Services,* 569.

5. Congress had allowed Arkansas and Tennessee back into the Union on June 22, 1868, and July 24, 1866, respectively. Under an omnibus bill of June 25, 1868, Alabama, Florida, Georgia, Louisiana, North Carolina, and South Carolina had also reentered on a provisional basis. Georgia, however, did not formally reenter until 1870, nor did Texas, Mississippi, and Virginia. On July 3, 1867, only Arkansas, Florida, and Tennessee had representatives in Congress. *Bio. Dir. U.S. Cong.,* 183–86; *Statutes at Large,* 14:364, 15:72–74, 16:62–63, 67–68, 80–81.

6. A sugar planter, Frederick H. Dupérier hailed from New Iberia, Louisiana. Writers' Program, Louisiana, *Louisiana: A Guide to the State* (New York, 1941), 313.

FROM ALEXANDER LONG

Autograph letter. Chase Papers, Historical Society of Pennsylvania (*micro* 38:0042).

New York Hotel
July 3rd. 1868

Hon. S. P. Chase
Chief Justice U.S.
My Dear Sir:

It is of the utmost importance that some one should hold authority from you to say that you will abide by the action of the convention and support its nominees.

The question will undoubtedly be asked when you are put in nomination and while I feel fully authorized in the premises, if the authority should be called for it is not such as could be used. In all probability the statement of whoever may nominate you will be sufficient, yet his authority to speak might be questioned and hense the necessity of being prepaired. A paper similar in import to that enclosed must be in the hands of whoever may be agreed upon to present your name, a question which has not yet been determined.[1] Gov. Seymour is the man if he can be prevailed upon to do it, but if not some one else will be selected.

You will of course employ such language as may be acceptable to yourself, making it as strong as you can & unmistakeable in meaning as to your intention. The question is frequently asked by the Pendleton men, "Will Mr Chase abide by the result of the convention and vote for the nominees?

We have deemed it most safe to send this by a messenger who will return with your reply and must leave Washington Sunday evening that we may have it Monday morning.

You can give it any date you prefer and should it become necessary to make it public the letter to which it is intended to be a reply we can prepare.

It is of the utmost importance that we have it, and unless we answer unhesitatingly for you all would be lost.

The prospect brightens and you are increasing in favor hourly.

Truly Yours
ALEXANDER LONG

P.S. The messenger that carrys this knows nothing about its character or object and will deliver your reply to myself in person.

Mr. Smith, Mr Craig, Mr & Mrs. Sprague and Schuckers with myself are all that have any knowledge of it.

LONG

1. According to an undated document copied in an unknown hand (Alexander Long Papers, Cinc. Hist. Soc.), Chase authorized his "most discreet friends"—Cisco, Long, Hamilton Smith, Van Buren, James Charles Kennedy, M.D. (b. 1809), a Democrat and former Ohio state legislator from Clermont County, "& any others that they may select"—to act for him. "I shall be entirely willing to be disposed of by them," added the message; "I can accept well enough the Platform." Similar wording appears in a letter that Chase wrote to his oldest daughter Kate on July 7 (below). Robson, *Biographical Encyclopædia,* 138.

TO FREDERICK A. AIKEN

Autograph letter. Chase Papers, Historical Society of Pennsylvania (*micro* 38:0046).

Private & confidential

Washington, July 4, 1868

My dear Sir,[1]

I was gratified by your note which came today.[2] Whatever the result I shall never forget your good will & good offices. The reports by letter, & telegram, & the press seem to warrant your hopes; but I do not forget the difference between outside speculation & inside decision. And shall acquiesce cheerfully whatever the event.

The assurance you give of the friendship of Mr V. affords me real satisfaction. He is a man of whose friendship one may well be proud. Even when we have differed & separated most widely I have always admired his pluck & constancy & have done full justice to his abilities & energies. The propositions you sent me as coming from him contain very little from which I dissent except on the one point of the reconstruction law. I have always favored the submission of the question of reorganization after disorganization by war to the entire people of the whole state; & whether right or wrong constitutions have been formed in eight of these states under which Senators & Representatives have been or shortly will be admitted to seats in Congress.[3] But there is no use in discussing this now

Dr. McIlhenny has taken some notes of conversation with me on this quest[ion] which he will send to Mr Long. You can see them of course: but I dont want to have them shewn to any body else except Mr. Van Buren.

I await the result very quietly—so quietly that I am almost ashamed of myself, when I think of your anxieties & labors in New York.

Yours most sincerely
S. P. CHASE

Fredk A. Aiken Esq

1. Democrat Frederick A. Aiken, "a good friend" of Chase, edited the *Washington Constitutional Union* and held the post of secretary for a committee of one hundred selected in Philadelphia on June 10 to promote Chase's candidacy. "I want you to hear his views as he will explain them," Chase instructed Hiram Barney on June 26, "& if you

approve, give him the benefit of your counsel & assistance." Recently, Aiken had established campaign headquarters for Chase at Chandler House, on 14th Street across from Tammany Hall in New York. Aiken to Chase, June 26, 1868 (Chase Papers, L.C.); Chase to Barney, June 26, 1868 (Chase Papers, Hist. Soc. of Pa.); Coleman, *Election of 1868,* 215.

2. Aiken's letter of July 3 reported "a marked improvement" in Chase's prospects over "the last forty eight hours." "My parlors are thronged all the time," he wrote. One recent visitor was Clement Laird Vallandigham, former antiabolitionist congressman from Ohio and Peace Democrat, who had discussed Chase's candidacy at length and given Aiken a copy of a platform that the Ohio delegation expected to consider. "I believe Mr. V. is a sincere friend of yours," ventured Aiken, "& any assurances I could give him that what he has written meets in any degree your views *may be* of vast importance." Aiken to Chase, July 3, 1868 (Chase Papers, Hist. Soc. of Pa.); *DAB,* 19:144.

3. Chase had discussed the readmission of southern states in correspondence to John D. Van Buren, July 3, 1868 (above).

TO ALEXANDER LONG

Autograph letter. Alexander Long Papers, Cincinnati Historical Society (*micro* 38:0047).

Private

Washington, July 4, 1868

My dear Sir,

I have seen the gentleman to whom you gave a letter of introduction to me; and he has made some notes of his conversation with me, which, so far as they purport to state my views, are correct[1]

Before making any use of these notes please see Col. Van Buren, & do nothing without his advice & consent. He resides as I presume you know at No. 11 West 9th Street.

I much doubt the expediency of making any use of them. The remarkable public sentiment which has so unexpectedly developed itself in favor of my nomination does not spring from any consideration of my particular views but from a confidence that I can be elected & if elected, will give to the country an honest & useful administration, with sincere good will to all, & without fear or favor toward any. If nominated I shall most earnestly endeavor not to disappoint this confidence, & especially not to disappoint the confidence of the great party which may put me in nomination. If not nominated I shall still try to do what good I can

What you & Col. Aiken say in your notes is very gratifying.[2] I hope you will be satisfied with what I have done. I could not do otherwise, & feel myself right.

Sincerely your friend
S P Chase

Hon. A. Long.

1. The "gentleman" was evidently Dr. J. S. McIlhenny, to whom Chase alluded in letters to Frederick A. Aiken, July 4, 1868 (above) and John D. Van Buren, July [4], 1868 (below).

2. See Alexander Long to Chase, July 3, 1868, and Chase to Frederick A. Aiken, July 4, 1868 (both above).

TO JOHN D. VAN BUREN

Autograph letter. Chase Papers, Historical Society of Pennsylvania (*micro* 38:0007).

STRICTLY CONFIDENTIAL

Washington, July 1, 1868.[1]

My dear Colonel,

At the urgent request of my friend Col Long I have written him a letter expressing my intention to support the nominees of the Convention, if the platform is such that I can honorably accept it.[2] He desired an unconditional pledge, but this I could not give. I have never in my life bound myself to the support of unknown candidates upon an unknown platform: nor have I asked such promises from any body.

I am now afraid that the letter goes a little too far in that direction: and I want you to protect me by your judgment from any mistake in this respect. I make no secret of my desire to be in perfect union & harmony with the party & to support its nominees if upright, honorable & capable men and on a right platform. The presumption is almost a certainty that a National Convention will nominate no other & I hope too that the platform will be one which I can accept without inconsistency. But I cannot assume this in advance; and I believe that there is no instance in which any pledge of any sort was asked or expected of any gentleman thought of for nomination

And the more I think of it the more unwilling I feel to make any pledge whatever.

I have enjoined on Mr. Long to make no use whatever of the letter or of some notes of a conversation to the same effect which I allowed to be taken,[3] except in a real exigency, and after full consultation with you & with your advice & consent. If he has not called on you please call on him at the New York Hotel—Hon. Alexander Long of Cincinnati—, & carefully consider both the letter & the notes and allow no mistake to be made.[4]

I see in the Messager-Américain of today that the Evg. Post had an article last Evening indicating some apprehension that I might be induced by desire for the nomination to pledge myself in advance to any platform & any candidate.[5] I would not on any account forfeit Mr Bryants good opinion. Between the good opinions of such men & the Presidency my choice would be easily made. The Presidency would kick the beam forthwith.[6] And I don't want even to seem to err in that way.

For this reason I invoke your judgment and friendship very earnestly in this matter. Suppress both letter & notes unhesitatingly if either even seems to make any pledge which you, with your knowledge of my antecedents & opinions, think I ought not to make.

Of course whether nominated or not myself my judicial position will forbid that I take any active part in the election. I can only cast my vote.

Faithfully your friend,
S P Chase

Col John D. Van Buren

Your telegram "letter recovered" was received today.

1. Chase actually wrote this letter on July 4, judging by the reference in this letter to a *New York Evening Post* article of July 3.

2. Chase's letter expressed the intention to support "all of the distinguished citizens" under consideration for the Democratic presidential nomination, unless the convention accepted a platform "to which I cannot yield my assent without disregard of my settled convictions of duty and of the whole tenor of my public life." Chase to Alexander Long, July 1, 1868 (Chase Papers, Hist. Soc. of Pa.).

3. The transcriber was Dr. J. S. McIlhenny, an acquaintance of Long. Chase to Frederick A. Aiken, July 4, 1868, Chase to Alexander Long, July 4, 1868 (both above); William B. Thomas to Chase, Aug. 26, 1868 (Chase Papers, Hist. Soc. of Pa.).

4. The New York Hotel was located at 721 Broadway. *New York Dir. (1864)*, 642.

5. The article that Chase read was published in *Le Messager Franco-Américain*. According to William Cullen Bryant's *New York Evening Post,* Chase had supposedly pledged himself "unreservedly to support the nominee of the Democratic Convention" in a letter to John J. Cisco. If so, claimed the paper, Chase "will lose every friend whom he should most value, and sacrifice, for the sake of an unworthy ambition, a name and fame which ought to be dear to him, and which might rank among the noblest in our history." Cisco later denied receiving such a letter. *New York Evening Post,* July 3, 6, 1868.

6. That is, upset the balance of a scale so that one end goes up and strikes the beam. *Oxford English Dictionary,* 2d ed. (Oxford, 1989), 2:15.

FROM HAMILTON SMITH

Autograph letter on stationery with monogram initials of Kate Chase Sprague. Chase Papers, Library of Congress (*micro* 38:0066).

Sunday noon[1]

My dear Chase— I am heated almost to the boiling point & so nervous that my writing will be almost as indistinct as yours— I am not up to the words—faces & trick of politicians & therefore can only give you the impressions of an honest country friend.

Save Mr. Cisco—I would trust any of your New York friends I have seen[2]— They want Seymour or somebody *less honest* than you— The Masses here are for you & their leaders must, *at first*—appear to be for you— They have, however, (unless a western friend lies like a New Yorker) made the strongest kind of overtures to the friends of Hendricks &, in consequence, those friends are in the highest spirits & feel entire confidence in the result—[3]

The Ind. Delegation *have agreed* to vote for Pendleton twice & longer if there is any probability of carrying that ticket—but the special friends of H. in that delegation, are as is believed by the Pendleton men—working hard to undo privately, what they do publickly— If P. cannot carry the 2/3ds., as is now highly probable, his friends—W. McLean & others will attribute the defeat to H. &, in order to punish him, will probably vote for you *in force.*[4] Ky. is *violent* for P. & will sympathise with the O. delegation & beyond this, J-D. Bright, would be glad of such an opportunity to pay off old scores he owes to H[5]— There are (I think) 4 or 5 of the Ky. delegation who will vote for you after the 1st. or 2d. ballot.

Vallandingham will probably take the place of a Delegate tomorrow—is (I think) in your favour & will use all his influence for you the moment P. is out of the way. Among those who advise me of these movements is Judge Key of O.[6] who, altho' he is obliged now to support P. is really very anxious that the contingency alluded to may happen & that Ohio may go for revenge if not for love. He urges me to suggest to you & your friends here the expediency of having the name of Gen. Franklin on your ticket: he has been offered the support of Pendleton—but says he will be second on no ticket but yours— His friends—Slocum—Morgan &c—promise (so says Key) the entire strength of the Soldiers Convention for that ticket[7]— In brief—that is the advice (entirely confidential) by Key & the others I am not authorised to name—Let Mr. Chase's friends press him strongly as possible—say nothing agst. Pendleton—& wait patiently for the contingency alluded to & be ready to take advantage of it— I shall only advise with Mr. Cisco for whom I am waiting now— What a Magnificent woman Kate has become— With her shrewdness & force, & with ninety days time, I could have you nominated by acclamation & elected by an overwhelming majority— These New Yorkers possibly may be trusted—but nobody will trust them— What you need is right down Western honesty & vigor—(not Pendleton bluster) but the hard working of honest men for an honest cause & an honest man.[8]

Ever yours
H. S.

1. The contents of this letter indicate that Smith wrote it on July 5, the weekend before the Democratic national convention cast ballots for a presidential nominee.

2. Subsequent comments in this letter indicate that Smith actually intended to express *distrust* for most of Chase's New York friends.

3. One interpretation of the convention suggests that the New York delegation planned to support Indiana senator Thomas A. Hendricks temporarily in order to dilute support for front-runner George H. Pendleton—who needed a two-thirds majority to be nominated—and then to promote Chase after Pendleton's support wavered. Coleman, *Election of 1868,* 207, 224–26.

4. Washington McLean, a leading Ohio Democrat, controlled the *Cincinnati Enquirer.* To solidify their power, Pendleton's partisans removed McLean and others from the Ohio delegation on July 5. Among the replacements was Clement L. Vallandigham. Ibid., 234; *New York Herald,* July 6, 1868; Thomas E. Powell, ed., *The Democratic Party of the State of Ohio . . . ,* 2 vols. ([Columbus, Ohio], 1913), 2:296.

5. Jesse David Bright had been elected to the Kentucky legislature in 1866. In 1862, the U.S. Senate had expelled him for alleged disloyalty while representing Indiana as a Democrat. *Appletons',* 1:376; *DAB,* 3:46.

6. Former Cincinnati jurist Thomas Marshall Key, an Ohio politician and legislator, had served as a colonel on the staff of Union general George B. McClellan. *Appletons',* 3:530; *Cincinnati Dir. (1849–50),* 162.

7. William Buell Franklin, a Connecticut firearms manufacturer, and Brooklyn attorney Henry Warner Slocum, held appointments as majors general of volunteers during the Civil War. William Henry Morgan (d. 1878) of Ohio had been a brigadier general. All three were attending the Soldiers' and Sailors' Convention. Coleman, *Election of 1868,* 192; *DAB,* 6:601–2, 17:216–17; Heitman, *Historical Register,* 1:726; *New York Herald,* July 5, 1868.

8. Smith added the latter portion of the sentence, beginning with *(not,* in the corner of the page after concluding the letter.

FROM KATE CHASE SPRAGUE

Autograph letter. Chase Papers, Historical Society of Pennsylvania (*micro* 38:0051).

New York.
5 July 1868.

Dearest Father.

I have just enclosed & addressed a letter from Mr. H—— Smith, who poor man is so overpowered by the heat he finds it hard to endure[1]— Day before yesterday, yesterday & to-day have been as hot as weather can well be, too hot by far, for the warm work on hand here— You will be sorry perhaps, to learn that I did not go to the country, as I had intended—but I really could not make up my mind, to leave just now. I am so comfortably established, & as I have to go to Washington again, in any event, I decided to postpone the visit to the boy[2]— Dear little fellow, I do long very much to see him.

There is a noble work being done here by your friends—& whether success or failure crowns their efforts, they will be always proud to have had a hand in it— I will not enter into details, but every thing, as far as developed looks well—only New York—friends inside that close corporation say, their action is cautious, those outside call it *timid.*

I am so glad that it does not fall to you to bear the burden & heat, & I love to think of you quietly at home, perhaps enjoying a game of Croquet or ten-pins—

Lovingly your child
KATIE

1. See Hamilton Smith to Chase, July 5 (above). On July 5, the temperature in New York peaked at ninety-four degrees Fahrenheit. *New York Herald,* July 6, 1868.

2. Kate had planned to visit her son William, Jr., at Narragansett, Rhode Island, on Sunday, July 5. Kate Chase Sprague to Chase, July 2, 1868 (above).

FROM JOHN D. VAN BUREN

Autograph letter. Chase Papers, Historical Society of Pennsylvania (*micro* 38:0055).

New York
July 6 1868

Dear Sir

Your letter about Mr. Long just received.[1] I have not yet seen him / We have hunted each other all day yesterday. I will protect your honor in the matter as my own & even if I am *too* rigid (which I shall not be) I know you would forgive me for erring on that side.

I am glad I had the good sense to withhold the assurances (personal) you authorised me to give Mr. T.[2] It was so much capital which I have used in the now important quarter.

As I said before Church's nomination is not a sham—it is accidental & unexpected—but the N.Y. delegates *must* stand by it now so long as there is hope.[3] He is an able vigorous man, equal to the station every way.

The EVG POST is no longer Mr. Bryant—he assured a gentleman he and *his paper* would support you. The juniors do not like you.

The article in the Herald yesterday morning was very ill-advised. It was the result of Mr. B's belief in his own great acuteness to see deeper than others.[4] I trust you & your friends have no belief of the kind. The Governor is under no sort of *obligation* to go a certain way which would justify any such charges of bad faith to you; and as for himself, there is no time in 6 months past when he has wavered in his resolution *not* to be the nominee

Yours truly
JNO D VAN BUREN

Chief Justice Chase

1. Chase to Van Buren, July [4], 1868 (above).

2. Chase may have authorized such assurances after a meeting with Van Buren and Samuel J. Tilden, which apparently occurred in Baltimore on June 27. "I have not thought it worth while to [connect] you to any promise to Tilden personally," Van Buren explained on July 2, "for he is setling back against you and is really *not* possessed of much actual power & I do not want to waste anything." Samuel Ward to Chase, June 26, 1868 (above); Van Buren to Chase, July 2, 1868 (Chase Papers, Hist. Soc. of Pa.).

3. In balloting on July 6 and 7, the New York delegation supported Sanford Elias Church (1815–80), a former lieutenant governor and comptroller of that state, possibly as part of a strategy to establish foundations for Thomas A. Hendricks's candidacy and thus split forces behind George H. Pendleton. *Appletons',* 1:613–14; Coleman, *Election of 1868,* 224–26, 237.

4. The article, which appeared in James Gordon Bennett, Jr.'s *New York Herald,* claimed that New York's delegation preferred Chase, but would vote for Church on the first ballot "in order not to be without a candidate." "An effort is being made to harmonize the New York, Ohio and Pennsylvania delegations upon the Chief Justice before presenting his name," asserted the piece, "which movement has every prospect of success." According to the *New York Herald,* former New York governor Horatio Seymour, who had repeatedly denied any interest in the presidency, would "be received with enthusiasm" if he nominated Chase. Coleman, *Election of 1868,* 178, 180, 182–83; *New York Herald,* July 5, 1868.

TO KATE CHASE SPRAGUE

Autograph letter. Chase Papers, Historical Society of Pennsylvania (*micro* 38:0063).

Washington, July 7, 1868.

Dearest Katie,

Your telegram about F.A.A. has just come & surprised me greatly.[1] There must be some mistake: for I have just received a telegram signed "Aiken" giving an account of the 6th ballot. "Pendleton 122½; Hancock

47[2]—two highest—name of Chief Justice not yet presented—all going well." I trust your informant was mistaken about him: but I shall be careful.

I also had a telegram signed J. P. Tucker giving the platform so far as adopted relating to debt & suffrage and asking if acceptable; to which I answered "Not prepared to say till I have seen the whole. Shall be gratified personally if friends will agree not to have my name presented to the Convention."[3]

My telegrams to you & to Prentice were sent to the Office not more than ten minutes ago.

I am glad that my name was not presented at first, & shall be better pleased if it is not presented at all. You know how little I have desired a nomination and how averse I have been to making any efforts to secure it. I have feared all along that it could not be tendered to me on any platform which would allow any hope of considerable accessions from the republicans; and without that hope any other person might as well be nominated as I. And I am entirely satisfied with the opportunities of usefulness which my present position afford.

I can accept well enough the platform so far as Prentice sent it to me. But I can't say that I like it, nor do I suppose that any body will like it. Every body will take, as every body will construe it. So I did not think it best to reply categorically to his telegram. Besides I thought that if any thing of the sort was thought necessary to be sent to me, it would come from Col. Van Buren & Mr. Long, one, or both of them, who have authority to represent me more fully than any other persons: and are perfectly well informed as to my views.

Another telegram from "Aiken" has just come "Convention has adjourned no nomination made—carried our point in gaining time."

You will get this therefore before the Convention meets. I wish a few of my most discreet friends could & would consult together— Say Col Van Buren, Mr. Long, Mr. Kennedy Amasa Sprague, Mr. Smith, Mr. Cisco, and any others that these might select and act for me.[4] I shall be entirely willing to be disposed of by them. But I must say that I think it will be much better not to have my name go before the Convention at all unless it goes upon such a demand as will ensure its acceptance by the necessary vote. Unless nominated now it is my fixed purpose to have nothing more to do with political life. I cannot think of any exigency that can arise in which I can forego this purpose. And I shall feel much more contented with the memory of the movement in my favor—so spontaneous & so remarkable though without results—than I shall with the reflection that I was made a candidate before a Convention & defeated.

If I vote at all this fall I shall in all probability vote for the democratic nominees.[5] No matter how the Convention goes, the manifestation of so great a sentiment in my favor, without asking any modification of my views on the questions of suffrage & debt—good faith to the laboring masses white or black & good faith to the National Creditors—this manifestation I say proves a vast advance in the sentiments of the party especially of its younger & more progressive wing; and if I were a little younger & unembarrassed by the gown I should like nothing better than to lead this wing to ascendancy & the party to glorious victory. With such an element in it the party seems to me worth more than the Republican Party as now constituted.

Mr. Barlow wrote to a friend here who showed me his letter today, that you were to have an interview with Mr McLean, my old friend today: and Mr Hamilton Smith writes with great admiration of your abilities.[6] I am afraid my darling, that you are acting too much the politician. Have a care. Don't do or say anything which may not be proclaimed on the housetops. I am so anxious about you that I cannot help wishing you were in Narragansett or here where I take all things very quietly & play croquet nearly every evening, & sleep as soundly as the heat will let me every night.

Most affectionately

Your father,
S P CHASE

Mrs Kate C. Sprague

1. A letter written by Chase's oldest daughter on the same date (Chase Papers, Hist. Soc. of Pa.) warned that Frederick A. Aiken, "who is too indiscreet to be trusted by you in any way," had disappeared for more than a day and recently resurfaced "still a good deal under the effects of his late intemperance." "He has done no good while pretending to be authorized by you," she warned. Kate continued: "The Comte. thought it best your letter of 'July 3.' should not be delivered to him, & propose to return it to you"—apparently a reference to Chase's response to Alexander Long's letter of July 3 (above).

2. Winfield S. Hancock, favored candidate of the Soldiers' and Sailors' Convention, had gained popularity through deference to civilian rule while commanding the fifth military district, which comprised Louisiana and Texas, from November 1867 to March 1868. Coleman, *Election of 1868,* 166–75.

3. In Chase's final platform, the fourth plank expressed faith in "the broadest basis of suffrage," but left implementation to the states. Plank thirteen straddled the greenback issue, calling for "honest payment of the public debt" and denying bondholders any special treatment. "The interpretation of laws, in cases of conflicting interests," it asserted, "belongs to the courts." Chase's telegram to Tucker is printed in Robert Bruce Warden, *An Account of the Private Life and Public Services of Salmon Portland Chase . . .* (Cincinnati, 1874), 706. Coleman, *Election of 1868,* 138–39; *Mr. Chase's Views,* 2, 3; Schuckers, *Life and Public Services,* 568, 569.

4. Chase employed almost identical language in the authorization evidently sent in response to Alexander Long's letter of July 3 (above).

5. Closer to the election, Chase expressed reluctance to support either the Democratic or Republican tickets. Chase to Gerrit Smith, Sept. 30, 1868 (below).

6. Samuel L. M. Barlow was a prominent New York attorney and Democratic activist. By July 7, George H. Pendleton's supporters had ousted Washington McLean from the Ohio delegation. For Smith's praise, see his letter of July 5 to Chase (above).

TO ELIZUR WRIGHT

Autograph letter. Elizur Wright Papers, Library of Congress.

Private Strictly

Washington July 9, 1868.

My dear Sir,[1]

I don't believe that you will be any wiser, because of my answer to your questions but I will answer them.[2]

And first I mean by "the people of the states" all the citizens, white & black; and suppose it is the right of these citizens to determine, either actively or passively, who shall exercise the right of suffrage. Either this or imposition of some external power: and what external power? Congress? I see no authority for intervention of Congress unless in the 13th Amendment; and the general opinion is that it cannot be found there, & this opinion seems to be confirmed by the 14th amendment now certain to be adopted.[3]

And, second, I see only "practically" that God has made the human mind & conscience, & that our only hope for security against abuses is in these trained & improved by reason & christianity. I see no greater *security* in placing the question of suffrage under the control of Congress than of the people of the states. It might do good so far as to make the rule uniform, if the Constitution allowed it.

You see the result of the Democratic Convention.[4] So far as I am personally concerned and so far as the great cause of freedom & justice is concerned I do not regret the use of my name. It has familiarized the younger & more progressive portion of the party to the idea of carrying democratic principles into honest practical application; and it has given me access to many minds in the south on which I constantly endeavor to impress ideas of justice to the colored man & votes for the colored man as both right & politic.

The effect on myself is of little importance. I was surprised by the extent and spontaneousness of the movement in my favor, especially among the younger men. They seemed to want my kind of democracy & I could not refuse the use of my name. But I have said to every one frankly that I had no desire for a nomination nor for any higher place than I now hold; and since the Convention met I have said constantly that I could not see how I could be nominated by it. There was in it too large a number of those with whom I have had to contend in times past & who could not put off their old hostility: too large a number also who, not content with opposition to the military & military commission features of the reconstruction laws which I never approved, were animated by a determination to overthrow the governments organized under them, &, for the sake of getting speedy possession of political power, those from the South were willing to plunge their states into new disorder & strife. Their will prevailed, & the democratic party will probably take another lesson from experience.

You know how I have longed for a genuine earnest, honest democracy amimated by a sincere love of exact & equal justice for all men. I believe you have shared this longing with me.

Shall we never see it?

I am now departed from all political aspiration. I resolutely & finally dismiss whatever hope I have had of using the powers of the highest office for realizing my idea of good for my country. It shall hereafter be the limit of all my ambition to do all the good I can in the sphere I occupy without a wish to enlarge it.

But enough. I am writing to an old friend or I would not write so freely. You will hold my confidence sacred

Faithfully yours
S P CHASE

Elizur Wright Esq.

1. Wright, a reformer and antislavery activist, worked in Boston as an actuary. A letterpress copy of this manuscript is in Chase's papers at the Library of Congress and appears at *micro* 38:0087. *DAB,* 20:548–49.

2. In a letter dated July 7, Wright had asked a series of questions about the fourth plank in Chase's platform, which left enforcement of suffrage to the states. *Mr. Chase's Views,* 2; Schuckers, *Life and Public Services,* 568; Wright to Chase, July 7, 1868 (Wright Papers, L.C.).

3. The Fourteenth Amendment became law on July 28, 1868. *Statutes at Large,* 15:708–11.

4. Alarmed at what seemed to be growing support for Thomas A. Hendricks, the New York and Ohio delegations had united behind an apparently reluctant Horatio Seymour, thus passing by Chase and starting a landslide that secured Seymour's nomination on the twenty-second ballot. Afterward, the convention chose Francis P. Blair, Jr., as Seymour's vice-presidential running mate. At no time during three days of balloting did Chase receive more than four votes out of a total of 317. Coleman, *Election of 1868,* 212–14, 238–45, 382; *New York Herald,* July 10, 1868.

FROM JOHN GLANCY JONES

Autograph letter. Chase Papers, Historical Society of Pennsylvania (*micro* 38:0090).

Private

Reading
9 July 1868

My dear Chief Justice

The nomination is made; The deliberate choice of the national will is not represented by the Convention; The times called for a man to meet a crisis & bridge a chasm; *Passion* not cool Judgment; has rushed in, & named *one antagonist,* in preference to *another,* because the one is *east* & not *West* & therefore preferable; for future contingencies;[1] alas how shortsighted; success never yet was known to be the logical sequence of *passion* / Ohio blinded by passion rushes to New York; to nominate, a highly estimable gentleman, unexceptionable in every particular, except that he is not just the man the *times* now call for, & she hopes by this step to call for a return in 1872—sad blunder; the nominee, can receive no aid from the friends of Ohios candidate;[2] It must come *now before* the election & *after* the election, from the friends of Chf Justice Chase who is this day the clear choice of [two thirds] of of the New York Convention, including New York and its gentlemanly & amiable candidate; The popular will, the speedy redemption of the Country, is at least put in Jeopardy; in order to appease personal ambition & provide for personal future interests— I like Pendleton, & only speak thus to deplore the consequences of foolish advisers; Now to be plain, Providence for good reasons, has *deferred* the day, you are young enough, plenty for 74 & 78, so am I to help you; Seymour is to fall into the *hands,* & must *lean upon him* who is able to help him nature decreed this when she made the man that man is you & you alone; for the Countrys sake help him, but *guide him*— He cannot *restore* this Country but he may pave the way, Heaven does not will that this thing shall be done as speedily as we had hoped / I regard Seymours election as entirely dependant upon the course of your friends so also if elected he is impotent without your aid; when you are called on respond but hold the reins in your own hands & take care of the *future.* You can if you will guide this whole affair & control it for the welfare of the country, out of your hands it will go under; will you do it? Write me at once;[3] I have devoted all my faculties for 18 mos. to secure your nomination not for selfish considerations for that might be secured at less cost, but because of solemn convictions; that you are the man to do the work; I could write more but it is needless now, Seymour cannot be elected without you, even if with you, If you help talk the reins in your own hands

Truly yours
J. Glancy Jones

1. Earlier in the day, delegates from New York and Ohio had successfully engineered the election of former New York governor Horatio Seymour as the Democratic presidential standard-bearer, largely in an attempt to prevent Thomas A. Hendricks of Indiana from securing the nomination. Coleman, *Election of 1868,* 238–45; *New York Herald,* July 10, 1868.

2. George H. Pendleton, the favored candidate of the Ohio delegation until July 8. Coleman, *Election of 1868,* 234–35.

3. Chase answered on July 11, noting with disapproval the Democratic candidates, a party platform that denounced the Reconstruction Acts, and a letter that vice-presidential nominee Francis P. Blair, Jr., had written on June 30 to delegate James O. Broadhead that advocated the reversal of Radical Reconstruction. All three factors, asserted Chase, "would deprive me of all power to be useful politically; Even if it were not plainly improper for one holding the judicial position I occupy to take an active political part." Ibid., 155–57, 204; Chase to Jones, July 11, 1868 (Chase Papers, L.C.); *New York Herald,* July 8, 1868; *New York Times,* July 3, 1868.

FROM KATE CHASE SPRAGUE

Autograph letter. Chase Papers, Library of Congress (*micro* 38:0113).

New York— 10 June 1868[1]

My dearest Father,

You have been most cruelly deceived & shamefully used by the man whom you trusted implicitly, & the *Country* must suffer for his duplicity. I would not write you yesterday, in the excitement of the result of the action of the Convention, & until I had carefully gone over in my mind all the circumstances that had come under my knowledge of the action of Mr. Van Buren. When I get comfortably settled at Narragansett, I will write out a full & detailed history of my *knowledge* of this matter that can not fail to convince you of his bad faith. Nothing more would be needed, than that since the result of the Nomination was announced Mr. Van Buren though constantly at the Manhattan Club, next door has not been near me,[2] & has passed both Mr. Kennedy & Mr. Schuckers this morning without a recognition / Had Mr. Kennedy had the authority to act for you, you would have been as certainly nominated on the wave of the enthusiasm created in the Convention by the ½ vote cast by California day before yesterday, as any thing could be— Mr. Van Buren's telegraph to you, "to answer no questions in regard to the Platform, was the block he put in the way of your Nomination—& when at the critical juncture he was at last found, (for he has scarcely been seen in the Convention) he refused to take the responsibility of speaking for you, & said he was not authorized. At 3½ P.M. when I finally saw him, he said he would divide the responsibility with Mr. Long—*but took no action,* & *the* moment had gone by— Had I received my letter at the hour it was due, or any time before 3½ P.M—I believe all would have been different.[3] Mr. Kennedy & Mr. Long were both true as steel, but neither of them were equal (or so situated as to be equal) to the combinations against them. Mr. Tilden & Mr. Kernan have done this work & Mr. Van Buren has been *their tool*[4]— This is my honest belief; but I will mite it out carefully— So dear Father in the future, be guided by the advice of some of those who are devoted to you, but who are more suspicious than your own noble heart will allow you to be—

With all this *you personally* can have nothing to regret. Your friends have worked noble—& the universal disappointment to-day is amazing— Not a flag floats nor, is the semblance of rejoicing visible anywhere.

Your name is a watch word with the people, & they have been outraged & deceived—

I am perfectly well, & go to the Country to kiss Willie & see the Governor. I may return, & think I shall, to Washington with the Governor, then I hope we can capture you & take to Narragansett. Mr. Cisco, is as true as tried steel, Mr. Long has gone home broken hearted. You can form no conception of the depression here

Your devoted
KATIE

1. Evidence in the body of this letter related to the Democratic national convention of 1868 indicates that it was actually written on July 10.

2. The Manhattan Club, 96 Fifth Avenue, was a center of Democratic political activity. During the convention, Chase's daughter stayed at 94 Fifth Avenue. Coleman, *Election of 1868,* 149. *New York Dir. (1872),* 19; Kate Chase Sprague to Chase, July 2, 1868 (above).

3. Kate apparently refers to Chase's letter of July 7 (above), which included authorization for a number of "discreet friends" to act on his behalf.

4. On July 9, former congressman Francis Kernan (1816–92), a delegate from New York, had announced the support of his delegation for Horatio Seymour. Moments later, Samuel J. Tilden formally cast the state's votes for Seymour. *DAB,* 10:356; *New York Herald,* July 10, 1868.

TO JAY COOKE

Letterpress copy of autograph letter. Chase Papers, Library of Congress (*micro* 38:0122).

Washington, July 11, 1868.

My dear Cooke,[1]

What do you mean? You have been neglecting me sadly for months and now you talk about my being your debtor to the [amount] of two letters. I don't believe it. Your bookkeeping is wrong—all wrong.[2]

However I will pay you for your last promptly. I was glad as I always am to see your honest & friendly—not face—but fist; and the pleasure was not at all diminished by the check for the first F. & W. dividend which it enclosed or by the expectation of future dividends which it encouraged. It will be charming when Sterling begins to pay as well. When do you think that will be?[3]

I have not had a look at you or a word from you since the impeachment began. Is it possible that your confidence also was shaken because I was simply honest and impartial? If ever in my life I acted conscientiously, in the fear of God, with a true reverence for the Constitution, & with genuine love for my country, I so acted in that business. But the cry went forth Crucify him!,[4] & hardly one Republican or Republican Press was bold enough to utter a word of remonstrance much less of defence. This sickened me of party: and I thought myself free of party obligations and connexions.

But at this time, to my great surprise, the movement for my nomination by the Democrats developed itself. Letters came to me from every quarter, north, south, east & west, from the Gulf, the Pacific & the Atlantic urging me not to decline the nomination if offered. Most of the writers were republicans—some democrats—some formerly rebels, but now willing to accept Universal Amnesty & Universal Suffrage.

It seemed to me, under these circumstances, a plain duty to let the movement take its course / I neither helped nor hindered it. I adhered to my own ideas & convictions. I never since the war closed believed in confiscation, disfranchisement, vindictive action of any sort; never in military government for states in time of peace, nor in military commissions; & I said so, but [made] no [speeches] nor any public proclamation of my opinions. On the other hand I did believe in universal amnesty & universal suffrage, & in complete removal of all political disfranchisements & disabilities; and longed for the restoration of good will between the south & the north, & for the renewal & increase of southern prosperity; and greatly desired that the democratic party might take advanced & liberal ground, and ensure itself a triumph honorable to itself & beneficial to the Union; and I said so when proper occasion offered.

This is all I did. The result is known. I should have been nominated on the 22d. ballot, had not Ohio brought forward Seymour.[5] That morning the New York delegation had determined to support me by a vote of 37 to 24, & Georgia, Wisconsin, R. Island Massachusetts Maine & New Jersey were ready to do the same thing. This prospect enraged some of the Ohio delegates, and those opposed to me were in the majority, & so it was agreed that Ohio should go solid for Seymour & this coup de main was successful in the Convention.

I am not sorry. The events of the last three or four [*illeg.*] have cut me off almost wholly from political [connexions, &c.] So [I am] independent of party. So I prefer to remain. Good bye politics—welcome jurisprudence for the rest of my life.

Faithfully your friend
S P Chase

1. Cooke, a close friend of Chase and a partner in the banking company of Jay Cooke and Co., had gained fame for his success as a government loan agent during the Civil War.

2. In a letter dated July 10, Cooke sent Chase a check of $22,500 for dividends from an investment in the Warren and Franklin Railroad of northwest Pennsylvania. Cooke to Chase, July 10, 1868 (Chase Papers, L.C.); Henrietta M. Larson, *Jay Cooke: Private Banker* (Cambridge, Mass., 1936), 153.

3. Cooke had apparently given Chase either a special deal or outright ownership of stocks and bonds from the Sterling Iron and Railway of Orange County, New York. Larson, *Jay Cooke,* 153; Chase to Cooke, Nov. 17, 1868 (below).

4. In accordance with the mob's cry prior to the crucifixion of Jesus. John 19:6; Luke 23:21; Mark 15:13.

5. Chase initially reacted to Horatio Seymour's nomination as the Democratic party's candidate for president on July 9 in correspondence of the same day to Elizur Wright (above).

TO MURAT HALSTEAD

Letterpress copy of autograph letter. Chase Papers, Library of Congress (*micro* 38:0145).

Private

Washington, July 14, 1868.

My dear Mr. Halstead

The Sunday Commercial contains an item from your New York Correspondent to the effect that I have written a letter thanking the Massachu[setts] delegates who voted for me & predicting the success of the democratic ticket.[1] It would be agreeable if there could be a little more truth in such reports,—especially if surmises could be stated as surmises & not as facts.

There is just as much truth in many of the stories set afloat about me in connexion with the New York Convention as in those connected with the Impeachment-trial. In this story there is none whatever

My name was brought forword spontaneously &, so far as I know, unexpectedly in various sections of the country some two months ago as that of a democrat in principle, not in mere party connexion, acceptable to great numbers outside of the democratic party, & likely therefore, if preferred by the Democratic Convention to unite most if not absolutely all who, for various reasons, are opposed to or dissatisfied with the nominations made at Chicago.

I thought it not [improper] nor unpatriotic to consent to this use of my name; but I never expressed any desire for the nomination; resorted to no efforts to secure it; nor ever except in one particular, even *seemed* to change or modify any views of public questions which I have heretofore avowed. I never gave any pledge or assurance, or authorized [any] support to nominees if nominated on a platform inconsistent [*two words? illeg.*] convictions & my life record; nor have I ever expressed any approval of the platform, beyond saying that it is in the main very good, unless interpreted as a commitment by the party [to] an aggressive assault upon the constitutions & governments established under the reconstruction acts, or of the nominees to special constructions of the constitution.[2] This you see opens a very wide margin of exception: and I would not have gone so far as this except in compliance with the wishes of valued and faithful friends, for whose sake I felt bound to say the most that conscience would allow.

The one particular just alluded to, in which I did really modify former views to some extent was this. I have been inclined to think that under the 13th amendment and as a means of assuring freedom under it Congress might provide by law for the extension of suffrage to all. But very few have accepted this view and the 14th amendment, now certain to be ratified, seems, by strong implication at least, to refer the whole suffrage question to the states. If this construction be the correct one the question is settled against the view I was disposed to adopt & I must needs submit.

So you see I am, in no wise, pledged or committed to any platform or any candidates or any party. I remain what I declared myself in the Senate to be "a democrat, by the grace of God, free & independent"; full of democratic sympathies & aspirations but the bondsman of no organization; a sincere lover of my country; a lover of all good & patriotic men whether they agree with me in my special views or not; a man who seeks no other position than that which he holds & who, now will accept no other; but, [*illeg.*] com[*illeg.*] & [*illeg.*] will do whatever he can to promote complete reconciliation between the sections, good will between the races, & the revival & increase of the prosperity of every section of the country & especially of that which needs it most, the theatre of the late rebellion, & who still believes that these great objects can be best promoted by universal suffrage & universal amnesty.

I regret exceedingly that the New York Convention committed itself to the folly or worse, of denouncing the reconstruction laws as unconstitutional "usurpations[",] revolutionary and void.[3] Senator Morton, who is among the wisest if not the very wisest of the Republican statesmen, saw at once the advantage to be taken of it: and the very next day after the adjournment of the Convention echoed the declaration of General Blair "that all that is said about greenbacks & bonds & questions of finance is mere nonsense," & added "The great issue is the question of overturning the new State Governments by fear, the restoration of the power of the rebels, or, as they call it the white man's government in those states—and all the rest is leather & prunella."[4] I warned gentlemen at New York against making this issue. I do not see how they can now escape from it; though I meet no democrat who does not disavow all intention of making war on the new State Governments. And certainly the interest of all is peace not discord.

But as usual I am making my letter too long. Don't believe any thing ill of me except on better evidence than rumor or report; & let me have still, though henceforth separated from politics the friend[ship] of the Commercial & its Editor. Especially contradict any story you see [that] [*illeg.*] am concerned, in any new political movement whatever. I [have] [*illeg.*] to do & shall have nothing to do with any such.

Faithfully your friend
S P Chase

M. Halstead, Esq

1. The notice appeared in the July 12 issue of the *Cincinnati Commercial.* Four delegates from Massachusetts cast their votes for Chase on July 9, during the twenty-first round of balloting. Coleman, *Election of 1868,* 239–40, 382.

2. Similar wording about the platform that the Democratic party officially adopted on July 7 appears in correspondence from Chase to John D. Van Buren, July 8, 1868 (Chase Papers, Cinc. Hist. Soc.). *New York Herald,* July 8, 1868.

3. As adopted, the Democratic platform expressed concern over the possibility of "a single, centralized and consolidated government." It asserted: "We regard the reconstruction acts, as so called, of Congress as such a usurpation and unconstitutional, revolutionary and void," it asserted. *New York Herald*, July 8, 1868.

4. Chase quotes from a speech that Senator Oliver Hazard Perry Throck Morton of Indiana delivered from the Senate floor on July 9. To Morton, the controversial letter of June 30 that Francis P. Blair, Jr., wrote to James O. Broadhead in opposition to Congressional Reconstruction indicated the Democrats' willingness to resist Congress "by force." The passage about "leather & prunella"—that is, a cobbler's leather apron and the material used to make clerical gowns—suggests indifference to superficial attributes. In this expression, Morton was quoting loosely from the fourth epistle of Alexander Pope's *Essay on Man* (1734), lines 204–5: "Worth makes the man, and want of it, the fellow: The rest is all but leather or prunella." *Congressional Globe*, 40th Cong., 2d sess., 1867–68, 3871–72; *New York Times*, July 3, 1868.

TO WILLIAM B. THOMAS

Letterpress copy of autograph letter. Chase Papers, Library of Congress (*micro* 38:0174).

Washington, July 17, 1868

My dear Sir,[1]

Pardon my delay in replying to your note of the 11th.[2]

I fear that the action and speech of Mr. Seymour was not entirely candid. A leading friend of Gov. Hendricks states to me that what he said & did, left upon his mind the assurance that the first choice of the N.Y. delegation was Gov. H.—— & that its vote would be given accordingly. Still I feel quite confident that Gov Seymours real preference was for my nomination, & that he would have declared it, had not the action of the Ohio delegation prevented; and I do not believe that the action of this delegation, though not wholly unexpected, was desired or approved by him. He simply yielded when almost any man would have yielded; but when his honor & duty required him not to yield.

I do not regret the result on account of myself: but I do on account of my friends & the country. My nomination wd. have practically disposed of the agitation which just now threatens most evil.

At present it does not seem to me best to print that letter.[3] I will think more of it & write you again.

I cannot express my gratitude to you for your noble & disinterested friendship. May God bless you

Faithfully your friend
S P Chase

Col. Wm B. Thomas

1. Thomas had served as U.S. collector of customs at Philadelphia and, during the Civil War, as an officer in Pennsylvania's 192d Volunteer Infantry Regiment.

2. Thomas's letter questioned the integrity of Horatio Seymour for accepting the Democratic presidential nomination. "He assured me at our first interview that the N Y. delegation would cast their vote for you," claimed Thomas; "Unless you can assure me that he was sincere in his disinclination to accept the nomination I must believe him to have been a party to the most contemptable doubledealing political tricksters were ever

guilty of." Thomas also asked for permission to publish a letter from Chase "about which Butler was so much concerned." Thomas to Chase, July 11, 1868 (Chase Papers, Hist. Soc. of Pa.).

3. Thomas most likely refers to correspondence from Chase of March 10, 1868, in which the chief justice admitted receiving "many" letters of advice about the impeachment proceedings and disavowed any interest in the presidential nomination. Thomas apparently shared the letter with Benjamin F. Butler, a congressional manager during the trial, for potential use as evidence of Chase's impartiality. Chase to Thomas, March 10, 1868 (Chase Papers, L.C.), *DAB*, 3:358; Thomas to Butler, May 19, 1868 (Butler Papers, L.C.).

TO GERRIT SMITH

Autograph letter. Chase Papers, Library of Congress (*micro* 38:0203).

Narragansett, July 26, 1868.

My dear friend,

It has been in my mind to write you ever since the New York Convention: and now I am going to do it. I have been here by the sea side, some five or six miles from Point Judith, and nearly opposite Newport for several days but must go away next Thursday to hold a Circuit Court on the shore of the Ohio at Parkersburg.

I never expected the nomination of the New York Convention; and think I said so to you.[1] But it did surprise me that so many wished it: and that even more seemed to expect it. Mr. Bryant wrote me apparently quite certain that it would be offered to me, and advising me to insist on a platform thoroughly identified with our most advanced views of the slavery question & the questions,—such as suffrage &c,—cognate to that. I replied that there seemed to me little ground for the opinion that the Convention would entertain the views he supposed, & that I should be very glad if it could be induced to take ground in favor of the principle of universal suffrage, leaving the application of the principle to the states, and of practically recognizing the work of reconstruction under the acts of Congress as accomplished by the admission of Senators & Representatives from the Southern States and not to be disturbed by any action of the National Government. Mr B—— wrote me afterwards declaring himself satisfied with my views[2]

When the Convention met there was undoubtedly a strong feeling—stronger than I had anticipated in favor of my nomination. It was much stronger however outside of the Convention, than inside. The delegates had been appointed long before the development of the popular desire for a new political departure to be represented by my name. Many of them had been instructed & many were already committed to particular candidates. Few comparatively shared the popular wish. This became manifest in the adoption of the platform. Those who earnestly wished my nomination desired that the selection of candidates should precede [*illeg.*] action. But a decided majority was of a different opinion, or rather saw no sufficient reason for departing from the usage. So the platform was adopted, and with very little apparent dissent—just as it would have been had it expressed fully my own views. But, though it was well enough in the main it was, in important respects, quite contrary to what I thought it ought to be. There was, however, so much that was good in it, that, although I wished & so said to my friends that my name should not be presented to the Convention, I did not feel at liberty,—considering how many had identified themselves with my nomination & how grievously a positive refusal of its use would disappoint them—to come out with any such refusal. Besides I was not a little influenced by your opinion that I ought to accept the nomination, if offered, without much regard to the platform unless compelled to profess unqualified assent to it;[3] & I felt sure that I could write a letter which would give an interpretation of it acceptable to the masses of the party, & not inconsistent with my own views of the practical questions of the time: So I let the matter go on: and I now think it certain that I should have been nominated on the 22d or 23d. ballot if a portion of the Ohio & a portion of the New York delegations had not concerted the nomination of Seymour. What the result of my nomination wd. have been it is impossible to say. I hoped it would be peace, enfranchisement without regard to color or political offences, harmony, between sections, harmony between races, Divine approval, & prosperity. God did not permit it, and I am personally something more than content.

To be sure it is somewhat painful to be misunderstood as I have been & am. Mr. Beecher's censures are perhaps the worst. I understand that some others have followed his example & among them Mr. Douglas.[4] They will see their mistake some day. You, my dear friend, with your characteristic greatness of soul, have vindicated me and I am sorry that I have nothing to offer you in return but my gratitude.[5]

In what has recently taken place I have simply acquiesced. And I simply acquiesce the result. I look forward to nothing but the performance of the duties which lie before me as a judge & a citizen: and regard myself as removed from all political responsibilities except those necessarily incident to these two characters. I cannot help however of looking forward with much anxiety / Has God more chastisement in reserve for our injustices to the colored people, or for our hardness towards those whose rebellion we have subdued? Is not our hardness towards these a natural &, perhaps, necessary consequence of their hardness toward those?

I think it not improbable that when released from Parkersburg, say three weeks hence, I may go to Cincinnati; take up my youngest daughter Nettie there, & come eastward again by the way of the Lake. In that case we may pass through New York by the Central Railroad, &, in that case, I mean to call on you at Peterboro. Please write me at P——g and let me know if you will be at home.[6]

With much kind remembrance of Mrs Smith, & Mrs Miller & the Colonel believe me my dear friend

Most faithfully yours
S P CHASE

Hon Gerrit Smith.

1. Examples of such disavowals appear in letters written to Smith on April 2 and June 17, 1868 (above).

2. See William C. Bryant to Chase, June 13, 1868; Chase to Bryant, June 19, 1868; and Bryant to Chase, June 23, 1868 (all above).

3. "If it shall nominate you," Smith had written anticipating the Democratic National Convention, "I hold that you should accept the nomination, whatever it may say in connexion with its nominations." Smith to Chase, June 20, 1868 (Chase Papers, Hist. Soc. of Pa.).

4. Henry Ward Beecher, the pastor of Brooklyn's Congregational Plymouth Church, had censured Chase in a recent letter to the *Boston Daily Advertiser.* "I have never been a Chase man," wrote Beecher in support of Republican candidate Ulysses S. Grant; "I have for years, as a leader in public affairs deemed him, like his greenbacks, as promising more on the face than they are worth in gold. . . . I have for years felt that Mr. CHASE's ambition was consuming the better elements of his nature." To black abolitionist Frederick Douglass, Chase's flirtation with the Democrats was "treachery": "His descent is from a point higher—he has fallen further—and he reaches a depth of infamy deeper, and hotter than that of any of his predecessors in treachery." *National Anti-Slavery Standard,* July 18, 1868; *New York Times,* July 11, 1868.

5. Smith's circular *Destroy Not Man's Faith,* written in June, included a defense of Chase's conduct during the impeachment proceedings. Chase to Smith, June 17, 1868 (above).

6. Chase's youngest daughter was sight-seeing in Minnesota. In the middle of August, Chase decided to travel directly from Parkersburg, West Virginia, to Narragansett, Rhode Island, since Nettie (Janet) had changed her itinerary and had gone to her sister's house without waiting for Chase in Ohio. Chase to Smith, Sept. 30, 1868 (below); Janet Chase to Chase, July 21, and Chase to Gerrit Smith, Aug. 13, 1868 (both Chase Papers, L.C.).

TO KATE CHASE SPRAGUE

Autograph letter. Chase Papers, Historical Society of Pennsylvania (*micro* 38:0247).

Parkersburg, West Va Aug. 6

My darling Katie,

I have had *such* a time getting here! Monday evening to Baltimore[1]—Tuesday Morning at 5 cars to Ellicotts Mills, and up an hour earlier & broken sleep before that I might not fail to be ready— On omnibus—crowded inside & four on top—three of the insiders babies—one crying almost all the time—slapped every now & then not hard but petulantly by the mother, & appealing with his two year old notes Mamma! pretty child! papa pretty child!—all this twenty miles, with a long delay at the crossing of the Patuxent on the Frederick Pike occasioned by the stalling of two Express Wagons till at length we reached the cars beyond the great break. This made us two hours behind time at Grafton, where I took a wash & got to bed about half past one Wednesday morning: to get up again at four—got ready to start at five,—but got breakfast instead & a start at six, on a freight train with a second class car attached, which brought us here a distance of a hundred & four miles in ten hours, at 4 in the afternoon.

Then all my troubles were over. Judge Jackson, one of the best sort once & very well to do, was waiting for me at the depot with a handsome carriage & handsome pair of horses, and a real old fashioned Virginia chunk of blackness for a coachman[2] / He took me to his house; a square old mansion with a very pleasant, who has been very pretty and is still very good looking, Mrs Jackson inside, and a fine young man of seventeen & a sweet young daughter of sixteen or eighteen I can't tell whether she is younger older than her brother.[3]

I am very pleasantly situated here indeed & Judge Jackson is full of all offers of kindness. He has *struck ile*—loosing at first very heavily, but now doing nearly well enough to make up all his losses. His income from his royalties on his wells is $70 a day. How long he can't say. But it is very well now.

He wants me to go with him and his family to Oakland;[4] but I advise him to take Mrs J. & Miss Lillie & go with me to Narragansett. I half hope he will.

In the cars from Baltimore I met Judge Erskine from Georgia, whom you perhaps remember as our guest at dinner one day. He is going to put a daughter at school in the north & I advised him to consult you.[5] I shouldnt wonder if he should come & advise with you. If he does receive him kindly & give him your best smiles & best advice. He is an excellent man & a warm friend of mine

I have charged the Grand Jury today & heard argument in one case & decided it with Judge Jacksons help.[6]

I wish you could see the Judge's father an old gentleman of 70—straight—active—clear headed—in every sense of the word a fine old gentleman'.[7]

Nettie will be with you next week perhaps this—& the week after—possibly next week. How pleasant it will be to see you all together again. Kisses for the boy—love for the Governor—love for Nettie when she comes.

Goodbye & God bless you & make you His own child.

Most affectionately
S P CHASE

Mrs K. C. Sprague

1. Chase wrote this letter on a Thursday. He had left Washington, D.C., on August 3. *Chase Papers,* 1:643.

2. John Jay Jackson, Jr., a former Virginia legislator, was judge of the U.S. District Court for the District of West Virginia. *Nat. Cyc.,* 11:521.

3. Jackson and his wife, Carrie C. Glime Jackson, had two children: Lily Irene and Benjamin Vinton. The Jacksons' daughter later became known for her skills as an artist and sculptor. Ibid.; *American Women: Fifteen Hundred Biographies with over 1,400 Portraits . . . ,* 2 vols. (New York, 1897), 2:415–16.

4. Possibly Oakland, Maryland, near the state's border with West Virginia.

5. John Erskine (1813–95) had been a federal judge for the district of Georgia since 1866. His only daughter later married Willard T. Ward. *DAB,* 6:180; William J. Northen, ed., *Men of Mark in Georgia,* 7 vols. (Atlanta, 1911; reprint, Spartanburg, S.C., 1974), 3:171.

6. Chase's charge suggests that he expected the jury to consider violations of laws that involved internal revenue, counterfeiting, and the post office. Johnson, *Cases Decided by Chief Justice Chase,* 263–66; *New York Times,* Aug. 10, 1868.

7. John Jay Jackson, Sr., an attorney and West Point graduate, had served on Andrew Jackson's staff. *Nat. Cyc.,* 11:521.

TO HIRAM BARNEY

Autograph letter. Chase Papers, Historical Society of Pennsylvania (*micro* 38:0250).

Parkersburg. Aug 9, '68

My dear friend,[1]

The mail travels slowly from New York here. Yours of the 4th came only night before last.

I am very sorry to read your account of your ill health; or *half health* as you call it. You must take care of yourself and *must not* allow business to deprive you of necessary relaxation. Because I am growing old myself, and feel the hold on life gradually relaxing, I am all the more easily alarmed about those I love and you are one of those I love best. So you must let me insist on your "knocking off work." Why cant you take up your quarters in a Narragansett or Newport comfortable house for a week or two. I expect to be at N. again about the first of next week say 17 or 18th.

I have read the Extract from S——'s letter to you & have destroyed it. He has himself destroyed all my power to be of service to him. He has my strong esteem; in many respects my full agreement & confidence. He is as much better than the platform as Blair is worse. But who will guaranty his life and health, if he & B—— are elected? I don't know a single Republican who would accept my assurance that the country will be safe in that event; nor do I see how I could conscientiously give it. What possessed the Convention to adopt the anti-reconstruction plank; & then give it the worst possible construction by the nomination of F.P. with his letter hardly dry from his pen?[2]

As things are now I find it difficult to take any side: and take none. I do not know that I shall vote: nor do I know how I shall vote if I do. If we meet I will talk the matter over with you. It looks to me as if Grant would carry every Western state except possibly this state of West Virginia & Indiana; not because *his* election is desired, but because people are afraid of violent & revolutionary measures in the south if he is not elected.[3] With a slight change in the platform, and a candidate for Vice President as good & acceptable as Gov. S—— and the result might be very different.

Yours faithfully
S P Chase

H. Barney Esq.

1. Barney, an attorney and collector of customs for the port of New York during the Civil War, had promoted Chase as the presidential nominee of the Democratic party. Barney to Chase, July 10, 1868, and Chase to Barney, June 26, 1868 (both Chase Papers, Hist. Soc. of Pa.); Coleman, *Election of 1868,* 216.

2. Chase refers to the plank that declared Congressional Reconstruction void. Francis P. Blair, Jr.'s, letter of June 30 to James O. Broadhead called for the "overthrow" of Radical reconstruction in the South. *New York Herald,* July 8, 1868; *New York Times,* July 3, 1868.

3. In voting on November 3, Ulysses S. Grant carried Indiana, West Virginia, and every western state except Oregon. His opponent, Horatio Seymour, won only in Delaware, Georgia, Kentucky, Louisiana, Maryland, New Jersey, New York, and Oregon. *Appleton's Annual Cyclopædia,* 8:753.

TO KATE CHASE SPRAGUE

Autograph letter. Chase Papers, Historical Society of Pennsylvania (*micro* 38:0255).

Parkersburg, Aug. 9. 1868.

My darling child.

Letters come slowly from Narragansett to Parkersburg. Yours of the 4th only reached me last night.

I am very sorry for your loss of the horse and don't wonder that the Governor was greatly provoked. The men deserved dismissal if the loss was through their carelessness, especially if they had been drinking to excess & driving too hard. But I fear you will have difficulty in replacing Edward.

Your letter makes me fear that you and your husband had some unpleasant words about his prompt action. It was quite natural doubtless that you should feel hurt by his sudden action in a matter which so nearly concerned your own comfort: but if you did I hope you suppressed any external manifestation of it as far as possible. You must reflect, my darling, that there can be but one head to a family, and that while a husband will always find the happiness of both increased by mutual counsels, yet that it is the wife's part when the husband chooses to act, in any matter upon his own judgment without asking hers, to acquiesce cheerfully and affectionately. This is a part of her marriage vow: and the best way, by all odds, to obtain & retain the confidence, affection, & consultation of her husband. Remember how cheerfully & beautifully Mrs Hamilton Smith yielded to her husband and how he devoted himself to her.[1] Few wives ever had a more indulgent husband, and a husband to be more justly proud of than you. You love & honor him I know; but sometimes you complain when he thinks it unreasonable & contend with him when duty & prudence require submission. You can conquer only by love & submission—not by argument & pertinacity. An end gained by pertinacity is really lost.

But here I am sermonizing away, & I fear you are impatient. But remember, my child, that it is your father who loves you beyond expression, and longs to see you perfect in every wifely & christian duty.

I think it *not impossible* that Judge Jackson & his daughter,[2] a sweet little girl, of sixteen, something of an invalid and a little deaf, but very cheery, bright, & pleasant may come with me. I am sure you will like her and the Governor will like the Judge. He knows all about these oil regions. I say not impossible, though it is hardly probable. It would be impossible for any one to be more kind to me than the whole family have been, & I want you to be as kind to them if they come.

Would you like to have Herbert come with me?[3] I will bring him if you wish. He can drive & do almost every thing; but would not like I suppose to be considered exactly as a coachman. He is with me here as my servant & if you dont want him will return to Washington. He has [no] wages, being under half pay as messenger at the request of the Judges whom he attended last winter. I shall not take him east, if you do not want him. Telegraph me if you do, if you get this on Wednesday. I expect to start on my return Thursday afternoon at 4.30. When I shall reach Nt.[4] will depend on the roads.

A letter from Nettie dated Frontenac, Aug. 2d came night before last.[5] She said she should write again before leaving. If only again I infer she would leave within ten or twelve days after the 21st—say 31st July or 3d Aug. If this inference is correct she is already with you or will be when I return. How glad I shall be to see her. Goodbye. Make the usual distribution of kisses, love, remembrances. Tell Willie to be a good boy. Try to make him know something of Christ.

Most affectionately your father
S P Chase

1. Hamilton Smith and Louise Rudd Smith, his second wife, married in 1846.
2. Lily Irene Jackson.
3. Ananias Herbert, evidently an African-American servant. Receipt to Herbert, Apr. 17, 1869 (Chase Papers, L.C.); *Wash. Dir. (1872)*, 233.
4. That is, Narragansett, Rhode Island.
5. Chase's youngest daughter was visiting Minnesota with relatives. Janet Chase to Chase, July 21, 1868 (Chase Papers, L.C.).

FROM HIRAM BARNEY

Autograph letter. Hiram Barney Papers, The Huntington Library (*micro* 38:0367).

Private!

New York
Sept. 7, 1868

My dear friend,

I shall probably leave for Iowa on the 9th. or 10th. instant, to be absent two months or more.

I wrote to you about two weeks ago at Narraganset—explaining my failure to go and see you and with a view to meet you before going west I asked where you cd. be found about this time / Having no reply I have no hope of being able to see you and do not know even how or where to send this letter— I visited Gov. S. on the 25th. August[1]— We own property together at the west and after talking business had some conversation on politics / He began the conversation by deprecating his nomination and saying that Hendricks would have been nominated on the 2d ballot afterwards if he had not received the nomination—that his nomination took him by surprise / That he had been faithful to his convictions that you ought to have been nominated and worked earnestly & persistently for that result—and then said that now he was the Candidate he desired to win and thought his chances good of success— He stated that if elected he shd. be powerless in the administration without the Co-operation of your friends and he wished their support. I told him that he would recollect what I said to him before the convention met—about the absolute necessity of their taking high radical democratic grounds on the equal rights of men & states and in referring to the rebellion should be particularly careful to use the most patriotic expressions of devotion to the principles which had been settled by the war— That he knew the character of democratic Republicans—and that they would never go back on their principles and the only way to win them was to acknowledge the correctness of their views and that by such a course alone could they divide the Republican party & ensure the triumph of the democrats— I said, your convention acted and spoke not to win republicans but to please southern democratic rebels, who do not regret their rebellion but glory in it. Under these circumstances he had no right to expect nor did I believe he would get many votes from dissatisfied republicans— I told him that he was personally popular, but his party had given such proofs of sympathy with the rebellion by the proceedings & Speeches at the convention & especially by the nomination of Blair with his letter before them that its patriotism was too much doubted to justify Mr Chase's friends in supporting it,[2] and he must not expect their votes—that I thought it very important to the welfare of the country that the democratic party should be beaten at this election— That they had bidden high for the support of the leading & unrepinting rebels and had shut their doors square in the face of Democratic Republicans / I told him also that this course had rendered it improbable that men of our way of thinking would ever trust the present leaders of the democratic party— I told him that I was going to the west & might not be able to return in time to vote; but that what I did in the way of politics at this election would be in the interest of Grant & Colfax / I said something about the platform, when he interrupted me by the remark that Mr. Chase approved of it as it is— I said I understand quite the contrary— He surely never approved of the clause declaring the reconstruction acts void. He did not answer / We parted friends as we have been for 30 years, in all things but politics— Did I talk right to him— I shall be at Keokuk Iowa two months and will be glad to have a letter from you while there— I send this letter to you through Mr Sprague as I know of no other way for it to reach you—

It really seems to me in view of the Condition of the southern states & of the Country generally of the highest importance that the democratic party should be severely beaten at this election.

I am faithfully Your friend
HIRAM BARNEY

Hon S. P. Chase

1. Democratic presidential candidate Horatio Seymour, former governor of New York.

2. Francis P. Blair, Jr.'s letter to James O. Broadhead, written on June 30, expressed hostility toward Radical Reconstruction. *New York Times,* July 3, 1868.

FROM JOHN D. VAN BUREN

Autograph letter. Chase Papers, Historical Society of Pennsylvania (*micro* 38:0388).

Newburgh
Sept 23 /68

Dear Sir

Thanks for your letter of 19th just received.

I did not hesitate to say when persons complained of the Brown, Long & Reed stories as coming from your special friends, that I was sure these things had, in no degree, your sanction.[1]

Much as, for many reasons, I would like to see you, with or without any followers, identified with the Democratic party now and for the future, I agree that you are not bound to support the nominations; you were never formally a candidate before our Convention; you had a few scattering votes but your name was never presented in form as a Candidate.

Certain features in the platform were, I doubt not, inserted with the purpose of making your nomination impossible.

I am glad you have the justice and the *charity* to recognise the difficulty of resisting the *pressure* that was suddenly brought to bear on Gov. Seymour. It was hard to resist; nevertheless he ought to have resisted & he knows plainly that I think so.

That bitter disappointment should make some men, like Col. Brown, guilty of harsh injustice & of indiscreet & hasty assumptions is very human-nature-like.

The whole affair impresses me with sad feelings; it is a great misfortune to the country to the party and to Gov. Seymour. We have lost an opportunity to obtain full control of the country & to save it from great evils. Our success now can be only partial; we cannot get Congress, if we do elect the President and restoration of the old-fashioned government will be therefore slow & difficult in the best event; but I am not so confident as I was that we shall even so far succeed. I shall be very much disappointed if Grant & those around him will pay any respect to the principles of our government.

I learned something new about the Convention the other day. The Ohio men had another card ready to play against you. If Seymour had refused, they had it all arranged to propose *John T. Hoffman;* what they wanted was to draw New York away from you. Hoffman would *not* have refused & the city delegation, your strongest friends, would have been demoralised. I have this from a sure source & I saw some things at the time which confirm it

Yours very truly
JNO D VAN BUREN

Chief Justice Chase

1. These men—Col. William Brown, previously a member of Kentucky's Union party state committee; Alexander Long, former Ohio legislator; and Cincinnati journalist Henry Reed—had supported Chase's bid for the presidency as a Democratic candidate. All three had recently written articles that depicted Horatio Seymour unfavorably and held him largely responsible for Chase's failure to secure the nomination and thus to promote the cause of what Brown called the "progressionists" within the party. Coleman, *Election of 1868,* 276–78; *New York Herald,* Sept. 6, 1868; *New York Times,* Aug. 26, 1868.

TO GERRIT SMITH

Autograph letter. Chase Papers, Library of Congress (*micro* 38:0424).

Private

Washington, Sep. 30. 1868.

My very dear friend,[1]

Nettie and I returned here Monday Evening. We gave up our project of visiting you very reluctantly. We were at Albany last week and I had thought we could run on to Peterboro and take a day or two more from the time I had appropriated to my cases here: but I saw in the papers that you were *on the Stump,* & so, not being certain of finding you at home, turned my face, & Nettie's southward.[2]

And here I found your note of the 5th with the generous gifts to the Howard university & the Freedman's Union Commission enclosed: $1000 for the former & $2000 for the latter.[3] I have handed the first to Gen. Howard who has no doubt written you; as he says in his note replying to mine that he would do so today.[4] The other check I retain for a few days that I may ascertain something more than I now know of the present operations of the Commission. I do this because your gift seems to have been somewhat influenced by the fact that I am President of the Commission, & yet I have known of late very little of its management. I am sanguine that the gift is a wise one but want to be *sure* that anything given, in any degree on my account, will be *well* applied.

I have read your letter to Gen. Lee and am very sorry that the occasion for writing it existed[5] / It does not seem to me that there is any danger of the reestablishment of Slavery in the event of democratic success; but it is infinitely to be deplored that the leading men of the South have not the wisdom & I may add the courage to recognize frankly and fully & finally the right of their colored fellow citizens to suffrage. I think that a good many of them are pretty well convinced on the points of duty & expediency; but these, with few exceptions, are afraid to face the reproaches of those of narrower & less discerning views. Social considerations govern. Social ostracism is the thing dreaded. If they could only be *forced* into doing what they know to be right & expedient they would be highly satisfied; for then they could avoid the ostracism; for all would be in the same condition, and the better sort could say to the others, "We don't like it any better than you, but we are forced into it, you see!"

If Gen. Grant is elected, I suppose they will get the force they want. But I cannot agree with your letter in the estimate it puts on the General. He may be all it represents him to be; and it is certainly better to be hopeful & generous as your letter is, than to exhibit the opposite qualities / So I will *hope* where you *believe*. But before I *believe* I must have better evidence that he sees the situation as you & I do than I have yet seen. I think him a brave & most deserving soldier, and a sincere patriot, and a man of good sense, and this is saying a good deal: but I have no knowledge that he has any more respect for the rights of American colored citizens or more real sympathy with them in their efforts to elevate themselves, than very many democrats who will vote for Seymour: and I have very little doubt that, if my friend Gerrit Smith were the Republican candidate for President, that Grant would vote for Seymour. So I cant get up any great amount of enthusiasm on either side, & very probably should not think it worth while to travel five or six hundred miles to vote in November even if my judicial duties did not call to a still greater distance from Ohio at that time / It is impossible for me to vote for Blair & the Broadhead letter & that plank in the democratic platform which countenances the Brodhead letter;[6] & I do not see my way clear to vote for Grant & the tendencies he represents; while I have no proof at all that on the point which I regard as vital, the colored citizens right to self protection by their own votes, he agrees with me more than he does with Blair.

The signs indicate that he will be elected & I hope the best. The people will keep the party leaders pretty near right [on this] point however.

Most faithfully your friend
S. P. Chase

1. The editors have inferred the recipient of this letter from its discussion of plans to visit Gerrit Smith's residence at Peterboro, New York, and because of themes common to Smith's correspondence to Chase of October 4 (below).

2. Originally, Chase and his youngest daughter planned to visit Smith en route from Cincinnati to Narragansett, Rhode Island. In Albany and nearby Troy, New York, Chase and Nettie stayed with Robert H. Pruyn and Amasa Parker, prominent Democrats, and visited the ironworks of former Democratic congressman Erastus Corning. Smith was stumping in support of the Republican presidential ticket. Chase to Smith, July 26, 1868 (above); Chase to Kate Chase Sprague, Sept. 29, 1868 (Chase Papers, L.C.); *New York Times,* Sept. 28, 1868; Smith to Chase, Oct. 4, 1868 (below).

3. According to the letter, Smith had recently sold a parcel of land and wanted to use the proceeds "for the benefit of the Freedmen." Howard University, named after Freedmen's Bureau commissioner Oliver Otis Howard, officially dated from March 2, 1867, when Congress granted the predominantly black institution its charter. Chase had served as president of the American Freedmen's Union Commission, product of a merger among numerous freedmen's aid societies, since October 1866. Ira V. Brown, "Lyman Abbott and Freedmen's Aid, 1865–1869," *Journal of Southern History* 15 (Feb. 1949): 27–29; Keim, *Keim's Illustrated Handbook,* 221; James M. McKim to Chase, Oct. 15, 1866 (Chase Papers, L.C.); Smith to Chase, Sept. 5, 1868 (Chase Papers, Hist. Soc. of Pa.); *Statutes at Large,* 14:438.

4. As promised, Howard thanked Smith in a note written on September 30. Howard to Smith, Sept. 30 (Smith Papers, George Arents Research Library, Syracuse University).

5. Smith's published letter reacted to a printed exchange of correspondence dating from August 26 between Lee and William S. Rosecrans, U.S. minister to Mexico at the time. In his letter, Rosecrans had asked for pledges of "chivalrous and magnanimous devotion to restoring peace and prosperity to our common country." Lee's response, which thirty other former Confederate leaders also signed, claimed that the South was resigned to emancipation, but that it opposed "any system of laws which would place the political power of the country in the hands of the negro race." To Smith, such a position put Lee and his cosigners in league with a policy of "bloody disenfranchisement," reflected in the platform and presidential ticket of the Democratic party. "In the election of those just and wise men, Grant and Colfax," countered Smith on September 25, "is the salvation of the South." Coleman, *Election of 1868,* 314–15; *New York Times,* Sept. 5, 1868; Gerrit Smith, *Gerrit Smith to General Lee,* ([Peterboro, N.Y], 1868), 1.

6. The platform denounced the Reconstruction Acts as "unconstitutional, revolutionary and void." Francis P. Blair, Jr.'s letter of June 30 to James Overton Broadhead (1819–98), a former Missouri state legislator and delegate at the Democratic national convention, called for the reversal of Radical reconstruction. *DAB,* 3:58–59; *New York Herald,* July 6, 8, 1868; *New York Times,* Sept. 5, 1868.

FROM GERRIT SMITH

Autograph letter. Schoff Civil War Letters and Documents, William L. Clements Library, University of Michigan (*micro* 38:0444).

Peterboro
Octr 4 1868

Chief Justice Chase,
My old & dear friend,

On my return home from one of my tours of speaking for Grant & Colfax, I find your letter.[1] Very welcome is the letter. But how much more welcome would have been yourself & Nettie! We are sad under the disappointment. But we hope to be made joyful by the presence of both of you under our roof next Summer. Oh how I *long to* have a *long* talk with you!

I thank you for giving the thousand dollar check to Genl Howard. He has written me a very pleasant note regarding it.[2] The two thousand dollar one I know you will dispose of in the *wisest* way—& therefore I sent it to *you.*

The train of thought in your letter, immediately following your reference to my Letter to Genl Lee,[3] interests me greatly—& greatly does it encourage me to hope that there will be Peace between the North & the South, the Black & the White.

You are probably, right in saying that social ostracism is the great dread at the South—& that the ostracism would cease when all were "forced into doing what they know to be right & expedient." They will be forced into this, if the Repn Ticket shall succeed—& it is well-nigh certain to succeed.

Now, to your character of Gen. Grant. What you say of him does, on the whole, afford me not a little satisfaction. Doubtless, you know him well—& knowing him well, your judgment of him is very valuable. You credit him, not only with bravery & patriotism, but with good sense. Here is a good foundation on which to build a pretty confident faith in him as the friend of equal rights. But this faith becomes very confident, when I see the happy influences brought to bear upon him by his being the candidate of the Republican Party—a Party, which is now so almost unanimously right on the question of equal rights. I am not surprised to find that the General's utterances at this point are improving—improving, perhaps as fast as did dear Lincoln's. But if the General is not all at this point that you desire him to be, how hopelessly far from it is his opponent, who would have the negro again in slavery! The "white mans government" I cannot make to mean any less than the black man's slavery—literal or virtual—[4]

I wish, with all my heart, that it were so that you could be spared from you official duties to go to Ohio & vote—& I wish, too, that you could vote for Grant with a cheerful spirit.

How many good men—how many eminent men of both Parties—I meet with who lament the foolish failure of the Dem Convention to put you in nomination!

We all join in love to youself & Nettie. I leave home again tommorrow—to work this time in the Northern part of our State to keep the Seymours & Blairs out of office.

Ever yours, my noble friend—
GERRIT SMITH

1. See Chase to Smith, September 30, 1868 (above).

2. Howard had thanked Smith in a note written on September 30. Howard to Smith, Sept. 30, 1868 (Smith Papers, George Arents Research Library, Syracuse University).

3. That is, *Gerrit Smith to General Lee,* Smith's published letter of September 25.

4. Among Democrats one of the major themes during the election of 1868 was the inappropriateness of black participation in politics and the need to disenfranchise newly-freed African Americans in the South who had secured the right to vote. William Ernest Smith, *The Francis Preston Blair Family in Politics,* 2 vols. (New York, 1933), 2:424–25.

TO JAMES B. CRAIG

Letterpress copy of autograph letter. Chase Papers, Library of Congress (*micro* 38:0500).

Washington, October 1 [6], 1868.

My dear Sir,

Perhaps you will remember the following sentence in a letter written by me to Colonel Van Buren just before the meeting of the Democratic Convention at New York;—

"A general declaration in the platform that the reconstruction acts are unconstitutional would doubtless suit a great many; but *it would be taken as a declaration of a determination to set aside by force* the Constitutions under which Senators of three of the Southern states have already been admitted to seats in Congress & will certainly be shortly admitted from six more; & probably before the election from all. *Success with such a declaration is simply impossible.* It would *band the whole republican party* in adhesion to the Chicago ticket, & *drive to their standards a large number of citizens,* north & south, who would *prefer Gen. Grant's platform "Let us have peace" to the platform which such a declaration would make "Let us have war."*[1]

It is now quite apparent that you & those who thought with you that the wisest as well as best course for the Convention was to meet the issues of the day in the spirit of the [day] and according to the old democratic ideas of progress, were wiser than those who actually controlled the Convention. It was not necessary to nomination but it was necessary to adopt a platform on which I and those who thought with me could support the nominees without inconsistency.

I do not know whether you have a copy of the platform which you approved & which I was willing to accept, & which, as I have understood was before the Committee on Platform; but set aside for a very different one which drove nearly every dissatisfied Republican, many Conservatives & some democrats to vote for Grant & Colfax tickets, & put me & some other good democrats hors du combat. If not you will probably like to have one, and I send you a copy, printed with [two] other statements which expressed my opinions / These have been printed,[2] not for general circulation; but to satisfy such individuals as care to be informed as to what I really was willing to be responsible for in connexion with the New York Convention

The past is without remedy; but is it not time that you and other young [men] of talent & energy should *take the lead* & bring the democracy out of the slough of [*illeg.*] anti-niggerism upon the solid ground of Equal rights & exact justice for all.

We might have had the democracy on such ground this fall and won a noble triumph: but let the past go: take occasion by the forelock now: sound the trumpet of resurrection & let democracy live as [*illeg.*].[3] If I were young & not trammeled by judicial position I [should] practice as I preach: and defeats should be transformed into victor[ies]

Sincerely your friend
S [P Chase]

James B. Craig, Esq

1. See Chase's letter of July 3, 1868, to John D. Van Buren (above).

2. Chase most likely enclosed a copy of the publication entitled *Mr. Chase's Views.*

3. According to the fables of Phædrus, opportunity was bald on the back of its head. Those who wanted to seize it needed to grasp it by the forelock. The phrase "trumpet of resurrection" alludes to a biblical passage from 1 Corinthians 15:52: "In a moment, in the twinkling of an eye, at the last trump: for the trumpet shall sound, and the dead shall be raised incorruptible, and we shall be changed." Phædrus, *The Fables of Phædrus,* trans. P. F. Widdows (Austin, Tex., 1992), 132.

TO THOMAS A. HENDRICKS

Autograph letter. Special Collections, The University of Chicago Library (*micro* 38:0516).

Washington Oct. 24, 1868.

My dear Sir,

Yours of the 20th did not reach me 'till today. As soon as I found that there was any serious thought of my name, in connexion with the change in nominations lately agitated, I wrote to New York that under no circumstances would I consent to the substitution of my name for that of Governor Seymour.[1]

The mistake at New York was not in his nomination though I believe your nomination would have drawn more votes. The mistake was in the sweeping denunciation of the reconstruction laws as unconstitutional, null & void usurpations, & in the nomination of Gen. Blair on the Brodhead letter.[2] That action shut the door in the face of mulitudes who wished to act with the democrats & were democrats. This mistake once made could not be retrieved by a change of candidates.

I thank you most heartily for your expressions of confidence and good will. They are cordially reciprocated. You made a splendid fight in Indiana, and the fact that you ran ahead of your ticket & came so near being elected shows what might have been easily accomplished on a larger scale had wisdom & liberality prevailed and the true issues been recognized at New York[3]

Yours most sincerely
S: P: Chase

Hon. T. A. Hendricks

1. Chase and Hendricks were two of several prominent leaders currently under consideration to replace Horatio Seymour in the wake of defeats that Democrats had suffered in state elections during September and October. Referring in part to the party's

official platform, Chase instructed John D. Van Buren on October 17: "I think it my duty to say to you distinctly, that under no circumstances would such a substitution be acceptable to me, & that, under existing circumstances it is impossible for me to consent to it." Despite Democratic forebodings, Seymour remained the party's nominee, losing to Grant in November by a margin 214–80 in electoral votes. Chase to Van Buren, Oct. 17, 1868 (Chase Papers, L.C.); Coleman, *Election of 1868,* 344–59, 384.

2. In his letter to James O. Broadhead, June 30, 1868, Francis P. Blair, Jr., had rejected the course of Radical Reconstruction and encouraged its reversal. *New York Times,* July 3, 1868.

3. On October 13, Hendricks had lost his second bid for the governorship of Indiana by 958 votes. Coleman, *Election of 1868,* 340.

TO JAY COOKE

Autograph letter. Jay Cooke Papers, Historical Society of Pennsylvania (*micro* 38:0581).

Washington, Nov. 17, 1868.

My dear Cooke,

Have you ever sent me the certificates of Franklin & Warren stock? If you have I have mislaid them. If not please send them, four $500 each & one $250 which I believe is the balance since consolidation. You wrote me there wd. [be] a dividend last month. I hope it did not fail.[1]

I enclose the Certificates of Sterling Stock.[2] I have never felt exactly satisfied about that matter. To be sure the transaction took place after I left the Department, & did not come within my rule against purchases for resale, & it would have been all well enough if you had made me take & pay for the bonds as well as the stock as I did more lately in the F. & W. subscription.[3] As it was I know nothing blameable in it. Still, as you did, in fact, sell the bonds & with the proceeds paid for the bonds & stock, & so let me have the stock without cost, the matter wears to much of the appearance of a present from yourself & Mr. M—— for my taste;[4] & I prefer not to have it transferred to me. Please therefore take the certificates back, and don't think me overscrupulous. If you do I know you will excuse me for wishing to err on that side if at all.

I appreciate fully your friendly intent in the matter and that of Mr. M——; and I acknowledge with pleasure your friendly services in investing my own small means, aided sometimes temporarily by your own, very much to my benefit; and particularly for allowing me an interest in the Franklin & Warren investment, which now promises to turn out so well.[5] That, I think, is the best investment I ever made, & I should like to make enough more of the same sort to enable me to pay for a good house here in Washington. You may help me in that way, by counsel & service, as much as you please.

I shall never cease to be glad & grateful that I laid down for myself the rule, after Congress gave me such great powers, enabling me to raise & depress values very largely at my discretion, that I would have nothing to do, directly or indirectly, with speculations or transactions, in gold or securities of any sort, for my own or any body's private benefit. You were well paid for your service as Government Agent for Loans; but it was by well e[ar]ned commissions, and not by any advantages which all might not equally have. If I was poorly paid, as Secretary, by a salary, insufficient to meet the expences of housekeeping which, in my position, could not be creditably avoided; I was nevertheless abundantly paid in the consciousness of good services, honestly & faithfully performed, not without benefits, both immediate & permanent, to my country and all my countrymen.

My separation from politics & parties seems now complete; but I earnestly hope that you who will now have great influence & be greatly responsible for it, will set your face like a flint against any modification of the funding system (which I established, and which I honestly believe cannot be materially improved,) impairing at all the great principle of controllability. Redeemability after five years for six per cents; after ten for five per cents;—& after not more than fifteen for four per cents is indispensable. I would undertake now to fund the whole of the 5–20 sixes into 10–40 fives of even date with those now outstanding, so as to be controllable after seven or eight years. If any thing will reconcile the American People to repudiation, direct or indirect, it will be perpetuity or approach to perpetuity of debt. Be sure of that.

Faithfully your friend
S P CHASE

Jay Cooke Esq.

1. Dividends on Warren and Franklin Railroad stock, in which Chase had invested, were payable quarterly and due on October 1. Chase to Cooke, July 11, 1868 (above); Cooke to Chase, July 10, 1868 (Chase Papers, L.C.).

2. As explained later in this paragraph, Chase had purchased shares of Sterling Iron and Railway of New York with financial assistance from Cooke.

3. Chase evidently refers to a passage in section 8 of legislation that established the Treasury Department in 1789. The law forbade any Treasury official appointed under that act to purchase "by himself, or another in trust for him, any public lands or other public property" while in office. Chase and Cooke had corresponded about the need to abide by this and other provisions of the statute as early as 1862. Chase to Cooke, Apr. 29, 1862; Cooke to Chase, Apr. 30, 1862 (both Cooke Papers, Hist. Soc. of Pa.); *Statutes at Large,* 1:67.

4. William G. Moorhead was Cooke's brother-in-law and business partner.

5. Cooke expected the investment, which yielded a dividend of 10 percent at this time, to increase to 15 or 20 percent. Cooke to Chase, July 10, 1868 (Chase Papers, L.C.).

TO JOHN C. UNDERWOOD

Autograph letter. John C. Underwood Papers, Library of Congress (*micro* 38:0588).

Washington, Nov. 19, 1868.

Dear Judge,

The papers say that you are holding the Circuit Court at Richmond with a Grand Jury, and are just now hearing an important habeas corpus case.[1]

If this is so you are holding, doubtless, an adjourned term, and the legality of it becomes important

There is no doubt of your authority, sitting alone in the Circuit Court, to adjourn any regular or regularly adjourned term to a future day, "exercising" as the Supreme Court said 6 Wheat 168, a power common to all courts unless "varied by act of Congress."[2]

The only question is whether this power is not *varied* as to the Circuit Court for the Virginia District by 14 Stat. 51, which provides for special & adjourned terms of that Court "at such time & on such notice as may be prescribed by the Chief Justice of the Supreme Court of the United States."[3]

I do not *think* that this statute was *intended* to limit or qualify the *ordinary* power of adjournment, but am by no means certain that such is not its legal effect: and as no time or notice has been prescribed by the Chief Justice as to the adjourned term it is not impossible that questions may not arise as to jurisdiction.

I have myself overlooked this question heretofore; but my attention being now directed to it I have thought it my duty to invite your consideration of it.

In the District Court or as District Judge you have undoubted jurisdiction of the Habeas Corpus Case: and perhaps the writ is returnable before that court, or before yourself at Chambers. If returnable to the Circuit Court would it not be best to postpone the decision till next week, & then we can confer on the subject.[4]

Yours sincerely
S P Chase

Hon. J. C. Underwood.

1. Recently, Underwood had agreed to accept under habeas corpus the appeal of Caesar Griffin, an African American convicted of assault with intent to kill. Chase was concerned that Underwood might release the petitioner—as he had in August with convicted arsonist Sally Anderson—citing provisions in the third article of the Fourteenth Amendment that supposedly disqualified Griffin's judge at the state level because of his prior allegiance to the Confederacy. Repeated application of this principle threatened to render Virginia's legal system inoperative. Fairman, *Reconstruction and Reunion,* 601–607.

2. Chase quotes from *Mechanics Bank of Alexandria v. Withers,* actually summarized at 6 Wheat. 108 (1821).

3. The legislation, which became law on May 22, 1866, set specific times and places for the U.S. Circuit Court to meet in Virginia.

4. In accordance with Chase's suggestion, Underwood proceeded to hear the case of Caesar Griffin in chambers and unilaterally overturned the conviction on December 7. Chase to Underwood, Jan. 14, 1869 (below); Fairman, *Reconstruction and Reunion,* 603–604.

TO JANET RALSTON CHASE

Autograph letter on letterhead stationery. Chase Papers, Library of Congress (*micro* 38:0594).

Richmond, Va. Decr 3, 1868.[1]

My darling Nettie,

I am really sorry that I did not carry into effect my purpose of two or three days ago and send for you & Sue to come down.[2] I did not, because I feared a change of weather & knew that, if the weather shd change, you might as well be in Libby as at the Spotswood.[3] Besides I did not expect that so far as the Court business was concerned there would be any thing that would interest you. But the weather continues splendid, & here today we have the Jeff Davis case on in one of its most interesting & important aspects—upon the question of the effect of the 14th Constitutional amendment upon the acts which provide for the punishment of treason & other offences supposed to be committed by being concerned in the rebellion.

And Mr. Ould has made this morning a very able & eloquent speech on the Davis side & is to be followed by Mr. Beach the District Attorney & Gov. Wells before adjournment. Mr. R. H. Dana Jr. of Mass will speak tomorrow, also, for the Government & Mr. OConor will close for Mr. Davis.[4] So you would not only have had fine weather, but might have heard if you chose, learned & eloquent advocates.

It is too bad to make you sorry in this way: but it has just come out. Perhaps, after all, you are so agreeably entertained in Washington that you don't feel a bit sorry.

What I really took my pen to say is that I shall not be able to come home tomorrow (Friday) as I intended; but you may expect me confidently the next day in the Evening of Saturday if I dont conclude to come up tomorrow night, in which case I shall be with you at breakfast Saturday Morning.[5]

Most affy your father
S P Chase

Miss Nettie Chase

1. Chase wrote on letterhead stationery of the U.S. District Court in the District of Virginia, but crossed out all but the city identification.

2. Susan S. Hoyt (b. 1845) was the sister of William S. Hoyt, Nettie's future husband. Chase had arrived in Richmond on or before November 25. Chase to Janet Chase, May 4, 1869 (Chase Papers, L.C.); *New York Times,* Nov. 27, 1868; *Representative Men and Old Families of Rhode Island . . . ,* 3 vols. (Chicago, 1908), 1:416.

3. That is, Richmond's notorious Libby Prison and the Spotswood Hotel, located at Eightieth and Main Street. Virginius Dabney, *Richmond: The Story of a City* (Charlottesville, 1990), 206–7.

4. Representing Davis were Richmond attorney Robert Ould (1820–81), former assistant secretary of war for the Confederacy, and Charles O'Conor of New York. On December 3, the team of prosecutors included S. Ferguson Beach, U.S. district attorney for the District of Virginia; Governor Henry H. Wells of Virginia; and Richard Henry Dana, Jr., former U.S. district attorney for the District of Massachusetts. Conflicting reports claim that either Ould or O'Conor had moved earlier to dismiss the case, arguing that the third section of the Fourteenth Amendment limited Davis's punishment to disenfranchisement. According to the prosecution, however, the amendment only created a disability—it did not supersede punishments already sought under Davis's indictment. On December 5, the district court issued a split decision, with Chase favoring dismissal, and referred the matter to the Supreme Court. Andrew Johnson's removal of exemptions to general amnesty on December 25 rendered the case moot, and the Court dismissed it on February 19, 1869. Fairman, *Reconstruction and Reunion,* 607–12; Johnson, *Cases Decided by Chief Justice Chase,* 82–124; *Nat. Cyc.,* 19:275; *New York Times,* Dec. 1. 1868; *Register of Officers (1869),* 304; *Richmond Daily Dispatch,* Dec. 4, 1868.

5. Chase returned to Washington, D.C., on the morning of Sunday, December 6. *New York Times,* Dec. 5, 1868.

TO SAMUEL H. WALLEY

Autograph letter. Washburn Collection, Massachusetts Historical Society (*micro* 38:0604).

Washington, Dec. 23, 1868

My dear Sir,[1]

I do not know that I can better respond to your requests for financial "hints" than by sending you a copy of a letter to Greeley in reply to one from him by the same mail which brought yours. You will observe that the letter is marked *private.* I don't propose to go into the public discussion.[2] Every body is too wise "by instinct." If I had time though I might be tempted to let the people see my views in a decent dress—not in the dressing gown habits of a hasty note.

By the way do you know that you are partly responsible for legal tender? Do you remember the conference at the Department when you represented the Boston Banks, & other gentlemen represented N. York & Phila & I urged the receipt & payment by the Banks of the United States notes, & we did come to a sort of understanding?[3]

Up to that time I had opposed legal tender. When our conference ended & you had returned to Boston you telegraphed me that the Boston Banks would not ratify. Immediately on receiving your telegram I wrote a note to the Chairman of the Com of Ways & Means giving in my adhesion to the legal tender law.[4] If the Banks had agreed to receive & pay out U.S. Notes I doubt much whether any legal tender provision would ever have been engrafted on the statute.

Not that I want my say for much; but the necessity which I recognized at once on the receipt of your telegram would not have been created.

I know nothing more interesting than this to you which I can write.

Sincerely your friend
S P Chase

Hon Sam W. Walley

1. Walley, president of the Revere Bank of Boston, had served in Congress from 1853 to 1855.

2. The Supreme Court currently had several cases on its docket with the potential of a decision that declared legal tender unconstitutional. Fairman, *Reconstruction and Reunion,* 700–704; *New York Tribune,* Dec. 15, 1868.

3. Chase refers to a conference on January 14 and 15, 1862, that addressed a range of issues related to U.S. finances. His diary identifies George S. Coe, president of New York's American Exchange Bank, as one of the other bankers. *Chase Papers,* 1:326–28.

4. Chase received Walley's telegram on January 20, and wrote to the chair, Thaddeus Stevens, nine days later. The First Legal Tender Act became law on February 25. Ibid., 1:328, 3:126–29.

TO THORNTON K. LATHROP

Letterpress copy of letter in clerk's hand, signed by Chase. Chase Papers, Library of Congress (*micro* 38:0614).

Washington Jany 2d 1869

Dear Sir[1]

I take pleasure in replying to your note of the 26th ult. Absence from the city will excuse a few days delay.

My impressions of Mr Hooper until Apl 1861, were derived almost wholly from the [opinions] of others. These gave me great confidence in his sagacity, integrity and patriotism.

I do not now recollect when our personal acquaintance commenced: but it was, I think not long before the 6th of April 1861. I then advertised for proposals for a loan of $14.901.000. in money (coin) in exchange for Treasury notes. The proposals were to be opened five days afterwards, on the 11th.[2]

This was at a time of great anxiety and depression. Before the day for opening the proposals arrived the expeditions for the reinforcements of Pickens and the provisionment of Sumter had already sailed; and on that day the correspondence between Beauregard commanding the rebels and Anderson commanding the Fort was going on in reference to the surrender of Sumter. The next day the rebel batteries opened fire.[3]

No time could be more unpropitious to the negotiation of a loan. Yet the advertisement could not be withdrawn without serious injury to the public credit, and a failure to obtain the amount advertised for would have had, perhaps, at that particular juncture, a still worse effect.

Mr Hooper happened to be in Washington for the purpose, I think, of making an offer for a part of the Treasury notes and was a subscriber for $100,000. On opening the proposals I found that the offers fell short of the amount required by almost a million of dollars. I sent for Mr Hooper, then personally almost a stranger to me, and asked him to take that sum assuring him that he should be protected from loss in the event of his being unable to distribute the amount in Boston. He complied with my request without hesitation and disposed of the whole amount without any aid from the Treasury. His readiness to come to the aid of the Government at the critical moment and the personal confidence he showed in me, made an impression [on my mind] which cannot be obliterated. The sum does not now seem large; but it was large then and the responsibility was assumed when most men would have shrunk from it.

On another and even more important occasion my obligations to Mr Hooper for support and còoperation were still greater.

Very few months had passed after I took charge of the Department before I became fully satisfied that the best interests of the people future as well as immediate, in peace as well as in war demanded a complete revolution in currency by the substitution of notes, uniform in form and in credit-value, issued under the authority of the nation, for notes varying in both respects issued under State authority; and I suggested to different financial gentlemen the plan of a National Banking System. The suggestion was not received with favor or any-thing like favor.

But my conviction of the necessity of some such measure both to the successful management of the finances during the war and to the prevention of disastrous convulsions on the return of peace, was so strong I determined to bring the subject to the attention of [Congress.]

In my report on the finances submitted on the 9th of December 1861, I therefore recommended the adoption of a National Banking System upon principles and under restrictions explained [partly] in the report and more fully in the Bill drawn up under my direction and either sent to the committee of Ways and Means or handed to one of its members—perhaps to Mr Hooper himself.[4]

However the Bill may have gone to the Committee I am not mistaken, I think in saying that Mr Hooper was the only member who gave it any support.

I am pretty sure that the only favor shown it by the Committee was a permission to Mr Hooper to report it without recommendation on his own responsibility.

He took that responsibility and the Bill was reported and printed.

No action was asked upon it at that session. If action had been asked it is not improbable that it would have been rejected with very few discenting votes; So powerful then was the influence of the State Banks, so reluctant were they to accept the new measure, and so strong was the general sentiment of the Members of Congress against it.

Before the next session a strong public opinion, in favor of a uniform currency for the whole country and of the National Banking System as a means of accomplishing that object, had developed itself; and Mr Hooper found himself able to carry the measure through the House of Representatives. It still encountered a formidable opposition in the Senate and I well remember the personal appeals I was obliged to make to Senators as I had already to Representatives in order to overcome their objections.[5]

The Bill found a powerful and judicious friend in Mr Sherman and at length passed by a close vote. It was approved by Mr Lincoln, who had [steadily] supported it from the beginning, on the 25th February 1863.

I think I cannot err in ascribing the success of the measure in the House to the sound judgment persevering exertions and disinterested patriotism of Mr Hooper.

The results of the measure during the war fulfilled and since the war have justified the expectations I formed.

It received valuable amendments in both Houses of Congress before its enactment and has since been further amended; and is I think still capable of beneficial modification[,] in points of much importance to the public interests.[6]

But this is not the place nor the occasion for the discussion of this matter; all that you desire is my estimate of the services of Mr Hooper.

I have mentioned only the two principal occasions on which I was specially indebted to him; but they were by no means the only occasions in which he aided me or rather the Department of the Government of which I then had charge both by personal counsel and by congressional support.

During the whole time I was at the head of the Treasury I constantly felt the great benefit of his wise and energetic coöperation.

It would be unjust saying this of Mr Hooper, not to say there were others in and out of Congress to whom in other financial relations the Treasury Department and the Country were very greatly indebted: but it is simple duty to add that the timely aid which he rendered at the crisis of the loan of April 1861, and in promoting the enactment of the National Banking law placed me, charged as I was with a most responsible and difficult task, under special obligations which I can never forget and shall always take pleasure in acknowledging.

With great respect

Yours very truly
S P Chase

Thornton. K. Lathrop Esq

1. Thomas Kirkland Lathrop, a former assistant U.S. district attorney, was the son-in-law of Massachusetts congressman Samuel Hooper. Most of this letter appeared in the *New York Tribune* soon after Chase's death with a note by William H. Barnes implying that Chase had addressed the letter to Barnes as he wrote the *History of the Congress of the United States,* 3 vols. (New York, 1870–72). The editors have used the *Tribune* version to help read faint spots in the letterpress copy. *New York Tribune,* May 10, 1873.

2. Chase had solicited bids under authorization granted by the loan acts of February 8 and March 2, 1861. *New York Times,* Apr. 9, 1861.

3. Federal reinforcements arrived at Fort Pickens, Florida, on April 13, 1861, but did not reach Fort Sumter, South Carolina, prior to the start of hostilities there on April 12. Correspondence of April 11, between Brig. Gen. Pierre G. T. Beauregard and Maj. Robert Anderson discussed Confederate demands for Fort Sumter's evacuation. Long, *Civil War Day by Day,* 56, 57; *OR,* ser. 1, v. 1:13–14.

4. Chase's annual report for 1861 recommended an association of banking institutions to redeem circulating notes backed by the federal government. Hooper introduced his proposal to Congress on July 11, 1862, and it was referred to the House Ways and Means Committee, where it died. *Congressional Globe,* 37th Cong., 2d sess., 1861–62, 3258; Bray Hammond, *Sovereignty and an Empty Purse: Banks and Politics in the Civil War* (Princeton 1970), 287; *Report of the Secretary of the Treasury, on the State of the Finances, for the Year Ending June 30, 1861,* 37th Cong., 2d sess., 1861, S. Ex. Doc., 2, 17–20.

5. Chase recruited Lincoln's help and is known to have lobbied William P. Fessenden and John Sherman, members of the Senate Ways and Means Committee, as well as Elbridge G. Spaulding of New York, a member of the House Finance Committee. The Senate passed the National Currency Act by a margin of 23–21 on February 13, 1863. The

House approved it 78–64 on February 20. Chase to Fessenden, Feb. 24, 1863, and Chase to Sherman, Feb. 9 (three letters) and 10, 1863 (all John Sherman Papers, L.C.).; *Chase Papers,* 3:366–68 371, 388; *Congressional Globe,* 37th Cong., 3d sess., 1862–63, 897, 1148; Fessenden to Chase, Feb. 23, 1868; and Sherman to Chase, Feb. 7, 1863 (two letters) (all Chase Papers, Hist. Soc. of Pa.); *Statutes at Large,* 12:665–82.

6. Hooper first introduced Chase's national bank bill (H.R. 567) in July 1862, but Congress rejected it. In January 1863, he proposed H.R. 656, which the Senate debated and amended on February 10 and 11, and which both houses passed in modified form later the same month. Congress repealed and replaced this measure on June 3, 1864, and then amended the replacement on March 3, 1865. *Statutes at Large,* 13:118, 498; *Congressional Globe,* 37th Cong., 3d sess., 1862–63, 113–19, 820–25, 840–52; Orig. Bills, 37th Cong., Recs. of U.S. House of Reps., Nat. Arch.

TO JOHN C. UNDERWOOD

Letterpress copy of letter in clerk's hand, signed by Chase. Chase Papers, Library of Congress (*micro* 38:0631).

Washington, January 14th 1869.

Dear Sir,

In our conversation some weeks ago, just after your decision in the case of Sally Anderson, I expressed my regret that you did not hear the case at Chambers, so that an appeal might have been taken as in the Cæsar Griffith case, and the case argued before us both in the Circuit Court.[1] I also stated that I entertained very serious doubts in regard to the correctness of the decision in those two cases, not being prepared to affirm that by the operation of the Fourteenth Amendment every Judge in the State, if not permitted by that amendment to hold office, was at once deprived of all judicial character and authority, so that judgments and decrees and sentences rendered by him became absolutely null and void. It is difficult to measure the consequences of such a determination, and the great probability that the most serious evils may result from it, though by no means proving its incorrectness, seem to justify and demand [great care] and circumspection in proceeding.

I have seen to-day a statement in the Richmond State Journal of yesterday that [an] application has been filed for an injunction restraining the Collection of a judgment on the ground that it was rendered by a Court the members of which were disabled from holding office under the Fourteenth Amendment. If any such application has been made I will join you in hearing it. It [*illeg.*] be heard here if you can attend. If not let it be postponed till I can [*illeg.*] Richmond.[2]

The best and quickest way of obtaining an authoritative and final decision of the point which has arisen is to certify to the Supreme Court a division of opinion between us in the Caesar Griffith case now in the Circuit Court on appeal. If you think as I do that it is proper and expedient to certify this division, you can have the necessary certificate made out and entered as of any day after the appeal when I was in Richmond in December last. As the division has arisen in a criminal case, the case can be heard here as soon after the record has come up as counsel are ready to argue it, and at any rate at some time during the present term.

Please give this whole matter your early and considerate attention.

Very truly yours,
S: P: Chase

Hon. John C. Underwood.

1. Chase had cautioned Underwood about his conduct in the cases of Anderson, an African American convicted of arson in August 1868, and Griffin, who faced charges of assault with intent to kill, in correspondence of November 19, 1868 (above).

2. On January 29, the Virginia state government filed a successful writ of petition in the U.S. Supreme Court to block Underwood from further proceedings in matters related to the cases of Anderson and Griffin. Authorized by the Supreme Court, Chase then reversed the *Griffin* decision on May 3, while presiding over the next session of the U.S. Circuit Court in Richmond. Fairman, *Reconstruction and Reunion,* 605–7.

TO WILLIAM M. BYRD

Letterpress copy of autograph letter. Chase Papers, Library of Congress (*micro* 38:0672).

Private

Washington, Apl. 3, 1869.

My dear Sir,[1]

My time has been too much occupied for more correspondence than has been absolutely necessary or I should have earlier acknowledged your letter of Xmas day & the paper which accompanied it: but I have not been unmindful of the views which you put in so clear a light.

Congress has not done all the good it might have done; but its measures have not been so extreme this Session as at the last. I hoped for the [*two words? illeg.*] a much more liberal measure of amnesty than has yet been proposed; and, I am sure that the sentiment [in] that direction is growing, and if nothing occurs to check its growth it will attain strength [enough] before next winter to ensure if not universal [amnesty] at least amnesty next to universal. [My judgment in favor] of making it universal is not [*illeg.*] but strongly [*illeg.*] on all proper occasions [*six words? illeg.*] [have peculiar] [*three words? illeg.*] exclude none. The [*illeg.*] gener[*illeg.*] [*several words illeg.*] both sides is the best.[2]

As to suffrage it was my opinion at the close of the war that the great needs of the South were first, contented and continuous industry & second reestablishment of such cordial relations between good men of both sections, divided by the war, as would ensure an [*illeg.*] supply of capital in your section. To the first I thought security to the laborers in their rights & in their wages indispensable, & I felt certain that, if suffrage could be accorded to them with the full consent of the educated classes, their votes would be given to the members of their classes whom they knew to be competent by intelligence & character to give them the needed security[.] In this way the educated classes would naturally & almost [*illeg.*]ly have been restored to lead; and this would have powerfully aided the reestablishment of good relations I have spoken of.

[I have no doubt] that all this could have been accomplished by [wiser] statesmanship here. Nor have I the least doubt that if universal suffrage had been accorded by the leaders of opinion in the south, or even impartial suffrage with modest educational qualification with a manifest disposition to protect all civil rights, that neither the 14th Amendment nor the reconstruction measures in their military government & military commission features would ever have been heard of.

It was ordered otherwise: and then came inevitably the 14th Amendment. It was harsher than I thought either wise or necessary: but I hoped for its ratification promptly by the Southern Legislatures. That would have averted reconstruction in all the harsh features: but counsels against ratification prevailed. Then came, also inevitably, military reconstruction. But I need not go on.

After the 14th Amendment was adopted I thought the suffrage should be left to the states after restoration. And I still think so. Centralization & consolidation have gone far enough & too far. And yet inasmuch as the proposed fifteenth amendment does not prevent the states from imposing reasonable qualifications, if qualifications should be found necessary, I incline to wish that it may be ratified.[3] I should have no reservation in that wish if the clause giving Congress power to legislate were left out. I want as little legislation by Congress in respect to the internal concerns of states as possible.

There is much more that I might say but I have no time; and, in fact, since I am no longer in a position to exert any influence on political measures, no inclination

Should business or inclination bring you to Washington I shall be very happy to see you. I notice your expression of regret concerning the action at New York. I have never regretted, but on the contrary have always been thankful for its action as far as I was concerned. After the platform, my nomination was quite undesirable. It was the first step that cost. The Bourbons cannot rule France! The Empire rather! was the irresistible fiat of the people.[4]

Very truly & respectfully yours
S P Chase

Hon Wm M Byrd

1. Byrd (1817–74) sat on Alabama's supreme court. Charles Lanman, *Biographical Annals of the Civil Government of the United States* (Washington, D.C., 1876), 63.

2. On March 31 and April 1, respectively, the House and Senate had considered resolutions to remove the political disabilities of loyal citizens in the former Confederacy, but neither chamber took formal action during the first session of the Forty-first Congress. The General Amnesty Act of May 22, 1872, restored political rights to most Confederates still excluded from office under terms of the Fourteenth Amendment. *Congressional Globe,*

41st Congress, 1st sess., 1869, 406, 410, 42d Congress, 2d sess., 1871–72, 3381–82; Edward McPherson, *The Political History of the United States during the Period of Reconstruction . . .* (Washington, D.C., 1875; reprint, New York, 1969), 393; James A. Rawley, "The General Amnesty Act of 1872: A Note," *Mississippi Valley Historical Review* 47 (Dec. 1960): 480–84.

3. The Fifteenth Amendment, which became law on March 30, 1870, prohibits denial or abridgement of voting rights "on account of race, color, or previous condition of servitude," and grants Congress authority to pass enforcing legislation. *Statutes at Large,* 16:1131.

4. The term *Bourbon* was often used to identify conservative Democrats during Reconstruction. Chase alludes to events at the most recent Democratic national convention, which took place in New York in July 1868, and to the popular revolution that overthrew the ineffective, conservative Bourbon rulers of France in February 1848, followed in 1852 with repression under the Second Empire and Napoleon III. J. P. T. Bury, ed., *The Zenith of European Power, 1830–70,* vol. 10 of *The New Cambridge Modern History* (Cambridge, 1960), 389–94, 399–401, 403–4, 407–8, 442–51; Thorne, *Chambers's Biographical Dictionary,* 932; Earle Dudley Ross, *The Liberal Republican Movement* (New York, 1919), 133–34.

TO JANET CHASE

Autograph letter. Chase Papers, Library of Congress (*micro* 38:0685).

Washington, Apl. 12, 1869.

My darling Nettie,

I am here at the Judge's reception room in the Capitol and the clock is striking ten—near an hour ahead of my usual time.[1] This apparent diligence like many other seeming qualities is not a virtue but a mistake / I *thought* I was late when I started from home.

Time has gone rather quickly by since you went away though I miss you sorely. The next Evening Friday I dined with the Cookes in Georgetown, and had the pleasure of being put between Mrs Cooke and Mrs Williams—(Douglas—) who was assigned to me.[2] Of course I was well placed. The guest of the evening was Gen Sherman who had Mrs Cooke's right. The table was very pretty adorned with flowers. A flat star shaped tray, with long single rays extending lengthwise and double rays extending crosswise each pair allowing just space enough to Mr. & Mrs. Cooke for their plates &c, was filled with the most beautiful flowers, resembling a small parterre. It interrupted no views & to my taste was just the thing—only a bit too mathematical. At either end of the long table, below a chandelier, hung a great flower tall like those we sometimes have—just like them. And all the table furniture was very handsome—and Mrs Cooke looked very young & sweet and Mr. Cooke performed the part of hospitable host very well—and Jay Senr. had come from Philadelphia & Mr. Fahnestock from New York and the guests were nice and made themselves agreeable & all went very well indeed.[3] Of course you & Katie were much enquired about

I must not forget to mention among the enquiries Mrs Marcy who with her husband the General were among the guests. She spoke of you in the kindest terms—*real* affectionate as Eliza Whipple would say.[4]

I had written thus far yesterday morning—today is the 13th—when the Judges began to come in and I was obliged to go in to Court / And at last my Texas opinion was read to a very intelligent & deeply interested audience—of lawyers almost exclusively—and you and Katie must pay me the compliment of reading it. I send you a copy in the Herald.[5]

And now I must go back to my history. The next great event of my life after the dinner at Mr. Cookes was the next Evening's dinner at Mr. Evarts.[6] It was quite a distinguished party at any rate so far as titles go. Gen. Sherman was again the honored guest; and then came Mr. Justice Nelson, Mr. Minister Thornton, Mr. President of the Senate Anthony, Mr. Speaker of the House, Blaine, Mr. Secretary Fish, Mr. Secretary Rawlins, Mr. Secretary Boutwell, Mr Secretary Cox, Mr. Postmaster General Cresswell, Mr Attorney General Hoar General Geo. H. Thomas,[7] Mr. Senator Sumner, Mr Senator Sherman to say nothing of a greater man than either of them Mr. Ex Secretary & Ex Senator Ewing, or of Mr. Chief Justice Chase.[8] There dont that list take away your breath. Gen Sherman had my usual place at Mrs Evarts[9] right, & I took the next place on Mr. Evarts right between him & Mr. Thornton. Next the last was Sumner, & he & Mr. Thornton tried to make themselves agreeable to each other but rather unsuccessfully I thought. Sumner could not talk of himself without bringing in the Alabama Treaty, & that of course would be a sore topic for the British Minister[10] / So the conversation had to be rather impersonal: which was a little hard on Sumner. Evarts was himself, intelligent, agreeable, wise & witty. Every thing went pleasantly around the round table. Towards the end of the dinner there was a stir. Somebody had come into the parlor. A figure could be seen, very imperfectly by my poor eyes, through the open doors. Presently it drew nigh & every body rose, except the awkward Chief Justice, who, not knowing what was the matter—only knowing that Mr Evarts had gone to meet somebody & was bringing in somebody—kept his seat. At last he also recognized the President, who took Mrs Evarts place, made pleasantly vacant for him, no doubt much to the satisfaction of the lady, by her graceful withdrawal from the room.[11] And then the mystery of the President's appearance was explained. "I knew," said Mr. Evarts to me "that it was not quite etiquette to invite the President to dinner, & that he would not come, & so I told him I wouldn't ask him, but mentioned that Gen Sherman was to be here, & said I thought he would take it as a compliment if his old Commander would come in & smoke a cigar". And thus it was that we enjoyed the unanticipated honor.

Well the President smoked & the other smokers smoked—not I am glad to say a majority of those at the table—when some of us at our side of the table thought it time to go & rose & broke up the sitting. I had a few moments pleasant talk with the President, & was glad to have it in my power to speak very cordially & with entire sincerity of what has thus far been done.

Today as usual when I have a great deal to do but nothing in particular which *must* be done at once, I have accomplished very little.

The Governor went to New York the morning after you left and only came back this morning. Tonight he was serenaded and made a speech in answer to an address: The Speech was well received by a considerable crowd.[12] Undoubtedly what he has been lately saying has attracted great attention, & has given him more reputation for ability as a public man & statesman than any thing in his past career. I don't exactly comprehend his views,—but shall try to make myself acquainted with them. Certainly he has gained an advantage, which wisely improved may have great results. And all who *try* to improve the condition of the masses deserve honor.

Mr. Wyman has just returned bringing Katies letter, but none from you.[13] On the contrary he says you took a bad cold through imprudence. This troubles me but I trust nothing serious will come of it: why cant you use foresight & care?

Most affectionately your father
S P CHASE

Love & kisses to Katie & Willie. I will write Katie very soon. Goodnight 11.25 P.M. We had a terrible storm of snow & sleet Saturday night & all Sunday. I was glad you were all out of its reach.[14]

1. Chase probably refers to the judges' robing room, on the main floor of the Capitol building across from the Supreme Court chamber. Fairman, *Reconstruction and Reunion,* 64.

2. Chase's youngest daughter was visiting her sister in Rhode Island. Laura S. Humphrey Cooke and her husband Henry David Cooke, Jay Cooke's brother and the president of Washington's First National Bank, resided at 170 Washington Street in Georgetown. Adèle Cutts Douglas, the widow of Stephen A. Douglas, had married U.S. Army officer Robert Williams in 1866. Chase to Kate Chase Sprague, Apr. 15, 1869 (below); Chase to Kate Chase Sprague, Apr. 8, 17, 1869 (Chase Papers, Hist. Soc. of Pa.); *Wash. Dir. (1869),* 76.

3. Harris Charles Fahnestock (1835–1914) presided over the New York branch of Jay Cooke and Co. *DAB,* 6:245–46.

4. Rudolph Barnes Marcy (1812–87), the husband of Mary A. Mann Marcy (d. 1878), had served in the U.S. Army for more than thirty years. During the Civil War, he was chief of staff under his son-in-law George B. McClellan and, at its end, received brevet commissions as brigadier general and major general. In 1869, he held a post as an army inspector. Eliza Whipple was the daughter of Chase's sister, Hannah Chase Whipple. Ibid., 12:273–74.

5. The April 13 edition of the *New York Herald* printed Chase's majority opinion in the case of *Texas v. White.* George W. White and John Chiles were military contractors from Texas. In 1865, Confederate state officials there had arranged what many later considered an unjust transaction that permitted White and Chiles to secure at a substantial discount U.S. government bonds held in the state treasury. The case reached the U.S. Supreme Court in February 1867, when officials from Texas, which had not yet been fully restored to the Union, filed a suit to prevent redemption of the bonds. In his opinion, Chase affirmed the state's membership in the Union despite recent acts of rebellion, affirmed the right of Texas to sue, and declared the arrangement with White and Chiles invalid. The United States, he declared, is "an indestructible Union, composed of indestructible States." Chase's opinion supported the position of Republicans who defined

Reconstruction as a political problem under congressional jurisdiction. Fairman, *Reconstruction and Reunion,* 628–48; Hyman, *Reconstruction Justice,* 140–50; 7 Wall. 700 (1869).

6. New York attorney William M. Evarts had left the office of U.S. attorney general in March. *DAB,* 6:216.

7. Chase's dinner companions included William T. Sherman, general commanding the U.S. Army; U.S. Supreme Court Justice Samuel Nelson; British minister Edward Thornton; Rhode Island senator Henry B. Anthony; and James Gillespie Blaine, speaker of the House. Also in attendance were members of Ulysses S. Grant's cabinet: Hamilton Fish, secretary of state, 1869–77; John Aaron Rawlins (1831–69), secretary of war, March to August 1869; George Sewall Boutwell, secretary of the Treasury, 1869–73; Jacob Dolson Cox, secretary of the interior, 1869–70; John Angel James Creswell, postmaster general, 1869–74; and Ebenezer Rockwood Hoar, attorney general, 1869–70. In June, Maj. Gen. George Henry Thomas would take command of the Military Division of the Pacific. *Bio. Dir. U.S. Cong.,* 19; *DAB,* 15:402–3, 17:97, 18:434.

8. Charles Sumner, John Sherman, and Thomas Ewing, Sr.

9. Helen Minerva Wardner Evarts.

10. Sumner was scheduled to deliver a speech in the Senate on April 13 prior to a vote on the Johnson-Clarendon Convention, a treaty intended to settle U.S. claims against Britain for Civil War damages, some inflicted by the Confederate raider *Alabama.* Sumner's speech opposed the treaty, which the Senate rejected on the same day by a margin of 54–1. Cook, *Alabama Claims,* 15, 73–76; U.S. Senate, *Journal of the Executive Proceedings,* 17:163; Charles Sumner, *The Works of Charles Sumner,* 15 vols. (Boston, 1874–83), 13:53–93.

11. Ulysses S. Grant's first inauguration had occurred on March 4. *Bio. Dir. U.S. Cong.,* 19.

12. In March and early in April 1869, William Sprague delivered a series of rambling speeches from the floor of the Senate that—among other things—assailed U.S. bankers, questioned the virtue of American women, and distanced him from Chase's political aspirations. Included also was a proposal to establish an official council of financial commissioners to disburse government income and provide cheap capital for large and small investors. A. T. Cavis, vice president of the National Labor Union in attendance with several hundred other serenaders from the Workingmen's Association of the District of Columbia, thanked Sprague for introducing the measure, which, in the opinion of Cavis, would "relieve the people, and rescue them from the clutches of rapacious banks and grasping money lenders." In response, Sprague underscored his "simple plan": "to use the great debt of the State, national and individual, that is crushing us as now managed, in the form of capital and power, against the combinations and unscrupulous power of the chartered enemy." *Congressional Globe,* 41st Cong., 1st sess., 1869, 64–66, 242–46, 358–62, 475, 612–20; *New York Times,* Apr. 14, 1869.

13. Perhaps Luther Boynton Wyman (1805–79), an acquaintance from New York and a founder of the Brooklyn Academy of Music who was known during the Civil War for his patriotic support of the Union cause. Wyman to Chase, Oct. 24, 1861 (Chase Papers, L.C.); *New York Times,* July 29, 1879.

14. Chase wrote to Kate on April 15 (below). The letter suggests that Chase's daughters were at Narragansett Beach, Rhode Island.

TO KATE CHASE SPRAGUE

Autograph letter. Chase Papers, Historical Society of Pennsylvania (*micro* 38:0692).

Washington, Apl. 15, 1869

My dearest Katie,

I was very glad to receive your letter and to note the indications in it of a more tranquil mind than you carried from Washington.[1] You have been sorely tried, my precious child; but much of your trial is as you acknowledge brought upon you & continued by yourself, and all is allowed to a wise & kind Father in Heaven who intends, I trust, to ensure your best happiness by it. Trust Him & love Him & follow Christ. I have great faith in the power of a truly Christian woman to overcome the greatest difficulties.

Have you written to the Governor? I hope you have and in the best spirit. He went to New York the evening after you left, and only returned day before yesterday morning. Since then he has been so busy with his speeches & letters[2] & I so busy with my records & opinions & the business of the Court that we have seen very little of each other, only meeting at table. The Court adjourned today, and I hope to have opportunities of conference with him before the week ends. I have no great expectation of benefit from what I can say: but what I can I will do. You can do more than any body else. Naturally you say "Must I do all?" It is hard to be loving & affectionate, when met by unkind words and unkind acts." I know it is; but I know too that she who thus acts will have her reward. There will come after a while a sweet internal serenity which will make duty easy & almost certainly ensure a return of love & affection.

The Governor's speeches have attracted great attention throughout the country. I have not considered what he proposes sufficiently to have any definite opinion as the merits of it; but undoubtedly he has gained a very prominent position; and, if your old mutuality of affection can be restored, you will be happier than ever; for, if I am not mistaken, you have been always ambitious for him. But, with his new position new responsibilities will come. How I wish you could be at his side bearing all things, believing all things, hoping all things,[3] a real helpmeet.

Tonight I am to have quite a company / The members of the Academy of Sciences are to call—Agassiz, Pierce, & Co—& I have invited a number to meet them. My heart is not much in it; but I will try to make myself agreeable.[4]

I have Netties letter today with the picture of the house and the story of Willie & mudpies & the garden & strawberries.[5] How I wish I could be with you. Tell Nettie that I will allow her any amount of money to spend on black ink, nice paper & good pens. I could with difficulty read her letter, the ink was so pale. Give my best love to her and dear little Willie. Either you or Nettie must write me every day, if only the briefest letters.

I began this expecting to be very short and *here I am!*

Most lovingly your father
S P Chase

1. A veteran of overseas travel, Kate evidently left Washington for Narragansett Beach shortly after William Sprague, who suspected his wife of infidelity, alluded in a Senate speech on March 30 to the immorality of "Americans who travel abroad, mix and mingle in that filth and come here to inculcate the immoralities that they have seen upon their own society." Thomas Graham Belden and Marva Robins Belden, *So Fell the Angels* (Boston, 1956), 227–29; *Congressional Globe,* 41st Cong., 1st sess., 1869, 361.

2. Sprague, who had received "bundles" of letters from supporters who wanted copies of his Senate speeches, visited New York to arrange for their publication, which occurred later in 1869. *The Civil Tenure Act: Speech of William Sprague in the Senate of the United States, March 24, 1869* (n.p., 1869); *The Financial Condition: Speech of William Sprague in the Senate of the United States, March 15, 1869* (New York, 1869); *National Affairs: Speeches of William Sprague, in the Senate of the United States, March 15, 17, 24, and 30, and April 8, 1869* (New York, 1869); *The National Currency: Speech of William Sprague, in the Senate of the United States, March 30, 1869* ([New York, 1869]); *New York Herald*, Apr. 16, 1869; and *The Tax Bill: Speech of William Sprague in the Senate of the United States, April 8, 1869* (New York, 1869).

3. A paraphrase of 1 Cor. 13:7.

4. The National Academy of Sciences assembled in Washington on April 12. Among its members were Swiss-American geologist Jean Louis Rudolphe Agassiz, the Academy's foreign secretary, and Benjamin Peirce (1809–80), a founder of the academy and, in 1869, superintendent of the U.S. Coast Survey. Chase's position as chancellor of the Smithsonian Institution since November 1868 probably accounts for his presence at the function. Rexmond C. Cochrane, *The National Academy of the Sciences: The First Hundred Years, 1863–1963*, (Washington, D.C., 1978), 634–37; *DAB*, 14:393–97; *Washington Evening Star*, Apr. 15, 1869; *Wash. Dir. (1868)*, 46.

5. The Spragues were building a sixty-eight-room mansion at Narragansett Beach, Rhode Island, named "Canonchet" after a seventeenth-century Narragansett Indian chief. Belden, *So Fell the Angels*, 218–20.

TO KATE CHASE SPRAGUE

Autograph letter. Chase Papers, Historical Society of Pennsylvania (*micro* 38:0707).

Washington, Ap. 26, 1869.

My dear child,

I was disappointed coming home, Saturday that I found no letter from you. I do not know whether you have written to your husband or not; nor whether you have had any letter from him since the letter in which you said he had not written you.

When I returned the affair in the Senate which has made so much noise—more here of course than anywhere else—had just occurred—the day before.[1] The attack on the Governor was a meanly concerted affair. When he replied the Senate went again into Executive Session, & then Abbott asked leave to make a personal explanation. The Governor said that if leave was given he should claim the right of replying in full, & the Senate refused to open its doors. The Governor then left the Chamber not supposing that anything more would be said of a personal nature. Abbott must have known this fact; and yet when the Senate shortly afterwards changed its mine & opened the doors to give him a chance to say his say, he charged the Governor with having skulked out of the Senate.[2] This was entirely untrue, and he must have known it. It was intended, probably, to force the Governor to take the offensive in a personal assault.

The Governor very properly has taken no notice of the matter. Mr. Sumner & Mr. Sherman have been here this morning as I suppose with a view to compose the affair with what result I do not know.

The Governor does not consult me at all in his matters; and I do not feel myself at liberty to obtrude unasked counsels: though I would not hesitate to volunteer, if I had any reason to believe that good would come of it. I fear the contrary.

Since I came back I have seen very little of him, He is visited a great deal & is almost constantly engaged. The newspaper men are, of course, eager to get something for their papers; and a great many want to see the man whose speeches have made such a stir. Besides callers he has ever so many letters. Mr. Halsted of New Jersey has been with him about two weeks giving him a great deal of aid in various ways.[3]

He does not seem as cordial towards me as formerly; but it may be that I am more sensitive to his natural reserve & abruptness.

I am anxious for a good opportunity for a frank conversation, and must have one before I leave for Richmond next Saturday or Monday.[4]

A letter from Nettie this morning mentions Mr. Charles Leary as staying with you for a day or two, and being your escort to Graniteville.[5] Does she mean that Mr. L—— is your guest? I hope not.

You cannot be too careful, my child. I have learned more of the slanderous propensities of men within the last few years than I ever knew before. Only this morning I received a most abominable note from New York. I seldom read these anonymous libels, but I read enough of this to find that it was full of the most detestable abuse of you & the Governor not sparing either me or our innocent Nettie. Of course I at once destroyed it. For Heaven's sake, for my sake, for your own sake avoid all possibility of occasion for evil eyes & evil tongues.

Your devoted father
S: P: Chase

1. On April 22, a heated exchange took place on the Senate floor between Sprague, on one side, and James Warren Nye of Nevada and Joseph Carter Abbot of North Carolina. According to later reports, a speech that Sprague delivered on that day about Gen. Ambrose Burnside included an illusion to Nye and Abbott as "the mastiff and the mongrel puppy dog." Taking exception, Abbott vowed to seek "satisfaction." Tensions eased with Abbott's disavowal of any intention to duel Sprague and with Nye's explanation that Abbott only wanted to "spank little Spraguey, spank him and send him to bed." *Congressional Globe,* 41st Cong., 1st sess., 1869, 744–45, 776–77; *DAB,* 1:23–24; *New York Herald,* Apr. 23, 1869.

2. According to the *New York Herald,* Sprague left the chamber either to avoid confrontation or to retrieve weapons for his own defense. *New York Herald,* Apr. 23, 1869.

3. During the Civil War, former congressman William Halstead (1784–1878) had raised New Jersey's First Regiment of Volunteer Cavalry. Reports from the *New York Herald* at this time suggest that Halstead was helping Sprague prepare his speeches for publication. Ibid., Apr. 16, 1869; *Bio. Dir. U.S. Cong.,* 1118.

4. Chase arrived in Richmond on May 3 to preside over the U.S. circuit court. Chase to Daniel Butterfield, July 2, 1869 (below); Chase to Janet Chase, May 4, 1869 (Chase Papers, L.C.).

5. Probably Granitville, Rhode Island.

TO ROBERT A. HILL

Letterpress copy of autograph letter. Chase Papers, Library of Congress (*micro* 38:0729).

Washington, May 1, 1869.

My dear Judge,

I send you a copy of the Texas opinion by mail.[1]

Never apologize for writing me. I am always glad to know your views, and to hear of your welfare. It is a special gratification to me that you have succeeded so well in the duties of your very important position.

I am not surprised that at last common sense & practical views recover their sway, and that so large a majority of the educated & intelligent recognize that suffrage for both whites & blacks is best for [*illeg.*]. If this simple truth had been recognized when I first urged its recognition on southern men in 1865 hundred of millions of dollars would have been saved & great suffering spared.

Faithfully your friend
S P CHASE

Hon R. A. Hill.

P.S. I may say to you that had the merits of the McCardle case been decided the court would doubtless have held that his imprisonment for trial before a military commission was illegal.[2]

1. That is, *Texas v. White.*

2. On April 12, the U.S. Supreme Court had dismissed *Ex parte McCardle* for want of jurisdiction after Congress revoked a provision of the Habeas Corpus Act of February 5, 1867, that permitted the Court to hear appeals on violations of constitutional rights. A decision in favor of the appellant, William H. McCardle, would have undermined the legality of the First Reconstruction Act, thus limiting the authority of Congress to protect former slaves and to proceed with Reconstruction. Fairman, *Reconstruction and Reunion,* 448–49, 492–93; 6 Wall. 318 (1868).

TO ELIZABETH SMITH MILLER

Letterpress copy of autograph letter. Chase Papers, Library of Congress (*micro* 38:0730).

Washington May 2, 1869.

My dear Mrs Miller,

My old affection for your honored father[1] & sincere respect & esteem for yourself [enforces] me to reply to your note[,] though my time is so entirely occupied by my special duties that I cannot write anything which I should be willing to have read in public.

Besides I have an extreme repugnance to even seeming to have any further connexion with political movements. I have done my share of work of that sort and prefer to leave future contests to younger folk.

But you will not be mistaken if you believe me heartily desirous of all things which will really improve the condition of woman. Among such things I count the increase of facilities for moral & intellectual culture; ample recognition & full protection to rights of property; and access to & perfect security in all employments for which she is qualified by strength, capacity & integrity. I am, also, so far, at least, in favor of suffrage for women, that I should like to see the experiment tried in one or more of the states, &, if found to work well, extended to all. I am [sufficiently] confident of good [results] to be willing to vote for it in the state where I reside.

I go tomorrow on my Circuit & shall not return to Washington probably for a couple of months: and may be still longer absent.[2]

With the greatest respect & esteem,

Yours sincerely,
S. P. Chase

Mrs. Elizabeth Smith Miller

1. Gerrit Smith.

2. Chase visited Richmond, Virginia; Charleston, South Carolina; and Raleigh, North Carolina, on circuit in May and June. In August, he evidently visited his oldest daughter in Rhode Island, then went to Parkersburg, West Virginia, where he attended circuit court. Chase returned to Washington sometime between September 15 and 20, after visiting friends and relatives in New England and Pennsylvania. Chase to Daniel Butterfield, July 2, 1869; Chase to William S. Rosecrans, Aug. 16, 1869; Chase to Kate Chase Sprague, May 4, Aug. 1, and Sept. 15, 1869; Chase to Jacob W. Schuckers, May 31, 1869; Chase to John E. Williams, June 10, 1869 (all below); and Chase to Flamen Ball, Sept. 20, 1869 (Chase Papers, Cin. Hist. Soc.).

TO KATE CHASE SPRAGUE

Autograph letter (incomplete). Chase Papers, Library of Congress (*micro* 38:0739).

Richmond, May 4, 69

My darling Katie.

Your letter by express came to me here by mail from Washington this morning. I read it with profound interest and the deepest sympathy for you. It is my firm faith that you have only to carry out the purpose you express, with patience and perseverance, to win a happy issue. Trust God, have faith in Christ, accuse no one but yourself, cherish every wifely sentiment whether now reciprocated or not, have no disguises with your husband, let your conduct be as the day, and all will come right. God is trying you severely now. I you take the trial as a loving child of God it will make you better & happier, & bring you nearer to Him where perfect safety is. Don't rebel, or let any impatience [be suffered in] your thoughts. Make all happy around you. Make Willie happy, & Nettie, and the domestics. Overcome your own temper, and be transparently truthful.

What I wrote you was in warning not in distrust.[1] You have very little idea what dreadful things are said; and you cannot be too careful. On the other hand let no despairing or even despondent thoughts find lodgment in your soul.

My advice to you is not to criticize your husbands public action even in your thoughts. Of course you say nothing to outsiders except all you can say honestly in agreement & approval. But you may write something else to him, which will do harm rather than good. He cannot take criticism from you now patiently. Let him take his own course without any words but cheer & support. His own judgment will correct what may prove erroneous.

As I wrote you he seemed gratified by something you had written; but I found afterwards that there was some admonition in the letter which he did not like, though he said nothing from which I could infer any thing more than this.

He went to New York last Friday by the noon train, and before he went I had a conversation with him. I found him under some excitement. He said he had been sincerely anxious to have peace & good will restored; but could not do any thing which was not misinterpreted by you, and that you seemed all the time to be wanting to make up a case against him or defend yourself against him. That very morning, he said that, having missed some things for several days, he had gone into your room & found the small trunk or box in which they & other things—papers I understood—were & packages taken out of it which [& been] sealed up and one in particular which contained your letters from Col Crosby broken open & the letters taken away.[2] He then spoke of your coming into his room when you thought he was asleep, & searching his pockets. This matter you had explained to me, & I tried to make the same explanation to him but what had just occurred made it impossible to get a hearing. He then went on to say that he could not be controlled by you &

1. See Chase to Kate Chase Sprague, April 26, 1869 (above).

2. Possibly John Schuyler Crosby (1839–1914), a wealthy socialite from Albany, New York. In 1869, Crosby was a lieutenant colonel and aide-de-camp to Philip Sheridan. Among Crosby's later accomplishments was service as a U.S. diplomat, territorial governor of Montana, and school commissioner for New York City. Belden, *So Fell the Angels*, 238, 382; *DAB*, 4:568–69.

TO HAMILTON FISH

Autograph letter. Hamilton Fish Papers, Library of Congress (*micro* 38:0749).

Charleston, May 26, '69

My dear Sir,

I am wholly out of all political connexions, and care very little about mere politics: but I do desire earnestly the success of the Administration, both because of personal good will to General Grant and to most of the members of his Cabinet,[1] and because of the importance of that success to the best interests of our country.

Feeling thus & seeing, in the public prints, an article from the London Times of the 11th an article relating to the suits prosecuted in England by the United States for property of the so called confederate government, I cannot help saying to you that I have regretted the whole action of our government, at home and abroad by which the National Government has advanced any claims as the successor of the so called government of which Jefferson Davis was the head.[2]

Unasked advice seldom is useful, and I offer none. But I hope that the subject may receive your careful consideration *in all its relations.*

No rhetoric is strong enough to make international law serve the convenience of any one nation however powerful.

With sincerest respect & regard

Your friend
S P Chase

Hon. H. Fish.

1. Grant's administration included two other members besides those who attended the dinner described in Chase's letter to Nettie on April 12, 1869 (above): Vice President Schuyler Colfax and Secretary of the Navy Adolph Edward Borie (1809–80), who resigned his post on June 25. *DAB,* 2:464.

2. The article of May 11 focused on *The United States v. Tait,* a case pending before the Court of Queen's Bench. The defendant, Sir Peter Tait, was a British army clothier who received a shipment of cloth shortly before the end of the Civil War to make Confederate uniforms. The arrival of peace, however, prevented him from filling the order. In its legal suit, the United States sought recovery of the property, claiming itself heir to the Confederacy. "At a moment when the relations between Great Britain and America are assuming a troublesome complexion," marveled the *Times* in regard to the U.S. claim, "the accidental course of a common lawsuit has placed one of the two governments in a position so strange as to be hardly imaginable."

TO JACOB W. SCHUCKERS

Autograph letter. Chase Papers, Library of Congress (*micro* 38:0754).

Charleston S.C. May 31, 1869.

My dear Mr. Schuckers,

I have been intending to write you for the last two or three weeks; but I was terribly driven in Richmond and have not been less so here.

And there is only one matter which I felt particularly anxious to write you about. For in my personal history there has been nothing but the dry discharge of judicial duties, enlivened somewhat by the constant kindness of the people among whom I have been.

The one thing I really wanted to say to you was about Young. Your note stating his thought that I ought to write him in vindication for the charge made against him of "living upon Salmon" embarrassed me. My first feeling was to write such a letter at once. Then I reflected that

Young had brought a suit for libel touching this very matter among others. And it seemed to me unwise on every account to write a note which would like volunteer testimony, and, worse than that, more like an endeavor to shield myself than to defend him. So I have foreborne to write. When the time comes I can testify. If the libel suit is abandoned I can then write.[1] Meantime assure Mr. Young of my constant esteem & good will. I trust most sincerely that every imputation upon him will prove as groundless, as the charge or intimation rather that he ever even intimated a wish for any aid to any paper in which he was concerned from me. Nothing could be more delicate & proper than his whole intercourse with me. I felt honored & gratified by his goodwill & respect, for I thought & still think him worthy of mine

I go to Raleigh—perhaps next Friday probably next Monday.[2]

Faithfully your friend
S P CHASE

J. W. Schuckers, Esq

1. John Russell Young had become managing editor of the *New York Tribune* in 1866. On April 27, 1869, he filed a libel suit of $100,000 in the Supreme Court of Kings County, New York, against Charles Anderson Dana, founder of the *New York Sun,* for an article of the same date suggesting that Chase and other prominent politicians had paid Young to write favorably about them. Young eventually dropped the suit but lost his position with the *Tribune* due to other allegations in the article that he had violated regulations of the Associated Press. Harry W. Baehr, *The New York Tribune Since the Civil War,* (New York, 1936), 73; *DAB,* 20:630–31; *The Nation,* May 6, 13, 1869; Candace Stone, *Dana and the Sun* (New York, 1938), 125; *New York Sun,* Apr. 27, 28, 1869; *New York Tribune,* May 1, 1869.

2. As in Charleston, Chase attended to circuit court duties while in Raleigh. Chase to Daniel Butterfield, July 2, 1869 (below).

FROM JOHN E. WILLIAMS

Printed copy. *New York Tribune,* May 14, 1873 (*micro* 38:0758).

NEW-YORK, June 4, 1869.

The Hon. SALMON P. CHASE.

DEAR SIR:[1] In this morning's paper I read with painful dissatisfaction the following lines in your letter of 29th ultimo, to Capt. H. H. Manning: "And may we not indulge the hope that ere long, we who adhered to the National cause, will be prompt also to join in commemorating the heroism of our countrymen who fell on the other side?"[2]

But I also read in the same paper, with lively satisfaction, the noble sentiments which follow from one of our brave Generals: "The Grand Army of the Republic seeks to honor and preserve the principles and institutions for which its members and their dead comrades fought. We strew flowers, therefore, on the graves of our comrades, and prevent their being strewn in the National Cemeteries, at the same time, on the graves of such Rebel dead as may be buried therein—not because we cherish any feelings of hate, or desire to triumph over individual foes, but because we seek to mark, in this distinction and manner, the feelings with which the nation regards freedom and slavery, loyalty and treason, republican principles and those of a slaveholding oligarchy. We are ready to forgive—we hold no malice—but we will never consent by public national tribute to obliterate the wide gulf which lies between the objects, motives, and principles for which we fought and our comrades died, and those for which the Rebel armies banded together, and for which their dead now lie in numerous graves."[3]

"Look on this picture and then on that,"[4] and then say which is most worthy and most becoming the position of the Chief-Justice of the free United States of America—aye, of a true, unambitious American citizen.

Your obedient servant,
J. E. WILLIAMS.

1. The letterhead of this note identifies Williams as president of New York's National Metropolitan Bank.

2. Chase's letter of May 29 to Capt. B. H. Manning declined an invitation to attend services in commemoration of slain Union soldiers at Magnolia Cemetery in Charleston, South Carolina. *New York Tribune,* June 4, 1869.

3. The author was Congressman John A. Logan of Illinois, a major general during the Civil War and, in 1869, commander in chief of the Grand Army of the Republic. An order by Logan issued on June 2 included an explanation of why the graves of Confederate solders in Arlington National Cemetery were not decorated during Memorial Day services on May 30. *New York Tribune,* June 1, 4, 1869; *DAB,* 11:363–64.

4. *Hamlet,* act 3, scene 4, line 53.

TO JOHN E. WILLIAMS

Printed copy. *New York Tribune,* May 14, 1873 (*micro* 38:0758).

RALEIGH, N.C., June 10, 1869.

DEAR SIR: I regret that the perusal of my letter to Capt. Manning caused "painful dissatisfaction" to you, for I am sure that you are patriotic and not intentionally unjust.[1] Doubtless you remember occasions upon which your active hostility to measures of finance which, as Secretary of the Treasury I thought indispensable to the success of the National arms and to the permanent welfare of the country, caused painful dissatisfaction to me. The present name of the institution which you manage with so much ability and success, shows that you have abandoned your opposition to one, at least, of those measures.[2] It is perhaps not impossible that you will change your mind as to the sentiment you censure. It seems to me that taken in connection with the context from which your quotation separates it, its sense cannot be mistaken. It is, that true patriotism requires that the close of a great civil war should be marked, not by proscription or disfranchisement but by manifestations of sincere good will, especially from the successful to the unsuccessful, and by generous recognition of whatever was really brave and earnest and noble in those who fought on the failing side. I have no sympathy with the spirit which refuses to strew flowers upon the graves of the dead soldiers who fought against the side I took; and I am glad to know there was no such spirit among those who joined in decorating the graves of the soldiers of the Union who lie buried at Magnolia Cemetery. The Magnolia lavishes its perfumes as freely, the pleasant air breathes as softly and the warm sun shines as brightly over Confederate as over Union graves.[3] In the letter which has incurred your censure, I sought to put into the hearts of my countrymen, something of the divine charity taught by the tree, the air and the sun, as well as by the precepts of our Savior. I believe it has done some good and I believe it will do more.

I have read your extract from the speech of "one of our brave Generals," whom you do not name.[4] There are some good sentiments in it and some not so good. On the whole, I prefer the letter to the speech, and I am sorry to differ from you so far as to think that of the two, the letter "is most becoming" the position which I hold. The Chief-Justice is, I think, not ill employed when he inculcates good will among men. I notice that you more than intimate that my letter was prompted by ambition. It certainly was not. I do not think I ever was so ambitious as some unambitious people have represented me. At any rate, I am now unconscious of any other ambition than that of doing as much good and as little harm as possible. I have no connection with politics. I neither seek nor expect any political position, content to leave to younger men all the contentions and distinctions of political life. I shall be fully satisfied with my share of the general welfare, which it may be hoped wise and generous statesmanship, with God's blessing, will secure for our country.

Very respectfully yours,
S. P. CHASE.

1. In correspondence to Chase on June 4, 1869 (above), Williams had discussed Chase's letter of May 29 to B. H. Manning and a related order written by Congressman John A. Logan.

2. Williams was known to write lengthy letters of advice to Chase during the Civil War. "You have always borne patiently my remarks and Comments," he observed in one. Earlier, Chase and Williams had disagreed over reluctance among bankers to loan specie, Chase's desire to minimize interest on federal loans, and legislation supported by Chase that established the national banking system. In 1869, Williams's bank was known as the National Metropolitan Bank—information displayed prominently on its letterhead, which suggested an acceptance of Chase's position on national banking. *Chase Papers,* 3:269; Williams to Chase, Dec. 13, 1861, and Dec. 12, 1863 (Chase Papers, Hist. Soc. of Pa.); Williams to Chase, June 4, 1869 (above).

3. The Charleston, South Carolina, city directory of 1866 described Magnolia Cemetery as a "beautiful City of the Silent," a "lovely retreat," whose "mingled woods and waters" overlooked the Cooper River. *Charleston Dir. (1866),* 61.

4. That is, the order that John A. Logan issued on June 2.

TO NATHAN CLIFFORD

Autograph draft. Chase Papers, Historical Society of Pennsylvania (*micro* 38:0772).

Richmond Va. June 22, 1869.

My dear Judge.

You are doubtless aware that a number of persons are imprisoned in Mississippi & Texas under sentences of Military Commissions. One of them, at least, is under sentence of death; and, I presume, you have seen the opinion of the Attorney General asserting the validity of this sentence, & the statement in the public prints that the President, whose sanction of such a sentence is made by law indispensable to the Execution of it has in this case given the required sanction.[1]

Quite recently E. M. Yerger of Mississippi has been arraigned before a Military Commission in that state upon a charge of murder & the trial is now proceeding.[2]

Application has been made in behalf of Yerger to Mr. Justice Swayne, who you remember was assigned by an order made last term to that Circuit in addition to his own regular Circuit for a writ of habeas corpus; but he has declined to allow the writ, expressing however to the gentleman who made the application his perfect willingness that the application should be made to me & granted or denied according to my views of the law.

An application has been made to me accordingly; and under the circunstances I have no doubt of my duty, if I have the power. I find no instance in which a Justice of the Supreme Court has ever allowed a writ of habeas corpus to bring before him a person imprisoned in any district not included in the Circuit to which he was allotted. Has or has not a Justice of the Supreme Court power to allow the writ for that purpose?

The gentleman Judge Fisher of Mississippi who represents Mr. Yerger brings me an opinion of Mr. Phillips, of Washington, in which Mr. Carlisle concurs, affirming the power.[3]

This opinion puts the power upon the ground that the constitutional privilege is universal & that the grant of the power to issue the writ to "either of the justices of the Supreme Court as well as judges of the district Courts" is without limitation in the act of 1789.[4] It puts the supposition that the laws providing for allotment to Circuits may be repealed & the Justices of the Supreme Court relieved of all Circuit Court duty, & asks would such repeal affect the power to issue writs of habeas corpus? It quotes the grant of jurisdiction in the act of Feb 5, 1867 "that the several Courts of the United States and the several justices and judges of such Courts within their respective jurisdictions, in addition to the power already conferred by law shall have power to grant writs of habeas corpus in all cases where a person may be restrained of his liberty in violation of the Constitution or any treaty or law of the United States"; and it interprets the description "within their respective jurisdictions" as applicable only to the "Courts"; and infers that as the jurisdiction of the Supreme Court is coextensive with the Union the power of its Justices to issue writs of Habeas Corpus must have the same extent.[5]

As I desire your judgment entirely irrespective of my own I merely state the question & what has been urged upon me, & beg your counsel.

With the greatest respect & esteem,

Most sincerely yours
S P Chase

Hon Nathan Clifford

Copy sent to Judges Nelson & Clifford June 22, 69 directed respectively to New York & Boston with requests to P.M. to forward.[6]

1. In Texas, a military commission had sentenced James Weaver to die for murdering a freedman. Fulfillment of the sentence, however, required the president's sanction in accordance with terms of the First Reconstruction Act. Andrew Johnson refused and returned the matter to the War Department. On March 24, soon after Grant's inauguration, Secretary of War John A. Rawlins referred the case to Ebenezer R. Hoar, the new attorney general, who issued his opinion on May 31. Fairman, *Reconstruction and Reunion,* 561–63; 13 Ops. Atty. Gen. 59, reprinted in McPherson, *Political History,* 475–78; *Statutes at Large,* 14:429.

2. A military commission sitting under authority of the First Reconstruction Act and relying on Ebenezer R. Hoar's opinion in *Weaver's Case* was trying Edward M. Yerger (d. 1875), a citizen of Jackson, Mississippi, for stabbing and killing Joseph G. Crane, a major in the U.S. Army. Fairman, *Reconstruction and Reunion,* 564–5, 591.

3. Yerger's attorneys were Ephraim S. Fisher, an associate justice of the High Court of Errors and Appeals of Mississippi from 1851 to 1858, and Philip Phillips of Alabama, a former congressman who practiced law in Washington. James Mandeville Carlisle, another Washington lawyer with no professional connection to Yerger, offered his unsolicited opinion in letters to Chase on June 21 and 22. Ibid., 566; Carlisle to Chase, June 21, 22, 1869 (Chase Papers, Hist. Soc. of Pa.).

4. The law of September 24, 1789, from which Chase quotes, established the U.S. judicial system. *Statutes at Large,* 1:81–82.

5. The quotation comes from legislation that amended the Judiciary Act of 1789. *Statutes at Large,* 14:385–87.

6. Chase's brethren, Samuel Nelson and Nathan Clifford, writing on June 28 and July 6, respectively, agreed with Yerger's attorneys that the chief justice was authorized to hear the appeal. Chase eventually agreed and issued the majority opinion of *Ex parte Yerger* on October 25, which extended the Supreme Court's appellate jurisdiction "to all cases of commitment by the judicial authority of the United States, not within any exception made by Congress." As for Yerger, he returned to civilian custody when Mississippi reentered the Union on February 23, 1870, and the state supreme court released him on bail in April. He remained free for the rest of his life. Clifford to Chase, July 6, 1869; Nelson to Chase, June 28, 1869 (both Chase Papers, Hist. Soc. of Pa.); Fairman, *Reconstruction and Reunion,* 582–83, 589–91; 8 Wall. 85 (1869).

TO DANIEL BUTTERFIELD

Copy in clerk's hand on letterhead stationery, signed by Chase. Chase Papers, Historical Society of Pennsylvania (*micro* 38:0798).

(Copy)
Greenbrier White Sulphur Springs[1]
Greenbrier County, West Va.
July 2. 1869.

Dear General:[2]

I have written to the Committee,—addressing Gen. Locke, the Secretary,—and expressing my regret that I cannot be present at the Reunion. The invitation was only received to-day, and the answer goes by the first mail; but will probably be too late for the occasion.[3]

This morning, and since my reply was written, I find, to my surprise, the enclosed in the Herald.[4] It is really painful to me to have all I do attributed to political motives; when I am utterly unconscious of such. My Southern journey has been one of laborious duty. My judicial circuit embraces Maryland, Virginia, North Carolina, South Carolina, and West Virginia. I began with Maryland in April; attended the courts in Virginia and South Carolina in May and June, and finished in North Carolina about a week ago. In August, I go to West Virginia. All this has nothing whatever to do with politics: nor have I had anything to do with any schemes or plans for the succession. Last year, had the Herald's views prevailed, it seems to me more than probable, that I should have been elected President.[5] I was not anxious for the nomination then, whatever folks may say: and all I have since heard and seen makes me heartily glad, on my own account, that I was not nominated. I hope, unfeignedly, that the nomination and election of General Grant will prove a real blessing to the country; and I shall be very glad if his administration proves so beneficial that the people will hear of nobody as his successor except himself.

Most certainly I don't. want to be. I feel that I am too old for these political contests; and that it is every way best for me to perform what public service remains to be performed by me, where I am, on the bench. I am *hors du combat,* politically.

I quite agree with the concluding sentence of the Herald's article: but it has no application to me, I am not a "Presidential candidate," and am not conscious of any political "ailment." So the advice in the next preceding sentence, though kindly meant, is of no practical importance.

You know Mr. Bennett, and the Herald folk generally. Wont you take the trouble to put them *au courant* upon the facts? I owe them all,—and above all Mr. B.,—very much for kind words last summer, and would not like to be misapprehended by them. Except as a basis for *conversation* of *this tenor,* this letter is private.

Yours always,
S P Chase

Gen. Butterfield.

1. On the morning of June 28, Chase departed Richmond for White Sulphur Springs, which is currently in Monroe County, one of several popular health resorts in southeastern West Virginia. *New York Herald,* June 29, 1869; Oren F. Morton, *A History of Monroe County West Virginia* (Staunton, Va., 1916), 205–6.

2. Maj. Gen. Daniel Butterfield served as Joseph Hooker's chief of staff in the Armies of the Potomac and the Cumberland. *DAB,* 3:373.

3. Brevet Brig. Gen. Frederick Thomas Locke (1826–93), former chief of staff for the Fifth Army Corps, had invited Chase to a meeting in New York on July 5 to organize a society for officers of the Army of the Potomac. Chase declined in another letter written to Locke on the same date. Chase to Locke, July 2, 1869 (Chase Papers, L.C.); *New York Times,* July 5, 6, 1869, and Feb. 7, 1893.

4. Chase might refer to an article in the July 30 issue of the *New York Herald* that the editors have not located. Earlier, the paper had accused Chase of launching a campaign to succeed Ulysses S. Grant in the presidency. "Chief Justice Chase, in his tour of the Southern States," asserted the paper on June 22, "is gaining golden opinions from all the anti-radical Southern elements, and, plank by plank, is building up a strong democratic platform for 1872."

5. In an article of May 18, 1866—which Chase discussed in a letter of May 22, 1866, to James G. Bennett, Sr., (above)—Bennett's *New York Herald* had supported Chase as the only potential presidential nominee capable of uniting members from both parties and winning the election of 1866 for the Democrats.

TO KATE CHASE SPRAGUE

Autograph letter. Chase Papers, Historical Society of Pennsylvania (*micro* 38:0824).

Parkersburgh Aug 1, 69.

My darling Katie,

My journey hitherto if not very pleasant was, at any rate, quite rapid enough. We just caught the train at the Kingston Station; but Noonan had time I suppose to put your letters on. I confess I did not think to ask him for them: but he had time enough to hand them to them in the car, if he could not get them off otherwise; which I remember you told him to do. I thought of them when I found Gen. Tomkins on the Boat, and it occurred to me how easy it would be for him to put them in the Post Office.[1] For that matter we reached New York so early that I could have done it myself. I had a full hour on my hands unoccupied. We arrived before six and did not leave till 8.40. From New York here my journey was a very rapid one, & the part from New York to Baltimore quite pleasant. I had a large room in a compartment car quite to myself except that now & then a gentleman would call to see me; and I never found conductors & baggage men more attentive & kind. We were a few minutes behind time & the Conductor telegraphed the Baltimore & Ohio to hold their train for me: and the baggage master had my trunk transferred & ticketed promptly & without detaining me a moment on arrival so that I had no difficulty in making the connexion.

Then came the fast running. Ed. Goldsborough was on the train to Frederick & urged me to stop but I felt so well & so little tired that I thought it best to keep on.[2] The road has ever so many curves & is not, by any means, the smoothest in the world. So we were strung to & fro & jolted up & down as Mr. Gallagher would say "to a degree"[3] / I got supper at Martinsburgh, & then had my bed made up in my section of quite a decent sleeping car—if *decent* describes any of that class—& laid down taking off hat, boots & coats only. And was I not tossed to & fro & up & down at a prodigous rate: the cars rushing on round the curves, through tunnels, over rough places at the rate of thirty miles an hour sometimes more sometimes less, making very few stops so that jolt & swing succeeded each other almost without intermission. I did not have any very refreshing sleep you may be assured but I did sleep some & the time passed more easily lying down than sitting up.

This morning at half past seven we were at the depot in Parkersburgh. From New York to Parkersburgh the distance is 569 miles and the time I took was 22½ hours a little more than 25 miles an hour the whole way including stoppages &c. I am afraid you will think that your father is getting to be a fast man in his old age.

My friend Judge Jackson[4] was waiting for me with his carriage at the depot, & in a few moments I was in my comfortable room under his hospitable roof. There was time for me to bathe, shave & dress before the other members of the family were ready for breakfast. Then came their welcome & then a nice breakfast, & I was almost as good as new.

We went to Church this morning, & this afternoon several gentlemen have called which hurries my writing a little that I may not miss the mail. The letter will go tomorrow morning.

I hope to get through in time to be with you on the 13th, but am not sure.[5] Dearest love to dearest Nettie & Willie & the Governor. May God bless you all.

Most affy your father
S P Chase

1. Chase's route probably took him by train from Kingston, Rhode Island, to Stonington, Connecticut, where he boarded a coastal vessel for New York. His companion might have been Charles Henry Thompkins (d. 1895) of New York and Rhode Island, a brevet brigadier general of volunteers during the Civil War. Chase to Jay Cooke, Sept. 9, 1869 (Cooke Papers, Hist. Soc. of Penn.); Heitman, *Historical Register,* 1:964–95.

2. Edward Yerbury Goldsborough had served as U.S. marshal for Maryland since April. In 1874, he married Chase's grandniece, Amy Auld. T. J. C. Williams and Folger McKinsey, *History of Frederick County Maryland* . . . , 2 vols., ([Frederick, Md.], 1910; reprint, Baltimore, 1979), 2:1241–42.

3. William Davis Gallagher of Ohio was a poet, journalist, and politician who worked under Chase during the Civil War as a commercial agent and special collector of customs in the upper Mississippi River Valley.

4. John Jay Jackson, Jr.
5. As planned, Chase returned to Narragansett on the morning of August 13. Chase to William S. Rosecrans, Aug. 16, 1869 (below).

TO WILLIAM S. ROSECRANS

Autograph letter. Rosecrans Papers, Department of Special Collections, University Research Library, University of California, Los Angeles (*micro* 38:0834).

Narragansett, Aug. 16, 1869.

My dear General,[1]

Some time last spring, just before I started to hold my southern courts I received at Washington, your very interesting letter by Consul Brink (if I rightly remember the name) and gave him the kindest reception I could. It so happened that no one was then in the city to whom I could beneficially introduce him with reference to the objects in view; but before I left town Mr. H. D. Cooke returned to whom I explained matters, & he promised to see the Consul, & consider the subject. Just, then, came the news of your recall & I presume that nothing was done.[2]

Afterwards some four or five weeks ago I received another letter from you; also written before your recall of which I need now say nothing except that I thank you for your kind remembrance & reciprocate most heartily every friendly sentiment.

Lately I had been hoping soon to see you; for I rejoiced with more in number than you have probably imagined in your nomination for Governor of Ohio. If I had known where to reach you I should certainly have strongly urged your acceptance. To be sure the platform was not one on which you could well stand: but it was not probably intended as a very positive or very permanent declaration of political faith; and your nomination qualified it largely. In fact your nomination was intended, so far as I gather, as a new departure in politics, and as a sort of reconciliation of Old Line Democracy with modern issues & duties: a reconciliation for which I have been longing for years. So I hoped your acceptance & rejoiced in the prospect of your election, which seemed to be sure. I do not doubt that in declining the nomination you were governed by sufficient reasons: but it was a great disappointment to me, and tens of thousands who felt as I did.[3]

The effect in Ohio has been very manifest. The democracy have for the time abandoned the forward movement & have nominated Mr. Pendleton, a gentleman every way worthy of their suffrages so far as capacity & character constitute worth, but representing very decidedly the rather remote past than the living present.[4] The general notion seems to be that the platform & the candidate represent each the other; and that the result of the election will determine what amount of strength the party can rally in its present position. I have no doubt it will be large; but I do not anticipate success. The party, occupying almost any position, is great & strong; but I doubt if it is great enough and strong enough to achieve a victory, without the help of advantageous position.

It is a long time since I have written so much about politics. It is not, now, a theme which has much attraction for me. I take very little interest in political movements except so far as general principles are involved, or friends. Events have placed me very much outside of political currents: and I am more than content that it is so. In principles & sympathies always earnestly democratic I have never been able to follow party leaders whithersoever they chose to go; & have been obliged, not unfrequently, to act in pretty decided opposition to them. Now I dismiss contentions, leaving them to younger men; and look to nothing except the discharge of my judicial duties.

Have you abandoned your purposes of good to Mexico? What are you about? What do you propose? I shall be very glad to hear of you and of your doings, and shall constantly desire your prosperity in all things.[5]

I held my last Circuit Court, week before last at Parkersburgh, West Virginia; and came here last Friday Morning, intending to make some brief visits during the next four weeks; & then to resume work at Washington. The Supreme Court will sit in adjourned Term on the first Monday of October, & will have some very important cases to decide—one involving directly the constitutionality of so much of the reconstruction laws as authorizes the trial of civilians by military commissions in Mississippi & states similarly situated.[6] You have seen perhaps the decision in the Case of Texas v Chiles & how entirely it sustains the views of reconstruction which I took last summer[7]

Faithfully & cordially your friend
S P Chase

Gen. Rosecrans

1. In 1868, Andrew Johnson had appointed Rosecrans, formerly a major general, as the U.S. minister to Mexico.

2. After his inauguration, Grant recalled Rosecrans from Mexico and appointed U.S. diplomat Thomas Henry Nelson in his place. *DAB,* 13:424–25; William M. Lamars, *The Edge of Glory: A Biography of General William S. Rosecrans, U.S.A.* (New York, 1961), 441.

3. Ohio's Democrats had nominated Rosecrans for governor in their state convention, which met in Columbus on July 7. The party's platform, adopted on the same day, included provisions that supported a policy of soft money by the federal government, denounced the national banking system and a high protective tariff, and urged rejection of the proposed Fifteenth Amendment. Rosecrans declined in a telegram written on August 7, citing his lack of sympathy with the party's position on major issues. *Daily Ohio Statesman,* July 8 and Aug. 12, 1869; Roseboom, *Civil War Era,* 469–70.

4. Ohio's Democratic central committee chose George H. Pendleton to replace Rosecrans on August 11. In the ensuing election, Pendleton lost to Republican candidate Rutherford B. Hayes, the presiding governor. *DAB,* 8:448; *Daily Ohio Statesman,* Aug. 12, 1869; Gilkey, *Ohio Hundred Year Book,* 328; Roseboom, *Civil War Era,* 470–71.

5. According to Rosecrans, Mexico's recent social and political turmoil would cease with greater immigration, commercial growth, and the development of railroads. In a letter written to Chase on August 27, he alluded to plans for proposing a solution to "the Mexican question" to Chase, to "other leading minds of the country, and . . . to the chiefs of the money and commercial interests of the country." Rosecrans later applied for a concession to build a telegraph line and narrow-gauge railroad across central Mexico,

but the scheme ended in failure. Lamars, *Edge of Glory,* 441–42; Rosecrans to Chase, Aug. 27, 1869 (Chase Papers, Hist. Soc. of Pa.).

6. That is, *Ex parte Yerger,* discussed in Chase's letter to Nathan Clifford on June 22, 1869 (above).

7. Chase probably meant *Texas v. White,* in which John Chiles was a defendant, discussed in correspondence to Janet Chase on April 12, 1869 (above). The Court did not hear *Texas v. Chiles,* a related case, until 1874. Chase's majority opinion in *Texas v. White* supported limited Congressional Reconstruction—a position he had taken in a letter to August Belmont on May 30, 1868 (above), which was later reprinted widely. Fairman, *Reconstruction and Reunion,* 534–35, 638–48, 669–70; 7 Wall. 700 (1869).

TO KATE CHASE SPRAGUE

Autograph letter. Chase Papers, Historical Society of Pennsylvania (*micro* 38:0859).

Philadelphia, Sep. 15, '69.

My dearest Katie,

We had a very pleasant journey from Narragansett to New York, and no very unusually unpleasant experiences in getting from the Steamer to the Ferry boat.[1] Our hackman did well—our express-man very badly—besides keeping for himself a couple of dollars I had given him to buy "compartment" tickets on the Railroad he was so long in getting our baggage from one Pier to the other that we just escaped missing the train.

Once in the cars, however on the Jersey side all went smoothly enough. The train was stopped to let us get off at Germantown—a great favor—where Mr. Cooke was waiting for us with a carriage to take us to Ogontz.[2] By this kindness we were saved the depot in Phila & some miles of driving and some hours of journeying. Our reception was most cordial, & so far our visit has been a most pleasant one.

The Church near Ogontz has been greatly enlarged & has an excellent rector. It will suit you that it is all of stone. Some months ago Mr. Cooke & Mr. Moorhead offered to build a parsonage & pay for the ground &c if the Congregation would pay for enlarging the Church &c.[3] The offer was accepted & the result is the Enlargement; the Parsonage with two or three acres I believe of ground; & a fine Hall (a separate building for meetings of all sorts connected with the Parish, for lectures &c &c. I know of nothing more complete in the Church way or that would suit you better.

I need say nothing of the House: you know all about it. The grounds are greatly improved, & undergoing constant improvement.

I suppose the Governor is in Maine, [&] trust that he will meet great success in all his objects including the fishing.

Day before yesterday Mr. Cooke & I went a fishing. We took the cars from Camden down the Peninsula of New Jersey towards Cape May, stopping at Cape May Court House with a Mr Beesly—(one of the quiet, good, efficient, kindly sort of men—a rare sort)—who unites in himself the capacities of Manufacturer Farmer, Fisherman, & Representative in the Legislature.[4] Yesterday Morning we went out with him in his boat to the fishing grounds, where we fished & fished & fished all day from eight oclock in the morning till six in the afternoon, catching altogether two hundred fish all with the hook, of which Mr. Cooke caught 84 & I 68 & Mr. Beesly the rest, besides attending to our lines, baiting my hook, taking off my fish &c &c. I just missed catching two prodigious fellows; but was very well pleased on the whole with my share of the work / Our fish were of several kinds poggies, most, next goodies;[5] then blue fish, mackerel, flying fish, a couple of sharks &c &c. I hope the Governors success will exceed ours.

This Morning (as well as yesterday) I was up at five and we returned by the 7 A.M. train to Phila. We have not yet been out to Ogontz & I have not seen Nettie.

It was a great delight to me to see the restoration of the old affection between you & your husband. God grant that it may never be interrupted again. How happy it seemed to make you both. It was wrong in you to leave me to be informed by others that you expect to be a mother again in October.[6] I cannot help being very anxious about you; but trust that our Heavenly Father, whose Mercies have ever exceeded our *ingratitude,* will give you safety and blessedness in your experience, and give us all love and obedience to Himself.

I wish you would write Nettie about the part of the *old* furniture you desire to retain. That in my Library room you know belongs to the Government. Keep what you please of the rest except the silver (not much) the pictures & the bust. It is painful to separate, but it will be little of separation after all, & doubtless is for the best.[7]

Most tenderly & affectionately your father
S P Chase

1. Chase and Nettie started their voyage on September 10, traveling by train from Kingston, Rhode Island, to Stonington, Connecticut, as probably happened during his trip early in August, and from there by ship to New York City. Afterward, they boarded a ferry to New Jersey, then took another train south to Philadelphia. Chase to Jay Cooke, Sept. 9, 1869 (Chase Papers, Hist. Soc. of Pa.); Chase to Kate Sprague, Aug. 1, 1869 (above).

2. Jay Cooke had built "Ogontz," a fifty-two-room mansion in Chilton Hills, north of Philadelphia, in 1866.

3. Cooke was a major benefactor of St. Paul's Episcopal Church, whose sanctuary dated from the early 1860s. The new parsonage housed Robert J. Parvin, St. Paul's rector. Cooke's brother-in-law and business partner, William G. Moorhead, also resided in Chilton Hills. Ellis Paxson Oberholtzer, *Jay Cooke: Financier of the Civil War,* (Philadelphia, 1907), 2:484.

4. In 1869, Republican Thomas Beesley held a seat in the New Jersey assembly. Lewis Townsend Stevens, *The History of Cape May County, New Jersey, from the Aboriginal Times to the Present Day* (Cape May, N.J., 1897), 452.

5. "Goodies," better known as "spots," are a type of croaker. "Pogy" is a common name for the Atlantic menhaden, of the herring family. C. Richard Robins et al., *A List of Common and Scientific Names of Fishes from the United States and Canada,* 4th ed., American Fisheries Society Special Publication No. 12 (Bethesda, Md., 1980), 17, 46, 129, 150.

6. Kate gave birth to her second child, Ethel Chase Sprague, late in October. William Sprague subsequently denied paternity. Belden, *So Fell the Angels,* 241, 291; Chase to Kate Sprague, Nov. 7, 1869 (below).

7. Earlier in the month, Chase and Nettie had decided to establish another household separate from the Spragues in a dwelling that the widow Anna P. Hoover owned at 1827 I Street. Chase to Hoover, Sept. 27, Oct. 26, and Dec. 9, 1870 (Chase Papers, L.C.); Chase to Richard C. Parsons, Sept. 26, 1870 (below); Chase to Kate Chase Sprague, Oct. 1, 1869 (Chase Papers, L.C.); *Wash. Dir. (1870)*, 69.

TO THOMAS H. YEATMAN

Autograph letter. Chase Papers, Cincinnati Historical Society (*micro* 38:0895).

Private Strictly

Washington, Oct. 19, '69

Dear Yeatman,[1]

I am glad to see that my "deacon" is to be Senator; and hope he will do a great deal of good as such & have all the enjoyment that is possible in Columbus.

Please let me know, if you can, what may be expected concerning the 15th Amendment.[2] Will you and the other Republicans elected from Hamilton County vote for it? Will the democrats or any considerable number of them vote for it?[3]

I am now as always—though practically out of politics—for universal suffrage & universal amnesty; and though I should have preferred to see the principles of the Amendment adopted by the states in their State Constitutions, I have become convinced that the best thing for the south & the whole country is to make sure of their adoption by ratifying the Amendment. I feel quite sure that its ratification will be followed very speedily by universal amnesty,—by which I mean removal of all disabilities,—and by a great increase of prosperity. Virginia has acted on this idea.[4]

The democrats cannot do a wiser thing than go for the Amendment as they went for the repeal of black laws in 1849. That action secured them the state for years, & like causes now will be apt to produce like effect.[5]

I write you freely as an old friend but I don't want to have any more letters of mine, written in the unreserve of private communication, get into print. So put this letter in the fire without letting any body see it: though you are quite at liberty to tell any body what I think, if it will do any good.

Yours sincerely
S P Chase

Thos. H. Yeatman Esq

Are you coming to Washington before January?

1. Ohio voters had recently elected Yeatman, Chase's former employee in the Treasury Department, to a seat in the state senate, where he served from 1870 to 1871. Gilkey, *Ohio Hundred Year Book*, 1:173.

2. In January 1870, the Ohio House of Representatives and Senate narrowly ratified the Fifteenth Amendment by a vote of 57–55 and 19–18, respectively. *Ohio State Journal,* Jan. 15, 21, 1870.

3. On October 12, a coalition of reformist Republicans and Democrats in Hamilton County—all of whom ran as Democrats—had swept elections for state officials. Thus, Democrats technically held all ten seats allotted to the county in the house and all four in the senate. In the lower chamber, four members from the county voted in favor of the amendment on January 14: Henry M. Bates, A. J. Cunningham, George H. Hill, and E. F. Kleinschmidt. Only Yeatman and Michael Goepper registered their approval in the senate on January 20. Ibid.; *Cincinnati Daily Enquirer,* Oct. 12, 1869, Jan. 21, 1870; Gilkey, *Ohio Hundred Year Book,* 173, 221; Roseboom, *Civil War Era,* 470–71.

4. The Virginia legislature had ratified the Fourteenth and Fifteenth Amendments on October 8. *Appletons' Annual Cyclopædia,* 9:714.

5. Democrats in the assembly tended to vote in accordance with their party's most recent platform, enacted on July 7, which opposed ratification of the Fifteenth Amendment. Ohio's black laws restricted the activities of African Americans. Democratic assemblymen helped repeal most of them as part of the political arrangement that yielded Chase's first election to the U.S. Senate. *Chase Papers,* 2:127–28, 236–41; *Daily Ohio Statesman,* July 8 and Aug. 12, 1869, and Jan. 15 and 21, 1870.

TO KATE CHASE SPRAGUE

Autograph letter. Chase Papers, Library of Congress (*micro* 38:0912).

Washington, Nov. 7, 1869

My darling child,

A letter from Eliza to Nettie last night gave us a great deal of pleasure. It was the first particular account of the baby we have have had.[1] In her note to me Eliza comforted me by the assurance that you are doing as well as could be expected, and I had the same from the Governor: though both charged you with some imprudence, from which I was delighted to learn you had escaped without serious consequences. But neither seemed to think it worth while to say much of baby. Now that defect in our information is supplied. And I congratulate you on being the mother of such a dear pretty little one. And I am glad that the baby is a girl. For my part I like girls rather better than boys though I would—I believe—have put up with one—perhaps two—for the sake of having a brother apiece for you and Nettie. But *girls* are *nice.* And it will be so good for Willie to have a little sister.

And now will come your additional responsibility. It is a great thing to have the charge of a little mortal, & to know that the character of all its life here below depends so largely on the direction given to the setting out. How much more to have the charge of young *immortals,* with all the influence which mothers necessarily possess. Let these things, my dear child, draw you close and closer to the Savior.

There is nothing new to tell you here. Our goings on are pretty much the same from day to day. Yesterday I varied the monotony a trifle by going out to my new purchase, after the conference was over, about half past four.[2] It was a bleak November afternoon. I thought of you and the Governor as we (Parsons & I) rode by the old Rhode Island Camping ground. The trees where Ballou lay with his regiment were almost bare / Wind & frost have dealt roughly with the foliage[3]

Parsons, always inclined to flatter, professed himself delighted with my place. But indeed it did look beautiful: except so bare & worn. The prospect of the Capitol & the Potomac beyond and the hills is splendid—nothing can be finer. If I were only able to get it up & put in order—that is if I had ten thousand dollars to spare—I really believe I would spend more than half the winter there. It is not too far for a good walk, for I tried it the other day with Mr. Hilliard. We walked out on the new railroad track till we came very near the house, & returned, in little more than an hour & a half.[4] It is certainly less than an hour walk either way. But no more of this. Good bye darling. I am half inclined to run on to Narragansett just to kiss you and the baby. Don't be *imprudent* again.

Your Affe. father
S P Chase

Mrs K. C. Sprague

1. The letter from Eliza Chase Whipple, Chase's niece, discussed the birth of Kate's second child, Ethel Chase Sprague, who had been born late in October. Belden, *So Fell the Angels,* 251.

2. In September, Chase had purchased "Edgewood," a dilapidated house with forty acres of land two and a quarter miles north of the Capitol. Chase renovated the structure over the next two years and occupied it in 1871. Chase to Flamen Ball, Oct. 4, 1869 (Chase Papers, Cinc. Hist. Soc.); Mary Merwin Phelps, *Kate Chase: Dominant Daughter* (New York, 1935), 230.

3. Richard C. Parsons, Sr., who oversaw renovations at Edgewood, had secured a appointment with Chase's help as marshal of the U.S. Supreme Court. Maj. Sullivan Ballou (1829–61), a former Rhode Island legislator, served in the Second Regiment of the Second Rhode Island Infantry until his death at the First Battle of Bull Run on July 21, 1861. Prior to the battle, Rhode Island troops under William Sprague occupied a site near Edgewood. Belden, *So Fell the Angels,* 247; Fairman, *Reconstruction and Reunion,* 85, 167, 171, 175; *Historical Catalogue of Brown University 1764–1914* (Providence, 1914), 451; Long, *Civil War Day by Day,* 98–100; *OR,* ser. 1, v. 2:400.

4. Chase probably refers to a segment of the Baltimore and Ohio Railroad's metropolitan branch, which was under construction in 1869. The new route ran north from Washington past Edgewood and Glenwood Cemetery, over hilly ground that required numerous "cuts, fills, and bridges." Belden, *So Fell the Angels,* 247; Edward Hungerford, *The Story of the Baltimore and Ohio Railroad, 1827–1927 . . . ,* 2 vols. (New York, 1928), 2:71–72; Keim, *Illustrated Handbook,* frontispiece; John F. Stover, *History of the Baltimore and Ohio Railroad,* (West Lafayette, Ind., 1987), 114, 142–43.

TO JOHN D. VAN BUREN

Letterpress copy of letter in clerk's hand. Chase Papers, Library of Congress (*micro* 38:0916).

Private

Washington Nov. 20. 1869.

My dear Sir:

It was pleasant to see your handwriting once more. My memory of all your kindness public and private is fresh and enduring.

I am now going to write what you may show to Gov. Hoffman if you think it best.[1] If not, you may burn this note.

To me, the Signs indicate that the Governor will be the next democratic candidate for the Presidency: and, he will, in that event, have my best wishes for his election, if I live.

But neither he nor any body else can be elected on the issues which have been hitherto presented by the democratic party. By hitherto, I mean for the last ten years. Much as the people dislike the policy or want of policy if you like it better of the Republican Party in many respects they like still less anything which smacks of repudiation or of oppression.[2] Certainly there is a great body of citizens, numerous enough to decide the result of any general election for some time to come, who have fixed opinions on these questions which will govern their votes.

Having reference to the future what is the line for a democratic statesman? The question of repudiation will, I think, take care of itself. Americans are an honest people in the mass whatever may be said generally of politicians. It is not in respect to this that damaging divisions need be seriously feared.

But the question of citizens rights for the enfranchised masses will remain a great and most troublesome question till it is finally settled. Once settled, and settled right by assuring to all the right to vote, I have no doubt that the democratic party will have a majority of the new voters on its side; although it must be confessed that thus far it has exhibited no very strong claims upon them. Now the only way of settling this question, permanently and satisfactorily is, as it seems to me, the adoption of the 15th. amendment. There is one feature in it which I do not like—the power of legislation given to Congress. But this power will hardly be exercised to any extent if at all; besides, the power will be nugatory if the states act impartially and fairly; for the rights of man once secured, the tide will set strongly in favor of the rights of states. And, the main principle of the amendment is right—equality of political rights for all citizens. It is the true basis of democracy.

I am glad to see that Gov. Hoffman transmitted the New York ratification promptly to the Secretary of State.[3] It was well and wisely done, though perhaps not overpleasing to some. He will do well and wisely if he prevents any legislative action looking to the rescinding of the ratification, and that without reference to the probable efficacy of such action. And he can use a great deal of quiet influence in favor of the ratification in other States—Ohio for example. And, all he does in this direction will, I am confident, redound to his honor and advantage in the future: as well as to the honor and advantage of the whole country.

I could say a great deal more, but I have not the time. If I could see you both & talk to you I could show more fully the grounds of my faith & judgment. But you will see all.

I need not add that in writing this letter I am stepping beyond the non-political line I present to myself general and write only in the confidence which reposed in you has never been disappointed

[*illeg.*] thfully your friend,

Col. Jno D. Van Buren

1. Tammany Hall politician John T. Hoffman had won election to New York's governorship in 1868. Despite Chase's predictions, explained in this letter, Hoffman's political career ended abruptly in 1871 after he defied his party's leaders. *DAB,* 9:114.

2. The Democratic national platform of 1868 had repudiated the Reconstruction Acts as "unconstitutional, revolutionary and void." *New York Herald,* July 8, 1868.

3. New York's legislature had ratified the Fifteenth Amendment on April 14, 1869, but neglected to send a certified notice to U.S. Secretary of State Hamilton Fish. On September 3, Hoffman agreed to forward the document at the urging of John Chandler Bancroft Davis, New York's acting secretary of state. Four months later, however, the legislature rescinded its approval after state elections gave Democrats majorities in both chambers. Despite this reversal, Fish declared the Amendment ratified by the necessary three-fourths majority on March 30, 1870. *Appleton's Annual Cyclopædia,* 9:486, 10:543; *DAB,* 5:134–35; *New York Times,* Sept. 3, 1869, Jan. 6, 1870; *Statutes at Large,* 16:1131–32.

TO JAMES SHEPHERD PIKE

Autograph letter. James Shepherd Pike Collection, Special Collections Department, Raymond H. Folger Library, University of Maine (*micro* 38:0931).

Washington, Decr. 24, 1869.

My dear Mr. Pike,

Your note did me good. It refreshed me to see your hand writing: even though it expressed dissent; in which, however, you are wrong. If there is any question on which Courts cannot revise legislative acts it is a question of measure in the exercise of acknowledged powers. If there is any question of discretion—any which can be properly called political—this is one.

But my *main* point—and the great value of the judgment to the Country is the assertion of the power of Congress to restrain the circulation as money of any notes not issued under National Sanction. This crowns the work of furnishing a National Currency. Without this that work would be vain. I shall ever count it the most valuable service I have been permitted to render our country to inaugurate, carry forward & crown that work.[1]

Nettie & I are keeping house on our own account at 1827 I Street where we should be *so* glad to have a visit from you & Lizzie.

I have just been surprised by a note from Mr. Hooper that "Mr Stanton died suddenly at 3 o'clock this morning. He was taken sick after midnight"

How sudden & how sad. Only yesterday Sumner & Hooper were here & we were talking of the prospect of perfect restoration, which we were all glad to think, his appointment to the Supreme Bench afforded to him. And already he is gone.[2]

Faithfully yours
S P CHASE

Hon. J. S. Pike

1. Pike's letter, which the editors have not found, evidently dealt with Chase's majority opinion in *Veazie Bank v. Fenno,* issued on December 13. In that case, a bank in Maine had challenged a 10 percent tax on state bank notes authorized by the Internal Revenue Act of July 13, 1866, as an unconstitutional restriction of state power and a direct tax in violation of the U.S. Constitution, art. 1, sec. 9, clause 4. Chase disagreed on both points, however, and sanctioned the authority of Congress to take a broad range of measures in exercise of recognized powers. Fairman, *Reconstruction and Reunion,* 711–13; 8 Wall. 533 (1869).

2. On December 20, Grant nominated Edwin M. Stanton to replace retiring Associate Justice Robert C. Grier. The Senate confirmed Stanton on the same day by a vote of 41–11. According to the December 25 edition of the *New York Times,* Stanton died from "congestion of the heart." U.S. Senate, *Journal of the Executive Proceedings,* 17:320, 322.

TO GEORGE H. HILL

Letterpress copy of letter in clerk's hand. Chase Papers, Library of Congress (*micro* 38:0947).

Washington, January 7. 1870.

Dear Sir.[1]

As a citizen of Hamilton County, and, therefore, one of your constituents, and also as a personal friend I suppose I may properly say what I think, about an important question on which you will have to vote—I mean the ratification of the 15th. Amendment.

Perhaps you know I have always thought, since universal emancipation became certain, that the new freemen must become citizens, and must have the right of suffrage sooner or later. I expressed these views at Charleston, South Carolina, shortly after the surrender of Lee, and they were sustained, as to citizenship, by the Supreme Court in the case of Texas v. White, a copy of which I send with this letter, and by the same mail. The address at Charleston you will find, if you have the curiosity to read it, in Whitelaw Reid's book, "After the War."[2]

I have always thought, too, that universal amnesty should be accorded, and the most liberal and generous policy should be adopted towards all who, having been enemies during the civil war, were willing to resume in good faith the relation of friends and fellow citizens when war was over.

Hence, I very early adopted the motto, Universal Suffrage and Universal Amnesty. I felt sure that this policy would secure the peace of the whole country, and the highest prosperity of all the South.

Unfortunately, universal amnesty has been slow to come; but the Fifteenth Amendment presents an opportunity for securing universal suffrage; and, I am very confident that universal amnesty will not stay far behind. Indeed, I believe that, the former having been secured by the adoption of the Amendment, we shall soon witness a competition among politicians for the honor of leading in securing the latter.

I have never heard of any substantial objection to the Amendment except two: the first being that it gives the right of suffrage to colored men who ought not to have it; and the second that it gives the regulation of suffrage to Congress, whereas it ought to remain with the states.

Events, I think, have disposed of the first objection. The number of adult colored male citizens in the United States must approach nearly a million.[3] It is simply impossible to exclude such a mass from the ballot box, with safety to our interests and institutions: and whatever inconveniences may attend their admission to the elective franchise are more than counterbalanced by its advantages and the consideration that it is right in itself.

As to the second objection, it strikes me as rather apparent than real. The Amendment gives no power to Congress to interfere with suffrage in any state unless it is denied or abridged by the state, on account of race, color, or former slavery. The full power of regulation, as it has existed heretofore will exist still in the states. The words of the Amendment are, "Sec. 1. The right of *citizens* of the United States to *vote* shall not be *denied or abridged* by the United States, or *by any state,* on account of *race, color,* or *previous condition* of *servitude.* Sec. 2. The Congress shall have power to *enforce* this article by appropriate legislation."[4] The power to *enforce* a right as against denial, or abridgement cannot arise until denial or abridgement has occurred. These, at least, are my present impressions, which I hold subject to correction if the question shall ever come before me for more deliberate consideration.

But, if these objections were more solid than they appear to me to be, still the advantages of the amendment seem to counterbalance them and more.

The advantages may be stated fairly, as I think, to be these[:]

First; It is *right* that in a republic suffrage should be [equal] to all citizens.

Second; It is expedient that the vexed questions arising from slavery and exclusion from franchise should be settled speedily and finally; and no mode of settlement seems so easy as by adopting the Amendment.

Thirdly; The recuperation of the South through a wiser, and more liberal policy than has been pursued is greatly to be desired, and the early adoption of such a policy will be made certain by the adoption of the amendment.

Fourthly; On this last point, the opinions of enlightened Southern men are entitled to great consideration, and it is no injustice to other states to say that no other state is entitled to more deference in this respect than Virginia, and Virginia has ratified the Amendment, not under coercion, or from any lower considerations than the best interests of the state and of the entire South, and [considerations] of right and justice.[5] But these opinions are not confined to Virginia. My duties required me to visit the other Southern states in my circuit last spring and Summer, and I can safely say that they are generally entertained by those whose judgments are most entitled to confidence.[6]

I might go on to state other advantages, but I have already written more than I intended. But, there is one which I must mention; not as *very* important; but still worth thinking of. The 14th. amendment, already ratified, reduces the basis of representation in proportion to the number of male citizens excluded from representation, except for participation in rebellion or other crimes, to the whole number of adult male citizens: and the census about to be taken will show what this proportion is.[7] I do not know the number of colored male adults in Ohio, but it is not at all unlikely that it may prove large enough, if the present statutes are not [superseded] by the [amendment], to deprive the state of a representative for a [fraction].[8] This is, at least, worth thinking of.

I did not mean to write all this when I began: and I write only for your own eye. My opinions as to the propriety and expediency, under existing circumstances, of ratifying the amendment, are no secret. They are not influenced [certainly] by personal or political considerations. I have no interest except that which all citizens have; and no political objects or aspirations. But I am not in the habit of writing letters about them. So please keep this letter to yourself.

Next summer I hope we shall meet again, if not before. I take if for granted that you will go to Narragansett, and try your luck at fishing as usual, and I hope to be there for a week or two. Meantime, if you can come to Washington, I shall be very glad to see you here.

Sincerely, Your friend,

Hon. Geo. H. Hill.

1. Hamilton County voters had elected Hill to the Ohio House in October 1869. Recently, "friends" had informed Chase that Hill's vote would most likely determine whether the House ratified the Fifteenth Amendment. "There was a little ripple of applause as Hill, of Hamilton, voted a strong 'Aye'" on January 20, reported the *Daily Ohio Statesman.* As Chase wanted, Hill's vote helped secure approval. Chase to Thomas H. Yeatman, Oct. 19, 1869 (above); *Chase Papers,* 1:646; *Daily Ohio Statesman,* Jan. 21, 1870.

2. Chase was traveling through the defeated former Confederacy when he delivered the speech in Charleston on May 12, 1865, one month to the day after Robert E. Lee surrendered to Ulysses S. Grant at Appomattox Court House. *Texas v. White,* issued on April 12, 1869, confirmed the duty of the national government to secure republican rights for all citizens, including former slaves freed as a result of the Emancipation Proclamation and Thirteenth Amendment. *Charleston Courier,* May 13, 1865; Chase to Andrew Johnson, May 17, 1865 (above); Fairman, *Reconstruction and Reunion,* 639; Long, *Civil War Day by Day,* 674; Reid, *After the War,* 581–86.

3. The 1870 census placed the total number of adult African American males in the United States at 1,032,475. U.S. Census Office, *A Compendium of the Ninth Census . . .* (Washington, 1872), 1:554.

4. The italics are Chase's. *Statutes at Large,* 16:1131–32.

5. Virginia had ratified on October 8, 1869. *Appletons' Annual Cyclopædia,* 9:714.

6. Chase, who presided over the Fourth Circuit, visited Maryland, North Carolina, South Carolina, Virginia, and West Virginia during the spring and summer of 1869. Chase to Daniel Butterfield, July 2, 1869 (above); Fairman, *Reconstruction and Reunion,* 2.

7. According to the 1870 census, emancipation increased the population base used to calculate congressional representation by 13.92 percent in the southern states and 4.6 percent throughout the nation. The editors have searched in vain for the proportion that Chase evidently expected to find in census publications. U.S. Interior Department, *Ninth Census, Volume 1* (Washington, 1872), xiii, xiv.

8. The 1870 census counted 15,614 adult African-American males in Ohio. U.S. Census Office, *Compendium of the Ninth Census,* 554.

TO ALEXANDER LONG

Autograph letter. Alexander Long Papers, Cincinnati Historical Society (*micro* 38:0968).

Washington Feb 10, 1870

Dear Colonel,

Thank you for sending me the slip from the Enquirer. It was a special pleaure to see your handwriting again & to be assured of your continued friendship.[1]

The article is founded wholly on misapprehension.

No doubt the Missouri Oath is detestable; but that was not the question: but Can the State regulate suffrage? There was so much injustice, & needless harshness in the extent of the right to challenge, & in the oath by which the challenged voter could relieve himself from the challenge that one was naturally inclined to go as far as possible against it: but I thought & still think it safer not to interfere with the right of the State to regulate her own internal concerns. I am glad to see that the People of Missouri are about to wipe out the blot from their constitution.[2]

As to being put in line with the Republican Party or any other party all that can be said is that I shall certainly try in every case that comes before me to decide exactly as the Constitution & law require, without the slightest reference to any political line. As I understand Democracy I am a democrat; but, God helping me, I will never swerve from the line which my own sense of duty prescribes for any personal or party advantage.

You remember what I wrote you in New York last July—that I would not compromise my principles for fifty Presidencies.[3] I am, of that mind still.

Faithfully yours
S P Chase

Col. Alexander Long.

1. On February 3, an article printed in the *Cincinnati Enquirer* had criticized the Supreme Court's decision in *Blair v. Thompson and Ridgely,* a case brought by Missouri democrat Frank Blair, Jr. The suit challenged provisions in the state constitution that required potential electors to take the same test oath at issue in *Cummings v. Missouri* before voting. In its judgment, issued on January 31, the Supreme Court sustained the

decision of a Missouri court that approved the oath, with Chase voting in agreement. According to the *Enquirer,* the Court acted in fear of legislation proposed by Senator Charles D. Drake, a Missouri Radical and a supporter of the oath, that threatened to strip the federal judiciary of jurisdiction in similar cases. Chase's vote, claimed the newspaper, "will put him in line with the Republican party again, and, perhaps, will make him its candidate for President in 1872." On February 14, the Senate Judiciary Committee postponed Drake's proposal indefinitely. Fairman, *Reconstruction and Reunion,* 151–52, 613–16; *Congressional Globe,* 41st Cong., 2d sess., 1869–1870, 87, 1250.

2. Missouri voters overwhelmingly rejected the oath in balloting on November 8. *Appletons' Annual Cyclopædia,* 10:516–18, 521.

3. The correspondence to which Chase refers actually dated from 1868. Chase to Long, July 4, 1868 (Long Papers, Cinc. Hist. Soc.).

TO EDWARD D. MANSFIELD

Autograph letter. Jared Mansfield Collection, Local History and Marine Room, Milwaukee Public Library (*micro* 38:0970).

Washington, Feb. 11, 1870

My dear Mr. Mansfield,

You must try again. The Princeton address has never come, and I always like to know what a thinker like yourself says to his countrymen.

As to the Blair case nobody has any right to say how the Court was divided. When no opinion is given it is not in rule to say what any body's opinion was.[1]

But I make no secret of mine / I hold and until convinced of error shall hold that the right to regulate suffrage is with the states: subject only to the conditions imposed by the 15th Amendment, soon to be declared ratified.[2] In the exercise of this power of regulation the Legislature may prescribe such causes of challenge as it sees fit if not prohibited by the Constitution / A fortiori may the People through their constitutions: and they may allow the citizen to free himself of the challenge by such oath as they see fit to direct. The Oath prescribed in the Missouri Constitution is simply detestable: but every thing detestable is not beyond the power of a state to do. If I could have regarded the provisions of the Missouri prohibition as punitive & not as precautionary & regulative my judgment would have been other than it was.[3]

I agree with you that the great error, especially of the South has been not accepting all the legal logical consequences of the War. On the other hand the great error of the North has been continuing war after war was over by test oaths, military commissions, military governments, & all sorts of hard usage / Hence bad passions inflamed on both sides

You have seen the opinion of the Court on legal tender in payment of pre[existing] contracts.[4] I knew it would not please paper money men: but I am sure it is right. The constititution does not permit robbery of citizens by citizens as an appropriate means of carrying on war. I thought I could so administer the Treasury as to protect the people against the worst evils of paper money; & I never meant that more than about five hundred millions should be in circulation. After I left the department the 300 millions of National Bank Currency was added to the 400 millions of Greenbacks, without any provision for retiring any part of the latter. Hence the great inflation, which prevented the return to payments in Specie when Grant entered Richmond & still prevents.[5] A Wise & bold admn. would have resumed at that time any how

I have never had but one thought about not being nominated in 1868. I was glad not to be and am still glad. The time was not for me, nor was I for the time: and now I regard myself as wholly out of politics & out of political possibilities.

We are both a good deal older than we were when we began to act together politically. I am sorry the Democrats had not sense enough to keep you where I put you.[6] But it matters little. I look for little more time: but I hope for Eternity, in Christ, our Savior, And cheerfully commit the Country I love & the dear ones whom I love to the care of our Father in Heaven.

Faithfully your friend
S P CHASE

1. In *Blair v. Thompson and Ridgely,* a divided Supreme Court sustained the ruling of a state court 4–4. Chase was under attack for his vote in support of the state decision. Chase to Alexander Long, Feb. 10, 1870 (above).

2. Secretary of State Hamilton Fish certified ratification on March 30. *Statutes at Large,* 16:1131–32.

3. The major effect of the test oath's "prohibition" was to deprive former Confederate soldiers of the elective franchise. *Appletons' Annual Cyclopædia,* 10:517.

4. Chase wrote the majority opinion in *Susan P. Hepburn v. Henry A. Griswold,* which the Supreme Court decided by the narrow margin of 4–3 on February 7. At issue was the authority of Congress to require acceptance of paper money (greenbacks) instead of specie in payment of debts, in accordance with the Legal Tender Act of February 1862. Chase had reluctantly endorsed the measure as a necessary expedient during the Civil War, but his opinion in *Hepburn* repudiated it in regard to debts that existed prior to the Legal Tender Act as a violation of the spirit of the Constitution and the Fifth Amendment's due process clause. *Chase Papers,* 3:126–27; Fairman, *Reconstruction and Reunion,* 713–15; *Statutes at Large,* 12:345–48; 8 Wall. 603 (1870).

5. Union troops occupied Richmond on April 3, 1865. From 1860 to 1865, wholesale prices rose 250 percent on average and the cost of living roughly doubled. In general, the price of goods declined over the next five years, but did not reach levels in existence before the Civil War. *Appletons' Annual Cyclopædia,* 9:264; Long, *Civil War Day by Day,* 665; Unger, *Greenback Era,* 16.

6. In 1858, Governor Chase had appointed Mansfield commissioner of statistics for Ohio. *DAB,* 12:256; Gilkey, *Ohio Hundred Year Book,* 328.

FROM I. C. MINTURN

Letter in clerk's hand, signed by Minturn. Chase Papers, Library of Congress (*micro* 38:0974).

New York *Feb. 12. 1870.*

Hon. Salmon P. Chase
Washington, D.C.
Dear Sir.

Your decision in regard to legal tenders, if not reversed, is likely to cause the greatest possible distress and ruin among a class of people already in debt—among the rest, very many widows & orphans owing money on Mortgage of Real Estate for a long date back.[1]

All over the State of New York, and elsewhere, there is a class of property owners among the most respectable in our Northern Cities, many of whom have found it hard work to pay their interest, and take care of the increased taxation and expenses of living to be able to stand up under any additional burden of Mortgages.

Ever since the decision has been made public, it has been the theme of general conversation thoughout the City with every Corporation, Savings Bank, Life Insurance Co. and Merchant, and while we New Yorkers have been strong advocates for Chief Justice Chase as our Chief Magistrate, without regard to party vote, it is to be hoped most sincerely that no such impediment as the late decision will be thrown in the scale of Justice against those who have so manfully stood up for your support as our candidate in this City

The whole Commercial Community are not prepared for any change in the Currency, and it would cause farspread ruin over the whole of the United States, as well to the Agriculturalist as the Merchant to have any change for the present.

One of the most favorable features in the prosperity and growth of the Western States has been the inflation of the Currency. It was not asked for, but has been forced on us as a necessity; but do not now take from us suddenly that which we have been taught to be the Legal tender of the Commerce and trade of the Country and adopt another currency—one for 1862 and previous, and another for 1862 and future. The confusion would be such as to completely paralyze trade, first destroying all the old and infirm folks, and next year finish up by taking the active business man.

If you are determined on Specie payments let it come together, but do not divide the Currency into two parts. The present Currency has built up the present Rail Road system of the Far West, and if it be permitted to remain until after the next Presidential Election, you will find the whole Western and Southern Country so much better prepared to contend against any such fatality as an attempt to force Specie Payments. There never was a Country made such rapid strides as we have made since the war, And why? Because of the aid the Currency has given us to develop its resources, which all Europe could not have done for us, without the aid of this Currency, so do not destroy the charm which you have so ingeniously built up. On the other hand, if we had 50 or $100,000,000. additional of Currency it would go far towards restoring the confidence which Commerical men, and the Agriculturalist just now require

Thousands of people are just on the brink of ruin by their losses in trade, caused by heavy taxation and the uncertainity of the future, and by the decline in Gold.[2]

Otherwise our farmers could have shipped their grain from the far West at reasonable prices, and formed a market in Europe at compensating rates

Excuse the haste with which this is written, while,

I remain,

Truly your Ob't. Servt.
I. C. Minturn

1. See Chase to Edward D. Mansfield, February 11, 1870 (above) for more on *Hepburn v. Griswold.*

2. From a peak of around 200 at the end of the Civil War, the price of gold had declined to highs of approximately 160 in 1869 and 120 in February 1870. *Appletons' Annual Cyclopædia,* 5:347, 9:265, 10:296.

TO CINCINNATI COMMITTEE

Letter in clerk's hand with Chase's signature and subsequent redrafting by Chase. Chase Papers, Historical Society of Pennsylvania (*micro* 38:0986).

Washington, March 2. 1870.

Gentlemen:—

Accept my thanks for the invitation you have tendered me in behalf of the Colored People of Cincinnati to attend their celebration of the ratification of the Fifteenth Amendment.[1] My duties here will not permit me to be present except by good will and good wishes.

Almost a quarter of a century has passed since some of you, probably, heard me declare, on the 6th. of May 1845, in an assembly composed chiefly of the people whom you now represent, that "All legal distinctions between individuals of the same community founded on any such circumstances as color, origin, and the like, are hostile to the genius of our institutions, and incompatible with the true theory of American Liberty:" that "True Democracy makes no enquiry about the color of the skin, or the place of nativity, or any other similar circumstance of condition;" and that "The exclusion of the colored people, as a body, from the elective franchise is incompatible with true democratic principles."[2]

I congratulate you on the fact that these principles not then avowed by me for the first time, nor ever since abandoned or compromised, have been at length incorporated into the Constitution, and made part of the Supreme Law of the land.

Many, no doubt, would have been glad, as I should have been, if the great work, consummated by the ratification of the Fifteenth Amendment, could have been accomplished by the states through amendment of state constitutions, and through appropriate state legislation; but the delays and uncertainties, prejudicial to every interest, inseparable from that mode of proceeding, seemed to necessitate the course actually adopted. Nor does the amendment impair the real rights of any state. It leaves the whole regulation of suffrage to the whole people of each state, subject only to the fundamental law that the right of no citizen to vote shall be denied, or abridged, on account of color, race, or previous condition of servitude. It is to be hoped that each state will so conform its constitution and laws to this fundamental law that no occasion may be given to legislation by Congress.

But the best indication of the wisdom as well as justice of the amendment must be found in the conduct of that large class of citizens whom you represent. On the occasion to which I have referred, I ventured to say that "the best way to ensure the peaceful dwelling together of different races is the cordial reciprocation of benefits, not the mutual infliction of injuries;" and I cannot now give you better counsel than I offered then: "Go forward, having perfect faith in your own manhood and in God's Providence, adding to your faith, virtue; and to virtue, knowledge; and to knowledge, patience; and to patience, temperance; and to temperance, brotherly kindness; and to brotherly kindness, charity."[3]

Every good man must rejoice in the progress which the colored citizens of the United States have made in education, in religious culture, and in the general improvement of their condition. Every good man must earnestly desire their continued and accelerated progress in the same direction. All public and all private interests will be promoted by it. And it will ensure at no distant day cordial recognition of their rights even from those of their fellow citizens, who have most earnestly opposed them.

No man can now be found who would restore slavery; a few years hence, if the colored men are wise, it will be impossible to find a man who will avow himself in favor of denying or abridging their right to vote

Very respectfully yours,
S P Chase

Messrs: Peter H. Clark,
T. N. C. Liverpool
J. C. Corbin,[4]
J. T. Troy,
Committee

1. The Ohio assembly had narrowly ratified the Fifteenth Amendment in January. Formal notice of ratification on the national level followed on March 30. *Ohio State Journal,* Jan. 15 and 21, 1870; *Statutes at Large,* 16:1131–32.

2. Chase quotes from a speech given in response to a testimonial from Cincinnati blacks thanking him for legal efforts in behalf of Samuel Watson, a fugitive slave. *Address and Reply, on the Presentation of a Testimonial, to S. P. Chase, by the Colored People of Cincinnati; With Some Account of the Case of Samuel Watson* (Cincinnati, 1845), 3–5, 10–12, 20–22; *Chase Papers,* 1:172, 2:113.

3. *Address and Reply,* 33, 35; 2 Pet. 1:5.

4. Clark taught school and Liverpool was a barber in Cincinnati. In 1873, Joseph Carter Corbin (1833–1911), an African-American educator from Ohio, won election as superintendent of public instruction for Arkansas. *Cinc. Dir. (1870),* 149, 387;

John F. Ohles, ed., *Biographical Dictionary of American Educators,* 3 vols. (Westport, Conn., 1978), 1:312.

TO FLAMEN BALL

Autograph letter. Chase Papers, Cincinnati Historical Society (*micro* 38:1001).

Washington, Mar. 7, 1870

My dear Mr. Ball,

I was much gratified by your kind & interesting letter which came yesterday.[1] The only drawback was your account of the physical suffering you have gone through and the fact that you still felt some of the effects of your rheumatism. I hope you have better weather than we & that you will soon be quite well.

My own health this winter has not been as good as formerly. In December I was quite unwell—a general nervous disorder with irregular action of the heart. I am not well now; but much better than I was. I attribute the improvement in great measure to the exercise which I take in walking daily between my house & the Capitol—a *strong* mile & a half—and to regular living[2]

But we have both lived to be old men, & cannot expect the vigor of youth. Let us look to the end of earth, & beyond to the blessed immortality which our Savior has revealed.

I enclose the authority duly signed. Every little helps. Please send me the back dividends & if you can get the present value of the future payments to be made on the stock get that too & add it. Whatever you think fit to take for the stock will be satisfactory to me & better the $50 in instalments.

Never was I so pinched as now for many years. I borrow nearly every dollar I use: hoping that I may be able to repay from income by & by; but I fear I shall be obliged to sell part of my income producing property; & I cannot afford to reduce my income. It takes all I have of my own & all I get from salary to get through

I wish I could sell my 6th St interest & Loveland place.[3] I bought here, as I told you, depending on this sale for means of payment

So you see if I consulted my own interest I should be an inflationist. But somebody must pay, & inflation would only put my burden on some other mans shoulders

Best remembrances to all.

Yours faithfully
S P Chase

P.S. Will draw for 120 dated 1 Jan at 6 mos—afterwords at 3 mos for $60 each.

1. Ball had written on March 3. "I am sitting up with my legs & feet in bandages," stricken with "my former complaint," he reported. Ball's letter thanked Chase for a copy

of *Hepburn v. Griswold,* evaluated a bust of Chase executed by medallionist Thomas Dow Jones, and told of dividends from an investment in the Cincinnati Fuel Company. "I enclose a power for you to sign to enable me to collect your money if you desire me to do so," suggested Ball. Ball to Chase, Mar. 3, 1870 (Chase Papers, L.C.).

2. Chase and Nettie still lived at 1827 I Street. Edgewood, his new house, remained unoccupied until renovations were completed in 1871. Chase to John A. Merideth et al., Apr. 8, 1870 (Vir. Hist. Soc.); Chase to Kate Chase Sprague, Sept. 15, 1869 (above); Chase to Ball, Oct. 4, 1869 (Chase Papers, Cinc. Hist. Soc.); Phelps, *Kate Chase,* 230–31.

3. According to Chase's income tax returns for 1870 (Chase Papers, L.C.), property that he owned on Sixth Street in Cincinnati and in Loveland, Ohio, yielded a yearly income of $2,143.33.

TO JAMES W. WARD

Autograph letter. Special Collections, Dartmouth College Library (*micro* 39:0027).

Washington May 15, 1870[1]

Dear brother Ward,

Your phiz & sig. came to a cordial welcome yesterday. I only wish the original had accompanied them: *that* would have been ample amends for delay. It would be a great delight to me if I could have visits from my classmates.

You mention Weeks, and say nothing of the manner of his death. I have seen it stated that he committed suicide. That you make no reference to it makes me hope that it was not so. It was very pleasant to meet him last summer at Dartmouth; and I don't want to have that agreeable memory darkened.[2]

I have not been so well as formerly during the past winter: but have been able to be in court every day & do a good deal of hard work. Through our Heavenly Father's goodness I find myself a good deal better this spring almost as well indeed as ever apparently. But as you say "we are among the gray haired fathers." We cannot do what we *"used to could"*. But there is a better land & better associations beyond. I thank God through Christ for that blessed hope. May we all meet again there? On earth there is not much ground for hope that our surviving classmates will meet again

You must never believe what you see about me in the newspapers: especially when they attribute designs of matrimony to me. It is possible that I might prefer to pass the rest of my life in those bonds, if all things concurred to make it right & pleasant. But at my time of life that is hardly to be hoped. Certainly I have no design such as is ascribed to me

xx I am glad to see that you *think* the legal tender decision correct.[3] I *know* it is. Honesty is always correct. Our constitution was made by honest men. No interpretation of it which makes it sanction dishonesty can be right. Our fathers did not believe in india-rubber yard sticks or in paper dollars. If you want to preach a Sermon on the subject let me give you a text, which, perhaps, having been so wonderfully delivered from British power, they had in mind. "Just balances, just weights, a just ephah & a just hin shall ye have: I am the Lord your God which brought you out of the land of Egypt." Lev. 19.36. The same thought is, again, expressed with somewhat more fullness (Deut. 25: 13–16.) by Moses;[4] and if you want to see what the old prophets thought of such things as false standards, either of weight or value, just read what Ezekiel says in the 45th chapter, v. 9–12. xx[5]

If I come to Providence this summer I will bear your invitation in mind, & hope I may be able to come and see you. I shall indeed be disappointed if I cannot. You and I & Blodgett at least must contrive to meet[6]

Goodbye. I shall be glad to have a letter from you whenever you can write. May every blessing attend you in life & beyond.

Affectionately & faithfully

Your Classmate & friend
S P Chase

Rev. James W. Ward.

P.S. If you want to print the paragraph xx—xx as "an extract from a letter from Chief Justice Chase to his Classmate Rev. J. W. Ward" I have no objection

You forgot to put the dates of sending your photo & of your birth, on the back.[7] If you will send them I will supply the omission.

1. Chase had attended Dartmouth College with Ward, a teacher and Congregational pastor.

2. William Pickering Weeks, a New Hampshire lawyer and politician, had died on January 8, 1870. The two classmates evidently met at Dartmouth's centennial celebration in July 1869, where Chase participated as president of the alumni association. Charles Franklin Emerson, ed., *General Catalogue of Dartmouth College* . . . (Hanover, N.H., 1910–11), 239; *New York Times,* July 22, 1870.

3. That is, *Hepburn v. Griswold.*

4. "Thou shalt not have in thy bag divers weights, a great and a small.

"Thou shalt not have in thine house divers measures, a great and a small.

"*But* thou shalt have a perfect and a just weight, a perfect and just measure shalt thou have: that thy days may be lengthened in the land which the Lord thy God giveth thee.

"For all that do such things *and* all that do unrighteously, *are* an abomination unto the Lord thy God."

5. "Thus saith the Lord God; Let it suffice you, O princes of Israel: remove violence and spoil, and execute judgement and justice, take away your exactions from my people, saith the Lord God.

"Ye shall have just balances, and a just ephah, and a just bath.

"The ephah and the bath shall be of one measure, that the bath may contain the tenth part of a homer, and the ephah the tenth part of a homer: the measure thereof shall be after the homer.

"And the shekel *shall be* twenty gerahs: twenty shekels, five and twenty shekels, fifteen shekels, shall be your maneh."

6. Chase visited Rhode Island in the middle of June 1870, but the editors have not found any evidence that he met Ward while there. Constantine Blodgett, another Dartmouth classmate, was a Congregationalist minister from Pawtucket, Rhode Island. Chase to Janet Chase, June 19, 1870 (Chase Papers, L.C.).

7. Ward was born on May 21, 1803. Emerson, *General Catalogue,* 239.

TO HENRY WILSON

Letterpress copy of autograph letter. Chase Papers, Library of Congress (*micro* 39:0035).

Washington, May 25, 1870

Dear Sir

I sympathize most truly with you in your grief on account of the illness of Mrs Wilson, and hope that you will soon have cause for rejoicing in her complete restoration to health.[1] There are no sadder trials than the sicknesses of those we love except their loss; which may God in His goodness avert from you.

I do not wish to write any thing for the public either in respect to Mr. Stanton or Mr. Cameron.[2] No one can reasonably [rate] the former's services higher than I do: and I have no doubt that he expressed a real feeling when he made the remark, I mentioned to you.[3] But the hope excited by the remark was never realized. I do not know that we ever agreed fully, either as to theory or practice, in respect to the rights of colored citizens, or as to the duties of the Government & the Nation to them. Before the war he was in intimate association with those most opposed to my views on this subject. After he came into the cabinet he adopted practical opinions *more* akin to mine especially on the subject of enlisting colored men as soldiers; but you doubtless remember the unjust discrimination as to pay. If he adopted finally the views I have so long held as to suffrage it was after the last conversation we ever had on that subject. You will see from this how difficult it would be for me to make a public statement which would not be misunderstood.

As to Senator Cameron what I said to you was true as what I said concerning Mr Stanton was also.[4] That he was dismissed is not only untrue; but seems to me ludicrously untrue. If I was not grossly mistaken in my knowledge of facts; and I thought myself well acquainted with them at the time, his retirement was wholly voluntary. Certainly it was never suggested to me by any body that any purpose of dismissing him from the cabinet was entertained by Mr. Lincoln; nor do I believe that any such purpose ever existed. Nor did I know of any fact, or believe that any fact existed which would justify such a purpose.

Of course I cannot tell what may have taken place without my knowledge. I did not suspect that any thing of importance in relation to this matter did.

I have no objection to have what I have now said stated in substance by you, if you think best; but let it be in your own words not mine; &, if you think it useful to do so you may vouch me as authority.[5]

Sincerely your friend
S P Chase

Hon H. Wilson.

1. Harriet Malvern Howe Wilson (c. 1824–70) died on May 28, evidently from cancer. Richard H. Abbott, *Cobbler in Congress: The Life of Henry Wilson, 1812–1875* (Lexington, Ky., 1972), 15, 230.

2. Edwin M. Stanton, secretary of war under Abraham Lincoln, had died on December 24, 1869. In 1870, Stanton's predecessor in Lincoln's cabinet, Simon Cameron, represented Pennsylvania in the U.S. Senate. Wilson had recently written a eulogy of Stanton for the *Atlantic Monthly* that included criticism of Cameron and members of James Buchanan's cabinet, in which Stanton also served briefly as attorney general. Chase to Jeremiah S. Black, July 4, 1870 (below); *DAB*, 17:517; Henry Wilson, "Edwin M. Stanton," *Atlantic Monthly* 25 (Feb. 1870): 234–46.

3. Chase evidently refers to the following anecdote about Stanton from Wilson's eulogy: "Nearly thirty years ago, in the streets of Columbus, Ohio, he familiarly accosted Mr. Chase and said to him, referring to antislavery sentiments the latter had just put forth, that he was in entire agreement with him, and hoped he should soon be able to take his place by his side." Wilson, "Edwin M. Stanton," 244.

4. The eulogy depicted Cameron and Stanton as pioneer advocates of emancipation and the arming of former slaves early in the Civil War. According to the piece, Cameron had resigned from Lincoln's cabinet with sensitivity to "adverse criticisms" and recommended Stanton as a successor "not unfriendly to his policy." Ibid., 238–39.

5. In October, Wilson published another article in defense of the eulogy and named Chase as a source. Wilson, "Jeremiah S. Black and Edwin M. Stanton," *Atlantic Monthly,* 26 (Oct. 1870): 463–75.

TO JEREMIAH S. BLACK

Autograph letter. Jeremiah Sullivan Black Papers, Library of Congress (*micro* 39:0063).

Sandusky, O. July 4, 1870

My dear Sir,[1]

Just before leaving Washington I received, through your kindness as I suppose, a number of the Galaxy for June. Your letter to Senator Wilson had already attracted my attention & I have since read it again.[2]

It is marked as every one who knows you would expect by great power; but there are, as I think some errors of fact in it which ought to be corrected.

What Senator Wilson said in the Atlantic Monthly for April about remarks made to me by Mr. Stanton nearly thirty years ago, at Columbus, is in substance, quite correct. Mr. Stanton, did, in 1842, express his concurrence in the views relating to slavery set forth in the Address & Resolutions of the Ohio State Liberty Convention of December 1841, of which I was the writer.[3] There was, I think, at that time, no material difference in political principle between us. But he was identified in party relations with the old line democracy, while I thought it my duty to act independently of both the then great political organizations. He urged me to join the party with which he was connected and declared with emphasis to stand by me in support of the principles I had proclaimed. And more than once on subsequent occasions, when withdrawn from active participation in politics and absorbed in professional labors he expressed his purpose to act whenever he should again engage in political action to unite with those, who like myself, were then known as Independent Democrats, against nationalized slavery.

And you are misinformed, also, in respect to the circumstances connected with his appointment as Secretary of War in place of Gen. Cameron. I then thought and still think I was well acquainted with them. Gen. Cameron had expressed a wish to retire & take the Mission to St. Petersburgh some time before he actually withdrew, and I believe he was the first to suggest to Mr. Lincoln the name of Mr. Stanton. I held myself several conversations on the subject of Gen. C——s retirement, his appointment to St. Petersburgh & the appointment of Mr. S—— as his successor both with Mr Lincoln & with Gen. Cameron, and I called on Mr. Stanton to ascertain if he would accept the post of Secretary if tendered. Ultimately, when, as I supposed, the matter was fully understood, Mr Lincoln addressed a note to Gen. Cameron tendering the mission to St. Petersburgh and signifying his willingness to accept his resignation. The note was brief & seemed curt. But Mr. Lincoln, on his attention being drawn to its terms, said that he intended to make it every thing it should be, and another note was substituted expressing what he declared to be his real sentiments.[4]

This is I believe as exact a statement as its brevity admits of Gen Cameron's retirement from Mr. Lincoln's cabinet. He was not removed; he resigned because as he stated at the time he preferred the Mission to the Secretaryship; & he did recommend the appointment of Mr. Stanton as his successor.

On one other point I wish to correct your information, lest, not mentioning it, I may seem to have admitted its exactitude. You state that "the Cabinet (Mr. Lincolns) voted six to one *in favor of surrendering Fort Sumter,*—Mr. Blair being the only dissentist": *I* never voted for the surrender of Fort Sumter. My grounds of opposition were not, perhaps, the same, nor so absolute as Mr. Blair's, but I was against it & so voted[5]

I make this statement not for the public but for yourself; because I was in a position to be well informed and am sure you would not willingly remain in error. Before all things, Justice.

With great respect & regard

Yours very truly
S P Chase

Hon. J. S. Black

1. Jeremiah Sullivan Black (1810–83) served as U.S. attorney general, 1857–60, and secretary of state, 1860–61, in James Buchanan's cabinet. In December 1861, Black was appointed reporter of the U.S. Supreme Court. The *New York Tribune* printed another version of this letter on November 11, 1870, without Chase's permission. Excluded from the published copy were passages which explained that Chase had discussed Simon Cameron's fate with Lincoln and Cameron and which identified the letter as a private communication. Chase to Black, Nov. 15, 1870 (Jeremiah S. Black Papers, L.C.); *DAB,* 2:310–12.

2. Chase left Washington sometime after May 31, and arrived in Philadelphia on the afternoon of June 7. Black's letter, published in the June edition of *Galaxy,* defended the Buchanan administration against criticisms that Henry Wilson had levied in February in

the *Atlantic Monthly* and disputed Wilson's depiction of Edwin M. Stanton. "His condemnation of the abolitionists was unsparing for their hypocrisy, their corruption, their enmity to the Constitution . . . ," asserted Black of Stanton. "Cameron did not resign," he added; "he was *removed* for good cause. He had not lot or part in naming his successor." Black rebutted Wilson in the October issue of the *Atlantic Monthly*, relying in part on observations that Chase included in this letter to Black. A compilation of the exchange between Wilson and Black was later published under the title *A Contribution to History: Edwin M. Stanton, His Character and Public Services on the Eve of the Rebellion* . . . (Easton, Pa., 1871). "Jeremiah Black to Henry Wilson," *Galaxy*, 9 (June 1870): 822–23, 827–28; Chase to Flamen Ball, May 31, 1870, and Chase to Janet Ralston Chase, June 10, 1870 (both Chase Papers, L.C.); Chase to Henry Wilson, May 25, 1870 (above); Wilson, "Edwin M. Stanton;" Wilson, "Jeremiah S. Black and Edwin M. Stanton," 463–75.

3. Chase refers to Henry Wilson's eulogy of Stanton, which actually appeared in the February issue of the *Atlantic Monthly*. For Chase's response to that piece, and for Stanton's remarks in Columbus thirty years earlier, see Chase to Wilson, May 25, 1870 (above). The Liberty convention met in Columbus, December 29–30, 1841, and proposed a separate political organization in opposition to slavery. *Philanthropist*, Jan. 5, 1842.

4. Both of Lincoln's letters bore the date of January 11, 1862. The second included an expression of confidence in Cameron's "ability, patriotism, and fidelity to public trust." For Chase's firsthand version of events related to Cameron's resignation on January 13, see *Chase Papers*, 1:324–26. Basler, *Collected Works*, 5:96–97.

5. Black apparently refers to a question that Lincoln submitted to members of his cabinet on March 15, 1861: "Assuming it to be possible to now provision Fort Sumter, under all the circumstances is it wise to attempt it?" Only Postmaster General Montgomery Blair supported the proposal without qualification. Chase favored provisioning if it did not lead to war. Basler, *Collected Works*, 4:284–85; *Chase Papers*, 3:53–55; David Potter, *The Impending Crisis, 1848–1861* (New York, 1976), 571.

TO RICHARD C. PARSONS

Letter in clerk's hand, signed by Chase (*micro* 39:0122).

Narragansett, R.I. Sept. 26. 1870.

My dear Parsons:—

I received your letter from Geneva, dated the 2nd., on yesterday. I was very glad to hear from you, and from Mrs. Parsons and the children.[1] I hope that notwithstanding the troubles in Europe, you will find your residence in Switzerland, and particularly in England, very agreeable.[2] There are such good accounts of Miss Julia that I shall expect wonders from her when I see her again.

You will see by the date of this that I am at Mrs. Sprague's. I have been here a month with Nettie. We went, as we designed, to St. Paul and Minneapolis and returned by the way of Niagara Falls.[3] On the journey from the Falls to New York, which we undertook to accomplish between 2 P.M. on the 16th. and 8 A.M. on the 17th., I was attacked without warning about 9 O'clock, by paralysis, which continued to increase until when I reached New York, my right side from the toe to the scalp was sensibly affected so that I could scarcely speak intelligibly. I could, however, get up stairs at the Hoffman House without very great difficulty. Dr. Clarke was immediately called in, and also Dr. Hammond. Dr. Clarke was my regular physician and, of course Dr. Hammond was merely advised with as consulting.[4] They both agreed as to the nature of the attack that it was paralysis of the right side, but unusually moderate.

I remained at the Hoffman House a week—arriving there Wednesday morning and leaving on Wednesday noon. Nettie was with me; and Mrs. Sprague and the Governor joined me there Wednesday evening. Since then I have been here, slowly, but as the doctor says, surely recovering. I could write this letter myself, but it would be a great labor, and the writing though plainer than common would be a good deal stiffer. How soon I shall get well, I can't. say. At present, I do not expect to be able to take my place in the court at the adjourned term; and I doubt very much whether I shall be able to take it at the regular term though it is quite possible that I may.[5] Of course, under existing circumstances, I shall want you to be here as early as possible, and am glad to know that your return is not to be postponed beyond the middle of November.

I have not been allowed to write or dictate until within a day or two. Mr. Didier has been with me for that time.[6] But I have been allowed, indeed, required, to take what exercise I could. I have walked more and more every day until at last, on yesterday I walked about a mile without resting. I can ride without difficulty eight or ten miles. This is a great improvement from the beginning. So, too, in respect to writing. At first, I could not use my right hand at all. I have recovered so far that I write a little every day.

I have been thus particular because you are at a distance, and may have heard incorrect accounts; besides, it is desirable that you should know the truth. I do not take the trouble to be as particular with anybody else upon this subject; and, perhaps, it will be well enough for you to keep what I write to yourself.

Give my best love to Mrs. Parsons and Julia, together with Master Richard. Nettie would join me, and so would Mrs. Sprague if they knew I am writing. Willie is grown to be a fine boy; and the little girl, who, perhaps, you remember is called Ethel, grows in beauty, and grace, and strength day after day.

Yours very cordially,
S P Chase

Col. Richard C. Parsons,
Paris.

1. That is, Sarah Starkweather Parsons, and the couple's two children: Julia and Richard C., Jr.

2. Chase alludes to the Franco-Prussian War, which started on July 19 and ended in French defeat on February 26, 1871. On September 19, 1870, German troops surrounded Paris, which, according to this letter's closing, was the Parsons' temporary home. *Appletons' Annual Cyclopædia,* 10:343, 358, 367; Bury, *Zenith of European Power,* 325–27, 596–600.

3. Chase started his voyage from St. Paul to Washington, D.C., sometime after August 4. Chase to William H. Seward, August 4 (Chase Papers, Hist. Soc. of Pa.).

4. New York's Hoffman House hotel stood at Broadway and Twenty-fourth Street. Alonzo Clark held an appointment on the faculty of the College of Physicians and Surgeons in New York. William Alexander Hammond (1828–1900), a pioneer neurologist, had taught in the same school and served as surgeon general of the U.S. Army. In 1870, he was a professor in New York's Bellevue Hospital Medical College. *DAB,* 8:210.

5. In 1870, the adjourned term lasted from October 31 to December 2. The regular term started on December 5. Chase presided over the Supreme Court intermittently throughout the remainder of his life. Fairman, *Reconstruction and Reunion,* 752–53; "Minutes Supreme Court U.S. 27 Apr. 1, 1870 to Mar. 24, 1871" (National Archives).

6. Eugene Lemoine Didier, who later gained notice as an author, had secured an appointment as deputy marshall of the U.S. Supreme Court in 1869 and worked as Chase's secretary. *Appletons',* 2:176.

TO RICHARD C. PARSONS

Letterbook copy in clerk's hand. Chase Papers, Library of Congress (*micro* 39:0273).

Narragansett, Dec. 26, 1870.

Dear Parsons,

I forgot to acknowledge the receipt of Mrs. Hoover in my last and thank you for your attention to that business. I am glad that you agree with me in your estimate of her.[1]

I have read with great interest the telegraphic as well as the Washington account of the debate on San Domingo. I think that very indecent passion was exhibited, but rather incline to the President's side. I believe I was born an annexationist.[2]

I am sorry that Fremont has done anything that will prevent the passage of the bill for his road. Apart from the interest I naturally felt for your success, I think the road itself deserves the recognition and support of the national government.[3]

Where did you get your Latin? *Fortuna,* &c. I don't remember it. I think, however, you have had your share of Fortuna's favours.[4]

Sometime next week I expect to go to New York.[5] My health mends, tho' slowly; the old story. Mrs. Spraque will go to Washington soon, and Nettie dont like this climate at this time, and it would not do either for me to keep her here or to stay myself without her. Besides it is very important for me to be near my physician. We shall be at No. 19 Fifth Avenue, just below the Brevoort House.[6] I wish you were here to accompany us to New York. But that is impossible now. We shall see you, however, on your eastward journey.

I have a letter from H. D. Cooke this morning, informing me that my account with him has been overdrawn by the $1500 check to the amount of $300. This rather surprises me, as I supposed my balance to be much larger. It will, however, be made all right on the first of January, when the salary and dividends together will more than make even the whole, including the memorandum note and the amount due you.[7]

I suppose I must give up the legal tender opinion, but I am sure that it is among my papers. There is quite a bundle relating to the same subject. I dare say that it looks very little like an opinion.[8]

I fear Marshall must have deceived you.[9] I know of no expenses paid by him, and he was with me 18 days and not 19. But he is gone and *that* is over, and I am grateful.

Since writing the foregoing part of this letter, it has been determined to go to New York, on Thursday or Friday.

Yours truly and always,
S. P. CHASE

Col. Parsons.

1. Chase and his daughter Nettie had rented Anna P. Hoover's house at 1827 I Street since 1869 and apparently vacated it in October 1870. Chase had commissioned Parsons to settle with Hoover, who claimed that Chase still owed her money. "She is a good woman," wrote Parsons of Hoover on December 22, "but I think had been badly advised—as you said—and only needed the complete explanation of a 'mild mannered' man (like me) to get her back into the straight path!" In the same letter, Parsons urged Chase to read recent debates in the Senate over proposals to annex Santo Domingo and reported the probable failure in Congress of a railroad bill that he supported. Chase to Hoover, Oct. 26, 1870, and Dec. 9, 1870; Hoover to Chase, Oct. 22, 1870; Parsons to Chase, Dec. 22, 1870 (second of the same date) (all Chase Papers, L.C.).

2. In June, Congress had considered annexation of Santo Domingo (the Dominican Republic) at President Grant's request, but Congress rejected the proposal under the influence of Charles Sumner, chair of the Senate Foreign Relations Committee. The measure under scrutiny in December was a joint resolution that authorized the formation of a presidential commission to negotiate acquisition, in accordance with a suggestion in Grant's annual presidential message of December 5. The resolution passed both houses of Congress on December 21, but failed to yield the results that Grant sought. *Message of the President of the United States,* 41st Cong., 3d sess., 1870–71, H. Ex. Doc. 1, 6–8; *Congressional Globe,* 41st Cong., 3d sess., 1870–71, part 1, 50–51, 53, 271, 479; Foner, *Reconstruction,* 494–97; U.S. Senate, *Journal of the Executive Proceedings,* 13:500–502.

3. "My railroad Bill will probably fail at last," Parsons predicted on December 22, "owing to the absolute folly of Gen'l Fremont in surrendering his powers to New York parties— And this is the end of all my labor!" In recent years, John C. Frémont, the famous Civil War general, had invested heavily in two proposed transcontinental railroads: the Memphis and El Paso, which failed in the summer of 1870, and the Southern Transcontinental Railroad Company, which Congress was considering for a charter later the same year. In the Senate, the Southern Transcontinental came into conflict with plans for another railway, the Southern Texas Pacific. A compromise melded the two proposals on March 3, 1871, and chartered the Texas Pacific Railway, which eventually absorbed the Memphis and El Paso. Parsons had invested in the Southern Pacific and counseled Frémont during Senate hearings. Cardinal Goodwin, *John Charles Frémont: An Explanation of His Career* (Stanford, 1930), 254–55; Allan Nevins, *Frémont: Pathmaker of the West,* (New York, 1955), 587–91, 603; Parsons to Chase, Dec. 22, 1870 (second of the same date) (Chase Papers, L.C.); *Statutes at Large,* 16:573–74; *In the Senate of the United States,* Sen. Misc. Doc. 121, 41st Congress, 2nd sess., 1869–70, 16, 45, 53–54, 67–70, 78–81, 100.

4. The aphorism "Fortuna nimium quem fovet, stultum facit" appeared at the conclusion of Parsons' December 22 letter. A mocking reference to Parsons' own railroad project, the quotation from *Publilius Syrtus* may be translated as "Fortune makes a fool of the man whom she favors overmuch." Parsons wryly concluded, "I am in no danger *that* way." Parsons to Chase, Dec. 22, 1870 (second of the same date) (Chase Papers, L.C.); Cree, *Dictionary of Latin Quotations,* 52.

5. Chase traveled to New York on December 30 to be closer to his physicians and stayed there until early March. Chase to Hamilton Smith, Dec. 26, 1870, and Chase to P. E. Jones, Feb. 24, 1871 (both Chase Papers, L.C.); Chase to Jay Cooke, Jan. 3, 1871 (Chase Papers, Hist. Soc. of Pa.).

6. Chase probably refers to his personal physician, Alonzo Clark. The Brevoort House hotel was located at 11 Fifth Avenue. Chase to Richard C. Parsons, Sept. 26, 1870 (above); *New York Dir. (1872),* 134.

7. In 1870, Chase received an annual salary of $6,500 as chief justice, despite longstanding efforts to secure a raise. According to another letter written on December 22, Parsons had recently written a total of $2,185 in notes for fifteen and a half acres of land

adjacent to Edgewood and incurred miscellaneous expenses of $1,040 in Chase's behalf. Chase to Samuel F. Miller, June 15, 1866 (above); W. W. Cox to Chase, Nov. 14, 1870, Chase to Parsons, Dec. 12, 1870, Parsons to Chase, Dec. 12 and 22, 1870 (first of two) (all Chase Papers, L.C.); Fairman, *Reconstruction and Reunion,* 68, 166–71; *Statutes at Large,* 10:655.

8. Chase had asked Parsons to find a misplaced segment of *Hepburn v. Griswold* deleted from the published opinion. Earlier, Parsons had reported defeat: "I am very sorry, but I do not know any where else to look." Chase to Parsons, Dec. 17, 1870, Parsons to Chase, Dec. 22, 1870 (second of the same date) (both Chase Papers, L.C.).

9. Marshall apparently worked in Chase's household.

FROM RICHARD C. PARSONS

Autograph letter on letterhead stationery. Chase Papers, Library of Congress (*micro* 39:0338).

Supreme Court of the United States,
Washington Feby 16th 1871

Dear C.J.

The Salary Bill has passed the Senate— The *CJ.* at *$8,500*—Justices at *$8000.*[1]

The Bill failed at $10,500. & $10,000. by *one* vote— What particularly grieves the Judges is, that, that vote was given by Gov Sprague—[2]

Why would he not help us in this emercency? Even had he left the Senate or *not* voted, we should have won the day.

I am really distressed about it—

Yours truly & affy
R C Parsons

Mr Chase.

1. Chase had lobbied for higher raises. The appropriations bill that passed Congress on February 15 increased the annual salaries of the chief justice and his brethren from $6,500 and $6,000, respectively. Chase to Samuel F. Miller, June 15, 1866 (above); *Congressional Globe,* 41st Cong., 3d sess., 1870–71, pt. 2:1256, 1262; Fairman, *Reconstruction and Reunion,* 68, 166–71; *Statutes at Large,* 10:655, 16:493.

2. The vote in the Senate on February 15 was 29–28. Congress finally raised the chief justice's salary to $10,500 per annum two months before Chase died in 1873. *Congressional Globe,* 41st Cong., 3d sess., 1870–71, pt. 2:1256, 1262; Fairman, *Reconstruction and Reunion,* 171; *Statutes at Large,* 17:486.

TO HENRY CLARKE

Letterbook copy in clerk's hand. Chase Papers, Library of Congress (*micro* 39:0351).

Washington— Mar. 22— 1871

Sir:[1]

I have received your letter and the copy of your testimonials. The cause of delay is doubt whether we shall suit each other. The only place I can offer is that of personal messenger or attendant upon myself: and I need some one who can accompany me on journeys, assist me in dressing and undressing and shave. I should like also in your case, seeing you write a good hand, to have you write short-hand. You could learn to shave in some shop and also under a competent instructor and with proper books and practice to write short-hand. It may be a difficulty with you that, when the Court sits, here or elsewhere it would be your duty to take my books and papers & docket to and from, and attend in Court—and all the other messengers are men of color—some light, some not so light. And then the smallness of the pay—($3 per day while the Supreme Court sits—say 5 months or 150 days—& $1.50 per day for 7 months or 215 days—in all $872.50 a year) might be another difficulty.

If with this plain statement you are inclined to take the place you may come. I shall expect you to do your best and to avoid all bad habits. Please let me know whether you will come or not as soon as you can.[2]

Your friend
S. P. CHASE

Mr H. Clark.

1. Clarke had served as Gen. Winfield Scott's personal attendant during the Civil War. At Scott's urging, Chase helped Clarke secure work in the 1860s as an assistant messenger in the Treasury Department and messenger in the New York Custom House. "He is quick, clearheaded, and obliging," wrote Chase of Clarke in 1863; "but unfortunately fallen into bad company and I fear is in danger of forming bad habits." Clarke experienced a religious conversion in 1865, much to Chase's approval. Chase to Hiram Barney, Sept. 15, 1863 (Chase Papers, Hist. Soc. of Pa.); Chase to Clarke, Aug. 26, 1865; Clarke to Chase, Aug. 25, 1865 (both Chase Papers, L.C.); *Register of Officers (1863)*, 18; *Register of Officers (1865)*, 99.

2. Clarke accepted Chase's offer and, among other duties, reported on work at Edgewood during Chase's absences from Washington. Clarke to Chase, June-Sept., 1872. (Chase Papers, L.C.).

TO EDWARD D. MANSFIELD

Autograph letter. Jared Mansfield Collection, Local History and Marine Room, Milwaukee Public Library (*micro* 39:0358).

Washington, Ap. 24, 1871

My dear Mr. Mansfield,

It gave me real pleasure to see your familiar hand once more, and to read the assurances of your continued interest and affectionate regard. You may depend upon it that they are fully reciprocated.

My health is a good deal improved as you rightly infer from my resumption of my place on the bench. I doubt however if I should have resumed it at this term; but the majority of the Judges had determined to reopen the questions adjudicated more than a year ago in the legal tender case, in connexion with the still more important question, as I think, whether the Constitution permits Congress to impose upon the Country irredeemable paper money as a standard of value;—and I did not feel at liberty to be absent from my post, if at all able to attend, when questions of such moment were to be argued, & for the present at least, decided. I say, for the present at least, for if a decision made by five to three can be reversed by five to four, it may happen that, under a new president, the later decision may be, itself, reversed, and the former one reinstated.[1]

Is it not possible that I may see you and have a talk with you before you go East with your daughters?[2] I think of taking Cincinnati in my way to the St Louis Springs near Saginaw in Michigan early in May.[3] If I do I shall count on that pleasure, may I not. I hope, at any rate, that your daughter's health will be renewed by her Eastern summer sojourn.

Tomorrow will complete three weeks since Nettie sailed for Europe. We heard of the safe arrival of the ship last Saturday week at Liverpool, and are now in daily hope of letters. Thanks for your good wishes for her. I remember, gratefully, the interest you and your excellent wife took in her.[4]

I am not so despondent in view of our situation and the men who make the largest figure politically as you seem to be. My faith is that Providence always provides suitable men for the work of each generation. Clay, Webster & Calhoun would hardly have suited the work of the war.[5] Lincoln & his coworkers might not have suited the work of reconstruction. They who have carried that work so near completion, will not, probably, be found competent to the work which the New Era will find for men to do. Men & their purposes change: God & his purposes change not.

You say you are still "a public writer." I wish you would send me, if you can conveniently, what you write: for it always interests and instructs me. I regret that you have not a periodical of your own, where one would always find whatever proceeds from your pen. If it were in my power the country would not fail of your services—in its statistics especially. I thought, indeed, at one time that you would be placed at the head of that bureau.[6]

Please make the assurance of my best wishes acceptable to your daughters. May our Father in Heaven bless and keep you.

Faithfully your friend
S: P: Chase

E. D. Mansfield, Esq

1. In *Hepburn v. Griswold*, decided on February 7, 1870, the Supreme Court held by the slender margin of 4–3 that the Legal Tender Act of 1862 was unconstitutional when applied to debts that existed before passage of the measure. Since then, President Grant had appointed two new associate justices under legislation enacted on April 10, 1869: Republicans William Strong of Pennsylvania, a former congressman and state supreme court judge, and New Jersey lawyer Joseph P. Bradley, both of whom united with the *Hepburn* dissenters to force another hearing shortly after they joined the Court in March 1870. In *William B. Knox v. Phoebe G. Lee and Hugh Lee* and *Thomas H. Parker v. George*

Davis—both announced on May 1, 1871—the Court upheld rulings at the state level, overruled *Hepburn*, and declared the Legal Tender Act constitutional by a vote of 5–4. *Chase Papers*, 1:650–51; Fairman, *Reconstruction and Reunion*, 713–15, 717, 732–46, 752–55, 759–63; *Statutes at Large*, 16:44; 8 Wall. 603 (1870); 12 Wall. 457 (1871).

2. Manfield's three surviving daughters were Elizabeth Phipps Mansfield Dudley, Eleanor Strode Mansfield, and Margaret-Edith Mansfield. Horace Mansfield, *The Descendants of Richard and Gillian Mansfield* . . . (New Haven, 1885), 133.

3. Various "magnetic springs" in St. Louis supposedly had "medical properties invaluable in the treatment of various forms of disease." Chase planned to visit the springs for treatment of paralysis at the recommendation of his physician. The trip started on June 7, with stops in Parkersburg, West Virginia, and Cincinnati, Ohio. Chase apparently arrived in Michigan sometime early in August and stayed several weeks. He returned to Washington, D.C., on October 13, after stopping in Rhode Island and New York. Chase to Janet Chase Hoyt, May 22 and Oct. 14, 1871, Chase to W. F. Dickson, Aug. 7, 1871, and Chase to Richard C. Parsons, Sr., Aug. 9, 1871 (all Chase Papers, L.C.); Chase to John W. Garrett, June 7, 1871 (Garrett Family Papers, L.C.); Chase to Jacob W. Schuckers, Oct. 3, 1871 (William Nelson Autograph Collec., Manuscript Group 23, N.J. Hist. Soc.); Charles Richard Tuttle, comp. *General History of the State of Michigan* . . . (Detroit, 1873), 658–60.

4. Nettie had married William Sprague Hoyt, a second cousin of Kate's husband, William Sprague, on March 23. The couple departed for Europe on April 5, aboard the British steamship *Java* and honeymooned in England, Wales, and Germany. Mansfield's wife was Margaret Worthington Mansfield, the daughter of former Ohio governor Thomas Worthington. Chase to Janet Chase Hoyt, May 22 and June 5, 1871, and Janet Chase Hoyt et al. to Chase, Apr. 30 (Chase Papers, L.C.); *DAB*, 12:256; *New York Times*, Mar. 24, 1871; *New York Tribune*, Apr. 6, 1871.

5. That is, Henry Clay, Daniel Webster, and John C. Calhoun.

6. Formerly commissioner of statistics for the state of Ohio, Mansfield had written newspaper columns in the *New York Times* during the Civil War under the pseudonym "Veteran Observer." *Chase Papers*, 4:245–46.

FROM JOHN RANDOLPH TUCKER

Autograph letter. Chase Papers, Library of Congress (*micro* 39:361).

Washington & Lee University—
Lexington *Apr.* 27. *1871*—

Hon. S. P. Chase
Dear Sir—[1]

You will excuse me for taking the liberty of calling to your attention an historic fact, which you have not referred to in your able and satisfactory opinion in Hepburn vs Griswold; and which may serve to shed light upon the question now under consideration before your Court again—[2]

You refer to the fact that the Articles of Confederation gave the power to Congress to borrow money or emit Bills of Credit—and that the words to emit Bills are omitted in Art. 1. § 8. c. 2 of the C.U.S.[3]

That the omission was not casual, but of purpose, is obvious from the fact, that in Mr Charles Pinkney's plan, presented May 29. 1787, the clause read—"to borrow money and emit Bills of Credit:" Journal of Fed. Conv. p. 75.—and that the Committee of five who reported the form (Journ. Conv. Aug 6, 1787, p. 221) had the clause in these words—"To borrow money and emit bills on the Credit of the United States."[4]

These words were therefore considered of importance— But on the 16th Aug. 1787—(Journal Conv. 256) it was moved to strike out these words—"and emit bills"—Yeas, 9 States— Nays two States— Carried by a strong vote—[5]

Why this was done is shown in the debates reported by Mr Madison—3 Mad. Papers—1343. to 1346—[6]

The fear was expressed with great emphasis, that to retain the words might afford a pretext to Congress to make its bills a *legal tender*—to which the people of the whole Country were very hostile— Mr Langdon of N.H. saying, he would reject the whole plan rather than retain it—[7]

A note on page 1346, states, that Mr Madison voted (and thus carried the vote of Va) to strike out—in order to prevent the "legal tender" consequence—but with an impression that to emit bills might be implied as a mode of borrowing money—his idea being, that the *implication* of a power to emit bills from the *express* power to borrow money, would not admit of *another* implication to make the Bills a legal tender—but that if the power to emit bills was expressly granted, the implication to make them a legal tender would be more readily made—[8]

Thus it appears, that the inference of right to make bills a legal tender from the power to borrow money is excluded, by the striking out of the words giving power to emit, lest it should have that effect— If cotemporaneous evidence of intent can avail, is it not conclusive here against the implication, from an *implied* power to emit; since the *express* power was refused, to prevent the very result which dissenting Judges in Hepburn vs Griswold insist is legitimate—[9]

It seems to me, that this fact supports very strongly your views, in which for many reasons I concur— The question is one, which very clearly calls for a distinction between the delegated & reserved powers in our System, and I was glad to see how well I could subscribe to the opinion you delivered in the case referred to—[10]

I hope your health is restored—and that your duties on the Bench you will now be able to perform without injury to yourself, and for the public good. I am

Very respectfully

Your ob. Serv—
J. R. Tucker

1. In 1870, Democrat John Randolf Tucker (1823–97), former attorney general of Virginia, taught law at Washington and Lee University. Tucker had appeared before Chase frequently in litigation before the Supreme Court. *DAB,* 19:34–35.

2. Chase had discussed the background of the Supreme Court's decision to reconsider the constitutionality of the Legal Tender Act of 1862 in correspondence with Edward D. Mansfield, April 24, 1871 (above).

3. "The old Congress," argued Chase in *Hepburn v. Griswold,* "under the Articles of Confederation, was clothed by express grant with the power to emit bills of credit, which are in fact notes for circulation as currency; and yet that Congress was not clothed with

the power to make these bills a legal tender in payment." Technically, Chase's opinion said nothing about deliberate omission of the phrase "emit bills" from art. 1, sec. 8, clause 2, of the U.S. Constitution. 8 Wall. 616 (1870).

4. Charles Pinckney (1757–1824) represented South Carolina in Congress under the Articles of Confederation and the Constitutional Convention of 1787. Pinckney's plan provided the framework for later discussions in the convention. The five members of the committee on detail were Oliver Ellsworth (1745–1807) of Connecticut, Nathaniel Gorham (1738–96) of Massachusetts, Edmund Randolf (1753–1813) of Virginia, John Rutledge (1739–1800) of South Carolina; and James Wilson (1742–1798) of Pennsylvania. Pinckney's plan is quoted at art. 6, clause 3. The committee's version of the phrase comes from art. 7, sec. 1, clause 8. *Bio. Dir. U.S. Cong.*, 1650; *DAB*, 6:111, 113, 433–34, 14: 611–13, 15:353–54, 16:258–59, 20:226, 329; U.S. Constitutional Convention, *Journal, Acts, and Proceedings of the Convention . . . which formed the Constitution of the United States* (Boston, 1819), 75, 221.

5. Supporting the proposal were Connecticut, Delaware, Georgia, Massachusetts, New Hampshire, North Carolina, Pennsylvania, South Carolina, and Virginia. Maryland and New Jersey opposed it. U.S. Constitutional Convention, *Journal, Acts, and Proceedings*, 256.

6. Henry D. Gilpin, ed., *The Papers of James Madison . . .*, 3 vols. (Washington, D.C., 1840), 3:1343–46.

7. John Langdon (1741–1819), a prosperous merchant from Portsmouth, had served as a legislator and chief executive of his state and attended the Continental Congress. Ibid., 3:1346; *DAB*, 10:587–88.

8. According to the note, delegate James Madison of Virginia, the future president, "became satisfied that striking out the words would not disable the Government from the use of public notes, as far as they could be safe and proper, and would only cut off the pretext for a *paper-currency* and particularly for making the bills *a tender*, either for public or private debts." Gilpin, *Papers of James Madison*, 3:1346.

9. Samuel F. Miller wrote the dissenting opinion, with Noah H. Swayne and David Davis concurring. In Miller's view, authority granted in the Constitution for Congress to regulate currency also implied power to issue paper money, and thus legitimized the Legal Tender Act of 1862. Fairman, *Reconstruction and Reunion*, 677, 714; 8 Wall. 626–39 (1870).

10. Unlike Miller, Chase claimed in *Hepburn v. Griswold* that the Constitution withheld the contested authority from Congress. Chase to Edward D. Mansfield, Apr. 24, 1871 (above); Fairman, *Reconstruction and Reunion*, 713–14; 8 Wall. 606–26 (1870).

TO JOHN R. TUCKER

Autograph letter. Tucker Family Papers (#2605), selected letter, Southern Historical Collection, Wilson Library, University of North Carolina at Chapel Hill (*micro* 39:0371).

Washington, May 1, 1871

My dear Sir,

The historical facts, mentioned in your welcome letter, were stated & commented on by counsel in the Case of Hepburn v. Griswold and the connected cases, and were considered in framing the opinion of the court.[1] But the general question of the Constitutionality of laws making promises to pay dollars a legal tender as real dollars did not necessarily arise in those cases; and of the five judges who concurred in the judgments & in the opinion, one at least (Mr. Justice Grier) regarded the act as constitutional in respect to Contracts made after its passage. Judge Field was then inclined to the same view. The opinion was, therefore, confined to the effect of the act on prexisting contracts. On this point the five judges had no doubt. The minority consisted of three judges. The full court then consisted of eight Justices[2]

Today the opinion in the case of Hepburn v. Griswold was reversed by five Judges against four.[3] The majority for it was two—the majority against it is one. The number of judges constituting the present is the same as the number constituting the former majority. The change is produced by the resignation of Judge Grier, & by appointments of the President under a law which had not gone into effect when the decision was made.[4]

Not only has the opinion in Hepburn v. Griswold been reversed today but the general constitutionality of the act as to legal tender has been affirmed. The court was divided as upon the more limited question—five to four the reflections of Judge Field having conducted him to the conclusion that the constitionality of no act making paper money a legal tender could be maintained. The four Judges sustained the doctrine of Mr. Madison that the Government might constitutionally issue its promises to pay, but could not constitutionally make them a legal tender, or, in other words compel citizens to accept them as money[5]

The opinions will be read during the last week of the adjourned term. If my health allows I expect to prepare a dissenting opinion: and I hope it will for I wish to leave my settled judgment on this great question upon the public records.[6]

I see from the date of your letter that you are in Virginia. Permanently? I take a warm interest in your movements: and expect much from you in jurisprudence

With Sincere respect & esteem,

Yours truly
S. P: CHASE

Hon. J. R. Tucker

1. Tucker had written to Chase on April 27 (above). In *Hepburn v. Griswold,* William M. Evarts and former Supreme Court justice Benjamin Robbins Curtis argued for plaintiffs Susan and Henry Hepburn. The defendant's attorney was Clarkson Nott Potter, a Democratic congressman from New York. Counsel in the related cases of *Knox v. Lee* and *Parker v. Davis,* the other two major legal-tender cases, included Washington, D.C., attorneys George Washington Paschal (1812–78), George Washington Paschal, Jr., and J. A. Wills, as well as several lawyers from Massachusetts, namely Representative Benjamin F. Butler, former congressman Benjamin F. Thomas, and brothers George Francis Richardson (1829–1912) and Daniel S. Richardson. Former commissioner of internal revenue George S. Boutwell also assisted the defense. Potter had referred to the debates of the Constitutional Convention in comments related to *Knox v. Lee,* even though he did not officially represent either party. *DAB,* 14:287–88; Fairman, *Reconstruction and Reunion,* 703–4, 757–63; *Nat. Cyc.,* 15:168–69; Clarkson Nott Potter, *Argument Against the Power of Congress to Make United States Treasury Notes a Legal Tender* (Washington, D.C., 1871); 8 Wall. 603 (1870); 12 Wall. 457 (1871).

2. In *Hepburn v. Griswold,* Chase, Nathan Clifford, Stephen J. Field, Robert C. Grier, and Samuel Nelson formed the majority. David Davis, Samuel F. Miller, and Noah H. Swayne dissented. Fairman, *Reconstruction and Reunion,* 713–14.

3. Chase refers to *Knox v. Lee* and *Parker v. Davis,* discussed in correspondence to Edward D. Mansfield on April 24 (above).

4. The two new members were William Strong and Joseph P. Bradley, appointed under legislation of April 10, 1869. The addition of Strong and Bradley raised the number of justices on the Supreme Court from eight to nine. Robert C. Grier had resigned on December 15, 1869, effective January 31, 1870. Chase to Edward D. Mansfield, April 24, 1871 (above); *Statutes at Large,* 16:44; Fairman, *Reconstruction and Reunion,* 716, 732–38.

5. Joseph P. Bradley, David Davis, Samuel F. Miller, William Strong, and Noah H. Swayne affirmed the constitutionality of legal tender in *Knox v. Lee* and *Parker v. Davis.* Chase, Nathan Clifford, Stephen J. Field, and Samuel Nelson dissented. Tucker had discussed James Madison's views on legal tender in correspondence to Chase on April 27 (above). Fairman, *Reconstruction and Reunion,* 759; 12 Wall. 457 (1871).

6. The Supreme Court's adjourned term started on October 16 and ran until November 27, 1871. December 4 marked the beginning of the regular term. "Minutes Supreme Court U.S. 28 Mar. 24, 1871 to Feb. 15, 1872" (National Archives).

TO CLEMENT LAIRD VALLANDIGHAM

Letterbook copy in clerk's hand. Chase Papers, Library of Congress (*micro* 39:0388).

Washington. May 20. 1871

My dear Sir:[1]

I have just read the resolutions of the Montgomery County Democratic Convention reported by yourself, together with your remarks and those of Mr. Howk.[2] You have rendered a great service to your country and to the party;—at least such is my judgment. May God bless you for it.

Nothing could be truer than your declaration that the movement contemplated by the resolutions is "the restoration of the Democratic Party to its ancient platform of progress and reform." I know you too well to doubt your courage or your fidelity to your convictions.

Very truly yours
S. P. Chase

Hon. C. L. Vallandi*n*gham. Dayton. Ohio.

1. The *New York Times* of June 20, 1871, published this letter as the last correspondence between Chase and Vallandigham, who died on June 17 from an accidental gunshot wound. *DAB,* 19:143, 145.

2. Vallandigham represented a movement of reformist Democrats—known as the New Departure—and Republicans increasingly disillusioned with the political and economic policies of the Grant administration. On May 18, Vallandigham proposed a platform of eighteen resolutions with bipartisan appeal to a local Democratic convention that met in Dayton, Ohio. Vallandigham's platform accepted the Thirteenth, Fourteenth, and Fifteenth Amendments and, among other points, expressed support for universal amnesty, taxation based on wealth, metallic currency, and civil service reform. "What we want now for this vigorous body of the young Democracy is not the dreamy contemplation of the past, but the energetic spirit of the present," challenged presiding officer George Washington Houk (1825–94), a future congressman. "It is not now a new departure," added Vallandigham, "but a return; the restoration of the Democratic party once more to the ancient platform of progress and reform. . . ." Democratic conventions on the state and national levels adopted most of Vallandigham's resolutions throughout the remaining months of 1871. *Bio. Dir. U.S. Cong.,* 1214; Foner, *Reconstruction,* 412–21, 505–6; *Daily Ohio Statesman,* May 19 and 20, 1871; Roseboom, *Civil War Era,* 475–77; Ross, *Liberal Republican Movement,* 68–69.

TO JANET CHASE HOYT

Autograph letter. Chase Papers, Library of Congress (*micro* 39:0520).

Washington, Feb. 16, 72

Dearest Nettie,

I was so glad to get the notes of your dear husband, and Aunt announcing your assured convalescence.[1] I am eager to be told now that you have been allowed to go down stairs and to ride out, and that you have taken no cold during the inclement weather we have had.

Last Thursday I was at Judge Bradleys dinner. There were twenty persons at table besides host & hostess; mostly people of note, such as the President & Mrs Grant the Vice President & Mrs Colfax &c.[2] I was assigned to Mrs Colfax, who is a sensible, good looking woman, but not a dinner table talker. My next neighbor was of the same type—the wife of an officer of our navy / So as I dont talk much now a days, and a total stranger to one, and almost a total stranger to the other I was not vastly annoyed. Still all went well enough / The company was merry and happy and the dinner was very good. You were frequently enquired for, as you always are.

Before going to the dinner from Katie's, (which I always do when I take dinner in the city) Mary Goldsborough, with her brother the marshal,[3] & young Mr Abbot from Baltimore called. She was full of enquiries about you and your baby; and just the same chatty, lively, inconsequential, & pleasant body she always was. They staid only a few moments having come over to attend Mrs Grant's last reception and returning to Baltimore the same afternoon.

Last evening Lellie Swayne was married at 6 o'clock to Mr Parsons of New York.[4] Gov. Sprague & I went. Katie thought it more prudent to stay at home, the weather being very inclement. Lellie made a very pretty, animated bride. My present to her was a basket of flowers & Katie a pretty piece of verse. Hardly more than fifty people were invited / Judge Swayne looked satisfied and I am told with reason. Mrs Swayne[5] looked sad & no wonder, for Lellie must have been the light of her house. They go at once to Egypt & the Holy Land sailing from New York tomorrow.

Every body is going to the first party given by the Japanese minister tonight,[6] except me and I am going to Edgewood.

Mr Pike went out with me last night, & breakfasted with me this morning. Mrs Pike is unwell from the effects of vaccination. She half promises a visit in the spring. Perhaps you and she will meet. Mr. P– was delighted with Edgewood. I want to see you so much that I begin to think I must go to New York[7]

Love to Will and Auntie & kisses for little Nettie

Your loving father
S. P. Chase

1. A telegram and a note had announced the birth of Nettie's first child, Janet. The author of the telegram, dated January 14, was William Sprague Hoyt. Chase received the letter from Charlotte Ludlow Jones, the sister of his third wife, on January 16. *Chase Papers,* 1:668, 670.

2. Joseph P. Bradley and his wife, Mary Hornblower Bradley, lived in Washington, D.C., at 201 I Street, N.W. Among Bradley's guests were Ulysses S. Grant, Julia Dent Grant, Schuyler Colfax, and Ellen Wade Colfax. *DAB,* 2:571, 4:298; *Wash. Dir. (1872),* 87.

3. Mary Goldsborough hailed from Frederick, Maryland. Edward Y. Goldsborough, a former state's attorney for Maryland, had become a U.S. marshall in 1869.

4. According to the *New York Times,* Mary Llewellyn Swayne (c. 1840–1913) had married Edwin Parsons (or Parsens) of New York "in the presence of a small but very distinguished company," at the residence of Noah Swayne in Washington, D.C. *New York Times,* Feb. 16, 1872; Norman Walton Swayne, *Swaynes Descended from Francis Swayne of East Marlborough Township, Chester County, Pennsylvania,* 2d ed. (Philadelphia, 1955), 64.

5. Sarah Ann Wager Swayne.

6. Chase meant the Japanese chargé d'affaires, Arinori Mori. *New York Times,* Feb. 17, 1872.

7. Chase finally visited New York on June 6 and spent the rest of the summer and part of the autumn in New England. He returned to Washington, D.C., early in October. *Chase Papers,* 1:687, 689; Chase to David Demerest Lloyd, Sept. 15, 1872 (below).

FROM S. BASSETT FRENCH

Autograph letter on letterhead stationery. Chase Papers, Library of Congress (*micro* 39:0540).

Senate Chamber,
Richmond, Va., *March 13 1872*

Hon Salmon P. Chase
Chief Justice of the U.S.
Washington D.C.
Honble & Dear Sir

Judge Joynes of the Co. of Appeals of Va has resigned his seat and it has devolved on the present Genl. Assy—to elect his successor. You are aware that nearly every lawyer in Va, whose elevation to the Supreme Bench would be proper, is labouring under disabilities growing out of the late unpleasantness; hence the line of selection is confined to a class unfitted for such pre-eminence either by talents or attainments.

Within the last day or two it has been asserted that the Supreme Court of the U.S. has rendered a decision which in effect relieves from all pains & penalties all such persons, who accepted the terms of the proclamations of Presidents Lincoln and Johnson; and so much of the best interests of Virginia are dependent on a certain knowledge of the true extent of the decision, that I have ventured upon an intrusion upon you, which I trust will not be deemed impertinent; trusting that in view of the high interests involved, it may be in accord with your judgement to advise us, whether the decision referred to grants the relief claimed by some.[1]

James Alfred Jones Esq of this City is named as Judge Joynes successor—and will accept if not under disabilities— He was *anterior to the war* a member of the Va Senate. Judge Robertson, formerly of the Co of Appeals is also mentioned. His disabilities depend on the fact of having occupied a seat on that bench *anterior to and during the war.*[2] Either of these gentlemen would be an honour to any Court & it is to be hoped that Virginia may now secure the service of one or the other

With high respect, I am,

Yr Obt. Servt.
S. BASSETT FRENCH

1. During and after the Civil War, a series of proclamations issued by Abraham Lincoln and Andrew Johnson offered pardons of various kinds to former Confederates. Johnson's most recent proclamation, dating from December 25, 1868, extended "a full pardon and amnesty" to anyone "who directly or indirectly participated in the late insurrection or rebellion." In *U.S. v. John A. Klein,* decided on January 29, 1872, the Supreme Court sustained the ruling of a lower court that affirmed the right of those granted clemency to recover property seized by the U.S. government during the Civil War. "The decisions to which you refer merely give effect to the amnesty proclamation by President Johnson in property cases . . . ," warned Chase in response to French; "It may become a judicial question whether any persons are relieved by the amnesty from the disabilities imposed by the Third section of the fourteenth amendment." Basler, *Collected Works,* 7:53–56, 269–70; Chase to [French], Mar. 19, 1872 (Chase Papers, L.C.); Fairman, *Reconstruction and Reunion,* 843–46; *Statutes at Large,* 15:699–700, 702–703, 711–12; 13 Wall. 128 (1872).

2. William Joseph Robertson (1817–98), a Charlottesville attorney, served on the Virginia Supreme Court of Appeals from 1859 to 1865. *DAB,* 16:29.

TO M. C. C. CHURCH

Letterpress copy of letter in clerk's hand, signed by Chase. Chase Papers, Library of Congress (*micro* 39:0546).

Washington, Mar. 2[0]. 72

My Dear Sir:[1]

Your letter, with its enclosures, is just received. My sincere thanks for your good-will. I am very sensible that your efforts are prompted by zeal for principle rather than by personal partiality. My thanks are the more earnest on that account. But will you pardon a few suggestions in reference to the circular?[2]

Its first sentence seems to place me in the position of a man desiring [the] nomination for the Presidency: I do not desire it. There has been a time when I did. I say this frankly: and say just as frankly that I have now no such desire. If those who agree with me in principle, think that my nomination will promote the interests of the country, I shall not refuse the use of my name. But I shall not seek nomination, nor am I willing to seem to seek it. I said this to you when you did me the honor to call upon me.[3]

I doubt the expediency of the remark in regard to the tendency of the Liberal Republican movement. Nothing, that I have seen, seems to warrant a doubt of the patriotism of its promoters.

Nor am I willing to be put in the attitude of rivalling Judge Davis. He is my friend and I hold him in the highest esteem as a man of honor and ability. I differ from him on some important points of principle, but do not question the integrity of his convictions; nor, I think, does he question mine.

And, finally, I doubt the expediency of suggesting any name for the second office. Let this be left to the Convention. Many will agree with you as to your first choice who may not agree in your second.

I enclose a draft which will show more clearly my views.

I have just been to New York, or rather to my daughter's in Astoria.[4] My visit was entirely to her but three gentlemen found their way out to see me. Two of these were Republicans and one was a Democrat. The Republicans were very much of your mind and seemed sanguine that their convictions were general. I learned from one of them that a call recommending attendance at the Cincinnati Convention was in preparation and already signed by some of the Republican electors at the last Presidential election

I showed your platform to them and also to the gentleman of Democratic connections / They all seemed to think very well of it, but suggested that the fifth and sixth paragraphs would meet with much objection.[5] The Democrat said he would be quite satisfied with the second paragraph as a platform and [marked] the first, second, third fourth, seventh, ninth, tenth, eleventh, twelfth, thirteenth and fourteenth as those which he thought might be safely adopted.[6] He himself agreed in the whole.

I requested a friend to show the platform to *The Tribune* people. The managing editor said to him that *The Tribune* would denounce a Free Trade plank. I suggest whether it would not be best to add to the fifth paragraph some words like the following: "Such discriminations as the general interests may require."[7]

I am glad to know that you expect soon to be in Washington. It will be a real pleasure to see you again[8] / I will bear in mind your suggestion as to a gentleman with whom you may correspond and write you again soon.

Yours, very [sincerely,]
S. P. Chase

Judge M. C. C. Church.

1. Church served as secretary for an alliance of Liberal Democrats and Republicans in Parkersburg, West Virginia, increasingly at odds with President Grant and his policies. In his biography of Chase, Robert B. Warden assigned a date of March 26 to this letter. A more plausible reading of the faint handwriting is March 20, since the New York trip to which Chase alludes in this correspondence ended on March 16 or 17. Chase to Hiram Barney, March 12 and 17, 1872 (Barney Papers, Huntington Lib.); *Parkersburg State Journal,* Apr. 25, 1872; Robert B. Warden, *An Account of the Private Life and Public Services of Salmon Portland Chase* . . . (Cincinnati, 1874), 728–29.

2. The editors have not located the letter. Another copy of the circular, which Church wrote to George W. Morgan on March 18, exists among the papers of David Davis at the Illinois Historical Society. "The friends of Cheif Justice Chase with his consent and with a

full knowledge of the present political situation are of opinion that now is a favourable time to bring forward his claims for the Presidency," wrote Church. According to the circular, "disorganization" and deflection threatened the Liberal Republican movement at its national convention, scheduled for Cincinnati in May, at which reformers hoped to select a challenger to President Grant. "The battle will be fought in the Cincinnati Convention between the friends of Judge Davis and the friends of Cheif Justice Chase," predicted Church. The circular enclosed a "Declaration of Principles," to which Chase had supposedly given "his unqualified endorsement," and ended with a recommendation that Massachusetts attorney and legislator John Quincy Adams, Jr. (1833–94), the son of Charles Francis Adams, be selected as the party's vice-presidential candidate. *Appletons'*, 1:13; Fairman, *Reconstruction and Reunion*, 1468–69; Foner, *Reconstruction*, 500–502; *Parkersburg State Journal*, Apr. 25, 1872; *Proceedings of the Liberal Republican Convention, in Cincinnati, May 1st, 2d and 3d, 1872* . . . (New York, 1872), 3.

3. Surviving evidence suggests that Chase consulted with Church on March 11 or 12. "A prominent distinguished citizen of West Virginia—a liberal Republican—showed me a printed platform a day or two since," wrote Chase to an unidentified correspondent on March 13; "It suits me." Chase to ———, Mar. 13, 1872 (Chase Papers, L.C.).

4. Chase had returned from New York on March 16 or 17. Chase to Hiram Barney, March 12 and 17, 1872 (Barney Papers, Huntington Lib.).

5. The editors have not located the early version of Church's platform. On April 18, at a meeting of Liberal Democrats and Republicans in Parkersburg, West Virginia, Church suggested a related series of resolutions in the form of paragraphs almost identical to the platform that Clement L. Vallandigham had offered to Democrats of Montgomery County, Ohio, in May 1871. Church's fifth paragraph called for tariff laws "adjusted to a revenue standard, with such discrimination only as the general interest may require." Paragraph six supported "the return of specie payments at the earliest practicable moment." Chase to Vallandigham, May 20, 1871 (above); *Parkersburg State Journal*, Apr. 25, 1872.

6. The second paragraph of Church's April 18 platform described powers delegated to the national and state governments under the U.S. Constitution. Paragraphs one, three, and four acknowledged the perpetuity of the Union, reaffirmed the separation of powers, and accepted the legitimacy of the Thirteenth, Fourteenth, and Fifteenth Amendments. In paragraphs seven and nine, Church opposed new land grants to railroads and welcomed "the accession . . . of neighbor states whenever they are willing to come in and can be received without breach of international obligations, or without corruption or fraud." According to paragraph ten, the U.S. government had an obligation to protect its citizens abroad. Paragraphs eleven, twelve, and thirteen expressed support for the rights of labor, criticized special treatment for creditors, and denounced wastefulness in government. "We invite and welcome the co-operation of all patriotic citizens who are willing to unite with us," read paragraph fourteen. *Parkersburg State Journal*, Apr. 25, 1872.

7. The managing editor of the *New York Tribune* at this time was Whitelaw Reid. The fifth paragraph in the April 18 version of Church's platform incorporated Chase's suggestion. Baehr, *New York Tribune*, 74.

8. Church apparently visited Washington early in April, but did not see Chase. Church to Chase, Apr. 8, 1872 (Chase Papers, L.C.).

FROM CHARLES I. GRADY

Autograph letter on letterhead stationery. Chase Papers, Library of Congress (*micro* 39:0555).

Office
Liberal Republican Press Association.[1]
Washington, D.C. March 29th, 1872

Dear Sir:

The enclosed editorial is the first pronounced expression of Liberal Republicanism at the capital.[2] Tomorrow it will appear in the "Transcript", and as you are the father of the party calling itself "Liberal", I desire to submit my views for your approval, as well as to obtain for publication—at such length as you may deem proper—your ideas on the situation political, and such advice as you are so capable of giving to an association formed for the purpose of promulgating Liberal Republican doctrines.

Our paper is not so widely circulated as it will be soon, but I have made arrangements to have your reply telegraphed throughout the country by the various correspondents.

Very Truly & Respectfully
CHARLES I. GRADY
Secty & Treasurer

Hon Salmon P. Chase
Prest.

1. The printed letterhead was of the Southern Republican Press Association; Grady struck through *Southern* and substituted *Liberal* by hand.

2. Attached to Grady's letter is a copy of the editorial, which the editors have not found elsewhere. The article compared Liberal Republicanism to the "moderation and wise statesmanship" that characterized the presidency of Thomas Jefferson. "So today, all who are liberal in sentiment may be as conservative or radical as they please, if they only agree in the policy of liberality," claimed the piece; "All sections of the country and men of all shades of opinion can unite on the platform of the liberal republicans as the only one that can bring the country together and restore harmony of feeling."

FROM ALEXANDER LONG

Autograph letter on letterhead stationery. Chase Papers, Historical Society of Pennsylvania (*micro* 39:0591).

Long & Kramer.[1]
Attorneys at Law,
25 West Third Street.
Cincinnati. April 22nd. 1872

Hon. S. P. Chase
Chief Justice U.S.
Washington D.C.
My Dear Sir:

Your kind favor of the 15th. came duly to hand and the information it contains on the much discussed questions of your health and physical condition is alike encouraging and valuable to your friends.[2]

As the convention approaches we see the necessity of action and a few of your friends in consultation this afternoon see the importance of securing the attendence of as many of your friends from abroad as possible[3]— Secure the attendence of as many as you can from Washington New York, Philadelphia, Richmond or any place where they can be induced to come and advocate your nomination. Senator Fowler of Tennessee heads that delegation and I telegraph him tonight to come on immediately.[4]

Much will depend upon creating an excitement in your favor and to that end we are organizing and appointing our men to visit the different hotels and press upon the delegates the necessity of your nomination as the only hope of securing the support of the democracy— Our ticket is Chief Justice Chase for President & Chas. Francis Adams for Vice-President— The Commercial this morning virtually rules Mr Groesbeck out and I will make an effort with Halstead on my way home this evening to say some thing in your favor— He too like many others is troubled about the condition of your health.[5]

The indications here are, that the democracy will support the nominees of the Cincinnati Convention whoever they may be.

The Enquirer has taken that position— Hence the necessity of action in your favor.[6]

Send out any of your friends that can exert an influence and we will assist them in operating on the convention.

Little or nothing has been said in the newspapers for some months past in your favor, indeed they seem to be acting on the presumption that you will not be a candidate before the convention— Can not some thing be done in New York or else where to bring out newspaper articles in your favor? If your nomination could be secured by the convention here it would be ratified by a democratic convention beyond a doubt, and the fear is that if you are not nominated and two republicans are that the democracy will either not hold a convention at all or if they do they will endorse the Cincinnati nominees. That there may be concert of action among your friends, you can indicate to any of them coming here from abroad whom you may see or communicate with to call upon us and we will be able to give some assistence and advice in the way of concert of action and the mode of operation—

If you can make any suggestions in the way of any publication in the papers here on the eve of the convention or other wise, that would in your judgment contribute to your nomination, you can entrust it in perfect confidence that your name will not be known in connection therewith.

Excuse this hastily written letter from your old

Friend
ALEXANDER LONG

1. A Cincinnati attorney, Long representated Ohio as a delegate to the Democratic national convention of 1872. Long's partner was Adam A. Kramer. *Bio. Dir. U.S. Cong.*, 1386; *Cinc. Dir. (1872)*, 520; Long to Jacob W. Schuckers, Aug. 12, 1873 (Jacob W. Schuckers Papers, L.C.).

2. "It would be presumptuous to predict the future, but my [severe] illness was eighteen months ago, and steady convalescence over fifteen months . . . seems to warrant the best hopes of my friends," wrote Chase; "I walk to the Capitol, two and a half miles, with

less fatigue, than most men after fifty." Chase to Long, Apr. 15, 1872 (Long Papers, Cin. Hist. Soc.).

3. Long anticipated the national convention of the Liberal Republican party, which opened in Cincinnati on May 1. On May 3, delegates chose Horace Greeley and Missouri politician Benjamin Gratz Brown as their presidential and vice-presidential candidates. Chase supporters known to be active at the Cincinnati convention included Hiram Barney; M. C. C. Church; David Demarest Lloyd, Chase's secretary at this time; and former Ohio congressmen James Mitchell Ashley and Edward Stowe Hamlin. Chase to Church, May 10, 1872 (below); *Chase Papers,* 1:676–78; *Proceedings of the Liberal Republican Convention,* 3, 29, 32.

4. Joseph Smith Fowler (1820–1902), an educator and attorney, served in the U.S. Senate from 1866 to 1871. *DAB,* 6:564.

5. Adams represented the United States at the Court of St. James, 1861–68, and in 1872 served as an arbitrator in disputes between the United States and Great Britain that arose from damages caused by the Confederate raider *Alabama.* The article from Murat Halstead's *Cincinnati Commercial* compared Adams with former Ohio congressman William Slocum Groesbeck. "The advantage that in our judgement Mr. Adams has," claimed the paper, "is that he can command the indispensable margin of Republican votes, because he has been a Republican, and as such has served the country conspicuously. . . ." On April 26, the *Commercial* published a letter that attempted to calm concerns about Chase's health. "I am assured from authentic sources that the health of the Chief Justice is restored, and that he still retains his intellectual powers unabated . . . ," wrote "Republican." Ibid., 1:42, 47–48, 8:14.

6. As predicted, the Democratic party chose Greeley and Brown as candidates at its national convention in Baltimore on July 9 and 10. "The GRANT dynasty see insurmountable objections to the union of the Democrats with the Liberal Republicans," claimed the *Cincinnati Enquirer* on April 10 in anticipation of the Liberal Republican convention. "They don't see how it can be done! But we see it, and we hope the Convention will see it. The Democracy are anxious for a union. They only ask fair terms." *Official Proceedings of the National Democratic Convention, Held at Baltimore, July 9, 1872* (Boston, 1872), 65, 71.

TO M. C. C. CHURCH

Letterbook copy in clerk's hand. Chase Papers, Library of Congress (*micro* 39:0599).

Washington. May 10. 1872.

My dear Judge:

It would be unpardonable if I should neglect to thank you for the interest you manifested in my behalf on a recent occasion. It does not diminish at all my sense of obligation that I know you were influenced in your action more by public than private considerations. Confidence in my personal character and appreciation of my public services formed the basis of your belief that the greatest number of Liberal Republicans and earnest Democrats would unite in my support and for this confidence and this appreciation I can never be sufficiently grateful.[1]

It does not at all surprise me that a majority of the Convention did not agree with you. I shall be glad if the necessary union can be secured by the nominations actually made. I am, as you are aware, a Democrat separated in nothing from the Democrats of the Jackson and Benton school,[2] except by my convictions on the slavery question, in times past and, now, by nothing. But, especially, since we came together in support of Mr Lincoln, Mr Greeley has given me a steady and generous support.

He advocated my nomination as Secretary of the Treasury and sustained my financial measures. After I retired from the Cabinet, he urged my appointment as Chief Justice. He agrees with me now on the questions of Finance and Amnesty—more important, as I verily believe, than any others now before the country. Why should I not then, though a Democrat and certainly not much of a Protectionist, give him the support which I believe he would have given me had I received the nomination?[3]

And why should you not support him? Why should not all Democrats support him? They will be sure of agreement upon the great questions of Amnesty and Currency and may rely with confidence from just consideration upon the impulses of gratitude for generous support given to an old antagonist. Division is defeat.

Are you coming to Washington? I need not say how much pleasure it will give me to receive you at Edgewood[4]

I am in very good condition now, and as I hope, constantly improving.

Remember me very kindly to Judge Jackson and Mrs Jackson and believe me[5]

Cordially yours
S. P. CHASE

Hon. M. C. C. Church.

1. Church had supported Chase as the presidential nominee of the Liberal Republican party, which passed over the chief justice on May 3 at its national convention in Cincinnati and selected Horace Greeley and B. Gratz Brown as candidates for the presidency and vice presidency, respectively. At no time during six rounds of balloting did Chase receive more than 32 of the 358 votes needed for the nomination. Chase to Church, Mar. 20, 1872 (above); *Proceedings of the Liberal Republican Convention,* 22–24, 26, 28, 29, 32.

2. That is, mainline Democrats Andrew Jackson and Missouri senator Thomas Hart Benton.

3. Lincoln appointed Chase to his cabinet on March 5, 1861, and Chase resigned on June 29, 1864. The appointment to the Supreme Court occurred on December 6, 1864. Chase and Greeley both favored universal amnesty and, as Chase demonstrated in *Hepburn v. Griswold,* a return to specie payments. Greeley was known to oppose free trade, though the Liberal Republican platform had avoided taking a stand on the issue. *Chase Papers,* 4:409–410, 445; Chase to William M. Byrd, Apr. 3, 1869; Chase to Horace Greeley, Mar. 14, 1867; Chase to George Hill, Jan. 7, 1870; Chase to Thomas H. Yeatman, Oct. 19, 1869; John Glancy Jones to Chase, June 7, 1867 (all above); Foner, *Reconstruction,* 502; *Proceedings of the Liberal Republican Convention,* 19, 20; U.S. Senate, *Journal of the Executive Proceedings,* 11:289.

4. Chase had lived at Edgewood since 1871. Phelps, *Kate Chase,* 230–31.

5. As with Church, Chase's friends John Jay Jackson, Jr., and Carrie C. Glime Jackson, lived in Parkersburg, West Virginia.

TO MURAT HALSTEAD

Letterbook copy in clerk's hand. Chase Papers, Library of Congress (*micro* 39:0602).

Washington, May 20. 1872

My dear Mr Halsted:

Your telegraphic correspondent "is at it again" in the Commercial of the 18th inst. and I beg you to insert the enclosed or its equivalent.[1]

I wish the Democrats could be persuaded to elect Greeley. Doubtless your ticket of Adams and Trumbull would have been best for the country, but it would have been less popular than Greeley and Brown, and the Democrats don't seem likely to accept that with unanimity sufficient to induce the Convention to nominate it or to recommend its support.[2]

Yours truly
S. P. Chase

Murat Halstead Esq.

"We are authorized to say in reference to so much of our special Washington telegram of the 17th instant as relates to

Chief Justice Chase

that he has no recollection of any conversation with any Senator or Representative about the bill, authorizing the President to accept the resignations of United States Judges, by reason of disability. He certainly has expressed no intention of resigning on the passage of such bill.

It is true that nearly two years ago, when suffering from severe and protracted illness, he desired the passage of a bill of that character concerning the Judges of the Supreme Court; but having so far regained his health as to resume his seat upon the bench last October and attend daily during laborious and protracted terms, performing a reasonable share of judicial duty not only without loss but with steady improvement of his health, he has ceased to take any personal interest in such legislation."[3]

1. According to the notice in Halstead's *Cincinnati Commercial,* dated May 17, Chase had expressed support "some time ago" for H.R. 1605, a proposal that would have allowed any federal judge "no longer able to perform the duties of his office" to retire with full pay. Chase, claimed the paper, "said he would at once place his resignation in the hands of the President, to take effect from the passage of the bill." The resolution passed the House on March 23, 1870, but failed in the Senate. *Cincinnati Commercial,* May 18, 1872; *Congressional Globe,* 41st Cong., 2d sess., 1869–70, 2181, 5357, 5406.

2. Charles Francis Adams and Illinois senator Lyman Trumbull were two favored candidates for president and vice president among Liberal Republicans prior to the Cincinnati convention. Despite Chase's doubts, the Democrats selected Horace Greeley and B. Gratz Brown as their nominees on July 9 and 10. *Official Proceedings of the National Democratic Convention,* 65, 71; Ross, *Liberal Republican Movement,* 85.

3. Chase evidently wanted such a bill around the time of his paralysis in August 1870. The May 23 issue of the *Cincinnati Commercial* included Chase's entire statement, with only minor variations in wording and punctuation. Chase to Richard C. Parsons, Sept. 26, 1870 (above).

TO DAVID DEMAREST LLOYD

Printed copy. Jacob W. Schuckers, *The Life and Public Services of Salmon Portland Chase* (New York, 1874), 593 (*micro* 39:0964).

Narragansett, R.I.,[1] *September* 15, 1872.

. . . . As to political matters, I have by no means lost heart, though results so far do not answer my hopes. The nomination was, in itself, the best that could be made; but it was an experiment, and a bold one. A Free-Trade convention nominated the ablest, after Mr. Carey, of American writers in support of protection; a Republican convention nominated a full Republican ticket for Democratic support, without which almost unanimously given, success was impossible; a Democratic convention, departing from all party usages, nominated for Democratic support Republican candidates![2] May it not well be said that it was an experiment, and a bold one? To me, knowing Mr. Greeley as I do, and feeling in him the confidence I do, it would be a pleasure to vote for him. I can postpone all differences in the full confidence that, practically, his administration will, in no respect, fundamentally clash with my views, while, in the important matters of currency, amnesty, and reform, it will thoroughly harmonize with them. It is not surprising that others think and will act differently. . . .

1. An advocate of free trade, Lloyd had recently joined the staff of the *Chicago Tribune* after quitting as Chase's personal secretary. Chase had been with his oldest daughter Kate since June 11, recovering from an illness that started in New York on June 6. From late June to September, he traveled elsewhere in New England and went back to Rhode Island on September 4. Chase returned to Washington, D.C., sometime between October 6 and 12, after visiting New York and Philadelphia. *Chase Papers,* 1:687–89, 692–93, 696, 699, 701–3; Chester McArthur Destler, *Henry Demerest Lloyd and the Empire of Reform* (Philadelphia, 1863), 65–71.

2. The "Free-Trade convention" was an assemblage of Liberal Republicans dissatisfied with the nomination of protectionist Horace Greeley at Cincinnati. On May 30, the dissidents gathered in New York and selected instead Ohio politician William S. Groesbeck, an authority on bimetallism and compared here to Philadelphia economist Henry C. Carey. Groesbeck, however, turned down the offer, as did his proposed running mate, New York landscape architect Frederick Law Olmsted. The Republican party, which met in Philadelphia on June 5 and 6, nominated Ulysses S. Grant and Massachusetts senator Henry Wilson for its ticket. At the Democratic national convention in Baltimore on July 9 and 10, delegates endorsed the nominees of the Liberal Republican party, Horace Greeley and B. Gratz Brown. *DAB,* 8:14; Foner, *Reconstruction,* 503; *Official Proceedings of the National Democratic Convention,* 65, 71; *Proceedings of the National Union Republican Convention Held at Philadelphia, June 5 and 6, 1872* . . . (Washington, 1872), 42, 55; Ross, *Liberal Republican Movement,* 112–13; 124–25.

TO CHARLES JEAN-MARIE LUCAS

Copy in clerk's hand. Chase Papers, Library of Congress (*micro* 39:0706).

Copy.

Washington, Nov. 19. 1872

My dear Sir:[1]

To receive your obliging letter and at the same time and from yourself, the various pamphlets written by you on the abolition of the death-penalty, together with the French edition of the writings of my illustrious countryman, Edward Livingston, was a gratification as unexpected as it was agreeable.[2] I found especial pleasure in the perusal of the preface in which you introduce the great jurist to the appreciation of French readers with such just discrimination and well merited eulogy. The part derived from your personal knowledge of Mr Livingston and from his correspondence with M. Taillandier was new to me and especially interesting.[3]

I thank you also for the pamphlets which you have so kindly sent me. Of these, your letter to Prince Bismarck and your observations relative to the Penitentiary Congress of London, have especially attracted my attention. Humanity owes you thanks for both.[4]

The whole American people feel a lively concern in the prosperity of your country. They deplore the misfortunes of France and admire the recuperative energy which she displays.[5] Far distant be the day when *"decadence"* will truthfully describe her condition.

I have not taken personally any part in the controversy concerning the abolition of the death penalty.[6] My sympathies are on the side of abolition; and my convictions are in favor of limiting it to the case of wilful murder. Such is the general conviction of my countrymen. In every, or nearly every State of the American Union, it is so limited. In some, it has been wholly abolished.

The time which I could spare from the professional labors, upon which I have depended for the support of myself and my family, has been given to two great and happily accomplished reforms, namely, the emancipation of four millions of my countrymen and the securing to my country the benefits of a uniform currency—not, I hope, without some influence upon the auspicious result in each case. My best wishes have attended those generous spirits who have endeavoured in other ways, to promote human welfare through Christian civilization; but I have been able to contribute little direct effort to the accomplishment of their excellent purposes.

It must be a great satisfaction to you that you have been able to do so much; and that, at an advanced age, you are still able to take an active part in a great reform. May your health and strength be long continued to you, and when your labors on earth close—as all our labors must,—may you receive the blessed welcome of "Well done, good and faithful servant; enter thou into the joy of thy Lord."[7]

With profound respect and esteem,
I have the honor to be

Yours faithfully
S. P. CHASE.

M. Ch. Lucas, Membre de l'Institut[8]
au Chateau de la Rougère près Bourges (Cher)

1. Lucas had written widely on French prison reform and abolition of the death penalty.

2. Included with Lucas's letter of introduction—which he wrote in French—was a copy of *Exposé d'un Système de Législation Criminelle pour L'État de la Louisiane et pour les États-Unis d'Amérique* (Paris, 1872), by former U.S. senator Edward Livingston, a French translation of a book first published in 1825 that discussed Louisiana's criminal law. Lucas to Chase, Oct. 8, 1872 (Chase Papers, L.C.).

3. Lucas's preface quotes from correspondence of 1826 and 1827 between Livingston and Paris trial lawyer, writer, and politician Alphonse-Honoré Taillandier (1797–1867). In

the 1870s, Chase wrote introductions for two English editions of Livingston's works: *A Code of Reform and Prison Discipline . . .* (New York, 1872), and *The Complete Works of Edward Livingston on Criminal Jurisprudence . . .* (New York, 1873). *Chase Papers,* 1:681, 684, 685; Lucas, *Exposé d'un Système de Législation Criminelle,* x–xiv, xvi; *Nouvelle Biographie Générale depuis les Temps les Plus Reculés jusqu'a Nos Jours . . .*, 46 vols. (Paris, 1853–66), 44:779–82.

4. Otto Edward Leopold von Bismarck, Prince Bismark, Duke of Lauenburg (1815–98), was the great unifier and reformer of the German empire. Lucas shared other copies of the same pamphlet with the International Penitentiary Congress in London, July 3–13, 1872. Thorne, *Chambers's Biographical Dictionary,* 132–33; Edwin Pears, *Prisons and Reformatories at Home and Abroad Being The Transactions of the International Penitentiary Congress Held in London July 3–13, 1872* (London, 1872), 534–37.

5. Under Bismarck, German military forces prevailed during the Franco-Prussian War, defeating France on February 26, 1872. *Appletons' Annual Cyclopædia,* 10:343, 358, 367.

6. In the United States, the antislavery movement had eclipsed agitation against capital punishment in the middle of the nineteenth century, but organized opposition to the death penalty surfaced again at the turn of the century. William J. Bowers, *Legal Homicide: Death as Punishment in America, 1864–1982* (Boston, 1984), 9–10.

7. Matt. 25:21, 23.

8. Lucas wrote his note of October 8 on letterhead of the Institut Imperial de France. Lucas to Chase, Oct. 8, 1872 (Chase Papers, L.C.).

TO HAMILTON FISH

Letter in clerk's hand, signed by Chase. Miscellaneous Letters of the Department of State, General Records of the Department of State (Record Group 59), National Archives (*micro* 39:0733).

Washington, Dec. 10. 1872

My dear Mr Secretary:

Absence in New York is my only excuse for delay in replying fully to your note of the 26th ultimo.

I have taken the liberty of consulting the two Senior Associate Justices on the subject of it.[1]

We agree in thinking that there is no impropriety in giving our impressions in regard to the article of the proposed treaty, which you have done me the honour of submitting to my consideration. These impressions may, of course, be changed upon argument and full consideration, should questions involving them ever be brought before us for judicial decision.

I proceed to state them.

1. The provisions touching admiralty jurisdiction to enforce the fines, penalties and forfeitures mentioned in the treaty, by proceedings *in rem* or *in personam,* seem to us unobjectionable.[2]

It may be well, however, to stipulate for legislation by Congress and also to give the choice of proceedings *in rem* or *in personam* or both, to the party instead of referring the question, which remedy shall be adopted, to the decision of the Court.

2. We all doubt the constitutionality of the provision which authorizes the examination of witnesses before the Commissioners and the

use of their depositions on the trial of citizens of the United States, charged with the offences described in the treaty. I incline to the opinion that the clause providing for the right to be confronted with witnesses before the Commissioners, is a substantial compliance with the constitutional provision on the subject, but my associates incline, and quite decidedly, the other way.

There is, of course, no objection as to any stipulation for such testimony to be used in civil suits, not criminal prosecutions.

3. We think the provisions in regard to the subjects of the Queen, especially where offences are charged to have been committed on the High Seas, are unobjectionable.[3]

I cordially agree with you as to the humane objects sought to be attained by the treaty and will gladly contribute, as far as I may, to the success of your efforts,—in all which my honored associates fully concur with me.

With great respect,

Faithfully yours
S: P: CHASE

To the Honorable
Hamilton Fish,
Secretary of State.

1. Chase had arrived in New York on or shortly before November 29, and returned to Washington, D.C., on December 5. While in New York, he served as a pallbearer at the funeral of Horace Greeley, who died suddenly on November 29, soon after suffering overwhelming defeat in the presidential election of 1872. Fish's letter solicited Chase's opinion of article 23 in a proposed treaty to protect emigrants in passage to the United States. One major provision created federal commissioners of emigration authorized to receive complaints and to facilitate judicial proceedings. For advice, Chase consulted with Nathan Clifford and Noah Swayne, the Supreme Court's two senior associate justices. *Chase Papers,* 1:707–9; *DAB,* 7:533–34; Fairman, *Reconstruction and Reunion,* 3, 657; Fish to Chase, Nov. 26, 1872 (Chase Papers, L.C.).

2. That is, proceedings against a thing (*in rem*) or person (*in personam*). Henry Campbell Black, *Black's Law Dictionary* . . . , 4th ed. (St. Paul, Minn., 1968), 899, 900.

3. Paragraph 3 of the proposed article called for local officers in dominions that Queen Victoria governed to enforce provisions of the treaty in consultation with the United States.

TO AUGUSTUS FRENCH BOYLE

Letterbook copy in clerk's hand. Chase Papers, Library of Congress (*micro* 39:0736).

Washington, Dec. 11. 1872

My dear Sir:

Thanks your kind words; though, in some respects, undeserved.[1]

There was, I think, no special act authorizing the employment of women, when I introduced them into the Department in 1861; but the law sanctioned the employment of *persons* to do the work committed to them and did not exclude females. My action was originally taken from motives of humanity mainly. There were many, refugees and others, deprived of the means of livelihood by the war & I gave them employment to enable them to provide for themselves and families. It is true, however, that I have always favored the enlargement of the sphere of woman's work and the payment of just compensation for it.

This is a private note, intended to correct any misapprehension you may be under and for no other use.

Yours truly
S. P. CHASE

1. Boyle (b. 1818), a writer, had enclosed "some papers" regarding "the progress of the 'Woman Movement'" and a discussion of plans to prepare a magazine article on the subject. "I have watched your course with much interest, and increasing faith in the wisdom of your purposes and the purity of your motives," wrote Boyle. Boyle to Chase, Nov. 8, 1872 (Chase Papers, L.C.); *The National Union Catalog: Pre-1956 Imprints,* 754 vols. (London, 1968–81), 71:89.

TO WHITELAW REID

Autograph letter. Whitelaw Reid Papers, Library of Congress (*micro* 39:0740).

Washington, Dec. 26, 1872

My dear Reid,

I trust you have had a happy Christmas & will have a prosperous & happy New Year. Since the death of Mr. Greeley—how sad an affliction to us all—you seem to have had a hard time; but the fiercer the battle the more welcome the triumph. And you seem to have triumphed if, in the distance, I read the indications aright[1]

But the price at which you are said to have bought the controlling interest strikes me as enormous, $550,000. But I know nothing of the real value of newspapers. If you have time & feel in the mood I should like to have the real facts? The effect of the late events upon the circulation & the business, and the prospect & the banking. I do not express a mere curiosity, but a real & deep interest not only in the paper but in you as a friend in whose welfare I feel a true concern.[2]

Your admirable article on taking the Chair marks out a difficult path. If any American journalist can tread it successfully you can. It is no flattery to say that you have great ability and of the varied sort required for your post. But is it possible for any man to be judicially impartial and at the same time successful? I hope it is.[3]

The Republican here the other day had a long article depreciatory of you in the course of which it charged you with defaming Mr. Lincoln in the interest of Mr. Chase. Did you see it? Have you any idea of what was intended? I have not.[4]

I think of much I should like to write. But it costs more labor than formerly & takes more time, and I have at present so little of the latter article that I must stop.

Faithfully your friend
S. P. CHASE

Whitelaw Reid, Esq

1. Reid, former managing editor of the *New York Tribune,* had found himself in the midst of a battle for control of the paper shortly after Horace Greeley's death on November 29. Reid and his allies had recently prevailed over a faction of stockholders who wanted to install former vice president Schuyler Colfax as editor. Baehr, *New York Tribune,* 119–23; *DAB,* 15:483.

2. Reid responded to Chase's request on December 27 (below).

3. On December 23, an article published in the *New York Tribune* promised a "frank and fearless" editorial policy in the tradition of Horace Greeley. "The *Tribune,*" it asserted, "is nobody's official advocate." *New York Tribune,* Dec. 23, 1872.

4. The article, which appeared on December 17 in the *Washington National Republican,* questioned the sincerity of a statement by Reid that implied support for Grant's second administration. The *New York Tribune,* asserted the *Republican,* "is owned by a gang of notorious jobbers and speculators, who have been partners, and accomplices with the worst men in Tammany Hall. . . . Mr. Reid's Republicanism has always been a matter of pay, always selling his services to the highest bidder." Continued the *Republican,* "We have again and again charged in these columns that he was paid in 1864 a monthly stipend to defame Mr. Lincoln in the interest of Mr. Chase, which he has not denied."

FROM WHITELAW REID

Letterpress copy of letter in clerk's hand. Whitelaw Reid Papers, Library of Congress (*micro* 39:0745).

Private

Dec. 27th. 2

Dear Mr Chase:

I owe you very many thanks for your pleasant letter of the 26th. inst, and hasten to return the congratulations of the season.[1]

Gossip slightly exaggerated the price at which I bought the controlling interest. Instead of $550,000 it was only $510,000. In other words I paid Mr Orton for 50 shares just what he had paid the week before for 51, making an allowance with him meantime which results in his coming into the Board of Trustees as one of my supporters.[2] The price seems large to you, yet in point of fact it is very low. The Chicago Tribune would sell at the same valuation at auction. The Cincinnati Commercial would come within a quarter of a million of it. The New York Herald would double or treble it.

Here is the substantial backing, which shows the real value of the property:

Real Estate (unencumbered),	$400,000.
Cash on hand	200,000.
Presses, Type, etc	100,000.
Associated Press Franchise	100,000[3]

The most of these items are valued very low. The presses and type would probably sell for more at auction; could hardly be replaced for double the price named.

I have no idea what the *Washington Republican* can have in its brain about my opposition to Mr Lincoln in 1864. It has been hammering on the same charge for six months, and I have seriously thought once or twice of bringing it up with a round turn by the suggestion that it either prove its charges or pay the penalty, under the law for libel in the district. You will probably have forgotten that in 1864, I said to you somewhat explicitly, that I considered the chairman of your Committee, Mr Senator Pomeroy, a dishonest man, and refused to even enter his committee-room. Whatever money was paid for the prosecution of the campaign against Mr Lincoln was paid there.[4]

But I think John Hay disposes of the charge more effectively than any body else. He says— "Well, somebody may have been fool enough to pay you for supporting Chase in 1864, but I shall expect next to see that same fellow around trying to bribe you to eat your dinner."[5]

At a time when the contest here was trembling between success and defeat I had some little correspondence with Gov. Sprague about it. He can tell you the particulars. I don't expect to make any money during the next year, but I do expect within three years to see the shares in *The Tribune* worth $15,000, instead of $10,000, at which I bought.[6]

Doubtless the role of honest independent journalism is a hard one. It is vastly easier to get the wheels of our chariot into the party rut, and keep them there; but I believe the future is with us; that honor now and profit hereafter belong only to those who honestly maintain their independence.

I hope you are to be soon in New York. Meantime I am with cordial regards always

Faithfully yours

Mr Chief Justice Chase
Washington D.C.

1. See Chase to Reid, December 26, 1872 (above).

2. In 1872, former commissioner of internal revenue William Orton was president of the Western Union Telegraph Company and served on the board of trustees for the *New York Tribune. DAB,* 14:65.

3. Connections between the *New York Tribune* and the Associated Press dated from 1849, when the syndicate came into existence. Baehr, *New York Tribune,* 14, 33–34.

4. In February 1864, Senator Samuel C. Pomeroy of Kansas spearheaded an unsuccessful movement to replace Lincoln with Chase as the Republican presidential candidate. Reid reported from Washington for the *Cincinnati Gazette* during the Civil War. *Chase Papers,* 4:303–5; *DAB,* 15:482–83.

5. John Milton Hay was one of Lincoln's personal secretaries during the Civil War, an American diplomat afterward, and an editor with the *New York Tribune* from 1870 to 1875. *DAB,* 8:431–32.

6. William Sprague helped finance Reid's recent takeover of the *New York Tribune.* Under Reid, the newspaper prospered after several years of retrenchment and by 1876

had a daily circulation of more than 60,000. Ibid., 15:483; Baehr, *New York Tribune,* 121, 124–28.

TO GERRIT SMITH

Autograph letter. Chase Papers, Library of Congress (*micro* 39:0762).

Washington, Feb. 13, 1873

My dear friend,

I was so glad to see your well known handwriting again, and that your interest in good works does not flag.[1] My opinions & feelings are in favor of woman suffage, but I would make haste slowly. It does well in Wyoming, and would probably work equally well in Ohio or Massachusetts; and might be adopted in other states progressively.[2] I am afraid that our friend Miss Anthony is a little too fast. Universal suffage & universal amnesty is my motto you know: but I am inclined to think that education in the duties & responsibilities of citizenship might well enough be made a prerequisite

Wont you come to the inauguration & bring Mrs Smith?[3] We shall all be most happy to see you and I tender you a most cordial invitation in the name of the Gov & Mrs Sprague as well as my own to our house on E St.[4] I have so many things to say which I have not time to write. With best regards to Mrs Smith

Most truly yours
S P Chase

Hon G. Smith

1. Smith's latest correspondence discussed Chase's health and included a copy of *Woman Suffrage Above Human Law* . . . (Peterboro, N.Y., 1873), a published letter in support of the female franchise that Smith had written to suffragist Susan Brownell Anthony (1820–1906). Anthony had recently been prosecuted for illegally registering to vote and casting a ballot in her hometown of Rochester, New York, during elections held in November 1872. Included in Anthony's unsuccessful defense was a strategy to appeal her case to the Supreme Court, claiming a right to vote under provisions of the Fourteenth Amendment. Kathleen Barry, *Susan B. Anthony: A Biography of a Singular Feminist* (New York, 1988), 249; *DAB,* 1:318–20; Smith to Chase, Feb. 9, 1873 (Chase Papers, L.C.).

2. "To hasten slowly" was supposedly the motto of Roman emperor Augustus. The phrase also appears (in Latin) in a letter that Stanley Matthews wrote to Chase on April 19, 1865 (above). Wyoming's territorial legislature granted women the right to vote and hold office on December 10, 1869. Women in Ohio and Massachusetts also received limited suffrage rights in 1894 and 1881, respectively. Taft A. Larson, *History of Wyoming* (Lincoln, Nebr., 1965), 79; Philip D. Jordan, *Ohio Comes of Age: 1873–1900,* v. 5 of Carl Wittke, ed., *The History of the State of Ohio* (Columbus, 1943, reprint, 1968), 310; Harriet Jane Hanson Robinson, *Massachusetts in the Woman Suffrage Movement* . . . (Boston, 1881), 103–4.

3. Chase anticipated the second inauguration of Ulysses S. Grant on March 4. Neither Smith nor his wife, Ann Carroll Fitzhugh Smith, attended. *New York Times,* Mar. 5, 1873; Octavius Brooks Frothingham, *Gerrit Smith: A Biography* . . . , 2d ed. (New York, 1879), 330.

4. Ill health had forced Chase back into the Spragues' residence at 601 E Street, where he remained until spring. Belden, *So Fell the Angels,* 271; Chase to Stephen J. Field, Apr. 13, 1873 (below).

TO WILLIAM P. MELLEN

Autograph letter. Clara Hawkins Mellen Papers, Bowdoin College (*micro* 39:0768).

Washington, March 6, 1873

My dear Mellen,[1]

Well, I have sworn in the President and now I begin to think on my search of health for next summer.[2] My mind turns towards Colorado. What think you. Can I hope to recuperate there? Sometimes I fancy that nothing ails me but debility proceeding from a torpid liver & deficient Circulation. Sometimes I think that the seat of the trouble is in the heart. People say I look much better than last winter, and sometimes I actually feel better. But I think there is no substantial difference. What do you advise? Give me your best thoughts

With kindest remembrances for Mrs Mellen and Queenie—I suppose I should say, Mrs Palmer,

Yours faithfully
S: P: Chase

W. P. Mellen Esq

1. In 1873, former special Treasury agent Mellen evidently lived in Colorado. *New York Tribune,* May 8, 1873.

2. Although "pale and feeble," according to one report, Chase administered the oath of office at Grant's second inauguration on March 4. *New York Times,* Mar. 5, 1873.

TO JANET CHASE HOYT

Autograph letter. Chase Papers, Library of Congress (*micro* 39:0579).

Washington, Apl. [12], 1872[1]

My darling Nettie

Your letter was written I suppose last Saturday, for that is its date, but I only received it this morning. I went to Richmond last week Friday and returned only yesterday.[2] The weather there was delightful. Peach trees and pear trees were in full bloom & the trees generally had begun to put forth their foliage. Vegetation seemed about in advance of vegetation here, as here it is in advance of vegetation in New York. And the kindness of my reception! I was the guest of Gen and Mrs Johnson who omitted nothing they could think of to render my stay pleasant. Gen J—— is engaged in preparing for the press a volume embodying my judicial administration in my circuit and my employment was aiding his revision of my decisions. So I was not altogether idle.[3] I could & would have done more and enjoyed more, if I had been in better health but I did very well for an invalid

Dont trouble yourself about your lady guests. Invite them if best suits you. I shall not come to New York for ten days yet, & perhaps not for a week later; and then if it is not entirely convenient for you to receive me I can easily find lodgings at the Hotel.[4] I cannot stop at any rate more than a day or two—just to look in upon you & to make the acquaintance of my new Grandson. By the way I am of Will's mind about the name, only I should give the first son the father's name—next to his I should take the paternal grandfather's, especially if one which the child would like when grown. And Edwin is just such a name. So, pet, I must vote against you.[5]

I had a letter from Mary Parker announcing her engagement. It was so kind of her to make me a sharer of her joy, I have thanked & congratulated her as well as I could[6]

I am quite prepared to admire your baby / Katie says he is splendid. Your letters make me a little afraid for your own health. Take care [*torn*] yourself. Goodnight— It is eleven o'clock & I must go to bed: Love to Will & kisses for the little ones[7]

Your loving father
S P CHASE

1. The date should be *1873*, given the letter's internal references to Janet Hoyt's son Edwin and to Chase's own travels.
2. Chase's trip to Richmond, Virginia, apparently started on April 4 and ended one week later on April 11.
3. In Richmond, Chase stayed with Bradley T. Johnson and his wife, Jane Saunders Johnson. Johnson was editing his *Cases Decided by Chief Justice Chase; DAB,* 10:91.
4. Chase went to New York on May 3 and stayed at Nettie's house on West Thirty-third Street, where he died on May 7. *New York Tribune,* May 8, 1873.
5. The Hoyt's first son, Edwin Chase Hoyt (1873–1954), later became an attorney in New York. His paternal grandfather was Edwin Hoyt, a New York merchant. *New York Times,* Oct. 22, 1954; *Representative Men,* 1:416.
6. Mary Parker was the daughter of New York attorney and politician Amasa J. Parker. Mary wed Erastus Corning, Jr. (1827–97), a New York businessman, sometime between the date of this letter and May 9, when she sent Nettie condolences on the death of her father. *Nat. Cyc.,* 9:533; *New York Times,* May 14, 1890; Mary Parker Corning to Janet Chase Hoyt, May 9, 1873 (Chase Papers, L.C.).
7. In addition to Edwin, their new child, the Hoyts also had a daughter named Janet, born in January 1872. Chase to Janet Chase Hoyt, Feb. 16, 1872 (above).

TO STEPHEN J. FIELD

Autograph letter. Stephen Johnson Field Letters (BANC MSS 71/34 c), The Bancroft Library, University of California, Berkeley (*micro* 39:0780).

601 E. St. Ap 13

My dear Judge,

Will you please say for me that I dissent from the opinion in Myra Bradwell v Illinois.[1] I think it better to dissent generally, than to dissent from the reasoning of the opinion

Your friend
S P CHASE

Mr. Justice Field

1. Myra Colby Bradwell (1831–94) had edited the *Chicago Legal News* since 1868. In 1869, she passed legal examinations and applied to the Illinois Supreme Court for admission to the state bar. Rejected, she appealed to the same court, which refused her

once more on account of her sex. Bradwell then took her case to the U.S. Supreme Court, where she argued that the Fourteenth Amendment protected her right to practice. On April 15, 1873, the Court sustained the lower court by a margin of 8–1. In 1885, Bradwell finally received a license to practice in Illinois and was admitted to practice before the U.S. Supreme Court in 1892. *DAB,* 2:581; Fairman, *Reconstruction and Reunion,* 1364–66; Jane M. Friedman, *America's First Woman Lawyer: The Biography of Myra Bradwell* (Buffalo, N.Y., 1993), 129; *Nat. Cyc.,* 2:137; 16 Wall. 130 (1873).

TO RICHARD C. PARSONS

Printed copy. *New York Tribune,* May 12, 1873 (*micro* 39:0794).

NEW-YORK, May 5, 1873.[1]

MY DEAR COLONEL: Since the adjournment, which came none too soon, I have made my way to New-York, and am passing three or four days with Mrs. Hoyt.[2] It seems odd to be so entirely out of the world in the midst of this great Babylon; but I am too much of an invalid to be more than a cipher. Sometimes I feel as if I were dead, though alive. I am on my way to Boston, where I am to try a treatment from which great results are promised; but I expect little. The lapse of 65 years is hard to cure. Mrs. Sprague is passing a week here with William and Ethel, at the Clarendon.[3]

Don't you want to go to Colorado? I think of going in late May or early June.[4]

Write me at Hotel Berkley, Boston. Love to Mrs. Parsons, and Julia and Richard.

Yours faithfully.
S. P. CHASE.

To Col. R. C. Parsons.

1. A statement that preceded the printed copy of this letter in the *New York Tribune* depicted this as the last correspondence that Chase ever wrote. According to Chase biographer Jacob Schuckers, however, Chase also wrote another letter around this time to niece Alice Nora Skinner Stebbins that discussed plans to visit Boston on May 7 or 8. Schuckers, *Life and Public Services,* 623–24.

2. In 1873, the Supreme Court adjourned on May 1. Chase arrived at his youngest daughter's house in New York two days later. *New York Tribune,* May 8, 1873.

3. Encouraged by Alice Stebbins, Chase intended to try "some new cure" in Boston "by the application of magnetism or electricity." Kate Chase Sprague and her children stayed at the Clarendon Hotel, 219 Fourth Avenue, in Manhattan. Alice Stebbins to Chase, May 6, 1873 (Chase Papers, L.C.); *New York Dir. (1872),* 200; *New York Times,* May 8, 1873.

4. Chase apparently planned to visit William P. Mellen while in Colorado. Chase to Mellen, Mar. 6, 1873 (above).

Bibliography

SOURCES CITED BY ABBREVIATED TITLES

Appletons'	James Grant Wilson and John Fiske, eds. *Appletons' Cyclopædia of American Biography.* 6 vols. New York, 1887–89.
Bio. Dir. U.S. Cong.	*Biographical Directory of the United States Congress 1774–1989 . . . Bicentennial Edition.* Washington, D.C., 1989.
Chase Papers	John Niven et al., eds. *The Salmon P. Chase Papers.* Kent, Ohio, 1993–.
DAB	American Council of Learned Societies. *Dictionary of American Biography.* 20 vols. New York, 1928–36.
DNB	Leslie Stephen and Sidney Lee, eds. *The Dictionary of National Biography.* Reprint ed., 21 vols. London, 1973.
Nat. Cyc.	*The National Cyclopaedia of American Biography.* 63 vols. New York, 1891–1984.
OR	*The War of the Rebellion: A Compilation of the Official Records of the Union and Confederate Armies.* 128 vols. Washington, D.C., 1880–1901.
ORN	*Official Records of the Union and Confederate Navies in the War of the Rebellion.* 30 vols. Washington, D.C., 1894–1922.
Register of Officers (1863)	*Register of Officers and Agents, Civil, Military, and Naval, in the Service of the United States, on the Thirtieth September, 1864.* Washington, D.C., 1863.

Register of Officers (1865) — *Register of Officers and Agents, Civil, Military, and Naval, in the Service of the United States, on the Thirtieth September, 1866.* Washington, D.C., 1865.

Register of Officers (1869) — *Register of Officers and Agents, Civil, Military, and Naval, in the Service of the United States, on the Thirtieth September, 1869.* Washington, D.C., 1870.

Who Was Who — *Who Was Who in America.* Chicago, 1943–.

CITY DIRECTORIES

Charleston Dir. (1866) — *Charleston Directory. 1866; Containing the Names of the Inhabitants, and an Appendix of Much Useful Information.* [Charleston], 1866.

Cinc. Dir. (1849–50) — *Williams' Cincinnati Directory and Business Advertiser, for 1849–50.* Cincinnati, [1850].

Cinc. Dir. (1870) — *Williams' Cincinnati Directory . . . June 1870.* Cincinnati, [1870].

Cinc. Dir. (1872) — *Williams' Cincinnati Directory . . . June 1872.* Cincinnati, [1872].

New York Dir. (1864) — H. Wilson, comp. *Trow's New York City Directory.* New York, 1864.

New York Dir. (1872) — H. Wilson, comp. *Trow's New York City Directory.* New York, 1872.

Phila. Dir. (1868–69) — Isaac Costa, comp. *Gopsill's Philadelphia City and Business Directory for 1868–69.* Philadelphia, 1868.

Wash. Dir. (1864) — Andrew Boyd, comp. *Boyd's Washington Directory. Containing Also a Business Directory of Washington, Georgetown and Alexandria.* Washington, D.C., 1864.

Wash. Dir. (1865) — Andrew Boyd, comp. *Boyd's Washington and Georgetown Directory.* Washington, D.C., 1865.

Wash. Dir. (1866) — Andrew Boyd, comp. *Boyd's Washington and Georgetown Directory.* Washington, D.C., 1866.

Wash. Dir. (1867) — William H. Boyd, comp. *Boyd's Directory of Washington and Georgetown; together with a Business*

Directory of Alexandria, Va., and a Compendium of their Government, Institutions, and Trades. Washington, D.C., 1867.

Wash. Dir. (1868) William H. Boyd, comp. *Boyd's Directory of Washington and Georgetown, together with a Compendium of their Government, Institutions, and Trades.* Washington, D.C., 1868.

Wash. Dir. (1869) William H. Boyd, comp. *Boyd's Directory of Washington and Georgetown, together with a Compendium of their Governments, Institutions, and Trades.* Washington, D.C., 1869.

Wash. Dir. (1870) William H. Boyd, comp. *Boyd's Directory of Washington, Georgetown, and Alexandria, together with a Compendium of their Governments, Institutions and Trades.* Washington, D.C., 1870.

Wash. Dir. (1872) William H. Boyd. *Boyd's Directory of the District of Columbia, together with a Compendium of its Governments, Institutions, and Trades.* Washington, D.C., 1872.

OTHER SOURCES CITED

Address and Reply, on the Presentation of a Testimonial, to S. P. Chase, by the Colored People of Cincinnati; with Some Account of the Case of Samuel Watson. Cincinnati, 1845.

Appleton's Annual Cyclopædia and Register of Important Events. . . . 42 vols. New York, 1862–1903.

Baehr, Harry W. *The New York Tribune Since the Civil War.* New York, 1936.

Basler, Roy P., ed. *The Collected Works of Abraham Lincoln.* 9 vols. New Brunswick, N.J., 1953–55.

Belden, Thomas Graham, and Marva Robins Belden. *So Fell the Angels.* Boston, 1956.

Berlin, Ira, et al., eds. *Freedom: A Documentary History of Emancipation, 1861–1867.* Cambridge, Eng., 1982–.

Brown, Alexander. *The Cabells and Their Kin.* Cambridge, Mass., 1895.

Bury, J. P. T., ed. *The Zenith of European Power, 1830–70,* vol. 10 of *The New Cambridge Modern History.* Cambridge, Eng., 1960.

Coleman, Charles H. *The Election of 1868: The Democratic Effort to Regain Control.* New York, 1933; reprint, New York, 1971.

Cook, Adrian. *The Alabama Claims: American Politics and Anglo-American Relations, 1865–1872.* Ithaca, 1975.

Cree, Anthony, comp. *Cree's Dictionary of Latin Quotations.* Topsfield, Mass., 1978.

Dictionary of North Carolina Biography. 6 vols. to date. Chapel Hill, 1979–.

Donald, David. *Charles Sumner and the Rights of Man.* New York, 1970

Emerson, Charles Franklin, ed. *General Catalogue of Dartmouth College. . . .* Hanover, N.H., 1910–11.

Fairman, Charles. *Reconstruction and Reunion, 1864–88, Part One.* Vol. 6 of Paul A. Freund, gen. ed., *The Oliver Wendell Holmes Devise History of the Supreme Court of the United States.* New York, 1971.

Foner, Eric. *Reconstruction: America's Unfinished Revolution, 1863–1877.* New York, 1988.

General Orders—Reconstruction. 40th Cong., 2d sess., 1867–68, H. Ex. Doc. 342.

Gilkey, Elliot Howard. *The Ohio Hundred Year Book: A Hand-Book of the Public Men and Public Institutions of Ohio. . . .* Columbus, 1901.

Gilpin, Henry D., ed. *The Papers of James Madison. . . .* 3 vols. Washington, D.C., 1840.

Graf, Leroy P., et al., eds. *The Papers of Andrew Johnson.* 13 vols. to date. Knoxville, 1967–.

Haskell, Monroe M., Jr., et al., eds. *The Papers of Jefferson Davis.* 9 vols. to date. Baton Rouge, 1971–.

Heitman, Francis Bernard. *Historical Register and Dictionary of the United States Army. . . .* 2 vols. Washington, D.C., 1903.

Hyman, Harold M. *The Reconstruction Justice of Salmon P. Chase:* in Re Turner *and* Texas v. White. Lawrence, Kans., 1997.

Journal of the Senate of the State of Louisiana. New Orleans, 1864.

Johnson, Bradley Tyler, ed. *Reports of Cases Decided by Chief Justice Chase in the Circuit Court of the United States Fourth Circuit. . . .* Intro. by Ferne B. Hyman and Harold M. Hyman. New York, 1876; reprint, New York, 1972.

Johnson, Rossiter, ed. *The Twentieth Century Biographical Dictionary of Notable Americans. . . .* 10 vols. Boston, 1904; reprint, Detroit, 1968.

Jones, Hugh Percy, ed. *Dictionary of Foreign Phrases and Classical Quotations.* Rev. ed. Edinburgh, [1963].

Keim, DeB. Randolph. *Keim's Illustrated Handbook: Washington and Its Environs. . . .* 4th ed. Washington, D.C., 1874.

Lamars, William M. *The Edge of Glory: A Biography of General William S. Rosecrans, U.S.A.* New York, 1961.

Larson, Henrietta M. *Jay Cooke: Private Banker.* Cambridge, Mass., 1936.

Long, E. B. *The Civil War Day by Day: An Almanac, 1861–1865.* Garden City, N.Y., 1971.

Lucas, Charles. *Exposé d'un Système de Législation Criminelle pour l'État de la Louisiane et pour les États-Unis d'Amérique.* Paris, 1872.

McPherson, Edward. *The Political History of the United States during the Period of Reconstruction. . . .* Washington, D.C., 1875; reprint, New York, 1969.

Mr. Chase's Views. N.p., [1868].

Official Atlas of the Civil War. Intro. Henry Steele Commager. New York, 1958.

Official Proceedings of the National Democratic Convention, Held at Baltimore, July 9, 1872. Boston, 1872.

Phelps, Mary Merwin. *Kate Chase: Dominant Daughter.* New York, 1935.

Proceedings of the Liberal Republican Convention, in Cincinnati, May 1st, 2d and 3d, 1872. . . . New York, 1872.

Reid, Whitelaw. *After the War: A Southern Tour. May 1, 1865, to May 1, 1866.* Cincinnati, 1866.

Report of the Secretary of the Treasury on the State of Finances, for the Year 1865. 39th Cong., 1st sess., 1865, H. Ex. Doc. 3.

Representative Men and Old Families of Rhode Island. . . . 3 vols. Chicago, 1908.

Robson, Charles, ed. *The Biographical Encyclopædia of Ohio of the Nineteenth Century.* Cincinnati, 1876.

Roseboom, Eugene H. *The Civil War Era, 1850–1873.* Vol. 4 of Carl Wittke, ed., *The History of the State of Ohio.* Columbus, 1944.

Ross, Earle Dudley. *The Liberal Republican Movement.* New York, 1919.

Schuckers, Jacob W. *The Life and Public Services of Salmon Portland Chase.* New York, 1874.

Shipherd, Jacob R., comp. *History of the Oberlin-Wellington Rescue.* Boston, 1859; reprint, New York, 1972.

Simpson, Brooks D., et al., eds. *Advice After Appomattox: Letters to Andrew Johnson, 1865–1866: Special Volume No. I of the Papers of Andrew Johnson.* Knoxville, 1987.

Smith, Gerrit. *On the Bailing of Jefferson Davis.* Peterboro, N.Y., 1867.

Sobel, Robert, and John Raimo, eds. *Biographical Directory of the Governors of the United States, 1789–1978.* 4 vols. Westport, Conn., 1978.

Taylor, Joel Gray. *Louisiana Reconstructed: 1863–1877.* Baton Rouge, 1974.

Thorne, J. O., ed. *Chambers's Biographical Dictionary.* Rev. ed. New York, 1969.

Trial of Andrew Johnson, President of the United States. . . . 3 vols. Washington, D.C., 1868.

Unger, Irwin. *The Greenback Era: A Social and Political History of American Finance, 1865–1879.* Princeton, 1964.

U.S. Census Office. *A Compendium of the Ninth Census. . . .* Washington, 1872.

U.S. Constitutional Convention. *Journal, Acts, and Proceedings of the Convention . . . which formed the Constitution of the United States.* Boston, 1819.

U.S. Department of Transportation. *Record of Movements: Vessels of the United States Coast Guard, 1790–Dec. 31, 1933.* Washington, D.C., 1989.

U.S. Senate. *Journal of the Executive Proceedings of the Senate of the United States. . . .* Washington, D.C., 1828–; reprint ed., New York, 1969.

Van Deusen, Glyndon G. *Horace Greeley: Nineteenth-Century Crusader.* Philadelphia, 1953.

Wilson, Henry. "Edwin M. Stanton," *Atlantic Monthly* 25 (Feb. 1870): 234–46.

———. "Jeremiah S. Black and Edwin M. Stanton." *Atlantic Monthly* 26 (Oct. 1870): 463–75.

Index

Page references for notes that identify individuals are in bold type (with **1**:, **2**:, **3**:, and **4**: indicating biographical references in Volumes 1–4 of the *Chase Papers*).

The Salmon P. Chase Papers, Volume 5
was designed by Will Underwood;
composed in 10/12 ITC New Baskerville
with Bulmer display type
on a Macintosh Power PC system in QuarkXPress
by The Book Page, Inc.;
printed by sheet-fed offset lithography
on 60-pound Glatfelter Supple Opaque Natural stock
(an acid-free, recycled paper),
with halftones printed on 70-pound enamel gloss stock,
Smyth sewn and bound over 98' binder's boards
in ICG Arrestox B grade cloth
by Thomson-Shore, Inc.;
and published by

The Kent State University Press
KENT, OHIO 44242